Health Informatics Research Methods

Principles and Practice

Elizabeth J. Layman, PhD, RHIA, CCS, FAHIMA, and Valerie J. Watzlaf, PhD, RHIA, FAHIMA
Volume Editors

American Health Information
Management Association®

ISBN: 1-58426-181-1
ISBN-13: 978-1-58426-181-0
AHIMA Product No. AB120908

AHIMA Staff:
Claire E. Blondeau, MBA, Senior Editor
Susan H. Fenton, PhD, MBA, RHIA, Director of Research
Katherine M. Greenock, Assistant Editor
Melissa A. Ulbricht, Editorial/Production Coordinator
Ken Zielske, Director of Publications

AHIMA strives to recognize the value of people from every racial and ethnic background as well as all genders, age groups, and sexual orientations by building its membership and leadership resources to reflect the rich diversity of the American population. AHIMA encourages the celebration and promotion of human diversity through education, mentoring, recognition, leadership, and other programs.

American Health Information Management Association
233 North Michigan Avenue, 21st Floor
Chicago, IL 60601-5800

www.ahima.org

Contents

Part III   Research Process

Part IV   Information to Knowledge

CD-ROM Resources

About the Authors

Elizabeth J. Layman, PhD, RHIA, CCS, FAHIMA, is professor and chair in the Department of Health Services and Information Management at East Carolina University, Greenville, NC. She previously worked at Hennepin County Medical Center and the University of Minnesota Hospitals, both in Minneapolis, from 1974 through 1990. Dr. Layman worked in several departments, such as third-party reimbursement, credit and collections, account auditing, outpatient registration, inpatient admissions, research studies, and quality management. In 1990, Dr. Layman joined the faculty of the Medical College of Georgia in Augusta, GA. While on the faculty, she also consulted for the Physicians' Practice Group. Dr. Layman successfully sat for the first CCS examination in 1992. In 2001, she was awarded the designation of Fellow of the American Health Information Management Association, one of the first two individuals in the country to receive this award. She is the coauthor of *Principles of Healthcare Reimbursement*, published by AHIMA in 2006, and for which she and her coauthor were recipients of AHIMA's Legacy Award in 2007. She was the first editor of *Perspectives in Health Information Management* and has delivered presentations at numerous AHIMA events. She earned her baccalaureate degree from the University of Minnesota. While working, she returned to school to earn her associate's degree in medical record technology. She completed St. Scholastica's progression program to earn her postbaccalaureate certificate in health information administration. She earned her master's degree in organizational leadership from the College of St. Catherine's and her doctorate in higher education from Georgia State University.

Valerie J. Watzlaf, PhD, RHIA, FAHIMA, is an associate professor within the Department of Health Information Management in the School of Health and Rehabilitation Sciences (SHRS) at the University of Pittsburgh. She also holds a secondary appointment in the Graduate School of Public Health. In those capacities, Dr. Watzlaf teaches and performs research in the areas of health information management, epidemiology, quality improvement, statistics, and long-term care. She has worked and consulted in several healthcare organizations in health information management, long-term care, and epidemiology. Dr. Watzlaf is very active in professional and scientific societies, having served on the Data Quality Task Force of the American Health Information Management Association (AHIMA), the Chairperson of the Coding, Policy, and Strategy Committee of AHIMA, the Research Committee of AHIMA, the Council on Accreditation of AHIMA, and most recently as a board member on the Foundation of Research and Education (FORE) of AHIMA. She is also on the Editorial Advisory Board for the Journal of AHIMA (JAHIMA) and for *Perspectives in Health Information Management*, a national peer-reviewed on-line journal within AHIMA. Dr. Watzlaf has published extensively in the field of health information management. She received the AHIMA Research Award in October 2001 and became a Fellow of AHIMA in April 2003. She received the SHRS Distinguished Alumni Award in 2005, was nominated for the Chancellor's Distinguished Teaching Award at Pitt in 1993 and in 1990 was elected to Delta Omega, the national public health honor society. Dr. Watzlaf received her bachelor of science degree in health records administration from the School of Health Related Professions; her master of public health and doctorate degrees in epidemiology from the Graduate School of Public Health; all from the University of Pittsburgh.

C. Andrew Brown, MD, MPH, is a professor of medicine and director of the University of Mississippi Medical Center (UMMC) Patient Safety Center. Dr. Brown has served as coinvestigator and principal investigator of clinical research trials since 1997, for such funding agencies as the National Institutes of Health; National Heart, Lung, and Blood Institute; Agency for Healthcare Research and Quality; and Health Resources and Services Administration. Dr. Brown's research interests include patient safety, the reporting of medication errors, and identifying causes of preventable healthcare errors and patient injury in healthcare delivery. Dr. Brown also serves as coeditor-in-chief of *Perspectives in Health Information Management*, the national journal of the American Health Information Management Association. Dr. Brown received a bachelor of science degree in Biology from Millsaps College in Jackson, master of science degree, and his doctor of medicine degree from the University of Mississippi School of Medicine. He completed his internship and residency in Internal Medicine at UMMC, where he served as a chief resident from 1992-1994. Dr. Brown completed the Clinical Effectiveness Program at Harvard University School of Public Health in 1995, and its masters of public health program in 1997.

John Eberhardt graduated Cum Laude from Duke Univeristy with a Bachelors in Economics and History. Mr. Eberhardt has spent his career in complex analysis for healthcare and financial institutions. A founder of machine learning company DecisionQ, Mr. Eberhardt is a recognized expert in data mining and machine learning.

Eric W. Ford, MPH, PhD, is the director of and an associate professor at The Center for Health Innovation, Education & Research, Health Organization Management, at Texas Tech University's Jerry S. Rawls College of Business. He is the endowed professor at Rawls College of Business, and also was the endowed professor and Humana Research Fellow at Penn State. In addition, Ford has held teaching positions at Tulane University in New Orleans, Louisiana; University of Alabama at Birmingham; and University of Alabama at Tuscaloosa. His research interests include strategic management, innovation diffusion, information systems and their effects on performance (both financial and population health outcome related). Ford has won several awards for his research articles; has authored or coauthored many refereed publications and other scholarly works; and has received several grants, contracts, and funded awards. He is a sought-after presenter and is active with several professional organizations. Ford was a doctoral fellow in the Department of Management/Health Services Administration, at the University of Alabama at Birmingham. Ford earned his MPH from the University of South Carolina in Columbia, South Carolina, and his bachelor's degree from Cornell University in Ithaca, New York.

Laurinda B. Harman, PhD, RHIA, is an associate professor and chair of the Department of Health Information Management at the College of Health Professions at Temple University in Philadelphia. She has been an HIM professional and educator for more than 35 years and has directed HIM baccalaureate programs at George Washington University in Washington, DC, and The Ohio State University in Columbus. Dr. Harman was a faculty member in the health information technology program at Northern Virginia Community College and served as director of education and human resource development for the Department of Health Care Sciences at George Washington University. She edited *Ethical Challenges in the Management of Health Information* and received the AHIMA 2001 Triumph Legacy Award for this important health information resource. The second edition was published in 2006. She contributed a chapter on Ethical Issues in Health Information Management to the second edition of *Health Information Management: Concepts, Principles, and Practice*, edited by Kathleen M. LaTour, MA, RHIA, FAHIMA, and Shirley Eichenwald Maki, MBA, RHIA, FAHIMA. Dr. Harman is a regular contributor to *Journal of American Health Information Management Association* and has delivered presentations at several AHIMA National Conventions. She received a bachelor of science degree in biology with a concentration in medical record administration from Daemen College in Buffalo, NY, a master of science degree in education at Virginia Polytechnic and State University in Blacksburg, and a PhD in human and organizational systems at Fielding Graduate University in Santa Barbara, CA.

Susan Hart-Hester, PhD, is a Professor in the Department of Family Medicine at the University of Mississippi Medical Center where she serves as the department's grantwriter. Dr. Hart-Hester has served as faculty at UMMC since 1992, bringing millions of dollars to the institution in grant funded research and training programs. Additional roles at UMMC include participation on the Informatics and Education and Awareness Cores of the Mississippi Institute for Improvement of Geographic and Minority Health, Center of Excellence in Womens Health, and the Patient Safety and Surveillance Center. Prior to her tenure at UMMC, she worked as a Student Field Placement Coordinator for the University of Southern Mississippi and as a Education Technologist for Planning and Policy with the Mississippi State Department of Education. Dr. Hart-Hester received her doctoral degree from the University of Virginia with an emphasis in Curriculum Development and Special Education. Her masters degree is in Psychology and was completed at West Georgia College. She has written for numerous refereed journals and served as the principal or coinvestigator on research grants, as well as serving as a reviewer for federal, state, and philanthropic grant funding agencies.

Jennifer Hornung Garvin, PhD, RHIA, CPHQ, CCS, CTR, FAHIMA, is a medical informatics postdoctoral fellow at the Center for Health Equity Research and Promotion sponsored by the Department of Veterans Affairs in association with the University of Pennsylvania School of Medicine. Her research interests center on the use of coded and administrative data and research methods in health information management (HIM) and health behavior, and her postdoctoral research focuses on the uses of coded data and its accuracy. Dr. Garvin has been a principal investigator funded by the AHIMA Foundation of Research and Education (FORE). Recent research includes ICD-10 and public health reporting, fraud and abuse prevention associated with computer assisted/auto coding, the preparedness of coding professionals for future roles in coding, and development of a public health Lyme disease prevention assessment instrument. She was awarded a National Library of Medicine fellowship in Woods Hole, MA for bioinformatics. She is also a lecturer in nursing informatics at the University of Pennsylvania School of Nursing. Dr. Garvin's professional HIM work includes such positions as professor and program director of HIM, director of HIM, director of QM, and consultant. She received her PhD from the Department of Public Health at Temple University, a postbaccalaureate certificate and associate degree from the HIM Program at Gwynedd-Mercy College, an MBA from St. Joseph's University, and completed the Clinical Research Certificate Program at the Center for Clinical Epidemiology and Biostatistics at the University of Pennsylvania School of Medicine.

Carol Nielsen, MLS, is the Senior Manager for Grants and Sponsored Programs in AHIMA's Foundation of Research and Education (FORE). Prior to coming to AHIMA/FORE, Nielsen was the Director of Research Administration at the Center for International Rehabilitation (CIR). In that position, she served as liaison on the federal grants received by CIR, managing budgets, coordinating new proposal submissions, and reporting on existing grants. She also coordinated the human subjects protection program for CIR. This included writing protocols and consent forms, managing submissions to the Institutional Review Board (IRB), and training research in ethics and humans subject protection issues. Prior to joining CIR, Nielsen served as the IRB Specialist in the Office for the Protection of Research Subjects (OPRS) at Northwestern University. While in the role of IRB Specialist, she drafted an extensive policy and procedures manual on human subjects protections issues for Northwestern faculty and researchers. She has also served as Director of OPRS and as Manager of Information Resources and Services in the Office of Research at Northwestern. At the American Library Association, Nielsen served as the Manager of the Office of the President. In that capacity, she contributed to national campaigns on reading, literacy, and the promotion of libraries; and worked in the Office of Research on a federal project coordinating statewide reporting of library statistics. She also served in the Office of Accreditation where she launched a major revision to standards for library education master's program. In addition, she has worked as a freelance editor, indexer, and database consultant. After earning her Masters in Library Science from the State University of New York at Albany, Nielsen worked at the School of Library and Information Science Library at the University of North Carolina.

William J. Rudman, PhD, is a Professor of Diagnostics and Clinical Health Sciences at the University of Mississippi Medical Center, where he has been on the faculty since 1995. Previous roles at UMC include Co-Director, Informatics Core—Institute for Improvement of Present Geographic and Minority Disparity, Co-Director for the Center on Patient Safety and Surveillance (CHIPS), Director of the Clinical Health Science Graduate Program, School of Health Related Professions. He was an Assistant Professor, Healthcare Supervision and Management, Health Information Management, School of Health and Rehabilitation Sciences, University of Pittsburgh, and Health Educator for the Illinois Cancer Council in Chicago. Other university appointments include Assistant Professor, Department of Health, Physical Education and Recreation, The Ohio State University, Columbus, OH; Assistant Professor, Department of Physical Education, Health and Sport Studies, Miami University, Oxford, OH. He also was a Graduate Teaching and Research Assistant, Sociology Department, University of Illinois, Urbana-Champaign, Illinois. Dr. Rudman is an active member of AHIMA and the Association of Management, and he serves in various high-ranking capacities for national entities such as the Department of Health and Human Services and the Agency for Healthcare Research and Quality. He has written for numerous refereed publications and is a sought-after speaker on health information-related topics such as ethics, technology and data mining, re-engineering and management-related issues including performance improvement and gender effects, domestic violence, medication errors, patient care reform, research and statistics, and sports and physical fitness. In addition, Dr. Rudman also has served as an editor for many publications, and has authored and reviewed several books. He has been awarded numerous grants that have funded millions of dollars in research. He holds two bachelors of science degrees, in health information management from UMC and liberal arts from Westminster College in Salt Lake City, and a masters of sociology and doctor of sociology, both from the University of Illinois, Urbana-Champaign.

Mark Weiner, MD, is an assistant professor of Medicine at the University of Pennsylvania School of Medicine and practices General Internal Medicine at the Hospital of the University of Pennsylvania in Philadelphia, PA. He is a Senior Fellow of the Leonard Davis Institute of Health Economics, Co-Chief of Data and Statistics Core at the Philadelphia VA Medical Center's Center for Health Equity Research and Promotion, and Associate Director of Patient Informatics in the Office of Human Research at the Hospital of the University of Pennsylvania. Dr. Weiner's interests help to bridge the gap between health services research and medical informatics. He has been integral in the development of the Pennsylvania Integrated Clinical and Administrative Research Database (PICARD) system that integrates clinical and administrative databases in support of the clinical research enterprise. Dr. Weiner also has experience in the practical aspects of research implementation within the community practice setting from technical, logistical, and legal standpoints. Dr. Weiner's research investigates the common themes that underlie the information needs of the research community with the goal of enhancing existing resources and developing new resources that address these needs. Dr. Weiner has a bachelor of science in engineering in computer science and earned his medical degree at the University of Pennsylvania School of Medicine. He completed his internship, residency, and fellowship at the Hospital of the University of Pennsylvania. Weiner is board certified in Internal Medicine and received training in applied medical informatics as a National Library of Medicine postdoctoral fellow.

Foreword

Research is critical in developing an understanding of how health information technology and systems support the delivery of quality, cost-effective, and safe healthcare. As the nation's healthcare system moves toward increased reliance on automation, electronic health records, and information technology, it is imperative that disciplines such as health informatics and health information management (HIM) validate their body of knowledge through systematic investigation and evaluation based on sound research methods.

Health informatics is a broad term that denotes disciplines that encompass the use of computer and information science to manage all aspects of healthcare data and information. HIM as a specific discipline, fits within the broader rubric of health informatics as does nursing, dental, public health, and consumer informatics, to name a few. These disciplines focus on the systems, applications, and technology used to collect, store, process, access, exchange, protect, and disclose healthcare data and information in electronic or paper form. Healthcare data and information are used for primary and secondary purposes such as direct patient care, reimbursement, patient safety, legal issues, healthcare policy, quality improvement, public health, biosurveillance, and healthcare cost containment.

As the cost of healthcare continues to rise, so does the demand and use of healthcare data and information to help control costs. What theories, systems, applications, and technologies best support the collection, use, and dissemination of data and information? What is the impact of health information technology on the quality, safety, and cost-effectiveness of healthcare? What is the perceived usefulness of health information technology and the satisfaction levels of its use among healthcare providers? To address these questions, health informatics professionals must have a solid background and under-standing of the various research practices and innovative approaches available to them. Until now, no textbooks have specifically addressed research related to health informatics.

Dr. Layman and Dr. Watzlaf along with their chapter authors have skillfully produced a book that provides a clear, distinct discussion of research methods particularly relevant to the HIM field. The book is divided into four sections. The first part provides a historical perspective of research in health informatics followed by an overview of research design methods. These two chapters set the stage for the remaining sections of the book. Part two focuses on the various research methods related to survey, observational, and experimental and quasi-experimental research design. The third part presents research methods related to epidemiology, informatics evaluation and outcomes, and research review and secondary analysis. The discussion of these research methods is followed by chapters devoted to research question development, data collection, and statistical approaches that translate data to information. The last part discusses the grant writing process as well as the organization and management of research protocol data. The last three chapters offer the reader an excellent discussion on grant and proposal writing, ethical considerations when conducting research, and the dissemination of research results.

What I particularly like about the book are the discipline-specific examples that are woven throughout the chapters. These examples illustrate and support how research methods may be used to address a variety of informatics-related questions. These examples are especially important for undergraduate students who are new to practice environments. They help to make the concept of research "real" to the reader. For the graduate student, and practitioner interested in research, this book provides an excellent view of the steps necessary to conduct quality health informatics research. It also supports the research endeavors of professional organizations such as the American Health Information Management Association (AHIMA), American Medical Informatics Association (AMIA), Health Information and Management Systems Society (HIMSS), and American Nursing Informatics Association (ANIA) by providing their members with a resource for conducting research vital to validating a profession's body of knowledge.

This book will become a significant resource to anyone interested in conducting research in health informatics. It will be a significant reference on my bookshelf as I continue to engage in health informatics research and advise undergraduate and graduate students in their quest for discovery and new knowledge.

Melanie S. Brodnik, PhD, RHIA
Director and Associate Professor
Health Information Management
The Ohio State University

Preface

Research in health informatics and health information management is critically needed. Now more than ever, applicable research methods and appropriate analyses are needed to support the development and the evolution of the electronic health record, the personal health record, computerized physician order entry, decision support systems, protocols for privacy and security of electronic health information, and other health information technologies and applications. Research can demonstrate why and where certain applications are most vital to improve the quality of healthcare. To support the development of health information technologies and applications and to advance the body of knowledge of health informatics, the authors have written this textbook.

Health informatics professionals can be the leaders in the advancement of health information technologies and applications by conducting effective research. These professionals provide a myriad of services to the health sector. They work throughout the healthcare delivery system in healthcare facilities, insurance companies, vendor settings, consulting companies, government agencies, and research and development firms. Health informatics professionals also teach and conduct research throughout university and college settings. To conduct effective research in the applied discipline of health informatics and information management, practitioners and educators must collaborate.

This textbook, *Health Informatics Research Methods: Principles and Practice,* supports seasoned and novice researchers, students, and educators. The textbook focuses on the practical applications of research in health informatics and health information management. It provides real-life examples of research with samples of survey instruments, step-by-step listings of methodology for several types of research designs, and examples of statistical analysis tables and explanations. The textbook's organization guides students through the process of conducting research specific to health informatics concepts and functions. This organization also assists faculty members in the teaching of health informatics research methods. Every chapter consists of the following features:

1. Learning objectives
2. Key terms with definitions embedded into the body of the chapter
3. Introduction of each chapter
4. Practical examples of research conducted
5. Samples of research applications

The textbook is presented in four parts. Part I introduces the history and paradigms of research and health informatics as well as the different research designs.

Chapter 1 introduces the history and background of research and health informatics. It also includes examples of early epidemiological studies as well as past and current studies that used medical and financial records in research. It also describes the research frame by explaining the definitions of research, the quantitative and qualitative approaches, and the differences between inductive and deductive reasoning as well as an outline of the research process.

Chapter 2 provides an overview of the research designs most commonly used in health informatics. It describes the research design, the process used to conduct this type of research, and examples of how it is used in health informatics. The research designs discussed include: historical, descriptive, correlational, evaluation, experimental, and causal-comparative.

Part II focuses on the research methods of common research types and describes each of them with samples of current research performed by health informatics researchers.

Chapter 3 centers on survey research and its importance in the development and design of the survey questionnaire. Steps taken to create surveys are explained and discussed, including the types of questions to use, pilot testing of the survey, testing for validity and reliability, choosing the sample, methods for improving the response rate, analysis of data, and dissemination of results.

Chapter 4 explains the purpose of observational research and how it is used in health informatics. It describes the different types of observational research: nonparticipant observation, participant observation, and ethnography as well as steps to use to conduct content analysis.

Chapter 5 contains information on the differences and similarities between experimental and quasi-experimental research. It walks one through the experimental designs: pretest-posttest control group method, Solomon four-group method and posttest-only control group method. Then, it describes the quasi-experimental designs: one-shot case study, one group pretest-posttest method, and static group comparison method. All designs include examples of research conducted that is related to health informatics.

Chapter 6 explains epidemiological research and how it can be used in health informatics. It describes the models of causation (infectious and chronic disease model) and how these models can be used when assessing health informatics applications. It then describes the types of epidemiological study designs: cross-sectional or prevalence, case-control, prospective, and clinical trials.

Chapter 7 provides a rationale for the practical applications of evaluation research in core health informatics functions. The scope, definition, and types of evaluation research are explained and discussed. Clinical practice scenarios are used to illustrate the various types of health informatics evaluation research.

Chapter 8 describes, in a step-by-step manner, how secondary analysis or the systematic research review process is conducted. The research question, research protocol, terms and scope of the project, inclusion and exclusion criteria, the mapping process, data extrac-

tion, and the final report are explicitly explained with examples.

Part III walks the reader through the research process by first identifying the research question, conducting the literature review, formulating the hypothesis, and identifying specific aims or objectives, selecting the research design, collecting data, and addressing proper sampling, data analysis, and presentation and discussion of results.

Chapter 9 addresses how to formulate the research question, conduct the literature review, develop hypotheses and test them for statistical significance, write specific aims or research goals, and choose an appropriate research design and methodology.

Chapter 10 focuses on data collection including instrumentation features such as validity and reliability, instrumentation scales, selection of the proper instrument to use, sampling types and size, and overall data collection procedures such as ensuring an adequate response rate.

Chapter 11 explains how to work with both quantitative and qualitative data in order to move it toward information. Descriptive, inferential, and test statistics are explained and discussed. How best to present the study results is also described.

Part IV discusses the grant writing process as well as the organization and management of research protocol data. It also explains the importance of the institutional review board (IRB) and its implications when conducting research involving human subjects as well as the overall ethical concerns and problems when conducting research. Part IV concludes with a formative analysis of how information collected from research should be properly disseminated through presentation and publication.

Chapter 12 describes the grant writing process with information about granting agencies and their applications and guidelines on why some grants are not accepted and funded. It also provides information concerning the proper management of research protocol data for intervention studies such as clinical trials.

Chapter 13 introduces the ethical principles as they relate to research. It also describes the research codes of conduct, protection of human subjects, the role and responsibility of the IRB, HIPAA, DHHS, and NIH.

Ethical research problems are discussed and examples are provided that relate to such things as informed consent, publication of accurate results, and integrity. It concludes by discussing the misuses of information and information technology.

Chapter 14, the final chapter of the textbook, concludes with a practical explanation on how to effectively present research findings through poster presentations, conference presentations, and publications.

Note to Educators

An instructor guide is available to instructors in online format from the AHIMA Bookstore or through the Assembly on Education (AoE) Community of Practice (CoP). The Instructor Guide contains suggestions for writing assignments and projects, as well as a test bank for each chapter. PowerPoint slides also are available for classroom lectures.

Access to the AoE CoP is limited to instructors who are AHIMA members. The instructor guide is available to others who are not AHIMA members by contacting the publisher at publications@ahima.org. The instructor materials are not available to students enrolled in college or university programs.

PART I

History and Paradigms

Chapter 1
Research and Health Informatics

Elizabeth J. Layman, PhD, RHIA, CCS, FAHIMA

Learning Objectives

- To provide a rationale for conducting health informatics research
- To show the relationship between research and professionalism
- To outline research frames within which to conduct investigations
- To explain the terms research, research methodology, theory, and model

Key Terms

Applied research
Basic research
Bayesian network
Cross-sectional
Data mining
Deductive reasoning
Empiricism
Generalizability
Hypothesis
Inductive reasoning
Longitudinal
Mixed methods research
Model
Naturalism
Paradigm

Positivism
Primary research
Prospective
Qualitative approach
Quantitative approach
Research
Research frame
Research methodology
Retrospective
Rigor
Scientific inquiry
Secondary research
Technology
Theory

Introduction

Health informatics **research** is the investigation of the process, application, and impact of computer science, information systems, and communication technologies to health services. Health informatics research covers a broad spectrum of topics, including:

- Principles of health information and communication systems
- Fundamental natures of health information and communication systems
- Factors that affect health information and communication systems
- Interventions capable of improving existing health information and communication systems
- Methods and principles of developing interventions
- Evaluation of interventions in terms of their effects on individuals, the organization, the work or its outcome, and societies (Coiera 2003, xxii)

Research is instrumental in the development of the field of health informatics into a professional discipline. This book explores the application of research concepts to concerns of health informatics professionals.

This chapter outlines the role of research in the field of health informatics. Research answers questions and provides solutions to everyday problems. It also provides clear, step-by-step methods that result in a comprehensive approach to questions and problems. These methods allow people to collect reliable and accurate facts that they can analyze and interpret. This analysis and interpretation becomes valuable information that can be used to draft policies, to respond to administrative and legislative queries, and to make decisions. Unfortunately, people wrongly believe that only scientists and policy analysts can conduct research. People also wrongly believe that research is vague and esoteric. In fact, the opposite is true. Practitioners and clinicians can use research because its logical, comprehensive approach results in usable, practical information.

In health informatics research, researchers and practitioners study questions and problems that involve

- Designing information systems to support decision making for clinicians, administrators, policymakers, researchers, patients and clients, and consumers

- Maximizing the functioning of information systems through their design, implementation, or use
- Creating and modeling systems to standardize, capture, store, organize, search, process, analyze, and communicate health data; and
- Understanding how individuals, organizations, and societies interact with systems and use health data

Health informatics is "the study, invention, and implementation of structures and algorithms to improve communication, understanding, and management" of health information (Warner 1995, 207). Friedman detailed areas of research or scholarly creative work in the field as:

- Formulating models for acquisition, representation, processing, display, or transmission of biomedical information of knowledge
- Developing innovative computer-based systems, using these models, that deliver information or knowledge to healthcare providers;
- Installing such systems and then making them work reliably in functioning healthcare environments
- Studying the effects of these systems on the reasoning and behavior of healthcare providers, as well as on the organization and delivery of healthcare (Friedman 1995, 65-66)

Knowledge built on information from health informatics research can increase the effectiveness and efficiency of healthcare delivery. For example, a comprehensive review of the literature found that clinical decision support systems improved health practitioners' performance in 64 percent of studies (Garg et al. 2005). Moreover, this same review showed that systems with automatic prompts were more likely to improve performance than systems requiring users' activation (Garg et al. 2005). Thus, health informatics research has the power to greatly enhance the quality of healthcare and to increase its cost-effectiveness.

Health informatics research has several names and subspecialties:

- Bioinformatics research
- Biomedical informatics research
- Clinical informatics research

- Consumer health informatics research
- Dental informatics research
- Healthcare informatics research
- Imaging informatics research
- Medical informatics research
- Nursing informatics research
- Pharmacy informatics research
- Public health informatics research
- Veterinary informatics research

Health informatics research is emerging as the most current and inclusive name.

Early History

In Germany, Karl Steinbuch first coined the term "informatik" for his computer science courses in 1957 (Widrow et al. 2005). Currently, informatik is still the term used in Germany for computer science. In France, in 1962, the term "informatique" came into usage to mean computer science and technology (Chamak 1999, 655). Concurrently, in the United States (U.S.), Walter Bauer named his new software company, Informatics (Bauer 1996, 76). The term "informatics" became widely used in the U.S. in the 1990s (Shortliffe and Blois 2006, 22–23).

Coiera writes that, although the term informatics is new, the study of health informatics dates to the very beginnings of medicine (Coiera 2003, xxi). He explains that health informatics began "the day that a clinician first wrote down some impressions about a patient's illness, and used these to learn how to treat their [sic] next patient" (Coiera 2003, xxi). As Coiera's comments suggest, health informatics is much more than the application of computers to health services delivery. Instead, health informatics is the systematic approach to the collection, organization, storage, use, and evaluation of health data, information, and knowledge.

Computers were introduced into medicine in the 1950s (Maojo and Kulikowski 2003, 515). Computers were seen as a natural match for healthcare because of the masses of data and the complexity of decision making. As early as 1971, Kaiser Permanente had compiled a data bank containing 1 million patient records (Fitzmaurice et al. 2002, 149).

One of the first persons to use the phrase "medical informatics" was Peter Reichertz, a German physician (Protti 1995, 441). An early theorist subsumed all health informatics under "medical informatics," stating that medical informatics dealt with "the systematic processing of information in medicine," with "medicine" in this context also meaning human science and healthcare organizations (Protti et al. 1994, 321). Some informaticians propose the term "biomedical informatics" as the current, accepted iteration of "medical informatics" (Shortliffe and Blois 2006, 23). However, just as the term "electronic health record" (EHR) has replaced the term "electronic medical record," so too has the term "health informatics" replaced the term "medical (biomedical) informatics". This text uses the term health informatics as the umbrella term for all the alternate terms and subspecialties.

Research activities, that currently would be classified as health informatics research, date to the 1800s. Thus, health informatics research actually preceded the introduction of computers into medicine and the coining of the term informatics. Health practitioners used the technology of the era to investigate health issues.

In 1854, Snow drew maps of a London district indicating the locations of cholera deaths and water pumps (Brody et al. 2000, 65). Snow was able to show that cholera mortality was related to the water source. (See figure 1.1 for Snow's map.) Current researchers also use maps—in the form of geographic information systems (GIS) and global positioning systems (GPS). Using mapping technologies, environmental and geospatial scientists and epidemiologists are researching relationships between exposure to environmental contaminants and health outcomes (Nuckols et al. 2004). For example, researchers in Alaska have investigated the association between exposure to traffic air pollution and the diagnosis of asthma in children (Gordian et al. 2006).

Also in the mid-1800s, Villermé analyzed French census data. Mortality was highest in areas where citizens paid the least in a special tax on the wealthy (Krieger 2001). Villermé concluded that variations in annual mortality rates were associated with economic status, even taking into account epidemics (Coleman 1982, 10). In another study based on the census data, Villermé looked at the relationship between the occupation of the head of the household and life expectancy (probable average years of life for a group). To study life expectancy, Villermé categorized all the members of a household as belonging to the occupation of the head of the household. Thus, if the head of a household was a manufacturer, all the infants, children, youth, and adults in that household were "manufacturers." If the head of a household was a spinner [person who spins cloth

Figure 1.1. Snow's map of cholera mortality and water pumps

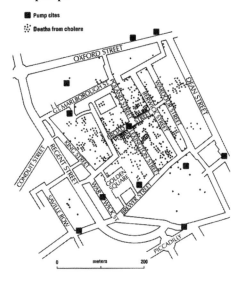

fabrics], all the members of the household were "spinners." In this way the short lives of infants and children, many of whom died very young in the past, were calculated into the life expectancies. Using this method of calculation, Villermé found the following life expectancies:

- 28.2 years for "manufacturers, merchants, directors, etc."
- 17.6 years for "factory workers, unspecified"
- 9.4 years for "day laborers"
- 1.3 to 1.9 years for "spinners, weavers, and locksmiths" [Villermé's classic 1840 work, *Tableau de L' État Physique et Moral des Ouvriers,* 251, 376-385 (Table of the Physical and Moral State of Workers) quoted in Antonovsky 1967].

Villermé concluded that members of households in some occupations lived longer than members of households in other occupations (1840, 251). Note that as this type of investigation was in its very rudimentary beginnings, terms such as "life expectancy" and "infant mortality" had not yet been clearly defined. However, in current terminology, Villermé was mining the census data.

Data mining is the extraction and analysis of large volumes of data with the intention of identifying hidden and sometimes subtle relationships or patterns and using those relationships to predict behaviors. Data mining can involve sophisticated statistical techniques. For example,

Stringham and Young mined Medicare Provider Analysis and Review (MedPAR) data to determine whether cases were being shifted to higher paying reimbursement categories because of nosocomial urinary tract infections (2005). Based on their study, the researchers recommended that the Centers for Medicare and Medicaid Services discontinue reimbursing hospitals for hospital-acquired infections.

In the US, the Agency for Healthcare Research and Quality (AHRQ) (and its predecessors) have funded research, development, and evaluation of health informatics since 1968 (Fitzmaurice et al. 2002, 144). The topics of funded research include:

- Health information systems, such as the automation of clinical laboratory, radiology, and critical care
- Decision support and quality assessment, such as computer-aided decision making and quality assurance and improvement
- EHRs and integrated information systems, such as standards and health information privacy (Fitzmaurice et al. 2002, 149).

For example, Lawrence Weed's work on the problem-based medical record was a funded project (Fitzmaurice et al. 2002, 149).

Records in Research

Recordkeeping has increased during the past 100 years in healthcare. Originally, physicians kept records to remind themselves of the care they provided to their patients. They believed that they could replicate the effective care of one patient in future patients with the same or similar condition. In 1918, as part of the hospital standardization program, the American College of Surgeons inspected the hospitals' patient records to evaluate the quality of care. Since then, health records have become the basis of communication among the healthcare, reimbursement, legal action, education, and research teams. In addition, other types of records have become common in healthcare and health-related organizations. These types of records include documents derived from data extracted from health records and documents of the organizations' operations and business transactions. The healthcare industry has a plethora of data waiting for analysis interpretation into information and knowledge. (See table 1.1 for sources of records.)

Health Records

Health records exist at individual and aggregate levels. At the individual level, health records are one practitioner's treatment of one patient or client. Health records can also represent a team of health personnel treating one patient or client, such as in a hospital. Aggregate records include registries, indexes, and administrative records derived from patient records.

Practitioners have used various terms for health records, such as case books, case histories, charts, clinical case histories, clinical charts, medical records, patient notes, and patient records. Clinicians use health records to document the care to individual patients or clients. In the modern continuum of care, this documentation serves as a means of communication for the healthcare team. Subsequently, the members of the team can use the records to replicate or improve the delivery of care to other patients.

The use of data in health records parallels the history of medicine. With the development of writing, ancient physicians and scribes could record diseases and their treatments. For example, as early as 3000 before the current era (BCE), scribes recorded on papyrus the medical and surgical treatments of Egyptian physicians (Haas 1999). The papyruses depict the

Table 1.1.   Sources of records

Health Records or Derived from Health Records	Healthcare Business, Operations, and Transactions Records
Health records	Claims and claims data
Disease index	Cost reports
Operation index	Chargemasters and superbills
Physician index	Health plan enrollment data
Cancer registry	Benefit administration reports
Disease registry	Remittance advices
Trauma registry	Adjudication decisions
Master patient (person) index	Contracts
	Patient accounts
	Accreditation surveys
	Certification surveys
	Quality and risk reports
	Credentialing reports
	Utilization reports
	Clinical pathways
	Emergency room and clinic logs
	Surgery schedules
	Obstetrical suite records
	Audit trails
	Supply catalogs
	Academic course catalogs
	Brochures and flyers

use of enemas and douches, with hydrotherapy being popular in Egypt (Todd 1921, 462). In the Ebers papyrus, dating to 1550 BCE, almost 900 prescriptions for various conditions are listed (Desnos 1972, 7). Several passages describe prescriptions of combinations of oatmeal, wheat, gum, honey, yellow ochre, and other substances for urinary retention and excessive urination (Desnos, 7–8).

Of special interest to health informatics professionals who study medical terminologies is the Edwin Smith papyrus. The Edwin Smith papyrus is a surgical textbook describing 48 surgical cases (Feldman and Goodrich 1999). As Atta explains, it is the first medical document to exhibit scientific methodology and systematic organization (1999, 1190). The writer used organizing principles, anatomical region, and severity to group and arrange the surgical cases (Atta 1999, 1190). Thus, a hierarchy was created. Furthermore, the writer structured each case in a specific order: Title, Examination, Diagnosis, Treatment, and Glosses (explanatory notes). This writer's order was the first example of structured data entry.

In 2700 BCE in China, Shen Nung studied the medicinal properties of plants, testing their actions on his own body. He is credited with recording 113 different prescriptions (Chan 1939, 563). In the seventh century of the current era (CE), Chinese authors, reflecting Indian medicine, also describe the surgical treatment of pterygium:

> Using a chicken (feather) turn and cut it, near the black part of the eye and that white part of the eye—, the membrane gets together on its own. With the help of a hook-shaped needle, cut it off and (then the patient can) see things (Sun Simiao quoted in Deshpande 2000, 377).

Writing in the Middle East in approximately 900 CE, the physician Al-Razi described clinical examinations in his text (Abdel-Halim 2006, 289). For example, to diagnose multiple bladder stones, he wrote, "and you detect that [presence of more than one stone] by your finger, because it will crackle so you then know it" (quoted in Abdel-Halim 2006, 289).

Individual health records, also known as case histories, are available from the 16th century through the present (Ackerknecht 1967, 213). Health records contain data on the patients' complaints and treatments rendered from the point of view of a practitioner. Often, health records include patients' complaints, in their own words.

In addition to the documentation about care and health status, health records contain demographic data such as gender; age; race, ethnicity, or nationality; marital status; residence; occupation; and religion. The details in these records provide insights into the practice of medicine, culture and customs, politics, economics, and technology. The insights can be used to create a snapshot of one decade or to create a longitudinal view of changing trends. Researchers can inspect one physician's practice, one hospital, one city, one region, or one country, or they can compare and contrast the various practices and trends of entities.

Published studies demonstrate the use of health records in research over time. These studies used paper-based records and EHRs from public health departments, insurance companies, sidelines of athletic fields, physician offices, and hospitals.

Sawyer reports on his review of one English physician's case histories (1983, 20). The physician, Richard Napier, practiced in the early 1600s. He kept unusually detailed and meticulous records of the more than 60,000 patients he treated. Of particular note, he recorded the patients' complaints in their own words and included their demographic data, such as age, residence, sex, major complaint, and past problems (Sawyer 1983, 20–21). From their comments, the previously unrealized proliferation and hierarchy of medical personnel can be discovered: "licensed and unlicensed doctors, clergymen-physicians, bonesetters, barbers, surgeons, apothecaries, wise men and women, herbalists, midwives, and gentle ladies" (Sawyer 1983, 20).

Public health records from 12 consecutive months in 1928 through 1931 were studied to obtain information on the rate of surgical procedures (Collins 1938, 124). At the time of the study, rates of surgical procedures per 1,000 persons were only available for Army and Navy service personnel (Collins 123). The study involved 8,758 white families (39,185 individuals) in 18 U.S. states and 130 localities, representing urban and rural communities from metropolises to unincorporated farming areas. Visiting public health nurses recorded data in their periodic visits (every two to four months; 124, 143). There were 65.0 surgical procedures per 1,000 persons with frequency of surgical procedure increasing with income and urban setting (143).

In the early 1930s, Britten and Goddard studied the health examinations of life insurance policy holders (1932). They looked at the frequency of certain diseases and conditions by age, gender, occupation, weight, and mortality. Of interest are some of the categories of "impairments," such as simple goiter, visceroptosis, nervousness, habitual use of laxatives, and weak rings (inguinal hernia; 1932, 238-240). The researchers concluded that health examinations could not serve as absolute measures of the health of a population. However, health examinations could provide information on relative comparisons of the rates of health conditions by groups in populations (Britten and Goddard 1932, 245–246).

Bolin and Goforth described how team physicians and athletic trainers documented the sideline care of athletes (2005, 405). They surveyed the 11 member schools of the Atlantic Coast Conference on the evaluation of injuries, dispensation of medications, availability of health records, and means and timing of documentation. Of the 11 schools, 5 had EHRs, 6 briefly documented on the sideline during the game and then composed a full note after the game, and all 11 had access to the athletes' key medical data (allergies) on the sideline (406). The researchers recommended two ways to manage clinical information on the sideline: laminated cards and EHRs on handheld computers (409).

Researchers investigated the feasibility of using a generic structured data-entry application in a general pediatrics practice (Roukema et al. 2006, 15). In the outpatient pediatric clinic, four pediatricians each entered data for eight new patients, first into the traditional paper record and then immediately into the electronic record. The researchers found that 44 percent of patient data was identical in the paper and electronic records, 25 percent was only in the paper record, and 31 percent was only in the electronic record. In the electronic record, the patient history lacked more data than the physical examination. They surmised that, because of the narrative nature of patient histories, writing in the paper record was easier than navigating the application (19). They concluded that a generic structured data-entry application appeared possible for a general pediatrics practice.

One researcher reported on an investigation that compared the capture of clinical information in two documentation systems (Silfen 2006). The sites of the investigation were two community hospital emergency departments. One hospital had a documentation system that was paper-based and template-driven and the other hospital had an EHR. The documentation systems were evaluated on their respective abilities to capture accurate data that could be subsequently coded to the American

Medical Association's evaluation and management codes. There was no statistically significant difference in the accuracy rates of the two documentation systems (665).

Retrospective review of health records, paper and electronic, is a common method of research in healthcare. However, researchers have found that key data are not documented (Watzlaf et al. 1996; Oral et al. 2003; Berner et al. 2005; Tully and Cantrill 2006). The absence of these data is a critical problem that researchers must consider as they design their studies.

For example, health information researchers found that data such as occupation, menopausal status, estrogen receptor and progesterone receptor values, and other items were not always documented in the health record or cancer registry abstract for African-American women diagnosed with breast cancer (Watzlaf et al. 1996). These data would be essential for studies of cancer.

Other researchers found that health records contained inadequate documentation to explain the cause of pediatric fractures and, thereby, to rule out abuse (Oral et al. 2003). This inadequate documentation is problematic for studies about abuse as a public health issue or as a legal issue.

Researchers assessed the completeness of documentation in electronic records (Berner et al. 2005). The performance of clinical decision support systems (CDSSs) depends on the data provided to the algorithms in the CDSS. The researchers specifically examined the support system's recommendations for therapy in gastrointestinal bleeding. The absence of key data "resulted in inappropriate and unsafe recommendations" in almost 77 percent of encounters (Berner et al. 2005, 43). The researchers concluded that missing data can affect the accuracy of clinical decision support systems that were designed to reduce medication errors.

Researchers assessed the content and operational validity of 14 indicators of prescribing appropriateness (Tully and Cantrill 2006, 87-88). Using the indicators, the study assessed the appropriateness of 132 new prescriptions for 61 patients being discharged from a hospital in the United Kingdom. Although the indicators were determined to have content validity, their operational validity, or capability of being implemented in practice, was questionable because necessary data were absent from the medical documentation (91). Of the 38 prescriptions (29 percent) for 13 patients who failed at least 1 appropriateness indicator, most failed because data were missing in the records. The researchers concluded that their findings had implications for evidence-based assessment as the physicians in the study stated that the missing data were unlikely to ever be documented in the records.

Some databases and most registries are derived from health records. Researchers can use these databases and registries to conduct primary or secondary research. The researchers who originally gathered the data conducted **primary research** and their data are primary data. On the other hand, analyzing the data of other researchers is known as **secondary research**.

Analysis of secondary data is a powerful tool because it allows researchers to mine large databases at the regional, state, and national levels. For example, Zhan and Miller (2003) analyzed 7.45 million uniform hospital discharge abstracts. The source of these data was the 2000 Healthcare Cost and Utilization Project Nationwide Inpatient Sample developed by the Agency for Healthcare Research and Quality. In this study, one finding among several was that excess length of stay attributable to medical injuries ranged from 0 days to 10.89 days.

Health information researchers used data from the 1994 Health Care Cost Utilization Project-3 (HCUP-3) study (Rudman and Davey 2000). The HCUP-3 data are medical record data from inpatient hospital discharges. The researchers were investigating the type of injury or illness and medical cost of domestic violence. They reported that for females, mental disorder, trauma, and pregnancy complications accounted for more than two thirds of the admissions, and for all victims the average cost of the hospitalization was $8,159.81 (6–7).

There are also obstacles in the use of databases and registries derived from health records in research. For example, researchers studied diagnostic tests to determine a prediction rule for the treatment of pediatric bacterial meningitis (Oostenbrink et al. 2003). The researchers asked, for which children should lumbar puncture be performed and empirical antibiotic treatment begun, so that no cases of bacterial meningitis are missed (502)? For diagnostic research, the researchers identified four problems with hospital databases: (1) selection of the subjects is biased because final diagnoses are recorded rather than the sign or symptom prompting the test; (2) selection of the subjects is also biased because not all patients receive the same work-up and subsequent diagnostic testing is predicated on results of earlier tests; (3) absence of blinding (see chapter 6); and (4) nonrandom missing data (501). In another investigation, researchers conducted a systematic review of studies, specifically those focusing on race or ethnicity, based on the administrative and secondary databases of the U.S. Veterans Health Administration (Long et al. 2006). There were 114 studies (1992–2004) that met the study's inclusion criteria (129–130). In 48 studies (42 percent), the researchers were unable to determine whether the data set included missing data on race or ethnicity (130). This absence is significant, given that in the studies for which missing data were reported, the rate ranged from 0 percent to 48 percent. Without explicit and clear information on the number of missing data, readers are unable to assess potential biases in the studies' results (130).

Despite the problems identified, thousands of studies have followed methods similar to these studies. They demonstrate the importance of health record data and health databases in research and their potential for improving the quality of patient care.

Financial Records

Financial records related to the delivery of health services exist at several levels: individual providers; local, state, and federal governmental agencies; and private insurers, payers, and professional associations. A prime example is the previously mentioned MedPAR data. Researchers should be aware that, in order to query the databases and to transform the data into information, they must understand the underlying structure of the data and how they were collected. Each data set has its own unique characteristics. Access to data sets, especially proprietary financial records such as the claims data of providers and insurance companies, is tightly controlled and may present an obstacle to researchers.

Finances affect the healthcare delivery system. Using financial records, researchers have studied the effects of payment systems and legislation on the financial viability of providers and the quality of patient care (Melzer et al. 2004; Cromwell et al. 2006; Seshamani et al. 2006). They have also investigated the economic impact that healthcare organizations have on their geographic localities (Holmes et al. 2006). Other studies have examined the internal operations of healthcare systems and the financial aspects of EHRs (Proenca et al. 2005; Hillestad et al. 2005). As representative examples of the myriad of topics that researchers could investigate, these studies will be briefly described.

Researchers studied the relationship between reimbursement under the resource-based relative value scale (RBRVS) and the costs of care for pediatric patients with diabetes mellitus (Melzer et al. 2004). Care was delivered through an endocrinology specialty practice using a multidisciplinary team. The researchers used financial data from billing records and income and expense reports of one physician practice. They found that the RBRVS payments covered the expenses for the physicians' time seeing the patients in the hospital and in the clinic. However, the reimbursement under RBRVS was insufficient for the expenses related to the nonphysician members of the team and the facility (138–139). They concluded that under RBRVS the model of multidisciplinary care may not be financially viable (140).

By reviewing Medicare cost reports, researchers studied the impact of the Balanced Budget Act (BBA) of 1997 on resident training in U.S. teaching hospitals (Cromwell et al. 2006). The researchers found that, despite a cap on the number of residents and reduction in the graduate medical education payment rates, the number of residents in training continued to increase after the passage of the act. The researchers noted that Congress made special exceptions to the caps and restored payment reductions, thus offsetting the effects of the BBA. The researchers concluded that resident training is profitable for teaching hospitals because the Medicare Graduate Medical Education (GME) subsidy generates almost $50,000 for one new resident after paying the resident's stipend and fringe benefits (126).

Another study involving the BBA of 1997 examined its financial strain on hospitals and their patients' mortality in one state (Seshamani et al. 2006). The researchers performed a statistical analysis of 30-day mortality rates, using hospital discharge and financial data and information from death certificates. The researchers concluded that lower Medicare reimbursement under the BBA did not result in higher 30-day mortality rates for four common, high-mortality conditions (697-698).

Researchers studied the economic impact of the closure of a rural hospital on its geographic location (Holmes et al. 2006). These researchers used U.S. census data; Medicare cost reports; the On-line Survey, Certification and Reporting System (OSCAR) Provider Service File of the Centers for Medicare and Medicaid services; and hospital data from the American Hospital Association (AHA). Economic health was determined by various measures, such as per-capita income, unemployment rates, the size of the labor force, and the county's population (471). The study's time period was 1992–1998 and involved 134 counties (475). The researchers found that closures of the only hospital in a county (sole hospital) decreased per-capita income by $703 and increased unemployment by 1.6 percentage points (477–478). Hospital closures in counties that had other hospitals did not adversely affect the county's economy (478–479). The researchers conclude that those who set health policy should consider the economic impact, especially on rural areas, of hospital regulations (481).

The effects of collaborations among hospitals on their costs was studied (Proenca et al. 2005). The researchers differentiated between collaborations through systems and collaborations through networks, with networks being the less stable relationship requiring more coordination. They used data from the American Hospital Association (AHA) on 1,338 private hospitals and Medicare cost reports. Hospitals that used systems to provide more services had lower costs (1254). For hospitals using networks, the costs initially decline, but then rose as the problems of coordination increased (1254–1255). The researchers concluded that their study had implications for hospital managers as they evaluate collaborative strategies (1255).

Researchers examined the potential health and financial benefits of EHRs (Hillestad et al. 2005). They used several sources of data including the following data sets: Medical Expenditure Panel Survey (MEPS) 1999 Inpatient File, 2000 AHA Hospital Survey, and the Healthcare Cost and Utilization Project (HCUP) 2000 National Inpatient Sample (1105). Using these data sources, the researchers calculated the savings related to increased efficiency in healthcare, reduced medication errors, improved preventive care, and management of chronic diseases and calculated the costs of adopting EHR systems for hospitals and physicians. They concluded that the potential cumulative net savings over 15 years was $371 billion for hospitals and $142 billion for physicians (1114).

These studies are only a mere indicator of the myriad topics and databases available to health informatics researchers. However, the studies do show that health informatics researchers have a fertile resource in financial records for topics and data. Moreover, the data that financial records provide are well worth the investment in learning their underlying structures and in expending the time to obtain the permission to use them. Exploring the relationships among health, finance, quality, policy, providers, and society builds the health informatics body of knowledge.

Research Frame

A **research frame** is the overarching structure of a research project. Another term for research frame is **paradigm**. A research frame comprises the theory or theories underpinning the study, the models illustrating the factors and relationships of the study, the assumptions of the field and the researcher, the methods, and the analytical tools. The research frame is a view of reality for the research and his or her discipline.

A field's body of knowledge is built on research. Research is conducted within frames. Each field has its own theories, models, assumptions, methods, and analytical tools. Fields even have preferred means of disseminating knowledge; some fields prefer books, others prefer journal articles.

Building a Body of Knowledge

A profession is defined as having a body of knowledge and an ethical code (Wilensky 1964, 138). The knowledge is coherent and systematic; it is acquired through an approved or predetermined educational program. An ethical code comprises professional norms. Professionals look to their colleagues or to their professional association for judgments of their ideas or work (Hall 1968, 93).

These characteristics are important to research because research builds a body of knowledge. Researchers follow ethical codes, as will be discussed in chapter 13. Moreover, research, prior to being accepted as part of the body of knowledge, is judged by professionals in the field. This judgment occurs in peer review and critical analyses. Thus, research in health informatics is fundamental to the field's evolution as a profession.

Professional Definition

Professionals' jobs are based on systematic knowledge that is attained through education (Wilensky 1964, 138). Professionals apply this body of knowledge as they complete their tasks and assignments. Researchers within a field consciously build and expand the field's body of knowledge. By definition, a field without a body of knowledge is an occupation. This body of knowledge gives a profession an exclusive area of competence (Wilensky 1964, 138).

Within a field's body of knowledge, there are underlying assumptions, key theorists, dominant theories, commonly accepted models and methods, operationalized and standardized definitions and measures, germinative articles, customary statistical approaches, and usual means of dissemination of information. Professionals within the field constantly manipulate these concepts as they conduct or read research. Through reading the articles in research journals, professionals become fluent and adept in the conceptual tools of their field. Continued exposure to the body of knowledge aids the new health informatics professional in this maturation. This text emphasizes the body of knowledge by providing examples of research and by summarizing research articles.

Knowledge of research supports evidence-based practice. Health informatics professionals can look at evidence-based practice from two points of view. They can be the persons using the evidence in their own practice or their systems can provide the needed evidence for the practice of other health personnel.

For example, in the first view, health informaticians can use the evidence provided by the study of Thakkar and Davis (2006). These researchers investigated the perceived benefits, risks, and barriers to the implementation of EHRs in hospitals. They found that the greatest perceived benefits of EHRs were interoperability and improved quality of care (5). They also found that as the size of the hospital increased, the perceived benefit of "medical staff's work efficiency and time management" decreased (5-6). In terms of evidence-based practice, health informatics professionals who are implementing EHRs in their hospitals should consider emphasizing, in their communications, the EHR's interoperability and improved quality and specifically addressing concerns about the medical staff's work efficiency and time management. Researchers also discussed the role of health informatics professionals as clinical informationists (Giuse et al. 2005). These researchers described a role that integrated expertise in clinical literature, querying medical databases, and linking expert systems to clinical information systems. The resulting integration and synthesis of the expertise of information specialists and informatics tools has the potential to deliver health information to the point of care.

Health informatics professionals can also support the evidence-based practice of other health personnel (Bakken 2001; Choi et al. 2005). Bakken contended that

an informatics infrastructure is essential for evidence-based practice (199). Moreover, she defined evidence as "synthesized information," including the practitioners' past experiences as information (199–200). In this perspective, expert systems would allow practitioners to analyze the health records of their former patients for applicable courses of care as well as clinical guidelines (Bakken 2001, 199–200). Researchers investigated how concept-oriented terminologies could support data exchange between home health and other sites of care in the continuum of care (Choi et al. 2005, 411). The researchers found that the data set used in home health, the Outcomes and Assessment Information Set (OASIS-B1) could be represented in the semantic structures of the Logical Observation Identifiers, Names, and Codes (LOINC; 414). The capability of integrating the data from the home health data set supports the creation of a comprehensive health record and, thus, evidence-based practice.

Research helps health informatics professionals be more effective and efficient as they perform their duties. Understanding research aids health informatics professionals whenever they use data or information to answer questions or to make decisions. Moreover, the step-by-step approach of research supports systematic gathering, analysis, and synthesis of data. Evidence-based practice and research are mutually supportive processes.

Research and Theories

Research is a way to create knowledge. Research is the systematic process of investigation that discovers, interprets, or revises data, such as facts, behaviors, or events. Research includes application such as development, testing, and evaluation. The purpose of research is to build **generalizable** knowledge.

Health informatics research includes the management of all aspects of health, health data, and health services through the application of computer science, information systems, and communication technologies to health service delivery. Health informatics research uses a broad meaning of the term **technology**, so the field includes practice guidelines; healthcare terminologies and standardized vocabularies, classifications, and nomenclatures; protocols; methods; and procedures (Coiera 2003, xxi).

A **theory** is the systematic organization of knowledge that predicts or explains behavior or events. Theories are the means to organize knowledge and explain the relationships among concepts. Present in all fields of study, theories explain what people have observed. In addition, they provide definitions, relationships, and boundaries. In other words, theories systematically organize everything that is known about a concept. Formally defined, theories are:

- Concepts that are abstract ideas generalized from particular instances
- Interrelationships that are assumed to exist among these concepts
- Consequences that are assumed to follow logically from the relationships proposed in the theory (Amatayakul and Shah 1992, 8)

The best theories simplify the situation, explain the most facts in the broadest range of circumstances, and most accurately predict behavior (Singleton and Straits 2005, 20).

In their practice, health informatics professionals draw on the theories from the many fields associated with healthcare, medicine, nursing, public health, and epidemiology; computer science, mathematics, engineering, and decision support; management and organizational behavior; sociology; physics; and psychology. Health informatics researchers use the theories from these fields to support and interpret their investigations from these fields. Some of the theories that these fields include are:

- Systems theory
- Information theories (Shannon and Weaver Information-Communication Model and Blum's model)
- Learning theories
- Behavioral theories
- Information processing or cognitive learning theories
- Adult learning theories
- Learning styles
- Change theories
- Diffusion of innovation (Englebardt and Nelson 2002, 5–25)

Each of these theories represents a perception of the world and an explanation of its phenomena. The theories provide different ways for health informatics researchers to understand the complex and turbulent healthcare sec-

tor in which they are attempting to describe and predict behaviors, actions, and outcomes.

Theories and research have a chicken-and-egg relationship. Theories are both the result and the foundation of research. Researchers begin with informed predictions or raw theories of what they believe will happen. As they collect observations and data, they refine their theories. Over time, the refined theories become more predictive of subsequent events than their previous embryonic versions.

Theories are practical and efficient. Theories allow researchers to explain and predict many events in simple and precise terms. In other words, theories organize knowledge. When knowledge is organized, both practitioners and researchers can access and use it. Without theories, health informaticians are merely speculating. Although speculation may be informed by experiences and some facts, it is nevertheless speculation. Thus, health informatics practitioners and researchers have a better understanding of their world through the concepts, interrelationships, and consequences that theories provide.

Research Methodology

Research methodology is the study and analysis of research methods and theories. Research methodologists tackle questions such as "What is research?" or "Which method of data collection results in the greatest, unbiased response rate?" For example, research methodologists examined various definitions of "scientifically based research" and how the definitions changed over time (Eisenhart and Towne 2003, 31, 35). In another example, research methodologists explored the desirability of combining methods from different research frames (Giddings and Grant 2007; Happ et al. 2006).

Generally, there are two types of research: **basic research** and **applied research**. These two types are ends of a continuum, not separate entities (Gay et al. 2006, 6). Therefore, the distinction between basic research and applied research is sometimes unclear. In essence, basic research focuses on the development of theories and their refinement. Applied research focuses on the implementation of the theories in practice. For example, as applied researchers, some health informatics professionals study questions they believe will improve the exchange of health data across the continuum of care. Another way to differentiate basic and applied research is that basic research answers the question "why" and applied research answers the questions "what" and "how."

Scientific Inquiry

Scientific inquiry involves making predictions, collecting and analyzing evidence, testing alternative theories, and choosing the best theory. Of primary importance is the testing of predictions using tight, well-designed research plans, and subjecting the results for external independent critique and replication. **Empiricism** is a concept related to scientific inquiry. Empiricism means "based on observed and validated evidence." For example, research based on experiments is empirical. Scientific inquiry and empiricism are the basis of many studies in health informatics research.

Combining scientific inquiry and empiricism to explain phenomena is the **quantitative approach**. As the word "quantitative" implies, the data often can be quantified and result in statistical or numerical results. In the quantitative approach, the desired outcome is objective knowledge. Another name for the quantitative approach is **positivism**. Researchers within the quantitative approach share assumptions about knowledge and reality. (See table 1.2 for assumptions.) A classic example of quantitative research is the Human Genome Project.

Another approach to scholarly inquiry is the **qualitative approach**. Researchers using the qualitative approach interpret nonnumerical observations. These nonnumerical observations include words, gestures, activities, time, space, images, and perceptions. These observations are placed in context. Another term for the qualitative approach is **naturalism**. Researchers using the qualitative approach share assumptions about knowledge and reality. (See table 1.2 for assumptions.) A classic example of qualitative research is Margaret Mead's anthropological study of the Polynesian culture of American Samoa in the early 1920s. Qualitative studies in informatics often involve assessing how patients and clinicians interact with EHRs, the Internet, or other electronic equipment. For example, using a qualitative approach, researchers described how patients with diabetes perceived their experience with an interactive, Web-based EHR (Ralston et al. 2004).

Mixed Methods Research

An emerging third approach is called **mixed methods research**. Mixed methods research is an approach in which researchers mix or combine quantitative and qualitative research techniques, methods, concepts, or language within one study and across related studies (Johnson and Onwuegbuzie 2004, 17). The mix or combination of approaches may occur either simultaneously or sequentially. For example, to collect data in a mixed methods approach, researchers may use both ethnographical observation and surveys to collect the data. Research supports that using mixed methods can increase the **rigor** (exactness or accuracy) of the findings (Moffatt et al. 2006, n.p.). Mixed methods researchers believe that the quantitative and qualitative approaches can be complementary.

Purists for both the quantitative and qualitative approaches strongly believe the opposite of the mixed methods researchers. Purists believe that the approaches should not be mixed (Johnson and Onwuegbuzie 2004, 14). For purists, the approaches' fundamentally different assumptions about knowledge and reality make them incompatible—the so-called "incompatibility thesis" (Howe 1988, 10). Giddings and Grant characterize mixed methods research as a Trojan horse for positivism (2007, 52). In essence, they believe mixed methods research undermines the philosophical foundations of the qualitative approach (2007, 52).

Mixed methods research may be suited to investigations into the complex phenomena in healthcare (McKibbon and Gadd 2004, n.p.). Multiple perspectives and types of evidence, such as sociobehavioral data, numerical outcome measures, and technical factors, may be needed to study the multifaceted interactions between persons and health information and communication technologies (Happ et al. 2006, S43). An example of mixed methods research is a study on the role of computerized

Table 1.2.   Comparison of assumptions in quantitative and qualitative research approaches

Quantitative	Qualitative
Single truth exists	Multiple truths exist simultaneously
Single truth applies across time and place	Truths are bound to place and time (contextual)
Researchers can adopt neutral, unbiased stances	Neutrality is impossible because researchers choose their topics of investigation
Chronological sequence of causes can be identified	Influences interact within one another to color researchers' views of the past, present, and future

physician order entry (CPOE) systems in introducing the risk of medication errors (Koppel et al. 2005, 1197). The researchers conducted a qualitative and quantitative study of the interaction between house staff and the CPOE system at a tertiary-care teaching hospital. They found that the CPOE system facilitated 22 types of medication error risks (1199).

The purpose of the research determines the approach. Research that investigates numerically measurable observations or tests **hypotheses** is often quantitative. Research that is exploratory and preliminary often begins with a qualitative investigation. Mixed methods research combines research techniques and concepts from both quantitative and qualitative approaches to investigate complex phenomena.

Relationship Among Theories and Models

A **model** is a representation of a theory in a visual format. Models can portray theories with objects, can be smaller-scaled versions, or can be graphic representations. A model includes all of a theory's known properties. An example of a model is the **Bayesian network** for the chief complaint of abdominal pain (Sadeghi et al. 2006, 406). The Bayesian network includes the complaintant's symptoms, medical history data, risk factors, possible diseases, and disposition. This model is a tool to support workers in emergecy departments as they make decisions about triage. (See figure 1.2 for the Bayesian network.) The data quality model of the American Health Information Management Association (AHIMA) is a less complex model. This model represents AHIMA's theory about what defines data quality. Experts at AHIMA have identified collection, analysis, application, and warehousing as the functions of data quality management and hypothesize that data quality will result if practitioners follow proper procedures within these activities. (See figure 1.3 for a model of the AHIMA theory.)

Reasoning

Researchers justify their decisions and conclusions through reasoning. They are arguing their case, in the manner of lawyers making a closing argument. To argue their cases, quantitative and qualitative researchers use two types of reasoning, **inductive** or **deductive**.

Inductive Reasoning

Inductive reasoning, or induction, involves drawing conclusions based on a limited number of observations. Inductive reasoning is "bottom up." Researchers using inductive reasoning begin with observations, detect patterns or clusters of relationships, form and explore tentative hypotheses, and generate provisional conclusions or theories.

Deductive Reasoning

Deductive reasoning, or deduction, involves drawing conclusions based on generalizations, rules, or principles. Deductive reason is "top down." Researchers using deductive reasoning begin with a theory, develop hypotheses to test the theory, observe phenomena related to the hypotheses, and validate or invalidate the theory.

Both inductive and deductive reasoning are important to research. Early exploratory research often takes an inductive approach. Once researchers have generated a theory, they use the deductive approach to prove or disprove the theory. Thus, the effective combination of induction and deduction is the basis of the research.

Timeframe

Another aspect of research is the timeframe of the study. There are two pairs of timeframes: **retrospective** versus **prospective** and **cross-sectional** versus **longitudinal**. Researchers select time frames based on the purpose of their study, practicality, and logistics. Researchers may combine the pairs of time frames. For example, a study may be described as retrospective and cross-sectional.

Studies within a retrospective timeframe look back in time. The retrospective reviews of health records previously discussed in this chapter are examples. In these studies, researchers:

- Recorded the number of surgeries that people recalled having

- Examined records of past health examinations to calculate the frequency of diseases for certain groups

- Requested that personnel on the sidelines during athletic events remember how they documented the injured athletes' care

Figure 1.2. The abdominal pain Bayesian network

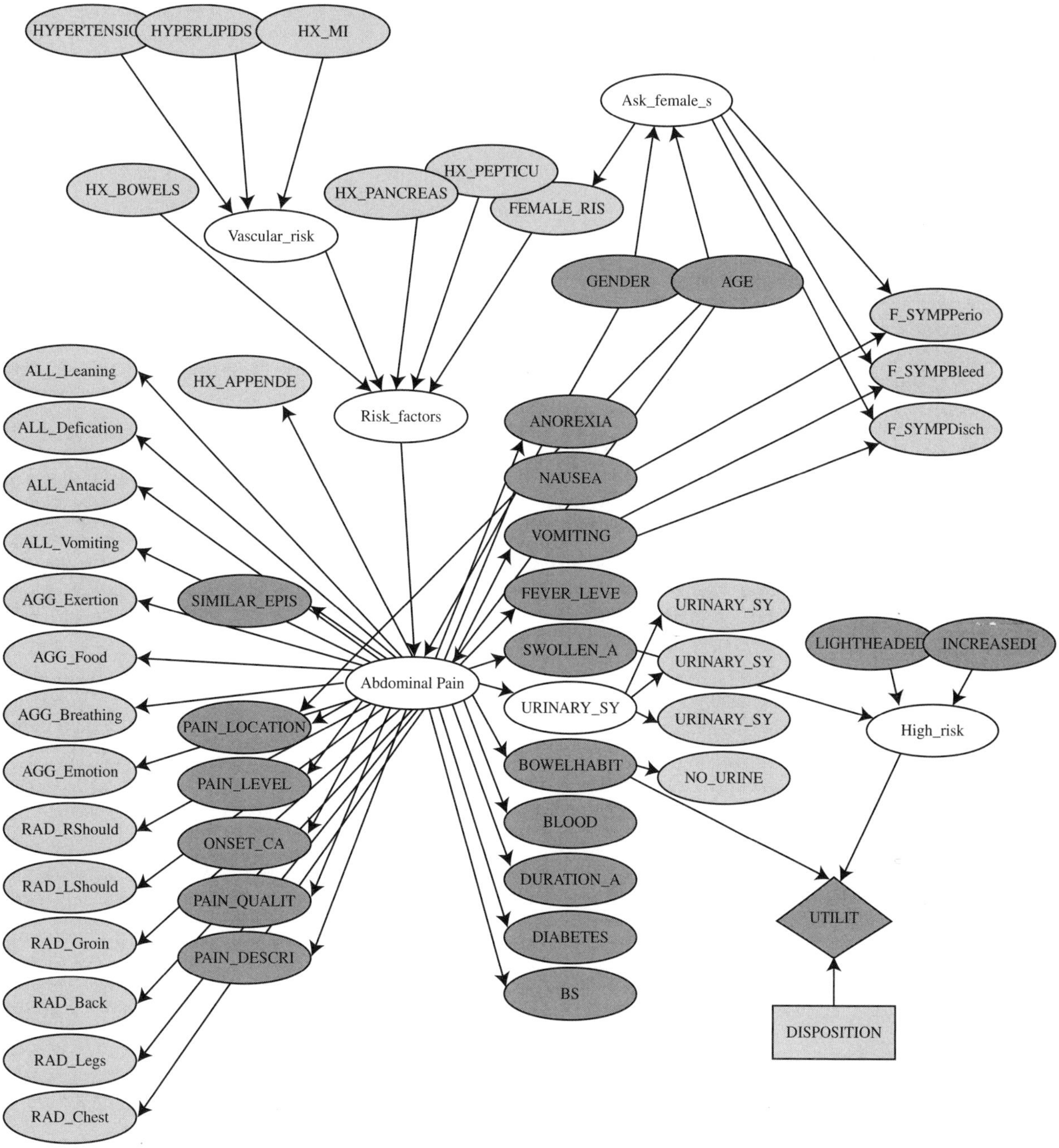

Figure 1.3.   AHIMA Data Quality Management Model

Source: AHIMA 1998.

Both the participants and the researchers were looking back in time. The studies were retrospective. For some types of questions, such as those related to historic events, a retrospective design is the only possible time frame.

In prospective research studies, participants are followed into the future to examine relationships between variables and later occurrences. For example, researchers identify individuals or subjects with certain risk factors and then follow these individuals or subjects into the future to see whether the disease, condition, or situation occurs. In health informatics research, investigators could identify risk factors for the implementation of EHR systems. They could identify hospitals with these risk factors and monitor the success or failure of the EHR implementation. Researchers conducted a study in which they prospectively assigned consecutively admitted patients to one of two groups (Oniki et al. 2003, 179). The nurses caring for one group of patients received periodic electronic reminders about the status of documentation of routine nursing tasks; the nurses caring for the other group did not (Oniki et al. 2003, 180). The researchers found fewer deficiencies in documentation for the group receiving an electronic reminder (Oniki et al. 2003, 181).

Research studies with a cross-sectional design collect data at one point in time. The previously described study of the documentation on the sidelines of athletic events was cross-sectional as well as retrospective. In another study, researchers investigated the role of EHRs in facilitating communications about medications between providers and patients (Arar et al. 2005). For the one point in time of the study, EHRs facilitated communication, especially among patients who took multiple medications (Arar et al. 2005, 19). However, cross-sectional studies

are snapshots and, as such, may collect data at an entirely unrepresentative point in time. The great advantage of cross-sectional studies is that they are efficient.

Longitudinal studies collect data from the same participants at multiple points in time. Researchers conducted two longitudinal case studies of the implementation of interorganizational clinical information systems (Sicotte et al. 2006, 558). They assessed risk factors over three years at one health information network composed of seven institutions and over two years at another (Sicotte et al., 560). The researchers found that the tool for risk analysis that they developed was useful and could increase the success of implementations of clinical information systems (Sicotte et al. 565). Longitudinal studies, while difficult to implement and time-consuming, avoid the problem of potentially capturing data at an unrepresentative point in time.

The time frame of a research study depends on the topic and the purpose of the researcher. Sometimes practical concerns, such as when the information is needed or the time available to the researcher, also affect the selection of a time frame. Time frames are often combined, such as retrospective and cross-sectional. Prospective and longitudinal studies, while more difficult to conduct, offer valuable insights and long-term perspectives.

Overview of the Research Process

Conceptually, researchers perform five major activities:

1. Defining the research question (problem)
2. Summarizing prior pertinent knowledge
3. Gathering data
4. Analyzing the data
5. Interpreting and presenting findings

However, because these major activities are so broad, most researchers divide them into more manageable components. Thus, the research process becomes orderly problem solving. In the verbal shorthand of researchers, these basic components are:

1. Defining the research question (problem)
2. Performing a literature review
3. Determining a research design and method
4. Selecting an instrument
5. Gathering data
6. Analyzing the data
7. Presenting results

The application of health information technology and systems should result in high-quality healthcare. To support this goal, researchers have identified future topics of health informatics research:

- Standardization of clinical vocabularies and coding

- Integration, comparability, and confidentiality of healthcare data across computer systems and sites of care

- Linkages of health data to support decision making, while protecting privacy and security

- Barriers and means to overcome barriers to the use of information technology and systems in the healthcare delivery system

- Best practices in information integration and in applications of computer and communication systems in the healthcare delivery system (Fitzmaurice et al. 2002, 157)

Summary

This chapter has introduced the health informatics professional to the foundations of health informatics research. It explained the importance of research to the future of the health informatics profession. Research frames within which researchers can conduct their research were described. Terms essential to understanding research, such as theory and model, were defined. Perhaps most important, examples of health informatics research were provided throughout the chapter so that readers can see concrete applications and also potential studies that they can undertake. The chapter closed with a discussion on directions in which current health informatics professionals can take future research.

References

Abdel-Halim, R.E. 2006 (February). Clinical methods and team work: 1,000 years ago. *American Journal of Surgery* 181(2):289–290.

Ackerknecht, E.H. 1967. A plea for a 'behaviorist' approach in writing the history of medicine. *Journal of the History of Medicine and Allied Sciences* 22(3):211–214.

AHIMA. 1998 (June 15). Practice brief: Data quality management model. Chicago: AHIMA.

Amatayakul, M., and M.A. Shah. 1992. *Research Manual for the Health Information Profession*. Chicago: American Health Information Management Association.

Antonovsky, A. 1967 (April). Social class, life expectancy, and overall mortality. *Milbank Memorial Fund Quarterly* 45(2, Part 1):31–73.

Arar, N.H., L. Wen, J. McGrath, R. Steinbach, and J. A. Pugh. 2005. Communicating about medications during primary care outpatient visits: The role of electronic medical records. *Informatics in Primary Care* 13(1):13–21.

Atta, H. M. 1999 (December). Edwin Smith surgical papyrus: The oldest known surgical treatise. *American Surgeon* 65(12):1190–1192.

Bakken, S. 2001 (May-June). An informatics infrastructure is essential for evidence-based practice. *Journal of the American Medical Informatics Association* 8(3):199–201.

Bauer, W.F. 1996 (April-June). Informatics: An early software company. *IEEE Annals of the History of Computing* 18(2):70-76 (Part of Biographies, E. Weiss, ed.: 67–76).

Berner, E.S., R.K. Kasiraman, F. Yu, M.N. Ray, and T.K. Houston. 2005. Data quality in the outpatient setting: Impact of clinical decision support systems. *AMIA Annual Symposium Proceedings*: 41–45.

Bolin, D., and M. Goforth. 2005, November. Sideline documentation and its role in return to sport. *Clinical Journal of Sport Medicine* 15(6):405–409.

Britten, R.H., and J.C. Goddard. 1932 (July). A new measure of the people's health: A critical summary of medical examination records. *Milbank Memorial Fund Quarterly Bulletin* 10(3):221–246.

Brody, H., M.R. Rip, P. Vinten-Johansen, N. Paneth, and S. Rachman. 2000 (July 1). Map-making and myth-making in Broad Street: The cholera epidemic, 1854. *Lancet* 356(9223):64–68.

Chamak, B. 1999 (October). The emergence of cognitive science in France: A comparison with the USA. *Social Studies of Science* 29(5):643–684.

Chan, L. 1939 (November). A brief history of Chinese herbs and medicine. *Bulletin of the Torrey Botanical Club* 66(8):563–568.

Choi, J., M.L. Jenkins, J.J. Cimino, T.W. White, and S. Bakken. 2005 (July-August). Toward semantic interoperability in home health care: Formally representing OASIS items for integration into a concept-oriented terminology. *Journal of the American Medical Informatics Association* 12(4):410–417.

Coiera, E. 2003. Guide to Health Informatics, 2nd ed. New York: Oxford University Press.

Coleman, W. 1982. *Death is a Social Disease*. Madison, WI: University of Wisconsin Press.

Collins, S.D. 1938 (April). The frequency of surgical procedures in a general population group: Based on records for 9,000 families in eighteen states visited periodically for twelve consecutive months, 1928-1931. *Milbank Memorial Fund Quarterly* 16(2):123–144.

Cromwell, J., W. Adamache, and E.M. Drozd. 2006 (Fall). BBA impacts on hospital residents, finances, and Medicare subsidies. *Health Care Financing Review* 28(1):117–129.

Deshpande, V. 2000. Ophthalmic surgery: A chapter in the history of Sino-Indian medical contacts. *Bulletin of the School of Oriental and African Studies, University of London* 63(3):370–388.

Desnos, E. 1972. Part I: The history of urology to the latter part of the nineteenth century. In the *History of Urology*, translated and edited by L.J.T. Murphy. Springfield, IL: Charles C. Thomas Publisher.

Eisenhart, M., and L. Towne. 2003 (October). Contestation and change in national policy on "scientifically based" education research. *Educational Researcher* 32(7):31–38.

Englebardt, S.P., and R. Nelson. 2002. *Health Care Informatics: An Interdisciplinary Approach*. St. Louis, MO: Mosby, Inc.

Feldman, R.P., and J.T. Goodrich. 1999 (July). The Edwin Smith surgical papyrus. *Child's Nervous System* 15(6-7):281–284.

Fitzmaurice, J. M., K. Adams, and J.M. Eisenberg. 2002 (March-April). Three decades of research on computer applications in health care: Medical informatics support at the Agency for Healthcare Research and Quality. *Journal of the American Medical Informatics Association* 9(2):144–160.

Friedman, C.P. 1995 (January-February). Where's the science in medical informatics? *Journal of the American Medical Informatics Association* 2(1):65–67.

Garg, A.X., N.K.J. Adhikari, H. McDonald, M.P. Rosas-Arellano, P.J. Devereaux, J. Beyene, J. Sam, and R. B. Haynes. 2005 (March 9). Effects of computerized clinical decision support systems on practitioner performance and patient outcomes: A systemic review. *Journal of the American Medical Association* 293(10):1223–1238.

Gay, L.R., G.E. Mills, and P. Airasian. 2006. *Educational Research: Competencies for Analysis and Applications*, 8th ed. Upper Saddle River, NJ: Pearson Prentice Hall.

Giddings, L.S., and B.M. Grant. 2007 (January-March). A Trojan horse for positivism? A critique of mixed methods research. *Advances in Nursing Science* 30(1):52–60.

Giuse, N.B., T.Y. Koonce, R.N. Jerome, M. Cahall, N.A. Sathe, and A. Williams. 2005 (May-June). Evolution of a mature clinical informationist model. *Journal of the American Medical Informatics Association* 12(3):249–255.

Gordian, M.E., S. Haneuse, and J. Wakefield. 2006. An investigation of the association between traffic exposure and the diagnosis of asthma in children. *Journal of Exposure Science and Environmental Epidemiology* 16(1):49–55.

Haas, L.F. 1999 (November). Payprus of Ebers and Smith. *Journal of Neurology, Neurosurgery and Psychiatry* 67(5):578.

Hall, R.H. 1968 (February). Professionalization and bureaucratization. *American Sociological Review* 33(1):92–104.

Happ, M.B., A.D. Dabbs, J. Tate, A. Hricik, and J. Erlen. 2006 (March-April). Exemplars of mixed methods data combination and analysis. *Nursing Research* 55(2 Suppl): S43–S49.

Hillestad, R., J. Bigelow, A. Bower, F. Girosi, R. Meili, R. Scoville, and R. Taylor. 2005 (October). Can electronic medical record systems transform health care? Potential health benefits, savings, and costs. *Health Affairs* 24(5):1103–1117.

Holmes, G.M., R.T. Slifkin, R.K. Randolph, and S. Poley. 2006 (April). The effect of rural hospital closures on community economic health. *Health Services Research* 41(2):467–485.

Howe, K.R. 1988 (November). Against the quantitative-qualitative incompatibility thesis or dogmas die hard. *Educational Researcher* 17(8):10–16.

Johnson, R.B., and A.J. Onwuegbuzie. 2004 (October). Mixed methods research: A research paradigm whose time has come. *Educational Researcher* 33(7):14–26.

Koppel, R., J.P. Metlay, A. Cohen, B. Abaluck, A.R. Localio, S.E. Kimmel, and B.L. Strom. 2005 (March 9). Role of computerized physician order entry systems in facilitating medication errors. *Journal of the American Medical Association* 293(10):1197–1203.

Krieger, N. 2001. Historical roots of social epidemiology: Socioeconomic gradients in health and contextual analysis. *International Journal of Epidemiology* 30(4):899–903.

Long, J.A., M.I. Bamba, B. Ling, and J.A. Shea. 2006 (February). Missing race/ethnicity data in Veterans Health Administration based disparities research: A systematic review. *Journal of Health Care for the Poor and Underserved* 17(1):128–140.

Maojo, V., and C.A. Kulikowski. 2003 (November-December). Bioinformatics and medical informatics: Collaborations on the road to genomic medicine? *Journal of the American Medical Informatics Association* 10(6):515–522.

McKibbon, K.A., and C.S. Gadd. 2004. A quantitative analysis of qualitative studies in clinical journals for the 2000 publishing year. *BMC Medical Informatics and Decision Making* 4(11):n.p.

Melzer, S.M., G.E. Richards, and M.L. Covington. 2004 (September). Reimbursement and costs of pediatric ambulatory diabetes care by using resource-based relative value scale: Is multidisciplinary care financially viable? *Pediatric Diabetes* 5(3):133–142.

Moffatt, S., M. White, J. Mackintosh, and D. Howel. 2006. Using quantitative and qualitative data in health services research – what happens when mixed method findings conflict? *BMC Health Services Research* 28(6):n.p.

Nuckols, J.R., M.H. Ward, and L. Jarup. 2004 (June). Using geographic information systems for exposure assessment in environmental epidemiology studies. *Environmental Health Perspectives* 112(9):1007–1015.

Oostenbrink, R., K.G.M. Moons, S.E. Bleeker, H.A. Moll, and D.E. Grobbee. 2003 (June). Diagnostic research on routine care data: Prospects and problems. *Journal of Clinical Epidemiology* 56(6):501–506.

Oniki, T.A., T.P. Clemmer, and T.A. Pryor. 2003 (March-April). The effect of computer-generated reminders on charing deficiencies in the ICU. *Journal of the American Medical Informatics Association* 10(2):177–187.

Oral, R., K.L. Blum, and C. Johnson. 2003 (June). Fractures in young children: Are physicians in the emergency department and orthopedic clinics adequately screening for possible abuse? *Pediatric Emergency Care* 19(3):148–153.

Proenca, E.J., M.D. Rosko, and C.E. Dismuke. 2005. Service collaboration and hospital cost performance: Direct and moderating effects. *Medical Care* 43(12):1250–1258.

Protti, D.J. 1995 (December). The synergism of health/medical informatics revisited. *Methods of Information in Medicine* 34(5):441–445.

Protti, D.J., J.H. Van Bemmel, R. Gunzenhuser, R. Vaux., H. Warner, J.V. Douglas, and E. Lang. 1994 (June). Can health/medical informatics be regarded as a separate discipline? *Methods of Information in Medicine* 33(3):318–326.

Ralston, J.D., D. Revere, L.S. Robins, and H.I. Goldberg. 2004 (May 15). Patients' experience with a diabetes support programme based on an interactive electronic medical record: Qualitative study. *British Medical Journal* 328(7449):1159–1163.

Roukema, J., R.K. Los, S.E. Bleeker, A.M. Van Ginneken, J. Van der Lei, and H.A. Moll. 2006 (January). Paper versus computer: Feasibility of an electronic medical record in general pediatrics. *Pediatrics* 117(1):15–21.

Rudman, W.J., and Davey, D. 2000. Identifying domestic violence within inpatient hospital admissions using medical records. *Women & Health* 30(4):1–13.

Sadeghi, S., A. Barzi, N. Sadeghi, and B. King. 2006 (May). A Bayesian model for triage decision support. *International Journal of Medical Informatics* 75(5):403–411.

Sawyer, R.C. 1983 (December). Ordinary medicine for ordinary people: Illness and its treatment in East Midlands, 1600-1630. *Society for the Social History of Medicine Bulletin* 33:20–23.

Seshamani, M., J.S. Schwartz, and K.G. Volpp. 2006 (June). The effect of cuts in Medicare reimbursement on hospital mortality. *Health Services Research* 41(3 Pt 1):683–700.

Shortliffe, E.H., and M.S. Blois. 2006. The computer meets medicine and biology: Emergence of a discipline. Ch. 1 in *Biomedical Informatics: Computer Applications in Health Care and Biomedicine,* edited by E.H. Shortliffe and J.J. Cimino. New York, NY: Springer Science+Business Media, LLC.

Sicotte, C., G. Pare, M-P. Moreault, and A. Paccioni. 2006 (September-October). A risk assessment of two interorganizational clinical information systems. *Journal of the American Medical Informatics Association* 13(5):557–566.

Silfen, E. 2006 (February). Documentation and coding of ED patient encounters: An evaluation of the accuracy of an electronic medical record. *American Journal of Emergency Medicine* 24(6):664–678.

Singleton, R.A., and B.C. Straits. 2005. *Approaches to Social Research,* 4th ed. New York: Oxford University Press.

Stringham, J., and N. Young. 2005 (Fall). Using Med-PAR Data as a measure of urinary tract infection rates: Implications for the Medicare inpatient DRG payment system. *Perspectives in Health Information Management* 2(12):1–14.

Thakkar, M., and D.C. Davis. 2006 (Summer). Risks, barriers, and benefits of EHR systems: A comparative study based on size of hospital. *Perspectives in Health Information Management* 3(5):1–19.

Todd, T.W. 1921 (October-December). Egyptian medicine: A critical study of recent claims. *American Anthropologist* 23(4):460–470.

Tully, M.P., and J.A. Cantrill. 2006 (April). The validity of explicit indicators of prescribing appropriateness. *International Journal for Quality in Health Care* 18(2):87–94.

Villermé, L.R. 1840. *Tableau de ÉtatPhysique et Moral des Ouvriers,* Tome Premier and Tome Second. Paris, France: Jules Renouard et. Cie.

Warner, H.R. 1995 (July-August). Medical informatics: A real discipline? *Journal of the American Medical Informatics Association* 2(4):207–214.

Watzlaf, V.J.M., A. Katoh, and F.D'Amico. 1996 (August). Obstacles encountered in the use of the medical record and cancer registry abstract in breast cancer research. *Topics in Health Information Management* 17(1):25–33.

Widrow, B., R. Hartenstein, and R. Hecht-Nielsen. 2005 (August). 1917 Karl Steinbuch 2005. *IEEE Computational Intelligence Society Newsletter* 3(3):5.

Wilensky, H.L. 1964 (September). The professionalization of everyone? *American Journal of Sociology* 70(2):137–158.

Zhan, C., and M.R. Miller. 2003 (Oct. 8). Excess length of stay, charges, and mortality attributable to medical injuries during hospitalization. *Journal of the American Medical Association* 290(14):1868–1874.

Chapter 2
Research Designs

Elizabeth J. Layman, PhD, RHIA, CCS, FAHIMA

Learning Objectives

- To provide overviews of the major research designs
- To differentiate the major research designs
- To discuss appropriate rationales that support the selection of a research design
- To provide relevant examples of the use of the research designs in health informatics research

Key Terms

Accuracy

Case mix

Case-control (retrospective) study

Causal-comparative research

Causal relationship

Central tendency

Confirmability

Confounding (extraneous, secondary) variable

Control group

Correlational research

Covariation

Credibility

Criterion variable

Dependability

Dependent variable

Descriptive research

Double-blind study

Ethnography

Evaluation research

Ex post facto

Experimental group

Experimental research

Exploratory

Feasibility

Generalizability

Historical research

Independent variable

Intervention

Interview

Natural (naturalistic) experiments (research)

Negative (inverse) relationship

Nonparticipant observation

Object

Observation

Observational research

Observer-expectancy effect

Outcome variables

Participant observation

Placebo

Positive (direct) relationship

Posttest

Predictor variables

Pretest

Primary source

Propriety

Quasi-experimental research

Random sampling

Randomization

Research design

Secondary source

Shallow data

Social desirability

Subject-expectancy effect

Survey

Transferability

Treatment

Triangulation

Utility

Variable

Introduction

Health informatics research is an intersection of the research from several disciplines—medicine, computer science, information systems, health information management, engineering, health services administration, nursing, and public health. Other disciplines with a connection to health informatics research include anthropology, biology, business and management, communications, economics, epidemiology, ethics, mathematics, organizational behavior, physics, psychology, sociology, and statistics. Many of the early and leading informatics researchers were trained in medicine, computer science, mathematics, and engineering. Consequently, the various methods of conducting research came about as a result of the varied experiences of researchers and practitioners. Moreover, research questions in health informatics cover a range of topics. Health informatics research is stimulating, dynamic, and endlessly varied. It is never dull.

Researchers can choose among many **research designs**. (See table 2.1 for a list of designs and corresponding examples.) Moreover, different disciplines, such as medicine, computer science, and nursing tend to emphasize and use different designs. Certain designs are better suited than others to answer certain types of questions or to solve certain types of problems.

Researchers can investigate the same broad question or problem using several different research designs. (See table 2.2 for a progression of studies on one topic.) The design chosen depends on the purpose of the research. How the problem or question is defined in the problem statement indicates the appropriate research design.

Again, the purpose of the research determines the appropriate research design. Thus, the choice of research design and research method depends on the research question or problem.

There are seven common research designs: **historical**, **descriptive**, **correlational**, **observational**, **evaluation**, **experimental**, and **quasi-experimental**. All of these designs have a role in health informatics research. Many research topics are suited to any one of these designs, whereas other research topics are more suited to one research design than another. Which design is appropriate depends on the problem and the researcher's definition of the problem.

Historical Research

Historical research investigates the past. Researchers examine **primary** and **secondary sources**. Primary sources are original sources, such as health records, patients' blogs, or eyewitness accounts. Secondary sources are derived from primary sources; secondary sources summarize, critique, or analyze the primary sources. This chapter is a secondary source because it describes and summarizes the original reports of others. (See table 2.3 for lists of sources.)

Process

Primary sources are superior to secondary sources. However, examining both primary and secondary sources lends credibility to studies. Multiple data sources that suggest the same chain of events are compelling evidence. For the reader, this convergence of evidence lends reasonableness and soundness to the researcher's conclusions.

Risse and Warner provided a list of several possible studies that could reconstruct clinical activities (1992).

- Reconstruct **case mixes** and physicians' criteria for admission from data in hospital admission records (Risse and Warner 1992,186)
- Identify, from the physicians' notes on the physical examination, key decision points in the physicians' decision-making processes (186)
- Identify, using health records, the diagnostic technologies, such as laboratory and pathology tests, radiologic films, stethoscopes, and electrocardiographs of the time period (186-187, 192, 194-195)
- Reconstruct referral patterns from health records and physicians' financial records (187-188)
- Trace shift from narrative descriptions of conditions and diseases to quantified physiologic signs (191-192)

Systematic entry of the data from these records would allow large-scale data mining and statistical analyses. Thus, Risse and Warner provide fertile grounds for future health informatics research.

The potential studies that Risse and Warner describe are based on data from health records and physicians' business records. These records exist in profusion from

Table 2.1. Designs of research and their applications

Design	Application	Method	Example in Healthcare
Historical	Understand past events	Case Study Biography	What factors led to the enactment of H.R.: Antitrust Criminal Penalty Enhancement and Reform Act of 2004 including the Standards Development Organization Advancement Act? How did Hurricane Katrina in 2005 advance the adoption of electronic health records in the United States?
Descriptive	Describe current status	Survey Observation	What barriers prevent the successful adoption of EHR systems in rural geographic areas? How do patients use health information on the Internet? How do health personnel respond to alerts?
Correlational	Determine existence and degree of relationship	Survey Secondary Analysis	What is the relationship between provider satisfaction and EHR systems? What is the correlation between the data in the OASIS B-1 data set and the semantic structures of LOINC?
Observational	Describe and detect patterns and regularities in existing situations or natural surroundings	Case Study Ethnography Nonparticipant Observation Participant Observation	How do providers interact with patients while using the EHR? How do nurses document in EHRs in intensive care units?
Evaluation	Evaluate effectiveness	Case Study	How has the implementation of an EHR system affected the enterprise's ability to deliver healthcare to underserved populations? Which implementation, incremental or systemwide, was most successful? What factors were predictive of successful implementations of clinical information systems for nursing documentation?
Experimental	Establish cause and effect	Randomized, Double-Blind, Clinical Trial Pretest-Posttest Control Group Method Solomon Four-Group Method Posttest-Only Control Group	Which interventions improved therapeutic monitoring? Does access to an EHR patient portal influence chronic disease outcomes? Does a clinical decision support system increase documentation of key data for patients with asthma when compared with usual practice?
Quasi-Experimental (Causal-Comparative)	Detect causal relationship	One-Shot Case Study One-Group Pretest-Posttest Static Group Comparison Nonparticipant Observation	What is the effect of structured data entry on the case-mix index? Does training on the Internet increase elder patients' search for and usage of online healthcare information?

the 16th century through the present (Ackerknecht 1967, 213). Based on daily documentation in health records, these studies provide data on actual events at the microscopic level rather than macroscopic overviews from idealized accounts. Generally, studies from health and business records could take snapshots at single points in time or could trace shifts over time.

Careful study of records from one era or decade would show for that single point in time the activities of:

- Clinical practice
- Perceptions
- Patient or client demographics
- Environments of hospitals or physician offices

Table 2.2.   Research designs in a progression of studies within one topic

Design	Example of Progression of Studies
Historical	The factors leading to the creation and expansion of The Medical Record (TMR) and the Regenstrief Medical Record System (RMRS) between 1970 and 1990.
Descriptive	A survey of physicians to determine how and to what degree they use the electronic health record.
Correlational	A study to determine the relationship among physicians' attributes, the setting, and the use of the electronic health record.
Observational	A study to observe how physicians actually document in an EHR in specific contexts, such as emergency departments, offices, or intensive care units.
Evaluation	A study to evaluate the efficacy of the implementation of an EHR in an academic health center.
Experimental	A study to compare the use of the EHR of two matched physician groups; one group trained in a low-barrier experimental computer laboratory and one group trained in a high-barrier experimental computer laboratory.
Causal-Comparative (Quasi-Experimental)	A study to compare the use of the EHR of a group of physicians in a low-barrier setting and of a group of physicians in a high-barrier setting.

To show shifts over time in these same activities, records from different decades could be dissected, analyzed, compared, and contrasted.

Health records are just one source of historiographic studies for health informatics researchers. Other examples of potential historical research in health informatics include investigations about the:

- Usage of the terms informatics, medical informatics, and health informatics

- Founding of informatics educational programs around the world

- Development of informatics codes of ethics

- Trends and development of standards organizations and their impact on the establishment of standards

- Development of individual terminologies and nomenclatures over time, especially those that no longer exist, such as the Standard Nomenclature of Diseases and Operations, and their influence on current terminologies and nomenclatures

In addition to using documents as a source of data, historians also use oral histories. Historians often

Table 2.3.   Primary and secondary sources

Primary Sources	Secondary Sources
Agency regulations Catalogs Charters Contracts Cost reports Curricular documents E-mail records Eyewitness accounts Handbooks Health records Laboratory reports Legislative bills, laws, or statutes Letters Logs Patient blogs Patient diaries Physician journals Physician accounting ledgers Reports	Disease index Operation index Physician index Cancer registry Disease registry Trauma registry Master patient (person) index Reviews Publicly available data sets: • HCUP • MEPS • NAMCS • NHAMCS and so on

interview individuals as a way of obtaining data, particularly to obtain eyewitness accounts. For example, researchers interviewed Seymour Rubinstein, one of the developers of WordStar, an early word processing software (Rubinstein 2006). Events associated with the company's rise and fall serve as caution signs to other software developers. Health informatics researchers may want to interview leaders in the field to record descriptions of key events in the leaders' own words.

Historical researchers also collect memoirs and autobiographies of leaders in health informatics. For example, one journal editor has published the memoirs of Mark Halpern, an early developer of hospital information systems, and the autobiography of Walter Bauer, one of the founders of Informatics, an early software company (Halpern 1994; Bauer 1996). These works serve to preserve the history of the field.

As a form of research, historical research is open to the scrutiny and critical assessment of the profession's members. Therefore, historical researchers must ensure the preservation of their source documents, such as tapes and transcripts of interviews, and make them available to other researchers (Kiple 1991, 566).

Perspective for Health Informatics

Historical research, while focused on the past, has truths for current practitioners. Moreover, practitioners currently can record and preserve their experiences to inform the practice of future health informatics professionals. A field's history is one aspect of its body of knowledge.

Descriptive Research

Descriptive research determines and reports the current status of topics and subjects. The focus of descriptive research is to accurately capture or portray dimensions or characteristics of people, organizations, situations, technology, or other phenomena.

Process

Descriptive research typically depicts the frequency of specific elements or individuals, the level or amount of **variables**, or the ranges of occurrences. This information is particularly important for policymaking or ongoing monitoring. For example, legislators need to know the number of people who would be affected by a decision, such as making electronic claims submission mandatory, before they enact the law. Information specialists need to know the clinicians' levels of familiarity with a technology before they implement it. Thus, an important function of descriptive research is to establish a benchmark against which future changes can be compared and contrasted.

Descriptive research is **exploratory**. In descriptive studies, researchers do not test hypotheses. Descriptive research is not explanatory. As such it is often a precursor to explanatory studies, such as **causal-comparative** and experimental studies.

Common tools used to collect descriptive data are **surveys**, interviews, and **observations**. The shortcomings of descriptive research include the *lack of*:

- Standardized questions
- Trained observers
- High response rates

Examples of descriptive studies include polls of citizens' opinions concerning the security of electronic health records (EHRs), surveys of practitioners on barriers to EHR adoption, surveys of chief information officers on the extent of computerization of their healthcare facilities, and compilations of standards currently in use. (See table 2.4 for a representative list of descriptive studies.)

Perspective for Health Informatics

Descriptive research is the preliminary work in building a body of knowledge in health informatics research, which is replete with descriptive studies. This disproportionate representation of descriptive studies may be related to the dynamic nature of the field and the ongoing attempts of its practitioners to describe the state of the industry. However, the advancement of the body of knowledge demands progression into studies that predict outcomes and that elaborate theories.

Correlational Research

Researchers who use correlational research study the existence, the direction, and the strength of relationships between variables. They also can compare the strength of relationships between different variables. Correlational research is exploratory and nonexperimental. This preliminary study is common in quantitative research and analysis.

Table 2.4.   Selected representative examples of descriptive research studies

Author	Year	Method	Time Frame	Sample & Response Rate	Analytical Techniques	Key Findings, Limitations, & Recommendations
Stausberg et al.	2003	Review of paper and electronic health records	Retrospective over 1 month	244 cases (response rate not applicable)	Descriptive statistics (frequencies, means, medians, modes, range, and Cohen's kappa)	Diagnosis coding from paper records showed minor qualitative advantages. Procedure coding from EHR showed potential quality and quantity advantages. Paper and electronic records are complementary. Limitations of one coder, limited generalizability, and restricted reproducibility. Recommend improvements in methods for comparisons of paper and electronic health records.
Helleso et al.	2004	Survey of nurses and review of hospital health records	Retrospective over months in early 2002	253 nurses (138 hospital and 115 home health), 68.4% total response rate 36 hospital health records, 100%	Descriptive statistics in SPSS, chi-square, Fisher's exact test Content analysis by coding and summing elements	Significant differences between hospital nurses and home health nurses in what data need to be exchanged. 21 of 36 (58.3%) patients discharged from the hospital and transferred to home health had a nursing discharge note. Content and completeness of the 21 notes varied. Limitation that records did not represent all units of the hospital; interpretations about exchange of information for the 15 patients without nursing discharge notes cannot be made. Recommend clarification of the information needs of all care providers.
Moen and Brennan	2005	In-person survey	Cross-sectional	49 recruited respondents representing 49 households (response rate not applicable)	Content analysis	Self-identified home managers of health information use variety of strategies. One individual manages information organized by household member. Paper-based tools are most common and information stored "just in case." Limitations include site of data collection; focus on tasks and tools, rather than other responsibilities; structured interview; not longitudinal; not generalizable. Recommend that PHRs align with the way people use health information and further analysis of storage.
Ferranti et al.	2006	Review of standards and characteristics	Retrospective	Two standards (response rate not applicable)	Comparison and analysis of standards and their characteristics	Clinical Document Architecture (CDA) and Continuity of Care Record (CCR) built on different information models. CDA offers greater interoperability than CCR. Limitations—none listed. Recommend that development organizations should collaborate, emphasizing each standard's strengths and avoiding overlap.

Humans naturally look for relationships to create order. A statement such as "Well, I just washed my car today; for sure it's going to rain" shows a tongue-in-cheek belief in a relationship between the activity of washing a car and the natural phenomenon of rain.

Process

Correlational research first seeks to determine whether a relationship exists between "things." Researchers in correlational studies ask how things relate to one another. These things can be phenomena, factors, attitudes, characteristics, indicators, performance measures, or any other item of interest. In correlational studies, the "things" are called variables. The relationship reflects how these variables change together or separately. The relationship between the variables' change is nonrandom.

Other terms may be used for variables. Variables that covary may be called covariables or covariates. In some correlational studies, the variables are known as **predictor variables (predictors)** and **criterion variables (or outcome variables)**. A canonical correlational study is an example that uses this alternate terminology. Prediction studies are another example. Such studies investigate strongly related variables. The strength of the relationship allows researchers to make predictions. In prediction studies, the predictor variables suggest scores on criterion variables. For example, the predictor variable of a mother's smoking predicts a low birth weight (criterion variable) in her baby.

First, how the variables occur or change together is called **covariation**. The verb is "covary"; the variables covary. Two or more variables may be involved. For example, early studies on cigarette smoking investigated the relationship between smoking and lung cancer. The researchers found that the two variables, smoking and lung cancer, covaried together.

Second, correlational research determines the direction of the covariation. A **positive (direct) relationship** means that the variables change in the same direction. For example, the *higher* the belief in personal computer fluency, the *higher* the use of handheld personal digital assistants (PDAs) for decision support (.822, the + is often assumed). Conversely, a **negative (inverse) relationship** means that variables change in opposite directions. The *lower* the belief in the dehumanizing attributes of computerization, the *higher* the use of handheld PDAs

for decision support. A negative relationship is indicated by the minus sign in front of the number (–.692).

Third, correlational studies show the degree (magnitude) or strength of relationships between and among variables. The degree of the relationship between the variables can range from .00 to 1.00 (or –1.00). This number is called a correlation coefficient. A correlation coefficient (or strength) of .00 means that absolutely no relationship exists. The closer the correlation coefficient is to 1.00 or –1.00, the more closely related are the variables. A strength of 1.00 or –1.00 means a perfect relationship—the changes in the variables match exactly.

Terms for the strength of relationships are perfect, strong, moderate, weak, and little or none. There are no set or exact cutoffs for strong, moderate, and weak. The designation as strong, moderate, or weak depends, in part, on the variables under study. For example, for variables about which little is known or are difficult to quantify, such as personality attributes or feelings, correlation coefficients .4 to .6 (–.4 to –.6) would be considered fairly strong, .2 to .4 (–.2 to –.4) moderate, and below .2 (–.2) weak. However, for variables that can be easily quantified, such as weight or height, correlation coefficients .75 to .99 (–.75 to –.99) would be considered strong, .45 to .75 (–.45 to –.75) moderate, and below .45 (–.45) weak. The interpretation of the strength of the relationship depends on the researcher's assessment of the findings in the context of the topic.

Bergman and Fors conducted correlational research (2005) to investigate the relationships among physicians' learning styles and the acceptance, use, and perceived usefulness of a clinical decision support system (CDSS) to make medical diagnoses. The researchers used a model with four learning styles: accommodating, diverging, converging, and assimilating. The CDSS was the Computer-Based Structured Clinical Interview for axis 1 of the *Diagnostic Statistical Manual*, version 4 (CB-SCID1). The subjects were 49 physicians (31 psychiatrists and 18 nonpsychiatrists) from three clinics. Key findings included:

- Across all styles, there was a negative correlation between computer skill and computer anxiety (–.51). This correlation means the higher the score on computer skill, the lower the score on computer anxiety. Equally, this correlation could mean the lower the score on computer skill, the higher the score on computer anxiety.

- Across all styles, there was a negative correlation between positive attitude toward computer-aided diagnostics and computer anxiety (–.48), and within the learning style of accommodating the negative correlation was even higher (–.80). This correlation means the lower the score on positive attitude toward computer-aided diagnostics, the higher the score on computer anxiety. Equally, this correlation means the higher the score on positive attitude toward computer-aided diagnostics, the lower the score on computer anxiety.

- Within the learning style of accommodating, there was a positive correlation between positive attitude toward computer-aided diagnostics and computer skill (.62). This correlation means the higher the score on positive attitude toward computer-aided diagnostics, the higher the score on computer skill. Equally, this correlation means the higher the score on computer skill, the higher the score on positive attitude toward computer-aided diagnostics.

- There was a negative correlation between perceived future usefulness and the dimension of perceiving information, Abstract Conceptionalization-Concrete Experience (converging and assimilating versus accommodating and diverging; –.32). This correlation means that the styles of converging and assimilating were associated with positive perceptions of the future usefulness of the CB-SCID1, whereas the accomodating and diverging styles were associated with negative perceptions of the future usefulness of the system.

The researchers concluded that:

1. Individuals' perceptions of their computer skills, computer anxiety, and attitude toward computer-aided diagnosing are related to learning styles, acceptance, use, and perceived usefulness of a CDSS.

2. CDSSs may favor the clinician whose learning style is abstract conceptualization (converging and assimilating).

Correlational research can only detect the existence, the direction, and the degree of relationship. Correlational research *cannot* detect cause and effect, also known as **causal relationships**. A causal relationship states that one factor or factors causes an outcome. Correlational research *cannot* state that one variable or vari-

ables caused another nor can correlational research state which variable came first. Correlational research can *only* state that variables are related to one another.

For example, in the Bergman and Fors study, the researchers could *only* state that:

- A relationship existed between computer skill and computer anxiety.

- The relationship was inverse (negative) in that the higher the score on computer skill, the lower the score on computer anxiety *or* the lower the score on computer skill, the higher the score on computer anxiety.

- A relationship existed between positive attitude toward computer-aided diagnosing and computer anxiety.

- The relationship was inverse (negative) in that the lower the score on positive attitude toward computer-aided diagnostics, the higher the score on computer anxiety *or* the higher the score on positive attitude toward computer-aided diagnostics, the lower the score on computer anxiety.

The researchers could have interpreted their findings in terms of strong, moderate, or weak relationships; however, they did not.

The researchers could *not* state whether:

- The score on computer skill caused the score on computer anxiety *or* the score on computer anxiety caused the score on computer skill

- The low score on positive attitude toward computer-aided diagnosing caused high computer anxiety *or* high computer anxiety caused decreased scores on positive attitude toward computer-aided diagnosing

The researchers could not conclude that a score on one variable caused the score on another variable. They could not state that a change in one variable caused the change in the other variable.

There are two reasons why researchers who conduct correlational research cannot make causal statements:

- Their research is not experimental (only experimental research, to be studied later in the chapter, establishes cause and effect)

- An unknown variable may be creating the phenomenon

The third (or fourth, fifth, and so forth) unknown factor may actually be involved in the occurrence under study. For example, in the Bergman and Fors study, another variable could be involved. Self-efficacy could affect any of the scores on positive attitudes toward computer-aided diagnosing, beliefs about computer skills, and feelings of computer anxiety. These additional, unlisted factors are called **confounding (extraneous, secondary) variables** because they confound (confuse) interpretation of the data.

Researchers conducting correlational studies use surveys, standardized tests, observations, and secondary data. Topics of potential correlational studies in health informatics include investigations of relationships between:

- Organizational attributes and utilization of EHRs
- Job satisfaction and utilization of EHRs
- Increased patient volumes and the level of organizational computerization

Perspective for Health Informatics

Correlational research is exploratory, quantitative research that identifies relationships among variables (see table 2.5). The movement of the variables may be in the same direction, which is a positive relationship. The movement of the variables may also be in opposite directions, which is a negative relationship. Correlational research also describes the strength of the relationship. The key point to remember is that correlational research never establishes causal relationships.

Observational Research

In **observational research**, researchers observe, record, and analyze behaviors and events. Observational research is exploratory research that identifies factors, contexts, and experiences. Highly descriptive, observational research provides insights into what subjects do, how they do it, and why they do it. Observational research is usually classified as qualitative research.

Process

Observational researchers strive for **credibility**, **transferability**, **dependability**, and **confirmability** (Guba and Lincoln 1989, 236–243; see table 2.6.). Focused on specific contexts, observational researchers do not attempt to attain **generalizability** (applicability) to other situations. Thus, characteristics of high-quality observational research are credibility, transferability, dependability, and confirmability.

Observational researchers in the qualitative tradition may also use **triangulation** to support their findings. Triangulation is the use of multiple sources or perspectives to investigate the same phenomenon. The multiple sources or perspectives include data (multiple times, sites, or respondents), investigators (researchers), theories, and methods (Ammenwerth et al. 2003a, 239). The results or conclusions are validated if the multiple sources or perspectives arrive at the same results or conclusions. This technique lends credence to the research.

The key characteristic of observational research is that researchers observe the subjects in their existing surroundings. The researchers are attempting to capture and record the natural, typical behavior of the subjects in their usual context. One advantage of observational research is that it records what actually occurred rather than what subjects report occurred. Therefore, observational research is also known as **natural** or **naturalistic research**. Observational research avoids the disadvantage of retrospective, self-report that can be colored by bias or social desirability. Observational researchers obtain data by observing rather than by asking.

There are three common types of observational research: **nonparticipant observation**, **participant observation**, and **ethnography**. In nonparticipant observation, researchers act as neutral observers who neither intentionally interact with nor affect the actions of the subjects being observed. Case studies often are examples of nonparticipant research. In participant observation, the researcher is a part of the group being observed—the researchers are participants in the observed actions. Participation can be overt (open) or covert (secret). Ethnography is a research technique widely used in anthropology. It combines participant and nonparticipant observation and quantitative and qualitative approaches. Typically, ethnographers exhaustively and thoroughly examine aspects of culture in naturalistic settings. Health informatics researchers could examine how the cultures of various health settings affect the acceptance of EHRs. Are work stations appropriately positioned with ergonomic chairs and privacy? Or are computer terminals crammed in noisy corners of nursing units without chairs? The common denominator in these three types of observational research is the natural setting.

Table 2.5. Selected representative examples of correlational research studies

Author	Year	Method	Time Frame	Sample and Response Rate	Analytical Techniques	Key Findings, Limitations, and Recommendations
Case and Paxson	2002	Secondary analysis (data mining)	Retrospective (1986–1995)	Database of National Health Interview Survey	Descriptive statistics (quintile, percentage) and regression	Correlate parental income and behaviors with children's health. Limitation was in understanding mechanics of household income's potential causal role in children's health. Recommend that policymakers consider focusing education and funding on altering parental behaviors with largest impact on children's health.
Wennberg et al.	2004	Secondary analysis (data mining)	Retrospective (1999–2000)	Databases Medicare Denominator file, Medicare Provider Analysis and Review (MEDPAR) file, Hospice file, Physician /Supplier Procedure Summary Master file, *U.S. News and World Report's* list	Descriptive statistics (percentage, average, quartile) univariate analyses using Pearson product moment correlation	Medicare claims data can be used to measure population-based, illness-adjusted utilization and costs for chronic illnesses (cancer, CHF, COPD). Limited to acute care hospital services, 18-month delay, and case-mix based on diagnoses on hospital discharge records. Extensive variation among hospitals on delivery of care in terms of use, technology, and number of providers.
Griffiths and Christensen	2005	Survey	Retrospective and cross-sectional (April 2003)	24 stratified and randomly selected sites from Depression Directory	Correlations and t-tests	Evaluations of health Web site quality using DISCERN by consumers and health professionals were correlated and the correlation between DISCERN scores and user satisfaction was higher than Google Page Rank and user satisfaction. Limitations included the strength of the correlation, small number of consumers, single field (depression), definition of satisfaction, and lack of expertise. Recommend further study to identify cutoff points and to identify means to automatically factor in relevance of multiple measures of quality.
Razavi et al.	2005	Secondary analysis (data mining)	Retrospective	Cancer registry data for 637 female patients in SE Sweden	Correlation (canonical correlation)	Canonical correlation of cancer registry data can be used to identify risk factors for breast cancer recurrence. Limitation is unfamiliarity with method of canonical correlation in medicine. Recommend use of canonical correlation to reduce the number of factors to the important ones as a step in creating models.

(continued)

Table 2.5. Selected representative examples of correlational research studies (*continued*)

Author	Year	Method	Time Frame	Sample and Response Rate	Analytical Techniques	Key Findings, Limitations, and Recommendations
Ray et al.	2006	Survey	Prospective and retrospective	82 internal medicine residents	Descriptive statistics (standard deviation), reliability coefficient, factor analysis, and correlations	The Attitudes Toward Handheld Decision Support Software Scale (H-DSS) is reliable, valid, and responsive. Limited by sample of residents in one specialty from one program. Recommend more assessments of impact of clinical decision support systems.
Sequist et al.	2007	Survey	Cross-sectional (study's duration unclear)	Champion of EHR at 26 health centers where implemented in June 2003 through December 2005, 73%; 223 primary care clinicians at 26 health centers, 56%	Descriptive statistics (frequencies, mean, standard deviation) and multivariate regression	Majority of clinicians in Indian Health Service where EHR implemented believe EHRs capable of improving care, but only one third believe the EHR actually improved care or patient safety. Process and structural measures were not associated with increased utilization. Clinicians' beliefs about importance of EHRs were strongest correlated with utilization. Limitations were the unique federal setting, subjects were early adopters, lack of information on usability of EHR, and no outcomes data available. Recommend additional studies in other underserved and rural settings and inclusion of actual outcomes and safety data.
Rangachari	2007	Analysis of secondary data	Retrospective (data from 2000 through 2004)	249 hospitals in NY State Dept. of Health administrative databases	Multivariate regression analyses	Relationship between hospital structure characteristics and coding accuracy. Smaller hospitals, nonteaching hospitals, and certain regions of NY were associated with higher coding quality. Limitations are reliance on secondary administrative data and exclusion of potentially important nonadministrative data and workforce data. Recommend use of its measure of coding quality (present on admission), replication in other states, evaluation of effects of policies.

Table 2.6. Criteria for quality observational research

Criterion	Definition
Credibility	Procedures of the study that support the accuracy and representativeness of the thoughts, feelings, perceptions, and descriptions of the subjects under study. Examples include involvement of appropriate duration and intensity; revision of hypotheses to account for facts; and ongoing review of data, analysis, and interpretation with participants.
Transferability	Degree to which key characteristics of contexts are similar and, thus, applicable to other contexts. Transferability affects the ability to apply the results of research in one context to other similar contexts. Detailed and extensive (rich) descriptions of the context are the primary way to establish transferability.
Dependability	Reliability of data achieved by being able to explicitly track and account for changes in the design and methods of the study occasioned by changing conditions, identification of gaps, or other important factors. Means to open decision making to public inspection is through the dependability audit.
Confirmability	Characteristic of data and their interpretation. Data can be traced to original sources and another person analyzing, categorizing, and interpreting the data based on the research's documentation would confirm the logic. Confirmability established by external reviewers conducting a confirmability audit.

Source: Guba and Lincoln 1989 (pp. 236–243).

Observational research uses a wide range of methods and may be combined with other designs, such as descriptive observational research. Observational researchers also come from both quantitative and qualitative approaches. Observational researchers do not conduct experiments, nor do they manipulate variables or conditions. Observational researchers record situations as they exist.

Common tools in observational research are case notes, check sheets, audiotapes, and videotapes. Observational research is intensive, and researchers amass vast volumes of details. Then, the researchers must compile, analyze, and interpret these masses of data.

Observational researchers conduct case studies. They also stage or participate in events where they observe the behaviors. For example, during a disaster drill, health informatics researchers could observe the exchange and transmission of health information throughout the drill. Did the information system support users unfamiliar with the system and provide information when and where it was needed? Researchers can also create their own vignettes and, thus, stage their own events. Health informatics researchers could create scenarios of medically complex diagnostic cases. They could then, using audit trails, track how clinicians queried health databases to gather information to diagnose the case. Observational researchers also wait for naturally-occurring events, such as hurricanes, floods, and fires. Health informatics researchers could observe and record the actual performance of postdisaster information recovery plans.

There are unique aspects of observational research. First, observational researchers form tentative or working hypotheses based on the literature, rather than testable hypotheses. Second, observational research is iterative or cyclical. As researchers gather and analyze data, they revise their working hypotheses and create new working hypotheses. Therefore, the researchers work in a cycle beginning with a working diagnosis, collecting data, revising hypotheses, and creating new working hypotheses, and then collecting more data about those new hypotheses. Finally, observational research is flexible. From questions raised or information learned in the first study, observational researchers investigate new topics. These aspects of observational research contrast with the other research designs that are more linear in their processes.

Observational research is not common in the healthcare body of knowledge. McKibbon and Gadd studied qualitative research published in 170 core clinical journals in 2000 (2004). Examples of core clinical journals are the *Journal of the American Medical Association*, *New England Journal of Medicine*, and *Lancet*. The 170 journals published 60,330 articles. Of these articles 367 were qualitative and, of those, only 355 were original studies (McKibbon and Gadd 2004,). Similarly, qualitative research is not common in health informatics research. (See table 2.7.)

Sørby and Nytrø conducted a study using nonparticipant observation (2005). The purpose of the study was to investigate how physicians used clinical information systems, both paper and electronic, in their tasks. In this study, physicians were observed as they processed patients discharged from the coronary care unit. The hospital used multiple clinical information systems. The researchers noted the following paper-based information systems (113):

- The chart of the current hospital stay
- The paper record assembling previous hospital stays
- The *Physicians' Desk Reference*
- Coding manuals
- Personal notes
- Patient lists

The electronic information systems included what the researchers called an electronic patient record (EPR) system [known in the U.S. as an electronic health record (EHR) system], the patient administrative system, an integrated interface to a Picture Archiving and Communication System, Laboratory Information Systems, and specialist systems. From March through June 2004, two nonparticipant observers (medical students) viewed 52 discharge processes. The nonparticipant observers had forms upon which to record their observations. The form included columns for each of the clinical information systems previously listed. As the physicians performed the discharge process, the nonparticipant observers marked the clinical information sources and described the information retrieved. The researchers found low reliance

Table 2.7. **Research articles and observational research articles: Representative numbers in health informatics journals January 1996 through May Week 5 2007**

Journal	No. of Articles	No. of Articles with Observational Research
BMC Medical Informatics and Decision Making	140	1
Health Informatics Journal	26	5
Health Information and Libraries Journal	305	8
Health Information Management	135	
Health Information Management Journal	245	1
Health Information on the Internet	174	
Health Information Systems and Telemedicine	2	
Healthcare Informatics	1167	
Healthcare Information Management	95	
Infocare	98	
Informatics in Primary Care	128	
International Journal of Medical Informatics	941	1
Journal of AHIMA	1540	
Journal of Biomedical Informatics	283	
Journal of Clinical Monitoring and Computing	369	
Journal of Medical Internet Research	254	1
Journal of the American Medical Informatics Association	783	10
Medical Informatics	94	
Medical Informatics and the Internet in Medicine	194	
Medinfo	851	
Methods of Information in Medicine	908	
Perspectives in Health Information Management	28	
Studies in Health Technology and Informatics	4036	1
23 journals	12,796	28

Source: CINAHL and MEDLINE Accessed 12 June 2007

on the EPR system, with the physicians using the paper chart for approximately 50 percent of the inquiries, the EPR system for approximately 10 percent, and human sources (physicians, nurses, and patients) for the remaining 40 percent (116–117). Moreover, the researchers found that the physicians actually used the EPR system less than they had reported on a survey (117). The researchers concluded that, to support physicians in their tasks, the EPR system could be improved, particularly the interfaces between applications.

Participant observation was used to examine participants' perceptions of the influences of a medical informatics course on their short-term and long-term knowledge, skills, and behavior (Patel et al. 2005, 257). Two phases of the research were conducted. The first phase was immediately before and after the course in Spring 2002. Surveys and interviews were conducted. Qualitative data were coded to reasons for taking the course, expectations, anticipated effects, satisfaction, and recommendations for change (257). The second phase involved surveying all participants in the course from 1990 through 2001. Qualitative data were coded according to how taking the course affected others' perceptions of the participants, their satisfaction, how aspects of the course affected them personally, and organizational influences from the participation in the course (257). The participants were satisfied with the course, considered their knowledge of medical informatics increased by the course, had a larger network of professionals than the nonparticipants, and believed that they could effect changes in their organizations in the area of medical informatics (261).

Winkelman, et al. (2005) conducted an ethnographic study to uncover chronically ill patients' language and perceptions in which they explored how patients living with a chronic disease valued Internet access to electronic patient records (EPRs). The researchers used the term EPR interchangeably with electronic medical record (EMR) (not using the more current term of electronic health record (EHR). The researchers believed that information and communication technology (ICT) should be developed as "systems and evaluation tools that capture this subjective reality of potential patient-users" (Winkelman, et al. 2005, 307). The researchers interviewed 12 patients with inflammatory bowel disease (IBD) present for 1 year or longer either as part of a focus group or individually in depth. The selection of interviewees and the interview questions evolved during the course of the study (307–308). Data analysis was simultaneous with data collection. Data were coded and grouped into ideas and themes. For patients with chronic IBD, merely providing access to an EMR portal was not sufficient. Instead, these chronically ill patients described useful EMRs as an integration of self-management data and templates, such as historical laboratory data and physician notes; communication tools such as e-mail; and personalized support, both from fellow patients as nurturing and from providers as informational (310–311).

Perspective for Health Informatics

Observational researchers focus on the participants' feelings, behaviors, and perceptions from the perspectives of the participants. (See table 2.8.) Data collection and analysis often are concurrent with additional participant interview questions to address perceived gaps or missing viewpoints. Iteration and evolution of the research process are common. The emphasis is on the richness and comprehensiveness of the descriptions and details. Through analysis, these descriptions and details are categorized into overarching themes. On the negative side, observational research can be time-consuming, human resource-intensive, and expensive. The findings of observational research may result in the testable hypotheses of quantitative research. Finally, observational research of high quality can be identified by its credibility, transferability, dependability, and confirmability.

Evaluation Research

Evaluation research is the systematic examination of the effectiveness of an **object** (described as "things" in the section on correlational research). Examples of evaluated objects include policies, programs, technologies (including procedures or implementations), products, processes, events, conditions, or organizations. The merit, worth, or quality of the object is assessed. This examination encompasses several aspects of the object, such as conceptualization, design, implementation, impact, and generalizability (Shi 1997, 390). Evaluation research is prevalent in health informatics research; it is a veritable "workhorse."

Process

"Systematic" is a key term in the definition of evaluation research. This characteristic of evaluation research differentiates it from the managerial function of control.

Table 2.8. Selected representative examples of observational research studies

Author	Year	Method	Time Frame	Sample and Response Rate	Analytical Techniques	Key Findings, Limitations, & Recommendations
Ely et al.	2005	Nonparticipant observation, interview, and audiotapes	Cross-sectional	56 invited general practitioners, general pediatricians, and family physicians younger than 45 years in eastern third of Iowa (46 random and 10 targeted)	Review and coding of field notes and interview transcripts by two researchers	The most common obstacle to finding an answer to patient-care questions is the physician's doubt that an answer exists. Other common obstacles include failure of selected resources to provide an answer. Limitations include small number of participants, small geographic area, wording of cover letter that focused on obstacles, and presence of observer. Recommend that clinical resource developers utilize information from physicians to improve content and access to information.
Saleem et al.	2005	Ethnography	Cross-sectional	35 nurses and 55 physicians and mid-level practitioners at 4 Veterans Administration medical centers	Field notes from observations on 2 days at each site were typed, coded, sorted into categories, observations integrated into meaningful patterns, and abstracted into themes	Use of clinical reminders was variable. Obstacles included unclear responsibility to clear clinical reminders, work flow, workload, inflexibility of application, and poor usability. Limitation was the convenience sample. Recommend redesign of clinical reminders, clarification of work assignments, and limits on number of reminders.
Adams et al.	2005	Ethnography including observations, informal meetings, interviews, and focus groups	Cross-sectional over 6 months	1 hospital	Grounded theory method in which data collection and analysis are concurrent identifying themes and gaps iteratively	How can awareness applications be adjusted to users' work patterns? Describes evolution of screensaver from privacy and security device to communication medium. General limitation of awareness applications that may devolve tasks into search and retrieval activities. Recommend ongoing and iterative user input in IT development and understanding of users' work practices.
Garrett et al.	2006	Literature review and case study	Cross-sectional over 2 years	8 rural hospitals in 1 state (response rate not applicable)	Review and analysis of case notes	Adoption of electronic medication error reporting system. 3 barriers (personnel, physical space, and Internet access) were identified in addition to 6 customary barriers listed in literature (cost, legality, time, fear, usefulness, and complexity). Limited to 8 rural hospitals in 1 state. Recommend means to mitigate barriers.
Bossen	2007	Participant observation and semistructured, open-ended interviews	Cross-sectional	4 hospitals in one county	Analysis, using grounded theory, of field notes taken during health informatics professional visits, observation of a department, committee meetings, pilot test, and semistructured, open-ended interviews	Technical, project management, and organizational problems adversely affect IT implementations, in this case the implementation of an electronic medication plan. Fit needs to be achieved between the IT, the work processes, and the organizational structures. No limitations were listed. Recommend creation of new organizational structures that cut across hospital divisions and support of informal work groups ("communities of practice") of engaged persons.

Evaluation research is conducted within the technical standards of research. Therefore, evaluation researchers follow an established protocol, utilize defensible analytic procedures, and make their processes and results available to other researchers. Evaluation research is reproducible by other researchers.

Examples from Health Informatics

Health informatics researchers conducting evaluation research might investigate the effectiveness of various applications of the EHR system in a healthcare enterprise. For example, for the Veterans Administration (VA), researchers evaluated the effectiveness of the different designs of information systems (IS) and results of different encoding software applications (Lloyd and Layman 1997). Eight VA medical centers tested encoding software applications from three vendors. The researchers found that the IS design was the crucial element in increasing coding speed.

Evaluation research is a diverse field (Shi 1997, 185). There are several types of evaluation research. Common types that health informatics researchers may encounter include:

- Needs assessment
- Process and implementation evaluation
- Cost effectiveness and cost-benefit analysis
- Outcome and impact evaluation
- Policy analysis

Each of these types of evaluations fulfills a different purpose (see table 2.9.)

Evaluation research overlaps with other research designs. Some evaluation research is experimental or quasi-experimental because some type of **intervention** (such as the effectiveness of a training technique) is involved. Other evaluation research is observational. For example, the research of Patel et al. (2005), using participant observation, described previously, also could be considered evaluation research because the study evaluated a medical informatics course and the extent to which the program's objectives were achieved (Patel et al. 2005, 256). Thus, the distinguishing factor that makes a study evaluation research is its focus. If the study's focus is evaluation, then the study is evaluation research.

In evaluation research, researchers ask three broad categories of questions:

Table 2.9.   Common types of evaluation research studies

Type	Description
Needs Assessment	Identification of needs that could be problems, weaknesses, or deficiencies. Data are also collected on the extent and severity of the needs of the targets
Process and Implementation Evaluation	Investigation of operations, such as providing or implementing an object, including alternate processes. Implementation evaluation investigates how closely the actual delivery or implementation followed the plan for the delivery or implementation (fidelity), including compliance with standards.
Cost-Benefit and Cost-Effectiveness Analysis	Economic analysis that: 1. Converts all effects, positive and negative, monetary and non-monetary (social, technological, competitiveness, etc.), into the same monetary term as the costs 2. Compares them Cost-effectiveness analysis is similar to cost-benefit analysis except nonmonetary benefits are not converted into the monetary term.
Outcome and Impact Evaluation	Investigation whether object achieved intended effect with an impact evaluation investigating both intended effects and unintended effects.
Policy Analysis	Exploration of means to achieve goals through policies and alternatives within constraints of time, information, and resources. Research determines options, identifies the optimal option, estimates costs, and predicts outcomes and consequences.

- Descriptive
- Normative
- Impact (Grosshans and Chelimsky 1991, 7)

Then, to answer these questions, the researchers systematically collect information about the characteristics and outcomes of objects. For example, researchers answering descriptive questions would compile data on numbers of people affected by a technology or by its ongoing costs. Normative questions address what should be or how things ought to happen. Actual results are compared against standards, levels of performance, or other expectations. In an evaluation study, a researcher asking a normative question about the utility of a data mining algorithm would compare the algorithm's output against expected output or the output of other algorithms. In another study, researchers could assess Web pages related to health issues against the requirements of Section 508 and the Americans With Disabilities Act of 1998 (PL 105-220). Impact questions investigate whether results can be attributed to the object. An example of an impact study would investigate whether an EHR improved clinicians' documentation.

Evaluation research is often retrospective. The research looks back at how an object occurred, such as how an application was rolled out in an implementation and the results of that particular method of rollout. Moreover, the study is often cross-sectional—focused on one point in time, a snapshot. However, prospectively, as organizations or entities consider new objects, leaders should consider how these objects will be evaluated. Planning for the evaluation of an object is as important as planning for its purchase or implementation.

Evaluation research is assessed against four overarching standards (Department of Health and Human Services 2005, 6–7):

1. **Utility**—right information to the right person at the right time

2. **Feasibility**—realistic likelihood of the evaluation's success given the time, resources, and expertise

3. **Propriety**—appropriate protections for participants are in place and the appropriate stakeholders are involved

4. **Accuracy**—probability that the evaluation's results will be accurate, valid, and reliable for their users

Evaluation researchers can invoke these standards at each step of their research to guide choices, embed quality, and strengthen credibility.

Kreps (2002, 209–210) identified specific flaws in the evaluation research of health information technologies. One major limitation of the evaluation studies in health information techology is overreliance on cross-sectional studies. For example, acceptance and utilization studies are often cross-sectional; they capture the situation at only one point in time. Acceptance and utilization during many months or years may present a very different picture. A longer timeline is needed to assess the totality of the technology's acceptance and usage. There is also overreliance on self-report data. Self-report

data are subject to biases, such as **social desirability** and **central tendency**. Another flaw is the focus on tangential variables, only indirectly related to the object's purposes, to measure the achievement of outcomes. This flaw occurs because data related to these tangential variables may be easier to collect and quantify than the data related to the relevant variables. The analyst also identifies **shallow data** as problematic. Shallow data are easily collected but are equivocal. The analyst provides the number of Web site hits on a health promotion site as an example of shallow data. The data are shallow because a visitor accessing a Web site does not necessarily mean that the visitor could navigate the site or use its information. Finally, evaluation researchers do not present their results in ways that communicate information to their readers. Too often, complex statistics are presented without explanations that are clear to practitioners, leaders, and policymakers. Kreps also recommends that evaluation researchers explicitly state the implications, applications, and limitations of their research (2002, 210). Thus, although evaluation research is common in health informatics research, its full potential has not been realized through flaws in design or presentation.

Researchers use various methods to conduct evaluation research (see table 2.10). These methods include case studies, field observations, experiments, and secondary data analysis.

Through a case study, researchers investigated the impact of an electronic order entry system at one academic health center (Georgiou et al. 2005, 130). The electronic order entry system for diagnostic test orders, medical imaging, diet, and transport services was implemented beginning in November 2003. In August and September 2004, the researchers conducted in-depth individual interviews and focus group interviews. Individual interviews, ranging between 15 and 30 minutes, were conducted with 16 physicians, 2 pathology laboratory manager-scientists, and 3 nursing unit managers. Focused group interviews, ranging between 40 and 70 minutes, were conducted with 4 additional nursing unit managers, 4 information service personnel, and 6 pathology laboratory and hospital scientists. The individual interviews and focus group interviews resulted in 9 hours of taped recordings and 118 pages of transcribed text. The researchers analyzed the text, field notes, and memoranda for themes with the assistance of computerized text analysis software. The researchers found that nurses and physicians commented positively on the effi-

Table 2.10. Selected representative examples of evaluation research studies

Author	Year	Method	Time Frame	Sample and Response Rate	Analytical Techniques	Key Findings, Limitations, and Recommendations
Zheng et al.	2005	Statistical modeling, structured interview, and survey	Longitudinal from February through November 2002	Usage data on 41 residents (response rate not applicable) 10 residents for structured interview Two surveys of residents with samples of 32 and 37 response rates to both of 78%	Group-based semi-parametric statistical modeling Content analysis	Usage of clinical reminder system. 3 types of user behavior identified (light, moderate, and heavy). Heavy users did not make qualitative comments about inefficiency and disruption of workflows. Preexisting perceptions affected adoption. Limitations—none listed. Recommend redesign reminder system to align with workflows and utilize mixed method research in the future.
Ahern et al.	2006	Semistructured qualitative interviews	Cross-sectional (May 2002 through September 2003)	38 representatives of sectors involved in the development, dissemination, or use of e-health technologies and representing entire U.S.	Content analysis assisted by computerized text analysis software	Study established areas of congruence and controversy among sectors involved in development, evaluation, dissemination, purchase, and use of e-health technologies. Consistent themes were identified with slight differences in emphasis. Limitations—none identified. Recommended improvement and formalization of development and evaluation standards, additional research on technological needs and preferences of underserved groups, and long-term epidemiological studies on the impact of e-health on outcomes and cost-effectiveness.
Zeng et al.	2006	Experiment with later analysis of computer log data and satisfaction survey	Cross-sectional during June and July 2004	213 English-speaking community college students who were not physicians or nurses	Descriptive statistics, multiple regression, and analysis of variance	Evaluation of a system that assists health consumers querying the Internet for health information by suggestion query terms. System led to a significantly higher rate of successful queries, but did not statistically increase user satisfaction. Limitations included difference between subjects and general population of healthcare consumers. Popular terms for health conditions did not map to UMLS concepts. Time spent querying was not an outcome in the study. Recommended continued refinement of the system.

(continued)

Table 2.10. Selected representative examples of evaluation research studies *(continued)*

Author	Year	Method	Time Frame	Sample and Response Rate	Analytical Techniques	Key Findings, Limitations, and Recommendations
Shah et al.	2006	Analysis of log data	Cross-sectional from August 5, 2004 through January 5, 2005	701 clinicians at 31 primary care practices in 1 integrated delivery system; 18,115 drug alerts	Descriptive statistics	Evaluation of computerized drug prescribing alert system.
						Selectivity, tiers of alert severity, and minimal disruption of workflow designed into the system resulted in higher user acceptance of alerts (67%) than reported previously in literature.
						Limitations included low numbers of alerts in some categories (drug-disease), lack of generalizability being performed in single healthcare system using one prescribing application, and internal determination of knowledge base for alert system.
						Recommended designing future prescription alert systems within similar parameters, externally validating knowledge base, correcting errors in clinical information systems that created false alerts, collecting reasons for clinician overrides as potential future enhancements, and future research on the balance between overalerting versus underalerting.
El Emam et al.	2006	Intrusion simulation (attack on research database)	Cross-sectional	Data sets: College of Physicians and Surgeons of Ontario (membership list), Law Society of Upper Canada (membership list), Ministry of Government Services' Personal Property Security Registration, and Canadian 411 Telephone Directory	Computations of risk using various identifiers and combinations of identifiers	Predicted the risk of re-identification in an attack on a research database that had been de-identified using HIPAA heuristics by linking it to public databases.
						Possibility exists to re-identify data that had been de-identified using de-identification heuristics. Re-identification performed for subpopulations, physicians and lawyers in Ontario, Canada. Re-identification not possible for the entire population of Ontario.
						Limited in that other types of attacks were not studied.
						Recommended that professional societies do not put membership lists on the Internet, researchers use statistical disclosure control rather than heuristics, and future research on other subpopulations that are at risk and other means of attack.

ciency and reliability of the new system. Pathology laboratory managers and hospital scientists, however, noted that the system resulted in reduced interdepartmental communication and their advisory roles. The researchers concluded that the electronic order entry system affected information management, communications, and work relations (132–133).

A time-and-motion study was conducted to compare the times required to use EHRs and paper-based health records (Pizziferri et al. 2005, 176). Physicians' beliefs that using EHRs took longer than paper records were an obstacle to adoption of EHRs. The researchers conducted the study in 5 primary care clinics and observed 20 physicians. Activities were timed both preimplementation and postimplementation of the EHR. In terms of physicians' time, there was no significant difference in time spent with patients in direct patient care (181). Moreover, similar amounts of time were used to perform activities related to indirect patient care (telephone, paperwork, etc.). From their observations, the researchers were able to conclude that EHRs did not require more time than paper records during the primary care session and that the benefits of EHRs could be realized without sacrificing time with patients (184).

Researchers conducted a quasi-experimental study to evaluate the acceptance of a computer-based nursing documentation system (Ammenwerth et al. 2003b, 71). The researchers conducted tests before, during, and after the implementation of the system (72). A computer-based nursing documentation system was implemented on four wards of an academic health center in Heidelberg, Germany. Previous acceptance of the nursing process and years of computer experience were positively associated with acceptance of the computer-based nursing documentation system (79). Complementary to the testing were focus group interviews. The interviews revealed that the ward with the lowest acceptance rates had the greatest volume of documentation because of the age of its patients and because of its patients' short lengths of stay (high patient turnover; 80). The researchers concluded that their results can be used to plan successful implementations of nursing documentation systems. They further note that information gained from evaluation studies can be used to design information technologies and systems that support the functions of health personnel (83).

Conducting a study using secondary analysis, researchers evaluated a tool to detect potential cases of inhalational anthrax (Chapman et al. 2003, 497). Early detection and antibiotic treatment are needed to reduce the 100 percent mortality rate (Chapman et al. 2003, 494). An early sign of inhalational anthrax is a widening of the mediastinum, which is visible on a chest x-ray. X-ray reports in free text are stored in hospital information systems. The researchers used a statistical text classifier to find x-ray reports describing mediastinal widening (Chapman et al. 2003, 495). The researchers created a model of terms positively and negatively associated with the target category (in this case inhalational anthrax). Then, using the model of terms, statistical classifiers compute probabilities whether a document belongs to the target category. The researchers tested the classifier tool on one hospital's x-rays (79,032) during 1 year (2000). The classifier tool attained a specificity of 0.99 (proportion of truly nondiseased persons) and a maximum sensitivity of 0.35 (proportion of truly diseased persons; 500). The researchers concluded that statistical text classifiers are useful complements to traditional disease reporting and that automated detection of mediastinal widening is useful in anthrax surveillance (500–502).

Perspective for Health Informatics

To be of more use to practitioners, leaders, and policymakers, Kreps recommended improvements in the design of future evaluation studies of health information technologies (2002, 210-211). These recommendations also apply to health informatics research in general:

- Longitudinal studies to show the acceptance and utilization of objects over time. These studies would address the issues of seasonal changes in the health sector and the evolution of users' skills, perceptions, and utilization.

- Studies using multiple methods. Studies that combine methods, such as survey and time-and-motion studies or case study and survey should be designed. Methods that offset their respective disadvantages should be selected.

- Studies combining quantitative and qualitative approaches. These approaches are complementary; the qualitative information could explain why the quantitative results occurred.

- Studies using nonobtrusive procedures to collect data. Nonobtrusive procedures include counters and trackers in software, feedback mechanisms, audit trails, response times, and observations. Researchers must be aware of the Hawthorne effect in which their mere presence affects the users' behavior.

- Reporting results on significant and meaningful factors. Reports of research on tangentially related factors diminishes the public's view of research relevance and reinforces the view of practitioners, leaders, and policymakers that research is immaterial and unrealistic. Important also is that the participants' time has been wasted on insignificant issues.
- Studies on important goals or issues. Evaluation research should contribute to the field's and the public's understanding of key objects.

Evaluation research is the systematic examination of effectiveness. It is an important component of the health informatics body of knowledge. Evaluation researchers describe what is; what ought to be; and what the impact has been, could be, or will be. Quality evaluation research has utility, feasibility, propriety, and accuracy. Common methods used in evaluation research include case studies, field observations, experiments, and secondary analyses. Evaluation research has great potential because of its capability of making a difference in the lives of practitioners, leaders, policymakers, and the public.

Experimental Research

Researchers conducting experimental research create environments in which to observe, analyze, and interpret the effects of treatments on phenomena. Experimental research discovers the causes of the phenomena under study. Therefore, experimental research establishes causal relationships. A causal relationship shows cause and effect. For example, smoking (the cause) results in lung cancer (the effect). Experimental research is the only research design that establishes causal relationships. It is the gold standard.

Process

Characteristics of experimental research include:

- Control (elimination to the best of the researchers' abilities of all potential sources of bias)

- Control groups
- Observation (pretest and posttest)
- Manipulation of treatment
- Random assignment of subjects to groups (randomization)

The hallmark of experimental research is control.

Researchers use the terms **pretest, posttest**, observation, and treatment broadly and generically, beyond their usual meanings. Pretest, posttest, and observation simply mean that the researchers have measured the variables in some way. A **treatment** is any action; it is not just a therapy. Therefore, treatment could mean a computer training program, an algorithm to extract medical abbreviations from bibliographic databases, a specific technology or application, or the procedure to implement health information and communication technologies.

Experimental researchers systematically manipulate factors of the treatments to test the factors' influences on the effects (outcomes). As they manipulate factors, experimental researchers are careful to fully control their environments and subjects. Variations are sources of bias in the experiment (investigation) and severely diminish its credibility and integrity.

Researchers conducting experimental research select both **independent variables** and **dependent variables** (see table 2.11). Independent variables are the factors that researchers manipulate directly. They are the interventions or treatments. Independent variables are antecedent or prior factors. Dependent variables are the measured variables and rely on the independent variables. The dependent variables reflect the results that the researcher theorizes. They occur subsequently or after the independent variables. Therefore, the independent variable causes an effect in the dependent variable.

In experimental research, researchers select subjects for comparison groups. The **experimental group** comprises the research subjects. Another group, the **control group**, comprises the control subjects. The experimental subjects undergo the intervention of the research study. For comparison, the control subjects do not. Thus, the researchers can compare the effect of the intervention on the experimental group against the status of the control group.

Important elements of experimental research are **random sampling** and **randomization**. Although the terms are similar, they represent two different procedures. Random sampling is the unbiased selection of subjects from the population of interest. (Random sam-

Table 2.11. Comparison of characteristics of independent variables and dependent variables

Independent Variable	Dependent Variable
Cause	Effect
Originates Stimulus or Is Treatment	Receives Stimulus or Treatment
Causes or Influences Change in Dependent Variable	Measured for Effect or Influence of Stimulus or Treatment
Manipulated	Measured for Effect of Manipulation of Independent Variable
Antecedent, Prior	Successor, Subsequent
Action	Consequence
Other Terms: Covariable or Covariate, Predictor, Predictor Variable, Treatment, Treatment Variable	Other Terms: Covariable or Covariate, Criterion Variable, Outcome, Outcome Variable

pling is discussed in greater detail in chapter 10, Data Collection.) Randomization is the random allocation of subjects between experimental groups and control groups. Thus, step one is to select subjects from the population using random sampling, and step two is to randomly assign the randomly selected subjects to experimental or control groups.

Random sampling and randomization characterize **double-blind studies**. A double-blind study is an extremely rigorous form of experimental research. In a double-blind study, neither the researcher nor the subject knows whether the individual subject is in the experimental group or in the control group. Therefore, neither the researcher nor the patient knows whether the patient is receiving the treatment. In double-blind studies, the random selection (random sampling) and the random allocation (randomization) eliminate the potentially biasing effects of expectations and perceptions.

Double-blind studies are rare in health informatics research. Research analysts point out that it is "almost never feasible to 'blind' a clinician" to the use of a new technology, such as an EHR (Lobach and Detmer 2007, 107). However, an example of a double-blind study related to health informatics is described on the Web site of the U.S. National Institutes of Health (Terrell 2006). In this study, the researcher is measuring the effect of information technology on patient care in the emergency department. Specifically, the researcher is studying the effects of a computer-alert system. In the study, the physicians are randomly (randomized) placed in the experi-

mental group (intervention group) and the control group. The study intends to compare the practice of the physicians in the experimental group who are receiving the reminders against the practice of the physicians in the control group who do not receive reminders.

Double-blind studies address the problem of potential bias from the expectations and perceptions of both researchers and participants. The effects of expectations and perceptions are known as **observer-expectancy effect** and **subject-expectancy effect**. The observer-expectancy effect is related to the researcher and the subject-expectancy effect to the participants (subjects). These effects are similar to self-fulfilling prophecies. In observer-expectancy effect, the researcher (observer) who expects a particular outcome unconsciously manipulates the experiment to achieve it. In subject-expectancy effect, a research participant (subject) who expects a particular outcome either unconsciously manipulates the experiment or reports the expected outcome. For example, a participant testing a new order-entry component may record on a satisfaction survey that the process takes longer because the participant expects the process to take longer. However, in actuality, when time-and-motion study data on the new order-entry component are compared against archival data on the old order-entry component, the new process takes no longer.

Classic double-blind studies come from the study of new drugs. In these double-blind drug studies, neither the researcher nor the patient knows whether the patient is receiving the new drug. The participants in the experimental group receive the new drug, and the participants in the control group receive a **placebo**. A placebo looks exactly like the new drug but, instead, contains harmless ingredients (sometimes called a sugar pill). Double-blind studies were necessary because both researchers and participants may have potentially biasing expectations about the effects of a new drug. For example, a researcher who knows that a participant is receiving the new heart medication may perceive that the participant's color has improved. Similarly, a participant receiving a new heart medication may expect to have more energy and actually believe that he or she does. Therefore, by creating an environment in which neither the researcher nor the participant knows who is receiving the new drug, the double-blind study controls for the potentially biasing expectations of researchers and participants.

Types of experimental research include pretest-posttest control group method, Solomon four-group method, and posttest-only group method (see chapter 5).

Common to these three types of experimental research is the use of randomization, observations (pretest and post-test), control groups, and treatments.

Perspective for Health Informatics

Unfortunately, in health informatics research, examples of studies using experimental research designs are few. Practical constraints and pressures of short timelines to implement new technologies often subvert efforts to conduct experimental research.

It is emphasized that the key defining characteristic of experimental research is control. Other key characteristics are manipulation of treatment and random assignment (randomization) of subjects to groups. Independent variables are causes, such as treatments or interventions, and dependent variables are effects, such as outcomes. Double-blind studies are a means to control the effects of observer-expectancy and subject-expectancy. The most important point to remember is that experimental research is the only research that establishes cause-and-effect relationships.

Quasi-Experimental Research

Quasi-experimental research searches for *plausible* causal factors. To conduct their investigations, quasi-experimental researchers *approximate* the environment of true experiments. In quasi-experimental studies, researchers investigate *possible* cause-and-effect relationships by exposing one or more experimental groups to one or more treatment conditions and comparing the results to one or more control groups not receiving the treatment. However, the phenomenon or variables under study do not allow the control, manipulation, or both of all their relevant aspects. Often, randomization, a key element of a true experimental design, is lacking. Therefore, as the term "quasi" implies, quasi-experimental research design is "similar to" or "almost" experimental research. Quasi-experimental research is only "similar to" experimental research because quasi-experimental research lacks the ability to establish causal relationships.

Process

Quasi-experimental designs suit phenomena for which true experiments are not feasible or ethical. Typically, in quasi-experimental studies, the researchers manipu-

late the independent variable, but they do not randomly assign participants to experimental or control groups or they may not have control over all variables, allowing introduction of a possible confounding variable. Thus, often, in quasi-experimental studies there are subjects, treatments, and nonrandomized groups.

Studies using quasi-experimental studies are common in health informatics research (Harris et al. 2006, 17). Some common types of quasi-experimental research are one-shot case study, one-group pretest-posttest method, static group comparison, **causal-comparative research**, field experiments, and natural experiments (see table 2.12 and chapter 5). Common to all these studies, the researchers relinquish control of the research environment.

In causal-comparative research, researchers investigate whether a particular cause (factor, event, situation, or independent variable) is associated with an effect (outcome, dependent variable). The data are collected after all the events of interest have occurred. The investigator then takes one or more effects (dependent variables) and examines the data by going back through time, seeking out potential factors or causes, relationships, and their meanings. The choice of a causal-comparative study is appropriate when one of the three following situations exist:

- The variables cannot be manipulated (gender, age, race, birthplace).

- The variables should not be manipulated (accidental death or injury, child abuse).

- The variables represent differing conditions that have already occurred (medication error, heart catheterization performed, smoking).

Causal-comparative studies are also referred to as "**ex post facto**," meaning retrospective. An example is the **case-control (retrospective) study**. In these studies, researchers investigate whether exposure to a factor or phenomenon is associated with an outcome.

Epidemiologists investigating the development of disease often use case-control studies. In case-control studies, the epidemiologists look for characteristics and occurrences related to the subsequent development of a disease. In these studies, epidemiologists collect masses of data from health records and through interviews with both persons with the disease (cases) and persons without it (controls). These case-control studies may involve

Table 2.12.   Selected representative examples of quasi-experimental research studies

Author	Year	Method	Time Frame	Sample and Response Rate	Analytical Techniques	Key Findings, Limitations, and Recommendations
Westbrook et al.	2005	One group pretest-posttest	Cross-sectional	Convenience sample of 75 clinicians who provided 600 answers to 8 scenarios	Descriptive statistics on demographics and search times from logs and statistical analyses of pretest and posttest answer using chi-square, analysis of variance, and other analyses for nonparametric statistics	Scenarios were used to investigate the impact of an online information retrieval system on clinicians' performance answering clinical questions. Information retrieval system resulted in significant improvement in the quality of answers. Limitations were that scenarios are more simplistic than actual practice, time, and volunteers as subjects. Recommended future investigations into the potential for automation bias and into the use of evidence from information retrieval systems.
Schmidt and Gierl	2005	Causal-comparative	Retrospective on 4-week periods over 5 flu seasons	Health data from one German state	Created model using temporal abstraction and case-based reasoning to calculate time points for warnings and consulted epidemiologists on accuracy of warnings	It is possible to create a prognostic model to determine optimal times to issue epidemiologic warnings (influenza forecast).
Chen et al.	2005	Before-after design	Cross-sectional	Nonrandomized experimental group with 30 subjects and control group with 30 subjects	Descriptive statistics; and chi-square test, t-test, and independent and paired t-tests	Multimedia video CD of patient-controlled pain analgesia increased patients' knowledge about pain, achieved better pain relief, and helped patients operate the devices. Limitations included self-selection of experimental group and small numbers of subjects at one medical center. Patient-subjects recommended that video CD be widely distributed to all patients. Researchers recommended additional research with larger sample and with randomization.

health informatics professionals because of their expertise in mining health databases, understanding the content of health records, and identifying cases and controls through the diagnostic and procedural codes. See chapter 6 for more information about epidemiological studies.

For example, researchers could examine the relationship between exposure to cockroaches and pediat-ric asthma. First, the researchers would identify *cases*, children with pediatric asthma (dependent variable, effect). Second, the researchers would identify *controls,* children without pediatric asthma. Third, they would look back in time (retrospective) to calculate the frequency and duration of exposure to cockroaches (independent variable, cause). Fourth, the researchers would compare the frequency and duration of the cases' exposure to cockroaches to the frequency and duration of the controls' exposure. Health informatics researchers would assist in this study by mining the databases and identifying cases.

Perspective for Health Informatics

Health informatics researchers could lead a causal-comparative study. Researchers could investigate the effect of an EHR on patient satisfaction in a hospital after an EHR system has been in place for five years. Researchers would go through survey data on patient satisfaction from time periods before and after the implementation of the EHR. In this case, the researcher is not manipulating any variables, only investigating the effect of the implementation of the EHR on patient satisfaction. However, other factors, such as downturns in the economy, changes in health insurance, differing populations of patients, changes in the composition of the medical staff, new features and upgrades in the EHR, and/or new facilities could affect the patients' satisfaction. Therefore, casual-comparative research must be closely examined to see how the researchers accounted for these other potential factors.

The next example illustrates the multitude and wide range of potentially confounding factors for which the researchers controlled. The researchers were mining data from inpatient cost reports to investigate whether hospitals' financial performance was associated with medical errors (Encinosa and Bernard 2005, 61). The researchers used data from the Healthcare Cost and Utilization Project (HCUP) State Inpatient Database for Florida from 1996 through 2000 and from the American Hospital Association's Annual Survey from 1996 through 2000. The sample consisted of 1,054,281 hospitalizations for major surgery at 176 hospitals. The researchers used an algorithm, the Patient Safety Indicator (PSI) developed by the Agency for Healthcare Research and Quality, to detect medical errors. The main independent variable was the hospital's operating profit margin. The researchers controlled for the lag time between the reduced operating profit margin and its effects on staffing, quality control, and other safety-related areas. The researchers controlled for unobservable factors, such as technological investments, differences in hospitals' patient populations and coding practices, and coding errors. To control for case mix, the researchers included variables on age (eight age groups), race, sex, insurance, indicators for transfer and emergency admissions, median household by zip code, indicators for 30 chronic conditions, major

diagnostic categories, and year indicators. The researchers concluded that reduced operating profit margins were associated with increased numbers of medical errors.

Health informatics researchers conducting a field experiment could observe how medical students use their laptops or PDAs. The researchers could accompany the medical students to class, on rounds, and in study sessions. Are the laptops password protected? Is the password robust? What are the Internet security settings? Have the students sent protected patient data across the Internet to another computer or device?

Researchers conducting **natural experiments** wait for the event to occur naturally. For example, health informatics researchers interested in the effectiveness of disaster recovery plans would wait for a disaster. Prior to the disaster, they would establish baseline data and tools for data collection. When the disaster occurred, they would record their observations of the actions and results.

Quasi-experimental studies are similar to experimental research. Quasi-experimental studies are common in health informatics research. Common types of quasi-experimental research include the one-shot case study, the one-group pretest-posttest method, the static group comparison, and the causal-comparative study. In quasi-experimental studies, there are subjects, treatments, and nonrandomized groups. Quasi-experimental research is valuable because in some situations it is the only design that is logistically and ethically feasible. For purists, however, the lack of randomization and control of treatment lessens the value of quasi-experimental research. It must be emphasized that quasi-experimental research can only identify possible causal factors; quasi-experimental research cannot establish causal relationships.

Summary

Experimental research is important because this major research category allows researchers to investigate cause and effect. It should be clear from these examples of research studies that true experimental studies are very difficult to conduct. Nevertheless, experimental research studies are extremely powerful research methods because only they can establish cause and effect (causal relationship). The types classified as quasi-experimental studies begin to determine that a causal relationship could exist. Some experts state that very large quasi-experimental studies weakly determine a causal relationship. However, to truly establish causal relationships, researchers must use one of the types classified as an experimental study.

The key to determining or classifying the design of a research study is to understand the purpose of the research. Historical research focuses on the past in order to inform future practice. Descriptive research depicts the current status or situation. This research is exploratory and provides useful baseline data. Correlational research is also exploratory and reveals relationships and associations between variables. Observational research, while again an exploratory research, uncovers underlying beliefs and meanings. Evaluation research is the systematic examination of the effectiveness of objects, such as policies, programs, technologies, or organizations. Experimental research is the gold standard of research because it can establish causal relationships. Quasi-experimental research, although very common, can indicate only potential causes. Health informatics researchers have a wide variety of designs with which to investigate the process, application, and impact of computer science, information systems, and communication technologies to health services.

The seven types of research designs described in this chapter are not rigid boxes. Researchers often combine designs to address their particular research questions or problems. For instance, many studies include both descriptive and correlational findings. In describing their study, researchers also often will state its time frame. Thus, a researcher would state that the study was descriptive, correlational, and cross-sectional. Moreover, there is considerable overlap among the designs—nonparticipant observation is very similar to field experiments and naturalistic experiments. Here the difference lies in the qualitative approach versus the quantitative approach of field and naturalistic experiments. The purpose of research study drives its design.

References

Ackerknecht, E.H. 1967. A plea for a 'behaviorist' approach in writing the history of medicine. *Journal of the History of Medicine and Allied Sciences* 22(3):211–214.

Adams, A., A. Blandford, D. Budd, and N. Bailey. 2005 (September). Organizational communication and awareness: A novel solution for health informatics. *Health Informatics Journal* 11(3):163–178.

Ahern, D.K., J.M. Kreslake, and J.M. Phalen. 2006 (January–March). What is e-health (6): Perspectives on the evolution of ehealth research. *Journal of Medical Internet Research* 8(1):e4.

Americans With Disabilities Act. 1998 (Aug. 7). Public Law 105–220, HR 1385, 112 Stat 936. Codified as: Section 504 of the Rehabilitation Act, 29 U.S.C. § 794d. Workforce Investment Act of 1998: Section 508, Electronic and Information Technology.

Ammenwerth, E., C. Iller, and U. Mansmann. 2003a (July). Can evaluation studies benefit from triangulation? A case study. *International Journal of Medical Informatics* 70(2–3):237–248.

Ammenwerth, E., U. Mansmann, C. Iller, and R. Eichstädter. 2003b (January-February). Factors affecting and affected by user acceptance of computer-based nursing documentation: Results of a two-year study. *Journal of the American Medical Informatics Association* 10(1):69–84.

Bauer, W.F. 1996 (April-June). Informatics: An early software company. *IEEE Annals of the History of Computing* 18(2):70–76 (Part of Biographies, E. Weiss, ed.: 67–76).

Bergman, L.G., and U.G.H. Fors. 2005 (January 7). Computer-aided DSM-IV-diagnostics—acceptance, use and perceived usefulness in relation to users' learning styles. *BMC Medical Informatics and Decision Making* 5:1.

Bossen, C. 2007 (January). Test the artefact—develop the organization: The implementation of an electronic medication plan. *International Journal of Medical Informatics* 76(1):13–21.

Case, A., and C. Paxson. 2002 (March-April). Parental behavior and child health. *Health Affairs* 21(2):164–178.

Chapman, W.W., G.F. Cooper, P. Hanbury, B.E. Chapman, L.H. Harrison, and M.W. Wagner. 2003 (September-October). Creating a text classifier to detect radiology reports describing mediastinal findings associated with inhalational anthrax and other disorders. *Journal of the American Medical Informatics Association* 10(5):494–503.

Chen, H-H., M-L. Yeh, and H-J. Yang. 2005 (July). Testing the impact of a multimedia video CD of patient-controlled analgesia on pain knowledge and pain relief in patients receiving surgery. *International Journal of Medical Informatics* 74(6):437–445.

Department of Health and Human Services. 2005 (August). Centers for Disease Control and Prevention. Office of the Director, Office of Strategy and Innovation. *Introduction to Program Evaluation for Public Health Programs: A Self-Study Guide*.

El Emam, K., S. Jabbouri, S. Sams, Y. Drouet, and M. Power. 2006 (October-December). Evaluating common de-identification heuristics for personal health information. *Journal of Medical Internet Research* 8(4):e28.

Encinosa, W.E., and D.M. Bernard. 2005 (Spring). Hospital finances and patient safety outcomes. *Inquiry* 42(1):60–72.

Ely, J.W., J.A. Osheroff, M.L. Chambliss, M.H. Ebell, and M.E. Rosebaum. 2005 (March-April). Answering physicians' clinical questions: Obstacles and potential solutions. *Journal of the American Medical Informatics Association* 12(2):217–224.

Ferranti, J.M., R.C. Musser, K. Kawamoto, and W.E. Hammond. 2006 (May-June). The clinical document architecture and the continuity of care record: A critical analysis. *Journal of the American Medical Informatics Association* 13(3):245–252.

Garrett, P., C.A. Brown, S. Hart-Hester, E. Hamadain, C. Dixon, W. Pierce, and W.J. Rudman. 2006 (Fall). Identifying barriers to the adoption of new technology in rural hospitals. A case report. *Perspectives in Health Information Management* 3(9):1–11.

Georgiou, A., J. Westbrook, J. Braithwaite, and R. Iedema. 2005. Multiple perspectives on the impact of electronic ordering on hospital organizational and communication processes. *Health Information Management Journal* 34(4):130–135.

Griffiths, K.M., and H. Christensen. 2005 (October-December). Website quality indicators for consumers. *Journal of Medical Internet Research* 7(5):e55.

Grosshans, W., and E. Chelimsky. 1991 (March). U.S. General Accounting Office, Program Evaluation and Methodology Division. *Designing Evaluations.*

Guba, E.G., and Y.S. Lincoln. 1989. *Fourth Generation Evaluation.* Newbury Park, CA: Sage.

Halpern, M. 1994 (July-September). Dreams that get funded: Programming rolls on its own reality. *IEEE Annals of the History of Computing* 16(3):61–69 (Part of Biographies, E. Weiss, ed.: 61–70).

Harris, A.D., J.C. McGregor, E.N. Perencevich, J.P. Furuno, J. Zhu, D.E. Peterson, and J. Finkelstein. 2006 (January-February). The use and interpretation of quasi-experimental studies in medical informatics. *Journal of the American Medical Informatics Association* 13(1): 16–23.

Hellesø, R., M. Lorensen, and L. Lorensen. 2004 (August). Challenging the information gap—the patients transfer from hospital to home health care. *International Journal of Medical Informatics* 73(7–8):569–580.

Kiple, K.F. 1991 (Winter). American Association for the History of Medicine: Report of the Committee on Ethical Codes. *Bulletin of the History of Medicine* 65(4):565–570.

Kreps, G.L. 2002. Evaluating new health information technologies: Expanding the frontiers of health care delivery and health promotion. *Studies in Health Technology and Informatics* 80:205–212.

Lloyd, S.S., and E. Layman. 1997 (February). The effects of automated encoders on coding accuracy and coding speed. *Topics in Health Information Management* 17(3):72–79.

Lobach, D.F., and D.E. Detmer. 2007 (May). Research challenges for electronic health records. *American Journal of Preventive Medicine* 32(5S):S104–S111.

McKibbon, K.A., and C.S. Gadd. 2004 (July 22). A quantitative analysis of qualitative studies in clinical journals for 2000 publishing year. *BMC Medical Informatics and Decision Making* 4:11.

Moen, A., and P.F. Brennan. 2005 (November-December). Health@home: The work of health information management in the household (HIMH): Implications for consumer health informatics (CHI) innovations. *Journal of the American Medical Informatics Association* 12(6):648–656.

Patel, V.L., T. Branch, A. Cimino, C. Norton, and J.J. Cimino. 2005 (May-June). Participant perceptions of the influences of the NLM-sponsored Woods Hole medical informatics course. *Journal of the American Medical Informatics Association* 12(3):256–262.

Pizziferri, L., A.F. Kittler, L.A. Volk, M.M. Honour, S. Gupta, S. Wang, T. Wang, M. Lippincott, Q. Li, and D.W. Bates. 2005 (June). Primary care physician time utilization before and after implementation of an electronic health record: A time-motion study. *Journal of Biomedical Informatics* 38(3):176–188.

Rangachari, P. 2007 (Spring). Coding for quality measurement: The relationship between hospital structural characteristics and coding accuracy from the perspective of quality measurement. *Perspectives in Health Information Management* 4(3):1–17.

Ray, M.N., T.K. Houston, F.B. Yu, N. Menachemi, R.S. Maisiak, J.J. Allison, and E.S. Berner. 2006 (September-October). Development and testing of a scale to assess physician attitudes about handheld computers with decision support. *Journal of the American Medical Informatics Association* 13(5):567–572.

Razavi, A.R., H. Gill, O. Stal, M. Sundquist, S. Thorstenson, H. Ahlfeldt, and N. Shahsavar. 2005. Exploring cancer registry data to find risk factors for recurrence of breast cancer—application of canonical correlation analysis. *BMC Medical Informatics and Decision Making* 5:29.

Risse, G.B., and J.H. Warner. 1992 (August). Reconstructing clinical activities: Patient records in medical history. *Society for the Social History of Medicine* 5(2):183–205.

Rubinstein, S. 2006 (October-December). Recollections: The rise and fall of WordStar. *IEEE Annals of the History of Computing* 28(4):64–72.

Ruland, C.M. 1999 (July-August). Decision support for patient preference-based care planning: Effects on nurse care and patient outcomes. *Journal of the American Medical Informatics Association* 6(4):304–312.

Saleem, J.J., E.S. Patterson, L. Militello, M.L. Render, G. Orshansky, and S.M. Asch. 2005 (July-August). Exploring barriers and facilitators to the use of computerized clinical reminders. *Journal of the American Medical Informatics Association* 12(4):438–447.

Schmidt, R., and L. Gierl. 2005 (March). A prognostic model for temporal courses that combines temporal abstraction and case-based reasoning. *International Journal of Medical Informatics* 74(2–4):307–315.

Sequist, T.D., T. Cullen, H. Hays, M.M. Taualii, S.R. Simon, and D.W. Bates. 2007 (April). Implementation and use of an electronic health record within the Indian Health Service. *Journal of the American Medical Informatics Association* 14(2):191–197.

Shah, N.R., A.C. Seger, D.L. Seger, J.M. Fiskio, G.J. Kuperman, B. Blumenfeld, E.G. Recklet, D.W. Bates, and T.K. Gandhi. 2006 (January February). Improving acceptance of computerized prescribing alerts in ambulatory care. *Journal of the American Medical Informatics Association* 13(1):5–11.

Shi, L. 1997. *Health Services Research Methods*. Albany, NY: Delmar.

Sørby, I.D., and O. Nytrø. 2005. Does the electronic patient record support the discharge process? A study on physicians' use of clinical information systems during discharge of patients with coronary heart disease. *Health Information Management Journal* 34(4):112–119.

Stausberg, J., D. Koch, J. Ingenerf, and M. Betzler. 2003 (September-October). Comparing paper-based with electronic patient records: Lessons learned during a study on diagnosis and procedure codes. *Journal of the American Medical Informatics Association* 10(5):470–477.

Terrell, K.M. 2006 (Feb. 27). Using informatics to enhance care of older emergency department patients.

Wennberg, J.E., E.S. Fisher, T.A. Stukel, and S.M. Sharp. 2004 (Oct. 7). Use of Medicare claims data to monitor provider-specific performance among patients with severe chronic disease. *Health Affairs* Suppl Web Exclusive: VAR5-18.

Westbrook, J.I., E.W. Coiera, and A.S. Gosling. 2005 (May-June). Do online information retrieval systems help experienced clinicians answer clinical questions? *Journal of the American Medical Informatics Association* 12(3):315–321.

Winkelman, W.J., K.J. Leonard, and P.G. Rossos. 2005 (May-June). Patient-percived usefulness of online electronic medical records: Employing grounded theory in the development of information and communication technologies for use by patients living with chronic illness. *Journal of the American Medical Informatics Association* 12(3):306–314.

Zeng, Q.T., J. Crowell, R.M. Plovnick, E. Kim, L. Ngo, and E. Dibble. 2006 (January-February). Assisting consumer health information retrieval with query recommendations. *Journal of the American Medical Informatics Association* 13(1):80–90.

Zheng, K., R. Padman, M.P. Johnson, and H.S. Diamond. 2005 (August). Understanding technology adoption in clinical care: Clinician adoption behavior of a point-of-care reminder system. *International Journal of Medical Informatics* 74(7–8):535–543.

PART II

Research Methods

Chapter 3
Survey Research

Valerie J. Watzlaf, PhD, RHIA, FAHIMA

Learning Objectives

- To describe survey research and how it is used in health informatics.
- To display and discuss examples of structured (closed-ended) and unstructured (open-ended) questions used in health informatics research.
- To demonstrate the appropriate organization of survey questions in relation to content, flow, design, scales, audience, and appropriate medium.
- To apply appropriate statistics in order to measure the validity and reliability of the questions.
- To plan and carry out the pilot testing of the questionnaire, whether it is used as a self-survey or interview instrument.
- To calculate the appropriate sample size in which to send the survey instrument.
- To provide appropriate follow-up procedures in order to retrieve a good response rate.
- To depict what statistics can be generated from collecting data via a survey instrument.

Key Terms

Advisory committee
American Hospital Association (AHA)
American Society for Testing and Materials (ASTM)
Census survey
Closed-ended (structured) questions
Cluster sampling
Computerized Physician Order Entry (CPOE)
Convenience sample
Cronbach's alpha
Face validity
Factor analysis
Health Information National Trends Survey (HINTS)
Healthcare Information and Management Systems Society (HIMSS)
Health Level 7 (HL7)
Institutional Review Board (IRB)

Interval
National Ambulatory Medical Care Survey (NAMCS)
National Center for Health Statistics (NCHS)
National Health Interview Survey (NHIS)
Nominal
Office of Measurement and Evaluation (OME)
Open-ended (unstructured) questions
Ordinal
Personal digital assistant (PDA)
Pilot test
Prevarication bias
Ratio
Reliability
Response rate
Sample size

Selection bias

Simple random sampling

Stratified random sampling

Structured questions

Survey research

Systematic random sampling

Test-retest

Unstructured questions

Validity

Web-based survey

Introduction

Survey research is one of the most common types of research used in health informatics because most of the research performed in health informatics is still new and emerging, and many times surveys are used when very little is known about a particular topic. It allows the researcher to explore and describe what is occurring during a particular point or period in time. Therefore, surveys are frequently used when conducting descriptive, cross-sectional or prevalence study designs.

In survey research, the researcher chooses a topic of study and begins to formulate criteria that will help develop questions he or she may have about that topic. The survey can explore a certain disease, community, organization, culture, health information system or software. A random sample of subjects from an appropriate population is chosen to answer the questions from a standardized format. The questionnaire or survey can be completed directly by the subject with directions included within the questionnaire or cover letter, or it can be administered by mail, online, by fax, or in person. Surveys also can be administered via an interview either by phone or in person. The researcher needs to weigh all the variables at hand to determine the best method of administering the survey questionnaire. The main goal of the researcher is to collect the most appropriate and accurate data that will answer the questions most pertinent to the research topic.

Survey Creation

Creation of surveys used for health informatics research is a very important step in the research process. However, it is important for the researcher to determine if a new survey needs to be created or if an existing survey can be used to answer the research questions. The health informatics researcher should decide this by searching the literature to determine if existing surveys are available that meet the needs of research goals. If, once the literature is exhausted and no appropriate existing survey is found, a new survey should be created.

Use of Existing Surveys

One of the first questions the researcher should ask is "What should the content of the survey include in order to effectively answer the research questions under study?" Also, the researcher should consider existing question-

naires and determine if they will be able to answer the questions under study.

For example, the goal of the National Cancer Institute's (NCI) **Health Information National Trends Survey (HINTS)** was to create a population-based survey that could be repeated biennially to track trends in the use of communication technologies such as the Internet as a source of cancer information (Nelson et al. 2004). HINTS examined several different types of existing surveys, such as the **National Health Interview Survey (NHIS)** from the **National Center for Health Statistics (NCHS)** as well as other survey research studies. However, the NCI concluded that, even though existing surveys provided some of the selected content, it was necessary for the researchers and the advisory board to develop a number of new questions and essentially a new survey.

However, in another study (Poole et al. 2004) an existing questionnaire, the Health Assessment Questionnaire (HAQ), was used to measure functional disability in women with scleroderma.

Still other studies (Aldosari 2003) have adapted existing surveys to better convey the purpose of their survey questions. For example, Aldosari, in his dissertation research, adapted several different existing surveys in order to develop a final survey that examined factors affecting physicians' attitudes about the medical information system and its usage and acceptance at the Saudi Arabia National Guard Health System. There were nine sections to the study survey, and different sections—such as the management support section—included questions modified from several other authors. For example, a statement such as "Management will provide or has provided me with the training that I need in order to use the MIS effectively," was modified from prior works. Aldosari also provides the **Cronbach's alpha** reliability coefficient for this work, which was 0.84. The Cronbach's alpha is a measure of internal consistency and determines whether all the variables within the instrument are measuring the same concept. Any value close to 1.00 is considered to have good reliability. The Cronbach's alpha will be discussed in more detail later in this chapter. Aldosari continues to examine and modify questions from several different researchers for each section of the questionnaire providing reliability coefficients for each of these sections.

Table 3.1 provides an example of how Aldosari organized each of the questions used for the management support section for this survey questionnaire.

Table 3.1.   Management support scale

Variable	Item	Source
MS2	The MIS project will be or has been introduced to me effectively by the management.	Current Study-Aldosari (2003)
MS4	Management will involve or has involved me in the implementation of the MIS.	Ivari (1996) Cronbach's alpha = 0.82
MS5	Management will provide or has provided me with the training that I need in order to use the MIS effectively.	Chau (1996) Cronbach's alpha = 0.84
MS7	Management expects me to use the MIS.	Moore (1991) Cronbach's alpha = 0.82

Source: Adapted from Aldosari 2003.

It is important to examine existing surveys to determine if they can be used as is or if they can be adapted by adding questions or rephrasing existing questions. The use of existing surveys can be advantageous because in many cases the validity and reliability of these surveys have been tested and shown to have a high validity and reliability score. (Validity and reliability are discussed in more detail later in this chapter.) However, in health informatics research, many new topics are explored for the first time and therefore, surveys that encompass a new topic are not available for use. It is still important to search the literature to make sure that additional surveys have not been developed that could be used to answer the research questions. Once the literature search has been exhausted, then the development of a new survey can begin.

The authors of the report "Health Information Technology: Information Base for Progress 2006" devote one chapter to determining whether existing surveys can be used or adapted for use to examine EHR adoption in all types of healthcare practices in the United States (RWJF 2006). Surveys such as the **National Ambulatory Medical Care Survey (NAMCS)** from NCHS or the **American Hospital Association (AHA)** annual survey are discussed for possible use by adding a section to the survey on EHR use. However, additional discussion in this report also centers on developing a new survey to collect this important information.

New Survey Development

If it is decided that a new survey is needed, there are several items to consider when building the new ques-

tionnaire. Table 3.2 provides the five different areas that should be considered before developing the questionnaire. They include:

1. The content
2. The audience or those individuals who will be responding to the questionnaire
3. The type or medium in which the questionnaire will be presented to the audience
4. Whether or not a sample or a survey of the entire population will be used
5. The statistics to be generated

All of these items are very important to consider because each has a very specific role to play in the development of the survey. Each of these items is explained in more detail throughout this chapter.

Advisory Committee for Survey Development

There are several areas to consider when building a new survey or questionnaire. First, it is important to form an **advisory committee** or focus group of experts with experience in survey design as well as the topic of study to assist in phrasing the questions in the appropriate manner. An advisory committee met to develop principles and selection of topics and questions for the survey instrument for the HINTS described above.

An advisory committee also participated extensively in the design and development of the survey questions for the Electronic Health Record (EHR) study (Watzlaf et al. 2004). In this study, the researchers' goal was to determine the awareness level of the **American Society for Testing and Materials (ASTM)** standards for health record content among individuals who work within a healthcare facility and use an EHR or are developing an EHR. The researchers also wanted to determine if vendors of EHR systems were aware of and knowledgeable about the ASTM standards. Therefore, the best way to determine this was to develop a survey and send it to these individuals. The full survey for this study can be found in Appendix 3A (pp. 75–87). Methods used to conduct this study will be referred to throughout this chapter so that these steps can be followed when performing survey research in health informatics and health information management.

Some universities and colleges have a separate department that provides assistance and guidance to students and faculty in the design and development of

Table 3.2.   Items to consider when building a questionnaire survey

Content	Audience	Type/Medium	Sample or Population	Statistics Generated
Consider existing surveys from the NCHS, AHA, and other health informatics researchers	Frame questions to level of audience, that is, children, elderly, CIOs	Electronic	Sample should represent population under study	Frequencies
Advisory committee or focus group of experts formed to make recommendations for survey content	Incentives	Mail	Population or census survey done on small populations	Percentages
Inclusion criteria developed to meet needs of research questions and specific aims	Confidential response	Fax	Random Simple Stratify Systematic	Confidence intervals
Open-ended or unstructured questions	Inaccurate response	Group administration or interview	Selection bias	Multivariate analysis (odds ratios, CIs)
Closed-ended or structured questions	Prevarication bias (exaggerate) Recall bias	Phone	Sample size calculation	Correlation
Scales—nominal, ordinal, interval	Follow-up via phone, e-mail, mail	Face-to-face	Convenience sample	
Pilot test		Available on-site	Response rate	
Incorporate changes from pilot test		Distribution	Collect demographic data on nonresponders to compare with that of responders	
Test for validity and reliability on pilot test data				
Factor analysis				

survey instruments. At the University of Pittsburgh, the **Office of Measurement and Evaluation (OME)** assists researchers and students in the development, design, and content of survey instruments. The OME reads or listens to the study objectives or specific aims, and strives to understand all aspects of the study to better assist in framing the survey questions. Also, once the survey is designed and data collected, the OME continues to assist in analyzing the data, if needed.

Once the advisory committee is formed, it makes recommendations for the survey content. The committee can start by developing inclusion criteria that should be developed with the research study objectives or specific aims in mind.

For example, the objectives and specific aims for the EHR study are listed in figures 3.1 and 3.2.

Inclusion Criteria

Some examples of inclusion criteria for the EHR study include the following:

- Use the ASTM standards minimum essential data elements when framing all questions.

- Organize the data elements similar to the ASTM minimum standards; that is, Administrative Patient Data, Encounter Entity, Problem Entity, Treatment Plan.

- Include a separate section on demographic data to include educational degree, major, credential.

- Include a section on Development of EHR or plans to develop an EHR as well as the stage of development/implementation.

- Include both closed-ended and open-ended questions so that additional data elements can be incorporated.

- Include a definition of the EHR for consistency.

- Include a question on the role/title of the person completing the survey.

- Include a section on the awareness of the ASTM standards and coded values

- Include each of the sections of data elements (closed-ended) and whether they should be part of the EHR, and if not, why not, as well as any additional data elements (open-ended).

Figure 3.1.   Objectives for the EHR/ASTM study

1. Measure the awareness of the ASTM E1384 Standard Guide on Content and Structure of Electronic Health Records and the corresponding ASTM E1633 Coded Values for Electronic Health Records.

2. Affirm the usage of the ASTM E1384 Standards and ASTM E1633 Coded Values in Electronic Health Records that currently exist or are being developed.

3. Validate the usefulness of the ASTM E1384 Standards and ASTM E1633 Coded Values in existing Electronic Health Records and identify areas of improvement for future revisions.

Source: Watzlaf et al, 2004.

Figure 3.2.   Specific aims for the EHR/ASTM study

The specific aims of this research study are to answer the following questions:

1. Are healthcare facilities and vendor organizations aware of the ASTM E1384 Standard Guide on Content and Structure of Electronic Health Records and the corresponding ASTM E1633 Coded Values for Electronic Health Records?

2. Are healthcare facilities and vendor organizations using or planning on using the ASTM E1384 Standard Guide on Content and Structure of Electronic Health Records and the corresponding ASTM E1633 Coded Values for Electronic Health Records in their EHR systems?

3. Do healthcare facilities and vendor organizations that use or plan on using the ASTM E1384 Standard Guide on Content and Structure of Electronic Health Records and the corresponding ASTM E1633 Coded Values for Electronic Health Records believe the standards meet their needs?

4. If healthcare facilities and vendor organizations do not believe the ASTM E1384 Standard Guide on Content and Structure of Electronic Health Records and the corresponding ASTM E1633 Coded Values for the Electronic Health Record are meeting their needs, what additions or changes in the standards are needed?

Source: Watzlaf et al. 2004, unpublished developmental material.

Figure 3.3 lists a sample of comments generated from the advisory committee after reviewing the first draft of the Web-based survey for the EHR study. Samples of the screens from the Web-based design are included in Appendix 3B (pp. 88–89).

Types of Questions

Open-ended (unstructured or qualitative**)** and **closed-ended (structured** or quantitative**)** questions usually comprise a survey questionnaire. Open-ended questions are used more often for phone or face-to-face interviews whereas closed-ended questions are used more for self-assessments, Web-based or e-mail surveys, or mail and faxed surveys. Open-ended questions are used when the

Figure 3.3.   Comments from the advisory committee regarding the EHR/ASTM survey

1. Add other credentials to describe job functions such as RN, MD, no credential, as well as health informatics, nursing informatics, health care professional.

2. At the top of each page on the survey, include "Standards from ASTM E1384—Table 6".

3. We need to think about adding an introductory page before all the tables describing all sections so respondents can click on the general section and they will then go directly to the data element section.

4. Define the electronic health record by using the definition on p. 2 of the ASTM E1384 standards.

5. Change patient data to "Administrative Patient Data".

6. Define "Data Elements" only if we can find a definition in the ASTM standards.

7. Advertise on Web sites and LISTSERV mailing lists, and in the journals that targeted facilities and vendors utilize.

8. Ask OME about response rate and how to compute with over sampling.

Source: Watzlaf et al. 2004, unpublished developmental material.

researcher may want to collect the "why" and "why not" that closed-ended questions may not answer. Sometimes surveys can be a mix of both closed-ended and open-ended type questions.

For example, in the EHR study, the researchers decided to use a mixed methodology to obtain results that quantify and thoroughly explain the validation of the data elements, users' needs, and the awareness and use of the ASTM standards. Many times with quantitative data alone, a survey may capture valid data that provide succinct numbers on a subject. However, a survey may not include the "why" and "why not" that more open-ended questions may answer.

Therefore, the EHR survey in Appendix 3A (pp. 75–87) was organized into the following six parts:

1. Demographic data on the facility and the individual completing the survey (closed-ended questions) (Page 75)

2. Awareness of ASTM E1384 standards and E1633 coded values (closed-ended questions) (Page 76)

3. Type of EHR system in place or in the development stage (closed-ended questions) (Page 76)

4. Minimum Essential Data Set—EHR Data View of All Settings—which data items are in place or will be put in place if in development stage (closed-ended questions) (Pages 77–83)

5. Data elements needed that are not included/data elements that should be eliminated (open-ended questions) (Pages 77–83)

6. Additional comments (open-ended questions) (Pages 77–83)

7. Definition of Terms (Pages 84–88)

Scales: Nominal, Ordinal, Interval, Ratio

It is also very important to decide the types of questions the researcher will create for the survey. Will the scale include the very simple, nominal, and ordinal types of questions or the interval and ratio scales?

Nominal Scale

Nominal scales assign a numerical value to a particular response. For example, the following nominal scale may be used for insurance type:

1 = Medicare

2 = Medical Assistance

3 = Private Insurance

A numerical value is assigned to the particular variable under study, but it does not have true meaning as far as the numerical value. It is only there to provide categorization. There are even simpler questions than nominal ones. The dichotomous questions provide two responses, such as "yes" and "no", "true" or "false," or "agree" or "disagree." For example, a dichotomous question may include:

In your opinion, is your Computerized Physician Order Entry (CPOE) system effective in preventing medication errors?

___ Yes

___ No

Ordinal Scale

The **ordinal** scale is used when a question can be rank ordered, such as with patient satisfaction surveys where 1 = not satisfied and 4 = very satisfied. The higher numbers mean greater satisfaction, but the distance from 1 to 2 may not be the same as the distance from 3 to 4. The numerical value assigned to each ranked response is not a true numerical value, just a method of ranked categorization.

For example, a two-part study (Watzlaf et al. 1995) conducted in one long-term care facility (LTCF) interviewed residents and healthcare providers and asked them to rank 25 clinical care topics in relation to how important they were in their life and care at this LTCF. Based on the results of the first part of this study, a more intensive review of the medical records was conducted to determine if those variables identified in the first part of the study could be retrieved from the medical record. The interview instrument consisted of 25 clinical care areas, and the residents were asked to listen to the clinical care area and state how important they believed this topic was in regard to their life and care. The residents also were told to not only think of their own situation, but of all residents in the LTCF. They were then asked to rank each topic discussed using a scale of 1 to 5 (1 being most important and 5 being least important). The healthcare providers were given the same clinical areas to rank but were told to think about them in relation to the residents' care.

A portion of the interview instrument and the ranked scale is provided in Table 3.3.

This instrument enabled the researchers to determine the most important clinical care areas for residents and healthcare providers. Based on this information, researchers could make comparisons between what the residents believed was important versus the healthcare providers. To do this, the researchers computed means for each of the clinical care topics and then rank ordered them for residents and healthcare providers. For example, it was found that residents ranked freedom of choice first (mean ranking = 2.05) whereas healthcare providers ranked it number 20 out of 25 (mean ranking = 2.19) clinical care topics. Therefore, because the value of 2.05 is a method of ranked categorization and not a true numerical value, it states that residents believe freedom of choice is very important. The healthcare providers agreed, but their mean of 2.19 falls much higher than their other rankings and therefore the researchers interpreted this to mean that freedom of choice is not as important as other clinical care areas.

Interval and Ratio Scales

Interval and **ratio** scales have true numerical meaning because the distance between the variables relates to the true numerical value assigned. The best example for interval scales is temperature, and the best example for ratio is weight, because in ratio scales the absolute zero is still meaningful.

Table 3.3.   Excerpt of interview instrument with ordinal scale

Topic	Scale 1 = Most Important 2 = Very Important 3 = Important 4 = Somewhat Important 5 = Least Important	Do you want to discuss your ranking?
1. Medications	1 2 3 4 5	
2. Use of Restraints	1 2 3 4 5	
3. Treatment Plan (aware of treatment plan and involved in process of developing treatment plan)	1 2 3 4 5	
4. Freedom of Choice (right to choose physician, participate in planning care and treatment)	1 2 3 4 5	

Source: Watzlaf et al. 1995.

Use of Appropriate Statistics with Different Scales

It is important to ascertain which types of scales will be incorporated into the questionnaire. Once this is determined, the researcher will be able to know which types of statistics to generate. For nominal data, frequencies and percentages are appropriate; for ordinal data, medians, percentages, and ranges are appropriate; but for interval and ratio scales, which have continuous variables, means, standard deviations, and variance are all appropriate to use. However, even though medians and ranges are best to use for ordinal data, many researchers will generate means or averages because they are easier to display in tables and graphs, and many readers are more familiar with means or averages. When using means for ordinal data, the means do not have true numerical value but demonstrate a method of ranked categorization in relation to the particular ranked scale.

Pilot Test Survey

Once the questions are framed and included into a first draft of the survey questionnaire, it should be **pilot tested** on a small group of individuals. These individuals should reflect the true sample of respondents as much as possible and provide an accurate simulation of administration of the survey questionnaire.

For example, in the EHR study, the survey was pilot tested by sending it to a random sample of 10 different healthcare facilities and organizations for their input on the content of the survey only. Also, a sample of three individuals was observed responding to the Web-based version of the EHR survey to obtain their feedback on the content as well as the ease of use in responding to

the survey online. Once their comments were received, changes to the survey were made.

The following list of comments is from the actual pilot testing of the EHR study survey and cover letter. A sample of the EHR cover letter can be found in Appendix 3C (pp. 90–91).

1. Survey confusing. We need to define what "Master Table" means. For example, the facility may have the data items in a facility-wide or department-specific policy but they might not be stored electronically.

2. We should also think about including how the EMR defines and uses consults or referrals. This is something important to ask about. But should we add this if it is not part of the ASTM standards? The respondent could include this under what other data elements should be included, correct?

3. Survey is fine and cover letter is fine. Both very clear and easy to complete.

4. Survey was long and boring and may have missed answering some of the data items because it was so long. Categories difficult. Yes/Planned, No, Not sure. There is a huge difference in what is planned with an EHR and a "Yes" we have that functionality. If company X completed the survey, everything would be a Yes/Planned and in reality it would have a "No" as of right now. As a result of those things I considered in Planning, I gave a "Not Sure" because I am not 100 percent sure we will have it functional. We need to really think about changing the categories here, especially if we are going to get a lot of not sures.

5. Provide a short definition of what ASTM is to clarify.

6. Include a question on the role of the respondent with the EHR, such as designer, coordinator, user, etc.

7. Split the long table into two pages so it can be seen on one screen.

8. "Not sure" may bias the result. This is important in relation to #4 comments also.

9. Good survey. Reset button should be located at top or somewhere more visible than the bottom right page.

10. Make sure that respondents must answer all questions without skipping ahead.

11. #2 on first page is a browser issue: the first answer runs into the question.

12. Should include the option of not applicable. Maybe we could include not applicable instead of not sure?

13. Change implementation in definition part to modular installation so that it matches what is on the table. Same thing for Fully in Place. In the definition it is stated as "Fully operational"—should state "Fully in Place."

14. Should include an answer of "no credentials" for those without credentials. Maybe we need to include something on job function or background as well as credentials?

15. The help button for provider/practitioner name is not correct. When the respondent clicks on help for this data item the correct definition does not come up.

16. Universal patient health number is misspelled in the text/definition section.

17. Page 11, when the respondent clicks on all three of the numerical measurements, it takes the respondent to the top of the page and not to the proper place for the proper definition.

18. History taking event date—no help next to it and the item is unclear. It needs a definition.

The researchers reviewed all of the comments from the pilot testing and discussed them with the advisory board to determine which changes should be made to the questionnaire. The comments were very helpful and tremendously improved the final questionnaire. For example, one of the possible responses was changed from "Not Sure" to "Not Applicable" based solely on the comments of the pilot study. It is extremely important to pilot test every questionnaire before it is distributed to respondents.

Validity and Reliability

Validity means the right thing was measured. Validity is accuracy. **Reliability** means the survey consistently produces the same results. Reliability is also referred to as reproducibility or repeatability. It is possible to have reliability without validity, but not validity without reliability.

Validity

For new surveys, it is important to test for validity and reliability.

There are several types of validity that can be examined for each survey developed. The four major types of validity include:

1. Face
2. Criterion-related
3. Construct
4. Content

Table 3.4 defines and provides examples of each type of validity. (Colorado State University, 1993–2007)

Because the EHR study survey included an advisory committee of EHR experts, content validity was achieved. Also, the survey contains **face validity** because it was used in a pilot study and was found to be understandable, flowed well, and most comments were incorporated into the final version of the survey.

Reliability

It is important to compute the reliability or consistency of the survey. This was performed in a study by Garvin and Watzlaf (2004) in which the researchers adapted the clinical data specialist section of the Evolving HIM Careers survey to assess whether coders and noncoders had the necessary skills. A sample of some of the survey questions can be found in Appendix 3D (p. 92).

Reliability was determined after the survey was provided to a group of 30 randomly selected credentialed HIM professionals and members of AHIMA. This sample

Table 3.4. Validity for survey research

Validity	Definition	Example
Face validity	On the surface, face validity examines how an instrument looks. Does it flow well? Is the survey the best method to capture the information needed for the research study?	Arranging questions in a certain order to measure the understanding of health informatics concepts. The first section may include demographics of the respondents and the second section may include questions related to health informatics concepts such as artificial intelligence, audit trail, and so forth.
Criterion-related validity	Measures accuracy of the intended survey instrument by comparing it to another method that has been shown to be valid.	Measuring computer skills of employees in a healthcare facility by providing both a hands-on computer skills test that is shown to be accurate and a written test on computer concepts.
Construct validity: Convergent validity Discriminate validity	Agreement between theoretical concept and the survey instrument. Can be separated into two parts: convergent validity (agreement among ratings collected independently on issues that should be agreed upon theoretically) and discriminate validity (disagreement upon issues measured that should be disagreed upon theoretically).	If seeking to study the concepts of what constitutes quality of healthcare, the researchers should first establish, in theory, the concepts of quality healthcare. Then, the practical relationships of these theoretical concepts can be measured. Next, the results from the practical data can be used to determine how well the survey instrument will collect quality of care data.
Content validity	The survey instrument captures the information the researchers intended to measure.	If researchers aim to study physicians' documentation practices in the EHR, but only examine this in the history and physical examination section of the EHR, this would not demonstrate content validity because it excludes other areas in which physicians conduct documentation practices.

Source: Adapted from information of Colorado State University 1993–2007.

of individuals completed the survey twice not knowing the purpose. The Cronbach's alpha was determined, and the reliability coefficient was 0.9285. The assumptions for the Cronbach's alpha include:

1. All items in the instrument should be measured on an interval or ratio scale
2. Each item should be normally distributed.

Reliability coefficients close to 1.00 have very high internal consistency or reliability and those close to 0.00 have very low internal consistency or reliability. Because the Cronbach's alpha for Garvin and Watzlaf's study was 0.9285, this shows high internal consistency and therefore demonstrates that all items in the instrument are measuring the same concept (Cronk 2006).

Garvin and Watzlaf also went on to measure the **test-retest** for reliability. The test-retest determines whether or not the instrument is consistent over time or when given multiple times. The assumptions for test-retest are the same as the Cronbach's alpha. The test-retest reliability coefficient is simply a correlation coefficient for

the relationship between the two total scores given on two different times to the same group of individuals. In Garvin and Watzlaf's 2004 study, the correlation coefficient for reliability was 0.908. Values close to 1.00 indicate strong reliability and those values close to 0.00 indicate poor reliability. The correlation coefficient of 0.908 indicates that the survey instrument is very reliable when administered multiple times (Cronk 2006).

Factor Analysis in Refining Survey Questionnaires

Sometimes researchers need to refine the number of questions that are used in a survey questionnaire. One way to do this is by using factor analysis. **Factor analysis** is a statistical technique in which a large number of variables are summarized and reduced down to a smaller number based on similar relationships among those variables. For example, researchers were interested in performing factor analysis to obtain a valid survey instrument for collecting information related to Lyme disease. The researchers administered the pilot survey to 743 participants and received a 45 percent response rate. Factor analysis was performed to reduce the number of items that were not associated with a common factor. Therefore, the factor analysis revealed that one question was not associated with a common factor and thus was eliminated from the assessment tool (Garvin et al. 2005).

Audience

It is extremely important to know the audience so that questions are framed to the level of that audience. Questions can be worded very differently depending on whether young adults or a group of chief information officers (CIOs) will be responding. The researcher should use clear, unambiguous terms when developing the survey questions because it is easy for the intended audience to misinterpret certain questions. For example, in the original draft of the EHR survey, a "not sure" response was included. This response was determined, through the pilot testing for the survey, to be unclear and therefore was not used in the final EHR survey. Therefore, it is also essential to pilot test the survey to a small sample of the intended audience before final distribution. By doing this, the researcher is better able to understand his/her intended audience and their ability to answer specific survey questions.

Framing of Questions

To obtain accurate data, it is also important to consider the order of the questions as well as the order of the response choices. For example, in one study (Firouzan and McKinnon 2004), questions were framed so that health information managers could easily respond regarding their role in Health Insurance Portability and Accountability Act (HIPAA) Privacy Rule implementation in Pennsylvania healthcare facilities. One of the questions provided the opportunity for the health information manager to describe who is responsible for developing/updating certain privacy practices. This was with a checklist of choices such as:

____Privacy officer

____Privacy staff

____Other: please list_____

By providing a clear method to answer these questions, it is easy for the intended audience to provide accurate information.

Incentives

It is also important to consider whether incentives will be provided to the audience for completing the survey. Although incentives such as the chance to win a $200 gift certificate may entice the respondents to answer all the questions, the researcher should consider that incentives may influence responses and that some respondents may hurriedly complete the survey to take part in the incentive. Therefore, the researcher should decide whether an incentive is really necessary and how effective it may be in increasing response rates compared with the possibility of an increase in inaccurate data.

Confidential Responses

The respondents expect that their responses will be kept confidential when completing a survey questionnaire. The **Institutional Review Board (IRB)**, from which the researcher(s) receives approval to conduct the research, also will want to know how the researcher maintains the confidentiality of the responses generated. The level of research in which the study is approved (exempt, expedited, full-board approval, and so forth) determines how the researcher will collect and maintain the data. (See chapter 13 for additional discussion of IRB approval.)

For example, in the EHR study, exempt approval from the IRB was received, which means that no identifying information could be linked with the survey responses. An e-mail was sent to each facility with the online survey URL included. Although some other studies require the users to log in, the researchers believed that this would discourage the user to proceed in the study and would produce errors as well. Therefore, an individual, nonidentifying number and password were included in the URL. A database separate from the survey responses was developed to include the ID number and facility name and was only used to determine who responded and who did not and therefore aid in the follow-up process. No identifying information could be linked with the survey responses, and all information that was reported in presentations and journal articles was reported in aggregate form so that no respondents could be identified. The facility was assured that their responses would remain completely confidential and that only aggregate data was used in the reporting of the results.

Limitations/Bias/Error

Error is something every researcher must deal with when conducting studies. There are times when respondents will not be able to provide an accurate response because they may not understand the question, may not have appropriate time to respond to the question, or may experience difficulty recalling past experiences in order to answer the question. For all of these reasons, it is important to ask questions that are unambiguous and that do not require extensive recollection. If the respondent needs to remember an experience to answer a question, a picture, graph, table, or other type of illustration can be used to help jog the respondent's memory and increase the chances of an accurate response. Sometimes respondents may exaggerate their responses to questions. This **prevarication bias** may occur when collecting salary information for a specific job title or when collecting other sensitive pieces of data. Therefore, it is important to phrase the questions clearly and give ranges to choose from to keep the respondents' answers as accurate as possible.

Type/Medium

There are many different ways to administer the survey. Web-based, mail, and fax are some of the different methods. The researcher should determine the best medium to use in order to obtain the highest response rate while still obtaining accurate response data. Each of the different mediums previously mentioned will be described in more detail.

Web-based

Once all aspects of the audience have been articulated, the researcher should determine the appropriate medium with which to administer the survey. For example, after the evaluation and modification of the EHR survey, it was decided to post the final version on a Web server for easy access by recipients. There are many advantages in using **Web-based surveys**. These include:

- Reduced cost in comparison with paper

- Less or no data entry (because data are automatically downloaded to a database or spreadsheet)
- Ease of data analysis
- The use of pop-up instructions and drop-down boxes
- Ability to present questions in random order (Gunn 2002).

There are also many disadvantages in using Web-based surveys. They include:

- Missing respondents who do not have a computer or access to the Internet
- Increased time in developing an effective questionnaire
- Difficulty hiring a person with skills in Web-based survey design and development
- Difficulty making changes to the questionnaire once on the Web
- Some respondents more reluctant to provide their responses over the Internet due to lack of confidence in privacy and security

It is best to provide the survey questionnaire in several media so that all respondents can reply. For the EHR survey, several important steps were conducted before the survey was in full use by respondents:

1. The online survey was tested intensively and extensively before its final release.

2. It was very convenient for respondents to complete the survey form, and this was one of the factors for the success of the survey. An e-mail including the survey URL was sent to each facility. Although some other studies require users to log in, the researchers believed that it would discourage users to proceed in the study and would produce errors as well. Therefore, an individual, nonidentifying number and password were included in the URL for the sake of the respondents. A database separate from the survey responses was developed to include the ID number and facility name, and this was only used to determine who responded and who did not and therefore aid in the follow-up process.

3. The length of the survey page was important for the users to finish the survey. If a survey is too long, respondents have to scroll down repeat-

edly to finish the survey, which could discourage the respondent in completing the survey. Therefore, the EHR survey was divided into pages of reasonable length, and the respondents could complete the form in the order that the pages were displayed.

4. Survey coding followed the HTML standard for compatibility with different end user browsers, allowing more respondents to participate despite their different browser environment.

Mail, Fax, and Group Administration

Even though the primary medium for administering the EHR survey was through the Web, researchers found that several facilities preferred the survey to be mailed or faxed, or for the information to be taken over the phone. Thus, researchers had to provide the survey in each of these media.

Other researchers have used mail surveys for health informatics research. For example, researchers used a mailed survey to determine if physicians in family practice residency programs across the U.S. used **personal digital assistants (PDAs)**. The response rate was 50 percent, and the researchers found that two thirds of the respondents used PDAs and an additional 14 percent planned to use them within the next two years (Criswell and Parchman 2002).

Other researchers (Murff and Kannry 2001) have used mailed surveys to internal medicine and pediatric medicine staff physicians to determine their satisfaction with using two different physician order entry systems. Again, the response rate was high (63 and 64 percent, respectively, for the two systems) and the researchers were able to determine that physicians were satisfied with one system but not the other. An existing questionnaire, the Questionnaire for User Interface Satisfaction (QUIS), was used. It contains a 27-question survey with five major categories (University of Maryland 1998). These categories included:

1. Overall reaction to the software
2. Screen design and layout
3. Terminology and systems information
4. Learning
5. Systems capabilities

Still other researchers (Patel et al 2005) used both survey questionnaires and face-to-face interviews to collect precoure and postcourse data on students enrolled in the Woods Hole Course in Medical Informatics. The goal of this study was to determine the students' knowledge of medical informatics and their involvement with medical informatics field work before taking the course as well as their reasons for enrolling in the course. Interviews supplemented the questionnaires in order to gain more elaborate responses on why students took the course, what they expected to achieve, how the course fulfilled their expectations, their recommended changes to future courses, and what new informatics-related activities the students participated in after finishing the course.

Some researchers (Couper et al. 2007) have used both mailed survey questionnaires and phone interviews to compare responses as well as to supplement data collected or to validate the responses received from the survey questionnaire. In a study by Couper et al. researchers used both phone and mailed surveys to collect data from respondents regarding their weight management. The researchers did this because in their original randomized controlled trial of weight management, 85 percent of the study subjects were lost to follow-up, and they wanted to find out which method of data collection was best. The response rate from the phone interview was 59 percent compared with 55 percent for the mail survey, although the mail survey was cheaper and the phone survey tended to provide more reports of weight loss than those reported from the mailed surveys.

Also, many times surveys can be made available for a particular group at one location, such as during a meeting or conference, or at a retirement community or physician practice, so that respondents can complete the survey and immediately submit it to the researchers.

Please see Appendix 3A (pp. 75–87) for the full EHR survey and Appendix 3B (pp. 88–89) for excerpts of the Web-based version.

Distribution of Survey

It is important to determine how the survey will be distributed. For example, in the EHR study, each of the facilities randomly selected was contacted by phone or e-mail to explain the study, determine if the facility was willing to participate in the study, and to obtain the name, address, e-mail address, fax, phone, and so on of the individual most capable and knowledgeable to answer questions related to the EHR standards. The participants were assured that their responses would remain completely confidential and that only aggregate data would be used in the results report. Identifying information related to the facility was stored separately from their responses. No identifying information was displayed on the survey form; only a coded number was used for follow-up purposes. The facilities received a copy of the results and a complimentary copy of the *Journal of American Health Information Management Association* for participating. The cover letter described information related to research study participation (Appendix 3C, pp. 90-91).

Once the names of the individuals who completed the survey were obtained, they were contacted via e-mail and were provided a copy of the cover letter and survey through a corresponding URL. If the participant did not have access to a computer, the cover letter and survey were faxed or mailed, whichever was preferred by the participating facility. The deadline date to return the survey was two weeks after receipt of the survey. After two weeks, if the facility did not respond, a follow-up e-mail (with follow-up cover letter attached) or phone call was made to request that a facility representative complete the survey. The importance of the study and its results were reiterated, and any questions regarding the survey were answered. See Appendix 3E (pp. 93–94) for a sample follow-up cover letter.

Sample and Sample Size

Most survey research in health informatics is performed on a sample of the population under study. A **census survey** surveys an entire population. If a sample is chosen, it is extremely important to make sure that it is an accurate representation of the population under study. In this way, the characteristics of the sample are then similar to the population characteristics. For example, if a researcher is interested in surveying physicians about their views on patients using a personal health record, it would be best to select physicians from many different specialties. Examining only pediatricians would not accurately represent the entire physician population and their specialties. Certain sample size calculations also should be used to determine the sample size to survey. Also, certain types of software applications can be used to generate an appropriate sample size. For example, sample size calculations can be performed using the SPSS statistical package.

Sampling Methods

Because most survey research is performed by using a sample, it is imperative to apply different sampling meth-

ods. For example, **simple random sampling** is the most common method used. It enables every member of the population under study to have an equal chance of being selected. Different software programs can easily provide effective random samples very quickly. Also, a table of random numbers can be used to select a good random sample. Other methods of random sampling include:

- **Stratified random sampling**—separate the population by certain characteristics, such as physician specialties, nursing units, or DRGs and then choose the random sample
- **Systematic random sampling**—draw the sample from a list of items such as diagnoses, ICD-9-CM codes, or discharges and select every nth case
- **Cluster sampling**—separate first into a city block and then sample everyone within that unit

Convenience samples are another method used to easily sample respondents to obtain quick results, but this type of sample is not random. An example of a convenience sample is surveying everyone in a particular HIT department to determine their knowledge of **Health Level 7 (HL7)**. It can generate quick results but it cannot be generalized to everyone in an HIT setting. In order to do that, a random sample should be chosen across all HIT employees in the United States, such as a sample of members of an HIT organization such as the **Healthcare Information and Management Systems Society (HIMSS)**. Please see chapter 10 for more specific information on sampling methods.

Example of Sample Size Calculation Used for the EHR Study

The discussion that follows is an example of how respondents were selected for the sample and the methods used to obtain the sample size.

Stratified random sampling was used to select a sample of healthcare facilities for the EHR study. The population of healthcare facilities in the United States that are identified in the American Hospital Association guide (numbering approximately 15,000) was stratified by state and by type of facility, such as acute, subacute, long-term care, ambulatory care, and so forth. Using a random number-generating procedure, a random sample was drawn from each subgroup of facilities formed by cross classifying the facilities according to both state and type. A subgroup was defined as all facilities of the same type within the same state. For example, one subgroup was made up of acute care facilities in Pennsylvania, and another subgroup was made up of long-term care facilities in West Virginia.

The healthcare facilities selected by this method comprised one of three components of the total sample. To be certain that facilities with an EHR in place are included in the total sample, the second component was made up of all healthcare organizations recognized by the Nicholas E. Davies EHR Recognition Program, a program sponsored by the Healthcare Information and Management Systems Society (HIMSS).

The third component of the total sample was made up of vendors of EHR systems. All information system vendors on the list published by Health Care Informatics magazine (approximately 100 vendors) and all 28 EHR vendors on the list of those reviewed by the American Academy of Family Physicians were included in the sample. Table 3.5 represents the composition of the total sample.

To determine the number of healthcare facilities to include in the first component of the sample, the following formula was used.

The bound for the error of estimate (B) was set at 5 percent, which is considered an acceptable margin of error for many studies. The value for p (the proportion of facilities that are aware of the standards) was set at 0.5 for the purpose of sample size determination, because this value produces the most conservative, or the largest, value for the required sample size. Substituting the appropriate values into the formula resulted in a sample size requirement of 390 facilities.

When stratified random sampling is used, the most typical way of distributing the total sample size among the subgroups (or strata) is for subgroups to be represented in the sample in the same proportion that they are represented in the population. To achieve this result, the same sampling fraction, 390/15,000 or approximately .03, was applied to each subgroup. For example, if there were 300 acute care facilities in Pennsylvania, 3 percent of them or 9 such facilities were selected; if there were 67 long-term care facilities in West Virginia, 3 percent of them or 2 such facilities were selected.

Therefore, the **sample size** was determined by using the following formula:

$$n = Npq/(N-1)D + pq$$

$$D = B\_/4 \text{ where } B = 0.05\_/4 = 0.000625$$

The total sample size for healthcare facilities was computed as follows:

$$n = (15,000)(0.5)(0.5) \underline{\hspace{1cm}} \underline{\hspace{0.5cm}3750\hspace{0.5cm}}$$

$$(14,999)(0.000625) + 0.25 = 9.624375$$

$$= 389.636 = 390$$

Therefore, when the other two samples (14 = Nicholas Davies Winners and 128 for Vendors) are included, the grand total sample size equals:

$$390 + 128 + 14 = \mathbf{532}$$

Each of the sample size estimates for the healthcare facilities was oversampled to allow for facility refusal, nonresponse, and so forth. There are limitations to the sample: It does not include all types of healthcare facilities in the United States, only those listed in the *AHA Guide to the Health Care Field: United States Hospitals, Health Care Systems, Networks, Alliances, Health Organizations, Agencies, Providers*, which also includes a convenience sample of "elite" facilities with EHR systems and the top 100 vendors.

Response Rate

The **response rate** is extremely important in survey research. Sometimes, however, even a low response rate in an area that has not been researched in depth before may prove beneficial. For example, this may prove true when researching the effectiveness of drug alerting in

Table 3.5.   Composition of the total sample for the EHR/ASTM study

Type of Facility or Organization	Total Population	Sample	Sample 2 (If Applicable)
Acute, sub-acute, rehab, and so forth	15,000	390	Approximately 3% per state and facility type
Nicholas E. Davies CPR Recognition Facilities	14 (could increase when 2001 winners are selected)	14	Not applicable
Vendors	128	All 128 except for any overlap between the two lists	Not applicable

Source: Watzlaf et al. 2004, unpublished developmental material.

the **Computerized Physician Order Entry (CPOE)** system, because at least some information is provided from which to answer the research questions.

In another study on HIM practices (Osborn 2000), 1,000 surveys were sent out to AHIMA members and only 200 were returned. Even though the 20 percent response rate may seem low, this study was one of the first of its kind to examine practices and productivity of health information management functions in acute care hospitals. Therefore, this study was able to provide some beginning and new information about HIM practices that was never before examined. It provided average completion times for chart assembly, chart analysis, coding, and billing, as well as mean turnaround time for release of information activities and other additional HIM functions.

One method used to increase the response rate is to follow up with the respondents to ask them if they could respond to the survey. However, the follow-up method should not be overly annoying or intrusive because this can affect the protection of research subjects (under IRB guidelines), and some IRBs will specifically ask the researcher to state the number of times respondents will be contacted to respond to the survey questionnaire. Still, follow-up can be very helpful in increasing the response rate. It can be performed by sending an index card via the mail, through e-mail, or by phone or fax. Follow-up should include the title of the research study, when the survey questionnaire was sent, the importance of the study and how important the respondent's reply is to the research study, as well as the maintenance of confidential responses and any incentives (if stated in the initial cover letter of the survey). The survey should be attached again so the respondent does not need to look for it in a previous email or letter.

In the EHR study, the researchers were planning to obtain a response rate of greater than 50 percent, and they believed that including different types of survey media as well as follow-up e-mails and/or phone calls were essential in obtaining this rate. See Appendix 3E (pp. 93–94) for a sample of the follow-up cover letter for the EHR study.

The researchers reported two response rates for the EHR study. A total of 1,129 surveys were sent out and the desired sample size was 390, based on the sample size calculation. There were 192 total surveys received for all pages completed, and 271 for at least one page completed. The response rate based on the desired sample size was between 49 percent for all pages completed to 69 percent for at least one page completed. Total response rate based on surveys sent was much lower at 17 to 24 percent.

Factors limiting the success of the response and completion rates included the length of the paper and Web-based survey, respondents not having an EHR on site and therefore not believing that they could continue to answer the questions, and not having the ability to use the Web to answer the survey.

There are some steps to follow if a response rate is very low. First, if it can be determined that the nonresponders are similar to the responders in relation to demographic characteristics such as age, gender, geographic region, and so forth, then it is safe to conclude that the responders are similar to the general population under study. However, this means that the researchers would need to collect this type of information on the nonresponders and compare it with that of the responders, and many times researchers do not have this data on the nonresponders. But if demographic data are available, then a comparison can be made and support given to a low but representative response rate.

Selection Bias

Researchers need to be aware of **selection bias,** which is the ability of some participants to choose to answer the survey questionnaire or to be part of the survey research study. This can bias survey results because responders may want to take part in the research study for different reasons. For example, some of the EHR responders may decide to respond to the survey because they have an EHR in place in their facility. However, some other potential participants may not have responded because an EHR was not in place in their facility. The researchers, then, may have missed this latter group of participants and their input into answers for the survey questions.

Statistical Analysis of the Survey Study Data

Statistical analysis of survey data is usually quite simple and includes calculating frequencies, percentages, correlation coefficients, tests of significance, or confidence intervals. It may also include graphs and tables that reflect these statistics. Also, each section of the open-ended or unstructured questions should be analyzed by reviewing each section and summarizing it into specific categories. Or, specific or additional comments can be reproduced in a separate section of the report so that no important information is missed.

Examples of statistical tables for the EHR/ASTM are shown in tables 3.6 through 3.12.

Table 3.6.   Stage of EHR system

	#	%
No plans/don't have one	24	10%
Development	28	11%
Fully in place	33	13%
Other	32	13%
Modular installation	66	26%
Planning	68	27%
Total	251	100%

Source: Watzlaf, et al., 2004.

Table 3.7.   Type of system

	#	%
Developed in-house	35	18%
Other	38	20%
Vendor	117	62%
Total	190	100%

Source: Watzlaf, et al., 2004.

Table 3.8.   Role with EHR system

	#	%
Designer	20	9%
Developer	20	9%
Coordinator	63	29%
Other	115	53%
Total	218	100%

Source: Watzlaf, et al., 2004.

Table 3.9.   Awareness of ASTM E1384 Standard Guide on Content and Structure of EHR

	#	%
Very much	8	3%
Enough	9	4%
Moderate amount	43	18%
No	81	34%
A little	97	41%
Total	238	100%

Source: Watzlaf, et al., 2004.

Table 3.10.   Awareness of ASTM E1633 coded values for EHR

	#	%
Very much	5	2%
Enough	10	4%
Moderate amount	38	16%
A little	84	36%
No	99	42%
Total	236	100%

Source: Watzlaf, et al., 2004.

Table 3.11.   Data elements for provider

	Yes		No		N/A		Total
	#	%	#	%	#	%	#
Provider agency ID code	97	51%	70	36%	25	13%	192
Admission surgeon role	121	62%	33	17%	41	21%	195
Practitioner current role	131	68%	47	24%	14	7%	192
Anesthesiologist	132	69%	24	13%	36	19%	192
Practitioner address	134	69%	47	24%	12	6%	193
Practitioner universal ID #	141	73%	39	20%	12	6%	192
Therapy performance practitioner	140	74%	26	14%	24	13%	190
Provider address	145	74%	40	21%	10	5%	195
Admission surgeon	151	76%	10	5%	37	19%	198
Practitioner profession	152	77%	37	19%	9	5%	198
Practitioner authentication	163	84%	23	12%	8	4%	194
Provider ID number	168	86%	16	8%	12	6%	196
Provider type	170	86%	19	10%	9	5%	198
Practitioner name	184	92%	7	4%	8	4%	199
Provider/ Practitioner name	196	97%	0	0%	7	3%	203

Source: Watzlaf, et al., 2004.

Table 3.12.   Open-ended responses for provider data

Provider Data Elements Added:	
All practitioners and appropriate information	Practitioner's status—active vs. inactive
	Practitioner's title—MD, FNP, MSW, PA, and so forth.
Other contact information-specifically, provider e-mail, phone number, fax number, beeper number (2)	Provider should always be identified with specialty and by role such as ordering or prescribing, attending, admitting, primary, interpreting, treating (3)
Name of consultant and specialty consultants during an episode of care. Type, date of order, date consultation completed, consultant's report (2)	Admission/encounter consultant; admission/encounter referring
DEA and state license numbers	Primary RN
Pharmacy provider information	Social Service provider information
Insurance plans providers participate with	Admission/encounter surgeon role
Include space for resident staff	Name of any laboratory or radiology services used
Provider Data Elements Removed:	
Provider agency ID code...goal should be to strive for a universal/ standard number for physicians and other providers	
Additional Comments:	
Would provider type be better served by provider taxonomy code? How/who will define provider type? Likewise for practitioner's profession.	

Source: Watzlaf, et al., 2004

Summary

There are several areas to consider when conducting survey research in health informatics. First and foremost is the development of the survey instrument. The researcher should decide whether a new survey instrument should be developed or whether an existing one can be used or adapted to fulfill the research study aim or focus. If it is decided that a new survey instrument should be developed or even if an existing one will be adapted, the researcher should address many areas such as the content of the survey, the audience or respondents, how the survey will be administered, whether to send it to a sample of the population or the entire population, and what type of statistics will be generated.

An advisory committee should be developed to provide feedback on the content of the survey questionnaire. The different types of questions and scales (nominal, ordinal, interview, and ratio) will need to be decided. Pilot testing of the survey questionnaire should always be performed, and feedback should be reviewed and discussed with the advisory committee to determine which of the survey questions may need to be adjusted or removed.

Validity and reliability testing of the survey instrument is essential and may consist of determining face validity, criterion validity, construct validity, and content validity, as well as reliability coefficients such as the Cronbach's alpha. More sophisticated assessment of the survey questionnaire may consist of factor analysis in order to determine which questions conform to a particular factor or area of interest. Then, the researcher should consider whether incentives will be used to increase the response rate, how to maintain confidentiality of the responses, and how to minimize selection bias, recall bias, and prevarication bias. Recall bias is discussed in detail in chapter 6.

Finally, once the data are collected, appropriate statistical analysis of the data should be performed and displayed in tables and graphs. Several different types of survey research studies were performed in order to assess many health informatics areas such as the EHR, privacy and security, use of PDAs in physician practices, comparing order entry systems, and so forth. Survey research in health informatics is necessary and will continue to be conducted with vigor as health informatics applications advance.

References

Aldosari, B. 2003. Factors affecting physicians' attitudes about the medical information system usage and acceptance through the mandated implementation of integrated medical information system at the Saudi Arabia National Guard Health System: A modified technology acceptance model. Doctoral dissertation, School of Health and Rehabilitation Sciences, University of Pittsburgh.

Colorado State University. 1993–2007. Writing Guides Reliability and Validity. Available online from http://writing.colostate.edu/guides/research/relval/pop2b.cfm.

Couper, M.P., Peytchev, A., Strecher, V.J., Rothert, K., and J. Anderson. 2007. Following up non-respondents to an online weight management intervention: Randomized trial comparing mail versus telephone. *Journal of Medical Internet Research* 9(2):e16.

Criswell, D.F., and M.L. Parchman, 2002. Handheld computer use in U.S. family practice residency programs. *Journal of the American Medical Informatics Association* 9(1):80–86.

Cronk, B.C. 2006. *How to Use SPSS*, 4th ed. Glendale, CA: Pyrczak Publishing.

Firouzan, P.A., and J. McKinnon. 2004. HIPAA privacy implementation issues in Pennsylvania healthcare facilities. *Perspectives in Health Information Management* 1(3).

Garvin, J., and V.J. Watzlaf, 2004. Current coding competency compared to projected competencies described in evolving HIM careers. *Perspectives in Health Information Management* 1(1).

Garvin, J.H., Gordon, T.F., Haignere, C., and J.P. DuCette. 2005. Development of a public health assessment tool to prevent Lyme disease: Tool construction and validation. *Perspectives in Health Information Management 2(11).*

Gunn, H. 2002. Web-based Surveys: Changing the Survey Process. *First Monday* 7(12). Available online from http://firstmonday.org/issues/issue7_12/gunn/index.html.

Murff, H.J., and J. Kannry. 2001. Physician satisfaction with two order entry systems. *Journal of the American Medical Informatics Association* 8(5):499–511.

Nelson, D.E., Kreps, G.L., Hesse, B.W., Croyle, R.T., Willis, G., Arora, N.K., Rimer, B.K., Viswanath, K.V., Weinstein, N., and S. Alden. 2004. The Health Information National Trends Survey (HINTS): Development, design, dissemination. *Journal of Health Communication* 9:443–460.

Osborn, C.E. 2000. Practices and productivity in acute care facilities. *Journal of the American Health Information Management Association* 2:61–66.

Patel, V.L., Branch, T., Cimino, A., Norton, C., and J. Cimino. 2005. Participant perceptions of the influences of the NLM-sponsored Woods Hole medical informatics course. *Journal of the American Medical Informatics Association* 12(3):256–262.

Poole, J., Watzlaf, V.J., and F. D'Amico. 2004. A five-year follow-up of hand function and activities of daily living in systemic sclerosis (scleroderma). *Journal of Hand Therapy* 17(4): 407–411.

Robert Wood Johnson Foundation, George Washington University Medical Center, and Institute for Health Policy at Massachusetts General Hospital. 2006. Health information technology: Information base for progress. Available online from http://www.rwjf.org/files/publications/other/EHRReport0609.pdf.

University of Maryland. 1998. Questionnaire for User Interaction Satisfaction (QUIS). College Park, MD: University of Maryland.

Watzlaf, V.J., Zeng, X., Jarymowycz, C., and P. Firouzan. 2004. Standards for the content of the electronic health record. *Perspectives in Health Information Management* 1(1).

Watzlaf, V.J., Mazzoni, J., and A. Pandolph. 1995. Quality assessment in a long-term care facility using the medical record as principal data source. *Journal of Health Information Management Research* 3(2):24–36.

Watzlaf, V.J. "Research and Epidemiology." In *Health Information: Management of a Strategic Resource,* 3rd Edition, edited by Abdelhak, et al., 418–419. Philadelphia: Saunders, 2007.

Appendix 3A
Survey to Measure the ASTM Minimum Content of the Electronic Health Record

1. What is your highest educational degree?
   - ☐ GED
   - ☐ High School Diploma
   - ☐ Bachelor's Degree
   - ☐ Master's Degree
   - ☐ Doctorate
   - ☐ Other (Please specify in text) _____

2. What is the major of your highest educational degree? (Select all that apply)
   - ☐ Computer Science
   - ☐ Information Science
   - ☐ Business
   - ☐ Healthcare Administration
   - ☐ Health Information Management
   - ☐ Nursing
   - ☐ Medicine
   - ☐ Other (Please specify in text) _____

3. What is your credential? (Select all that apply)
   - ☐ Registered Health Information Administrator (RHIA)
   - ☐ Registered Health Information Technician (RHIT)
   - ☐ Certified Coding Specialist (CCS)
   - ☐ Certified Coding Specialist—Physician-Based (CCS-P)
   - ☐ MD
   - ☐ Registered Nurse (RN)
   - ☐ Health/Medical Informatician
   - ☐ No Credential
   - ☐ Others (Please specify in text) _____

The definition of the Electronic Health Record (EHR) from the American Society for Testing and Materials (ASTM) is an electronic record of any information related to the past, present, or future physical/mental health, or condition of an individual. The information resides in electronic system(s) used to capture, transmit, receive, store, retrieve, link, and manipulate multimedia data for the primary purpose of providing healthcare and health-related services.

4. What is the current stage of your EHR system?
   - ☐ **Planning** (Initial stage of EHR implementation and involves identification of the purpose and features of the proposed system)
   - ☐ **Development** (Involves design of the EHR system and includes both the conceptual design and the physical design)
   - ☐ **Modular Installation** (Implementation of the EHR system that can include portions of the entire system and add components over time or implement the entire system at once)
   - ☐ **Fully In Place** (The EHR system collects data from multiple sources throughout the organization, provides decision support, and is used by all caregivers at the point of care as the primary source of information)
   - ☐ **Other** (Please specify in text) _____

5. If you are developing or have an EHR, what type of system is it?
   - ☐ Developed in-house
   - ☐ Vendor
   - ☐ Other (Please specify in text) _____

6. What is your role with the EHR in your facility?
   - ☐ Designer
   - ☐ Developer
   - ☐ Coordinator
   - ☐ Other (Please specify in text) _____

The rest of this survey will include data items from Table 6 of the E1384 ASTM Standards for the Minimum Content of the Electronic Health Record.

1. Are you aware of the ASTM E1384 Standards—Standards for the Structure and Content of Electronic Health Records (EHR)?
   - ☐ No
   - ☐ A Little
   - ☐ Moderate Amount
   - ☐ Enough
   - ☐ Very Much

2. Are you aware of the ASTM E1633 Standards—Standard Specification for Coded Values Used in the Electronic Health Record?
   - ☐ No
   - ☐ A Little
   - ☐ Moderate Amount
   - ☐ Enough
   - ☐ Very Much

1. Below is a list of data elements related to the **Administrative Patient** entity for the EHR. Administrative Patient entity includes personal data elements, data elements indicating legally binding directions or restraints on patient healthcare, release of information and disposal of body or body parts, or both, after death and financial data elements.

   Please indicate which of those data elements you already include or will include in your existing system.

Elements of Patient Data	Already Included / Will Include in EHR?		
	Yes	No	Not Applicable
Patient name	☐	☐	☐
Universal patient health number	☐	☐	☐
Record-holding location ID	☐	☐	☐
Date of earliest held entry	☐	☐	☐
Date of latest held entry	☐	☐	☐
Date-time of birth	☐	☐	☐
Birthplace	☐	☐	☐
Sex (gender)	☐	☐	☐
Race	☐	☐	☐
Ethnic group	☐	☐	☐
Religion	☐	☐	☐
Marital status	☐	☐	☐
Educational level	☐	☐	☐
Occupation	☐	☐	☐
Family member name	☐	☐	☐
Family member relationship	☐	☐	☐
Patient permanent address	☐	☐	☐
Consent signed/admit agreement	☐	☐	☐
Patient rights acknowledgment	☐	☐	☐
Directive to physician	☐	☐	☐
Release of information	☐	☐	☐
Action date	☐	☐	☐
Type of record action	☐	☐	☐
Personnel authorizing release	☐	☐	☐
Payment source	☐	☐	☐
Payer group number	☐	☐	☐
Payer ID number	☐	☐	☐
Principal payment sponsor	☐	☐	☐
Address of principal	☐	☐	☐
Payment sponsor	☐	☐	☐

2. What other data elements related to Administrative Patient do you believe should be included in the standard dataset?

3. What data elements related to Administrative Patient do you believe should be removed from the standard dataset?

4. Do you have additional comments on the listed data elements related to Administrative Patient?

1. Below is a list of data elements related to the **Encounter** entity for the EHR. Encounter entity captures the facts relating to the events that took place in the healthcare environment. Certain information that characterizes the time, place, and circumstances of the initiation of the encounter are required.

   Please indicate which of those elements you already include or will include in your existing system.

Elements of Encounter Data	Already Included / Will Include in EHR?		
	Yes	No	Not Applicable
Date and time of encounter/admission	☐	☐	☐
Treatment facility name	☐	☐	☐
Encounter type	☐	☐	☐
Episode ID	☐	☐	☐
Episode diagnosis (es)	☐	☐	☐
Disposition date-time	☐	☐	☐
Disposition type	☐	☐	☐
Disposition destination	☐	☐	☐
Disposition patient instructions	☐	☐	☐
Text of note/report	☐	☐	☐
Authentication/signature	☐	☐	☐

2. What other data elements related to Encounter do you believe should be included in the standard dataset?

3. What data elements related to Encounter do you believe should be removed from the standard dataset?

4. Do you have additional comments on the listed data elements related to Encounter?

---

1. Below is a list of minimal data elements related to the **Problem** entity for the EHR. The Problem entity includes specified clinical problems, a diagnosis summary and stressor exposure, and an ongoing list of clinically significant health status events and factors, resolved and unresolved, in a patient's life.

   Please indicate which of those elements you already include or will include in your existing system.

Elements of Problem Data	Already Included / Will Include in EHR?		
	Yes	No	Not Applicable
Problem number(s)	☐	☐	☐
Problem name	☐	☐	☐
Problem date of onset	☐	☐	☐
Problem current status	☐	☐	☐
Problem name at encounter	☐	☐	☐
Problem name at care/treatment plan/order	☐	☐	☐

2. What other data elements related to PROBLEM do you believe should be included in the standard dataset?

3. What data elements related to Problem do you believe should be removed from the standard dataset?

4. Do you have additional comments on the listed data elements related to Problem?

---

1. Below is a list of data elements related to the **Order-Care/Treatment Plan** entity for the EHR. The Order-Care/Treatment Plan entity includes data entries that direct a patient's treatment and detailed data on deliverance of orders and compliance with any diagnostic or therapeutic treatment plans, whether written, oral, or standing.

   Please indicate which of those elements you already include or will include in your existing system.

Elements of Order-Care/Treatment Plan Data	Already Included / Will Include in EHR?		
	Yes	No	Not Applicable
Treatment plan	☐	☐	☐
Treatment plan ID	☐	☐	☐
Date-time	☐	☐	☐
Care/treatment plan (text)	☐	☐	☐
Clinical order(s) (full text)	☐	☐	☐
Date-time of order	☐	☐	☐

2. What other data elements related to the Order-Care/Treatment Plan do you believe should be included in the standard dataset?

3. What data elements related to the Order-Care/Treatment Plan do you believe should be removed from the standard dataset?

4. Do you have additional comments on the listed data elements related to the Order-Care/Treatment Plan?

---

1. Below is a list of data elements related to the **Provider** entity for the EHR. The Provider entity contains in one place the descriptive data about each provider/practitioner and may then be referenced when recording data about the events of healthcare.

   Please indicate which of those elements you already include or will include in your existing system.

Elements of Provider Data	Already Included / Will Include in EHR?		
	Yes	No	Not Applicable
Provider/practitioner name	☐	☐	☐
Provider address	☐	☐	☐
Provider type	☐	☐	☐
Patient ID number	☐	☐	☐
Provider agency ID code	☐	☐	☐
Practitioner name	☐	☐	☐

	Yes	No	Not Applicable
Practitioner's universal ID number	☐	☐	☐
Practitioner's profession	☐	☐	☐
Practitioner's address	☐	☐	☐
Practitioner's current role	☐	☐	☐
Practitioner's authentication (signature)	☐	☐	☐
Admission/encounter surgeon	☐	☐	☐
Admission/encounter surgeon role	☐	☐	☐
Therapy perform practitioner	☐	☐	☐
Anesthesiologist/Nurse anesthetist	☐	☐	☐

2. What other data elements related to the Provider do you believe should be included in the standard dataset?

3. What data elements related to the Provider do you believe should be removed from the standard dataset?

4. Do you have additional comments on the listed data elements related to the Provider?

---

1. Below is a list of data elements related to the **History** entity in the EHR. The History entity includes the long-term relevant natural family and patient history and signs that would aid practitioners in predicting or diagnosing illness, or actual or potential alterations in health, or in predicting outcomes of the patient's care.

   Please indicate which of those elements you already include or will include in your existing system.

Elements of History Data	Already Included / Will Include in EHR?		
	Yes	**No**	**Not Applicable**
Health history—previous illnesses	☐	☐	☐
History taking event date	☐	☐	☐
Source of history/contact name	☐	☐	☐
History relationship to patient	☐	☐	☐
History—social	☐	☐	☐
Current habits/oral health practices	☐	☐	☐

2. What other data elements related to the History do you believe should be included in the standard dataset?

3. What data elements related to the History do you believe should be removed from the standard dataset?

4. Do you have additional comments on the listed data elements related to the History?

---

1. Below is a list of data elements related to the **Observation-Assessment/Exams** entity for the EHR. The Observation-Assessment Exams entity characterizes the patient's health status in tandem with the history. This entity may include a general or specialty medical or dental exam or assessments by nursing, dietary, social service, therapy or dental hygiene specialists, or all of these.

Please indicate which of those data elements you already include or will include in your existing system.

Elements of Observation Data	Already Included / Will Include in EHR?		
Assessment/exams	**Yes**	**No**	**Not Applicable**
Date-time of exam	☐	☐	☐
Health assessment/exam present illness/injury history	☐	☐	☐
Exam review of systems	☐	☐	☐
Exam finding (s)	☐	☐	☐
Exam finding comment (s)	☐	☐	☐
Patient generated functional health status	☐	☐	☐
Exam summary (text)	☐	☐	☐

2. What other data elements related to the Observation-Assessment/Exams do you believe should be included in the standard dataset?

3. What data elements related to Observation-Assessment/Exams do you believe should be removed from the standard dataset?

4. Do you have additional comments on the listed data elements related to Observation-Assessment/Exams?

---

1. Below is a list of data elements related to the **Diagnostic Tests** entity for the EHR. The Diagnostic Tests entity includes the documentation of the results from the clinical laboratory, radiology, nuclear medicine, pulmonary function and any other diagnostic examinations.

Please indicate which of those elements you already include or will include in your existing system.

Elements of Diagnostic Test Data	Already Included / Will Include in EHR?		
	Yes	**No**	**Not Applicable**
Test requests	☐	☐	☐
Test/exam/spec-collection date time	☐	☐	☐
Test request ordering treatment facility	☐	☐	☐
Test request performing facility	☐	☐	☐
Test date-time result reported	☐	☐	☐
Test report text	☐	☐	☐
Test comment	☐	☐	☐
Numeric measurement/analyte name	☐	☐	☐
Numeric measurement/analyte value	☐	☐	☐
Numeric measure/analyze interpretation	☐	☐	☐
Test request microbial organism	☐	☐	☐
Microbial organism attribute	☐	☐	☐
Microbiological organism resistant pattern	☐	☐	☐
Microbiological organism specification comment	☐	☐	☐

2. What other data elements related to the Diagnostic Tests do you believe should be included in the standard dataset?

3. What data elements related to the Diagnostic Tests do you believe should be removed from the standard dataset?

4. Do you have additional comments on the listed data elements related to Diagnostic Tests?

––––––––––––––––––

1. Below is a list of data elements related to the **Encounter/Episode Detail** entity for the EHR. The Encounter/Episode Detail entity includes detailed information about the healthcare events.

   Please indicate which of those elements you already include or will include in your existing system.

Elements of Encounter/Episode Detail data	Already Included / Will Include in EHR?		
	Yes	No	Not Applicable
Chief complaint (text)	☐	☐	☐
Reason for visit (master table)	☐	☐	☐
Clinical progress note	☐	☐	☐
Date-time (text)	☐	☐	☐
Clinical progress note (encounter)	☐	☐	☐
Authenticator/signature	☐	☐	☐

2. What other data elements related to the Encounter/Episode Detail do you believe should be included in the standard dataset?

3. What data elements related to the Encounter/Episode Detail do you believe should be removed from the standard dataset?

4. Do you have additional comments on the listed data elements related to the Encounter/Episode Detail?

––––––––––––––––––

1. Below is a list of data elements related to the **Service Instance** entity for the EHR. The Service Instance entity includes instances of services such as immunization, medication, and anesthetic treatment.

   Please indicate which of those elements you already include or will include in your existing system.

Elements of Service Instance Data	Already Included / Will Include in EHR?		
	Yes	No	Not Applicable
Immunization name	☐	☐	☐
Immunization date	☐	☐	☐
Medication prescription/order date time	☐	☐	☐

Medication name	☐	☐	☐
Medication prescriber	☐	☐	☐
Medication dose	☐	☐	☐
Medication vehicle (table)	☐	☐	☐
Medication route (table)	☐	☐	☐
Medication frequency	☐	☐	☐
Medication instruction (text)	☐	☐	☐
Medication date of last refill	☐	☐	☐
Medication notes	☐	☐	☐
Name of therapy/service	☐	☐	☐
Therapy start date-time	☐	☐	☐
Therapy finish date-time	☐	☐	☐
Therapists' response assessment (text)	☐	☐	☐
Therapists' recommendations	☐	☐	☐
Operations date-time	☐	☐	☐
Post-operation diagnosis	☐	☐	☐
Operative procedure name	☐	☐	☐
Anesthetic agent	☐	☐	☐
Post-anesthesia assessment	☐	☐	☐
Operation complication	☐	☐	☐

2. What other data elements related to Service Instance do you believe should be included in the standard dataset?

3. What data elements related to Service Instance do you believe should be removed from the standard dataset?

4. Do you have additional comments on the listed data elements related to Service Instance?

Definition of Terms

Data Item	Definition
Address of principal payment sponsor	The mailing address of the principal payment sponsor.
Admission/ Encounter surgeon	The surgeon participating in the principal operative procedure of this admission.
Admission/ Encounter surgeon role	The role of the surgeon principal operative procedure of this admission.
Anesthesiologist/ Nurse anesthetist	The name of the practitioner responsible for the induction and maintenance of anesthesia during the surgery.
Anesthetic agent	Type of agent used to induce diminished, or loss of, feeling or sensation
Authentication/ signature	An electronic unique signature of the physician identifying that individual.
Birthplace	The city, state, and nation where the patient's birth records may be found.
Chief complaint	The reason for the episode/encounter and patient complaints and symptoms reflecting his/her own perceptions of needs.
Clinical order(s)	The textual content of the order detailing what action should be taken and the means to go about it.
Clinical progress note	A textual description of the physician's observations, his or her interpretations and conclusions about the clinical course of the patient or the steps taken, or to be taken, in the care of the patient.
Clinical progress note date-time	The time point that the physician's textual assessment was composed or written.
Consent signed/admit agreement	Patient indicates in writing that he or she has been informed of the nature of the treatment, risks, complications, alternative forms of treatment, and treatment consequences.
Current habits/oral health practices	A current statement of personnel habits at the time of the health history updating.
Date of earliest held entry	The least recent date within the record of a datum about the patient.
Date of latest held entry	The most recent date within the record of a datum about the patient.
Date Time Encounter/ Admission	The month, day, year, and hour that patient began episode/encounter of care.
Date-time	The date the treatment plan was started using the initial phase.
Date-time of birth	The exact time of birth event.
Date-time of exam	The date on which a physical examination and attendant history update was conducted.
Directive to physician	A living will written by the patient to give further instructions to the physician in case of incapacitation.
Disposition date time	Date-time of formal release from, or termination of, an episode of care when discharged alive.
Disposition destination	A description of the actual destination of the patient upon leaving the facility.
Disposition patient instructions	The instructions for care or follow-up issued to a patient who left the facility.
Educational level	The highest level, in years, within each major education system, irrespective of any certifications achieved.
Episode diagnosis (es)	A list of all conditions coexisting at the time of the episode that affect the treatment received or length of stay (LOS).

Data Item	Definition
Episode ID	An identifier code of the sequence of encounters relating to a single health problem.
Ethnic group	That cultural group with which the patient identifies himself/herself either by means of recorded family data or personal preference.
Exam findings	A term for an observation name made by the examiner.
Exam findings comment	A textual remark about the particular finding.
Exam review of systems	This data element contains the textual summary of the systematic review of the status and functioning of the body's systems and regions.
Exam summary	A textual narrative of the observations made by the examiner.
Family member name	The name of each family member.
Family member relationship	A term denoting the relationship of the family member to the patient.
Health history—previous illnesses	A statement of the illness experienced since the last history updating.
History relationship source to patient	The relationship of the data source used in updating the health history of the patient, if it is not the patient.
History—social	A statement of the current social aspects of the patient's functioning.
Immunization date	The date the immunization procedure was conducted.
Immunization name	The name or identifier of the immunization procedure conducted.
Marital status	Marital status of the patient at the start of care.
Medication date of last refill	The date of each refill of the prescription.
Medication dose	The strength, dosage, or concentration
Medication frequency	The number of doses to be administered per day or the interval between doses.
Medication instruction	Signature: prescription part that gives directions on how to take the medication.
Medication name	Description of the current product.
Medication notes, for example, patient response	The effects/results of medication administration or a change in the patient's clinical status and/or lab findings caused by drugs.
Medication prescription/ order date-time	The date-time the prescription or medication order was initiated.
Medication prescriber	The identity of a person with prescribing authority who wrote the prescription/order.
Medication route	The term identifying the route of administration.
Medication vehicle	The form of the medication, including the vehicle.
Microbial organism attribute	A list of attributes for a microbiological organism.
Microbiological organism resistant pattern	A list of therapeutic agents for which the microbiologic organism is resistant.
Microbiological organism specification comment	A remark about the microbiologic organism tested.
Name of therapy/service	The identifier or name of the therapeutic service conducted.
Numeric measure/analyze interpretation	A term of interpretation for the measurement
Numeric measurement/analyte name	The name of the exact measured species or measurement during the test or examination

Data Item	Definition
Numeric measurement/analyte value	The numeric value of the measurement.
Occupation	The employment, business, or course of action in which the patient is engaged.
Operation complication	A textual account of surgical misadventures.
Operations date-time	The date-time at which the operative procedures commenced during the surgery.
Operative procedure name	The unique name of the procedure conducted during surgery
Patient name	Person receiving healthcare services and whose records containing data about those services are collected.
Patient permanent address	The usual residence and/or address of the patient as defined by the payer organization.
Patient rights acknowledgment	A text stating the patient's understanding of his/her rights and the rights associated with the information in the record of care.
Payment source	Responsible for the largest percentage of patient's current bill.
Payer group number	An identification number, control number, or code assigned by the carrier or administrator to identify the group under which the individual is covered.
Payer ID number	The identifier of the patient's insurance policy.
Personnel authorizing release	The name or identifier of the individual authorizing the release of the type of information.
Postanesthesia assessment	A textual synopsis of the effectiveness and adverse affects of the anesthesia.
Postoperative diagnosis	Determination of the case after operating.
Practitioner's authentication signature	The electronic signature of the practitioner.
Practitioner name	The name of the practitioner; structure in common person name format.
Practitioner's address	The usual or principal place of practice.
Practitioner's current role	The role that the practitioner plays with this patient.
Practitioner's profession	The profession in which the practitioner is currently engaged.
Practitioner's universal ID number	The universal numeric identifier, which will be used to link services for a provider across care systems.
Principal payment sponsor	The name of the person responsible for the bill or whose insurance provides coverage for the patient.
Problem current status	The activity category of the problem, for example, inactive, active.
Problem date of onset	The estimated date that the problem first occurred.
Problem name	A term uniquely identifying the nature of the problem.
Problem number	The problem identifier for this unique problem.
Provider address	The complete address to which the provider wishes the payment sent.
Provider agency ID code	The agency associated with this unique identifier of this provider.
Provider type	The particular branch of medicine, dentistry or surgery; by virtue of advanced training certifies individual to be qualified to so limit his/her practice.
Provider/Practitioner name	The name of the facility or practice submitting the bill.

Data Item	Definition
Race	The region of the world from which the patient's ancestors originated, generally indicating possible inherited biologic diversity.
Record-holding location ID	Code identifier of a healthcare site that maintains a primary record of care about this patient.
Release of information action date	The date of each instance when any data from the patient record is released to other than authorized persons caring for the patient.
Religion	A term denoting the current religious affiliation of the patient at the start of care.
Sex (gender)	Distinction of gender.
Source of history—contact name	The name of an individual who relates the patient's history to the practitioner.
Test comment	Textual remarks on the test or examination.
Test date-time result reported	Date-time that the results were reported from the performing facility.
Test report text	The body of the report on tests producing the narrative.
Test request microbial organism	The name of the microbiological organism evaluated in the test.
Test request ordering treatment facility	The name or identifier of the facility from which the test was requested in a clinical order.
Test request performing facility	The name or identifier of the facility performing the test or examination.
Test requests	The name of the diagnostic test.
Test/exam/spec-collection date-time	The date and time when the specimen was collected from the patient or the measurement was made.
Text of note/report	The textual content of the report.
Therapist recommendations	Further plans for continued treatment and/or services, including an assessment of patient's ability to improve and to what level.
Therapist response assessment	Therapist documentation of patient's attitude toward the plan, including estimates of further therapeutic potential.
Therapy finish date-time	The time point that the service was ceased.
Therapy start date-time	The time point that the service was commenced.
Treatment facility name	The name of the facility at which treatment is rendered.
Treatment plan	A human readable name of the treatment plan.
Treatment plan ID	Identifier of a specified treatment plan.
Type of record action	A code that identifies the type of action involved in the release of information from the patient's record.
Universal patient health number	Permanent, unique number used by all providers and third party payers in conjunction with establishing and using the longitudinal record. It will link services for the individual across care systems.

Source: Watzlaf et al. 2004, unpublished, developmental material.

Appendix 3B

Samples of the Web-based Version of the EHR/ASTM Survey

AHIMA SURVEY TO MEASURE THE ASTM MINIMUM CONTENT OF THE EHR/CPR

Page 5 of 13 —   print the entire survey

1. Below is a list of data elements related the to ENCOUNTER entity for the CPR/EHR. ENCOUNTER entity captures the facts relating to the events that took place in the health care environment. Certain information that characterizes the time, place and circumstances of the initiation of the encounter are required.

Please indicate which of those elements you already include or will include in your existing system. Click ►HELP for detailed explanations.

Elements of Encounter Data	Already Included/will include in CPR/EHR?		
	Yes	No	Not Applicable
Date time encounter/admission ►HELP	○	○	○
Treatment facility name ►HELP	○	○	○
Encounter type	○	○	○
Episode ID ►HELP	○	○	○
Episode diagnosis (es) ►HELP	○	○	○
Disposition date time ►HELP	○	○	○
Disposition type (master table) ►HELP	○	○	○
Disposition destination ►HELP	○	○	○
Disposition patient instructions ►HELP	○	○	○
Text of note/report ►HELP	○	○	○
Authentication /signature ►HELP	○	○	○

2. What other data elements related to ENCOUNTER do you believe are needed to be included in the standard dataset?

3. What data elements related to ENCOUNTER do you believe should be removed from the standard dataset?

4. Do you have additional comments on the listed data elements related to ENCOUNTER?

Thank you for finishing page 5 of 13. Please click here to [Submit and Go to Next Page] or click here to [Reset]

SURVEY TO MEASURE THE ASTM MINIMUM CONTENT OF THE EHR/CPR

print the entire survey

The rest of this survey will include data items from Table 6 of the E1384 ASTM Standards for the Minimum Content of the Electronic Health Record

1. Are you aware of the <u>ASTM E1384 Standards</u> **-- Standards for the Structure and Content of Electronic Health Records (EHR)?**

- ○ <u>No</u>   ▶ HELP
- ○ <u>Little</u>   ▶ HELP
- ○ <u>Moderate</u> ▶ HELP
- ○ <u>Enough</u>   ▶ HELP
- ○ <u>Very Much</u> ▶ HELP

2. Are you aware of the <u>ASTM E1633 Standards</u> **-- Standard Specification for Coded Values Used in the Electronic Health Record?**

- ○ <u>No</u>   ▶ HELP
- ○ <u>Little</u>   ▶ HELP
- ○ <u>Moderate</u> ▶ HELP
- ○ <u>Enough</u>   ▶ HELP
- ○ <u>Very Much</u> ▶ HELP

Thank you for finishing page 3 of 13. Please click here to   Submit and Go to Next Page   or click here to   reset

Source: Watzlaf et al. 2004.

Appendix 3C
Sample of Cover Letter for EHR Study

IRB#

Dear (Insert participant's name):

Thank you for agreeing to participate in the research study entitled *"Standards for the Content of Electronic Health Records"* **sponsored by the American Health Information Management Association (AHIMA) Foundation of Research and Education (FORE) and conducted by the University of Pittsburgh, Department of Health Information Management.**

As we described to you previously on the telephone, your participation in this study is **extremely important** since your responses could lead to the uniform data standards for the electronic health record/computer-based patient record (EHR/CPR), which HIPAA is recommending.

The focus of this research study is the American Society for Testing and Materials (ASTM) E1384 Standard Guide on Content and Structure of Electronic Health Records and the corresponding ASTM E1633 Coded Values for Electronic Health Records. We are investigating the level of awareness and usage of the standards for the content of electronic health records. We are also collecting feedback on how the content for the standards for the EHR/CPR meet users' needs. The primary method of data collection for this research study is through a Web-based survey.

Your prompt participation is extremely important and will aid in the next revision of the standards.

For your efforts in completing the survey, we are offering an opportunity for your name to be entered into a drawing to win $200.00! There will be two $200.00 prizes awarded from the pool of people completing the survey by the due date listed below!

In addition, you will receive the overall results of the survey as well as a complimentary copy of the most recent edition of the *Journal of the American Health Information Management Association*, or, if you already receive that journal, another comparable AHIMA journal of your choice.

Your responses will be kept completely confidential and will only be reported in aggregate form. Completion of the survey will take approximately 20 minutes. Please <u>click here</u> to start the survey.

Once you access the Web site, please follow the directions included on the survey.

Please provide your responses to us no later than _____ to be eligible for the drawing.

Your responses will be kept completely confidential.

If you have any questions or concerns regarding completion of the survey, please contact: Valerie Watzlaf or Patti Anania-Firouzan at e-mail_____ or phone _____.

Thank you so much for taking the time to complete this important survey. You are helping to make a difference in the health information field.

Sincerely,

Valerie J.M. Watzlaf, PhD, RHIA, FAHIMA
Associate Professor and Principal Investigator

Patricia Anania-Firouzan, MSIS, RHIA
Assistant Professor and Co-Investigator

Xiaoming Zeng, MD
Doctoral Student in HIS and Research Assistant

Department of Health Information Management
School of Health and Rehabilitation Sciences
University of Pittsburgh

Source: Adapted from Watzlaf 2007, pp. 418–419.

Appendix 3D
Excerpt of Survey on Current Coding Competency

Are you aware of the skills identified in *Evolving HIM Careers: Seven Roles for the Future* for the clinical data specialist (check one)?

☐ Yes

☐ No

As you complete each question in the enclosed survey please use the following definitions for the numbers representing the level of competency:

1 = **awareness**, introductory recall and recognition

2 = **literacy**, knowledge of framework and content

3 = **concept**, comprehensions, translation, extrapolation, and interpretation of meaning

4 = **detailed understanding**, appropriate application of knowledge in a structured and controlled context

5 = **skilled use**, application using analysis, synthesis, and evaluation in new situations

Please answer the following questions based on how competent you believe you are in each of the following categories using the levels of competency provided above.

1. Understanding of current clinical coding systems relevant to the organization

A. ICD-9-CM	5	4	3	2	1
B. CPT	5	4	3	2	1
C. DSM-IV	5	4	3	2	1
D. SNOMED	5	4	3	2	1
E. ICD-O	5	4	3	2	1
F. ICD-10	5	4	3	2	1

2. Ability to gather clinical data from primary data sources   5   4   3   2   1

3. Understanding of the elements required for research and outcomes   5   4   3   2   1

4. Ability to participate in the design of studies   5   4   3   2   1

5. Ability to collect, analyze, and interpret medical information for quality and accuracy   5   4   3   2   1

6. Ability to design specifications for study around outcomes   5   4   3   2   1

7. Ability to review data and identify patterns, trends, and so on   5   4   3   2   1

8. Ability to design audit tools   5   4   3   2   1

9. Ability to perform quality audits   5   4   3   2   1

10. Ability to identify the problems and issues suggested by audits   5   4   3   2   1

Source: Garvin et al. 2004

Appendix 3E
Sample of Follow-Up Cover Letter for EHR/ASTM Study

IRB#

Dear (Insert participant's name):

Recently we sent you an email and Web-based survey for the research study entitled *"Standards for the Content of Electronic Health Records"* **sponsored by the American Health Information Management Association (AHIMA) Foundation of Research and Education (FORE) and conducted by the University of Pittsburgh, Department of Health Information Management.**

Since we sent the survey, we have not heard from you and we truly need and value your input. **We have attached the survey again and we would greatly appreciate your prompt response. If you are having problems accessing the survey or experience any problems at all, please contact us and we will do everything we can to enable you to complete the survey.** Please complete all pages of the survey and click the Finish button at the end to send it to us.

Remember that your prompt participation is extremely important and will aid in the next revision of the standards. You do not have to have an EHR in place to complete the survey.

For your efforts in fully completing the survey, we are offering an opportunity for your name to be entered into a drawing to win $200.00! There will be two $200.00 prizes awarded from the pool of people fully completing the survey.

In addition, you will receive the overall results of the survey as well as a complimentary copy of the most recent edition of the *Journal of the American Health Information Management Association,* or, if you already receive that journal, another comparable AHIMA journal of your choice.

Your responses will be kept completely confidential and will only be reported in aggregate form. An ID number will be used for follow-up purposes only. Completion of the survey will take approximately 10 to 20 minutes. You may also download and print the entire survey in Microsoft Word format on any page by clicking the printer icon on the upper bar of the questionnaire. You can also choose to complete the survey via the attachment and fax or e-mail it back to us. Please click here or use the address 136.142.142.146/astm/survey01?userid=1001 to start the survey.

Once you access the Web site, please follow the directions included on the survey. If you choose the paper-based survey, please **fax it to (412) 383-6655** or **mail it to the following address:**

Valerie J.M. Watzlaf
Department of Health Information Management
University of Pittsburgh
Pittsburgh, PA 15260

If you have any questions or concerns regarding completion of the survey, please contact: Valerie Watzlaf or Patti Anania-Firouzan at (e-mail)_____ or at (phone)_____.

Thank you so much for taking the time to complete this important survey. You are helping to make a difference in the health information field.

Sincerely,

Valerie J.M. Watzlaf, PhD, RHIA, FAHIMA
Associate Professor and Principal Investigator

Patricia Anania-Firouzan, MSIS, RHIA
Assistant Professor and Co-Investigator

Xiaoming Zeng, MD
Doctoral Student in HIS and Research Assistant

Department of Health Information Management
School of Health and Rehabilitation Sciences
University of Pittsburgh

Source: Watzlaf et al. 2004, unpublished, developmental material.

Chapter 4
Observational Research

Valerie J. Watzlaf, PhD, RHIA, FAHIMA

Learning Objectives

- Explain the purpose of observational research and how it is used in health informatics.
- Describe the different types of observational research: nonparticipant observation, participant observation, and ethnography.
- Determine how to record and collect data for each type of observational research.
- Conduct the constant comparative method of analysis for observational research.
- Discuss which type of observational research is most appropriate for health informatics.

Key Terms

Case study observation
Content analysis
Direct observation
Ethnography
Field notes
Focus group
Focused interview
General interview guide
Grounded theory
Group case study
Indirect observation

Individual case study
Informal conversational interview
Institutional case study
Naturalistic observation
Nonparticipant observation
Observational research
Participant observation
Qualitative research
Simulation observation
Standardized open-ended interview
Triangulation

Introduction

Observational research or **qualitative research** allows the investigator to get to know the nuts and bolts of the study subject, program, or facility. This type of research strives to examine the perceptions, interactions, feelings, and attitudes rather than the progression of a particular disease or system. By collecting these types of data, observational or qualitative research also adds depth, substance, and meaning to the results.

There are many reasons for a researcher to conduct observational research. Observational research is usually conducted when there is little known about the study subject; when the researcher is studying relationships between the research subjects and the setting; or when the researcher is studying a transitional program and the change or impact it may have on study subjects, attitudes, feelings, and behaviors. It also can be used as a background for larger quantitative studies or it can stand alone, especially when studying a topic for the first time.

Observational research may use several different methods to obtain the robust, rich data that is needed. Some observational research studies use a combination of observation, field interviews, medical record reviews, and ethnographic methods in order to fully conduct a study. There are several different observational research methods that should be considered when conducting this research. It is important to pay particular attention to the observation site, time period, what will be observed, how it will be recorded, who will conduct the observation, how the data will be analyzed, and how the results will be disseminated.

Nonparticipant Observation

Field observation may include direct observation or indirect observation. **Direct observation** is when the researchers conduct the observation themselves, whereas **indirect observation** is when researchers use audio or video recording so that the environment is not changed in any way from the norm. In direct observation, researchers spend time in the environment they are observing and may record observations by taking extensive and meticulous notes related to the observations.

During observational research, the researcher may influence the actions of the individuals being observed. Therefore, it is important for the researcher to determine which type of observational method is needed for a specific research topic and how important it is to determine whether to use nonparticipant or participant observation. **Nonparticipant observation** is when the investigator observes the actions of the study subjects with limited interference. In **participant observation** (which will be discussed in more detail later in this chapter), the researcher is also a part of the environment he or she is observing. The influence of the researcher on specific observations is necessary to discuss and consider when determining which method to use (Giacomini and Cook 2000). Nonparticipant observation can be used to examine, for example, how employees react to a new documentation software system by observing their education and training with the system, their collection or use of data with the new system, and with their use of the results that the system provides. The investigator is a neutral observer who should not become involved in the discussions, actions, or issues of the study subjects. The investigator is there to record the feelings, behaviors, attitudes, and perceptions of the employees regarding the new documentation software system. By using nonparticipant observation, the investigator is able to determine where the problems in the software system may be and begin to correct them. Non-participant observation usually includes three different types: **naturalistic observation, simulation observation,** and **case study.**

Naturalistic Observation

Researchers use naturalistic observation when recording behaviors or events that occur naturally in the normal environment. They may choose this type of observation when they want to know if individuals are following a specific procedure, rule, law, or policy. Another concern of the naturalistic observation method is that the study subjects normally should not know what researchers are observing or when they will be observing them. This ensures that the study participants or events that are being observed are as similar as possible to the real or natural environment, and allows the study participants to display behaviors that tend to occur in their normal environment.

Example of Naturalistic Observation in Health Informatics

Watzlaf and Katoh (1989) investigated the reasons for underutilization and lack of visibility of a cancer registry in a 500-bed inner-city tertiary care teaching facility. The purpose of the study was to determine why the cancer registry was underutilized and to determine if a new automated cancer registry system would enhance its utilization.

- First, informal discussions with several hospital physicians involved in the diagnosis and treatment of oncology patients showed that few used the cancer registry.

- Second, visits and nonparticipant naturalistic observations of the cancer registry were conducted to determine what data are collected, how the cancer registry operates, and what its potential is in terms of the newly automated cancer registry software system. Another goal of the study was to expand the types of information inserted into the registry software so that meaningful information and statistics can be generated.

- Third, semistructured interviews were conducted with physicians and nurses who care for cancer patients, as well as with administrators. Subjects were asked whether they use the cancer registry and if not, why not; and also to establish their information needs in relation to diagnosis, treatment, prevention, research, and planning. The researchers conducted the interviews together and encouraged the participants to discuss their views candidly and openly.

- Fourth, data collected from the interviews were compared with the data collected in the nonparticipant naturalistic observations of the cancer registry. Any additional information analyzed from all the sources of data collection was used to enhance the new software system that was used for the cancer registry.

Another example of nonparticipant naturalistic observation in health informatics was conducted by researchers from Sweden when investigating patients' experiences of care before, during, and after a hip fracture. The major goal of this study was to examine the patients with hip fractures to determine their pain and nutrition needs (Hallstrom et al. 2000). Nonparticipant observation, informal field interviews, and abstraction of nursing notes and medical records with patients and relatives were conducted. Patients were followed throughout their care for their hip fracture to include time spent in the emergency department (if applicable), hospitalization, and rehabilitation throughout their arrival at home and 4 months after. Observation periods lasted between 1 and 4 hours, and approximately 20 hours were used per patient. A total of nine patients were observed. Field notes were recorded either immediately after the observation or during short breaks between observations. The observer's role was more of a listener while patients created the topics for conversation. Observers were registered nurses, did not have any personal or medical involvement with the patients, and wore street clothes during all observations. No information collected from the observers was given to hospital staff at any time, which is the normal procedure when naturalistic observation methods are used. Analysis of the data collected was reported in stories based on the transcribed field notes, interviews, and data from medical records. The researchers used open coding to determine themes from the data collected. A theme was found when a response appeared many times or if it could lead to major changes although it was only mentioned once. The researchers found that the most important method of data collection used in this study was nonparticipant naturalistic observation. "Observations revealed information that would not have been obtained from interviews or questionnaires" (Hallstrom et al. 2000, 644). Their research found that nursing care could be improved with a focus on pain needs and nutritional protocols for hip fracture patients.

Simulation Observation

The simulation observation method is another type of nonparticipant observation used by researchers. It is usually conducted by observing study subjects in an environment created for them instead of in their natural environment.

Example of Simulation Observation in Health Informatics

Hackett (2007) observed individuals with visual disabilities using the Internet in a simulated setting by choosing which Web sites the study subjects will examine. The researchers have the study subjects answer questions about the Web sites to determine how well they can navigate through each Web site and how accessible it is to persons with visual disabilities. The researchers do this while subjects use a transcoding technology and again without the new technology. The researchers find where specific problems may lie with the Web sites and provide this information to the webmasters so that their Web sites will be fully accessible to persons with visual disabilities. This is one example of simulation observation because the events or questions that the study subjects answer are simulated. If the researchers observed the study subjects in their natural environment, perusing the Web at their leisure, and recorded their behaviors, feelings, and perceptions without any interference, then this would have been considered naturalistic observation. This is also an example of a usability study because the researchers record how the subjects use a new technology. Usability outcomes include the time to complete a specific task, number of user errors, severity of the errors, and the ability to recover from the errors, user satisfaction, the length of time it takes to complete a task (efficiency of use) and how fast a user can learn a new system (ease of learning). Usability studies are very common in health informatics.

Case Study

The case study method is another example of nonparticipant observation. It is used when the researcher wants to know more about a particular individual; group of individuals; or a particular facility, organization, or institution. Each of these levels is examined in great detail and includes collecting specific characteristics (demographic, disease, religious, social, cultural, technological system and software, community) about the individual, group, or institution. Each type of case study (individual, group, and institutional) will be discussed in more detail.

Individual Case Study

The **individual case study** is one of the oldest methods used within observational research. Its roots stem from physicians and other healthcare providers yearning to learn more about a new disease that has afflicted certain individuals. Therefore, the researcher records (field notes, tape recording, images, video recording) and collects everything they can on this particular individual as he or she progresses through a certain disease, procedure, treatment, cultural, or health information system change.

Example of Individual Case Study

For example, in order to determine the feasibility of a 74-year-old man to swim the English Channel, an indi-

vidual case study was conducted (Kanaar and Hecht 1991). The researchers were interested in determining whether the individual could swim for 21 hours in water as cold as the English Channel and not become unconscious from hypothermia as he did twice earlier in his life. They also wanted to test two thermal protective suits and to offer advice from his experience. Therefore, the researchers observed his long-distance training three times a week for several months. The swimmer's body temperatures, water temperatures, types of body covers used, length of swims, diet, and general comments on the swimmer's attitude were recorded. It was found that this individual should not attempt to swim the English Channel because he could not tolerate the cold water. The study also provided some very interesting information for marathon swimmers such as the length of time swimmers should spend in cold water if planning on doing longer swims.

Case studies are also performed in health informatics at the individual level, although it is not as common. For example, individual patients may be followed closely and their actions recorded as they use a specific assistive technology device. Other examples may include observing healthcare providers as they proceed throughout their work day to determine which technological devices may increase their work productivity. Still other examples may focus on an administrator of a large healthcare facility, observing his or her interactions with healthcare employees, patients, and family to determine current communication techniques used, and to see how communication can be improved with health information technology systems.

Group Case Study

The **group case study** is quite similar to the individual case study except the interviews or observations are performed on a group of individuals instead of just one individual.

Example of Group Case Study

For example, the group case study method was used when researchers assessed the need to improve the moral reasoning skills of medical students (Self et al. 1998). Small groups of 8 to 10 students and 2 faculty members were used to discuss clinical cases that contained many different types of ethical issues. The faculty group leaders were asked to encourage students to take a stand on each of the ethical issues and defend it. Moral reasoning skills were assessed by using standardized tests and tabulated results, both before and after the students participated in medical ethics education classes. It was found that teaching medical ethics can significantly increase medical students' moral reasoning skills.

Institutional Case Study

The **institutional case study** is another method used within observational research. It includes observing a particular healthcare institution or facility to determine how it conducts a particular process, system, or procedure. Individual case studies may be included within the institutional case study, but the focus should be on the institution wide system, process, or procedure.

Example of Institutional Case Study

For example, the Department of Veterans Affairs (VA) healthcare system used the institutional case study method to describe how its electronic health record (EHR) system is used in home-based primary care programs (Shea 2007). The researchers began by describing how the EHR can be accessed remotely by the home and hospice care team whenever a patient referral occurs. They also explain that the historical medical record of any patient within the VA healthcare system can be accessed from anywhere in the United States. The researchers continue to explain how the record is accessed in a matter of minutes by simply keying in the name and identifying number. They also discuss how patient information is kept confidential and can be accessed only by selected employees who need to use the healthcare information. Also, each user has an identifying code number that is changed every three months. The researchers continue to explain the importance of the institution wide EHR in relation to traumatic events such as Hurricane Katrina by discussing the importance of a backup system should the electronic system become inoperable. They succinctly explain how the backup system was helpful in retrieving health history information on their patients during Hurricane Katrina when asked by family members to retrieve it. The researchers go on to describe the parts of the EHR and how the tabs at the bottom of the computer screen are similar to information found in paper-based record. Sections include the cover sheet, problems, order, medications, notes, surgery reports, labs, discharge summary, and so forth. Home healthcare providers click on one of these tabs and peruse the data before making a home visit. The researchers then provide a case report on one particular patient and how the use of the EHR enhanced their care. The case report discusses patients' healthcare problems as well as their need for home healthcare, but it also describes how other healthcare providers can use the EHR to prepare for their home healthcare visit. For example, it shows how the nurse can review the medication list, which includes medications currently taken as well as over-the-counter (OTC) medications that are self-reported. Also, alerts are provided from the pharmacy when OTC medications are not compatible with prescribed medications. The nurse can further assess the patient's blood pressure over time through past readings as well as with graphs. The social worker, dietician, and occupational therapist can review specific parts of the EHR at the same time to include advance directives, diet education history, and fall history. The institutional case study report provides a complete overview of the institutionwide EHR system at the VA and how it is used successfully within home and hospice care. Other organizations can review the report and develop similar institutional case studies to determine the effectiveness of other health information technology systems from the standpoint of ease of use. It also would be interesting to examine how the use of the EHR improved patient care by using the institutional case study method.

Focused Interview

The **focused interview** is used extensively in observational research. It is used when the researcher wants to collect a more in-depth, hearty type of information that would not be obtained from close-ended questions. Focused interviews normally use three types of interviews: **informal conversational**, **standardized open-ended**, and the **general interview guide**.

Informal Conversational Interview

The informal conversational interview moves forward as the subject discusses certain topics of conversation. No specific topics or questions are developed or used, and the researcher is trying to learn about a particular setting, culture, system change, or person. It is used most in participant observation, and its main goal is to learn as much as possible about the particular situation as the subject or group of subjects discuss a particular topic of interest to them in their own words or terms.

Example of Informal Conversational Interview

Graneheim and Jansson (2006) used the informal conversational interview method when assessing the lives of individuals living with dementia in a nursing facility in Sweden. The focus of the informal conversational interview was on the residents' experiences of an ordinary day. Examples of questions include:

1. How are you getting along?
2. What are you engaged in and with whom?
3. What do you feel or think?

A total of three interviews (30 to 45 minutes long) were conducted with two of the residents, and four interviews were conducted with one resident. All interviews were tape recorded and transcribed into text. Even pauses, sighs, and laughter were included in the text. Extensive content analysis was performed on all text.

Standardized Open-ended Interview

The standardized open-ended format is when specific questions written by the research team are used to ask respondents questions. The questions used are the same across participants, and the interviewer should probe all respondents the same way. Standardized open-ended interviews are not used as much in observational research because questions are framed by the researchers. This does not always allow the subject to speak freely. Because the questions are designed by the researcher, the subject may be led to answer in a certain manner inconsistent with their own experiences.

Example of Standardized Open-ended Interview

The standardized open-ended focused interview was used extensively in a 2005 study to examine automated coding software and its development and use to enhance antifraud activities (AHIMA/FORE 2005). This study examined the types of automated coding software available across healthcare settings, vendors, and users, as well as the software's ability to reduce fraudulent activities by preventing errors, increasing the accuracy of coded data, and detecting false claims.

The objectives of this descriptive research project were:

- To identify the characteristics of automated coding systems that have the potential to detect improper coding.
- To identify the components of the coding process that have the potential to minimize improper or fraudulent coding practices when using auto-

mated coding and to determine their effectiveness with the use of the EHR.

- To develop recommendations for software developers and users of coding products to maximize antifraud practices.

This descriptive research study included several parts, but two parts of the methodology included the use of focused interviews (standardized open-ended questions). First, focused interviews were used with appropriate federal agencies regarding their experience with improper reimbursement or potential fraud involving automated coding software. The interview form shown in figure 4.1 was developed by members of the research team.

The second part of the research study included an evaluation of automated coding software, coding optimization software, anti-fraud software, and coding application tools such as bar codes, pick or lookup lists, and so forth to determine their use as well as the cost of these systems. The number of vendors that participated in the development of coding optimization, coding automation, and anti-fraud software was determined by sending each vendor a product information form to complete. (See figure 4.2.) An extensive search of coding vendors and users was conducted via both the Internet and telephone interviews. Approximately 40 vendors were contacted and given the opportunity to complete the product information form. Once the form was received, it was reviewed by the research team who then determined whether an interview was needed. Following the format shown in figure 4.3, interviews were conducted with all vendors who had the specific coding-related software necessary for this research.

Next, three product matrices that demonstrate the extent of use and cost of these systems were developed.

The third part of the research study included describing the available automated coding software tools, how these tools are being used in the coding and billing process, the impact of these tools on coding and billing accuracy, and the characteristics and limitations of anti-fraud features now available in automated coding software. Special attention was paid to "weak links" in automated coding and fraud and abuse software, user education, and compliance practices. This section of the research study will be discussed in more detail under content analysis.

Figure 4.1.   Government interview form

The following questions were used during interviews with members of the federal government:

1. In your view, what are the best processes to prohibit fraud and abuse?

2. What problems do you foresee in relation to fraud and abuse when the Electronic Health Record (EHR) is used?

3. As discussed in an AHIMA practice brief, automated coding was defined as the use of computer software that automatically generates a set of medical codes for review, validation, and use based upon clinical documentation provided by healthcare practitioners. Are you aware of specific facilities or settings that use automated coding systems or automated coding? Have you found patterns of abuse with automated coding?

4. Are you aware of incorrect coding or abuse detected with Natural Language Processing (NLP)? If you are familiar with the approach of the NLP, was it a rules-based approach or data-driven approach? Please describe.

5. Have you found a pattern of abuse with any particular commercial software product that assists in the determination of codes? Examples of products include: bar codes, pick or lookup lists, coding templates or coding protocol, automated superbills, logic or rules-based encoders, groupers, imaged and remote coding applications, hard coding via charge master tables. Please describe any patterns found.

6. According to *Managed Healthcare Executive,* the most effective antifraud and recovery programs include elements of process assessment, both retrospective and prospective technology, and investigations and resolutions. Do you agree? Please discuss.

7. With the proliferation of EHRs with embedded reference terminology, such as SNOMED CT, do you envision this to affect fraud and abuse in automated coding systems? Please discuss.

8. What in your view are the weak links in antifraud software, education, and compliance practices?

9. What general patterns of abuse have you found by setting (for example, physician office, SNF, hospitals, and so forth) with services that:

   • Were never rendered, either by adding charges to legitimate claims, or by using actual patient names and health insurance information to fabricate claims.

   • Were upcoded (second most common).

   • Were a deliberate provision of medically unnecessary services, which include tests, surgeries, and other procedures?

10. Are you aware of programs in which consumers have been educated to alert governmental agencies of fraud? If yes, how has it worked? What is the extent of fraud found by this means and are there any patterns of reporting by setting, diagnosis, or procedure?

Source: AHIMA/FORE et al. 2005, 37.

The fourth part of the research study included an extensive search of users of automated coding systems. Focus interviews following the format presented in figure 4.4 were conducted by telephone and in person to augment the information that was found via the Internet and literature searches and to determine the effectiveness of the automated systems currently in use.

Content analysis of the interview data (discussed later in this chapter) was performed, and results were categorized into common themes related to strategies for reducing the fraud and abuse risk. Guidelines for developers and best practices for users of automated coding products were developed. Also, detailed recommendations regarding the development of automated coding tools and their use were compiled.

Use of standardized open-ended interviews for this study enabled the researchers to compile important recommendations regarding automated coding software that is now being used by system developers, users, and federal agencies. Without the use of the focused interview as a data collection technique, many of the candid and open remarks regarding the automated coding software may not have been recorded and used to develop recommendations.

General Interview Guide

The general interview guide is a bit more structured than the informal conversational interview. Here the researcher uses an outline of issues that he or she may want to explore during the interview process. The outline is used as a checklist, and as each topic is discussed during the interview, it is checked off on the outline. Interviews conducted with the general interview guide tend to be very long. Therefore, they are tape recorded so that none of the information is lost and so that the researcher has time to focus on the interview process while all important information is recorded. Also, questions may be listed on one section of the guide with additional prompts listed across from the questions.

Example of General Interview Guide

Researchers from several different medical schools across the country used the interview guide to reassess team-based learning (TBL) among 10 medical schools since the initial evaluation in 2003 (Thompson et al.

Figure 4.2.   Product information form

Vendor Name:	
Address:	
E-mail Address:	
Phone:	
Contact Person:	
Title of Respondent:	

Place an X in the appropriate setting for each product listed that your company provides. The following definitions are from the *Coding (AHIMA Practice Brief) Glossary:* ED = Emergency Department; SDS = Same Day Surgery; Other OP = Other Outpatient; HH = Home Health, LTC = Long-Term Care; ASC = Ambulatory Surgical Center; PO = Physician Office

	ED	SDS	Other Outpatient	X-ray	HH	LTC	Acute	Physician Office	Hospice
Coding optimization software									
Antifraud Software: software that provides aggregate data analysis and record-specific audits									
Antifraud software									
Automated coding: Software that automatically generates a set of medical codes for review/validation and/or use based upon clinical documentation provided by healthcare practitioners									
Automated coding with NLP									
Automated coding with structured text									
Automated coding products									
Coding Tools: Tools used by coding professionals in the code assignment process									
Bar codes									
Pick lists or lookup lists									
Automated superbills									
Logic or rules-based encoders									
Groupers									
Imaged coding applications									
Remote coding applications									
Hard coding via chargemaster tables									
Automated coding-NLP system									
Automated coding-structured text									
Other automated coding systems									
Maintenance									

Source: AHIMA/FORE et al. 2005, 40–41.

Figure 4.3.   Vendor interview form

As discussed in AHIMA's practice brief, automated coding is defined as the use of computer software that automatically generates a set of medical codes for review, validation, and use based upon clinical documentation provided by healthcare practitioners.

1. What type of automated coding system do you provide?

2. When was your first installation of the automated coding system? How many installations (users/clients) do you have and in what settings?

3. What is the average installation and training time?

4. Did coder quality change with the use of your automated coding system? Please describe what occurred in terms of coding quality and define how you evaluated coder quality. If coder quality was affected, by what percent was it affected?

5. Do you provide a remote coding application? Has this application improved coding productivity? Please describe what occurred in terms of productivity and by what percent the productivity changed. Please describe the number of outpatient records and inpatient records per hour before and after use of the remote coding application. What was the percent change?

6. How is the automated coding system used with the EHR? What are your thoughts regarding automated coding systems and what will transpire when the EHR is fully implemented?

7. How is the automated coding system used within the coding and billing process? Include the workflow from the coder assigning codes to billing to the payer.

8. What are the antifraud features available and how do they link to the automated coding system? Do you have future recommendations for antifraud features within automated coding systems?

9. How do you use the coded data in your analytics? Please elaborate on rules-based vs. statistics-based approach, as well as statistical modeling applications you may be using with the automated coding software.

10. Can you recommend any users of automated coding systems or vendors who are using or developing automated coding applications that we can also interview?

11. What do you believe are the weak links in fraud/abuse software, education, and compliance practices?

Source: AHIMA/FORE et al. 2005, 38.

2007). Faculty members using the TBL approach were interviewed using the interview guide. Parts of the interview guide are listed below to demonstrate how this method of observational research is used:

Sample Questions:

Has team learning been introduced into new courses?

Prompts:

Why? (Explore specific enablers and inhibitors)

When and how did it happen?

What elements of team learning are used?

What unexpected outcomes have occurred?

Focus Group

A **focus group** is a group of subjects, usually experts in the particular area of study, who are brought together to discuss a specific topic using the focused interview. A focus group consists of approximately 6 to 12 people and usually has a moderator other than one of the members of the research team. The moderator is there to make sure that all members of the focus group have equal time to discuss the issue as well as record important information through audio or video recording. The group then discusses issues as they are presented by the moderator. This allows the focus group members to hear one another's opinions and to comment on them. The focus group provides an excellent way for the research team to learn

Figure 4.4.   User interview form

1. What type of automated coding system do you use within your facility?

2. Is the automated coding system natural language processing (NLP) or structured text?

3. What is the approximate cost of the automated coding system (including education and training)?

4. When was the automated coding system developed?

5. How long did it take to implement the automated coding system on-site, including education and training?

6. What is the level of accuracy in coding and billing?

7. How is the automated coding system used with the EHR?

8. How is the automated coding system used within the coding and billing process?

9. What are the antifraud features available and how do they link to the automated coding system?

10. What do you believe are the "weak links" in fraud/abuse software, education, and compliance practices?

Source: AHIMA/FORE et al. 2005, 39.

more about the area of study because a group of experts is brainstorming together about it. It also enables the researcher to see how the group interacts and responds to particular study participants. Some studies may have more than one focus group, if necessary (Shi 1997).

Example of a Focus Group

Watzlaf et al. (2007) examined the effectiveness of ICD-10-CM in capturing public health diseases by conducting a focus group with experts in ICD-10-CM, public health, and classification systems. For example, members of the research team developed a listing of required reportable diseases to the Centers for Disease Control and Prevention (CDC) and state departments of health. The researchers coded each of the diseases using ICD-10-CM and ICD-9-CM. The principal investigator and co-investigators provided rankings for each of the disease categories. The rankings ranged from 1 = "Coding system does not capture the disease" to 5 = "The coding system fully captures the disease." The focus group then came together to discuss each of the rankings and to determine where changes need to be made. The use of the focus group in this capacity provided the researchers with validated information that was used to clarify many of the final rankings.

Participant Observation

As discussed previously under nonparticipant observation, participant observation is when the observer may actually be a part of the observed environment. They may be the researcher or an actual working member of the healthcare environment. What is important to determine with participant observation is whether the openness, attitudes, feelings, and behaviors will truly be observed when the participant is also the observer. The example that follows shows how participant observation, as one method in assessing compliance with Health Information Portability and Accountability Act (HIPAA) regulations, works well for one healthcare facility.

For example, healthcare facilities that are interested in how well their employees abide by the HIPAA may use the participant observation method. Investigators may observe employee's behavior on the elevators of the healthcare facility to determine if patient-specific information is kept confidential. Investigators may also observe health information management employees as they process requests for medical record information, observing whether they checked for completeness of the request form, including appropriate signatures, dates, and medical record forms. To record the behaviors, the researchers will record the information using check sheets, audiotapes, or videotapes. Because much of the information they are recording is confidential, researchers should take additional steps to maintain the confidentiality of the data collected, which includes keeping the information in secure systems, whether on paper or electronic, and abiding by any other requirements that the Institutional Review Board (IRB) may determine necessary. The researchers, who also may be employees within the facility, may use the information collected to improve the processes and systems related to compliance with HIPAA regulations.

Example of Participant Observation

Hofler et al. (2005) used the participant method of observational research when examining HIPAA compliance activities at the University Health Systems of Eastern Carolina (UHSEC). They used several elements when conducting this participant observational research method. Their study included physical inspection or observation, staff interviews, review of the information related to privacy and security, and observation and review of automated system activity. The privacy officers conducted the physical observations or "walkabouts," which included elevator observation, cafeteria conversation observation, trash-can content review, and informal interviews with staff. Walkabouts were unannounced, and reports of results were provided to managers so that they could fix any noncompliance problems. Conversations with staff included education as well as problems found. The privacy officers who were also the observers used what was found to provide education and training to staff so that compliance of HIPAA regulations could be maintained. Site visits at each of the UHSEC facilities examined the physical layout, operations, and privacy issues of each of the sites. Audits of specific practices revealed that some patients' notice of privacy practices (NPP) was needed on a consistent basis. A report generated from the automated patient admission system verified whether the NPP was provided to patients upon admission. Further review and analysis of the data collected led the privacy officers, IT security officers, and risk management staff to develop and implement an activity review process that identified the greatest risks first. A matrix was developed that outlined which activity should be monitored, who should be responsible for the review, how often it should occur, and what should be reviewed. An excerpt of the matrix is provided in table 4.1 using IT Infrastructure Activity as an example.

The participant observational method that UHSEC researchers used as part of their process to analyze HIPAA compliance is an excellent way to address this most complex and ongoing issue. Although the authors

Table 4.1. Excerpt of the HIPAA Activity Monitoring Matrix with IT Infrastructure Activity as an example

IT Infrastructure Activity		
Responsible Party	**Frequency**	**Reviewed**
IT security	TBD	• Network traffic activity • Firewall activity • Intrusion detection system activity • Wireless activity • E-mail activity • File transfer activity • Virus management • Internet activity • Remote activity • Software licenses

Source: Adapted from Hofler et al. 2005.

know that this will be a "process in evolution," their creative methods to assess it and to develop articulate tools for evaluation and analysis will certainly aid in their ability to consistently examine this extensive requirement.

Ethnography

Ethnography is the personal touch of research. It includes delving into a particular culture or organization in great detail in order to learn everything there is to know about a population and to develop new hypotheses. Ethnography can be broken up into two parts. The first part includes the method of cultural anthropology in which the researcher seeks to answer questions concerning the ways of life in living human beings. Ethnographic questions include the links between culture and behavior and how the cultural processes develop over time. The second part includes the writing up and reporting of results. Researchers or field workers tend to live among the people they are studying and participate in as much of the day-to-day activities as possible. Even mundane events, such as preparing meals and eating, provide pieces of information that field workers may use in their data collection process. This emersion into a particular culture is part of participant observation and provides what is called an "emic" perspective or the "native(s) point of view" without imposing the researchers' own views or opinions (Hall 2007).

Unique Characteristics

Ethnographic research tends not to be objective, and researchers who conduct ethnographic research may have different conclusions about the same population studied. This is all part of the unique characteristics of ethnography. This is because every ethnographer has different backgrounds and ideas and therefore no two ethnographers will examine a specific culture or organization the same way. Ethnography is not replicable like other types of research, and does not collect large numbers, rates, or percentages, or focus on trends of large databases, but instead focuses on people and insights into their culture and life.

Field notes are an important part of ethnographic research. Field notes should be written immediately after leaving the field site and should include the following four parts:

1. Jottings or brief notes written at the field site that will be expanded when the full field notes are written

2. Description of everything the researcher can remember about the observation event such as a meeting, an encounter, and so forth

3. Analysis or the ability to use what you have documented from 1 and 2 above and link it back to the specific research questions as well as the culture, policy, or regulation

4. Reflection or what the researcher learned in doing the observation from a personal viewpoint such as how comfortable you felt in collecting the information (Hall 2007)

Ethnography is different than observational research because it can include both qualitative and quantitative approaches. It can include both the participative and nonparticipative methods, although the participative approach is used more often. When the participative approach is used, researchers collect extensive field notes, conduct open-ended and unstructured interviews, and review and collect documents that are pertinent to the particular setting. Review of certain ethnographic books and articles enable the researcher to better understand how to conduct ethnographic methods (Hall 2007; Savage 2000).

For example, ethnographic methods are used to better understand different aspects of gender discrimination and the use of sex-selective abortion in Asia (Miller 2001). The author explains how ethnographic methods are used, starting with the examination of quantitative data to compare data across Asia in the trends of sex-selective abortion. Next, the dynamics of the Asian culture are discussed that support a strong son preference. Then, the author reviews technological availability for prenatal sex selection and national policies of sex selection. Last, the author discusses several positions on female selective abortion and how cultural anthropology and the use of ethnographic methods may help in the understanding of prenatal gender discrimination in Asia.

Cyclical

Ethnographic research tends to move in a cycle. Figure 4.5 demonstrates how this occurs. First, the researcher begins by reviewing the literature and developing tentative hypotheses rather than one that is easily tested. Second, the researcher collects data through field notes, interviews, and documents, and then analyzes and organizes the information. As this occurs, the ethnographic researchers revise their tentative hypotheses and create new hypotheses. Once the new hypotheses are created, the researcher sets out to collect more data to answer questions about the new tentative hypotheses. This cycle continues until the entire culture or organization is known extremely well, and developing hypotheses and research questions are answered. This method of using several different approaches to collect data and to answer the research questions and support the conclusions made is called **triangulation**.

Figure 4.5.   Cycle of ethnographic research

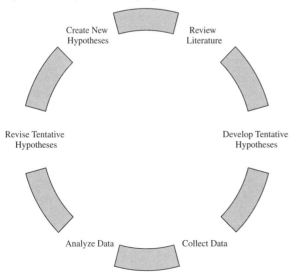

Example in Health Informatics

Ethnography was used as the core research method in assessing physicians, patients, and the EHR (Ventres et al. 2006) in four primary care practices in Oregon. Eighty hours of participant observation was conducted in which researchers observed interactions with the EHR among physicians and patients. Observations consisted of examining the physical layout of the office including the waiting rooms, reception areas, medical assistant stations, exam rooms, and physician work areas, as well as shadowing patients, medical assistants, and physicians. Also, participants were asked open-ended questions about their experiences, and researchers collected extensive field notes and drawings showing the positions of physicians and patients in relation to the exam room computer. Seventy-five open-ended interviews and five focus group interviews (most were audiotaped) were conducted with three main groups:

1. Professionals with knowledge about the use of EHRs
2. Randomly selected patients
3. Randomly selected physicians

The focus of the interviews centered on the participants' perspectives of their experiences with the EHR. Also, 29 convenience sample clinical encounters were videotaped to observe physician-patient interactions with EHR use. After each videotaped visit, physicians were interviewed about the impact the EHR has on physician-patient behavior. Also, physicians were asked to review one videotaped visit thought by researchers to best reflect his or her clinical behavior in relation to the EHR and write down their thoughts on the major aspects of the visit. Data continued to be collected until the researchers were assured that the observed patterns were valid. The analysis of the data collected consisted of several different steps and techniques. First, the audiotaped transcripts from the individual and focus group interviews were reviewed independently from the field notes. Prominent factors were highlighted and descriptive quotations were recorded. The researchers then discussed the factors and themes jointly and the interpretations had to be agreed upon by all members of the research team. The researchers identified data to confirm or refute the interpretations, and then themes were categorized. Videotapes were reviewed and discussed similarly to the audiotape interviews, and interpretations were agreed upon by all members of the team. Field notes from observations and brief interviews were

analyzed, and prominent factors listed and themes categorized. All results were reviewed with a medical anthropologist. Study results were reviewed by four key participants,
their comments were reviewed, and results were changed
based on these comments. Four themes emerged with 14
factors identified by which EHR use influenced physician-
patient encounters. The four themes include:

1. Spatial or geographical: how the physical presence of the EHR influenced behavior between
   physician and patient.

2. Relational: how patients and physicians perceived
   and used the EHR for each specific clinical visit.

3. Educational: how proficient the physician is in
   using the EHR and how well the patient understands the use of the EHR for a medical visit.

4. Structural: institutional and technological forces
   that influence how the physician perceives their
   use of the EHR

Examples of factors for each of the themes include
the following:

1. Spatial: position and size of computer monitor
   (many physicians positioned the monitor so the
   patient could see it to bring the patient into the
   interaction rather than the computer pulling the
   physician away).

2. Relational: benefits of use of EHR were context-
   dependent because some diagnoses (such as upper
   respiratory infection) could be documented easily
   using a drop-down menu whereas others (such as
   depression) needed extensive documentation.

3. Educational: patients were uninformed as to
   how the EHR could benefit them and how it
   was used in their medical care, and these feelings were not expressed to their physicians.

4. Structural: EHR notes are concise but lack
   depth and tend to look similar due to menus and
   protocols.

Content Analysis

Observational or qualitative methods result in the collection of large volumes of textual information such as
notes, recordings, and existing documents. The methods
used to analyze all of this data in order to answer research
questions and finalize conclusions are performed quite
differently than in quantitative research. **Content analy-**
sis is the ability of the observational researcher to examine all textual data collected and detect the number of
recurrent terms to determine emerging themes and factors reflective of the culture or institution examined.

Content analysis was performed in the 2005 AHIMA/
FORE computer-assisted coding (CAC) fraud and abuse
study. Table 4.2 summarizes the themes seen from interviews with the federal government, vendors, and users
of CAC systems. An antifraud model (table 4.3) was
developed to summarize all of the data collected and
to provide methods used to combat fraud in the coding
industry.

The constant comparative method is another method
used to analyze observational or qualitative data (Glaser 1965). It, however, uses **grounded theory**, which
seeks to examine what is actually going on instead of
what should go on, in the ability to analyze qualitative
data. The constant comparative method is made up of
four stages:

1. Comparing incidents applicable to each
   category

2. Integrating categories and their properties

3. Delimiting the theory

4. Writing the theory

The constant comparative method was used by
researchers examining patients with colorectal cancer
(Tang 2007). Respondents were interviewed using the
semistructured interview guide and focused on four
domains:

1. Cancer experiences: when and how they discovered the cancer and what treatment was received

2. Physical and emotional distress: emotional feelings when they were informed of the diagnosis,
   during treatment, and about the future after
   treatment

3. Coping strategies: ways they coped with the
   physical discomforts and emotional stress

4. Meaning searching pathways: cancer attributable to possible causes and any positive
   implications or benefits from cancer experiences, further probing guided by respondents'
   responses

The constant comparative method was used and
began with open coding of the interviews. All transcripts
were read and words that reflected respondents' ideas

Table 4.2.   Weak links

The following table summarizes weak links in fraud and abuse software, user education, and compliance practices.

Respondent	Software	Education	Compliance
Federal Government	Incident of fraud with autocoding software, so it can facilitate fraud Access to the data can be inhibited because of the type of software used. For example, if the coding system is proprietary, it may be difficult to obtain access to the data. Most individuals in crime detection and compliance are not technologically savvy so may not be able to deal with the increased technological patterns. Antifraud software is turned off, ignored, or the issues detected are not addressed—it is a disincentive, if not a deterrent.	There is ignorance of automated coding and technology and fraud More education is needed regarding EHRs and how they will work. Further, it is important to know how interoperability will come into play. It is important to teach law enforcement professionals and investigators how it will work; the more that investigators understand, the more they will be able to apply their knowledge to ongoing work in the area of concern. Educate beneficiaries about fraud. With more awareness comes help with antifraud activities. Provide education about how to report inaccuracies on the Medicare Summary Notices (MSN) and especially the medication report.	Compliance staff will need to understand automated coding, EHR technology, and how it impacts fraud. More education about EHR is needed so that compliance staff can use appropriate software within the context of interoperability of systems. There are mechanisms provided in HIPAA to allow beneficiaries to report fraud (Beneficiary Incentive Program from HIPAA 63FR31123 published June 8, 1998, 42CFR420.400).
Vendor	Rules may be inconsistent when audits are conducted because software edits are bypassed or software is not used. Difficult to cross-check the accuracy of information from system to system. Retrospective and prospective designs, prospective good but difficult to do because of prompt payment laws. All vendors require a final evaluation by an experienced or expert coding professional. Coding accuracy of automated coding alone would be problematic. Much of the software is rules-based or statistics based; need a combination of both to improve accuracy. Loose standards and poor data quality, especially for claim elements that aren't tightly linked to payment.	Inaccuracy of clinician dictation or documentation but coder should be able to confirm whether information is correct. Lack of education of fellows and interns on how language used changes code. Lack of education for providers, government personnel, payers, and consumers regarding what constitutes fraud and how to detect it. Lack of HIM education on how the coded data interfaces with revenue cycle. Lack of reminder systems in dictation and autocoding systems for physicians on what to include in their documentation.	Tension between the payer and provider communities. Limited administrative power leads to not monitoring medical necessity. Not always done correctly or consistently even though they have compliance officer. No aggregate data evaluation capabilities a payer can query regarding a claim's accuracy. Lack of incentives for insurance payers to pursue and eradicate fraud.
User	Inaccuracy of automated coding systems; none 100% accurate. Don't know the weaknesses of the automated coding system. Don't know if automated coding software improved coding quality. Have capabilities to cut and paste the documentation and need to change content to show what was done that day.	Automated coding systems not used correctly by physicians. Education and background of coder, if lacking, can make a huge difference in the quality of coded data. Proficient coders more scarce, which can also impact cost and quality of coded data. Reliance on physicians to code without appropriate coding education background.	Inaccuracy of codes of the automated coding product. Whether compliance is being done consistently everywhere. No benchmarking standards. Control of whether test is necessary, ordered appropriately, or completed as ordered is much bigger underlying issue than whether software is effective.

Source: AHIMA/FORE et al. 2005, 50–51.

Table 4.3.   Antifraud model

The following table summarizes features, processes, and staffing for the ideal antifraud system or model.

Features	Processes	Staffing
Automated coding with NLP with a rules-based and statistics-based combination	Prepayment fraud detection using data profiling, advanced analytic models, and rank scoring	Advanced coder analyst to edit and check all processes for accurate code assignment IT staff for maintenance of current technology and HIS staff to train office staff and physicians
A standardized system of data (based on a representative sample of standardized claims information) for statistical reference Private development of software for code assignment facilitated by the federal government; which may also establish criteria or certification procedures for software.	Prepayment fraud detection by using a standardized method to derive the statistical aspects of code assignment and data analysis	Payer, provider, vendor all working together to combat fraud through education and incentives
ANN and predictive modeling to determine where potential for fraud lies	Postpayment fraud detection	Consumer involvement and education
Audit trails		

Source: AHIMA/FORE et al. 2005, 52.

and thoughts were labeled. Codes were derived from the actual wording. Categorizations were developed from interpretation and grouping of the codes applied in the first stage of analysis. Codes sharing similar meanings were grouped into categories for further analysis. Grouping categories were developed for clearer and easier analysis. All information was then reflected back to the theory or objectives. Objectives included:

1. To characterize the disorientation experiences
2. To explore the factors that foster the process of sense making and benefit finding
3. To examine the growth through meaning searching, and the results or new theory were reported

Software is available to assist the researcher in conducting content analysis. Several different types of software are available depending on what types of textual documents will be analyzed. These programs count word frequencies, category frequencies, concordance (each word on the document in alphabetical order), cluster analysis (groups together words used in similar contexts), and co-word citation (examines occurrence of pairs of words). However, the software can be expensive and it is not easy to use and may require extensive training. The researcher must weigh the risks and benefits in order to determine whether to use a software program for content analysis (Audience Dialogue 2007).

Summary

Observational research is a very important method used to assess or evaluate aspects of health information. There are several different types of observational research methods, which are summarized in table 4.4. This method provides the researchers with in-depth observations, interviews, or ethnographic accounts of what occurs in healthcare facilities among interactions between patients and physicians, as well as the feelings of patients diagnosed, for example, with dementia or colon cancer. Health informatics researchers should use this method whenever they want to obtain a qualitative aspect to a particular problem. It provides extensive amounts of data that need to be evaluated using content analysis and other more complex methods, but it can provide the researcher with the feelings, perceptions, attitudes, and thoughts of patients that quantitative research methods will not provide.

Table 4.4.   Summary of Observational Research Methods

Method	Definition and Example in Health Informatics
Nonparticipant observation	Observes actions of study participants with limited interference. Example: Observing how employees react to a new documentation software system.
Participant observation	Researcher is a part of the environment he or she is observing. Example: Used to assess how well employees in healthcare facilities abide by HIPAA.
Naturalistic	One example of nonparticipant observation in which behaviors and events are recorded as they occur naturally in the normal environment. Example: naturalistic observations conducted to determine whether the cancer registry is underutilized.
Simulation	Observing participants in an environment that has been created for them rather than their normal environment. Example: observing individuals with visual disabilities use different Web sites to determine if the Web sites are accessible.
Case study	Nonparticipant observation when the researcher wants to thoroughly assess an individual, group, or institution.
Individual case study	Researcher records and collects as much information as possible about a particular individual as he or she progresses through a certain disease, procedure, treatment, cultural, or system change. Example: individual patient is followed and evaluated to determine how he or she uses an assistive technology device.
Group case study	Very similar to individual case study except that interviews or observations are conducted on a group of individuals instead of one individual. Example: Assessing the moral reasoning skills of medical students using ethical issues.
Institutional case study	Observing a particular healthcare institution or facility to determine how it conducts a particular process, system, or procedure. Example: Department of Veterans Affairs healthcare system used the institutional case study method to describe how their electronic health record system is used in home-based primary care programs.
Focused interview	An interview used in observational or qualitative research in which the researcher wants to collect in-depth, rich, robust information. Three types of focused interviews include: focus group, informal conversational, and standardized open-ended.
Focus group	A focus group is a group of subjects, usually experts in the particular area of study, who are brought together to discuss a specific topic. Example: Focus group of experts used in evaluating ICD-10-CM and its effectiveness in capturing public health-related diseases.
Informal conversational	No set questions developed, moves forward based on what the study participant would like to discuss. Example: What is the meaning of living with dementia while in a nursing facility?
Standardized open-ended	Specific questions are used to interview the study participants. Example: Used to study automated coding software and the potential to decrease fraud and abuse.
General interview guide	Outline of issues is used to conduct the informal interview. Examples: Medical schools used the general interview guide to reassess team-based learning.
Ethnography	Delving into a particular culture or organization in great detail in order to learn everything there is to know about them and to develop new hypotheses. Example: Used to assess interactions between physicians and patients when using the EHR.

References

Audience Dialogue. 2007. Software for content analysis. Available online from http://www.audiencedialogue. org/soft-cont.html.

AHIMA/FORE, University of Pittsburgh, HHS, and ONC. 2005 (July 11). Automated coding software: Development and use to enhance anti-fraud activities. HHS Contract Number: HHSP23320054100EC. Available online from http://www. hhs.gov/healthit/documents/AutomaticCodingReport.pdf.

Giacomini, M., and D.J. Cook. 2000. A User's Guide to Qualitative Research in Health Care, Evidence Based Medicine Informatics Project, Centre for Health Evidence. Based on the Users' guide to evidence-based medicine from *JAMA* 284(4):478–82 Available online from http://www.cche. net/userguides/qualitative.asp

Glaser, B. 1965. The constant comparative method of qualitative analysis. *Social Problems* 12(4):436–445.

Graneheim, U., and L. Jansson. 2006. The meaning of living with dementia and disturbing behaviour as narrated by three persons admitted to a residential home. *Journal of Nursing and Healthcare of Chronic Illness* 15(11):1397–1403.

Hackett, S. 2007 (December) An exploration into two solutions to propagating Web accessibility for blind computer users. PhD dissertation, University of Pittsburgh.

Hall, B. 2007. How to do ethnographic research: A simplified guide. Available online from http://www.sas.upenn. edu/anthro/CPIA/methods.html.

Hallstrom, I., Elander, G., and L. Rooke. 2000. Pain and nutrition as experienced by patients with hip fracture. *Journal of Clinical Nursing* 9(4):639–646.

Hofler, L.D., Hardee, J., Burleson, D., and J. Grady. 2005. HIPAA audit and system activity review: Developing a process that focuses on the greatest risks first. *Journal of American Health Information Management Association* 76(3):34–38.

Kanaar, A.C., and M.W. Hecht. 1991. Marathon swim training in a 74-year-old man: Personal experience. *Medicine and Science in Sports and Exercise* 24(4):490–494.

Miller, B.D. 2001. Female selective abortion in Asia: Patterns, policies, and debates. *American Anthropologist* 103(1):112–33, Abstract only.

Savage, J. 2000. Ethnography and health care. *British Medical Journal* 321:1400–1402.

Self, D.J., Olivarez, M., and C.B. DeWitt. 1998. The amount of small-group case study discussion needed to improve moral reasoning skills of medical students. *Academic Medicine* 73(5)521–523.

Shea, D. 2007. Use of the electronic record in the home-based primary care programs at the Veterans Affairs Health Care System. *The Journal for the Home Care and Hospice Professional* 25 (5):323–326.

Shi, L. 1997. Health Services Research Methods. Chapter 6 (pp.125–141) in Qualitative Research. Albany, NY: Delmar Publishers.

Tang, V.Y., Lee, A., Chan, C., Leung, P., Sham, J., Ho, J., and J. Cheng. 2007. Disorientation and reconstruction: The meaning of searching pathways of patients with colorectal cancer. *Journal of Psychosocial Oncology* 25(2):77–102.

Thompson, B.M., Schneider, V.F., Haidet, P., Levine, R., McMahon, K., Perkowski, L., and B. Richards. 2007. Team-based learning at ten medical schools: Two years later. *Medical Education* 41:250–257.

Ventres, W., Kooienga, S., Vuckovic, N., Marlin, R., Nygren, P., and V. Stewart. 2006. Physicians, patients, and the electronic health record: An ethnographic analysis. *Annals of Family Medicine* 4(2):124–131.

Watzlaf, V.W., and A. Katoh, 1989. The tumor registry— Unrealized potential: One hospital's experience. *Topics in Health Records Management* 10(1):43–50.

Watzlaf, V.W., Garvin, J., Moeini, S., and P. Firouzan. 2007. The effectiveness of ICD-10-CM in capturing public health diseases. *Perspectives in Health Information Management* 4(6):1–31.

Chapter 5
Experimental and Quasi-Experimental Research

Valerie J. Watzlaf, PhD, RHIA, FAHIMA

Learning Objectives

- Describe the different types of experimental and quasi-experimental research and its use in health informatics
- List and explain the different components that comprise each of the methods involved in experimental and quasi-experimental research
- Describe the pretest/posttest control group method and how it can be used in health informatics
- Describe the Solomon four-group method and how it is used in health informatics
- Explain when the posttest-only control group method should be used
- Discuss the differences between quasi-experimental research and experimental research
- Provide examples of when to use the one-shot case study
- Demonstrate when to use the one-group pretest/posttest method and when to use the static group comparison
- Summarize the key elements of the experimental and quasi-experimental methodology

Key Terms

Attrition
Comparison group
Confounding variable
Control group
Crossover design
Dependent variable
Experimental group
Experimental procedures
Experimental research
History
Independent variable
Instrumentation
Interaction of factors
Intervention
Maturation

Midtests
One group pretest-posttest method
One-shot case study
Posttest-only control group method
Pretest-posttest control group method
Quasi-experimental research
Randomization
Selection
Selection bias
Solomon four-group method
Static group comparison method
Statistical regression
Testing
Time-series tests

Introduction

A patient walks into a physician's office and hypothesizes that the first question the medical receptionist may ask her is about her insurance information. The medical receptionist asks her to check the insurance information on a sheet of paper and to sign the bottom of the form if the information is still accurate. A co-payment of $15 is requested. She checks the information on the form and it is accurate so she signs her name at the bottom and pays the $15 co-payment. She takes a seat in the waiting room and hypothesizes about the amount of time she will wait until she sees the doctor. She waits about 20 minutes and is taken into the examination room where she is told that the doctor will be right with her and she hypothesizes that she will wait more than 30 minutes in the exam room before she actually sees the doctor. The doctor arrives in about 15 minutes and the medical exam begins.

This is an example of an experiment. The patient started with a hypothesis about a request for insurance information as she entered the physician's office and she was correct. She continued to hypothesize about the amount of time it would take before she actually saw her doctor, thinking it would be longer than it actually was, so she was incorrect about the waiting time. She continued to develop hypotheses and test them and reach conclusions in her experiment, trying to establish cause and effect (Barnes et al. 2005, 1).

Experimental research studies are considered the most powerful when trying to establish cause and effect. **Experimental research** studies expose participants to different **interventions** (**independent variables**) in order to compare the result of these interventions with the outcome (**dependent variables**).

The independent variable is the intervention or factor you wish to measure in order to determine if it will have an effect on the dependent variable or the disease or outcome under study. Examples of independent variables are medications, diet, exercise, education, or health information systems. Examples of dependent variables include increases in survival time for patients with cancer, reduction of pressure sores in patients using a wheelchair, decrease in the number of adverse events in healthcare facilities that utilize a computerized physician order entry system (CPOE), and so forth. Experimental research also tries to determine how much the independent variable will have an effect on the dependent variable. Therefore, if the researcher uses a new medication

and finds that it has slowed the progression of cancer, if the dose of the medication is increased, it may slow the progression even faster. A dose-response relationship may be determined from experimental research studies. Also, sometimes researchers find that if they remove a specific variable from the environment, it decreases the incidence of certain outcomes. For example, if radon is removed from certain homes or if the level is decreased significantly, the incidence of lung cancer decreases. It is sometimes difficult for the researcher to prove, however, that the specific independent variable caused the dependent variable without any interference from other factors or events. This is one example of problems with internal validity and there are certain things the experimental researcher can do to reduce the amount of internal validity. This will be discussed later in this chapter.

When deciding whether to use the experimental research design, the researcher should consider the following issues:

1. Eligibility of appropriate participants
2. Randomization (discussed later in this chapter)
3. Ethical issues

Ethical issues pose the greatest problem against using the experimental method because it would be unethical to withhold a particular treatment from one group of patients who might benefit from it, while administering it to another group. Sometimes comparison groups are used that receive some other type of intervention or sometimes the intervention under study is provided to all participants once the study is completed. (See chapter 13 for a discussion of ethical principles in research.)

Quasi-experimental research is similar to experimental research but does not include randomization of participants. The independent variable may not be manipulated by the researcher, and there may be no control group (Barnes et al. 2005, 3). It also may be used over time and with something other than individual participants. For example, a researcher may study the effects of an automated coding system to determine if there is an increase in hospital reimbursement before and after the system is implemented. Health informatics researchers use quasi-experimental research designs more than experimental research designs. The quasi-experimental design tends to be more prominent because of the ethical concerns in withholding a particular health information system from a specific group of patients. However, there are some situations where an experimental design can be used. For example, if different types of educational techniques are used to improve a patients' use of the personal health record, an experimental design may be appropriate because withholding a specific educational technique is not considered life-threatening.

Overview of the Types of Experimental Study Designs

There are many different types of experimental and quasi-experimental study designs. The most common experimental study designs as described by Campbell and Stanley (1963) include the pretest-posttest control group method, Solomon four-group method, and posttest only control group method. The **pretest-posttest control group method** (classic experimental design) is when participants are randomly assigned to either the intervention (experimental) or a nonintervention (control) group. However, those participants assigned to the control group may receive a different intervention other than the one under study. Pretests are given to both groups at the same time to assess their similarities and differences. Posttests are given to both groups to determine the effect of the intervention. The **Solomon four-group method** is similar to the pretest-posttest design but includes two intervention or experimental groups and two control groups. Pretests are used for one of the intervention groups and one of the control groups. Posttests are used for all groups. Therefore, four groups are included in which the first experimental group receives a pretest, an intervention, and a posttest. The first control group receives a pretest, no intervention, and a posttest. The second experimental group receives the intervention and a posttest only. The second control group receives no intervention and a posttest only. The extra groups are included to neutralize the effect of the pretest because sometimes it may influence the responses of recipients on the posttest. The **posttest-only control group method** is similar to the pretest-posttest control group method except that no pretest is used. **Randomization**, which is the random assignment of participants to the intervention or control group, is used in all of the experimental study designs briefly described above (Shi 1997). Each of these designs will be described in more detail later in this chapter. Table 5.1 provides a brief summary of each experimental study design.

Overview of the Types of Quasi-experimental Study Designs

Common quasi-experimental study designs as described by Campbell and Stanley (1963) include the one-shot case study, one group pretest-posttest method, and the static group comparison method. The **one-shot case study** is a simple design in which an intervention is provided to one group and they are followed forward in time after intervention to assess the outcome (posttest). The **one group pretest-posttest method** is similar to the one-shot case study except that the pretest is used before the intervention. The **static group comparison method** is when two groups are examined; one with the intervention and one without, and then a posttest is given to assess the result of the intervention. Randomization is not used in any of the quasi-experimental study designs, and most of the quasi-experimental designs are used on units or groups, so randomization can be quite difficult to execute (Shi 1997). Each of these designs will be described in more detail later in this chapter. Table 5.2 provides a brief summary of each quasi-experimental study design.

Differentiating Elements

When conducting experimental research, important elements should be addressed and described. These elements include: randomization, crossover design, observation, control group, and treatment.

Randomization

Randomization is when study participants or groups of participants are randomly assigned to one type of intervention or no intervention. The intervention group is called the **experimental group,** and the group with no intervention is called the **control group.** Sometimes other groups called **comparison groups** are used when a different intervention is used as a comparison. For example, a researcher may be interested in determining whether individuals retain more if they do higher levels of exercise before they learn how to use the personal health record (PHR). Therefore, three different groups of participants could be established. The first group will run for 30 minutes before sitting down in front of the computer to learn to use their PHR, the second group will walk for 30 minutes before learning to use the PHR, and the third group will not do any type of exercise before learning to use the PHR. Therefore, the first group

Table 5.1. Summary of experimental research designs

Study Design	Characteristics	Diagram
Pretest-posttest control group method	Randomly assigned to intervention or nonintervention (control) group Pretests given to both groups Posttests given to both groups after intervention	R---O---X---O R---O--- ---O
Solomon four-group method	Two intervention groups Two control groups Randomization used to assign to all four groups Pretest for one pair of intervention and control groups Same intervention used in both groups Posttest used in all four groups	R---O---X---O R---O--- ---O R--- ---X---O R--- --- ---O
Posttest-only control group method	Randomization used for assignment into intervention and control groups No pretest given Intervention given to one group only Posttest given to both groups	R--- ---X---O R--- --- ---O

R = randomization
O = observation
X = intervention

Table 5.2. Summary of quasi-experimental research designs

Study Design	Characteristics	Diagram
One-shot case study	Simple design One group Intervention Posttest	---X---O
One group pretest-posttest method	One group Pretest Intervention Posttest	O---X---O
Static group comparison method	Two groups Intervention No intervention Posttest for both groups	---X---O --- ---O

R = randomization
O = observation (pretest or posttest)
X = intervention

is called the experimental group, the second is called the comparison group, and the third is called the control group. Randomization will need to be employed for this study. This is not the same as random sampling. Randomization is when a group of participants are randomly chosen to be in the experimental, control, or comparison group using a random method, such as probability sampling, so that each participant has an equal chance of being selected for each of the groups. This can be done by developing a list of all the study participants, numbering them and putting all their numbers in a hat. Each of the numbers are picked out and allocated to a particular group. For example, the first number drawn will go into the experimental group, the second number to the control group, the third number to the comparison group, and so forth until all the numbers are drawn and participants allocated. The goal is to have the experimental, control, or comparison groups as similar as possible except for the intervention under study.

Because it may be unethical to withhold a certain intervention from one group of participants, some experimental research studies do not contain a control group but instead use two comparison groups. In this way, the intervention under study still is used, but all members of the study are receiving some type of intervention. For example, if researchers are assessing the effect of using regional health information organizations (RHIOs) to decrease the incidence of nosocomial infections in four nursing facilities in a particular region, then two of the nursing facilities will use the RHIO-based data, and the other two nursing facilities will utilize some other type of database to minimize the unethical consequences of not providing any type of data.

Crossover Design

A **crossover design** also can be used to minimize the unethical effects of not providing certain types of interventions. It includes using one group of participants as both the experimental group and the control group. A group of participants start out by being assigned to the experimental group and receive this intervention for a certain period of time, such as 6 months or 1 year. After they receive the intervention, they cross over to receiving no intervention or another comparison intervention for another 6 months to 1 year. For example, the crossover design may be used when studying whether certain types of telerehabilitation will improve the outcomes of patients with multiple sclerosis. Patients may start out using sensors and body monitoring and then cross over to using a personal digital assistant (PDA) or the traditional in-house therapy monitoring in order to monitor their functional levels after treatment. The same group is used as the comparison group and the experimental group, but the researcher must be careful with this design because the use of one group for both the intervention and the comparison may bias the results.

Observation

Observation, or pretest and posttest, includes observing the experimental and control groups before (pretest) or after (posttest) the intervention. Pretest and posttest is used as common terminology to describe the observations but the observation may not always include a test. It may be, for example, blood pressure taken before and after the administration of a certain medication, exercise, or diet. Or it may be a questionnaire given to determine levels of depression before and after a medication intervention. Still other observations may include observing a group of individuals before the administration of a policy or procedure change and then observing them again after the change has been in place for one month. Other types of observations are not administered before or after the intervention but during the middle of the particular study. These observations are called **midtests**. Other observations may be conducted several months or years after the intervention ends to determine its long-term impact. Observations may be conducted throughout the study period as a new policy or law is implemented. These are called **time-series tests**. For example, a researcher might use the time-series test to examine the number of breaches of confidentiality after the implementation of the Health Insurance Portability and Accountability Act (HIPAA). These rates could be compared to rates before HIPAA was implemented.

When pretests and posttests are used in educational intervention studies, the same pretest and posttest is usually administered so that the researcher can determine if the study participants improved their performance after the intervention. However, using the same test may bias the results because some participants may remember the questions when responding the second time. Therefore, researchers will control for this bias by adding a group that will not take the pretest but just the posttest. The Solomon four-group method employs this design. Internal and external validity issues in experimental and quasi-experimental research and how to control for them is discussed later in this chapter.

Control Group

The control group is the group of individuals who will not receive the intervention or will receive an alternative intervention. They then may be referred to as a comparison group. This enables the researcher to determine if the intervention or treatment used has made an effect in one group (treatment or intervention group) more so than in another group (control group). The use of the control group allows the researcher to determine if the effect seen is really due to the intervention and not other extraneous factors or **confounding variables**. Sometimes, especially in clinical trials when medication is being tested as the intervention, the control group is given a placebo so that they are as similar as possible to the intervention group but are not receiving the medication under study.

Treatment

In experimental and quasi-experimental research, the treatment is the intervention. Treatments or interventions are also the independent variable. They may include a variety of different components depending on what the researcher wants to test in the particular experiment. Therefore, treatments or interventions may include use of experimental medications, changes in an individuals' behavior such as smoking or alcohol cessation, or changes in a particular assistive device, technology, software, or system. Whatever treatment is administered, it must be administered in the same way for all participants in the experimental group. For example, if physical therapists are going to be educated and trained online in using a new rehabilitation electronic health record (EHR) system, the level (hours of training), quality (content of the online education and training), and hands-on application (amount of time using the EHR system) should be the same for all physical therapists in the experimental group. The control group may consist of physical therapists who will receive traditional in-class education and training. The hypothesis is that the physical therapists trained online or with distance education will be the same or better than those trained using the in-class method.

Experimental Studies

There are several different types of experimental study designs. Three of the most common experimental designs

will be discussed in the following paragraphs and an example related to health informatics will be described for each of the different experimental designs.

Pretest-Posttest Control Group Method

The pretest-posttest control group method is similar to the randomized controlled trial (RCT) or clinical trial discussed in chapter 6, Epidemiological Research. The RCT is more appropriate for testing interventions such as medications or other medical treatments on individuals while the pretest-posttest control group method focuses more on providing an intervention that may include a specific program or system change than a medication or treatment. The pretest-posttest control group method randomly assigns participants to either the intervention (experimental) or a nonintervention (control) group. However, those participants assigned to the control group may receive a different intervention other than the one under study. Pretests are given to both groups at the same time to assess their similarities and differences. Posttests are given to both groups to determine the effect of the intervention.

Examples in Health Informatics

For example, an experimental pretest-posttest control group design was used to assess the impact of a computer-assisted education program on factors related to asthma self-management behavior (Shegog et al. 2001). The Watch, Discover, Think, and Act (WDTA) computer-assisted instruction program was used to teach children in inner-city elementary and middle schools who have asthma how to manage their care. The authors hypothesized that children using the intervention would experience improvement in certain cognitive variables that provide success with asthma self-management. The study included 76 children from six clinics and seven schools in a large urban area. Five subjects were lost to follow-up and one refused to participate further, so the final sample included 71 children ranging in age from 8 to 13 years with a diagnosis of asthma. Children were randomly assigned to either the intervention or control group. Those in the intervention group played the WDTA and those in the control group received no intervention. The goal of the WDTA game is to help the main character get to a castle by managing asthma in a positive way.

The participants must make sure that the main character adheres to four self-regulation steps, which include:

- Watching
  - —Monitoring symptoms
  - —Taking preventative medications
  - —Keeping appointments
- Discovering
  - —Deciding whether an asthma problem exists and its probable cause
- Thinking
  - —Deciding on a list of possible actions
- Acting
  - —Choosing an action such as medicine, avoiding environmental triggers such as dust and fur, and getting additional help

The game includes 18 real-world and 4 castle activities that have specific problems that inner-city children with asthma must deal with on a daily basis.

Baseline data were collected from all children on their asthma self-management skills in session one. Session two included having children in the experimental group use the WDTA. Session three began 1 week later and included the collection of posttest data, which again included the assessment of asthma self-management skills as well as attitudes toward computer-assisted instruction. The instrument used to test knowledge of asthma management was pilot tested before implementation and was found to have a Cronbach's alpha of 0.86.

Results of the study indicate that children using the WDTA program scored significantly higher on questions about steps of self-regulation components, treatment decisions and greater self-efficacy. The WDTA program needs to have a more thorough evaluation of how it can best be adopted and disseminated in clinics, but for the most part it was found to be a positive component of asthma self-management education.

Another example of an experimental pretest-posttest control group method was conducted by researchers trying to improve the outcomes of older adults with Type II diabetes mellitus (Miller et al. 2002). In this study, an information processing model was used to teach older adults how to better manage their diabetes. Education instruction included how to evaluate nutrition information on food labels when purchasing food for meal planning and preparation. Researchers used the steps of the information processing model (which include steps used to acquire and process information that leads to decisions), to teach participants how to assess nutritional information over a 10-week period. All participants received an examination to assess their cognitive ability. Researchers collected data related to their medical and diet history. These data helped the researchers develop an education intervention specific to their needs. Participants were then randomized to the intervention or to the control group. Those in the control group did not have any further contact with the researchers until the posttest data were collected. Blood tests were given at pretest and posttest to determine cholesterol, triglycerides, glucose, and hemoglobin levels. Results showed that the fasting glucose and hemoglobin levels of the experimental group were significantly more improved than those in the control group. Also, the total cholesterol values at posttest for the experimental group were closer to their treatment goals than those in the control group ($p < 0.05$).

Solomon Four-Group Method

The **Solomon four-group method** includes two intervention groups and two control groups. Pretests are used for only one of the intervention groups and only one of the control groups. Posttests are used for all groups. Therefore, the Solomon four-group has two experimental groups, both of which receive the intervention, but one receives a pretest and posttest while the other experimental group receives a posttest only. Two control groups also are used in this design in which one control group receives a pretest and posttest while the other group receives the posttest only. All participants are randomly assigned to the groups. This method controls for pretest exposure but also requires more time, effort, and cost due to the additional groups. There are some modifications in the Solomon four-group design in which three groups are used instead of four. An example of that modification is discussed below.

Examples in Health Informatics

An adaptation of the Solomon four-group design was used by researchers evaluating the effectiveness of a multimedia tutorial in the preparation of dental students to recognize and respond to domestic violence (Danley et al. 2004). The first experimental group of dental students was randomly assigned to take the pretest, the tutorial (intervention), and then a posttest. The second experimental group first took the tutorial and then the posttest. The third group (control group) took the pretest and then the posttest. The control group did receive the tutorial after the posttest in order to provide them with useful information, but this had no effect on the results. The fourth group (posttest only with no pretest and no tutorial) was excluded because the authors believed the addition would not serve any purpose in the study. The tutorial was developed based on an approach that includes asking, validating, documenting, and referring (AVDR). Asking refers to asking the patient about abuse; validating refers to providing support to the patient that abuse is wrong while still verifying the patient's self-worth; documenting refers to writing in the dental record signs and symptoms with photos; and referring includes making sure patients are properly referred to domestic violence experts. The tutorial is 15 minutes long and shows interaction between a dentist and a patient who shows signs of domestic abuse during her dental visit. The tutorial works through the four stages of AVDR in referring to the specific patient example. The pre- and posttests were developed by the researchers and included 24 online questions related to the AVDR approach. For example, a question under the documentation section included:

> "If I identified a patient as being abused, I would document the abuse in the patient's chart. How much do you believe you know about how to document abuse in the dental chart?" Items were scored on a Likert scale from 1 = none to 4 = a lot.

The pretest and posttest had the same questions but in a different order.

Results showed that of the 161 dental students and 13 dentists that completed the study, those in the experimental groups who used the tutorial had significantly higher mean scores than those in the control group on most of the test items.

In another example, researchers used the Solomon four-group design in assessing how well health education increases screening for cervical cancer among Lumbee Indian women in North Carolina (Dignan et al. 1998). Here, researchers randomly assigned women into one of the following four groups:

1. Pretest/health education program/posttest (Experimental Group 1)
2. Pretest/posttest (Control Group 1)
3. Health education program/posttest (Experimental Group 2)
4. Posttest only (Control Group 2)

The pre- and posttest face-to-face interview questions centered on perceptions of health status, use of healthcare services, healthcare behaviors, knowledge, attitudes, and behaviors related to cervical cancer and demographic data. A total of 854 women were involved in all phases of the study. Those who received the health education program improved their knowledge about the Pap smear more than those in the control group, whether they received the pretest or not. The researchers concluded that the health education program improved knowledge about cervical cancer prevention and led to higher percentages of Lumbee Indian women receiving the Pap smear in the past year.

Posttest-Only Control Group Method

The experimental posttest only control group design is when participants are randomly assigned to an experimental group or a control group and posttests are the only means of observation. No pretests are used. This is done to reduce the effect of familiarity with exposure to a pretest. By eliminating the pretest, the researcher reduces the amount of recall that may influence responses on the posttest. However, not using a pretest eliminates the ability to assess an improvement in test or observation scores from before the intervention to after the intervention. Therefore, only an assessment of current utilization of the effectiveness of the intervention can be assessed.

Example in Health Informatics

The experimental posttest-only control group method was used by researchers assessing the effect of community nursing support on clients with schizophrenia (Beebe 2001). Twenty-four participants were randomly assigned to the control group (routine follow-up care and informational telephone contact at 6 and 12 weeks) and the experimental group (weekly telephone intervention plus routine follow-up care for 3 months). All participants were followed for 3 months after hospital discharge to determine the length of survival in the community setting as well as frequency and length of stay for rehospitalizations. Fifteen participants from the experimental group and 22 from the control group fully completed the intervention and follow-up phase. The treatment intervention consisted of a 10-minute telephone call with questions such as "Are you having problems with your medication?" or "Did you have any follow-up appointments scheduled this week? How did that go?" Also, the researchers asked participants about specific symptoms related to their illness based on review of their medical records from previous hospitalizations. This treatment intervention was performed weekly for 3 months. Control participants received 1- to 3-minute phone call to collect data on any previous hospitalizations. If readmissions were found, medical records were reviewed for length of stay data. This phone call was provided only twice during the study, at 6 and 12 weeks. Outcome measures included the following:

1. Community survival: number of days in community before rehospitalization or until end of study
2. Length of rehospitalization
3. Frequency of rehospitalizations: number of admissions to inpatient psychiatric units

Other confounding variables also were collected such as demographic characteristics, symptoms leading to hospitalization, alternative care sought before hospitalization, and so forth.

Results showed that overall the experimental participants survived in the community longer than the control participants. When a readmission occurred, the experimental group also had a 27 percent reduction in length of stay.

Another example of the experimental posttest only control group method was conducted in hospitals and healthcare centers in Greece (Saounatsou et al. 2001). Researchers were interested in assessing how well hypertensive patients improve in their compliance with medication and overall self-care when given direct education from public health nurses. Forty total hypertensive patients participated in the study, with 20 randomly assigned to the intervention group, and 20 randomly assigned to a control group. The intervention group received education from a public health nurse through four to five individual visits and phone contacts twice per week, emphasizing the importance of compliance with their medications and the risks involved when not taking their medications as prescribed. The control group did not receive the educational contacts from the public health nurse, but after the study they did receive educational instructional kits regarding compliance. The dependent variable or the outcome measure was compliance and was measured on a 5-point Likert scale ranging from 1 = noncompliant to 5 = full compliance. Compliance was based on the number of monthly doses taken. For example, if patients took between 21 to 30 doses in 1 month, they would be considered in poor compliance,

whereas if patients took 51 to 60 doses in 1 month, they would be in full compliance. The results support the hypothesis of the study in that hypertensive individuals who are educated about the importance of their medication will show improved compliance with their medication use than those who do not receive this education.

Quasi-Experimental Studies

There are several different types of quasi-experimental study designs. Three of the most common designs are discussed in the following text and examples specific to health informatics are described.

One-Shot Case Study

The quasi-experimental one-shot case study is a simple design in which an intervention is provided to one group and they are followed forward in time after intervention to assess the outcome (posttest). No randomization, no control group, and no pretest are included and so there is no baseline measurement to provide a comparison to the intervention outcome.

Examples in Health Informatics

Researchers conducted a quasi-experimental one-shot case study to determine if an automated two-way messaging system will help human immunodeficiency virus (HIV)-positive patients comply with complex medication treatments (Dunbar et al. 2003). Nineteen HIV-positive patients were enrolled and completed the study, and were provided with two-way pagers that included reminders to take all medication doses and follow any dietary requirements. Additional messages provided information on the importance of medication compliance, adverse effects, sleeping patterns, mood, any stressful events, drug use, and any difficulties with the messaging system. Examples of messages included: "Good morning, JT, time for your indinavir" or as a question: "Any problems with your medications over the weekend?" and so forth. Respondents then received a multiple choice of possible responses to choose from, such as "Took all but not all on time" and so forth. There was no control group in this study design, and outcome measures or the dependent variables consisted of the number of times participants reported missing one or more medication doses or reported medication side effects. Other outcome variables included the participants' satisfaction level in using the messaging system. Overall results showed that the two-way messaging system was very favorable to participants and that it did help with medication compliance.

One-Group Pretest-Posttest Method

The one group pretest-posttest method is similar to the one-shot case study except that the pretest is used before the intervention. The limitation of this study design is that there is no control group and no randomization. However, the quasi-experimental one-group pretest-posttest method is used when it is unethical or inappropriate to withhold the intervention from a group of participants.

Examples in Health Informatics

For example, researchers assessed the timeliness and access to healthcare services using telemedicine in individuals aged 18 and younger in state correctional facilities (Fox et al. 2007). Data were collected 1 year before implementation of a telemedicine program and 2 years after implementation. The telemedicine intervention consisted primarily of remote delivery of behavioral healthcare services as well as other types of care. Timeliness of care and use of healthcare services before and after telemedicine implementation was examined. The timeliness of care was measured by examining the time from referral to date of service at a behavioral healthcare facility. Healthcare use was measured by recording the number of outpatient, emergency, and inpatient visits per month per person. The data were collected primarily from medical records and other claims and information assessment logs. Results showed that the average wait time from referral to date of service decreased by 50 percent after 1 year of implementation of telemedicine and by 59 percent after 2 years of implementation. Outpatient visits increased by 40 percent after implementation of telemedicine. However, some healthcare facilities did not show significant improvements, and it was thought that this was due to difficulty in implementing the telemedicine program.

Another example of the quasi-experimental one-group pretest-posttest method is seen when researchers examine the clinicians' response to computerized detection of nosocomial infections (Rocha et al. 2001). An expert reminder system was provided to clinicians, and a pretest and posttest observation was provided before and after implementation of the system, Computerized Pediatric Infection Surveillance System (COMPISS). COMPISS is a rules-based system used to generate alerts and reminders that are divided into three areas: educational, managerial, and therapeutic. An educational reminder may refer to notify-

ing infection control about a reportable disease, whereas the managerial reminder may refer to medical management of the infection (other than appropriate medication), such as use of an isolation room. Therapeutic reminders include suggesting what medications should be prescribed to patients. COMPISS was implemented in three units within the hospital setting. All clinicians were trained on using COMPISS. The main outcome measures were the number of suggestions to treat and manage infections that were followed before and after implementation of COMPISS. Results failed to show a statistically significant difference between the clinicians' treatment patterns before and after implementation of COMPISS. The authors did state that this could be due to lack of documentation in the medical record, showing that the clinician had followed the reminders as well as other problems such as incomplete specimen location descriptions and misleading preliminary culture results.

Static Group Comparison

The static group comparison method is when two groups are examined—one with the intervention and one without—and then a posttest is given to assess the result of the intervention. There are no pretests and no randomization but a control group is used.

Examples in Health Informatics

An example of the static group comparison design can be found when researchers assessed the use of alcohol in patients after a traumatic brain injury (TBI) based on patients' and relatives' reports (Sander et al. 1997). This study examined the validity of patients' reports by comparing them to relatives' descriptions of postinjury alcohol use. In this design, researchers use the TBI as the intervention and then assess, via a postinjury questionnaire, whether drinking habits as perceived by the patient with the TBI and the close relative are similar or different. Results show that of the 175 patients and family members, a high rate of agreement was found for each of the alcohol use measures. Lesser rates of agreement were found for those with more severe TBIs.

An adaptation to the static group comparison method is seen when researchers investigate whether cooperative learning (small group learning) techniques with case study are effective for nursing students' problem-solving and decision-making skills when compared to other learning techniques (Baumberger-Henry 2005). This study used one experimental and three comparison groups with no randomization of the groups. The experimental group was taught using cooperative learning and case study. The first comparison group was taught using lecture and large group case study; the second comparison group was taught using lecture only; and the third comparison group was taught using lecture and case study, and was used as the posttest only control group. Therefore, each student group was tested at the beginning and end of the semester except for the third comparison group, which was tested only at the end of the semester (posttest only). Most static group comparison methods do not use a pretest. A convenience sample of 123 students participated in the study. Two different instruments were used to assess self-perception of problem-solving inventory (PSI) and clinical decision making in nursing scale (CDMNS) skills before and after the different teaching interventions except for the third comparison group in which the instruments were given only at post intervention. Both instruments had Cronbach's alpha ranging from 0.82 to 0.88. Results show that no significant differences were found across the groups, indicating that the different teaching methods had no effect on the self-perceptions of problem-solving and decision-making skills in nursing students.

There are several different adaptations of quasi-experimental study designs. Even though a researcher may categorize the study design into one of the methods discussed above, they may add certain attributes to the study design, such as an additional control group or pretest. Also, there are several flaws with each of the experimental and quasi-experimental study designs described here. Internal and external validity measures are major concerns of these study designs and will be discussed in more detail in the next section.

Internal and External Validity

A research study is internally valid if the study demonstrates that the dependent variable (outcome measure) is only caused by the independent variable (intervention) rather than other confounding variables. External validity is concerned with being able to generalize the results to other populations (Campbell and Stanley 1963).

History

There are several factors that can play a part in reaching internal validity. These include **history,** or the events

happening in the course of the experiment that could impact the results. For example, a researcher collects level of functioning data on hip replacement patients before and after the use of a new physical therapy device. During the time that this device is being used, the developer becomes ill and is unable to fully train all physical therapists in its proper use. Therefore, the study may be affected by inadequate time in training rather than the device itself (Key 1997, Shi 1997).

Maturation

Maturation, another factor affecting internal validity, refers to the natural changes of research subjects over time due to the length of time that they are in the study. For example, older individuals may become very fatigued after completing a training session on using a computer to manage their finances. Their fatigue could then affect their responses on the posttest (Key 1997, Shi 1997).

Testing

Testing is the effect created once exposed to questions that may be on the posttest. For example, participants of a study to assess whether a course module on the use of privacy and security within the EHR improves their knowledge content of this subject use a pretest and posttest to assess whether there is improvement after taking the course module. However, because the students are already exposed to the pretest and are able to think of some of the test questions, they may change their answers on the posttest and do better by learning from the pretest. Therefore, the use of the pretest is what may be causing the improvement in test scores more so than the course module on privacy and security of the EHR (Key 1997, Shi 1997).

Instrumentation

Instrumentation also may affect internal validity. Changes in instruments, interviewers, or observers all may cause changes in the results. For example, interviewers may probe for answers more from one individual they are interviewing than others they interview if training is not performed consistently across all interviewers (Key 1997, Shi 1997).

Statistical regression

Statistical regression (regression toward the mean) is when extreme scores of measurement tend to move toward the mean because they have extreme scores, not because of the intervention under study. For example, coders who performed inadequately on an ICD-10-CM coding examination are selected to receive training. The mean of their posttest scores will be higher than their pretest scores because of statistical regression, not necessarily because of the ICD-10-CM training session (Key 1997, Shi 1997).

Selection

Selection is when there are systematic differences in the selection and composition of subjects in the experimental and control groups based on knowledge or ability. For example, one group of subjects who viewed an instructional video on how to give themselves insulin injections is compared to another group that has not watched this video but received other materials to read regarding insulin injection. Because the groups were not randomly assigned to the different interventions, the researcher is unable to determine that the groups would have been the same or different (Key 1997, Shi 1997).

Attrition

Attrition (also called mortality) is the withdrawal of subjects from the study. Those individuals who leave a study can be very different than those who remain and the characteristics of these individuals can affect the results. For example, a study over a 1-year time period on how to reduce the number of incomplete medical records due to incomplete nursing documentation have 15 nurses leave the experimental group and 2 nurses leave the control group. The 15 nurses who leave the group may be very different than those who remain in the experimental group. Also, the difference in attrition between the experimental and the control group may be a problem (Key 1997, Shi 1997).

Interaction of Factors

An **interaction of factors** or a combination of the factors discussed here may also lead to bias in the final results. Therefore, the researcher needs to be aware of the effect of a combination of some of the factors discussed here and their impact on internal validity (Shadish and Cook 1998, Key 1997, Shi 1997).

Selection Bias

Factors affecting external validity or generalizability include testing, because individuals who are pretested are different

from the general population as they may have learned information from the pretest that may influence their decisions and therefore not make them a good representation of the population under study. Other concerns for external validity are **selection bias.** How subjects are selected to be part of a study is very important when generalizing the results of the study to an entire population. Sometimes, in health informatics, subjects are chosen who are frequently under medical care and they are actually different from the general population. Also, volunteers and subjects who receive compensation for participating in a study are different than the general population. Volunteers may want to be part of the study because they are interested in the study topic or are interested in improving their health moreso than the general population. This makes them different from the general population. Subjects who are compensated for being in the study may choose to be in the study for the compensation and this again makes them different from the general population.

Experimental Procedures

Still other concerns include poor **experimental procedures** that may lead to the control group being exposed to part of the intervention under study; multiple treatment interference, which is when subjects are given several different interventions at one time; the length of time of the program or treatment intervention because time may affect the study outcomes more so than the intervention itself; attrition rates or loss of subjects because subjects who then remain in the study are different than those who leave and therefore may be different than the general population; and other potential confounding variables that may influence the outcomes of the study (Key 1997, Shi 1997, Shadish and Cook 1998).

There are several tools that can be used to control for internal and external validity concerns. Randomization is probably the most powerful tool to use to control for selection, regression to the mean, and interaction of factors. It also improves external validity because subjects are not preselected to join a certain group but uses random assignment of subjects to an experimental and control or comparison group. Use of groups that are not pretested or not given an intervention help to control for the use of pretests and experimental procedures because they provide a good control for some of the issues that arise when using a pretest as well as the effect of the intervention. Use of a control or comparison group may help control for the effects of history, maturation, instrumentation, and interaction of factors because the control group serves as a buffer to much of the effects consumed by the experimental group (Key 1997, Shi 1997)

Summary

Experimental study designs are one of the most powerful designs to use when trying to prove cause and effect. Quasi-experimental study designs also are very effective but tend to have many more problems with external validity because most quasi-experimental designs do not include randomization of subjects. However, they do aim to evaluate interventions and their effectiveness in causing a particular outcome. Quasi-experimental designs are quite common in medical informatics literature. Researchers in health informsatics choose to use the quasi-experimental design for many reasons, such as ethical considerations, the difficulty in randomization of subjects, and small sample size (Harris et al. 2006). Even though there are concerns regarding internal and external validity issues for experimental and quasi-experimental designs, the concerns can be controlled by utilizing different types of experimental and quasi-experimental methods as described in this chapter. Several examples of experimental and quasi-experimental studies and the methodology used in the health informatics and healthcare setting demonstrate that this study design is a viable option for health informatics research.

References

Barnes, L., Hauser, J., Heikes, L., Hernandez, A.J., Richard, P.T., Ross, K., Yang, G.H., and M. Palmquist. 2005. *Experimental and Quasi-Experimental Research*. Writing@CSU. Colorado State University Department of English. http://www.writing.colostate.edu/guides/research/experiment/p.1.

Baumberger-Henry, M. 2005 Cooperative learning and case study: does the combination improve students' perception of problem-solving and decision making skills? *Nursing Education Today* 25(3):238–246

Beebe, L.H. 2001. Community nursing support for clients with schizophrenia. *Archives of Psychiatric Nursing* XV(5):214–222.

Campbell, D.T., and J.C. Stanley. 1963. *Experimental and Quasi-Experimental Designs for Research*. Chicago: Rand McNally.

Danley, D., Gansky, S.A., Chow, D., and B. Gerbert. 2004. Preparing dental students to recognize and respond to domestic violence: The impact of a brief tutorial. *Journal of the American Dental Association* 135:67–73.

Dignan, M.B., Michielutte, R., Wells, H.B., Sharp, P., Blinson, K., Case, L.D., Bell, R., Konen, J., Davis, S., and R.P. McQuellon. 1998. Health education to increase screening for cervical cancer among Lumbee Indian women in North Carolina. *Health Education Research* 13(4):545–556.

Dunbar, P.J., Madigan, D., Grohskopf, L.A., Revere, D., Woodward, J., Minstrell, J., Frick, P.A., Simoni, J.M., and T.M. Hooton. 2003. A two-way messaging system to enhance antiretroviral adherence. *Journal of the American Medical Informatics Association* 10(1):11–15.

Fox, K.C., Somes, G.W., and T.M. Waters. 2007. Timeliness and access to healthcare services via telemedicine for adolescents in state correctional facilities. *Journal of Adolescent Health* 41:161–167.

Harris, A.D., McGregor, J.C., Perencevich, E.N., Furuno, J.P, Zhu, J., Peterson, D.E., and J. Finklestein. 2006. The use and interpretation of quasi-experimental studies in medical informatics. *Journal of the American Medical Informatics Association* 13:16–23.

Key, J.P. 1997. Module R13 Research Design in Occupational Education. Oklahoma State University. Available online from http://www.okstate.edu/ag/agedcm4h/academic/aged5980a/5980/newpage2.htm.

Miller, C.K., Edwards, L., Kissling, G., and L. Sanville. 2002. Nutrition education improves metabolic outcomes among older adults with diabetes mellitus: Results from a randomized controlled trial. *Preventive Medicine* 34: 252–259.

Rocha, B.H., Christenson, J.C., Evans, R.S., and R.M. Gardner. 2001. Clinicians' response to computerized detection of infections. *Journal of the American Medical Informatics Association* 8(2):117–125.

Sander, A.M., Witol, A.D., and J.S. Kreutzer. 1997. Alcohol use after traumatic brain injury: Concordance of patients' and relatives' reports. *American Journal of Physical Medicine & Rehabilitation* 78:138–142.

Saounatsou, M., Patsi, O., Fasoi, G., Stylianou, M., Kavga, A., Economou, O., Mandi, P., and M. Nicolaou. 2001. The influence of the hypertensive patient's education in compliance with their medication. *Public Health Nursing* 18(6):436–442.

Shadish, W.R., and T.D. Cook. 1998. Donald Campbell and evaluation theory. *American Journal of Evaluation* 19:417–422.

Shegog, R., Bartholomew, K., Parcel, G., Sockrider, M., Masse, L., and S. Abramson. 2001. Impact of a Computer-assisted education program on factors related to asthma self-management behavior. *Journal of the American Medical Informatics Association* 8:49–61.

Shi, L. 1997. Health Services Research Methods. Chapter 7 (pp. 143–164) in *Experimental Research*. Albany, NY: Delmar Publishers.

Chapter 6
Epidemiological Research

Valerie J. Watzlaf, PhD, RHIA, FAHIMA

Learning Objectives

- To explain the purpose of epidemiology and how it is important in health informatics
- To use epidemiological principles and models to examine health informatics topics
- To describe the different types of epidemiological study designs and how they can be used in health informatics research
- To discuss the impact of confounding, recall bias, and other types of bias in epidemiological studies
- To determine which statistical tests should be used for each study design, such as the odds ratio for the retrospective study and the relative risk for the prospective study
- To list and explain the rules of evidence when considering whether an association is causal
- To summarize how epidemiology and its study designs are used in health informatics and link with the FORE research priorities

Key Terms

Agent

American Hospital Association (AHA)

Analytical study

Blinding

Case-control study

Cases

Chronic disease model

Clinical trial

Cohort study

Community trial

Confounding variables

Controls

Crossover design

Cross-sectional study

Dependent variable

Descriptive study

Diagnostic trials

Environment

Epidemiologists

Epidemiology

Experimental study

Health informatics systems

Historical-prospective study

Host

Incidence cases

Incidence rates

Independent variable

Infectious disease model

Kappa statistics

Life table analysis

Masking

Matching

Models of disease causation

Multivariate analysis

National Cancer Institute (NCI)

Odds ratio (OR)

Phase I

Phase II

Phase III

Phase IV

Prevalence rate

Prevalence study

Prevention trials

Prospective study

Protocol

Quality of life (QOL) trials

Randomization

Randomized controlled trials (RCTs)

Recall bias

Relative risk (RR)

Retrospective study

Screening trials

Sensitivity rates

Specific aims

Specificity rates

Survival analysis

Treatment trials

Univariate association

Introduction

Epidemiology examines the patterns of disease occurrence in human populations, and the factors that influence these patterns in relation to time, place, and persons. **Epidemiologists** determine if there is an increase or decrease in the disease over time, if one particular community has a higher incidence of the disease than another community, and if individuals with the disease have certain characteristics or risk factors more so than individuals without the disease (Lilienfeld and Stolley 1994, 3). Based on this information, epidemiologists can then determine ways to prevent the disease from occurring.

Therefore, even though epidemiology is linked more to public health than healthcare informatics, it is an essential tool when developing specific research methodologies in health informatics. This chapter provides examples of epidemiological principles to study disease and health informatics.

Types of Epidemiology and its Effectiveness in Eradicating Disease

Epidemiology began with the study of epidemics to determine what caused them and how they could be controlled and prevented. The field expanded rapidly beyond the study of infectious diseases into the study of all types of illnesses. Many different types of epidemiology currently exist, such as cancer epidemiology; pharmaco-epidemiology; environmental epidemiology, nutritional epidemiology; chronic disease epidemiology, and health services epidemiology.

The methods epidemiologists use have helped to eradicate several diseases. As mentioned in chapter 1, John Snow, in 1854, used epidemiological principles and methods to determine the cause of cholera. He found that several water companies supplied water to different parts of London, so he used maps to determine how the water was distributed to certain houses. He found that some houses on the same street received their water from different sources. Cholera death rates per 10,000 houses for the beginning weeks of the epidemic were computed and compared with those of the rest of London. Snow found that the mortality rates of the houses that were supplied water by one particular company were eight to nine times higher than those supplied by other water companies. Snow's quantitative approach in analyzing the data revealed the cause of the epidemic. His findings led to legislation that all water companies in London filter their water by 1857 (Lilienfeld and Stolley 1994, 28).

Epidemiology and Health Informatics

Epidemiological principles can be used to study any type of behavior, outcome, occurrence, community, or healthcare system. The key is to know which epidemiological study design to use to inspect a particular problem. These study designs are used in health informatics because they study the distribution and determinants of disease or events in populations, and the ability to prevent and control public health problems.

Many **health informatics systems** need to be researched fully to determine if they are effective in the delivery of healthcare services or if they improve patient outcomes. Epidemiological principles and its basic study designs and methods are used to examine many of the health informatics systems and structures that currently sustain the healthcare system.

For example, researchers (Bell et al. 2003) used a **cross-sectional study** to determine whether physician offices located in high-minority and low-income neighborhoods in southern California have different levels of access to information technology than offices located in minority and higher-income areas. The received response rate of 46 percent found that 94 percent of physician offices in both populations had at least one computer, 77 percent had Web access, 29 percent had broadband Internet access (487), and 53 percent used a computerized practice management system to include computerized scheduling and billing systems (488). The researchers found that physician offices surveyed in both categories had high levels of interest in using online clinical systems but also had concerns regarding the security and confidentiality of online patient information systems (489).

This example shows that researchers continue to use epidemiological principles similar those that Snow developed. They researched physician offices in targeted geographic areas and neighborhoods to determine the use of different types of health information technology. Even though they did not establish the cause of any particular disease, they determined whether or not socioeconomic demographics play a part in the use of information technology.

Epidemiological Models of Causation

Epidemiologists use models of potential influences that affect disease occurrence. The infectious disease model examines disease causation and occurrence by examining infectious agents, the host or person, and the environment and how each plays a part in disease development. The chronic disease model examines how combinations of risk factors influence the severity of chronic illnesses.

Infectious Disease Model

Two **models of disease causation** have evolved from epidemiology. The first model discussed here is the **infectious disease model** (figure 6.1). It demonstrates how infectious disease is influenced by three factors: the agent, the host and the environment.

The **agent** of the disease is the actual cause of the disease. Examples include:

- Nutritional agents (deficiencies in calcium or overabundance of saturated fat)
- Chemical agents (lead, pesticides, and medications)
- Physical agents (noise, vibration, hot or cold temperatures)
- Infectious agents (bacteria, viruses, and so forth)

Factors that can affect agents include the severity of the disease or illness, the speed in which the disease multiplies within the host, the capability of the agent to cause disease, and antibody production within the host. The **host** is the person itself. Anything that influences the development or immunity of disease is considered a host factor—including age, gender, race, religion, marital status, family history or genetics, ethnicity, anatomy and physiology, social behaviors, and prior illness or chronic disease. The host is affected by its resistance to the agent, and its portal of entry (intact skin or open wound). The **environment** of the host and agent include the physical environment or environmental influences, such as disasters (tornado, flood, hurricane, war), crowding, neighborhood density, housing, and occupation. Factors affecting the environment include the balance between an individual's immunity as well as the opportunity for exposure. For example, a large deer population can increase the chance of contracting Lyme disease, whereas open water can breed mosquitoes and increase the chance of contracting West Nile virus (Gordis 2004, 16; Lilienfeld and Stolley 1994, 37–38).

Chronic Disease Model

The second model, the **chronic disease model** (figure 6.2), is quite similar to the infectious disease model except that it focuses on the fact that the host may have several risk factors that can lead to disease.

One risk factor may not lead to disease, but the combination of several may increase the chance of contracting a chronic disease. For example, if this model is used to examine lung disease (figure 6.3), it is apparent that several factors influence the development of lung disease, such as smoking, passive smoking, air pollution, family history or genetics, respiratory infections or congenital lung problems, and occupational hazards. The chronic disease model demonstrates that a mix of risk factors may cause the disease, and that the presence of

Figure 6.1.   Epidemiological model

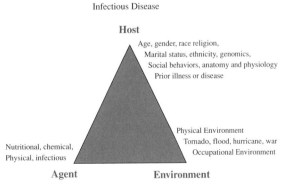

Source: Adapted from Gordis 2004 and Lilienfeld and Stolley 1994.

Figure 6.2.   Chronic disease model

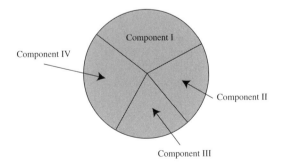

Figure 6.3. Chronic disease model: Example of lung disease

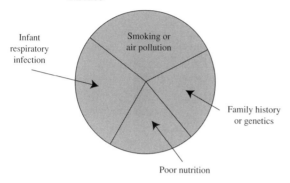

Figure 6.4. Epidemiological model: Health informatics example—Computer-assisted coding (CAC)

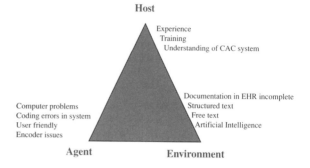

several risk factors over a long period of time may cause the disease (Schlomo and Kuh 2002, 286).

Using the Epidemiological Models of Causation in Health Informatics

Epidemiological models of causation can be used as a logical framework when examining concepts within health informatics. For example, coder resistance to computer-assisted coding (CAC) systems may help a researcher to consider the reasons for resistance and to study it in relation to epidemiological models of causation. What agent is causing the resistance? Is the computer-based system capable of accurate coding? Is the system user-friendly or is it easier for the coder to perform the coding manually? How is the host (the coder) responding and why? Is the response related to the level of the host's experience, amount of training, and understanding of the system? Does the environment aid in the use of the CAC system, or does incomplete documentation in the electronic health record (EHR) hamper the CAC's ability to code correctly? (Figure 6.4)

The chronic disease model could be used to examine why certain individuals do not use a personal health record (PHR). There may be a combination of reasons why the PHR is not used, and determining which combination of reasons may be helpful in attracting more individuals to use a PHR (figure 6.5).

Epidemiological Study Designs

Epidemiologists use three types of study designs—descriptive, analytical, and experimental—to examine disease prevalence and incidence as well as the ability to

Figure 6.5. Chronic disease model: Example of reluctance to use PHR

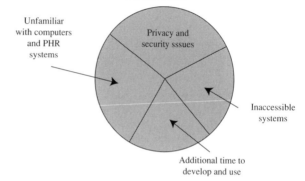

control the spread of disease, and eventually to prevent the disease from occurring.

1. The **cross-sectional** or **prevalence study** explores a disease, first by determining the prevalence in a community or geographic area. This is a **descriptive study** in which new ideas are generated rather than existing hypotheses proven.

2. The two types of **analytical study** designs are the **case-control** or **retrospective study** design, and the **cohort** or **prospective study** design. Both of these epidemiological study designs are used to determine whether an independent variable (defined below) or risk factor causes a particular disease.

3. **Experimental studies** comprise the third type of study design and include the **clinical** and **community trial**. In this design, the epidemiologist intervenes to determine if the intervention improves the spread of the disease or prevents the disease from occurring.

Figure 6.6 provides a progression of the epidemiological study designs previously described. Each of these study designs are subsequently described in detail, as are their uses in health informatics.

Descriptive Study Design

The cross-sectional or prevalence study describes disease or health characteristics at one particular point or period in time such as 1 month or 1 year. It usually does not follow health characteristic or determine whether a host may develop a disease, but instead determines if the host already has the disease when the study is performed. These studies are also called prevalence studies. Prevalence studies examine existing diseases, whereas incidence studies (described later) examine new cases of a particular disease. The prevalence study does not answer questions regarding causation or whether one particular risk factor led to the development of the disease, rather it is used to generate new hypotheses rather than to prove existing hypotheses. It strives to describe what is present in a particular environment at a specific point in time. This design can be extremely effective if very little is known about the particular topic or disease because it describes the topic's prevalence in the environment at a specific time. Components of the cross-sectional or prevalence study are listed in table 6.1.

For example, a health informatics professional may be interested in determining the prevalence of digital radiology systems across acute care hospitals. The cross-sectional or prevalence study design can be used to assess the use of the digital radiology system across ambulatory care facilities within the U.S. To do this, the condition under study, (that is, digital radiology) must be defined prior to undertaking the study.

Figure 6.6.   Progression of epidemiological study designs

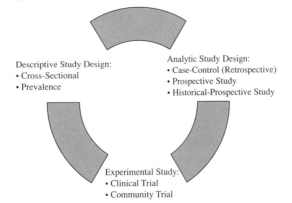

Descriptive Study Design:
• Cross-Sectional
• Prevalence

Analytic Study Design:
• Case-Control (Retrospective)
• Prospective Study
• Historical-Prospective Study

Experimental Study:
• Clinical Trial
• Community Trial

Table 6.1.   Components of the cross-sectional or prevalence study

Describes health characteristic at one point or period in time	Generates hypotheses
Determines whether the disease or health characteristic currently exists	Generates new ideas
Performed when very little is known about a topic	Excellent design when studying new concepts in health informatics
Leads to analytical studies	

The purpose of digital radiology systems is to provide the radiologist, physician, and other healthcare providers the ability to view images immediately within the EHR. The advantages are many, such as decreasing the amount of effort and cost for radiology services whether in-house or outsourced, but the cost of the digital radiology system may still tend to be higher than many facilities will pay. Therefore, as part of the prevalence study, it may be important to determine not only the amount of use of these systems but also the start-up and maintenance costs, including those costs among several types of systems offered by multiple vendors. Then, the researcher can compare these costs to a facility's current radiology costs to determine if a digital radiology system is a good alternative.

Inclusion criteria related to the digital radiology system are developed to be certain that similar systems are collected. Criteria may include whether or not the system is:

1. Used for at least 75 percent of all radiology reports within the healthcare facility
2. Provided by a vendor or developed in-house
3. Able to be used with the EHR
4. Able to provide final validation checks on the quality of the image or for false-positive reports

Prevalence Rate

Below is an example of how a **prevalence rate** is determined:

$$\frac{\text{Number of U.S. ambulatory healthcare facilities that use digital radiology systems}}{\text{Number of ambulatory care facilities in the U.S.} \times N}$$

where N = 1000 if expressing the rate per 1,000 facilities, 10,000 if expressing the rate per 10,000 facilities, and so forth

With this study design, the researcher can make statements of association, such as that ambulatory care facilities use digital radiology more (or less) than other healthcare facilities. From this assessment, the researcher may be able to generate new hypotheses based on the findings. For example, the researcher may develop a new hypothesis that digital radiology systems are more prevalent than speculated because of better quality of the images when compared with an x-ray. Additional research may be needed to determine if this is true by comparing digital radiology images with radiology film.

Cross-sectional or prevalence studies are very important within health informatics because much of what is done in this area is new and emerging and needs a basic assessment of many of the components of health informatics to move the field forward. The cross-sectional or prevalence study design can provide that initial assessment.

For example, Linder et al. (2006) used a cross-sectional design to examine whether electronic diagnoses of acute respiratory infections (ARI) and urinary tract infections (UTI) and electronic prescribing of antibiotics is accurate when compared with the electronic clinical record. The researchers compared the electronic claims data to abstracted clinical records. The clinical records abstracted by the researchers were considered the gold standard. This cross-sectional study took place at nine clinics in Brigham and Women's Primary Care Practice Based Research Network in the Boston area. During the study, which took place from 2000 to 2003, there were 65,285 visits with a primary diagnosis of ARI or UTI. One thousand visits were randomly selected and stratified by calendar year, but only 827 visits were used due to the following: no clinical note found (68), duplicate encounters (3), or the clinic was not using an EHR (102). Because the study was a descriptive, cross-sectional design, descriptive statistics were generated to include the mean age (37 years); race and ethnicity (43 percent white, 29 percent Hispanic, 10 percent black, and 18 percent other); gender (79 percent women); and insurance type (26 percent HMO, 21 percent private, 15 percent Medicaid, 12 percent self-pay, 7 percent Medicare, and 19 percent other or missing) of the beneficiaries in the study (63). **Sensitivity and specificity rates** were then determined for each of the electronic diagnoses collected. The sensitivity

and specificity rates for ARI were 98 percent and 96 percent, respectively. The sensitivity and specificity rates for the UTI were 100 percent and 87 percent, respectively. When comparing electronic prescribing of antibiotics to data abstracted from the visit notes (gold standard), the sensitivity and specificity rates were 43 percent and 93 percent, respectively (64).

Sensitivity and specificity rates as used in the previously described example refer to measures of validity when assessing correct measurement or correct labeling. In order to understand sensitivity and specificity, it is important to know the following definitions:

- True Positives (TP): Correctly categorize true cases as cases (cases are individuals with the disease or outcome) = VALID labeling

- False Negatives (FN): Incorrectly label true cases as noncases (noncases are those individuals without the disease or outcome = INVALID labeling

- True Negatives (TN): Correctly label noncases as noncases = VALID labeling

- False Positives (FP): Incorrectly label noncases as cases = INVALID labeling

- Sensitivity = Percentage of all true cases correctly identified where TP/(TP+FN)

- Specificity = Percentage of all true noncases correctly identified where TN/(TN+FP) (Lilienfeld and Stolley 1994)

Using these terms in the example provided above, the sensitivity rate of 98 percent suggests that the electronic diagnosis system correctly identified cases of ARI 98 percent of the time, and incorrectly identified individuals without ARI when they did have it only 2 percent of the time. However, even though 2 percent of the cases missed is small, these patients would not have received proper treatment. The specificity rate of 96 percent suggests that the electronic diagnosis correctly identified individuals without ARI 96 percent of the time, and incorrectly identified 4 percent of those patients with ARI when they did not have it. The sensitivity rate of 100 percent states that the electronic diagnosis system correctly identified cases of UTI every time; however, the specificity rate was much lower, at 87 percent. This means that the electronic diagnosis system labels patients with a UTI 13 percent of the time even though they do not have a UTI. This may not be as severe as missing a patient's other, more serious illnesses, but could still result in inappropriate treatment which can lengthen hospital stays and increase costs.

The **American Hospital Association (AHA)** (2007) conducted a prevalence study by surveying AHA member hospitals to determine their use of health information technology. Survey instruments were sent to hospital chief executive officers (CEOs) from all types of hospitals and from different geographic areas across the country. The survey yielded a 31 percent response rate (1,543 hospitals). Hospitals that responded were very similar in relation to location, teaching status, geographic location, ownership, and system membership when compared with the overall hospital population (4,936 hospitals). The survey included questions related to the use of specific health information technologies (IT) such as the EHR, computerized physician order entry (CPOE), and clinical IT functions such as access to medical history, radiology images, drug alerts, and so forth. It also requested information about the costs of health IT, barriers to use, and sharing of clinical information. (Hospitals share clinical data most often with physician offices.) Results from this prevalence study show that more than two thirds of hospitals had implemented an EHR, and larger hospitals (92 percent) were more likely to have an EHR than smaller hospitals (46 percent). It also found that hospitals increased the use of decision support functions, electronic record management functions, bar coding, telemedicine, personal digital assistant (PDAs), and administrative systems (patient scheduling, patient accounts). The cost of health IT is high, with average operating costs per bed count reaching more than $12,000, and capital costs more than $5,000. Therefore, cost was reported as being the greatest barrier to health IT adoption. These results showed progress in health IT adoption when compared in a 2005 AHA survey.

The AHA 2007 study demonstrates how a prevalence, cross-sectional study design can be used to examine a new area in health informatics and use it to generate new hypotheses and new areas for further study. For example, the study found that smaller and rural hospitals had more problems in adopting health IT. Based on this information, researchers may decide to conduct additional studies, such as a prospective study, to determine what the barriers are for smaller hospitals and to compare the barriers to larger hospitals by following them over time. Based on the results, researchers may be able to determine how adoption of health IT may affect patient outcomes and develop ways in which smaller rural hospitals can combat the adverse outcomes.

Analytic Study Designs: Case-Control (Retrospective) and Cohort (Prospective)

In the **analytic study** design, the epidemiologist determines whether there is a relationship between two variables, the **independent variable** and the **dependent variable**. The exposure or risk factor is normally considered the independent variable, and the disease or health outcome is the dependent variable. One method used to determine the relationship between these two variables is the case-control or retrospective study design. In this design, epidemiologists look back in time to determine if the independent variable is causing the dependent variable (the disease). Another method is the prospective or cohort study design. In this design, epidemiologists follow participants with the independent variable (risk factor) and those without it, over time, to determine if the participants develop the dependent variable or disease.

Case-Control (Retrospective) Study Design

In case-control design, the researcher chooses the **cases**— those individuals who have the disease, and compares them to the **controls**—those without the disease, to determine if the independent variable is more prominent in the cases than in the controls. This is done by looking back in time. For example, if the researcher is interested in determining the cause of melanoma, individuals with melanoma (cases) could be compared with individuals without melanoma (controls). The controls should be very similar (in age, gender, treatment facility, geographic location, and other demographic components) to the cases in everything except the disease under study. Therefore, the controls may include friends or siblings of the cases, or even individuals that have another type of cancer other than melanoma. Then, the researcher interviews the cases and controls to determine their health history and other health characteristics, such as the number and severity of sunburns. The researcher asks the subject to think back about something that may have happened several years ago, so **recall bias** is a problem with this study design. (Recall bias refers to the fact that the respondent's answer may be affected by the respondent's memory and therefore not completely accurate.) Examples of methods used to decrease the amount of recall bias include showing subjects lists of medications so that they can choose those medications they have taken, pictures of sunburn exposure to determine severity, and so forth. Table 6.2 provides steps to follow when conducting a case-control study.

Interview Instrument for the Case-Control Study

Some researchers design the research instrument to collect both interview-related data and medical record data. Watzlaf (1989) did this in a study in which the research instrument was designed and used to collect data via face-to-face interview and the subjects' medical records when examining risk factors related to ovarian cancer. The full research instrument is provided in appendix 6A (pp. 151–159). It is extremely important that the researcher choose appropriate data sources so that information related to both the cases and controls can be found.

Odds Ratio

The **odds ratio (OR)** is a very useful statistic that can be used in conjunction with the case-control study design because it quantifies the differences in exposure for the cases vs. the controls. One way to demonstrate this is to design a 2X2 table as shown in table 6.3.

The first group to consider is the one most important to what one is trying to seek out, which is the proportion of cases exposed to the risk factor. This is = A/(A+C). The proportion of cases not exposed to the risk factor

Table 6.3.   Example of 2X2 table to calculate odds ratio

	Disease (Cases)	No Disease (Controls)
Exposure	A	B
No Exposure	C	D
	A+C	B+D

= C/(A+C). The odds of exposure is the ratio of these two proportions. It is simplified to A/C. the odds that the person with the disease was exposed to the independent variable or possible risk factor. The odds of exposure for the controls are B/D. To determine if the odds of exposure for the cases are greater than the odds of exposure for the controls, a ratio of the two groups is needed (Friis and Sellers 2004):

$$\frac{(A/C)}{(B/D)}$$

which is reduced to:

$$\frac{(AD)}{(BC)}$$

Table 6.2.   Steps to follow when conducting a case-control (retrospective) study

Step 1	Determine the hypothesis and decide whether to use prevalence (existing cases of disease) or incidence cases (new cases of disease).
Step 2	If prevalence, seek out cases from the state or hospital-based cancer registry. If incidence cases, have healthcare facilities provide new cases as they are treated.
Step 3	Decide who will be part of the study by using inclusion criteria such as ICD-9-CM codes, laboratory reports, radiology reports, medical records, and so forth, which all validate the disease under study.
Step 4	Randomly select the cases by obtaining a list of possible cases (either from the state or hospital-based cancer registry or from a list of ICD-9-CM codes and so forth) and use a systematic sample by choosing every fifth case.
Step 5	Choose controls from siblings or friends who are the same gender and of similar age, and socioeconomic status, or from the same hospital. Controls should be similar to the cases for all characteristics except the disease under study. For example, if studying melanoma, choose controls from the same hospital-affiliated cancer registry as the case but who have another type of cancer such as colon cancer or lung cancer. Select these controls from a list of cancer cases identified by their ICD-9-CM code and validate the diagnosis through pathology reports and medical records. Also, choose controls from this list who are similar in age by at least five years.
Step 6	Decide whether matching of the cases and controls will be used on certain variables. **Matching** on variables such as age, gender, race and so forth should only be used when the researcher is certain that there is a relationship between that variable and the dependent variable. For example, age is always related to cancer because during the aging process, our likelihood of developing cancer increases. Therefore, age becomes what is called a **confounding variable** because it may be the underlying factor that is leading to the development of the cancer instead of the specific risk factor that one is trying to prove is related. Therefore, when studying cancers, matching should be done for age.
Step 7	Design the instrument used to collect the exposure or risk factor data. Collect it through phone or in-person interviews, self-report questionnaires, abstracts from existing sources such as the EHR, cancer registry, birth certificates, death certificates, financial records, and so forth.
Step 8	Analyze the data to include the appropriate statistics.
Step 9	Summarize the results and determine if they support or refute the hypothesis.
Step 10	Publish the results.

In order to prove that exposure to tanning lamps increases the risk of melanoma, the data collected can be inserted into the 2X2 table to determine the odds ratio as shown in table 6.4.

The odds ratio for this example is:

$$\frac{AD}{BC} = \frac{(200) \times (100)}{(500) \times (10)} = \frac{20,000}{5,000} = 4$$

The value of 4 means that those individuals who use tanning lamps are 4 times more likely to develop melanoma than those individuals who do not use tanning lamps. If the odds ratio for this particular example equaled 1, then it means that the risk for melanoma is actually equal for the cases and controls and that use of tanning lamps is not a risk factor for melanoma. If an odds ratio is less than 1.0, this means that the factor (the use of tanning lamps) actually decreases the risk of disease and provides a protective effect.

Examples of Case-Control Studies Related to Health Informatics

A case-control study conducted by Watzlaf (1989) examined not only the cause of epithelial ovarian cancer, but also the ability of the medical record to provide access to the independent variables or possible risk factors associated with this cancer. Ovarian cancer can be difficult to diagnose early because it tends to contain combinations of mild symptoms (such as backache, bloating, and nausea) that when observed singly may signify other less-severe illnesses. Therefore, if a specific risk factor associated with ovarian cancer can be found, it could be used to prevent the disease from occurring.

Ten hospitals' medical record departments and/or cancer registries were contacted (after IRB approval) to obtain the number of patients in whom epithelial ovarian cancer was diagnosed.

The study used patients newly diagnosed with the ovarian cancer (**incidence cases**) because the researchers thought that the medical record should provide a more complete history of medical information when a patient is newly diagnosed. Once the patients agreed to be part of the study and consent forms were signed, their medical record was abstracted, the interview conducted, and a control was randomly selected from the same healthcare facility as the case but for reasons unrelated to cancer: Each control was matched by age (within 5 years), discharge date, and hospital.

Research assistants with backgrounds in health information management abstracted data from the medical records and conducted telephone interviews using the ovarian cancer study questionnaire presented in appendix 6A (pp. 149–157). These research assistants were trained in abstracting medical records and interviewing techniques. The emphasis in the training sessions was that the entire medical record should be examined for the research assistant to record a "no" on the abstract. For example, the research assistants looked for "no history of cervical fibroids" before a "no" could be recorded. If there was no mention of the risk factor anywhere in the medical record, then it was considered "not documented." The same questionnaire format was used for interviewing and abstracting.

The telephone interviews were necessary in cases where the medical records lacked some of the necessary information. However, the fact that many of the participants were too ill to be interviewed lessened the sample size and hindered the ability to examine the risk factors related to ovarian cancer. Therefore, the researchers decided to focus on the medical record, examining which risk factors were found in the medical record and which were not, across three different individuals conducting the abstraction of information from the medical records. Percentages of agreement and Kappa statistics were computed. The percentage of agreement is the number of occurrences in which abstractors agreed on the recording of a particular risk factor within the medical record. **Kappa statistics** provide a value that states whether the levels of agreement seen across abstractors are real or due to chance. Kappa values >0.60 show good agreement. History of any cancer was found to be documented 50 percent of the time (84 percent agreement, Kappa = 0.67), whereas smoking and alcohol use was documented 94 percent of the time (80 percent agreement for alcohol, Kappa = 0.68; 86 percent agreement for smoking, Kappa = 0.69). Oral contraceptive use was found to be documented only 15 percent of the time (96 percent agreement, Kappa = 0.71).

Table 6.4.   Example of odds ratio in 2X2 table for melanoma study

	Melanoma (Cases)	No Melanoma (Controls)
Tanning Lamp Exposure	200 (A)	500 (B)
No Tanning Lamp Exposure	10 (C)	100 (D)
	210	600

In order to collect and document these risk factors, all healthcare providers should include an epidemiological approach in assessing health status as outlined in figure 6.7. This approach improves the quality of documentation in the medical record, whether it is paper-based or electronic, and in turn leads to better diagnosis, treatment, and prevention of disease.

Hippisley-Cox and Coupland (2005) used the case-control design to examine the relationship between myocardial infarction (MI) and use of nonsteroidal anti-inflammatory drugs (NSAIDs). The authors of this study used a research database called QRESEARCH to examine this relationship. This clinical database contains more than 9 million clinical records of patients seen in more than 525 practices during a 16-year period. Information recorded in the database includes:

1. Year of birth
2. Gender
3. Socioeconomic status
4. Region
5. Height
6. Weight
7. Smoking status
8. Symptoms
9. Clinical diagnoses
10. Consultations
11. Physician referrals
12. Prescribed drugs
13. Results of investigations

Data within this database were tested and analyzed, and found to be valid in more than 90 percent of the cases

when compared with paper-based records. Cases registered by August 1, 2000 were selected from the United Kingdom's Egton Medical Information Services computer system. Cases were patients age 25 to 100 years identified as having an acute MI for the first time recorded from Read Codes (similar to SNOMED codes) during a four-year study period. Controls were those individuals with a diagnosis of coronary heart disease, but without an MI, matched to each case by age, year, gender, and physician practice. Cases and controls that had less than three years of electronic prescribing data available were excluded so that the prescribing data were consistent. Exposure assessment was based on electronic data extracted from codes in the medical history and use of prescribed drugs before the registration date for each set of cases and controls. The researchers identified all prescriptions for NSAIDs in the three years before their registration date. Twenty-seven different NSAIDs were found to be used. The number of prescriptions was categorized for each drug group as zero, one to three, and more than three prescriptions. Odds ratios were computed. **Confounding variables** also were collected and controlled for, and include smoking and comorbidities such as diabetes, hypertension, coronary heart disease, osteoarthritis, rheumatoid arthritis, and obesity. The results show that 9,218 cases were identified with 63 percent of them being male. They were matched to 86,349 controls, approximately nine controls per case. They found a significantly increased risk of MI associated with current use of the NSAID rofecoxib (marketed under the brand name Vioxx) with an adjusted odds ratio (OR) of 1.32 compared with no use of Vioxx within the previous three years. They also found this to be true for use of diclofenac (Voltaren or Cataflam) (OR 1.55), and current use of ibuprofen (many brand names) (OR 1.24). (See chapter 13 for an ethical discussion of Vioxx research.)

This research study demonstrates how healthcare informatics can be used effectively to examine important epidemiological relationships. Without the use of the QRESEARCH database, which is an example of healthcare informatics and epidemiology working together to build an effective database system, the cases and controls and the prescribing data could not have been retrieved in such large volume with complete and consistent data content. Because electronic clinical databases are available across large geographic regions such as this one in the United Kingdom, epidemiologists and other clinical researchers are able to conduct effective, efficient, case-control studies.

Figure 6.7.   Epidemiological approach in assessing health status

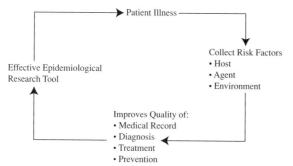

Cohort (Prospective) Study Design

The analytic study design known as **cohort or prospective study** also is referred to as the incidence study. This study design has two groups of study participants: one with the exposure (independent variable) and one without the exposure (dependent variable). Both groups are then followed forward in time to determine if and when they develop the disease or outcome variable under study.

Therefore, the prospective or incidence study starts by identifying individuals with the exposure of interest, such as alcohol use, and ones without the exposure, such as those who do not drink alcohol. Both groups are followed to determine if one group, the alcohol users, develops liver disease at a greater rate than the group that does not use alcohol.

This study design generates **incidence rates** of disease occurrence because the researchers are able to document new cases of the disease as they occur. The incidence rate of the disease in the exposed group is then compared with the incidence rate of disease in the unexposed group to obtain the relative risk.

Relative Risk

The **relative risk (RR)** is very similar to the odds ratio in the case-control study design, except that the odds ratio is an estimate of the relative risk. The magnitude of the relative risk measures the strength of the association. Thus, the greater the relative risk, the greater the association between the exposure and the disease (Lilienfeld and Stolley 1994). Therefore, a relative risk of 3 will have a stronger association between the exposure and the disease than a relative risk of 2, and so forth. In addition, those relative risks of less than 1 demonstrate a protective effect between the exposure and the disease.

This was seen in a study (Manson et al.1999) in which the authors examined exercise and heart disease in women and found that brisk walking and vigorous exercise decrease the risk of coronary heart disease. Age-adjusted relative risks in this study ranged from 0.77 in the least physically activity group (0 to 2 hours per week) to 0.46 in the highest physical activity group (>21 hours per week) (652). When the authors controlled for other confounding variables, walking was found to be inversely related to coronary heart disease. In addition, women who walked more than 3 or more hours per week at a brisk pace were found to have a RR of 0.65 when compared with women who walked infrequently (655).

Calculating the Relative Risk The calculation for the relative risk is:

$$\frac{\text{Incidence rate of the exposed group}}{\text{Incidence rate of the unexposed group}}$$

The incidence rate is:

$$\frac{\text{Number of new cases of a disease over a period of time}}{\text{Population at risk} \times N}$$

where N = 1000 if expressing the rate per 1,000 people, or N = 100,000 if expressing the rate per 100,000 people and so forth.

Population at risk refers to those free of the disease at the start of the study.

If the researcher is interested in determining whether there is an increased risk of migraine headaches in children after playing video games, the exposure is the video games and the disease is the migraine headache. Two groups of children will be followed forward in time, one group that plays video games at least three times per week, four hours per day and one group that does not play video games, to determine their incidence in developing migraine headaches. The framework for the 2x2 table should look like table 6.5.

The calculation for the relative risk is:

$$\text{Incidence Rate of Exposed} = \frac{A}{(A+B)}$$

$$\text{Incidence Rate of Unexposed} = \frac{C}{(C+D)}$$

$$\text{Relative Risk:} \ \frac{[A/(A+B)]}{[C/(C+D)]}$$

The numbers are put into the table to determine the relative risk as shown below in table 6.6:

The relative risk for this example is:

$$\text{Incidence Rate of Exposed} = \frac{200}{275}$$

$$\text{Incidence Rate of Unexposed} = \frac{25}{325}$$

$$\text{Relative Risk:} \ \frac{[0.727]}{[0.077]} = 9.4$$

In this hypothetical example, the relative risk of 9.4 is very high for the association between use of video

Table 6.5.   Relative risk 2x2 table

Exposure	Disease	No Disease	Total
Yes	A	B	A+B
No	C	D	C+D

Table 6.6.   Odds ratio for hypothetical example: Video games and migraine headaches

Exposure	Disease	No Disease	Total
Yes	200	75	275
No	25	300	325

games and migraine headaches, and those children who play video games are almost nine times more likely to develop migraine headaches than those who do not play video games.

Prospective Study Example in Health Informatics

Baxt and Skora. (1996) conducted a prospective study that compared the accuracy of physicians diagnosing patients with acute MI with an artificial neural network. This prospective study design compared data collected by physicians when evaluating 1,070 patients who entered the emergency department of a teaching hospital in California with anterior chest pain with the neural network diagnosis of the same patients. Patients were also followed over time by review of their medical records in the outpatient department or via telephone to determine their final diagnoses, which were validated by serum creatine kinase levels and EKG evidence. Results indicated that the physicians had a diagnostic sensitivity rate of 73 percent compared with 96 percent for the neural network. The specificity rate for the physicians was 81 percent compared with 96 percent for the network. Although this study had limitations, it demonstrates that the use of artificial neural networks can assist physicians when diagnosing conditions in patients with symptoms related to acute MI. (Limitations included the fact that the study was performed at one healthcare facility and network accuracy needs to be transportable to different data sets and sites, small sample size of 75 patients with acute MI in 19 months, and errors in physician data entry). Also, the article did state that the neural network will suffer if there are extensive inaccuracies in the data entry and that if neural networks are to be used as clinical aids, data entry will need to be consistently accurate.

Historical-Prospective Study Design

The **historical-prospective study** design is used when existing data sources can be used to identify characteristics pertaining to the study groups. The groups are followed over time, usually from the time the data are first collected to the present or into the future, to examine their outcomes.

For example, two studies used the historical-prospective design to examine the association between obesity and breast cancer recurrence, and survival in postmenopausal Caucasian and African-American women in two studies. Katoh et al. (1994) examined this relationship primarily in Caucasian women. Data from 301 postmenopausal women in whom breast cancer was diagnosed between 1977 and 1985 were collected. The primary source of the study population was obtained from women in whom breast cancer was diagnosed at a local hospital in Pittsburgh and who had estrogen receptor (ER) and progesterone receptor (PR) analyses performed on breast cancer tissue. Watzlaf et al. (2002) examined this relationship in African-American women because the researchers did not find a significant association between obesity and recurrence or death from breast cancer in the first study. Also, only 18 postmenopausal African-American women were examined. Of these 18, 12 (67 percent) were obese, and of these 12, 7 (58 percent) had documented recurrences. Therefore, the researchers tried to determine if the association between obesity and breast cancer recurrence and survival could be more prominent in African-American women than in Caucasian women (Watzlaf et al. 2000). If a relationship was found, then diet intervention studies could be provided and possibly a reduction in the development of breast cancer recurrence and mortality.

Data for both studies were collected using the medical record and cancer registry. Because some of the data from the 1994 study could not be found, researchers could not use those cases in the 2002 study, which limited the sample size.

Data collected for both studies is shown in table 6.7.

Postmenopausal status was determined in patients older than 55 years and in patients younger than 55 years by reviewing the medical record, cancer registry data, and physician office records. Obesity was determined by using the body mass index, which is weight divided by height squared given in metric units:

$$\frac{kg}{m^2}$$

Table 6.7.   Data items collected for the historical-prospective study on breast cancer recurrence and mortality

Age	Number of positive nodes
Age at diagnosis	**Estrogen receptor (ER)** and **progesterone receptor (PR)** analyses
Weight	Site of distant metastasis
Height	First course of treatment
Date of diagnosis	Additional treatment
Menopausal status	Five-year recurrence and survival
Diagnosis and coding of tumor (histopathology and topography)	Stage and size of tumor

Values >27 were considered to indicate obesity. Recurrence and survival classifications are shown in table 6.8.

Tables 6.9 and 6.10 demonstrate the statistical analyses used to determine if obesity is related to mortality in African-American women with breast cancer (Watzlaf et al. 2002). The OR is used instead of the RR for two reasons. First, the OR should be used when performing logistic regression analyses. Second, it is best to use the OR when conducting a historical-prospective study because the exposure is an estimate of the true exposure retrieved from past data, and the outcome (death due to breast cancer) is considered rare.

The **univariate association** between each variable and case fatality is shown in table 6.9. For each variable, the specific (univariate) associations analyzed are indicated. Variables that were found to be significant ($p < 0.05$) include the following:

Table 6.8.   Recurrence and survival classifications for recurrence and survival for the breast cancer study

Recurrence:	Survival:
Never free of disease	Alive
No recurrence	Death from other causes
Alive with recurrence	Death due to breast cancer
Death due to breast cancer recurrence	
Breast cancer recurrence at the time of any cause of death	

- PR negative vs. positive
- Level of treatment: surgery and therapy vs. surgery
- Stage II vs. I, stage III vs. I, and stage IV vs. I
- Size of tumor (2.0 cm vs. 2.0 cm)
- Nodal status (1 to 3+ vs. 0 and (4 vs. 0)

The ORs were consistent for these associations. Associations that lacked significance consisted of age, ER, and obesity.

The statistical analysis was expanded by using multiple logistic regression for predicting death from breast cancer while simultaneously controlling for the independent variables. The results of a **multivariate analysis** for predicting death from breast cancer are shown in table 6.10. In this analysis, multiple logistic regression was used with case fatality as the dependent variable and

Table 6.9.   Univariate association between each variable and case fatality*

Variable	P-value	Odds ratio	95% Confidence Interval
Age ≥63.2 vs. <63.2	0.475	1.16	[0.77, 1.76]
ER Negative vs. Positive	0.079	1.57	[0.95,2.59]
PR Negative vs. Positive	0.037	1.72	[1.03,2.88]
Level of Treatment Surgery + therapy vs. surgery alone	0.000	8.07	[4.04,16.11]
Obesity Yes vs. no	0.364	1.21	[0.80,1.85]
Stage II vs. I	0.002	2.97	[1.51,5.85]
III vs. I	0.000	12.62	[5.53, 28.80]
IV vs. I	0.000	88.31	[23.9,326.5]
Size of Tumor ≥2.0 cm vs. <2.0 cm	0.000	4.15	[2.30, 7.50]
Nodal Status 1-3+ vs. 0	0.016	2.21	[1.16,4.21]
≥4 vs. 0	0.000	7.56	[4.02,14.20]

*Derived using logistic regression.

Table 6.10. Multivariate analysis for predicting case fatality*

Variable	P-value	Odds ratio	95% CI
PR	0.036	2.23	[1.05,4.73]
Level of Treatment	0.002	8.91	[2.27,34.90]
Obesity	0.362	1.41	[0.67,2.94]
Stage II III IV	0.345 0.310 0.514	1.85 2.25 13.38	[0.52,6.66] [0.47,10.75] [0.98,181.9]
Size of Tumor	0.594	1.38	[0.42,4.47]
Nodal Status 1-3+ vs. 0 ≥4+ vs. 0	0.756 0.028	0.86 2.86	[0.33,2.23] [1.12,7.34]

*Derived using multiple logistic regression analysis. The appropriateness of fit of the model was evaluated using the Hosmer-Lemeshow chi-square statistic.

Table 6.11. Data items not documented in the medical record and tumor registry

Demographic Items (N=493)	# Not Documented	% Not Documented
Birth Date	0	0%
Age at Diagnosis	1	0.2%
Date of Diagnosis	0	0%
Marital Status	27	5.5%
Occupation	68	13.8%
Diagnostic Items (N=493)		
Height	49	9.9%
Weight	42	8.5%
BMI (Body Mass Index)	57	11.6%
ER Value	181	36.7%
ER (+/-)	120	24.3%
PR Value	210	42.6%
PR (+/-)	175	35.5%
Summary Stage	27	5.5%
Tumor Size	44	8.9%
Number of Positive Nodes	112	22.7%
Number of Nodes Examine	103	20.9%
Site of Distant Metastases	294	59.6%
Family History of Cancer	127	25.8%
First Course of Surgery	5	1.0%
Surgery Date	12	2.4%
Survival Items		
N = 493		
Reference Status	39	7.9%

PR, level of treatment, obesity, stage, size of tumor, and nodal status as the independent variables. These variables were chosen because they were significant ($p<0.05$) from the univariate analysis, except for obesity. PR, level of treatment, and nodal status (4+ vs. 0) emerged from this analysis as significant predictors. All other variables, including obesity, failed to show significance.

The 2002 study indicated that obesity is not related to fatality because the p value is not <0.05, and therefore the OR of 1.21 could be due to chance. This may have occurred because of the small sample size. or because obesity was differentiated by just two categories: Obese= BMI >27 and Not obese=BMI<27. However, even when the authors calculated the BMI values into quartiles and ran the analysis again, obesity was not found to be related to case fatality or breast cancer recurrence.

It can be seen from tables 6.9 and 6.10 that obesity is not related to case fatality in both the univariate and multivariate analyses. This was seen for both Katoh and Watzlaf's 1994 study, which examined primarily Caucasian women, and for Watzlaf et al.'s 2002 study, which examined African-American women.

Furthermore, because of the lack of certain data such as height and weight, the total number of cases that could be used in this study was much less than anticipated (table 6.11). Recording a simple but important variable such as height or weight is necessary if the medical record and cancer registry are to be considered reliable data sources for epidemiological research. Also, other important vari-

ables such as ER and PR values, stage of cancer, number of positive nodes, and so forth must be documented 100 percent of the time to improve the quality of patient care as well as the advancement of breast cancer research.

Data capture in breast cancer research can be improved if health informatics professionals:

- Work closely with administration, the medical staff, and other direct healthcare providers
- Demonstrate the importance of proper and complete documentation
- Develop documentation policies and procedures specific to breast cancer

- Assist in developing electronic databases specific to breast cancer risk factor data so healthcare providers know what risk factors are important and which ones should be documented

- Assist in the development of a standardized breast cancer registry abstract

- Move toward concurrent record analysis to capture missing, incomplete, or incorrect data quickly

- Assist in developing methods to encourage direct data capture through Palm Pilots, Web-based access, voice recognition, and so forth

- Encourage the use of national and state breast cancer registries and databases to enhance local data

- Stay informed of the most effective methods of data capture for breast cancer research which in turn leads to improvements in the quality of patient care

- Learn the data mining/data warehousing capabilities for breast cancer databases that can then be linked with local cancer registry data

- Strive toward the development of an electronic health record but make sure that the data are of good quality, can be easily accessed, and can be linked to other important databases throughout the healthcare facility

- Encourage standard setting organizations to include height, weight, menopausal status, and hormone receptor analysis as required data elements

- Encourage registry software vendors to include specific risk factors related to breast cancer as required data elements

---

Analytic study designs are excellent tools to establish an association between two variables. Epidemiologists use the case-control study design when the disease or outcome is rare and when the independent variable can be assessed fairly easily by looking back in time. The prospective or cohort study design allows the researcher to see how the relationship between two variables comes about because the participants are followed over time to determine if and when they develop the disease or health outcome. A more time-efficient version of the prospective design is the historical-prospective design, which allows the researcher to use existing information found in past records or vital statistics to establish the independent variables. Then, participants are examined in the present time and possibly forward in time to determine their health outcomes. Each of these epidemiological study designs allows researchers to support cause and effect between two variables.

Experimental Study Designs

Experimental research studies are considered the most powerful designs to establish cause and effect. Experimental research studies expose participants to different interventions (independent variables) to compare the result of these interventions with the outcome (dependent variables). Two examples of experimental research studies in epidemiology are the clinical and community trial.

Clinical trials are designed to help healthcare professionals test new approaches to the diagnosis, treatment, or prevention of different diseases. Patients who are at high risk for developing these diseases are often the ones who participate in the clinical trial. The information that researchers obtain from the clinical trial have enabled them to make true differences in the advancement of these diseases. Community trials are very similar to clinical trials except that they take place in a particular community and therefore have less control over the intervention than one would have with the clinical trial. The clinical trial is designed to test new medications (most common) and surgical procedures, as well as new treatments or combinations of treatments to prevent disease. The community trial's goal is to produce changes in a specific population within a community, organization, or association. The participation for the clinical trial can be very selective to individuals with disease, those at high risk of developing the disease, or volunteers, whereas in the community trial, the participation includes all members of the community and the intervention tends to be provided throughout the population with less control than in the clinical trial. (Friis and Sellers 2004, 322–323; UPMC 2008).

Clinical and Community Trial Protocol

Every clinical and community trial should follow a **protocol**—a step-by-step plan on how the trial will be conducted. It should include the components detailed in the next paragraphs.

Rationale and background: This section should describe the reason for conducting the clinical or community trial as well as the background of the disease under study and the particular intervention that will be used in the trial.

Specific aims: This is the purpose or goal of the particular trial. Both long- and short-term goals may be provided and should explain the major aim of the study. For example, if a community trial is examining whether use of a PHR by parents is better in treating childhood asthma than not using a PHR, one such specific aim may include determining if PHR use by parents to manage asthma care in their children is more effective in reducing the number of asthma emergency room visits than in those who are not using a PHR.

Randomization: Patients who agree to participate in a clinical trial may be randomized to one of two groups: the control group (no intervention or receive placebo) or the intervention group. Randomization is achieved by using statistical techniques to prevent preselection of patients into one of the groups. Each group is followed over time, and the outcomes of both groups are measured to determine if the group receiving the intervention fared better than the control group. Sometimes a **crossover design** is used, in which one group of patients starts out in the intervention group for a specified time and then that group crosses over into the control group. This switch of treatments allows the patient to serve as his or her own control. Normally the switch is planned, but sometimes it can be unplanned due to changes in a patient's condition or reluctance to participate in a certain procedure (Friis and Sellers 2004).

Blinding or **masking:** In order for the clinical or community trial to be objective, study participants may not know to which group (intervention or control) they are assigned. This is called single-blind design. In double-blind design, neither the participant nor the researcher knows the group assignment. In triple-blind design, the subject, researcher, and statistician do not know the group assignment. However, the triple-blind design may vary across **randomized controlled trials (RCTs)** and sometimes it may mean that the participant, researcher, and person administering the treatment (nurse, pharmacist) are blinded to what is being administered.

Types and duration of treatment: The protocol should explain all types of interventions (treatments) used in the clinical or community trial. Types of treatments may include medications, surgery, vaccines, dietary changes, exercise intervention, smoking cessation, use of a particular software system, education intervention, and so forth. The dose and duration of treatment must be specified.

Number of subjects: The number of subjects needed for the clinical or community trial to be valid should be explained. A sample size calculation may need to be performed to determine the best sample size necessary to see differences between the intervention group and the control group.

Criteria for including and excluding participants: Researchers list the criteria needed to enroll participants such as: age older than 50 years, familiarity with using a personal digital assistant, and so forth, as well as criteria that excludes participants from entering the study, such as no evidence of heart disease, diabetes, or hypertension.

Outline of treatment procedures: Treatment procedures should be specified to include the dose and duration of medications, how follow-up will be conducted, and any additional tests or use of interviews or questionnaires.

Procedures for observing and recording side effects: The protocol should state how observations will be made, how side effects will be documented, and what will be done to treat the side effects of certain patients. Also, specific procedures should be outlined to explain how side effects and other problems related to the trial will be handled. Patients are free to leave the trial at any time and this should be explained in the protocol and informed consent.

Informed consent: Every clinical and community trial must be approved by the Institutional Review Board (IRB). The IRB reviews all research studies to make sure that the patient or participant is protected and that all procedures within the trial are ethical and appropriate for the patient. (See chapter 13 for additional information about IRBs.)

Analysis of data: Once data are collected, it should be analyzed by calculating the relative risk, survival analysis, number needed to treat (NNT), and tests of significance.

Dissemination of results: Results may be provided before the study is completed if it can be seen that a particular medication or other intervention is significantly improving a disease. The possibility of stopping the trial and providing the intervention to both groups must be considered. After the study is completed, results should be disseminated to both groups, and further treatment options may be discussed as well.

Types of Clinical Trials

The many different types of clinical trials include treatment, prevention, diagnostic, screening, and quality of life (QOL) trials. The types of clinical trial are explained below, and an example of each is provided.

Treatment trials test experimental treatments, new combinations of medicines, different types of surgery, radiation or chemotherapy. For example, an ongoing treatment trial (UPMC 2008) includes the comparison of cisplatin with three different types of new chemotherapy combinations (cisplatin plus vinorelbine [Navelbine], cisplatin plus gemcitabine [Gemzar], or cisplatin plus topotecan [Hycamtin]) compared with cisplatin plus paclitaxel [Taxol] in order to detect differences in how each improves survival in Stage IVB cervical cancer patients. Another goal of the study is to compare the toxicities of these four different therapies and to compare quality of life across the four treatment groups through four cycles of therapy, and again nine months later (UPMC 2008; clinicaltrial.gov 2007).

Prevention trials aim to prevent disease in a person who has never had the disease or to prevent it from advancing or recurring. Some of these trials may use vitamins, diet, vaccines, medications, or lifestyle changes such as smoking cessation or exercise.

For example, the goal of the Alzheimer's Disease and Depression trial sponsored by the National Institute of Mental Health (Clinicaltrials.gov 2005) is to determine if treating individuals with Alzheimer's disease and depression using the antidepressant medication setraline (Zoloft) as well as caregiver support and education is helpful to people with Alzheimer's disease, their families, and caregivers. In this study, subjects are randomly assigned to taking the medication (25 to 125 mg/day) or an identical-dose placebo for approximately six months. Eight in-person visits are scheduled within the six-month trial period for neuropsychological testing. Caregivers keep a daily effect diary for six weeks during the study period. Telephone follow-up is done at nine months and one year. Both groups receive caregiver support and education for Alzheimer's disease.

Each clinical trial has inclusion and exclusion criteria. For example, for the Alzheimer's Disease and Depression study, two of the inclusion criteria state that participants must have dementia due to Alzheimer's disease and stable treatment for Alzheimer's disease. One of the exclusion criteria includes the presence of a brain disease that might mimic dementia. This is necessary so that subjects with a brain disease other than Alzheimer's disease are not included in the study.

Diagnostic trials are conducted to find better tests, procedures, or screenings to detect a disease or condition. For example, one diagnostic trial sponsored by the **National Cancer Institute (NCI)** (Clinicaltrials.gov 2006) compares computed tomographic colonography (CTC) with colonoscopy to determine if it is as effective in screening health subjects for colon cancer. If this is found to be true, then CTC may provide a better and less-invasive alternative to colon cancer screening. The trial also will examine the interobserver variation in the accuracy of interpreting the CTC examinations and its ability to detect flat lesions in the colon. It compares the participant's willingness to have a repeat CTC when compared with a colonoscopy.

Screening trials examine the best method to detect diseases or health conditions. One such trial sponsored by the NCI evaluates the patient's ability to use the clinic computer system to record symptoms and ability to carry out activities of daily living (ADLs) (Clinicaltrials.gov 2007). The purpose is to help physicians understand how patients use a computer to report their symptoms. This screening trial is studying how well the Internet can be used to collect symptoms and ADLs in patients with metastatic prostate cancer that has not responded to hormone therapy. Patients will be trained to use the Symptom Tracking and Reporting (STAR) database to record their symptoms through several courses of chemotherapy. Physicians also will record their perceptions of the patient's symptoms, and then researchers will assess levels of agreement on the severity of symptoms reported by the patient and physician.

Quality of life (QOL) trials explore methods used to improve comfort and the QOL for individuals with a chronic disease. For example, one such QOL trial sponsored by Odense University Hospital is exploring the QOL for individuals with thyroid disease in Denmark (Clinicaltrials.gov 2007). They hypothesize that the QOL is decreased for patients with thyroid disease despite successful treatment. A valid and reliable questionnaire to collect QOL data in patients with thyroid disease will be developed by searching the scientific literature, and through interviews with 13 physicians and 100 patients. Once developed, it will be tested with 100 new patients. After revision, it will be answered by 1,000 patients.

Phases of Clinical Trials

Most clinical trials are categorized as phase I, II, III, or IV based on the size of the population and the intervention being tested. The Food and Drug Administration

(FDA) provides guidelines for the different types of clinical trials. According to the FDA, **Phase I** clinical trials usually test a new drug or treatment in a small group of people (20 to 80) for the first time to evaluate its safety, determine a safe dosage, and identify any side effects. **Phase II** clinical trials study the intervention in a larger group of people (100 to 300), and in **Phase III** the study drug or treatment is given to even larger groups of people (1,000 to 3,000) to confirm its effectiveness, monitor side effects, compare other treatments, and collect data to affirm that the drug or treatment can be used safely. **Phase IV** clinical trials include studies that collect additional information after the drug has been marketed, such as the drug's risks, benefits, and optimal use.

The principles relative to clinical and community trials can be used when examining health information systems. For example, Shea et al. (1996) examined several different experimental studies comparing computer-based clinical reminder systems with manual reminder card-type systems in ambulatory preventive care settings. They found 16 different randomized controlled trials from 1975 to 1994 in which computer-based clinical reminders were used for several different preventive services such as hypertension follow-up, influenza vaccine, pneumococcal vaccine, mammography, fecal occult blood test, Pap smear, tetanus vaccine, dental screening, smoking assessment, dietary assessment, and so forth. They found that computer-generated reminders when compared with manual reminders increased preventive practices by 77 percent. The use of the experimental study to examine the effectiveness of the computer-based clinical reminder system provided thorough evaluation of this system.

Statistical Analysis

Statistical analysis used in clinical trials may include RR, survival analysis, or basic statistics such as the gain in a specific score from before the intervention to after the intervention. **Survival analysis** or **life table analysis** examines survival of study subjects over time and compares whether the intervention group survived longer than the control group. It is used when there is a loss of subjects due to follow-up because it takes into account those subjects who withdrew from the study before it was completed. Survival curves are developed to estimate survival over time between the two groups.

Rules of Evidence for Causality

In order to prove that one particular variable led to another endpoint or outcome, the nine specific rules of evidence detailed below are necessary (Lilienfeld and Stolley 1994):

1. **Strength of association:** The strength of the association is measured by the RR. A strong RR is important, and those >2 are effective to show causality. However, repeated findings of weak RRs may be of equal importance if it is found in studies with reliable methodology.

2. **Consistency of the observed association:** Consistency of the observed association includes confirmation of results in many different types of epidemiological studies in different populations and different settings. This can be seen in the study by Shea et al. (1996) in which upon review of 16 RCTs, computer-generated reminder systems improved preventive practices over time.

3. **Specificity:** A one-to-one relationship between an independent variable and a dependent variable, or between the exposure and the disease is necessary to add weight to causality. However, because some exposures may lead to many different adverse outcomes, if specificity is not found this does not mean an association is not causal.

4. **Temporality:** The independent variable must precede the dependent variable, not follow it. For example, in order to state that decision support systems decrease medical errors, the use of the decision support system must precede the development of the medical error. Sometimes this is not easy to determine. A prospective study design can help support this rule.

5. **Dose-response relationship:** As the dose of the independent or exposure variable is increased, it strengthens the relationship with the dependent variable or the disease. In epidemiology, this can be demonstrated for smoking, in which dose and duration increase risk of disease. In health informatics, if clinical reminder systems for colonoscopy reduce the likelihood of developing colon cancer, increasing the use of the clinical reminder systems for other types of cancer screening can be assumed to also reduce the development of cancer.

6. **Biological plausibility:** The relationship must make sense in relation to what is known about it in the sciences, animal experiments, and so forth.

7. **Experimental evidence:** A well-conducted RCT may confirm the causal relationship between an independent variable and a dependent variable.

8. **Coherence:** Association should be in accordance with other factors known about the disease.

9. **Analogy:** If similar associations have demonstrated causality, then the more likely this association is probably causal.

Summary

Epidemiology and its principles can be used effectively when studying health informatics. Researchers can use infectious disease or chronic disease models of causation to do this. Many different types of epidemiological study designs can also be used to examine health informatics. These include the descriptive (prevalence or cross-sectional), case-control (retrospective), prospective, and the experimental (clinical and community trial) study designs. Most epidemiologists conduct research by beginning with the cross-sectional or prevalence study, and then move forward to the case-control, prospective, and experimental study designs.

The prevalence study is performed when little is known about a particular disease or health characteristic. The case-control (retrospective) and prospective study designs are usually performed when the researcher is trying to support cause and effect or when one variable leads to a particular outcome. Experimental studies confirm causality by intervening with some type of medication or treatment to improve a disease or outcome. However, experimental studies such as clinical trials are not always the most appropriate designs to use when investigating disease. Prevalence (existing cases of disease) rates are computed from prevalence studies, whereas incidence rates (new cases) are generated from prospective and experimental studies.

The odds ratio (an estimate of the relative risk) is computed from the case-control study, whereas the relative risk is generated from the prospective and experimental studies. Table 6.12 summarizes the epidemiological study designs in relation to their usefulness in health informatics. The table also provides health informatics

Table 6.12.   Summary of epidemiological study designs and their effectiveness in health informatics

Study Design	Useful in Health Informatics	Examples in Health Informatics	Links to AHIMA Research Priorities
Descriptive Study: Cross-Sectional Prevalence Study	When studying new ideas, concepts or systems to determine their use in a community, particular practice or region	AHA study to examine the prevalence of health information technology in the US.	Explore EHR workflows, processes, and content to reengineer the way in which health information is created, utilized, exchanged, and maintained to improve quality of care and patient safety
Analytical: Case-Control (Retrospective) Prospective/ Cohort/ Longitudinal Historical-Prospective	To examine a particular system over time to determine its effectiveness when compared with another system or when comparing computer-based analysis to human analysis	Case-control study to examine NSAID and MI using the QRESEARCH database Prospective study to compare accuracy of physicians' diagnosis of AMI to an artificial neural network diagnosis Historical-prospective study to examine breast cancer recurrence and mortality in post-menopausal women using the cancer registry, medical record, and existing clinical databases	Study interrater reliability agreement rates at the disease condition, clinical service for current or pending national standard terminology and classification systems such as ICD-9-CM, ICD-10-CM, SNOMED CT and so forth
Experimental: Clinical Trial Community Trial	When studying an intervention or treatment over time to test its impact	Clinical/community trial to examine the patient's ability to use computers to record symptoms and their ability to do ADLs using the STAR database	Examine best practices for efficient, effective, and legal EHR management for the following: Authentication Authorship Corrections Retention Downtime Procedures

examples for each of the study designs and demonstrates how these examples are linked to the American Health Information Management Association's (AHIMA) research priorities. In order to provide evidence that a causal association is exhibited, the nine rules of evidence should be examined. The researcher does not need all nine rules to achieve causality, but it helps to have most of them for final results of the epidemiological study. Epidemiology and its study designs provide an effective way to aid in the study of health informatics.

References

American Hospital Association. 2007 (February). Continued progress Hospital use of information technology. Available online from http://www.aha.org/aha/content/2007/pdf/070227continuedprogress.pdf.

Bell, S.B., D.M. Daly, and P. Robinson. 2003 Is there a digital divide among physicians? A geographic analysis of information technology in southern California physician offices. *Journal of the American Medical Informatics Association* 10(5):484–493.

Baxt, W.G., and J. Skora. 1996. Prospective validation of artificial neural network trained to identify acute myocardial infarction. *Lancet* 347(8993):12–15.

Friis, R.H., and T.A. Sellers. 2004. *Epidemiology for Public Health Practice.* Sudbury, MA: Jones and Bartlett Publishers.

Gordis, L. 2004. *Epidemiology.* Philadelphia: Saunders.

Hippisley-Cox, J., and C. Coupland. 2005. Risk of myocardial infarction in patients taking cyclo-oxygenase-2 inhibitors or conventional non-steroidal anti-inflammatory drugs: population based nested case-control analysis. *British Medical Journal* 330:(7504)1366. Available online from www.bmj.com/cgi/content/full/330/7504/1366.

Katoh, A., Watzlaf, V.W., and F.D'Amico.1994. An examination of obesity and breast cancer survival in postmenopausal women. *British Journal of Cancer* 70:928–933.

Lilienfeld, D.E., and P.D. Stolley. 1994. *Foundations of Epidemiology*, New York: Oxford University Press.

Linder, J.A., Bates, D.W., Williams, D.H., and M.A. Connoly. 2006. Acute infections in primary care: Accuracy of electronic diagnoses and electronic antibiotic prescribing. *Journal of the American Medical Informatics Association* 13(1):61–66.

Manson, J.E., Hu, F.B., Rich-Edwards, J.W., Colditz, G.A., Stampfer, M.J., Willett, W.C., Speizer, F.E., and C.H. Hennekens. 1999. A prospective study of walking as compared with vigorous exercise in the prevention of coronary heart disease in women. *New England Journal of Medicine* 341(9):650–658.

National Cancer Institute. 2006. Study of computed tomographic colonography in screening healthy participants for colorectal cancer. Available online from http://www.clinicaltrial.gov/ct/show/NCT00084929?order=23.

National Cancer Institute. 2007. Study on using the Internet to collect symptoms and the ability to carry out daily activities from patients with metastatic prostate cancer that has not responded to hormone therapy. Available online from http://www.clinicaltrial.gov/ct/show/NCT00417040?order=96.

National Institute of Mental Health 2005. Study of Depression in Alzheimer's Disease. Available online from http://www.clinicaltrial.gov/ct/show/NCT00086138?order=8.

Odense University Hospital. 2007. Study on Health related quality of life for thyroid patients. Available online from http://www.clinicaltrial.gov/ct/show/NCT00150033?order=343.

Schlomo, Y.B., and D. Kuh. 2002. A life course approach to chronic disease epidemiology: conceptual models, empirical challenges, and interdisciplinary perspectives. *International Journal of Epidemiology* 31:285–293. Available online from http://arctichealth.oulu.fi/suomi/documents/Life-course_2.pdf.

Shea, S., DuMouchel, W., and L. Bahamonde. 1996. A meta analysis of 16 randomized controlled trials to evaluate computer-based clinical reminder systems for preventive care in the ambulatory setting. *Journal of the American Medical Informatics Association* 3(6):400–09.

University of Pittsburgh Medical Center (UPMC) Hillman Cancer Center website. 2008. Available online from www.upmccancercenters.com/trials/trialDisplay.cfm?id=4114&type=D.

Watzlaf, V.W. 1989. Is the medical record an effective epidemiological data source? *Proceedings of the National Center for Health Statistics Public Health Conference on Records and Statistics*, pp.57–60.Washington, DC

Watzlaf, V., Katoh, A., and F.D'Amico. 2002. Obesity and breast cancer recurrence: Obstacles/improvements in data capture and results. *Proceedings of the AHIMA National Meeting.*

Appendix 6A
Telephone Interview Questionnaire/Abstract

A–C. ID #_____

D. Group _____

E. Hospital No. _____

K–P. Medical Record No. _____

F. Abstractor No. _____

G. Method _____

TELEPHONE INTERVIEW QUESTIONNAIRE/ABSTRACT

H. Marital Status: _____ Single   _____ Married
                       _____ Divorced   _____ Widowed
                                          _____ ND

I. Race: _____ White _____ Black _____ Other: _____
           _____ ND

J. What is your nationality/ethnicity?   _____ Slovak   _____ British
                                           _____ Russian   _____ Italian
                                           _____ German   _____ Middle-Eastern
                                           _____ Irish   _____ Czech
                                           _____ Other: _____
                                           _____ ND

1. What is your highest education level?   _____ High School
                                             _____ Baccalaureate
                                             _____ Master
                                             _____ PhD
                                             _____ Other
                                             _____ ND

2. Yearly Household Income: _____ < 10,000
                                _____ 10,000–19,999
                                _____ 20,000–29,999
                                _____ 30,000–39,999
                                _____ 40,000–49,999
                                _____ > 50,000
                                _____ ND
                                _____ NA

3. If retired, yearly household income prior to retirement?
                                _____ < 10,000
                                _____ 10,000–19,999
                                _____ 20,000–29,999
                                _____ 30,000–39,999
                                _____ 40,000–49,999
                                _____ > 50,000
                                _____ ND
                                _____ NA

What is your date of birth? _____   _____ ND

149

4–8. What is your height? _____ weight? _____   _____ ND

9–12. When were you diagnosed as having ovarian cancer? _____
                                                          mo./yr.

13. Stage _____   14. Histology _____
     _____ ND   _____ ND
     _____ NA

15. Do you know of any other blood relatives in your family who have or have had ovarian cancer?

     _____ Yes   _____ No   _____ ND   If no, go to No. 18

16. If so, what relation?   _____ Mother
                                _____ Aunt
                                _____ Grandmother
                                _____ Sister
                                _____ Great-Grandmother
                                _____ Niece
                                _____ ND   _____ NA

17. Do you know the specific type of ovarian cancer your relative had?

     _____ Epithelial
     _____ Germ Cell
     _____ Teratoma
     _____ Fibrosarcoma
     _____ ND
     _____ NA

18. Do you know of any blood relatives in your family who have or have had any type of cancer?

     _____ Yes   _____ No   _____ ND   If no, go to No. 23–25

19–20. What relation?   _____ Mother   _____ Sister
                            _____ Father   _____ Brother
                            _____ Aunt   _____ Grandfather
                            _____ Uncle   _____ Grandmother
                            _____ Niece   _____ Nephew
                            _____ Other: _____
                            _____ ND
                            _____ NA

21–22. Type: _____ Lung   _____ Liver   _____ Lymphomas
               _____ Brain   _____ Breast   _____ Colon
               _____ Skin   _____ Pancreas   _____ Blood-related (Leukemia)
               _____ Other: _____
               _____ ND   _____ NA

150

23–25. Which of the following describes the status of your menstrual periods:

a. they have ceased/stopped—what age?

_____ 40–44
_____ 45–50
_____ 51–55
_____ 56–60
_____ > 60
_____ ND
_____ NA

b. they are present but irregular—at what age did irregularity begin?

_____ 40–44
_____ 45–50
_____ 51–55
_____ 56–60
_____ > 60
_____ ND
_____ NA

c. they are present and regular

26. At what age did your period begin?

_____ < 9
_____ 10–12
_____ 13–15
_____ 16–18
_____ > 18
_____ Other
_____ ND

27. Have you had any interruptions in your menstrual period due to the following:

_____ excessive weight loss
_____ pregnancy
_____ birth control pills
_____ other
_____ ND
_____ No

28. Have you ever been pregnant?

_____ Yes   _____ No
_____ ND

29–30. If yes, number of full-term pregnancies? _____

_____ ND   _____ NA

31–38. Age at each pregnancy: _____ _____ ND _____ NA
                                  _____ _____ ND _____ NA
                                  _____ _____ ND _____ NA
                                  _____ _____ ND _____ NA

39. Have you ever had any miscarriages? If no, go to 44–45.

_____ Yes   _____ No   _____ ND

40. If yes, how many miscarriages have you had? _____ 1
                                                 _____ 2
                                                 _____ > 2
                                                 _____ ND
                                                 _____ NA

41–43. How many months were you pregnant before the miscarriage?

_____   _____ ND   _____ NA
_____   _____ ND   _____ NA
_____   _____ ND   _____ NA

44–45. What is your occupation?_____ _____ ND
                                                       _____ NA

46–47. If retired, what was your occupation prior to retirement?

_____   _____ ND   _____ NA

48–49. How many years have you performed this occupation?

_____   _____ ND   _____ NA

51–52. Did you have any other occupations prior to this one?

_____   _____ ND   _____ NA

53–54. If yes, number of years employed?

_____   _____ ND   _____ NA

55–56. What is your husband's occupation?

_____   _____ ND   _____ NA

57–58. If retired, what was his occupation prior to retirement?

_____   _____ ND   _____ NA

59–60. How many years had he performed this occupation?

_____   _____ ND   _____ NA

61–62. Did he have any other occupations prior to this one?

_____   _____ ND   _____ NA

63–64. If yes, number of years employed?

_____   _____ ND   _____ NA

65. Have you ever been exposed to asbestos? (See attached sheet for definition of asbestos)

  _____ Yes _____ No _____ DK _____ ND

66. If yes, where: _____ House
 _____ School
 _____ Occupation/workplace
 _____ other
 _____ ND
 _____ NA

67. What is your blood type? _____ A Pos _____ O Neg
 _____ A Neg _____ AB
 _____ O Pos _____ Other _____
 _____ DK
 _____ ND

68. Did you ever have x-rays taken of your pelvic organs? (below waist, above knees)

  _____ Yes _____ No
  _____ DK _____ ND

69–73. If yes: when? _____ month/year _____ NA
 how many times?_____ _____ NA

Do you have a history of:

74. Cervical cysts/tumors/fibroids	_____ Yes	_____ No	_____ DK	_____ ND
75. High blood pressure	_____ Yes	_____ No	_____ DK	_____ ND
76. Gallbladder disease	_____ Yes	_____ No	_____ DK	_____ ND
77. German measles (year _____) (see attachment A)	_____ Yes	_____ No	_____ DK	_____ ND
78. Premenarchal mumps (year _____) (see attachment A)	_____ Yes	_____ No	_____ DK	_____ ND
79. Hypothyroidism (see attachment A)	_____ Yes	_____ No	_____ DK	_____ ND
80. Endometriosis (see attachment A)	_____ Yes	_____ No	_____ DK	_____ ND
81. Ovarian cysts	_____ Yes	_____ No	_____ DK	_____ ND
82. Benign breast disease (i.e., Breast tumors, cysts)	_____ Yes	_____ No	_____ DK	_____ ND

Have you ever experienced:

83. Abnormal breast swelling	_____ Yes	_____ No	_____ ND
84. Pain associated with menstruation	_____ Yes	_____ No	_____ ND

85. Have you ever used?:

Talc (Body Powder) _____ Yes _____ No _____ ND

If so, did you use it on your:

86. vaginal/rectal area? _____ Yes _____ No _____ ND _____ NA

87. sanitary napkins _____ Yes _____ No _____ ND _____ NA

88. other _____ Yes _____ No _____ NA

Have you ever used any of the following:

89. Noncontraceptive estrogen/diethylstilbestrol _____ Yes _____ No _____ ND

90. Birth control pills _____ Yes _____ No _____ ND

91–92. If yes, what type? (read attached list) _____

_____ DK _____ ND _____ NA

(If no to 89 and 90 above, go to question 103)

(If yes to 89 above, ask questions 93–98)

(If yes to 90 above, ask questions 93–102)

93–96. What types of estrogen were used and what dosage (in micrograms?) (see attached list) _____

Type: _____ DK _____ ND _____ NA

Dosage: _____ DK _____ ND _____ NA

97. How long did you take this medication/birth control?

_____ 3–6 months
_____ 6–12 months
_____ 1–3 years
_____ 4–6 years
_____ > 6 years
_____ DK
_____ ND
_____ NA

98. What was the pattern of use: _____ constant
_____ interrupted
_____ discontinued
_____ ND
_____ NA

99–102. What type of progestogen was used and dosage in micrograms? (see attached list)

_____

_____ DK   _____ ND   _____ NA

103. Do you smoke cigarettes?

_____ Yes   _____ No   _____ ND   If no, go to No. 105

104. If yes, how many cigarettes do you smoke each day?

_____ 1/2 pack or less
_____ 1 pack
_____ 1 to 2 packs
_____ more than 2 packs
_____ ND
_____ NA

105. Have you ever smoked?

_____ Yes   _____ No   _____ ND   If yes, go to question 107.

106. How long has it been since you quit smoking?

_____ 3 months
_____ < 3 months
_____ 4–6 months
_____ 7 months - < 1 year
_____ 1–5 years
_____ Specify
_____ ND
_____ NA

107. Do you drink or have you ever consumed alcohol?

_____ Yes   _____ No   _____ ND

108. If yes, which of the following groups do you believe most accurately depicts your alcohol use:

a. _____ 2 or more drinks/day
b. _____ 5–10 drinks/week
c. _____ 1–4/week
d. _____ 1–3/month
e. _____ < 1 a month
f. _____ ND
g. _____ NA

109. Do you drink coffee?

_____ Yes   _____ No   _____ ND   _____ NA

110. If yes, which: _____ Decaffeinated _____ Regular _____ Both _____ ND

111. How many cups of regular coffee do you drink per day?

_____ < 2

_____ 3–5

_____ 6–8

_____ > 9   Specify _____

_____ ND

_____ NA

112–113. How many years have you consumed regular coffee?   _____

_____ ND

_____ NA

114. How many cups of decaffeinated do you drink per day?

_____ < 2

_____ 3–5

_____ 6–8

_____ > 9 Specify _____

_____ ND

_____ NA

115–116. How many years have you drank decaffeinated coffee?   _____

_____ ND

_____ NA

117. Do you normally drink the same number of cups of coffee each day?

_____ Yes   _____ No   _____ ND   _____ NA

118–119. If no, what does your weekly consumption of coffee include?

_____   _____ ND   _____ NA

Any general questions/comments about study: _____

_____

_____

*ND = Not documented

*DK = Don't know

*NA = Not applicable

Attachment A

1. Hypothyroidism:

   The thyroid gland will not function up to its normal potential. Marked by tiredness and drowsiness, and so forth.

2. Endometriosis:

   Abnormal occurrence of tissue (which more or less perfectly resembles the endometrium, the mucous membrane lining the uterus) in various locations in the pelvic cavity.

3. Premenarchal Mumps:

   Contagious disease seen mainly in childhood (before the start of the female menses or period). It involves the salivary glands (parotid) but other tissues (meninges) may also be affected.

4. German Measles:

   Rubella. A mild viral infection marked by a pink rash, fever, and lymph node enlargement.

5. Asbestos:

   Soft fibrous mineral made into fireproof material or used for heat insulation. If inhaled, may cause asbestosis, a lung disease caused by inhaling asbestos fibers.

Chapter 7
Informatics Evaluation and Outcomes Research Related to Core HIM Functions

Jennifer Hornung Garvin, PhD, RHIA, CPHQ, CCS, CTR, FAHIMA and Mark Weiner, MD

Learning Objectives

- Provide a rationale for conducting evaluation research
- Show the relationship between core health information management functions and research
- Outline important research methods pertaining to evaluation research
- Explain terms related to evaluation research and theory

Key Terms

Cost-benefit analysis

Cost-effectiveness

Evaluation research

Formative evaluation

Impact evaluation

Implementation evaluation

Needs assessment

Objectivist

Outcome evaluation

Process evaluation

Subjectivist

Summative evaluation

Introduction

The health information management (HIM) department performs many significant functions that require evaluation. These include the release of information, coding and abstracting, transcription, filing, scanning, master patient index maintenance, and chart completion functions. Quality improvement initiatives such as analyzing the quality of data contained within registries and elements used for performance assessment may also fall within the purview of HIM. In addition, HIM departments are responsible for the education of internal and external staff regarding issues related to important departmental functions. For organizations that have electronic health records (EHRs), HIM professionals may be involved in the implementation or redesign of electronic records or development of software programs that interface with them. All of these areas can be examined using evaluation research techniques.

Scope of Evaluation Research

Evaluation research consists of a set of methods to explore the impact of new or existing processes. The determination of whether or not the evaluation constitutes traditional research requiring institutional review board (IRB) approval depends on the motivation and approach to these analyses, and the intended application of the results. In addition to traditional research, the evaluation may be considered quality improvement, or an analysis of the return on investment of a project or process. If the evaluation is seeking to gain generalizable knowledge or to formally compare two processes using experimental methods, especially when the processes involve human subjects, then that defines the evaluation as true research and requires IRB approval. If the intent is to improve local processes or demonstrate financial benefit, generally this does not constitute traditional research and therefore does not require IRB approval (Baily et. al. 2006) However, the institutional policy of the organization conducting the research should be considered as well as the source of the funding in this determination.

Evaluation Research Defined

Although evaluation research could be defined in several ways, Trochim and Donnelly (2006) provide a useful definition. They note that "evaluation [research] is

the systematic acquisition and assessment of information to provide useful feedback about some object." The term "object" in this context refers to a program, policy, technology, person, need, activity, and so on. They further discuss the goals of evaluation, namely, to provide "useful feedback" to a variety of audiences such as sponsors, donors, administrators, staff, and other relevant stakeholders. Generally, feedback is considered useful if it aids in decision making.

Types of Evaluation Research

Trochim and Donnelly (2006) discuss the many different types of evaluations. The two broad categories are **formative** and **summative.** Formative evaluations are conducted during the course of development or implementation of a new program or method to provide iterative feedback on the process.

Some examples of **formative evaluations** are to measure or assess:

- Improvement in delivery methods with regard to technology used
- The quality of implementation of a new process or technology
- Information about the organizational placement of a given process
- The type of personnel involved in a program
- Other important factors such as the procedures, source, and type of inputs

Summative evaluations are conducted after implementation and are designed to examine areas such as the effects or outcomes of a program. Some examples of summative evaluations are to:

- Determine whether the program had the intended effect it was designed to have
- Determine the overall impact of a project or program
- Evaluate the cost-effectiveness of the program

Potential Applications of HIM— Clinical Practice Scenario

A clinical practice scenario is used to illustrate the various types of HIM-related evaluation research applied to a common process of clinical program development that requires workflow changes and more systematic data collection than currently exists. In this example, a hypothetical facility is assessing whether or not to implement an American College of Surgeons (ACS) approved cancer program. Although the program does appear to be beneficial, there are a number of other potential initiatives competing for a limited set of funds. The HIM department was asked to participate in the advance analysis of the ACS program with a special focus on the requirements for a tumor registry, as well as to participate in the ongoing evaluation efforts of the ACS approved program should it be implemented.

Needs Assessment

Altschuld and Witkin (2000, 253) define **needs assessment** as "the process of determining, analyzing, and prioritizing needs, and in turn, identifying and implementing solution strategies to resolve high-priority needs." Within the context of the clinical practice scenario described here, the first step is determining if the development of an ACS-approved cancer program is desirable with respect to competing alternatives. How do researchers determine if it is? The following types of steps in a needs assessment will help to answer the question.

- A planning committee composed of relevant stakeholders must be established to conduct the needs assessment and recommend action following the study.
- The health problems of the patient population and the related treatment services must be analyzed.
- The potential solutions are determined, including requirements of the ACS for various types of cancer centers.
- The potential solutions and requirements of the ACS programs must be weighed against the needs of the patient population to determine which type of program, if any, is desirable to institute.
- An action plan is developed, if applicable, and the priority next steps are established.

A variety of data and processes can be used to undertake the needs assessment. For example, the costs of establishing the various types of ACS programs can be determined, including a breakdown of costs of software, personnel costs, office space required, and materials needed to establish the registry. In addition to evaluating the requirements of a tumor registry, information from potential patients and other stakeholders should also be obtained. A description of clinical needs of the patient population associated with the facility should include information such as tumor type and stage, general treatments applied (surgery, chemotherapy, radiation therapy), and outcome. Other areas of interest to major stakeholders may also include:

- Specifics regarding the nature and duration of the chemotherapy
- Details regarding the radiation therapy
- Number of patients with "remission" as an outcome
- Functional outcomes of patients who have been treated at the facility

To obtain needed information, a variety of research methods could be used, including patient and staff focus groups, surveys, and descriptive data providing the incidence of various types of cancer that have been diagnosed at the facility based on medical data that can be obtained from the patients' medical record. Demographic data for the patients currently and potentially served by the program also should be considered as part of the assessment.

Within this context, the evaluation would not be designed to be generalizable and therefore would not require IRB approval. Even though this is the case, sound research methods can be used. For example, a survey can be undertaken to determine patient needs and preferences. It is important to ensure that the survey instrument is valid and reliable and that population sampling was done in such a way as to engender confidence in the results of the evaluation. To assess current cancer patient health conditions and treatments, a cross-sectional analysis of the current cancer cases and treatment methods should be obtained from secondary data such as those in coded and abstracted data. Significant stakeholders inside and outside the healthcare facility can be interviewed. In this way, although the research is not intended to extend outside of the context of the given healthcare facility, the quality of the evaluation still must be high so that optimal decisions can be made for the healthcare organization.

Implementation and Process Evaluation

The needs assessment determines if the creation of a new program is an appropriate course of action, and helps to set priorities and schedules for an implementation plan. Through the course of implementation, **implementation evaluation** essentially consists of monitoring how well the planned events are actually occurring and whether the implementation is meeting the expected time frames. **Process evaluation** measures the effectiveness of the program. In the current hypothetical case, the effectiveness of the tumor registry would be evaluated. In order to do this, the goals and objectives established for the program of interest would be examined against the outcomes established for the registry. For example, the outcomes of accessioning 90 percent of eligible cases that are abstracted within 6 months of contact would be evaluated (ACS 2006).

While evaluating the process associated with implementing the tumor registry, the HIM department may be asked to use the tumor registry to find information that pertains to a process evaluation of the cancer program itself. For example, the tumor registry may be asked to provide data about the number of patients within a given primary cancer site who have been seen at the facility within a given time period. This data will help the Cancer Committee evaluate if the program is being initiated as designed in the original program plan. Alternatively, the tumor registry could be used to generate patient lists for surveys or focus groups so that feedback can be gained to enhance such aspects of the program as patient satisfaction and ease of use. Findings from this type of research can help researchers make informed changes to the implementation of programs and patient-related processes.

Summative Evaluation

Trochim and Donnelly (2006) further discuss the focus of various types of formative and summative evaluation research. *Summative evaluation* can also be subdivided into several areas. Areas important to HIM are **outcome evaluations** to determine if the program or technology has caused demonstrable effects as defined in the project goals; **impact evaluation** to assess the intended or unintended net effects of the program or technology; and **cost-effectiveness** and **cost-benefit** analyses to deter-

mine if the project has a positive financial impact (Trochim and Donnelly 2006).

Outcomes Evaluation

In addition to evaluating the outcomes related to the clinical case scenario, the HIM department and associated tumor registry may be asked for information pertaining to outcomes of the use of the registry and the cancer program. For example, the tumor registry may be asked to provide data about how often the registry is used to identify patient cases for concurrent multidisciplinary treatment discussion. Or the registry can be used to determine the use of a given treatment of patients with a given primary site before and after the institution of the cancer program. These data will help the Cancer Committee evaluate if the program is meeting program objects as originally designed.

Impact Evaluation

To determine if the program has had a beneficial effect on the healthcare organization and the associated patient population, the Cancer Committee may evaluate aspects such as access to treatment options in a given primary site compared to the treatment outcomes of the patients in the same facility before the ACS-approved cancer program was instituted. For example, prior to the development of the cancer program, access to treatment programs and participation in clinical trials of patients with late-stage cancer may have been suboptimal because patients may have had to travel significant distances. If during the time period after implementation of the cancer program, patients with this same stage of cancer were able to enroll in a clinical trial despite geographic barriers, this provides evidence that the cancer program is effective in improving patient access to both state-of-the-art care and novel experimental therapies. Studies of patient access to care is commonly conducted with ACS registries and because of this, it is relatively easy to benchmark the results of the newly developed program with the findings from studies undertaken in similar types of facilities with equivalent program offerings.

Cost-effectiveness and Cost-benefit Analysis

One of the goals of the ACS-approved cancer program may have been to increase the number of cancer patients treated in the inpatient and outpatient settings of the facility. As part of the new program evaluation, the financial impact of an increasing number of new patient referrals and improved patient outcomes can be measured. A **cost-effectiveness** analysis (Russell et al. 1996) can help explore the value of the program in terms of the quality-adjusted years of life gained by patients attributed to the investment in the program. A **cost-benefit analysis** would show the financial benefits of the program from an institutional or a societal perspective. These evaluations require an analysis of the costs associated with the program as well as the associated revenues and patient outcomes. The program can be evaluated on whether or not the predetermined financial and patient care goals are being met.

Informatics and HIM Research Found in the Scientific Literature

The prior section provided a synopsis of the categories and characteristics of evaluation research as applied to internal quality improvement initiatives at one facility. The current section provides examples of studies from the HIM and informatics scientific literature that illustrate a more broad application of evaluation research principals meant to be generalizable outside a single facility. The various types of evaluation research methods presented in the preceding section are also applied in clinical research. The studies illustrate how several topics related to informatics and HIM are assessed. These topics include: the process of coding, clinical alerts, outcomes measurement, impact of missing information in primary care, and return on investment of electronic health records in physician offices.

Needs Assessment

As health and healthcare needs continue to expand, the classification systems used to support these efforts need to expand as well. It is important for HIM professionals to anticipate changes in classification systems and their uses. Research by Garvin and Watzlaf (2004) established a need for further preparation of coders with the goal that coding staff will have the professional competencies required for future work. Garvin and Watzlaf determined this need by evaluating the degree of alignment of current HIM skills with the projected coding competencies of the future. In essence, this research evaluated the readiness of the coding workforce in comparison with future work requirements.

This research measured key areas related to anticipated future skills of coding professionals that would be examined in a formal needs assessment process. Coding competency is extremely important to the HIM profession and to healthcare in general. This research evaluated coding skill and competency using practice-based research. The projected skill set for the clinical data specialist and future coding roles set forth in the publication *Evolving HIM Careers* (AHIMA 1999) was used to determine how prepared current coders are in terms of projected competencies. In this investigation, a random sample of coders and noncoders were surveyed to determine how well the current level of skills related to the skills described for the clinical data specialist. The findings from the research suggest that there are many skills projected for the clinical data specialist that are shared by both coders and noncoders. Also, neither coders nor noncoders reflected the level of competence in their self-assessed skills in many areas, such as understanding coding and classification systems other than ICD-9 and CPT, designing audit tools, performing quality audits, and selecting statistical software applications appropriate to the data to be captured. The research also suggests that coding professionals who wish to prepare for the future should acquire more communication, research, and management skills.

Based on this evaluation research, a plan to provide training to the current coders could be developed. This kind of evaluation was undertaken in order to prepare the coding professional for work with EHRs. The findings from the research revealed that coders did not reflect the level of projected competence in their self-assessed skills in many areas, such as understanding coding and classification systems other than ICD-9 and CPT, designing audit tools, performing quality audits, and selecting statistical software applications appropriate to the data to be captured. The research also suggested that coding professionals who wish to prepare for the future should acquire more communication, research, and management skills.

The data for the study was gathered with a survey tool for which reliability and validity was established. Further research could be undertaken using the same tool to evaluate the current skills of HIM professionals. This data could then be used to substantiate the need for a given set of education to address the projected needed skills. Because there are ever-greater numbers of coding professionals working in facilities with an EHR, it would also be interesting to determine if there is a correlation between individuals with the future anticipated skills and the adoption of an EHR.

Process Assessment

One extremely significant research study by O'Malley et al. (2005) examined key areas related to the use of coded data. In this study, the process of inpatient coding was examined via a review of the literature, flow charting the process, interviews, and discussion with coders and the users of the coded data. By virtue of this close examination, the potential error associated with each step in the process was identified. The statistical method by which code accuracy is determined also was evaluated. This thorough review of the literature provided greater clarity regarding the ways that coding accuracy was measured. This research serves as an excellent starting point for HIM researchers.

O'Malley et al. (2005) provides an overview of research studies that have quantified error rates from studies done in the 1970s to 2003. Although these studies discuss varying amounts of coding accuracy, O'Malley et al. (2005) noted caution in several areas, including the following: these studies were conducted with different data sets, multiple versions of the ICD system were used because of annual modifications, differing conditions were studied, and the number of digits in the codes that were compared and the actual codes examined varied.

Though the error rates must be viewed within the context of a study's design, many sources of errors were identified. A critical contributor to error is the inherent influence of uncertainty in the diagnostic process. A coder is trained and educated to classify conditions into categories such as ICD. The clinician, however, is primarily concerned with gathering clinical data to monitor and treat the patient's aggregate symptomatology, which is labeled with a diagnosis. O'Malley et al. go on to note that the quality and quantity of communication between patients and providers, the state of scientific understanding regarding various presentations and etiologies of diseases, and the utility of the tests and procedures available to the clinician are critical determinants of diagnostic and coding accuracy. Although this finding may be true, Lloyd and Rissing (1985) conducted a study in which many potential errors originate with the coder. They found that 11 experienced medical coders had differences in one or more data fields for more than half of the records. It should be noted that the study was conducted in the early 1980s before the widespread use of diagnosis-related groups and the resulting attention paid to assigning codes based on increased use of the Uni-

form Hospital Discharge Data Set (UHDDS). Clearly, it is important to measure coding accuracy in a way that contributes to the scientific literature. Figure 7.1 depicts the steps in the coding process with the associated potential sources of error. This flowchart reveals how the coding process is impacted by many factors, most of which are not within the purview of the coding staff. Further, that error in coded data results from the variability inherent in the patient care processes as well as the variability of training and experience of coding professionals.

O'Malley et al. (2005) provide a useful guide to how accuracy measures for coding can be calculated. The most common statistics are sensitivity, specificity, positive predictive value, negative predictive value, and the kappa (κ) coefficient. However, although these statistics are simple to compute, determining what the answers mean is not a straightforward process. Sensitivity and specificity require a gold standard, but the authors note that there is no standard for the diagnostic labeling associated with coding. However, if the research question is, "In medical chart reviews, how well do medical coders' ICD code assignments match those of physicians?" then a true standard exists for medical presence of disease. In such a situation, the researcher might prefer to calculate specificity, sensitivity, and predictive values using the physicians' reviews as the gold standard. However, the reliability of medical diagnoses is not being measured. The authors estimate, in the context of medical chart review, the corroboration between physician and medical coders' ICD classifications. In addition to what is stated by O'Malley et al. (2005), it is also important to note that the gold standard can change. For example, if the statistical comparison is between an expert coder and a less-skilled coder, in this case the standard is the expert coder. The comparison relates to the accuracy of the coding in terms of the medicolegal aspects of coding for payment and compliance. This comparison is different from the one that establishes medical presence of disease, which occurs based on a comparison between a physician and a coder.

O'Malley et al. (2005) also note that another way to measure accuracy would be to compare the diagnoses established by two or more peer experts (for example, physician to physician or coder to coder) evaluating the same sample of patients. In this instance the κ coefficient would be a good statistic to use. This statistic quantifies beyond-chance agreement among peer reviewer experts, and it would be an appropriate estimator of the reliability of diagnoses made by expert peer reviewers. This type of

Figure 7.1.   Overview of the inpatient coding process

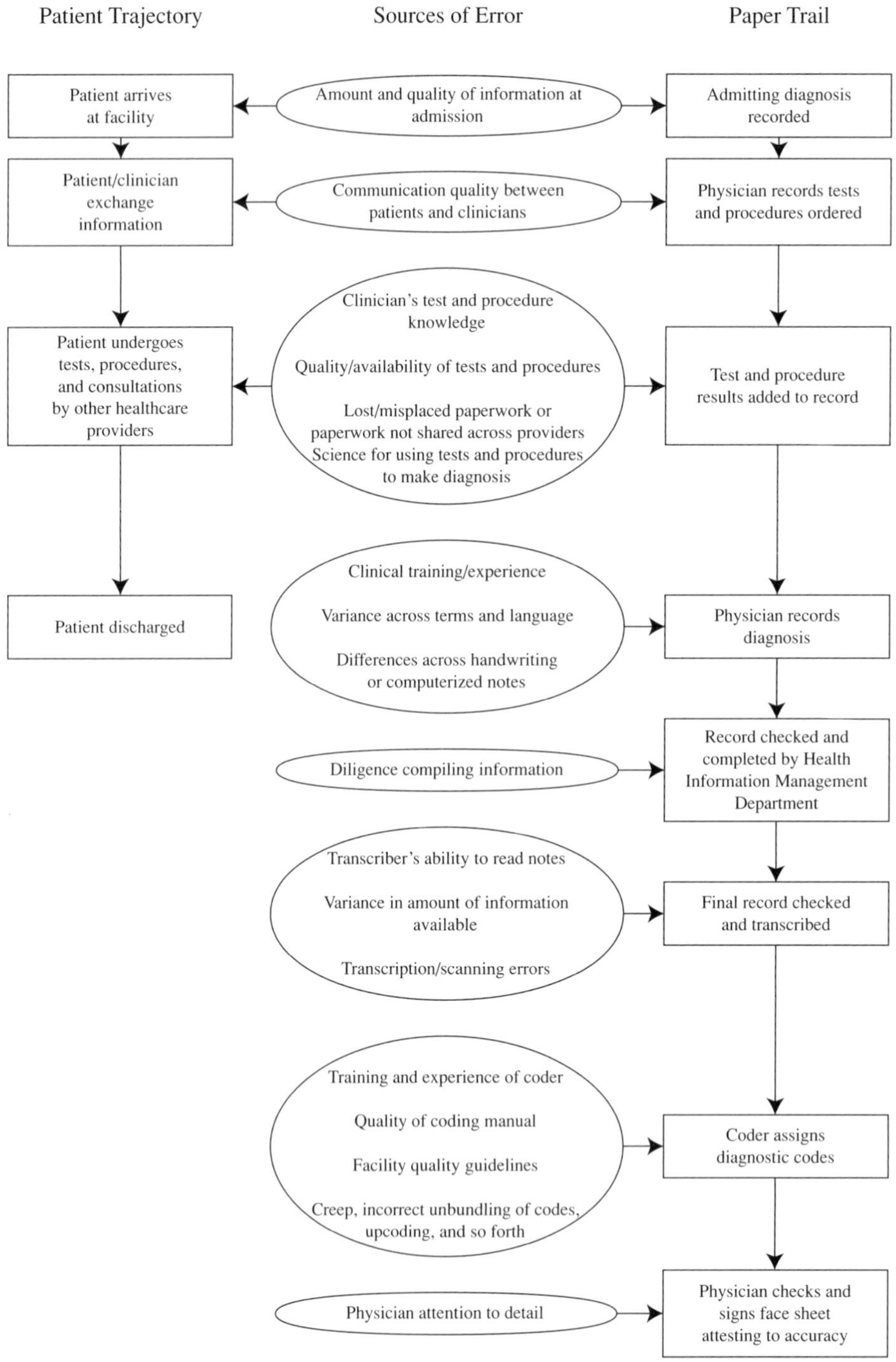

Patient Trajectory	Sources of Error	Paper Trail

Patient arrives at facility
← Amount and quality of information at admission →
Admitting diagnosis recorded

Patient/clinician exchange information
← Communication quality between patients and clinicians →
Physician records tests and procedures ordered

Patient undergoes tests, procedures, and consultations by other healthcare providers
← Clinician's test and procedure knowledge
Quality/availability of tests and procedures
Lost/misplaced paperwork or paperwork not shared across providers
Science for using tests and procedures to make diagnosis →
Test and procedure results added to record

Patient discharged
Clinical training/experience
Variance across terms and language
Differences across handwriting or computerized notes →
Physician records diagnosis

Diligence compiling information →
Record checked and completed by Health Information Management Department

Transcriber's ability to read notes
Variance in amount of information available
Transcription/scanning errors →
Final record checked and transcribed

Training and experience of coder
Quality of coding manual
Facility quality guidelines
Creep, incorrect unbundling of codes, upcoding, and so forth →
Coder assigns diagnostic codes

Physician attention to detail →
Physician checks and signs face sheet attesting to accuracy

statistic measures the agreement between peers and the concordance between nonpeers. So, if the accuracy of coding between a physician and a coder was assessed, the measure would constitute the degree of concordance (similarity) between them rather than the degree of agreement. This is because the physician—unless also a coding expert with regard to knowledge of coding rules—is coding based on medical presence of disease, whereas the coding professional is using the medicolegal standards of coding guidelines in order to determine codes. There is no true gold standard, and peers are not evaluating each other using the same knowledge base. These are important distinctions because they inform the meaning of the accuracy statistics.

ICD codes are important because their use allows research in healthcare, policy, and monitoring of disease. It is also important, however, to monitor and critically evaluate the accuracy of code assignment. Code accuracy is improved when there is an awareness of the sources of potential error. Future areas of research could include determining what factors have the greatest influence in coding accuracy, quantifying them, and instituting potential interventions to increase accuracy.

Assessing Implementation

A computerized medication alert system was designed to decrease patient safety events. However, it was found that the alerts often were overridden because of poor specificity and alert overload. Shah et al. (2005) redesigned drug alerts to improve clinician acceptance. The key factor in the redesign was the modification of the revised design, which used a selective set of drug alerts that denoted the potential of a high-severity event. The system was designed this way in order to minimize interruptions to clinician workflow. The new design was tested with presentation of alerts to clinicians using a commercial knowledge base modified to include a subset of only the most clinically relevant contraindications. The alerts were used with computerized prescribing in an EHR. The revised design was used in 31 Boston-area practices. During the use of this modified system, there were 18,115 drug alerts during the six-month study period. Of these, 5,182 (29 percent) were high-severity, and 67 percent of these alerts were accepted by clinicians.

The reasons for overrides were collected, and they varied for each drug alert category. In addition to evaluation of the new design, potentially useful information for future alert improvement also was gathered. These data suggest that a computerized prescribing decision support can be devised so that there is a higher rate of acceptance of clinical alerts. The researchers contrast their findings to those of Weingart et al. (2003), in which physicians accepted only 11 percent of high-severity drug interaction alerts. In Weingart's study, an inclusive commercial knowledge base was used as the basis of the alert generation. In contrast, Shah et al. (2005) started with a modified commercial knowledge base that used a subset consisting of only the most clinically relevant contraindications. The researchers believed that there was high clinician acceptance of alerts due to presentation of fewer but more meaningful alerts. More research is needed to find the optimal balance between overalerting and underalerting.

It is important to capture potentially adverse drug effects (ADEs). HIM professionals are trained to undertake quality improvement, assist accreditation processes, utilize coding systems, and improve documentation and computer systems. All of these areas are related to the aforementioned research. More research could be undertaken to determine how ADEs are being captured in EHRs, how the capture varies based on the type of EHR, the functional requirements that could be used to facilitate capture, and quantification of the sensitivity and specificity of ADEs in various practice settings.

Evaluating Outcomes

Jha et al. (2007) undertook research to evaluate the outcomes associated with the Hospital Quality Alliance (HQA) program. This program provides the opportunity to systematically monitor the quality of hospital care nationwide. The study was designed to gauge the importance of the HQA indicators and how an outcome such as mortality relates to the HQA indicators. In order to do this, the researchers used study data from the December 2005 release of the HQA program and limited the research to using 10 measures designated as the starter set. The HQA performance scores for 4,048 acute-care hospitals were linked to data from the American Hospital Association (AHA) and with the 2003 Medicare Provider and Analysis Review (MedPAR) Part A data set.

The data were risk-adjusted using the Agency for Healthcare Research and Quality (AHRQ) Elixhauser comorbidity scheme (Elixhauser et al. 1998). The researchers evaluated the relationship between hospital performance as expressed by the HQA quality indicators and mortality data for Medicare enrollees admitted for acute myocardial infarction, congestive heart failure, and pneumonia. The researchers found that higher condition-specific performance in the national quality reporting program was associated with lower risk-adjusted mortality for each of the three conditions. A summary of these findings is presented in figure 7.2. The relationship between high HQA performance and lower risk-adjusted mortality was thought to be an important validation for this national hospital quality rating program. This research is based on data provided by HIM professionals and raises the issue that data quality evaluation is critical to maintain credibility within a healthcare organization as well as within the national research and payer arenas.

Evaluating Impact

Smith et al. (2005) studied the impact of missing clinical information in primary care practice. This research provides insight regarding the lack of patient information in primary care at the time of the patient visit. The researchers described the amount of missing information reported by clinicians. The researchers used a cross-sectional survey in 32 primary care clinics within State Networks of Colorado Ambulatory Practices and Partners (SNOCAP). Between May and December 2003, 253 clinicians were surveyed about 1,614 patient visits. For every visit during a half-day session, each clinician completed a questionnaire about patient and visit characteristics, and stated whether important clinical information had been missing. Clinician characteristics also were recorded.

Summary reports generated include missing clinical information frequency, type, and presumed location; perceived likelihood of adverse effects, delays in care, and additional services; and time spent looking for missing information. Multivariate analysis was conducted to assess the relationship of missing information to patient, visit, or clinician characteristics, adjusting for potential confounders, and effects of clustering.

Clinicians reported missing clinical information in 13.6 percent of visits. This missing information included laboratory results (6.1 percent of all visits), letters/dictation (5.4 percent), radiology results (3.8 percent), history and physical examination (3.7 percent), and medications (3.2 percent). Missing clinical information was frequently reported to be located outside the clinical

Figure 7.2.   Adjusted odds ratio of in-hospital mortality, by Hospital Quality Alliance (HQA) performance quartile

HQA performance[a]	Adjusted odds ratio (95% confidence interval)		
	AMI	CHF	Pneumonia
1st quartile	0.89 (0.85, 0.94)	0.93 (0.88, 0.98)	0.85 (0.81, 0.89)
2nd quartile	0.93 (0.89, 0.98)	0.99 (0.94, 1.04)	0.87 (0.83, 0.92)
3rd quartile	0.96 (0.91, 1.01)	1.01 (0.96, 1.07)	0.90 (0.86, 0.95)
p value for trend	<0.001	0.005	<0.001
HQA performance[b]			
1st quartile	0.91 (0.86, 0.96)	0.92 (0.88, 0.98)	0.90 (0.86, 0.95)
2nd quartile	0.95 (0.90, 1.00)	0.98 (0.93, 1.04)	0.91 (0.87, 0.96)
3rd quartile	0.97 (0.93, 1.02)	1.00 (0.94, 1.05)	0.92 (0.88, 0.97)
p value for trend	0.0002	0.0056	<.0001

Source: Authors' analysis of HQA data, December 2005 release, and Medicare data.
Notes: AMI is acute myocardial infarction. CHF is congestive heart failure.
[a]Adjusted for patient age, sex, race, and the presence or absence of each of thirty comorbidities.
[b]Adjusted as in Note a, as well as for teaching status, bed size, for-profit status, and region of the country.

system but within the United States (52.3 percent), to be at least somewhat likely to adversely affect patients (44 percent), and to potentially result in delayed care or additional services (59.5 percent). Significant time was reportedly spent unsuccessfully searching for missing clinical information (5 to 10 minutes, 25.6 percent; 10 minutes, 10.4 percent). After adjustment, reported missing clinical information was more likely when patients were recent immigrants (odds ratio [OR] 1.78; 95 percent confidence interval [CI], 1.06 to 2.99), new patients (OR 2.39; 95 percent CI, 1.70 to 3.35), or patients who had multiple medical problems compared with no problems (1 problem: OR 1.09; 95 percent CI, 0.69 to 1.73; 2 to 5 problems: OR 1.87; 95 percent CI, 1.21 to 2.89; 5 problems: OR 2.78; 95 percent CI, 1.61 to 4.80). Missing clinical information was less likely in rural practices (OR 0.52; 95 percent CI, 0.29 to 0.92) and when individual clinicians reported having robust electronic records (OR 0.40; 95 percent CI, 0.17 to 0.94).

This research found that primary care clinicians commonly report missing clinical information. It also was found that the missing information is likely to consume time and other resources, and may adversely affect patients. The researchers suggest that further research is needed to build on this initial study so that the clinicians' perceptions found in this study could be validated. It also was suggested that prospective study design could be used to determine the causes of missing information as well as its sequelae. Areas could include evaluating the ambulatory EHR functional requirements associated with provider perception of complete information, and significant differences in patient outcomes when ambulatory Commission for Certification of Health Information Technology (CCHIT) EHR products are used.

Cost-benefit Analysis

Miller et al. (2005) conducted a retrospective qualitative study of 14 solo or small-group primary care practices in 12 states to determine the return on investment of installing an EHR in physician practices. Initial EHR costs averaged $44,000 per full-time-equivalent (FTE) provider, and ongoing costs averaged $8,500 per provider per year. The average practice paid for its EHR costs in 2.5 years and profited handsomely after that; however, some practices could not cover costs quickly, most providers spent more time at work initially, and some practices experienced substantial financial risks.

The researchers selected practices from customer lists provided by two leading vendors of EHR software for the solo/small-group market. In this study, primary care practices were selected that:

- Used an EHR for one to three years when first contacted
- Had full practices prior to implementation
- Had relatively stable complements of billing providers
- Could provide needed data

Approximately 20 percent of practices meeting these criteria agreed to participate. The research involved the use of semistructured interviews of self-identified physician and office manager EHR champions. The providers were observed in their use of EHRs and vendor contracts, and practice reports were reviewed. Data also were obtained on practice operations, EHR-related hardware and software, selection and implementation processes, costs, financial benefits, use of EHR capabilities, quality improvement (QI) efforts, and barriers and facilitators for achieving benefits. Data were obtained on one-time and ongoing EHR-related costs for hardware, software, information systems staffing and external contractor services, installation, training, abstraction, productivity loss, and telecommunications, as well as on efficiency savings (decreases in compensation for medical records and other support staff FTE positions and overtime, and decreases in transcription and paper supply costs), efficiency financial gains (increased visits due to reduced provider time per visit), and efficiency nonfinancial gains (decreased provider time at work). Further, researchers considered data on revenue enhancement from higher payment for increased levels of coding for visits, and more complete documentation of visit activities, substantiating higher coding.

The researchers focused on key EHR-enabled QI activities that might lead to improved patient outcomes, delivered reminders at the point of care, generated lists of patients needing services and follow-up services, created QI performance reports, provided patient self-management aids, or participated in QI collaboratives. They also examined external performance reporting and financial incentives to improve quality. The study findings revealed that most providers used the EHR for common tasks, including prescribing, documenting, viewing, and within-practice messaging, and almost all used it to assist with billing. Providers typically used templates (electronic forms) to document activities; they also used electronic forms to generate prescription and laboratory orders that were printed out for patients. Transcription was rare, and 10 of the 14 practices no longer routinely pulled paper charts. Few practices used the EHR for reporting patient lists or provider performance, patient-provider communication, or communication from providers within the practice to those outside it. The spread of financial costs reflected variation in small practices in pre-EHR hardware and in technical and negotiating skills.

HIM professionals could pursue further research in this area, including which negotiation skills reduce costs, whether or not the use of management tools such as workflow analysis during implementation reduce costs and improve profit, and an evaluation of data quality capture for performance measures.

Evaluation Research Questions

As was discussed earlier, there are two general areas of evaluation research: formative and summative research. The following research questions are pertinent to evaluation research in HIM and informatics.

In formative evaluation research, the research questions would consist of issues such as:

- What is the issue or problem that should be addressed?
- What is the scope of a given problem or issue?
- What is the ideal design of a process or program that will address the problem or issue?
- How well is a process or program delivered?

Summative research questions would relate to the following aspects:

- What is the effectiveness of the program or project?
- What is the impact of the program or project?

Research Methods

As illustrated by the research presented earlier, the issues or problems that would be addressed by the HIM department may require a variety of research methods. These research methods can be determined based on the research questions for the study, the data available, and

the outcomes evaluated. This said, research methods could include all of the following:

- Brainstorming
- Focus groups
- Nominal group techniques
- Delphi methods
- Concept mapping

Similarly, determining the scope or important aspects of needed work may require undertaking a needs assessment. Researchers undertaking a needs assessment may use a range of research methods, including an analysis of existing data sources such as:

- Surveys
- Interviews of stakeholders
- Focus groups

To evaluate the delivery of a program, research methods may include the use of:

- Surveys
- Simulations
- Focus groups
- Flowcharting
- Work analysis
- Evaluation of existing data

As discussed earlier, the methods appropriate for the evaluation of the effectiveness and impact of a program or project could be selected from quantitative research methods such as surveys, correlational analysis, case control or cohort studies, or randomized controlled trials. Alternatively, qualitative techniques, such as focus groups, also can be used.

Other issues include considering the appropriate theory or theories underpinning the areas of investigation. The models illustrating the factors and relationships of the study, the assumptions of the field and the researcher, the methods, and the analytical tools also can be part of the evaluation research design. As was mentioned in other areas of this chapter and book, some databases and most registries are derived from health records. Researchers undertaking evaluation research can therefore use these databases and registries for their studies. Similarly, the time frame for the studies can be retrospective or prospective, and cross-sectional or longitudinal. The time frame will be based on the purpose of the study, the data available, and other factors. There are many types of evaluation research possibilities, and many of the research methods stem from the discipline that originates the research question. For example, if the financial impact is studied, a cost/benefit analysis will be important in the evaluation. In contrast, if the research question has to do with ease of use of a given software product, surveys, focus groups, direct observation, and interviews may be required.

Adapting Research Methods to Biomedical Informatics

In the biomedical informatics realm, Friedman and Wyatt (2006) have written extensively about the use of evaluation research in informatics. Evaluation research is complicated because the intersection of computer science, evaluation methodology, and medicine and healthcare delivery must be considered (see figure 7.3). They provide five major aspects of research related to evaluating biomedical informatics applications:

1. Need for the resource
2. Design and development process
3. Resource static structure
4. Resource usability and dynamic functions
5. Resource effect and impact

Figure 7.3.   Complexity of evaluation in biomedical informatics

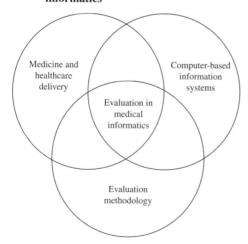

They further designate nine study types:

1. Needs assessment: the need for the resource and what is the problem

2. Design validation: design and development process relative to whether the resource is appropriately designed

3. Structure validation: resource static structure regarding whether the resource is appropriately designed to function as intended

4. Usability test: resource dynamic usability and function (can intended users navigate the resource so that it carries out intended functions)

5. Laboratory function test: resource dynamic usability and function (does the resource have the potential to be beneficial in the real world?)

6. Field function study: resource dynamic usability and function (does the resource have the potential to be beneficial in the real world?)

7. Lab user effect study: resource effect and impact (is the resource likely to change user behavior?)

8. Field user effect study: resource effect and impact (does the resource change actual user behavior in ways that are positive?)

9. Problem impact study: resource effect and impact (does the resource have a positive impact on the original problem?)

In addition to considering the intersection of several disciplines, it is also important to consider that there are multiple perspectives from which to examine the questions just discussed (see figure 7.4).

Joan Ash, PhD and her research team have conducted several studies that evaluated the use and impact of computerized physician order entry (CPOE). She has used both qualitative and quantitative methods. Success factors for implementing computerized physician order entry (CPOE) were identified in a study reported in 2005 (Ash et al. 2005) A multidisciplinary team of five qualitative researchers conducted observations, interviews, and focus groups. Data were analyzed using a combination of template and grounded theory approaches. The result was a description of 14 themes clustered into technology, organizational, personal, and environmental categories. An interesting finding was that although the results were

**Figure 7.4.   Differing perspectives on a clinical
information resource**

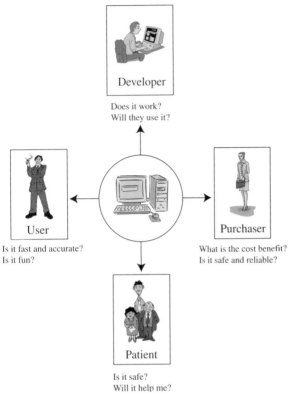

Copyright 2006 Springer Science and Business Media. Adapted with
kind permission

similar to inpatient study results, the outpatient investigation generated subtly different themes.

In another study (Ash et al. 2004), the implementation and use of CPOE were evaluated. A combined mail and telephone survey were used. The study concluded that despite the desirability of CPOE use, the data from the research indicated that at the time of the study only 9.6 percent of U.S. hospitals had CPOE completely available. Further, in those hospitals that had CPOE, its use was frequently required.

Ash and her team (2004) have studied unique and illuminating psychosocial issues in evaluation research. For example, a study reported in Ash et al.'s 2006 study found that an unintended consequence of CPOE implementation is "changes in the power structure" of the organization. The research resulted in recommendations for improved management of implementations. The shifts in power were related to work redistribution and safety initiatives. These issues were found to be related to a perceived loss of control and autonomy by clinicians.

The investigators concluded if the extent of these shifts are recognized, clinicians can anticipate these changes and not be surprised by them. The study recommendations also included involving providers in planning, quality initiatives, and the work of clinical information coalitions/committees.

In the book *Evaluation Methods in Biomedical Informatics*, Friedman and Wyatt (2006) discuss the use of a wide range of research constructs within the context of health informatics. In this text, both objectivist and subjectivist research approaches are considered and discussed. Further, in the book *Computer Applications in Health Care and Biomedicine*, Friedman et al. (2001) define these two terms.

- *Objectivist* is a term related to but distinct from "objective" and refers to philosophy of evaluation, which suggests the merit and worth of an information resource can, in principle, be measured with all observations yielding the same result and that a quantitative gold standard for performance can be identified and agreed upon.

- *Subjectivist* is a philosophy that suggests that what is observed about a resource depends in fundamental ways on the observer and the context of the observation, that observations may be more qualitative, and that legitimate disagreements can exist. They assert that both approaches are necessary because the research methods must follow from the research questions and the context of the evaluation. In addition to providing guidance on the design of evaluation studies, Friedman and Wyatt (2006) also examine how concepts such as measurement and observation can be used within the context of biomedical informatics.

Another excellent resource for evaluating a wide range of health information technology is the AHRQ's Evaluation Toolkit (Cusack and Poon 2007). This toolkit provides a user-friendly, step-by-step guide to evaluating health information technology. The toolkit helps in the development of evaluation goals, metrics, and methods to carry out the study. It also suggests that both quantitive and qualitative research methods be used to assess the technology.

Consumer Health Informatics Evaluation

The amount of health information and healthcare processes being published on the Internet is increasing.

Healthcare organizations may have routine forms on Web sites to facilitate such processes related to obtaining medical records. Some of the processes that may be explained on a Web site are:

- What is a valid authorization?
- Is there a fee to obtain medical records?
- Which records should be requested?
- Who can sign for a patient's medical records?

Other information related to the HIM department could include a map to locate the department, a discussion of the Health Insurance Portability and Accountability Act (HIPAA), and privacy statements.

HIM researchers can evaluate the design of the Web-based presentation of this material based on the model of consumer informatics presented in figures 7.5 and 7.6.

Lewis et al. (2005) also discuss methods to evaluate Web sites from the consumer perspective. Important aspects of Web site evaluation concern ethics, privacy, and accessibility. There also are specific criteria in use that guide evaluation, such as those developed by the Health Summit Working Group (HSWG) (Health Summit Working Group 1998) and Silberg et al. (1997). An important aspect of evaluating Web sites is the perspective of the site users. Both patients and nonpatients may

be frequent users. For example, physician office staff may use a site related to information release to teach patients how to request their own records. Or they may use it to design their own processes for release of information. When undertaking a formal evaluation of a Web site, it is important to consider all of the types of users in the evaluation design.

The HSWG developed criteria that can be used to assess a Web site for HIM practices. These criteria include:

- Credibility
- Content
- Disclosure
- Links
- Design
- Interactivity
- Caveats

Utilizing these criteria will help design Web sites that provide quality and accuracy of information in a format that allows easy and informed use of the content of the Web page. These aspects of quality were further reduced to a set of four criteria by Silberg et al. (1997):

1. Authorship: the authors, their credentials, and affiliations should be provided

2. Attribution: references, sources, and copyrighted material should be noted

3. Disclosure: the Web site ownership should be clearly denoted as should any sponsorship, advertising, underwriting, commercial funding arrangements, and potential conflicts of interest

4. Currency: the dates that content was posted and updated should be indicated

The use of evaluation to assess a given health or healthcare-related Web site is similar to the types of quality improvement efforts used to better meet the needs of those who use the services of the HIM department. It is important to evaluate a Web site that is related to the HIM department to make sure that it is user-friendly, accessible, up to date, and has the content that patients and their caregivers need. Individual organizations may have design criteria that can be combined with what is presented in this chapter. Common techniques used to evaluate a given Web site include using Web-based or paper-based survey tools, or by conducting focus groups. Marketing departments of organizations

Figure 7.5. A model for consumer health informatics.

(The consumer in this figure is meant to represent persons of all genders, races, and ethnicities.)

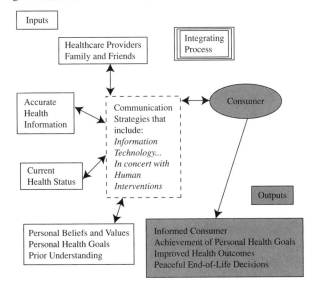

Copyright 2006 Springer Science and Business Media. Adapted with kind permission.

Figure 7.6.   Levels of accessibility barriers

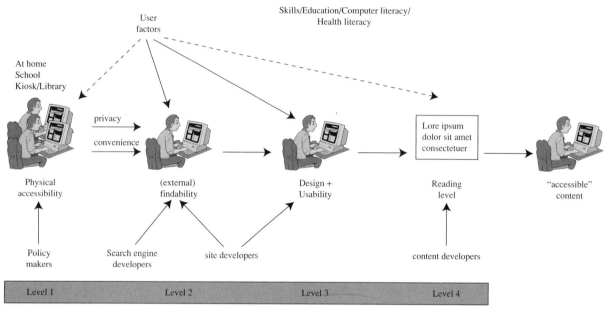

may have ongoing efforts to evaluate Web applications. Becoming involved in these efforts may be welcomed by those conducting the evaluations. This type of collaboration results in efficient use of resources and allows HIM professionals to gain greater understanding of consumer informatics evaluation research.

Evaluation Research in Informatics Education

An important area of evaluation research for education is outcomes assessment. Many accrediting agencies and organizations require that education outcomes be evaluated. The specific method used to assess outcomes may be specified by the accreditation organization (AHIMA 2005) or may be up to the institution of higher learning (Middle States 2005). An example of the evaluation of an informatics educational program is presented in an article by Patel et al. (2005). In this evaluation both qualitative and quantitative methods were used to determine the impact of a short course sponsored by the National Library of Medicine. The course and the extent to which the objectives of the program were achieved were measured. Studies were conducted to examine the participants' perceptions

of both the short-term and the long-term influences on knowledge, skills, and behavior. The methods used were questionnaires, semistructured telephone interviews, and participant observation methods. Many of the participants feel and show evidence of becoming effective agents of change in their institutions in the area of medical informatics, which is one of the objectives of the program.

Summary

Evaluation research has broad applications in the work that HIM professionals undertake. Given their broad training in clinical practice workflow and information flow from the point of care, to clinical documentation, to coding of clinical encounters, HIM professionals have a great deal to contribute to evaluation research techniques in existing areas of investigation such as those discussed in this chapter, as well as in new areas. The easiest way to get started in evaluation research is to partner with individuals who have expertise in the chosen area, followed by applying the principles learned to new areas. Evaluation research does not have to be complex or extensive. Important areas in which to pursue this type of research include coding accuracy, implementation of EHRs, and consumer informatics.

References

American Health Information Management Association. 1999. *Evolving HIM Careers: Seven Roles for the Future.* Chicago: AHIMA.

American Health Information Management Association, Commission on Accreditation for Health Informatics and Information Management Education. 2005. 2005 Interpretation of Standards and Items of Evidence (Baccalaureate Degree). Chicago: AHIMA/CAHIIM.

Altschuld, J.W., and B.R. Witkin. 2000. *From Needs Assessment to Action: Transforming Needs into Solution Strategies.* Thousand Oaks, CA: Sage Publications.

American College of Surgeons, Commission on Cancer. 2006. http://www.facs.org/cancer/coc/programstandards.html

Ash, J.S., Sittig, D.F., Campbell, E., Guappone, K., and R. Dykstra. 2006. An Unintended Consequence of CPOE Implementation: Shifts in Power, Control, and Autonomy. *American Medical Informatics Association 2006 Symposium Proceedings,* Washington, DC, p. 11.

Ash, J.S., Chin, H.L., Sittig, D.F., and R. Dykstra. 2005. Ambulatory Computerized Physician Order Entry Implementation. *American Medical Informatics Association 2005 Symposium Proceedings,* Washington, DC, p. 11.

Ash, J.S., Paul, N., Gorman, N., Seshadri, V., and W.R. Hersh. 2004. Computerized physician order entry in U.S. hospitals: Results of a 2002 survey. *Journal of the American Medical Informatics Association* 11(2): 95–99.

Ashish, K., Jha, E., Orav, J., Li, Z., and A.M. Epstein. 2007 (July/August). The inverse relationship between mortality rates and performance in the hospital quality alliance measures. *Health Affairs* 26(4):1104–1110.

Baily, M.A., Bottrell, M., Lynn, J., and B. Jennings. 2006. The ethics of using QI methods to improve health care quality and safety. Hastings Center Report. S1–40.

Cusack, C.M., and E.G. Poon. 2007 (June 19). Evaluation Toolkit, Version 3. Washington, DC: AHRQ.

Elixhauser, A., et al. 1998. Comorbidity measures for use with administrative data. *Medical Care* 36(1):8–27

Friedman, C.P., and J.C. Wyatt. 2006. *Evaluation Methods in Biomedical Informatics,* 2nd ed. New York: Springer.

Friedman, C.P, Owens, D.K., and J.C. Wyatt. (2001) Evaluation and technology assessment. In *Medical Informatics: Computer Applications in Health Care and Biomedicine,* edited by E.H. Shortliffe and L.E. Perreault. 2nd ed., New York: Springer.

Garvin, J., and V. Watzlaf. 2004 (Spring). Current coding competency compared to projected competency. *Perspectives in Health Information Management* 1(2):19–29.

Health Summit Working Group. 1998. Policy paper: Criteria for assessing the quality of health information on the Internet. Agency for Health Care Policy and Research, confer-

ence grant R13 HS09549-01. Falls Church, VA: Mitretek Systems (Noblis). Available online from http://hitiweb.mitretek.org/docs/policy.pdf.

Jackson, L.A., et al. 2003. Effectiveness of pneumococcal polysaccharide vaccine in older adults. *New England Journal of Medicine* 348(18):1747–55.

Jha, A.K., Orav, E.J., Li, Z., and A.M. Epstein. 2007 (July/August). The inverse relationship between mortality rates and performance in the hospital quality alliance measures. *Health Affairs* 26(4):1104–10.

Lewis, D., Eysenbach, G., Kukafka, R., Stavri, P., Zoe, P., and H. Jimison, eds. 2005. *Consumer Health Informatics: Informing Consumers and Improving Health Care.* New York: Springer Science+Business Media.

Lloyd, S.S., and J.P. Rissing. 1985. Physician and coding errors in patient records. *Journal of the American Medical Association* 254 (10):1330–6.

Middle States Commission on Higher Education. 2005. *Assessing Student Learning and Institutional Effectiveness: Understanding Middle States Expectations.* Philadelphia: Middle States Commission on Higher Education.

Miller, R.H., West, C., Brown, T.M., Sim, I., and C. Ganchoff. 2005 (September/October). The value of electronic health records in solo or small group practices. *Health Affaire* 24(5):1127–37.

O'Malley, K.J., et al. 2005 (October). Measuring diagnoses: ICD code accuracy. *Health Services Research* 40(5):1625. In Measurement challenges in health services research: Population, setting, and methodology considerations, Kuykendall, D.H., and A.L. Siu, guest editors. A special issue of *Health Services Research* 40(5):Part II.

Patel, V.L., Branch, T., Cimino, A., Norton, C., and J.J. Cimino. 2005. Participant perceptions of the influences of the NLM-Sponsored Woods Hole medical informatics course. *Journal of the American Medical Informatics Association* 12:256–262.

Russell L.B., Gold, M.R., Siegal, J.E., Daniels, N., and M.C. Weinstein. 1996. The role of cost-effectiveness analysis n health medicine. Panel on cost-effectiveness in health and medicine. *Journal of the American Medical Association* 276:1172–77.

Shah, N.R., Seger, A.C., Seger, D.L., Fiskio, J.M., Kuperman, G.J., Blumenfeld, B., Recklet, E.G., Bates, D.W., and T.K. Gandh. 2005. Improving acceptance of computerized prescribing alerts in ambulatory care. *Journal of the American Medical Informatics Association* 13:5–11.

Silberg, W., Lundberg, D., and R. Musacchio, R. 1997. Assessing, controlling, and assuring the quality of medical information on the Internet: Caveant lector et viewor-Let the reader and viewer beware. *Journal of the American Medical Association* 277:1244–45.

Smith, P.C., et al. 2005. Missing clinical information during primary care visits. *Journal of the American Medical Association* 293:565–71.

Trochim, W., and J.P. Donnelly. 2006 (Oct. 20). The Research Methods Knowledge Base. Web Center for Social Research Methods. Available online from socialresearch-methods.net/kb/index.php.

Weingart, S.N., et al. 2003. Physicians' decision to override computerized drug alerts in primary care. *Archives of Internal Medicine* 163:2625–31.

Chapter 8
Research Reviews and Secondary Analysis

William J. Rudman, PhD, Susan Hart-Hester, PhD, and C. Andrew Brown, MD, MPH

Learning Objectives

- Understand basic concepts of the systematic research review process.
- Understand the steps and techniques in conducting various types of qualitative analysis such as meta-analysis and the constant comparative method.
- Understand how qualitative theory, for example, grounded theory, is used to guide the research process.

Key Terms

Acyclic graph
Area under the curve
Binning
Confusion matrix
Constant comparative method
Cross-validation
Data extraction
Defining the project scope
Defining the terms
Descriptive map
Documentation
Epistemological assumptions
Feature analogs
Focused modeling
Gap analysis
Global modeling
Inclusion/exclusion criteria
Integrative analytical methods
Interim report
Interpretive analysis

Iterative modeling process
Literature reviews
Machine learning
Manual modeling
Meta-analysis
Naïve modeling
Narrative analysis
Ontological assumptions
Positive predictive value
Preliminary modeling
Probabilistic models
Quality appraisal
Queue learning
Receiver-operator characteristic
Research protocol
Screening process
Semantic ontology
Stepwise modeling process
Synthesis of data
Systematic research review (SRR)

Introduction

In this current age of information overload, it is estimated that:

- 3,000 new books are published every day
- 800 megabytes of information per person are stored every year
- 2.7 billion Google searches are performed every month
- The amount of information doubles every 2 years and is expected, by 2010, to double every 72 hours

It is estimated that the United States produces approximately 40 percent of the world's new stored information. As information expands at an exponential rate, it has become increasingly clear that not all information is knowledge. One way that researchers can judge the value as well as organize the volume of information produced every day is through systematic research reviews.

Traditionally, reviews of research evidence have taken the form of literature reviews; however, such reviews are prone to bias and random error (chance errors). These limitations may surface throughout the review process in the selection of search databases, indexing terminology, and/or study selection (EPPI-Centre 2007, South African Medical Research Council 2007). The more rigorous systematic review addresses these limitations through several key features:

- Identifying a specific research question
- Utilizing explicit methods and process stages
- Utilizing methodology and results that are transparent, replicable, and updatable
- Utilizing empirical research evidence
- Utilizing consumers/users in the review process

The systematic method of gathering, synthesizing, and evaluating evidence has evolved greatly over the past half century. Formally termed **meta-analysis** by Glass in 1976, the systematic review of evidence was applied to areas such as psychotherapy, public policy, and social interventions. Ultimately, this systematic approach to the review of research evidence moved further into the healthcare arena and provided the foundation for the practice of evidence-based medicine. This systematic approach is known as **systematic research review**

(SRR) (Stevens 2001). In general, SRR has become the method by which policy decisions are often based. For example, the Institute of Medicine's (IOM) 2001 report, *Crossing the Quality Chasm*, became the primary data source for patient safety initiatives, integration of health information technology (HIT), and eventually, the National Health Information Network (NHIN) architecture as defined by the Department of Health and Human Services (HHS).

The goals of SRRs are twofold:

1. Compile an exhaustive literature review
2. Determine best practices in a relevant work area

The aims of SRRs are to:

1. Reduce evaluator bias
2. Create greater transparency and replicability of prior research
3. Provide a consistent overview of prior work

SRR is a dynamic process that changes as the literature in a specific area grows and changes. SRR can be applied to any research question or method of analysis.

This chapter will detail 10 elements surrounding the process of systematic reviews. Steps involved in a systematic review discussed in this chapter are shown in figure 8.1.

Figure 8.1.   Systematic review process

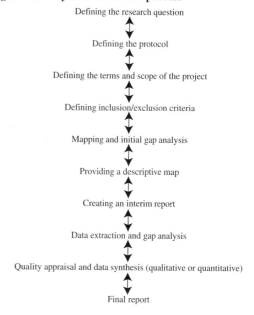

Defining the research question

Defining the protocol

Defining the terms and scope of the project

Defining inclusion/exclusion criteria

Mapping and initial gap analysis

Providing a descriptive map

Creating an interim report

Data extraction and gap analysis

Quality appraisal and data synthesis (qualitative or quantitative)

Final report

In order to understand the evolution of the movement toward evidence-based decisions, it is important to understand the features of an SRR. Specifically, the process of an SRR as presented in this chapter will be developed through answering questions surrounding EHR integration in small physician offices, using a quantitative data synthesis, and employing Bayesian Belief modeling networks (see chapter 1).

Defining the Research Question

The systematic review process shown in figure 8.1 identifies the methodological processes involved in a systematic review. Systematic review methods involve comprehensive coverage of current knowledge that exists to answer specific questions; therefore, the first step (that is, identifying a research question or identification of the problem) lays the foundation upon which the review is built (Russell 2005).

The most important step in any research process is explicitly defining the research question. Because defining the research question is based on an iterative process, the research question may develop further over time, as presented in figure 8.1. The research question determines the configuration of the research review team. The research review team should consist of experts in the field who provide complementary knowledge. In this chapter's example, integration of EHRs in small physician offices, the research review team consists of physicians, economists, academics who conduct research on EHR adoption/benefits/barriers, HIT experts, and statistical modelers. Members of the research review panel bring an interdisciplinary knowledge base that will help refine the research question, develop the protocol, and define the inclusion/exclusion criteria for the literature review.

Defining the Research Protocol

The **research protocol** defines the methodology that will be followed in collecting, synthesizing, and analyzing the research literature review or data. The protocol enables the research review team to address potential bias because it is developed a priori (not based on a prior example). Guidelines for how the review will be carried out are established prior to the beginning of any work. The establishment of review guidelines in advance of actual work maintains focus on the actual research question and reduces the potential for research review team

members to reframe the initial question but provides the option of expanding the scope of the question based on ongoing research findings. The review protocol includes a brief introductory narrative that links the research question to an identified need or gap in existing knowledge.

Defining Terms and Scope of the Project

Defining the terms to be used in the SRR is an essential step in the process. Although this step may seem simple and straightforward, it is often the step where the greatest amount of controversy and debate exists. In the example, the first two terms to be defined are: small physician office and EHR. Intuitively, each member of the research review team had preexisting definitions of each term. However, as the research review team began discussing appropriate definitions, it became apparent that definitions varied by discipline and even geography. Research review team members who lived in urban areas defined small physician offices as those having fewer than 10 physicians whereas those living in rural states defined small physician offices as three or fewer physicians. In fact, for research review team members who live in rural states, most of the critical-care hospitals have five or fewer physicians. Similarly, there is no consensus on what defines an EHR. After much debate and controversy, small physician offices were defined as those having fewer than 10 physicians and EHR definitions were based on functionality.

Defining the project scope began by developing a directed literature review on background issues, significance of the problem, and legislative or regulatory issues. The scope is not a comprehensive literature review but is used to develop a framework on which the inclusion and exclusion criteria may be based. In the example, little if any research had been conducted on EHR or HIT integration in small physician offices. Most of the work focused on large urban areas and hospitals. This finding significantly impacted the inclusion/exclusion criteria, which is the next step in the review process.

Defining the Inclusion/Exclusion Criteria

Defining the inclusion/exclusion criteria should evolve from the research question, the definition of terms and background provided in the directed review. **Inclusion/ exclusion criteria** explicitly define parameters for including or excluding studies as part of the comprehensive literature review. Along with the criteria, the process for determining these criteria will be part of the protocol. Given the lack of quantitative research studies on EHR or HIT integration in small physician offices, the inclusion criteria expanded to include EHR or HIT integration in healthcare facilities regardless of type or size. The primary exclusion criteria applied in the example focused on studies that did not use accepted quantitative methods of data collection and analysis. In other words, qualitative research designs were excluded from the SRR.

Literature Review and Mapping Process

The purpose of the literature review is to identify current knowledge that addresses the research question. **Literature reviews** are independent scholarly works, published as articles or entire books. Search strategies may involve the use of applicable information and/or data sets from electronic databases such as PubMed (http://www.ncbi. nlm.nih.gov/sites/entrez), the Internet (government white papers and reports), and consumer expertise/information, as well as data not yet in published format such as conference presentations and foundation white papers. The inclusion/exclusion criteria will determine the type and scope of literature to be included in the review process. Searches based on broad inclusion criteria may identify a larger number of studies/information; however, broader search criteria may lead to a number of studies that lack scientific rigor. On the other hand, narrowing the search criteria to quantitative studies published in peer-reviewed journals may limit the amount of information relevant to the research question. Based on the preagreed inclusion/ exclusion criteria established in the protocol by the research review team, the search strategy will be limited by terminology specific to the databases, language restrictions for studies included in the search, and timeframes (for example, 2000–2007). Typically, "goodness of fit" search criteria determine where the initial search is conducted and define the time frame during which data are to be collected. An important part of this process is to determine a cutoff date on which data to be used in framing the research question and the database will be completed.

The **screening process** begins by a review of study abstracts followed by a second screening of complete articles. In order to address the possibility for error and bias, more than one reviewer is required to be involved in the screening process. At this point an initial **gap analysis** is performed. The research review team examines the collected literature and data to assess whether gaps exist, and then provides guidance to those conducting the literature review on additional literature and data sources missed during the initial review.

Descriptive Map

In order to organize the information obtained through the literature searches and other relevant databases previously identified, a descriptive map is developed. The **descriptive map** usually takes the form of a matrix where predetermined criteria are identified. This process identifies relevant studies by specific keywords or codes developed by the research review team; for example, authors, publication date, type of publication, topic, research design, outcomes, population, or data source.

Descriptive maps provide a structured view of selected studies and/or user information. Descriptive maps using a category keyword or code provide a method that allows the research review team to quickly navigate a complex and in-depth literature review. The descriptive map does not provide an in-depth review of studies within the literature review. In-depth reviews provide added details pertaining to relevant studies and involve the identification of specific data to be extracted and further synthesized for selected studies. The utilization of descriptive maps enables the research review team to summarize information within the matrix by (quantitative) numerical measures and/or (qualitative) interpretive themes.

Creating an Interim Report

The **interim report** allows the research review team to summarize precise details that have provided the framework for the SRR; for example, the selection of the research question, selection of the research review team, protocol guidelines, definition of terms and inclusion/exclusion criteria. This report allows the research review team to periodically self-assess the methodology appropriateness and continued relevance of the research question. In the analysis of the impact of HIT in small physician offices, the interim report provided the opportunity to share ideas and findings with other experts in the field and to begin the initial gap analysis. This process provides validation of the initial report as well as data to begin the formal gap analysis process.

Data Extraction

Once the screenings and descriptive mapping have enabled the research review team to identify a selected number of studies for more in-depth analysis, **data extraction** can begin. At this stage of review, the full study text is reviewed for selected articles and/or information from other data sources. Specific information is extracted in a manner that fosters consistency and reliability among reviewers.

Formats for data extraction may vary from handwritten forms to review software. Because a major advantage of SRR is transparency, uniformity of interpretation on elements identified on the data extraction form is essential. The assignment of more than one person to extract data strengthens the review against bias and error. Data extracted from the studies are vital to the synthesis of information that addresses the initial question/topic.

After the initial data extraction, formal gap analysis begins. Gap analysis is used to identify areas of deficiency in both prior research and theory. Whether utilizing quantitative or qualitative data, two methods are generally used to close gaps in current research. Based on the scope of the project (money and time), either new data are collected or statistical modeling methods are used to predict missing data. In the example, very little is known about deadoption of HIT among healthcare providers. To overcome this gap in knowledge, a survey was used to collect data on reasons why healthcare providers stopped using EHR in their practices. These data were then placed into the data modeling algorithms to provide a more complete picture of HIT utilization among small physician offices. If it is not feasible to collect new data, various inferential methods (for example, multivariate regression, logistical regression, Bayesian analysis) may be used to predict missing data points.

Quality Appraisal and Data Synthesis

An important ingredient in the SRR is the **quality appraisal** of studies included within the review. This appraisal identifies research methodology within the study that either strengthens or weakens the credibility of the outcomes. Therefore, quality appraisal of included studies (qualitative or quantitative) involves weighting so that their level of significance to the research question can be assessed. Studies may be deemed weaker in design due to such factors as sampling bias, number of participants, lack of statistical power, missing data, or statistical errors. Such factors affect the relevance of study results to the initial research question.

This **synthesis of data** may utilize two basic forms, interpretive (qualitative) approaches and integrative (quantitative) methods. Interpretive research approaches information synthesis based on **epistemological** (origins of knowledge) or **ontological** (existing) **assumptions** concerning the nature of knowledge and socially constructed relationships. An interpretive approach employs qualitative methods and theory generally derived from phenomenology, or more recently, grounded theory. Grounded theory is important in that it allows a researcher to focus on interpreting relationships and examining the underlying belief systems that define an individual response and motivation (see chapter 4). **Interpretive analysis** allows for a more rigorous interpretation of data in that it forces researchers and participants to not only examine themes and patterns, but to recognize and identify relationships.

The most commonly used method of interpretive analysis, and perhaps the most scientifically rigorous, is the constant comparative method (see chapter 4). The constant comparative method is used to extract, identify, and structure themes utilized in data analysis. The **constant comparative method** (figure 8.2) is an iterative methodology that allows researchers to compare and refine results as data are mined.

Figure 8.2.   Constant comparative method

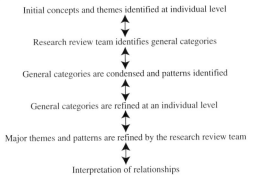

Initial concepts and themes identified at individual level

Research review team identifies general categories

General categories are condensed and patterns identified

General categories are refined at an individual level

Major themes and patterns are refined by the research review team

Interpretation of relationships

Step 1: The research team identifies concepts and themes.

Step 2: The research team is brought together to compare initial analysis of concepts/themes, and to develop categories.

Step 3: The research team members reanalyze concepts and themes within the context of categories identified by the group.

Step 4: The research review team meets for a second time, categories are condensed, and major themes and patterns are further refined.

Step 5: Categories and themes are reanalyzed independent of the group in order to assure validity and, finally, researchers are brought back together, relationships are discussed, and underlying themes identified.

Narrative analysis offers researchers an opportunity to demonstrate thorough analysis of personal accounts or themes within an individual's experiences. Narrative analysis is best used in qualitative research by recreating the individual's experience and allowing the researcher to identify empathetically with the person and their social context. Although narrative analysis cannot solely prove theoretical or scientific truth, it can illustrate points more thoroughly and vividly than can other avenues of analysis. Narrative analysis captures a narrative, or story, of a person that illustrates a particular social, clinical, or medical point and analyzes that story for its instructional value. Narrative analysis *suggests* causal links between ideas and allows the discovery of particular themes in an individual's experiences, framing the experience in its social setting.

On the other hand, **integrative analytical methods** combine data through a number of mechanisms, for example, meta-analysis, modeling, consensus development (group judgments), systematic literature reviews, unstructured literature reviews, and expert opinions (National Information Center on Health Services Research and Health Care Technology 2004, Dickersin and Berlin 1992). Meta-analysis joins systematic qualitative analysis with statistical quantitative methods to provide a structure for in-depth research reviews. Meta-analysis may combine studies with smaller sample sizes and less statistical power with more definitive studies in an effort to pool data, identifying an actual treatment effect. Techniques associated with meta-analysis adjust for biases such as those based on weak study design, limited data, publication bias, and/or

insufficient number of studies related to the research question. However, utilizing meta-analysis within a systematic approach can reduce these potential biases and minimize their effects on results. In the example, quantitative integrative analysis is used to synthesize data. Specifically, a full Bayesian Belief network analysis was used to synthesize the various quantitative data sources.

Final Report

Ultimately, data extracted from the included studies will be analyzed and synthesized into a final report. The final report is comprehensive and provides explicit details about the review process from the steps involved in the identification of the research question to data extraction and synthesis.

The example presented in the next section is intended to provide information on how systematic review is used on quantitative data using a Bayesian modeling technique. The discussion starts with a data set on EHR adoption using data from the Texas Medical Association (TMA 2005); how other data sets are mapped to fill in gaps and complement the existing data; modeling methods used in this example; and validation methods.

Step One: Single Set Example

Results of a 2005 TMA survey consisting of 1,772 responses from small ambulatory care practices across Texas are used for this example. Figure 8.3 is an example model based on a subset of the TMA data. In this model, the primary predictors of adoption are the cost of the system, benefits of the system, and the status of the practice (that is, active practice and time to retirement). As the network is examined more closely, it is clear that benefits and cost are related to concerns about system reliability, data entry issues, and implementation time.

Using the model, how observed factors influence outcomes of interest can be calculated. Table 8.1 details how various combinations of system cost perceptions, system benefits perceptions, and practice status influence probable EHR adoption attitudes.

Those physicians who are close to retirement are unlikely to have any plans to implement an EHR, whereas those active practices in which costs are perceived as low and benefits as high either have implemented or plan to implement an EHR. In preliminary cross-validation, this network generated an area-under-the curve for nonimplementation of 93.5 percent and an overall

Figure 8.3.   Bayesian network of Texas Medical Association data subset

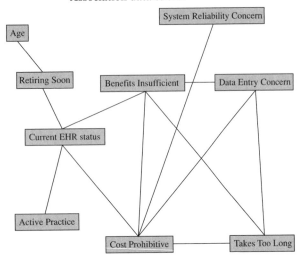

predictive value of 70.2 percent. Interpretation of these cross-validation statistics will be discussed later.

Step 2: Mapping Other Data Sets for Systematic Review

The TMA data set is one of several available to study clinician perceptions and actions relating to EHR adoption. In order to develop the most globally applicable model, a researcher must try to account for as many factors as possible as universally as possible. This should support the development of a more robust model. In order to

assess and incorporate additional data sets into a model, the researcher must perform three functions:

1. Feature set selection
2. Data set selection and quality assessment
3. Development of a semantic ontology

Researchers must first identify pertinent features of the problem or domain to be modeled. These features support the distinct elements to be used for model prediction/estimation of outcomes as well as the semantic structure of these elements. A feature is a specific element of the domain that can be used either as an independent variable (predictor) or a dependent variable (prediction). Each feature represents an individual element that can be quantified or described for the purpose of calculating an outcome. It is unique from all other features, but not necessarily mutually exclusive. Each feature must have a concise description, data type, and listing of allowable values.

To identify and specify features, the researcher should use a three-tier method. The first tier is to conduct a literature/data review in order to identify those features specified/studied in the literature and in existing data sets. The second tier is research team input—what feature does the team think is missing from the domain? The third and final tier is expert review; using thought leaders and acknowledged domain experts to refine the specified features by adding, deleting, and refining the list of features and their acceptable values and data types.

One critical element of feature specification is the development of a semantic ontology to support domain

Table 8.1.   Texas Medical Association data inference table, frequency of case, and current EHR status

Probability of case	Drivers			Target			
	Benefits Insufficient	Cost Prohibitive	Retiring Soon	Current EHR status			
				Currently use	No plans	Plan to impl...	MISSING
75.284%	No	No	No	34.4	4.1	58.7	2.9
2.619%	Yes	No	No	2.1	88.5	2.1	7.2
4.828%	No	Yes	No	0.6	93.3	0.6	5.6
10.266%	Yes	Yes	No	0.3	95.5	0.3	3.9
1.471%	No	No	Yes	3.8	67.8	3.8	24.6
0.782%	Yes	No	Yes	0.0	96.0	0.0	4.0
1.503%	No	Yes	Yes	0.0	97.0	0.0	3.0
3.243%	Yes	Yes	Yes	0.0	97.9	0.0	2.1

modeling. The researcher needs to develop a standard **semantic ontology**, or system of describing knowledge, for the integration of heterogeneous data sets to be used in modeling. These semantics will allow the researcher to normalize all of the data sets to a common set of features and values that can support modeling. In order to ensure that the ontology used is as representative of the domain as possible, researchers should use widely accepted sources for their ontology development, such as existing ontologies, benchmark surveys, and the literature.

Once a set of features is identified and a semantic ontology designed, the researchers need to identify survey data and map this data to the common semantic ontology in a database. Each data set should be assessed for data quality, survey method, and statistical power. Those data sets that are of sufficient quality need to be mapped to the semantic ontology. As these data sets are mapped, researchers need to be aware of several common data quality pitfalls:

- Sparse data. Data sets that have very few respondents create features with very sparse data and tend to be unrepresentative.

- Numeric fields. Many surveys collect numeric values in the form of ranges rather than specific values. Researchers must identify the optimal way to normalize these values.

- Qualitative answers. Mapping differing semantic ontologies to a common ontology can be very difficult. Often, words of a similar meaning, such as "unknown," "no answer," and "indifferent" must be effectively mapped.

Step 3: Modeling Method

The TMA data in this example was modeled using a Bayesian Belief network (BN). In dealing with the problem of missing data in meta-analyses, BN techniques present methods for assessing the relative contribution of features to the domain. These network meta-analysis techniques allow estimation of both heterogeneity and inconsistency (incoherence) in the evidence from different pairs of treatments (Owens et al. 1997). This is known as probabilistic inference. Given a set of observations of the values of some of the domain attributes, the conditional probability distributions of one or more of the remaining attributes can be calculated. The BN allows researchers to predict the likelihood of the vari-

ous states in nonobserved variables based on the states of observed variables. BNs derived from such meta-analyses are **probabilistic models** that can represent complex interrelationships between variables. It is an intuitively appealing structure for reasoning with probabilities that can be used for interpretation and prediction purposes. BNs are graphical models capable of encoding probabilistic relationships among elements in a domain (Miller and Sim 2004). What makes this methodological approach advantageous in the context of systemic review are the following concepts:

1. BNs are known for their transparency, so the model is easily interpreted.

2. BNs are designed to deal with uncertainty.

3. BNs are characterized as having an intuitive usage, which is attractive in complex modeling problems such as systematic review.

4. The probabilistic inference capability of BNs facilitate predictions about unobserved data that could allow for the filling of data gaps.

5. BNs and machine learning technology support complex optimizations.

BNs encode the information structure of the problem using conditional dependence relationships between variables (for example, the statistical likelihood of an outcome given the presence or absence of other factors) in a directed acyclic graph. The networks are directed **acyclic graphs** that incorporate parent-child relationships between nodes. The structure of the network provides the user with immediate knowledge about the nature of the problem set and the hierarchy of features to the outcome of interest. By entering current knowledge into the model, the user obtains a probability of outcome, and relative risk in real time. Further, the graphical representation of the network also provides the user with likely rationale for the outcome and knowledge about additional information required to confirm or refute the predicted outcome.

The BNs created using the TMA data were developed using machine learning technology. **Machine learning** is a field of computer science that uses intelligent algorithms to allow a computer to mimic the process of human learning. The learning algorithm allows the computer to learn dynamically from the data that reside in the database. Prior probabilities are derived from the data to be modeled by calculating a distribution of discrete states or using equal area binning in the case of continuous variables. The machine learning algorithms automatically detect and promote significant relationships between variables, without the need for human interaction. This allows for the processing of vast amounts of complex data quickly and easily. This type of high dimensionality analysis is well suited to systematic review and meta-analysis.

BNs are developed and maintained using an ongoing cyclical process of data collection, classifier training, validation and deployment, use and verification, and retraining, as described in figure 8.3 (p. 186). It is important to note models are, by definition, not static. As new data are collected from a variety of sources, they can be used to enhance the richness and predictive accuracy of the model. Initial classifier training and subsequent retraining should be performed using a **stepwise** or **iterative modeling process** to ensure the highest quality model (see figure 8.4). The modeling process is an iterative process consisting of several steps. The goal of the process is to streamline variable selection and preparation to produce the optimum outcome by selecting the best model, performing rigorous validation, and providing thorough documentation. The process for creating a model is:

1. **Preliminary modeling**

   Identify appropriate machine learning parameters.

   Identify base level of correlation in the dataset.

   Identify obvious correlations that are interfering with the base level (confounding features).

   Identify and remove **feature analogs** (features that are proxies for one another and reduce accuracy).

2. **Global modeling**

   Set appropriate machine learning parameters.

   Make appropriate changes to data set, including removal of analogs and confounding features and further **binning** (categorizing).

   Run full **queue learning** to observe global data structure and strong meaningful correlations. Explore model relative to literature and domain expertise as a "sanity check" and to analyze relationships.

3. **Naïve Modeling**

   Perform linear naïve modeling on dependent outcomes of interest to identify relative contribution of features

   Develop quantitative contribution report

4. **Focused Modeling**

   Run "queue learning" using only subsets of variables identified in prior steps to obtain a more focused network than the one obtained in global modeling. By excluding certain variables the remaining ones are explored more exhaustively.

   Focused modeling is superior to a naïve model as interdependence among features related to the target(s) is taken into account when analyzing the combined effect of several features on the target(s).

   Explore focused model and automatically create preliminary reports.

5. **Manual Modeling**

   Enhance focused modeling by changing structure of relationships and manually incorporating expert information beyond what the data contains using appropriate user interface in software.

6. **Cross-Validation**

   A global or focused modeling classifier will be trained on each of the 10 training sets created in the data preparation step using the same data discretization and modeling parameters.

   Each corresponding test set is used to create a set of case-specific predictions.

   A **receiver-operator characteristic (ROC)** curve is plotted for each test exercise to calculate classification accuracy.

Figure 8.4.   Iterative model development

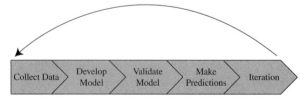

7. **Documentation**

Upon completion, the best model is documented in XML format for deployment into the predictive pathology platform.

The relevant learning parameter and modeling log files will be stored for future audit purposes if required.

Once the best classifier for each training set is selected, the network will be validated using a train-and-test cross-validation methodology. For this example 10-fold cross validation was used, wherein the data set will be randomized into ten separate and unique train and test sets, each set consisting of a training set consisting of 90 percent of records and a test set consisting of the remaining 10 percent. A model is trained on each of the 10 training sets. The test set corresponding to each training set is input into the model to generate a case-specific prediction for each test record for variables of interest. The test set predictions are then used to calculate a ROC curve and **confusion matrix** by threshold for each test set by feature of interest. (See sample ROC curve in figure 8.5.) The curve is calculated by comparing the predicted value for each feature of interest to the known

Figure 8.5.   Sample ROC curve

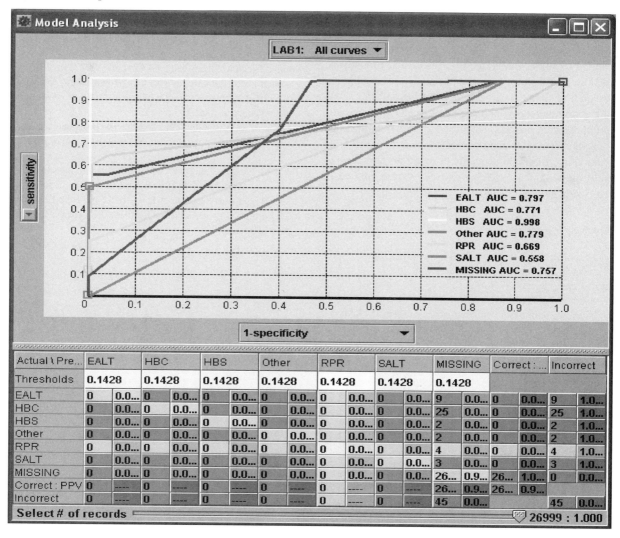

value in the test set on a case-specific basis. This curve is then used to calculate the **area under the curve**, a metric of overall model quality, and **positive predictive value**, a measure of the probability that a positive result is a true positive given a specified probability threshold for the variable of interest.

Summary

As the amount of scientific information grows at an exponential rate, it becomes increasing important to rigorously analyze and use this information. SRR methodologies provide techniques that allow researchers to collate, map, and analyze disparate data in a meaningful way. SRR is a process that provides a structure upon which researchers can systematically evaluate literature in a specific area in a dynamic manner. SRR can be applied to any research question or method of analysis. SRR is useful in eliminating researcher bias, allowing research findings to be extrapolated beyond the scope of the original study; and provides greater transparency in the research process. By providing this much-needed transparency, SRR methodologies provide a reliable method in critiquing the quality of research. This is especially important when research findings are applied in real-world situations to meet real-world needs.

References

Dickersin, K. and J. Berlin. 1992. Meta-analysis: State of the science. *Epidemiologic Reviews* 14:154–76.

EPPI-Centre. Systematic Research Synthesis. London: Social Science Research Unit, Institute of Education. Available online from http://eppi.ioe.ac.uk/cms/Default.aspx?tabid=67.

Glass, G.V. 1976. Primary, secondary and meta-analysis of research. *Educational Researcher* 5:3–8.

Institute of Medicine. 2001. *Crossing the Quality Chasm: A New Health System for the 21st Century*. Washington, DC: National Academies Press.

Miller, R., and I. Sim. 2004. Physicians' use of electronic medical records: Barriers and solutions. *Health Affairs* 23(2):116–26.

National Information Center on Health Services Research and Health Care Technology. 2004 (August). Primary data and integrative methods. Bethesda, MD: NICHSR. Available online from http:www.nlm.nih.gov/nichsr/hta101/ta10105.html.

Owens, D.K., Shachter, R.D., and R.F. Nease. 1997. Representation and analysis of medical decision problems with influence diagrams. *Medical Decision Making* 17(3):241–62.

Russell, C. 2005. An overview of the integrative research review. *Progress in Transplantation*. 15:8–13.

South African Medical Research Council. 2007 (Jan. 29). What is a systematic review? Cape Town: South African Cochrane Centre. Available online from http://www.mrc.ac.za/cochrane/systematic.htm.

Stevens, K. 2001. Systematic reviews: The heart of evidence-based practice. *AACN Advanced Critical Care* 12:259–538.

Texas Medical Association. 2005. *TMA Special Survey, Electronic Medical Record System Implementation*. Eric Ford, Ph.D. and Lori Peterson at Texas Tech, and John Eberhardt and Phil Kalina at DecisionQ. Austin, TX: Texas Medical Association.

PART III

Research Process

Chapter 9
Identifying and Delineating the Research Question or Problem

Elizabeth J. Layman, PhD, RHIA, CCS, FAHIMA

Learning Objectives

- To formulate research problems in terms of research questions
- To search knowledge bases such as bibliographic databases
- To synthesize information in articles and other scholarly sources into logical, precise, and succinct literature reviews that present compelling rationales
- To articulate clear hypotheses related to research questions
- To specify unambiguous purposes of the research
- To select designs and methods for research projects appropriate to the research questions

Key Terms

Abstract
Accepted theory
Alpha levels (α)
Alternative hypothesis (H_A)
Beta (β)
Confidence interval (CI)
Confidence level
Equitable coverage
External validity
Generalizability
Hypothesis
Internal validity
Literature review
Meta-analysis
Mortality (attrition)
Null hypothesis (H_0)
One-tailed (directional) hypothesis
Operationalize
ρ value
Parsimony
Peer

Peer review
Peer reviewed
Peer reviewer
Power
Primary source
Purpose statement
Research problem
Research question
Sample
Secondary source
Significance
Significance level
Significance (hypothesis or null hypothesis) testing
Statistical significance
Systematic review
Transparency
Two-tailed (nondirectional) hypothesis
Type I errors
Type II errors
Validity

Introduction

Research is the systematic process of investigation that discovers, interprets, or revises data, such as facts, behaviors, or events. Research applications include development, testing, and evaluation. The purpose of research is to build new knowledge.

This chapter is the first chapter of Part III, the Research Process. The research process is both linear and nonlinear. The research process is linear in that researchers follow plans and methods. For example, quantitative researchers follow strict timelines once the research has begun. However, the research process is also nonlinear. For example, the research question that begins the investigation guides the researchers' review and analysis of the literature. However, researchers will return to their research questions and revise and refine them as they collect information from the literature. Thus, the research process takes on a cyclical and iterative nature. Therefore, researchers who are new to the process are advised to read the remaining chapters before beginning an investigation.

This chapter presents information on identifying and delineating the research topic. The chapter begins with an explanation on how to develop a research question. Information on conducting and writing a literature review follows. Essentials about hypotheses are then reviewed. The chapter concludes with an examination of the impact of the research's purpose and of other key factors on the selection of the research's design and method.

Research Question or Problem

Research is a systematic investigation that builds new knowledge or refines current knowledge. The word "investigate" in the definition of research implies that questions or problems exist about a topic or subject. The **research question** is an interrogative sentence (question) about the specific issue that the researcher is investigating. A **research problem** is the same as a research question except that it is stated in a declarative sentence. The issues may be processes, phenomena, or relationships among variables. It should be emphasized that a research question involves an issue that lends itself to systematic investigation through research. This chapter uses the terms research question and research problem interchangeably.

Issues that lend themselves to empirical investigation are:

- Ongoing controversies in a field
- Debates about unresolved issues
- Gaps in the body of knowledge
- Flaws in previous research (such as a limited **sample**)
- Unquestioned assumptions
- Contradictory or ambiguous findings
- Extensions into new areas of practice
- Recurring problems

Researchers develop these types of topics into research questions. Research questions guide researchers' investigations.

Steps to develop a research question are:

1. Become familiar with the research topic
2. Identify the topic in the researcher's area of interest or expertise
3. Define the issue
4. Refine the question
5. Ensure that the question is significant, relevant, and of merit to the field

Become Familiar With the Topic

As researchers develop the research question, they narrow and focus their topic to result in a manageable and researchable issue. A helpful metaphor is the funnel. Researchers begin with a broad, general topic, gradually pinpoint the issues, and then pinpoint the question or problem.

Developing a research question begins during higher education, when students gain familiarity in an area of the field's literature, such as decision support systems or data search algorithms. They may have written a paper for a course on a topic that piques their interest. Additionally, most health informatics professionals are familiar with issues in their work settings. For example, a recurring problem in the work setting's information systems may be the impetus to conduct research to find solutions. Attitudes toward information systems or communications technologies may be another source of questions. Usually a research question will address a recurring or widespread problem. However, the singular importance of a sentinel event (an unexpected serious occurrence, such as death resulting from medication error) or the attitude of one or two positional (influential) leaders may justify a research study. In this step, researchers explore the topic's viability as an issue that can be investigated empirically.

Identify Area of Interest or Expertise

In the second step, researchers identify areas of special interest or expertise within the research topic. Specialties exist in all fields. For example, a graduate student working in a hospital's health information management department could find many issues of special interest (see figure 9.1).

At this point, researchers determine during the literature review whether information exists about their specialty or expertise. Moreover, at this step, researchers also determine whether a resolution to the research problem or an answer to the research question will be of interest to external constituencies such practitioners, researchers, decisionmakers, policy analysts, or government agencies.

Figure 9.1.   Examples of special interests in health information management

- Concordance of electronic and paper records
- Personal health records
- Coding; diagnostic, procedural, and specialty
- Voice recognition software and other specialized applications
- Claims data and concordance between claims data and health records
- Point-of-service data entry
- Authentication
- Technology training
- Components of electronic health records, such as problem lists and abbreviation lists
- Nomenclatures and nosology
- Data crosswalks
- Security and privacy
- Data capture and transfer
- Release of records and required (mandated) release
- Technology diffusion
- Quality and productivity
- Organizational leadership and behavior

Define the Issue

In the third step, defining the issue, researchers clarify the question or delineate the problem. Establishing the boundaries of the problem is critical to its definition. Researchers also decide in this step whether the issue lends itself to research. Thus, researchers determine whether the research is feasible. Establishing the boundaries includes:

- Setting the parameters of the issue
- Quantifying and describing the extent of the problem
- Distinguishing (demarcating) the constituencies affected by the problem

Establishing boundaries is important. Researching the universe of possibilities in one topic is impossible.

In setting the parameters, researchers decide in which setting to investigate the topic. For example, decision support systems can be investigated in clinics, hospitals, nursing homes, or health maintenance organizations, or other healthcare settings. Researchers also could investigate the use of one application of a decision support system across all the sites in an integrated health delivery system. However, investigating a research topic across multiple sites is more suited to a series of studies by coordinated teams of investigators than a single study by one or a few researchers.

As a part of establishing boundaries, researchers quantify or describe the extent of the problem. They explain the scope of the problem. How many sites, practitioners, or technologies are involved? How many different decision support systems could be evaluated? How much time or money is involved? Researchers with a qualitative slant would describe how the issue affects culture or acceptance. For example, a qualitative researcher could describe how a technology affects a core value of the nursing profession. Quantifying or describing the problem explains the extent or pervasiveness of the issue.

Finally, in establishing boundaries, the researcher demarcates how the issue affects various groups. Based on his or her interests and expertise, the researcher determines which group will be the focus of the research study. For example, physicians and patients have different views of the personal health record and how its data are incorporated into health records. The researcher would need to determine which group's perspective to study, or whether to study both and compare the results.

Establishing boundaries is important because the process helps clarify the focus of the investigation. Moreover, the process is important because it may reveal to researchers the amount of time and work the research study is likely to require. Quantifying or describing the extent of the problem provides supporting documentation about organizations and persons who, besides the researcher, may be interested in the research. Clarity assists researchers in determining what the investigation *is* and *is not*.

Refine the Question

In the fourth step, researchers refine the research question by examining details about the topic. This step includes:

- Identifying an underlying or related model or theory and its components (factors and relationships)
- Determining the appropriate approach
- Identifying gaps in the body of knowledge and determining whether those gaps can be filled by descriptions, relationships, or differences

Details are important because they add another level of clarity to the question.

Utilizing theories and models explicitly links the study to a larger body of knowledge. Research models show all the factors and relationships in a theory. Researchers must consciously identify factors and relationships affecting their research question, and deliberately determine which factors and relationships to study. For example, researchers may select one or two factors that other researchers have questioned or have found problematic. They also specify the factors and relationships that are outside the scope of their study. Using models also is advantageous because they may propose relationships among factors. Moreover, by explicitly linking to theories or models, researchers demonstrate the value of their study by showing its effect on the larger body of knowledge. For example, researchers could use the Triad Model to show the overlapping interests of software developers, patients, and molecular biologists, particularly in the areas of ethics and social policies (see figure 9.2). Finally, theories and models are useful because they show all the factors and relationships, many with which the researchers were familiar and some with which they were unfamiliar and may have inadvertently ignored.

Figure 9.2.   The Triad Model

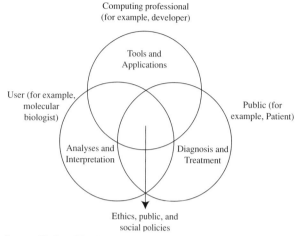

Source: Kesh and Raghupathi 2004.

Researchers develop the research question by conducting a literature review. As they read, the researchers recognize that their question or problem may be more amenable to one approach than another. For example, exploratory studies in ill-defined topics related to perceptions or acceptance are more amenable to a qualitative approach than a quantitative approach. Or, for example, studies related to a topic for which survey instruments already have been developed may be more amenable to a quantitative approach than a qualitative approach.

Identifying the gaps in the body of knowledge helps researchers develop their research question. In incipient areas of the body of knowledge, basic descriptive data may be scarce and thus critically needed. Other areas may need to establish the relevant factors the relationships among them. Still other areas could benefit from building predictive models.

Refining the research question provides information about its depth. This process is complementary to establishing boundaries, which provides information about the scope of the research question. The details determined in refining the research question focus the research study.

Ensure the Question's Significance

In the fifth and final step of developing the research question, researchers ensure that the research question is significant. To justify the investment of time and resources, the research question should have merit.

Research on a trite issue is a waste of time, money, and energy. Significant issues are those that other researchers have identified as problematic, affect many groups, or consume many or scarce resources. Information from the previous steps also contributes evidence supporting the importance of the research question.

A field's literature provides sources of research questions (see table 9.1). For example, journal articles and presentation proceedings provide discussions of relevant theories and models. Literature includes journal articles, abstracts and papers from proceedings, and doctoral dissertations and master's theses. In these scholarly works, authors detail their investigations. Occasionally, authors reveal methodological flaws or errors in their own studies or in other researchers' studies. Current researchers can correct these flaws or errors. An important tool for researchers as they develop their research questions is the **systematic review,** a specialized type of journal article that summarizes, synthesizes, and critiques all

the literature on a topic (see chapter 8.) One purpose of the systematic review is to identify gaps in the body of knowledge and areas needing research. Table 9.2 mentions some of the health informatics research systematic reviews. Authors in journals outside health informatics also recommend research questions. For example, Lobach and Detmer (2007, S105) recommend research questions for evaluation research on the development, deployment, and clinical implementation of electronic health records (EHRs). Thus, with existing sources and their own experiences, health informatics researchers can craft meaningful research questions. Table 9.3 illustrates the development of a research question for a study in health informatics.

The importance of investing time and effort in developing the research question cannot be overstated. Experts "agree that the key element, the starting point and the most important issue in developing research, is the research question" (Metz 2001, 13). Characteristics of a well-written research question are presented in figure 9.3. As a general guide to writing a good research question, researchers should find a meaningful problem that needs a solution or an important question that needs an answer.

As a result of developing the research question, the researchers should be crystal clear about what they are investigating. They should be able to explain to an informed layperson the purpose and the focus of their research. They should be able to describe what they expect to learn. A well-written research question is important because its content underlies and guides subsequent decisions about the research's design and method. A vague, poorly written research question does not guide decisions about design and method. Moreover, clearly written research questions help researchers later in the research process when writing the hypotheses. Hypotheses (discussed later in this chapter) are written after researchers complete the literature review. Clear,

Table 9.1.   Literature that provides sources of research questions

Source	Aspects
Theories and models	Factors and variables Relationships
Systematic reviews and meta-analyses	Gaps in the literature Debates Controversies Contradictory or ambiguous findings Methodological flaws Unquestioned assumptions
Journal articles and presentation proceedings	Recommendations for future research Methodological flaws
Dissertations and theses	Recommendations for future research Methodological flaws
Annotated bibliographies	Alphabetical summaries of scholarly sources

Table 9.2.   Selected systematic reviews in health informatics research

Researcher	Year	Topic
Kaplan, B., and N. T. Shaw	2004	Evaluation literature on applications of medical informatics concerning people, organizational, and social issues. Recommendations for future research.
Ammenwerth, E., and N. de Keizer	2005	Trends in evaluation research of health information technology between 1982 and 2002. Helps researchers avoid replicating available studies.
Pluye, P., R.M. Grad, L.G. Dunikowski, and R. Stephenson	2005	Quantitative, qualitative, and mixed-methods studies on impact of clinical information-retrieval technology on physicians and medical students.
Poissant, L., J. Pereira, R. Tamblyn, and Y. Kawasumi	2005	Impact of electronic health records on documentation time of physicians and nurses. Identifies factors that may explain efficiency differences across studies.
Sanders, D.L., and D. Aronsky	2006	Identification of computerized applications for clinical asthma care and of gaps in the research, such as variety of clinical settings.

well-written research questions are one step on the way to efficient use of time and energy, complete data, and quality research.

Literature Review

A **literature review** is a systematic and critical examination of the important information about a topic. The sources of information for the literature review include articles in peer-reviewed journals and in magazines, books, book chapters, conference papers, and governmental documents. Typically, the authors of the articles, books, and other documents are recognized researchers, scholars, and experts on the topic. Excluding irrelevant or tangential studies distills the literature review to only what is relevant. The examination results in a synthesis of current, important information about a topic.

Literature reviews trace the development of the accepted knowledge base and identify gaps in the body of knowledge. Moreover, literature reviews identify competently conducted research and inadequately conducted research.

Good literature reviews are characterized by:

- Comprehensiveness
- Exhaustiveness
- Relevance

Figure 9.3.   Characteristics of well-written research questions

- Clarity, exactness, and objectivity
- Theoretical significance, practical worth, or both
- Obvious and explicit linkages to a larger body of knowledge, such as a theory or a research model
- Advancement of knowledge in a definable way
- Utility

Adapted from Metz 2001, 13.

These characteristics result in a literature review that is a distillation and synthesis of the current status of knowledge on a topic.

Literature review has three meanings (see table 9.4). In the first meaning, a literature is a process, and in the second and third meanings, it is a product:

1. Process—identifying, reading, analyzing, summarizing, and synthesizing information

2. Product (1)—paragraphs of a manuscript, article, or grant proposal in which researchers record their synthesis of the literature that they have read

3. Product (2)—independent and separate scholarly work of research (See chapter 8 for information about this type of research.)

   —Literature review article

   —Annual review (entire book)

Table 9.3.   Example of the development of a research question

Step	Effect on research question
1. Become familiar with the research topic	The hospital's risk manager believes the incident reporting system is missing medical errors and has asked the information systems and technology (IS&T) department to automate the identification of medical errors.
	The graduate student in health informatics asks, "Is it possible to use data mining to identify medical errors?"
2. Identify in the research topic an area of interest or expertise	The graduate student in the IS&T Department is interested in surgical errors.
	The graduate student focusing on surgical errors asks, "Is it possible to use data mining to identify inpatient surgical errors?"
3. Define the issue	The graduate student, after reading articles on surgical errors, realizes that many types of errors exist. Based on the numbers of errors and current popular interest in gastric bypass surgery, the graduate student decides to narrow the study to bariatric surgery.
	The graduate student establishing a boundary asks, "Is it possible to use data mining to identify inpatient surgical errors during bariatric surgery?"
4. Refine the question	The graduate student has become interested in fuzzy logic, automatic cluster detection, and linkages and affinity models. This interest leads the graduate student to wonder whether a linkage and affinity model and the text of the hospital's surgery reports could be used to identify surgical errors during bariatric surgeries.
	The graduate student asks, "Is using a linkage and affinity model on inpatient surgery reports more sensitive and specific for bariatric surgical errors than the incident report system?"
5. Ensure that the question is significant	After reviewing the hospital's trend data showing increased numbers of bariatric surgeries and seeing blogs online publicizing negative outcomes of bariatric surgeries, the graduate student decides the study has merit.

Both as a process and as a product, literature reviews distill and synthesize what is known and what is not known about a topic.

Purpose

The purpose of a literature review is to develop and present a strong knowledge base. The strong knowledge base can be used to:

- Conduct research
- Analyze and generate theories
- Develop evidence-based practice guidelines
- Develop curricula

- Conduct strategic planning
- Develop white (position) papers

To achieve these purposes, literature reviews should be organized in ways that identify areas of accepted knowledge, issues of controversy, and gaps in the body of knowledge.

Process

As stated in the definition, literature reviews are systematic. Therefore, researchers follow an orderly and organized process as they conduct literature reviews. The process encompasses identifying, reading, analyzing, summarizing, and synthesizing knowledge and research

Table 9.4.   Three meanings of phrase "literature review"

Meaning	General Description	Example
One	Process	Identifying, reading, analyzing, summarizing, and synthesizing the works of researchers and experts.
Two	Product (Dependent Part) Poster Presentation (1 to 3 paragraphs) Proceedings or Conference Paper (1 to 5 paragraphs) Grant Proposal (1 to 2 paragraphs) Journal Article (1 to 5 paragraphs) Term Research Paper for Course (3 to 7 pages) Master's Thesis or Doctoral Dissertation (1 chapter)	Excerpt from research article, Kesh, S., and W. Raghupathi. (2004). Critical issues in bioinformatics and computing. *Perspectives in Health Information Management* 1(9):1–8. "Bioinformatics" is defined by the National Institutes of Health as the "research, development, or application of computational tools and approaches for expanding the use of biological, medical, behavioral, or health data, including those to acquire, store, organize, archive, analyze, or visualize such data."[1] The exponential growth in the amount of such data has necessitated the use of computers for information cataloging and retrieval, whereas a more global perspective in the quest for new insights into health and disease and the resulting data mining also underscore the need for bioinformatics.[2] Both sophisticated hardware and complex software play an increasingly critical role in the analysis of genomic data, and the accelerated maturation of the field of bioinformatics has implications for computing and life sciences professionals as well as the general public. Like computational biology, bioinformatics is anchored in the life sciences as well as computer and information sciences and technologies. Its interdisciplinary and integrative approach draws from fields such as mathematics, physics, computer science and engineering, biology, and behavioral science. The generally accepted subdisciplines include (1) development of new algorithms and statistics with which to assess relationships among members of large data sets; (2) analyses and interpretation of various types of sequences, domains, and structures; and (3) development and implementation of tools that enable efficient access and management of different types of information.[3–5]
Three	Product (Separate and Independent Entire Work) Review Article (7 to 30 pages) Annual (Book) (150 to 200 pages)	Citation in bibliographic databases includes publication type of "review" and number of references Mendonca EA. Cimino JJ. Johnson SB. Seol YH. Accessing heterogeneous sources of evidence to answer clinical questions. [Review] [92 refs] *Journal of Biomedical Informatics. 34(2):85–98, 2001 Apr.* Barrows RC Jr. Clayton PD. Privacy, confidentiality, and electronic medical records. [Review] [42 refs] *Journal of the American Medical Informatics Association. 3(2):139–48, 1996 Mar-Apr.* Systematic (Integrative) Review or Overview Meta-Analysis Annual Review

[1–5]Superscripts appear as in original article. See original article for references.
Source: Adapted from Kesh and Raghupathi 2004.

on a topic and closely related topics. The process of a literature review consists of four steps:

1. Determining the literature to review
2. Identifying, categorizing, organizing, and obtaining the literature
3. Analyzing the research questions, methods, and results presented in the literature
4. Synthesizing the information in the literature

Researchers proficient in reviewing literature have two skills. First, they seek information efficiently through quickly searching reference databases, skimming articles, and identifying relevant information. Second, they critically appraise research and information. Analyzing the existing studies and articles, they determine which research studies are important, and key points, patterns, and gaps in the information (See table 9.5 for complete list of information to capture.). Skills in information seeking and critical appraisal are essential for researchers.

Sources of Information

In the first step, researchers determine the literature to review. Sources of information (detailed in figure 9.4) include journals; periodicals; books, brochures, and book chapters; technical and research reports; proceedings of conferences; doctoral dissertations and master's theses; unpublished works; reviews; audiovisual media; and electronic media. These sources can be found in indexed reference databases.

Health informatics researchers need to search a wide variety of databases because the field combines theories from many academic disciplines. These databases represent the disciplines of:

- Healthcare, medicine, nursing, public health, and epidemiology
- Computer science, mathematics, engineering, and decision support
- Management and organizational behavior
- Sociology
- Physics
- Psychology

To assist users, librarians typically organize the reference databases by subject. Subjects particularly related to research in health informatics are business and economics, health and medicine, science and technology,

and social sciences (see table 9.6). However, researchers should consider all databases as potentially related to their topic, even though the database may be categorized within another subject. For example, health informatics researchers investigating health informatics education would also want to query education databases.

Recent advances in computer applications have created software that allows users to concurrently search across multiple databases. These federated search products make use of a library's current subscriptions for databases and online journals. Researchers should check whether their library has this current software.

Researchers should be aware that these databases may be quirky. Even though databases are under the same subject, they may not index the same journals. For example, under the subject of health and medicine, the HealthSTAR and MEDLINE databases index *IEEE Transactions on Information Technology in Biomedicine*, but CINAHL does not. In another instance, the content of journals overlaps, but the indexing does not. An article about a survey and analysis of EHR standards was published in *ACM Computing Surveys* (Eichelberg et al. 2005). *ACM Computing Surveys* is indexed in the business and economics databases and in the science and technology databases, but not in any of the health and medicine databases. Researchers accustomed to searching the health and medicine databases for EHR standards would have missed this article if they did not search the other databases. In any event, to ensure that all the relevant articles are captured, researchers must scrupulously search all potentially relevant databases.

Web sites also may contain helpful information. For instance, Web sites may provide access to valuable government reports, policy papers, and other documents. The Institute of Medicine's influential 2001 report, *Crossing the Quality Chasm*, is available online. Google Scholar is an Internet resource that researchers can use to access documents that may be absent from the reference databases (Steinbrook 2006, 5). These documents include theses, books, preprints, and technical reports (Steinbrook 2006, 5). However, researchers must use Web sites with caution. Their content typically has not been peer reviewed nor checked for accuracy. Thus, as information sources for literature reviews, Web sites have less credibility than academic or professional sources.

The literature comprises **primary** and **secondary sources**. Primary sources are the original works of the researchers who conducted the investigation, such as research-based articles in the *Journal of the American*

Table 9.5.   Literature review: Data, information, and knowledge to capture

General Area	Details to Capture
History of topic	• General timeline • Development of the topic • Key occurrences (theory, discovery, events) that advanced or halted the topic • Turning points • Patterns and trends over time • Scope, significance, and relevance
Orientation	• Ontological and epistemological beliefs of researchers in field and topic • Predilection for quantitative approach, qualitative approach, or mixed methods research • Acceptance of quantitative approach, qualitative approach, or mixed methods research • Disputes between researchers in different approaches
Theoretical foundation	• Mainstream and lesser-known theories • Evolution of mainstream and lesser-known theories • Discredited theories and their devolution • Theorists associated with theories • Applicable models • Related concepts and constructs • Relevant and irrelevant variables, factors, predictor variables, criterion variables (outcomes), covariates, and confounding variables • Operational and standardized definitions and measures • Germinative articles or books
Designs and methods	• Major and accepted designs • Typical and accepted methods and their comparative advantages and disadvantages • Populations and accepted sampling techniques • Types of interventions • Accepted and commonly used research instruments or measures and their respective strengths and weaknesses • Methodological weaknesses or errors in past researchers' studies
Current knowledge base	• Relevant reference databases and sources of data and information • Key researchers and their contributions • Current trends in the topic • Commonly accepted information and knowledge • Unquestioned or untested assumptions • Controversies and debates in the topic • Controversial, contradictory, or ambiguous findings and why they are problematic • Disputed findings and the basis of the dispute • Gaps in the body of knowledge • Weaknesses, gaps, and errors in past researchers' studies • Researchers' recommendations for future research
Analytical techniques	• Customary and accepted statistical techniques • Customary and accepted nonstatistical techniques • Analytical and interpretative weaknesses, gaps, or errors in past researchers' studies
Dissemination	• Preferred means of dissemination (book, white paper, journal article, practice brief) • Field's most respected journals • Journals matching the topic and study's design and method • Style of writing in journals

Figure 9.4.   Sources of information

Periodicals	Books, Brochures, and Book Chapters	Technical and Research Reports
Abstract Annual review Cartoon Journal Magazine Monograph Newsletter Newspaper Press release	Book or book chapter Brochure Dictionary Encyclopedia Legal citation Letter: Published or archived Manual Map or chart Pamphlet Product insert	Government bulletin or report Industry report Issue brief Monograph Nongovernmental agency report Position paper Reference report University report White paper Working paper
Proceedings of Meetings Conference Meeting Poster session Symposium Unpublished proceeding paper	**Doctoral Dissertations and Master's Theses** Dissertation or dissertation abstract Thesis or thesis abstract	**Unpublished Works** Submitted or unpublished manuscript Unpublished letter Unpublished raw data
Reviews Book Film Video	**Audiovisual Media** Oral address Audiotape Chart Film Interview: Published or unpublished Lecture Music recording Performance Recorded interview Slide Speech Television broadcast, series, or transcript Work of art	**Electronic Media** Abstract on CD-ROM CD-ROM Computer program Computer software Electronic database Online abstract, book, or journal Software manual Web site

Table 9.6.   Representative reference databases by subject

Subject	Representative Database
Business and Economics	ABI/INFORM Complete Business Source Premier Emerald
Health and Medicine	CINAHL HealthSTAR MEDLINE
Science and Technology	ACM Digital Library Compendex IEEE Xplore MathSciNet SIAM Journals Online
Social Sciences	PsycINFO Social Sciences Citation Index

Medical Informatics Association or *Information Retrieval* (See also table 2.7, p. 36.). Secondary sources are summaries of original works. Encyclopedias and textbooks are familiar secondary sources. Other examples of secondary sources are annual reviews (also sometimes called tertiary sources). Annual reviews synthesize current and recent knowledge on a topic. They may be special issues of print or electronic journals or entire books (See chapter 8 and table 9.2, p. 196, and examples of annual reviews at http://www.annualreviews.org/.). For literature reviews, primary sources are preferable to secondary sources.

An example of a primary source is an article in *BMC Health Services Research*. The researchers reported on a study that described access to electronic health knowledge in five African countries (Smith et al. 2007, n.p.). The researchers found that 70 percent of the postgraduate doctors at four teaching hospitals used textbooks as their main source of information, and 66 percent of the total surveyed used the Internet for health information in the past week (Smith et al. 2007, n.p.).

A **meta-analysis** is an example of a secondary source. Haque and Srinivasan (2006, 52) conducted a meta-analysis using statistical techniques to combine the findings of 16 studies on the training effectiveness of virtual reality (VR) surgical simulators. As customary in meta-analyses, the researchers explained how they identified the 16 studies and what outcomes they collated and analyzed (52). The researchers found that VR surgical simulator training lessened the time to complete the task (54). They concluded that VR simulation training "is highly effective in . . . the transference of skills from the simulation environment to the operating room" (52).

The gold standard for a literature review is primary research in peer-reviewed journals. Journals may be **peer reviewed** (also called research, refereed, academic, and professional) or nonpeer reviewed (also called popular). In peer-reviewed journals, there is an official and publicized process of review and approval. There is also an editorial review board composed of experts in various fields and subjects related to the journal's focus. These experts are **peer reviewers** (or **peers**). Peers evaluate manscripts in their subject area or field. Peers evaluate the quality of the manuscript. The peers and the journal editor determine whether to publish a manuscript. The **peer review** process ensures that the information reported in the journal is of the highest quality (Colaianni 1994, 156).

Both print and electronic journals may be peer reviewed (see table 2.7, p. 36, for examples of peer-reviewed journals in health informatics). Information about the status of a journal as peer-reviewed is found on a journal's Web site and in the citation information for articles. Researchers must distinguish between research (scholarly) literature and popular literature. Properly conducted and written literature reviews focus on primary sources in peer-reviewed journals.

Search Techniques

In the second step, researchers identify, categorize, organize, and obtain the literature. A systematic plan identifies the databases to search as well as all the terms used to query the databases. Categorizing includes listing types of sources of information. Although traditional literature may constitute the major portion of the plan, other sources (such as videos, newscasts, and the Internet) can contribute and should be considered. Tables and lists are essential tools to achieve thorough search techniques. The plan also includes organizing the documentation of the terms used in the queries, the search terms, the results of the queries for each database, and the literature itself as it is received. This section focuses on the search techniques.

As a means to organize the literature review, researchers are strongly encouraged to invest in reference (citation) management software (personal bibliographic management software) before beginning their

research. This type of software greatly assists researchers by allowing them to:

- Create their own citation databases
- Utilize the softwares' search engines that directly download citations into the researchers' citation databases
- Import the contents of databases into word-processing software
- Transform citation entries into the required style of the journal (styles editor)

There are several commonly used reference management software packages, including Reference Manager, EndNote, RefWorks, and ProCite. Reference management "freeware" includes BiblioExpress and Scholar's Aid 2000 Lite.

Procedure

The following steps describe the search procedure for refereed journal articles. Researchers can use similar tactics in other media and for popular literature.

1. Generate a list of key terms.
   (**Note:** Key terms have different names in the various databases. A key term may be called a key word, index term, classification, classification code, subject, or subject category. The databases of medical literature use key words and medical subject headings [MeSH headings]. Include synonyms, abbreviations, and alternative formats and spellings [clinical information system, CIS; computer-based patient record, CPR, electronic health record, electronic healthcare record, EHR, electronic medical record, EMR, electronic patient record; manage, management; meta-analysis, metaanalysis].)

2. Generate a list of target databases (such as Business Source Premier, CINAHL, MEDLINE, PsycLIT, and Social Sciences Citation Index).

3. Search each database with each term. Use both a key word search and an advanced "all fields" search and document each search. Save search histories.

4. Use the "limit" function to narrow the searches to refereed journals (also sometimes called

academic journals). Other useful limits include specifying human subjects, English language, and time periods.

5. Pull up the complete reference. The complete reference includes information such as the author, journal, key terms (see figure 9.5), and abstract. Note whether the journal is peer-reviewed and add any new relevant key terms to the search strategy.

6. Scan the **abstracts** of the articles to determine whether the articles are applicable. Abstracts summarize of research studies' major parts:

   —Context

   —Objective

   —Design, setting, and participants

   —Interventions

   —Main outcome measures

   —Results and conclusions

7. Import relevant citations into the personal citation database.

8. Print articles from online journals or save them electronically. Researchers are cautioned to print or save PDFs rather than text files so the page numbers are accurate for proper citations.

9. Obtain articles from print journals. (**Note:** Although it may be convenient [expedient] to use only online articles, the resulting literature review is likely to be incomplete and biased. Some libraries require a special application to request articles. Library personnel obtain an electronic version of the article from another library or they make a PDF from the article in the print journal. Fees may be as high as $11 for normal processing and $25 for "rush" jobs. Other libraries may require researchers to make the photocopies themselves with copy cards. Therefore, researchers must make every effort to obtain all relevant articles, both in electronic and print format.)

10. Read and analyze the literature obtained to date.

11. Identify key journal articles.

12. Obtain the references cited at the end of the key articles. Track their order and receipt.

13. Note the key words of the key articles. If the original list missed these terms, rerun the searches of the databases on the new terms.

14. Identify key researchers in the topic. Run advanced searches on "author." Obtain all their articles and books on the topic.

15. Alphabetize all the copies of the articles (electronic or print) by author. This strategy avoids duplication and allows prompt access.

To avoid rework during the manuscript's composition, researchers should capture all data about the source when they first obtain it. The various style manuals have different requirements. To meet all the requirements,

Figure 9.5.   Generic sample of complete reference in citation database

Number	2003092126 2004091216
Author	Researcher E
Organizational Affiliation	Department of Research and Health Information Management, SomewhereUniversity, ATown, XX
Title	Health informatics: managerial issues
Source	HealthLeadership Today. 2004 Jan; 22(1): 2-15. (100 ref)
Category	Health Administration
Key Words	Information Technology/Health Services Administration Telehealth/
Abstract	Managing resources is a component of the education of healthcare managers and supervisors. Recent advances in the technologies of health informatics present these leaders with new challenges. Managing these evolving technologies requires new tools. A multipronged solution that incorporates adherence to regulations and standards, promotion of professional guidelines, and creation of a culture of continuing education is recommended.
Publication Type	Journal Article.
Language	English

researchers should be sure to capture all the data listed in figure 9.6.

Library Research

Library research requires skills in information seeking. Therefore, although library research no longer requires long hours in the stacks of brick-and-mortar libraries, researchers must build their skills in querying electronic databases, the Internet, and reference management software. Libraries often offer workshops or tutorials to build electronic research skills. For example, the University of South Carolina Beaufort Library developed an online tutorial, "Bare Bones Web Searching," that explains the features of various Internet search engines (Chamberlain 2007). Utilizing the unique features of search engines makes online research more efficient. Thus, although the computerization of library holdings puts these resources at the researchers' fingertips, they need to have the information skills to fully delve into the holdings and capture all relevant information.

Students and instructors have access to sources of information and bibliographic databases through the holdings of their educational institutions' libraries. Libraries have extensive holdings that include books, reference manuals, maps, videotapes, audiotapes, and literary and other databases. Many libraries list their holdings on the Internet. Book holdings can typically be accessed through the library's catalog, and databases and online journals usually can be found in a library's electronic resources. Libraries purchase licenses that allow their users access to the various databases. Just as different libraries have purchased different books, different libraries have purchased different licenses.

Practitioners may access sources of information and databases through their workplaces. Healthcare organizations have libraries or possibly arrangements with institutions that provides access to libraries. As employees, practitioners may access these resources.

Members of professional associations and societies have access to information resources through their organizations. Members of the American Health Information Management Association (AHIMA) have access to the holdings of the Foundation Of Research and Education (FORE) Library in the Body of Knowledge (BoK) of the Communities of Practice (CoP). These holdings include:

- Full text articles from the *Journal of the American Health Information Management Association* since 1998

- Recent white papers about electronic health information management (e-HIM) and practice briefs on the transition from paper health records to EHRs (http://www.ahima.org/infocenter/ehim/)

- 125 leading journals in healthcare and HIM

- 1,000 books related to healthcare and HIM

- Limited access to some propriety bibliographic databases

- Document delivery for a fee that varies by availability

- Full text or links to external and governmental sources

Members of the American Medical Informatics Association (AMIA) have access to

- *Journal of the American Medical Informatics Association* both in print and online

- Proceedings of the AMIA annual symposium in CD-ROM format

- Electronic resources including MD Consult, FirstConsult, and Thomson Clinical Xpert (formerly MobileMICROMEDEX)

Professionals are encouraged to contact their professional association or society for details about their benefits. Some resources may be available to nonmembers.

Now, the researchers' energies are focused on analyzing, interpreting, and synthesizing the information they have obtained. The literature review is one of those

Figure 9.6.   Citation data to capture on all sources

- Full name of the author, including first name, and middle initial or name (Some entries in Web sites have authors.)
- Full title of the article, book chapter, or Web page
- Full name of the journal, book, video, or Web site
- Complete information about dates of publication, including year, month, and season (Some entries in Web sites are dated.)
- Complete name and address of the publisher (relevant for most sources other than periodicals and unpublished works)
- Inclusive page numbers
- Volume and issue number (These data may be only on the front of the publication, and some publications may use only volume number.)
- Accurate Internet URL and access date (date last updated as noted at bottom of page may also be acceptable)

tasks in research, as discussed at the beginning of the chapter, that is nonlinear. The brevity of this step of the process in no way represents the amount and intensity of the work involved in a critical reading and analysis of the literature.

Researchers can use table 9.5 (p. 200) as a guide to identify trends, common characteristics, and gaps. Table 9.7 presents a tool that researchers can use to record and summarize the key features of each article, book, or other source of information in a table.

The transparency required by peer review also assists the researchers as they conduct the literature review. Published articles and scholarly works must explain and detail every step of the research. Those explanations and details include both the positive and the negative. For example, in journal articles, master's theses, and doctoral dissertations, researchers often will identify unintentional flaws in their studies that later researchers could correct in a replication study. Therefore, it is valid to conduct research that corrects flaws in an original study. Moreover, in journal articles, master's theses, and doctoral dissertations, researchers will discuss the additional questions that their investigations raised and that later researchers could address. They specifically make recommendations for future research. Thus, by closely and thoughtfully reading the articles and other resources, researchers will discover that the articles' authors reveal much helpful information.

Development

As noted in the process, the fourth step of the literature review is to "Synthesize the information in the literature review." Researchers began synthesizing the data and information into knowledge as they were analyzing the literature in step three. For example, they noted major trends and advances in their topic. The focus in step four is to condense and distill the information.

However, the word *synthesize* cannot be emphasized enough. In the current world of data and information overload, narrative reviews that summarize previous studies are not adequate. Readers require the knowledge resulting from the analysis, summary, interpretation, and synthesis of the literature.

After completing the literature review (process), researchers develop its products. These written products record the researchers' synthesis of the literature that they have read (also known as "literature reviews"). As previously discussed, there are two types of products:

- Dependent part of a larger work; such as paragraphs of a manuscript, journal article, grant proposal, or presentation; pages of a term paper; and a chapter of a master's thesis or a doctoral dissertation (chapter 10 focuses on the dependent parts of larger works.)

- Independent article or annual review (book) (See chapter 8 for information about this type of research.)

The purpose of a literature review (product) is to convey to readers and other researchers the established knowledge about a topic. In a few paragraphs or pages, researchers persuade the reader or audience of the study's necessity. The literature review guides the audience to raise the same questions and reach the same conslusions of the researchers. Moreover, the audience also will recognize the importance of the research question being asked. The audience

Table 9.7.   Tool to record summarize articles, books, or other sources

Fictitious Author and Citation	Research Design, Method, Time Frame, Sample, and Response Rate	Research Question and Hypothesis	Analytical Technique	Key Findings, Limitations, and Recommendations
Johnson, A.J. 2004, March. Advanced Topics in Health Informatics 17(3):15-30	*Correlational* *Survey* *Cross-sectional* *30 nurses in convenience sample from four nursing wards* *100%*	*Will a training session on the EHR increase nurses' confidence in its efficacy?* *Nurses' feelings of confidence in the efficacy of the EHR will be positively related to participation in 3-hour training session*	*Descriptive statistics and bivariate correlation*	*No statistically significant relationship demonstrated (but approaching statistical significance at .06)* *Small convenience sample limited generalizability* *Recommend using larger random sample*

should conclude that the logical and necessary next step is the proposed research. A secondary purpose is to ensure the audience that the researcher conducted a thorough and diligent review of all aspects of the topic. The thoroughness of the literature review lends credibility to both the researcher and the entire investigation. Finally, the literature review should conclude with a clear and exact statement of the hypothesis (discussed later in this chapter).

The characteristics of a good literature review are:

- Comprehensiveness that is also relevant and focused
- Critique that includes strengths, weaknesses, limitations, and gaps
- Analysis
- Summary that is succinct and logical and comprising mainly primary sources
- Interpretation that highlights major ideas, trends, and developments
- Synthesis

Procedural conventions that characterize good literature reviews are detailed in the following paragraphs. Good literature reviews deliver concentrated knowledge to the reader.

Literature reviews are guided by several conventions, including transparency in content, organizational structure, progression, equitable coverage, pertinence, and style. These conventions are detailed in the following paragraphs.

Transparency

Literature reviews are **transparent**. Being transparent means that someone else could replicate the researchers' process. Therefore, researchers briefly describe the strategy used to identify the literature. In addition, they explain the scope of the literature review by explicitly stating both their inclusion and exclusion criteria. For example, a researcher could state:

The topic of decision support systems is broad. This literature review focuses on applications to support emergency physicians' diagnostic decision making. Empirical research studies were included; reports in trade journals were excluded.

Organizational Structure

An explicit or obvious organizational structure helps readers follow the researchers' logic. Therefore, research-

ers should make a conscious effort to identify, consider, and use an organizing function for the literature review. In a literature review organized by the research model, each component is discussed in turn. The components of the model directly related to the researchers' study are discussed in greater detail. A literature review can also be organized by issues in the topic. Chronology is yet another organizing function. Explicitly stating the order helps to guide and direct the reader. A coherent and logical order clarifies the topic.

Progression

Literature reviews follow a progression. The progression parallels the development of the knowledge base of a topic. For example, researchers identify the key points or turning points in the history or background of the topic. Therefore, literature reviews include research studies that moved the topic forward or that added new factors to the topic. The literature review moves from older studies to more current studies. The review should end at the problematic or ambiguous findings, unresolved problem, or other issue that the researchers' study addresses. This progression results in readers understanding the need for the study.

Equitable Coverage

Equitable coverage means that the literature review includes points of view contrary to the researchers' points of view. Credible literature reviews are unbiased. Therefore, important studies supporting the researchers' premises are included as are nonsupportive studies. Readers could perceive the absence of contradictory studies as bias. Evidence of bias detracts from the credibility of the literature review. Explanations of the contradictory findings, based on evaluation and analysis, might be suggested.

Pertinence

Studies included in the research study should be pertinent. Similar to the development of the research question, the metaphor of the funnel is again useful. The review should move from the most broadly related studies to the most closely related studies. When tangential studies are included, their relevance should be explicitly stated. Generally, the least-related studies should be discussed first and the most-related studies discussed last. If the researchers are rectifying errors in prior studies, those that either were conducted inadequately or resulted in gaps or conflicts are included. To justify their study, researchers should specify the inadequacies, gaps, or conflicting results. The pertinence of the studies should be evident to the readers or audience.

Style

Stylistically, key research studies or turning-point studies should be described in greater detail than replication or duplicative studies. Key studies make major contributions to the body of knowledge. Turning-point studies, a subset of key studies, are those that sent the research on topics in new directions. Enough information about the key studies and turning-point studies (design, time frame, method, sample, response rate, statistical techniques, and findings) should be included so the reader can evaluate their quality. Research that has the same findings with the same factors should be bundled. For example, the author could state:

Research (citation one, citation two, citation three, and so on) has shown that smoking is bad for skin tone.

Verb tense also should be considered. Tradition and logic demand that researchers pay close attention to verb tense when they write literature reviews. The tense of the verb situates the event or idea in time. Present tense expresses truths, accepted theories, and facts. Recent, valid studies also are explained in the present tense. For example:

- **Accepted theory:** Specific goals motivate employees more than vague goals
- **Recent study:** Researcher X's results illustrate the importance of specific goals

Past studies with continued historical value can be described in the past tense. Including the date to situate the study is a common practice. For example:

- Study of historical importance: In 1972, the study of Smith et al. showed the importance of expectancy in motivation.

Generally, the safest rule is to use present tense for published studies and theories.

Researchers should consider creating a table that highlights the important features of the studies in the literature review. (See table 9.8.) This effective tool distills the information and helps readers quickly see trends and gaps in the literature.

In literature reviews, researchers produce a synthesis of information from various sources. The purpose of literature reviews is to identify areas of accepted knowledge, issues of controversy, and gaps in the body of knowledge. Literature reviews are organized in ways that create information from voluminous data and information. The process of reviewing the literature is systematic and results in a comprehensive knowledge of the topic. Researchers use literature reviews to make compelling arguments that justify their research studies. In conclusion, literature reviews are syntheses representing the researchers' analysis, summary, and interpretation of relevant and key information from reliable sources.

Hypothesis

A **hypothesis** is a statement that predicts the relationship among variables. The relationship should be capable of being expressed in measurable data. A hypothesis is based on:

- Theory
- Model
- Observation
- Researchers' expectation from their analysis and interpretation of studies in the literature

Hypotheses are written in quantitative research because they are associated with measuring and testing researchers' predictions.

In hypotheses, researchers state their research questions in measurable terms. Therefore, hypotheses are more specific than research questions because they are measurable. Some experts explain that hypotheses **operationalize** (define) research questions. Hypotheses are also the bases of which statistical tests are conducted in the analysis of the data. As such, hypotheses guide research investigations because they state the the study's predicted outcomes.

Hypotheses are clear, simple, and precise refinements of the research question. (See table 9.9.) Writing clear and simple hypotheses is hard work. Surprisingly, clarity and simplicity require work and careful thought to achieve. As they formulate hypotheses, researchers use the operational definitions of the variables that they learned in the literature review. They also incorporate what they believe are the relationships or differences among the variables. Researchers must avoid writing an ambiguous or untestable hypothesis. Finally, they must ensure that the hypotheses reflect the intent of their research.

Table 9.8.   Literature summary for literature review

Fictitious Author	Year	Research Design, Method, and Time Frame	Sample and Response Rate	Analytical Technique	Key Findings, Limitations, and Recommendations
Author Last Name, First and Middle Initials	*2004*	*Descriptive and mixed-methods research* *Survey and focus groups* *Retrospective*	*30 hospital nurses and 15 nursing nurses (65% response rate)*	*Descriptive statistics, chi-square,* *Content analysis of discussions of focus groups*	*Significant differences in levels of confidence about relevant transfer of information between hospital nurses and nursing nurses* *Limitations were that all types of patient discharges were not included and that all nurses used the same EHR (one health system)* *Recommendations included different types of patients (that is, surgical) and nurses from different health systems using different EHRs*
Author Last Name, First and Middle Initials	*2006*	*Correlational* *Survey* *Cross-sectional*	*45 occupational therapists in convenience sample from single rehab center* *(100% response rate)*	*Descriptive statistics and biivariate correlation*	*No statistically significant relationship demonstrated (but approaching statistical significance at .06)* *Small convenience sample limited generalizability* *Recommend using larger random sample*
Author Last Name, First and Middle Initials	*2007*	*Quasi-experimental* *One group pretest-posttest* *Cross-sectional*	*Convenience sample of 28 medical residents* *(52% response rate)*	*Descriptive statistics, chi-square, ANOVA, and analyses for non-parametric statistics*	*Scenarios in simulation (3) used to investigate impact of clinical decision support system on residents' diagnosing of patient complaints* *Limitations were the simplistic nature of complaints, lack of time constraints of simulation* *Recommend using more complex scenarios, time constraints, and other types of health personnel*

Table 9.9.   Sample of actual hypotheses from health informatics research

Research Question or Topic	Hypothesis
"Determine clinicians' . . . 'actual' and 'reported' use of a point-of-care online information retrieval system; and to make an assessment of the extent to which use is related to direct patient care. . . ." (Westbrook et al. 2004, 113)	"Hypothesis 1: Clinicians use online evidence primarily to support clinical decisions related to direct patient care" "Hypothesis 2: Clinicians use online evidence predominantly for research and continuing education" (Westbrook et al. 2004, 114)
"To (1) establish a parsimonious and valid questionnaire instrument to measure credibility of Internet health information by drawing on various previous measures of source, news, and other credibility scales; and (2) to identify the effects of Web site domains and advertising on credibility perceptions" (Walther et al. 2004, n.p.)	"H_1: Different top-level domains (*.org, .com, .edu, .gov*) influence the credibility of the Web site" "H2: The *.com* domain reduces the credibility of a Web site" "H3: The presence of advertisements reduces the credibility of a Web site" (Walther et al. 2004, n.p.)
"The aim of the present study was to explore whether lay people are able to understand information on intervention effectiveness in the sense that they are able to discriminate between different magnitudes of postponement" (Dahl et al. 2007, n.p.)	"Increasing the magnitude of postponement of the heart attack would increase the respondents' consent to therapy" (Dahl et al. 2007, n.p.)

Alternative and Null Hypotheses

Researchers write two types of hypotheses: **alternative hypotheses** and **null hypotheses** (see table 9.10). The **alternative hypothesis** states the predicted association or difference between the independent and dependent variables. Alternative hypotheses are symbolized as H_1 (H_A) for the first alternative hypothesis, H_2 for the second alternative hypothesis, and so on. The null hypothesis states that there is no association between the independent and dependent variables. The word null means none. The null hypothesis is symbolized as H_0. Typically, a colon follows the symbol, such as $H_{1:}$ (see table 9.10, p. 209). Alternative and null hypotheses are matched pairs.

Direction of Hypothesis

Alternative hypotheses are **one-tailed (directional)** or **two-tailed (nondirectional).** In one-tailed hypotheses, researchers predict the direction of the relationship between the variables. The direction is one way. For example, if the researcher states that the association is "more," "higher," or similar language; the alternative hypothesis is a one-tailed hypothesis, as shown in table 9.10. In another study, a researcher also could write a one-tailed hypothesis in which the association is "less," "lower," or similar language. The point is that the relationship or difference is one way. In two-tailed hypotheses, researchers do *not* predict the direction of the relationship or difference among the variables. For example, if the researcher makes no prediction about whether the association is "more or less," or "higher or lower," the alternative hypothesis is a two-tailed hypothesis. (See table 9.10.) In two-tailed hypotheses, research-ers simply state that there is either an association or a difference. For each alternative hypothesis, researchers choose whether they will use a one-tailed hypothesis or a two-tailed hypothesis. They do not use both.

The word "tail" in one-tailed and two-tailed hypotheses refers to the bell-shaped (normal) curve (see figure 9.7). Two-tailed hypotheses have tails on both ends of the bell-shaped normal curve. One-tailed hypotheses contain a tail only on one end. Two-tailed hypotheses are more conservative than one-tailed hypotheses.

Researchers state their existing beliefs in alternative hypotheses. The alternative hypothesis is formulated first. If the alternative hypothesis is a one-tailed hypothesis, it includes the predicted direction. If the alternative hypothesis is a two-tailed hypothesis, there is no direction, and the hypothesis just states that there is an association or a difference. After the alternative hypothesis is formulated, its matching null hypothesis is formulated. The alternative and null hypotheses are mutually exclusive and incorporate all possible outcomes of the research.

Figure 9.7.   Tails of hypotheses

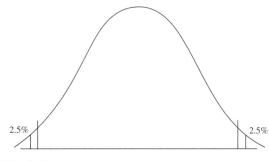

2.5%   2.5%

5% probability in two-tailed test

Table 9.10.   Example: Null hypothesis and alternative hypotheses

Hypothesis	Symbol	Sample Text
Alternative (one-tailed)	H_1	The use of the prescribing decision support system in the group of clinicians receiving the tailored alerts will be 10 percent higher than the use of the system by the group receiving the generic alerts.
Null	H_0	There is no difference in the use of the prescribing decision support system between the group of clinicians receiving the tailored alerts and the group receiving the generic alerts.
Alternative (two-tailed)	H_1	There is a 10 percent difference in the levels of utilization of voice recognition software between the group of physicians receiving the training and the group not receiving it.
Null	H_0	There is no difference in the levels of utilization of voice recognition software between the group of physicians receiving the training and the group not receiving it.

Researchers must write both alternative and null hypotheses to use statistical techniques and conduct statistical analysis. The logic of the statistical techniques is based on a choice between two hypotheses. Moreover, the properties of statistical techniques do not allow researchers to directly test the accuracy of the alternative hypotheses. Instead, statistical techniques test null hypotheses. If the null hypothesis is rejected, the alternative hypothesis is accepted. The researchers' predictions are supported when the null hypothesis is rejected and the alternative hypothesis is accepted.

Significance

Significance is related to the likelihood that the relationships or differences that researchers found in their data are pure, random chance. Researchers want to avoid situations in which there are no real relationships or differences. In such situations, what may have occurred is that the researchers' sample is not representative of the population (entire group). However, statistical techniques exist to investigate this issue. These techniques related to significance, though, are appropriate only with random samples (Baird 2006, 1). Therefore, researchers should carefully consider their research design so that they do not inadvertently select a biased sample (see chapter 10).

Researchers begin to lay the groundwork for using statistical techniques as they write the hypothesis. Researchers establish various criteria to determine significance. These criteria *must* be established before any data are collected. There are several key terms associated with these statistical techniques.

Confidence Interval

A **confidence interval (CI)** is a range of values inferred for a characteristic within a sample that has a possibility of including the characteristic's true value for the population (Riopelle 2000, 203). **Confidence levels** represent the probability that the confidence interval includes the population's value. Confidence levels are usually set at 95 percent or 99 percent.

Significance Testing and Significance Level

Significance (hypothesis or null hypothesis) testing analyzes the study's data to obtain the probability value and then compares that probability to a preestablished significance level (Riopelle 2000, 199; Watson 2006, 1). This comparison establishes whether the study's findings are **statistically significant**. With significance testing, researchers determine whether data are due solely to random chance. If results are not due solely to random chance, the null hypothesis is rejected in favor of an alternative hypothesis.

A **significance level** is the criterion used for rejecting the null hypothesis. The significance level is a prestablished cutoff that determines whether the null hypothesis is rejected. The significance level is also known as the **alpha level (α)**. The alpha level is set at a probability level, such as .001, .01, or .05. A probability of .001 is more stringent (lower) than a probability of .01. Common alpha levels are .05 and .01. Researchers set the lower alpha level when they want to minimize the chance that they might erroneously reject the null hypothesis when it is actually true. Moreover, the more severe the consequences of being wrong about whether or not the findings are random chance, the more stringent (lower) the probability is set. The level of significance is established prior to conducting statistical techniques.

Statistical tests for significance result in a **p value**. A p value indicates the probability of obtaining the result by chance if the null hypothesis is true. Therefore, if the p value is 0.05, the probability that the difference occurred by pure chance is 5 percent. If the p value obtained from the statistical test is less than or equal to the level of predetermined alpha value, the study's results are considered unlikely to be mere chance and the null hypothesis is rejected.

Power

Power is the probability of identifying real differences between groups (Goodman and Berlin 1994, 200). Specifically, power is the likelihood of failing to reject a false null hypothesis. Power is usually set at .80 or higher (Goodman and Berlin 1994, 203). If power is set at .80, there is a 20 percent chance that the researcher will wrongly determine that no relationship or difference exists in the results, when in actuality, there is a relationship or difference. For example, the researcher could falsely state that a training workshop made no difference in the utilization of the decision support system, when in fact the training workshop *did* make a difference. The cutoff set for power depends on the research. Power is less stringent than significance level because failing to assert a relationship or difference is less serious than falsely asserting a relationship or difference when none really exists.

Types of Errors

Researchers can make two types of errors associated with significance (null hypothesis) testing (see table 9.11). A **type I error** occurs when the researcher erroneously rejects the null hypothesis when it is true; in actuality, there is no difference. Alpha levels are associated with type I errors. A **type II error** occurs when the researcher erroneously fails to reject the null hypothesis when it is false; in actuality, there is a difference. **Beta (β)** designates the probability of making a type II error. Power is associated with type II errors.

For example:

- Alternative hypothesis (one-tailed): The mean time to triage HMO patients on the call line (medical help line) will be less for nurses who participate in a 3-hour workshop on the clinical diagnostic decision support system than for nurses who do not participate in the workshop.

- Null hypothesis: There is no difference in the mean times to triage HMO patients on the call line between the nurses who participate in a 3-hour workshop on the clinical diagnostic decision support system and the nurses who do not participate in the workshop.

A researcher committing a type I error would reject the null hypothesis. Rejecting a null hypothesis that states there is no difference means there is a difference. Thus, the researcher is reporting a false positive, that there is a difference in the performance of the two groups. Continuing in the error, he or she would report that the workshop reduced the nurses' triage time. However, the fact is that there is no difference between the performance of the two groups of nurses; the 3-hour workshop does not affect performance. Researchers who set the alpha level at 0.05 have a five percent chance of making this error, whereas those who set the alpha level at 0.01 have a one percent chance of making the error. Researchers, cautious about reporting on the efficacy of the workshop, should select the lower alpha.

In the previous example, the researcher would make a type II error if he or she failed to reject the null hypothesis and it was indeed false. This error is a false negative. The researcher would erroneously state that there was no difference between the performance of the nurses who participated in the workshop and the nurses who did not participate. In fact, there was a difference, and the workshop did reduce the triage time as predicted.

The language associated with significance testing is "rejecting or failing to reject null hypotheses." For purists, the logic of null hypothesis testing makes using the language of "accepting the null" inappropriate. However, researchers will see statements about "accepting the null" in the literature.

In conclusion, the statement of the hypothesis is a crucial step in the development of the research plan. Hypotheses are statements of the researchers' predictions on the outcome of the study. Hypotheses are testable. Formulating good hypotheses requires attention to operational definitions and clarity of writing. The statement of hypothesis leads to the establishment of the appropriate statistical techniques and the determination of the level of significance and power. The level of significance and power are established prior to conducting statistical techniques. Researchers performing significance testing can make either type I or type II errors. Thus, establishing the hypothesis affects the analysis of the study's data and the interpretation of the consequences of the treatment.

Table 9.11.   Type I and type II errors in significance testing

Error	Truth or actuality
Fail to reject null hypothesis	Incorrect: Type II error (β) (false negative)
	Difference or association between groups' performance
	Correct
	No difference or association between groups' performance
Reject null hypothesis	Incorrect: Type I error (α) (false positive)
	No difference or association between groups' performance
	Correct
	(power)
	Actual difference

Specific Aims, Objectives, or Purpose

The **purpose statement** clearly states what the researchers are attempting to achieve. Similar terms are aims or objectives. The choice of term and use often is dictated by the format requirements of funding agencies and journals. For example, some funding agencies require both goals and objectives, with the latter being measurable and time-limited. To orient the reader, the purpose statement is placed near the beginning of the article or grant proposal.

In grant proposals, researchers should follow the instructions of the granting agency. For example, some granting agencies require that the purpose incorporates a needs assessment. In this case, researchers provide data on the scope of the problem, its economic and social impact, and the populations and factors involved. Other granting agencies have word or page restrictions. In such instances, the purpose must be succinct and precise. Moreover, the statement of purpose becomes the basis of outcomes assessment. Therefore, the purpose would need to identify essential research activities, such as "evaluate, develop, and compare." The outcomes measures then are explicitly linked to these activities. Outcomes assessment is especially prevalent when researchers are implementing programs or projects. A well-constructed purpose statement is critical to the success of the grant proposal.

In other instances, purpose statements or objectives are written to conform to the required format of a journal. In this case, researchers restate their research question in a declarative sentence as a purpose statement, or as a list of objectives.

Absent external requirements, the purpose should reflect the researcher's overarching goal. Thus, the purpose may be broader than the research question. The purpose is oriented to the interests of the reader, audience, or funding agency. The purpose should make clear how the research will advance the goals or knowledge of the reader, audience, or funding agency (see table 9.12).

Selection of Design and Method

Researchers weigh many factors when selecting the design and method of a research study. The most important factor is the purpose of the research. Other factors are associated with the researchers' expertise and resources. Finally, researchers weigh issues associated with validity and the impact of these issues on their design and method.

Factors

Researchers should establish a match among the design, the method and the following factors:

- **Purpose:** The purpose of the research is the first and foremost factor to consider when determining the design and method of a research study. This purpose is reflected in the research question. If researchers want to establish a causal relationship,

Table 9.12.   Examples of statements of purpose

Use	Content
Reader or audience of a journal article	"The purpose of this study was to evaluate completeness, level of granularity, multiple axial content, and clinical utility of the ICNP-beta in order to study the ability of the ICNP to express nursing content in different settings.... The specific research questions were: What is the level of domain completeness with respect to nutrition and skin care, of the ICNP-beta, based on examination of nurses' recordings in a practical setting? What characterizes granularity (that is, level of detail) of the ICNP-beta in relation to nurses' recordings in a practical setting? What is the correspondence between the axial structure of the ICNP-beta and nurses' recordings in a practical setting?" (Ehnfors et al. 2003, 9)
Reader or audience of a journal article	"The purpose of this study was to address the absence of information in administrative databases relevant to nursing in acute care and long-term-care (LTC) settings to determine (a) the reliability of the instruments measuring nursing-sensitive outcomes, (b) whether the outcome measures are sensitive to changes in patients' health, and (c) whether the outcome measures are associated with nursing interventions" (Doran et al. 2006, S76).
Reader or audience of a journal article	"The aim of this study is to assess the effectiveness of an online evidence retrieval system (QC) in improving clinical decision-making processes in general practice" (Coiera et al. 2006, n.p.).
Funding agency (Agency for Healthcare Research and Quality, AHRQ)	"The study uses a randomized, prospective cohort design to assess the impact of shared online health records on 1) patient safety, 2) health goal adherence and outcomes, 3) documentation of family history, and 4) barriers to the adoption of patient-physician communication technology" (Middleton 2005, n.p.).

they should conduct one of the experimental studies. If they are breaking new ground in a poorly understood area of practice, they may want to consider an exploratory study in a qualitative design.

- **Expertise:** The researchers should determine whether they can conduct, interpret, and explain sophisticated statistical techniques or whether more basic statistical techniques are within their comfort zone.

- **Skills:** The researchers should determine whether they can conduct the laboratory experiments necessary for the research. For example, to investigate physicians' utilization of clinical guidelines, the researchers should be able to insert a code into a computer-based patient record. The researchers should be able to insert a time clock into the software and design a query mechanism.

- **Personal attributes:** If the researchers are considering interviewing people, they should determine whether they are able to easily establish a rapport with people. If conversations with strangers make the researchers feel awkward, they should consider a way to collect data other than interviewing people.

- **Time:** The researchers should determine whether they have the time to devote to conduct the research plan well. For example, conducting a longitudinal investigation of the long-term effects of a health informatics workshop on the career patterns of its participants is a meritorious idea. However, graduate programs have time frames within which students must complete their studies. A longitudinal study may not fit the time frame.

- **Money:** The researchers should determine whether they can afford the fee to use a proprietary survey or software.

- **Potential subjects:** The Solomon four-group method (discussed in chapter 5) is excellent and beautifully controlled; however, it requires double the number of subjects. If subjects are in short supply, this method is most unlikely to be feasible.

Validity

Two types of **validity** are associated with the research design and method: **internal validity** and **external validity**. They underlie the integrity of the research plan.

Internal validity represents the bare minimum because it involves the accuracy of the data. As the importance of the application of the research findings to practice increases, the importance of external validity increases. Thus, internal validity combined with external validity is the ideal.

Internal validity is an attribute of a study's design that contributes to the accuracy of its findings. Threats to internal validity are potential sources of error that may contaminate the study's results. These sources of error come from factors outside the study (confounding variables). Therefore, if internal validity is breached, researchers cannot state for certain that the independent variable caused the effect. In their classic text, Campbell and Stanley (1963) identified eight threats to internal validity. (See figure 9.8.)

For example, a natural disaster caused one pair of researchers to experience **mortality (attrition)** within their study. Mortality, as it relates to validity, is the loss of research subjects. These researchers were evaluating the use of encoding software in the medical centers of the Department of Veterans Affairs (VA) (Lloyd and Layman 1997, 75). Eight VA medical centers tested encoding software from three vendors. During the course of the study, an earthquake damaged one of the VA medical centers to the extent that it never reopened. Therefore, no final data on the software were available from that

Figure 9.8.   Threats to internal validity

1. History	Events occur during the research and affect the results
2. Maturation	Subjects grow or mature during the period of the study
3. Testing	Taking the first test affects subsequent tests; also known as "practice effect"
4. Instrumentation	Lack of consistency in data collection
5. Statistical Regression	Subjects selected because of their extreme scores
6. Differential Selection	Control group and experimental group differ and that difference could affect the study's findings
7. Experimental Mortality	Loss of subjects during the study
8. Diffusion of Treatment	Members of the control group learn about the treatment of the experimental group

Source: Campbell and Stanley 1963.

center. This event represents mortality as a threat to a study's internal validity.

External validity refers to the extent to which a study's findings can be generalized to other people or groups. **Generalizability** is the term that researchers use to mean the ability to apply the results to other groups, such as hospitals, patients, and states. Generalizability was questionable in Lloyd and Layman's 1997 encoding software study. The VA centers were not covered by Medicare's inpatient prospective payment system (PPS) at the time. Thus, the findings could not be generalized to most U.S. hospitals because they were using Medicare's PPS at that time. This uniqueness of the VA site represents a threat to generalizability. Thus, the findings lacked external validity.

Both internal validity and external validity are important considerations for researchers. However, achieving both internal and external validity becomes a balancing act for researchers as they design their studies. Studies high in internal validity may not reflect the external environment; thus, their external validity is compromised. On the other hand, to achieve external validity, researchers give up control necessary for internal validity. As a rule of thumb, researchers should strive for **parsimony** or elegance. Parsimony means that the researcher has eliminated extraneous or unnecessary complications. Just as the simplest theory is the best, the simplest research design and method also are best.

Summary and Conclusions

The commitment of time and effort on the parts of both researchers and participants (subjects) demands that a research study advance the body of knowledge. Clarity about an important and meaningful research question leads to efficient and effective use of the researchers' time, effort, and energy. A well-developed literature review concisely and logically states what is known and unknown about a topic, and results in a hypothesis. A hypothesis is a testable, theory-based prediction about a set of measurable data. Finally, internal validity and external validity are key issues when implementing a research plan.

References

Ammenwerth, E., and N. de Keizer. 2005. An inventory of evaluation studies of information technology in health care: Trends in evaluation research 1982-2002. *Methods of Information in Medicine* 44(1):44–56.

Baird, D. 2006 (Aug. 15). Significance tests, history and logic of. *Encyclopedia of Statistical Sciences*:1–5.

Barrows, R.C., and P.D. Clayton. 1996 (March-April). Privacy, confidentiality, and electronic medical records. *Journal of the American Medical Informatics Association* 3(2):139–148.

Campbell, D.T., and J.C. Stanley. 1963. *Experimental and Quasi-Experimental Designs for Research*. Chicago: Rand McNally.

Chamberlain, E. 2007 (May 30). Bare bones 101: A basic tutorial on searching the web. Available online from http://www.sc.edu/beaufort/library/pages/bones/bones.shtml

Coiera, E., Magrabi, F., Westbrook, J.I., Kidd, M.R., and R. O'Day. 2006 (Aug. 24). Protocol for quick clinical study: A randomized controlled trial to assess the impact of an online evidence retrieval system on decision-making in general practice. *BMC Medical Informatics and Decision Making* 6:33. Available online from http://www.biomedcentral.com/1472-6947/6/33.

Colaianni, L.A. 2004 (July 13). Peer review in journals indexed in Index Medicus. *Journal of the American Medical Association* 272(2):156–158.

Dahl, R., Gyrd-Hansen, D., Kristiansen, I.S., Nexøe, J., and J.B. Nielsen. 2007 (March 29). Can postponement of an adverse outcome be used to present risk reductions to a lay audience? A population survey. *BMC Medical Informatics and Decision Making* 7:8. Available online from http://www.biomedcentral.com/1472-6947/7/8.

Doran, D.M., Harrison, M.B., Laschinger, H.S., Hirdes, J.P., Rukholm, E., Sidani, S., Hall, L.M., and A.E. Tourangeau. 2006 (March-April). Nursing-sensitive outcomes data collection in acute care and long-term-care settings. *Nursing Research* 55(Supplement 2S):S75–S81.

Eichelberg, M., Aden, T., Riesmeier, J., Dogac, A., and G.B. Laleci. 2005 (December). A survey and analysis of electronic healthcare record standards. *ACM Computing Surveys* 37(4):277–315.

Ehnfors, M., Florin, J., and A. Ehrenberg. 2003 (January-March). Applicability of the International Classification of Nursing Practice (ICNP) in the areas of nutrition and skin care. *International Journal of Nursing Terminologies and Classifications* 14(1):5–18.

Goodman, S.N., and J.A. Berlin. 1994 (Aug. 1). The use of predicted confidence intervals when planning experiments and the misuse of power when interpreting results. *Annals of Internal Medicine* 121(3):200–206.

Haque, S., and S. Srinivasan. 2006 (January). A meta-analysis of the training effectiveness of virtual reality surgical simulators. *IEEE Transactions on Information Technology in Biomedicine* 10(1):51–58.

Institute of Medicine, Committee on Quality of Health Care in American. 2001. *Crossing the Quality Chasm: A New Health System for the 21st Century*. Washington, DC:

National Academy Press. Available online from http://www.iom.edu/?id=12736.

Kaplan, B., and N.T. Shaw. 2004. Future directions in evaluation research: People, organizational, and social issues. *Methods of Information in Medicine* 43(3):215–231.

Kesh, S., and W. Raghupathi. 2004 (Fall). Critical issues in bioinformatics and computing. *Perspectives in Health Information Management* 1(9):1–8. Available online from http://www.ahima.org/perspectives/.

Lloyd, S.S., and E. Layman. 1997 (February). The effects of automated encoders on coding accuracy and coding speed. *Topics in Health Information Management* 17(3):72–79.

Lobach, D.F., and D.E. Detmer. 2007 (May). Research challenges for electronic health records. *American Journal of Preventive Medicine* 32(5S):S104–S111.

Mendonça, E.A., Cimino, J.J., Johnson, S.B., and Y-H. Seol. 2001 (April). Accessing heterogeneous sources of evidence to answer clinical questions. *Journal of Biomedical Informatics* 34(2):85–98.

Metz, M.H. 2001 (June-July). Intellectual border crossing in graduate education: A report from the field. *Educational Researcher* 30(5):12–18.

Middleton, B. 2005 (Nov. 9). Shared online health records for patient safety and care. Agency for Healthcare Research and Quality, ClinicalTrials.gov Identifier NCT00251875. Available online from http://www.clinicaltrials.gov/ct/show/NCT00251875?order=6.

Pluye, P., Grad, R.M., Dunikowski, L.G., and R. Stephenson. 2005 (September). Impact of clinical information-retrieval technology on physicians: A literature review of quantitative, qualitative and mixed methods studies. *International Journal of Medical Informatics* 74(9):745–768.

Poissant, L., Pereira, J., Tamblyn, R., and Y. Kawasumi. 2005 (September-October). The impact of electronic health records on time efficiency of physicians and nurses: A systematic review. *Journal of the American Medical Informatics Association* 12(5):505–516.

Riopelle, A.J. 2000 (April). Are effect sizes and confidence levels problems for or solutions to the null hypothesis test? *Journal of General Psychology* 127(2):198–216.

Sanders, D.L., and D. Aronsky. 2006 (July-August). Biomedical informatics applications for asthma care: A systematic review. *Journal of the American Medical Informatics Association* 13(4):418–427.

Smith, H., Bukirwa, H., Mukasa, O., Snell, P., Adeh-Nsoh, S., Mbuyita, S., Honorati, M., Orji, B., and P. Garner. 2007 (May 17). Access to electronic health knowledge in five countries in Africa: A descriptive study. *BMC Health Services Research* 7:72. Available online from http://www.biomedcentral.com/1472-6963/7/72.

Steinbrook, R. 2006 (Jan. 5). Searching for the right search: Reaching the medical literature. *New England Journal of Medicine* 354(1):4–7.

Walther, J.B., Wang, Z., and T. Loh. 2004 (July-September). The effect of top-level domains and advertisements on health web site credibility. *Journal of Medical Internet Research* 6(3):e24. Available online from http://www.pubmedcentral.nih.gov/articlerender.fcgi?artid=1550615.

Watson, G.S. 2006 (Aug. 15). Hypothesis testing. *Encyclopedia of Statistical Sciences*: 1-10. Available online from http://www.mrw.interscience.wiley.com/emrw/9780471667193/ess/article/ess0978/current/abstract.

Westbrook, J.I., Gosling, A.S., and E. Coiera. 2004 (March-April). Do clinicians use online evidence to support patient care? A study of 55,000 clinicians. *Journal of the American Medical Informatics Association* 11(2):113–120.

Chapter 10
Data Collection

Elizabeth J. Layman, PhD, RHIA, CCS, FAHIMA

Learning Objectives

- To select instruments of data collection appropriate to the research

- To collect data using standard and suitable tools and techniques

- To determine sampling techniques appropriate to the research

- To articulate an effective plan of data collection

Key Terms

Census survey

Cluster sampling

Concurrent validity

Construct

Construct validity

Content validity

Content validity index (CVI)

Content validity ratio (CVR)

Convenience sampling

Convergent validity

Coverage error

Criterion validity

Divergent (discriminant) validity

Face validity

Factor analysis

Focus group

Heterogeneity

Instrument

Instrumentation

Internal consistency

Interrater reliability

Interval

Interview guide

Intrarater reliability

Likert scale

Nominal

Nonrandom sampling

Operational definition

Ordinal

Pilot study

Primary source

Probe

Purposive sampling

Questionnaire

Quota sampling

Random sampling

Rater reliability

Ratio

Reliability

Reproducibility

Response (nonresponse) bias

Response rate

Rich data

Sample

Sample size

Sample survey

Sampling

Sampling error

Sampling frame

Secondary source

Semantic differential scale

Semistructured interview

Simple random sampling

Snowball sampling

Stability (test-retest reliability, reproducibility)

Stratified random sampling

Structured (closed-ended) question

Systematic sampling

Target population

Test-retest reliability

Theoretical sampling

Unstructured (open-ended) question

Validity

Introduction

"One of the cardinal ways the quality of any research is assessed is by noting how rigorously the data were collected" (Rowan and Huston 1997, 1445). Therefore, planning the process of data collection is critical. This plan should be comprehensive. Researchers should write a step-by-step, day-by-day plan for gathering data prior to implementation.

Failure to plan can result in violation of the study's internal validity. This violation is **instrumentation**, which is the lack of consistency in the collection of data. Researchers who make this error may collect contaminated data and may compromise their ability to analyze their data.

This chapter encompasses selection of **instruments**, techniques and tools to gather data, and **sampling**. The chapter concludes with a detailed list of issues that researchers should consider as they develop their research plans.

Selection of an Instrument

An **instrument** is a standardized, uniform way to collect data. Figure 10.1 lists some of the many types of instruments.

Researchers can find standardized instruments in electronic databases and in reference books, such as those included in figure 10.2. These databases and reference books provide descriptions and critiques of the instruments. The databases can be searched for relevant instruments. For example, querying the database of

Figure 10.1.   Types of measurement instruments

- Checklists
- Coding schemes and manuals
- Clinical screenings and assessments
- Educational test
- Index measures
- Interview guides (schedules)
- Personality tests
- Projective techniques
- Psychological tests
- Questionnaires
- Rating scales
- Scenarios
- Vignettes

Health and Psychosocial Instruments (HaPI) for instruments with the term "computer literacy" resulted in more than 40 possible instruments.

Features

Several features of instruments lead researchers to determine which instrument to use in their studies. These important features are **validity**, **reliability**, mode, and format.

Validity

Validity is the accuracy and truth of the data and findings that research produces. Validity, as it relates to instruments, means the extent to which the instrument measures what it is intended to measure (see chapter 9 for the meaning of validity in relationship to the research design).

Validity and reliability are two important features of instruments. Electronic databases and reference books that are sources of instruments list the validity and reliability of the instruments, if available. Researchers who are using an existing instrument should state in the study the instrument's **content validity**, **construct validity**, and reliability.

Acceptable levels of validity and reliability vary by the type of instrument and the type of research. Instruments measuring attitudes, perceptions, and personality traits tend to have lower levels than standardized aptitude tests. Moreover, newer instruments initially tend to have lower reliability than older instruments. As the instruments are further developed, tested, and refined, their levels of validity and reliability increase.

The four types of validity associated with instruments are discussed below.

Face Validity

Face validity is the extent to which the instrument appears to measure what it says it measures. Face validity is related to the instrument's apparent coverage of the topic upon an expert's cursory review. Thus, a quick scan of the content to reveal that the instrument appears to measure the phenomenon sought. Basically, the expert makes an intuitive and subjective judgment that an instrument has merit. The term face validity is related to the phrase "at face value." The connotation is that, upon delving into the instrument, this appearance may not be true. Technically, face validity is superficial and is a weak measure of validity.

Figure 10.2.   Sources of measurement instruments

Electronic Databases
Health and Psychosocial Instruments (HaPI, through OVID reference database)
Buros Institute of Mental Measurements (http://www.unl.edu/buros/)
Reference Books
Bowling, A. 2005. *Measuring Health: A Review of Quality of Life Measurement Scales,* 3rd ed. New York: Open University Press.
Chun, K-T, Cobb, S., and J.R.P. French, Jr. 1975. *Measures for Psychological Assessment: A Guide to 3,000 Original Sources and Their Applications.* Ann Arbor, MI: Survey Research Center, Institute for Social Research.
Herndon, R.M., ed. 1997. *Handbook of Neurologic Rating Scales.* New York: Demos Vermande.
Keyser, D.J., and R.C. Sweetland, eds. 1991. *Test Critiques.* Kansas City, MO: Test Corporation of America.
Maddox, T., ed. 2003. *Tests: A Comprehensive Reference for Assessments in Psychology, Education, and Business,* 5th ed. Austin, TX: Pro-Ed.
McDowell, I., and C. Newell. 1996. *Measuring Health: A Guide to Rating Scales and Questionnaires,* 2nd ed. New York: Oxford University Press.
Murphy, L.L., Spies, R.A., and B.S. Plake, eds. 2006. *Tests in Print VII: An Index to Tests, Test Reviews, and the Literature on Specific Tests.* Lincoln, NE: University of Nebraska Press.
Redman, B.K., ed. 2002. *Measurement Tools in Clinical Ethics.* New York: Springer.
Redman, B.K., ed. 2003. *Measurement Tools in Patient Education,* 2nd ed. New York: Springer.
Spies, R.A., and B.S. Plake, eds. 2005. *The Sixteenth Mental Measurements Yearbook* (Buros Mental Measurements Yearbooks). Lincoln, NE: University of Nebraska Press.
Spreen, O., and E. Strauss. 1998. *A Compendium of Neuropsychological Tests: Administration, Norms, and Commentary,* 2nd. ed. New York: Oxford University Press.

Content Validity

Content validity is the rigorous determination that the instrument represents all relevant aspects of a topic. Content validity concerns whether all the content of an instrument is related to its topic and that none of the content is unrelated (extraneous) to its topic. Thus, both relevance and irrelevance must be considered. Content often is represented by the instrument's items. For example, an instrument about usage of the components of an electronic health record (EHR) should contain an item about each component of an EHR. One way to assess an instrument's content validity is to have experts in the field review it and provide their opinion. In his classic 1975 article, Lawshe provides a method to quantify the experts' opinions (567–569). In Lawshe's method, researchers query each expert about the essentiality of each item on the instrument. Experts independently score each item as:

- Essential
- Useful but not essential
- Not necessary

The next step is to calculate the **content validity ratio** (CVR). The CVR is based on the items that experts score as essential. For each item, the CVR represents the experts' level of agreement in numerical terms, as cal-

culated in figure 10.3. Lawshe's minimally acceptable values for CVRs are listed in table 10.1. The underlying concept of his method is that the greater the strength of the experts' consensus on items' essentiality, the greater the content validity.

A final step is to calculate the overall content validity of the instrument. The **content validity index** (CVI) is a numerical representation of the experts' aggregate level of agreement for the entire instrument (Polit and Beck 2006, 492–493). One way to determine the CVI is to calculate the mean (average) of the individual item's CVRs. (See table 10.2.)

Construct Validity

Construct validity is the degree to which an instrument measures the **constructs** that it claims to measure. Constructs are theoretical, nonobservable concepts. Being nonobservable, constructs are "constructed" in language and graphics. Classic examples of constructs are psychological concepts, such as intelligence, motivation, and anxiety. For example, although intelligence itself is not visible, its effects are. Similarly, although satisfaction itself is not visible, its effects are. Therefore, if an instrument is intended to measure users' satisfaction, it should include measurable aspects associated with users' satisfaction.

Figure 10.3. Formula and example: Content validity ratio (CVR)

$CVR = \dfrac{n_e - (N/2)}{(N/2)}$	n_e = number of experts indicating "essential" N = total number of experts
Example 1 $CVR = \dfrac{9 - (14/2)}{(14/2)}$ $CVR = \dfrac{9-7}{7}$ $CVR = \dfrac{2}{7}$ $CVR = .28$	$n_e = 9$ $N = 14$
Example 2 $CVR = \dfrac{15 - (20/2)}{(20/2)}$ $CVR = \dfrac{15-10}{10}$ $CVR = \dfrac{5}{10}$ $CVR = .50$	$n_e = 15$ $N = 20$

Table 10.1. Minimum values of content validity ratio (CVR)[1]

No. of Experts	Minimum CVR value
5	.99
6	.99
7	.99
8	.75
9	.78
10	.62
11	.59
12	.56
13	.54
14	.51
15	.49
20	.42
25	.37
30	.33
35	.31
40	.29

[1]One-tailed test, $p = .05$
Source: Adapted from Lawshe 1975.

Construct validity is assessed by evaluating the degree of correlation between the instrument and the variables it purportedly measures. The three components of construct validity are **convergent validity**, **divergent (discriminant) validity**, and **concurrent validity**.

1. Convergent validity is the degree of correlation between the instrument and other instruments designed to measure similar constructs.
2. Divergent validity is the degree to which the instrument does *not* correlate to instruments measuring dissimilar constructs.
3. Concurrent validity is the instrument's ability to discriminate between groups it should differentiate.

For example, an instrument with concurrent validity would be able to discriminate between expert users and novice users of computer code. **Factor analysis** is a statistical technique that analyzes the correlations and is used to assess construct validity. Factor analysis identifies the underlying set of relationships (factors) in an instrument.

These factors comprise variables that are highly correlated among themselves, but lowly correlated with other variables (Gay et al. 2006, 204). In addition to identifying the underlying factors, it is used to reduce the factors to the fewest number. The relationships are reported as eigenvalues and factor loadings. Minimum values are typically 1 and 0.30 (Kim and Mueller 1978, 44, 70). Numerous studies, showing high degrees of correlation between the instrument and the variables it purportedly measures and showing common factors, build evidence supporting the instrument's construct validity.

Criterion Validity

Criterion validity is the assessment of an instrument against another established instrument. The validity and reliability of the established instrument are known and accepted. Thus, the established instrument is the "gold standard" and the criterion. The researchers' instrument is checked against the established instrument, the criterion.

Reliability

Reliability is the extent to which a procedure or an instrument yields the same results over repeated trials,

Table 10.2.   Calculation of content validity index (CVI): Sample ratings on a 10-item instrument by 14 experts

EXPERT	ITEM 1	ITEM 2	ITEM 3	ITEM 4	ITEM 5	ITEM 6	ITEM 7	ITEM 8	ITEM 9	ITEM 10	OVERALL CVI
A		x							x	x	
B	x	x	x	x	x	x	x	x	x	x	
C	x	x	x	x	x	x	x	x	x	x	
D	x	x	x	x	x	x	x	x	x	x	
E		x	x	x	x	x	x		x	x	
F	x	x	x	x	x	x	x	x	x	x	
G	x	x	x	x	x	x	x	x	x	x	
H	x	x	x	x	x	x	x	x	x	x	
I		x	x	x	x	x	x		x	x	
J	x	x	x	x	x	x	x	x	x	x	
K	x	x	x	x	x	x	x	x	x	x	
L		x	x	x	x	x	x		x	x	
M		x	x	x	x	x	x		x	x	
N	x		x	x	x	x	x	x	x		
No. in Agreement	9	13	13	13	13	13	13	9	14	13	
CVR	0.29	0.86	0.86	0.86	0.86	0.86	0.86	0.29	1	0.86	0.76
											(mean of CVRs)

x = rated as "essential"

over time, across similar groups, within individuals, and across raters (administrators). Reliability means that, over time, a test or observation is dependable and consistent in its measurement. Consistency, dependability, and reproducibility characterize reliable instruments. Three aspects of reliability are **stability**, **internal consistency**, and **rater reliability**.

Stability

Stability is also known as **test-retest reliability** or **reproducibility** (Lohr 2002, 199; Osborn 2006, 73). Test-retest reliability means that repeated tests will result in reasonably similar findings. One caveat is that this stability depends on constancy in the object being measured. If changes occur in the intervening period between tests, the results may be different (see chapter 9, threats to internal validity). Two statistical techniques to assess test-retest reliability are the Pearson *r* correlation coefficient (**sample** size >15) and the intraclass correlation coefficient (ICC, sample size ≤15) (Hopkins 2000, n.p.). A perfect correlation is 1.0; no correlation is 0. The

minimally acceptable coefficient for groups is ≥ 0.70 and for individuals 0.90 to 0.95 (Lohr 2002, 199).

Internal Consistency

Internal consistency is the homogeneity of an instrument's items. An instrument with internal consistency measures a single construct, a single characteristic, a single skill, or a single quality. Three statistical techniques are used to assess internal consistency:

1. Split-half reliability (two halves of the test are correlated and then the Spearman-Brown correction formula applied)

2. Kuder-Richardson formula

3. Cronbach's alpha (Gay et al. 2006, 141) (see chapter 3)

Cronbach's alpha (α) is common in health informatics research. The minimum level of acceptability varies by the type of instrument and number of test takers. For most instruments in health informatics, an acceptable

Cronbach's alpha for groups is ≥0.70 and for individuals 0.90 to 0.95 (Lohr 2002, 199).

Rater Reliability

Rater reliability involves the scoring of tests. The scoring of tests, by one rater or multiple raters, should be consistent. Subjectivity should be eliminated. **Interrater reliability** means that different persons scoring the test will have reasonably similar results. **Intrarater reliability** means that the same person scoring the test at different times will have reasonably similar results. For continuous data (see chapter 11), the ICC is used to assess interrater reliability and intrarater reliability (Shrout and Fleiss 1979, 421). For categorical data (nominal and ordinal, (see chapter 11), the kappa coefficient (sometimes called Cohen's kappa) is used to assess interrater reliability and intrarater reliability (Landis and Koch 1977, 159; Sim and Wright 2005, 258). The kappa coefficient (κ) measures the strength of agreement among raters. (See table 10.3.)

Some researchers conduct studies aimed at developing and validating instruments. In these studies, the researchers describe the statistical tests or other procedures that they used to assess their instrument's validity and reliability. Usually, the researchers provide details about their instruments' content validity, construct validity, and reliability. Instruments developed by health informatics researchers are described in the following paragraphs and in table 10.4.

In the first example, researchers developed a scoring index (also called a metric or instrument) to be used as an outcome measure for studies evaluating diagnostic decision support (Ramnarayan et al. 2003, 564). The purpose of the instrument was to simultaneously measure changes in diagnostic quality and clinical management as a result of the diagnostic decision support system (DSS). The instrument comprised 24 pediatric cases with appropriate diagnoses and clinical management. A panel of two pediatricians reviewed the cases twice to determine the appropriate diagnoses and clinical management. The researchers assessed intrarater reliability by checking the panel members' two sets of scores. Intrarater reliability was determined to be acceptable. Content validity was assessed by having consultants (10 pediatricians) review the instrument. The researchers assessed the instrument's construct validity by comparing the mean scores of medical students and consultants. Supporting the instrument's construct validity, the mean scores of medical students were much lower than the mean scores of consultants. In terms of interrater reliability, the intraclass coefficient correlation was acceptable at 0.79 for diagnoses and 0.72 for clinical management (568).

Another set of researchers developed and validated a scale (instrument) to assess physicians' attitudes about using handheld DSSs (Ray et al. 2006, 568). They reported that content validity was assessed by a panel of researchers (themselves). The test-retest reliability was 0.71. A Cronbach's alpha reliability coefficient was computed to assess the scale's internal consistency. The Cronbach's alpha was 0.73. The researchers also assessed the instrument's construct validity by conducting a factor analysis and a multiple regression (multiple correlations and cross-correlations in one statistical analysis). Moderate correlations were found between attitude scores and usage of the handheld DSSs, supporting the instrument's validity. The researchers concluded that the instrument could be used for future development and implementation of handheld DSSs.

Bakken et al. developed and validated a telemedicine satisfaction and usefulness instrument (2006, 661). The instrument was developed in both English and Spanish and at a reading level of eighth grade or lower. The researchers assessed construct validity through a factor analysis. Two factors—Video Visits (home telemedicine visits) and Use and Impact—accounted for 63.6 percent of the variance in satisfaction scores. For internal consistency, Cronbach's alpha was 0.96 for Video Visits and 0.92 for Use and Impact (663). The researchers concluded that analyses supported the construct validity and internal consistency of the instrument (666).

Researchers developing new instruments and researchers using existing instruments pay attention to their instruments' validity and reliability. Validity and reliability are important aspects of research throughout a

Table 10.3.   Interpretation of kappa statistic

Kappa Statistic	Strength of Agreement
<0.00	Poor
0.00–0.20	Slight
0.21–0.40	Fair
0.41–0.60	Moderate
0.61–0.80	Substantial
0.81–1.00	Almost Perfect

Source: Adapted from Landis and Koch 1977.

Table 10.4.   Selected examples of the development of instruments

Attribute	The Development and Initial Testing of the Internet Consequences Scales (ICONS) (Clark and Frith 2005)	Testing the Reliability and Validity of Computer-Mediated Social Support Measures among Older Adults (Nahm et al. 2004)
Validity		
• Face		Instrument given to two experts (informatics and sociology) who rated each item's relevance
• Content	Team of 3 Internet communications and 1 instrument development expert assessed each of the scale's items Each item rated on its relevancy with 4 being very relevant and 1 being not relevant Items with mean ratings >3 were retained	Content validity index (CVI) were 0.90 for modified-Lubben Social Network Scale (LSNS) 0.90 and 0.80 for modified-Medical Outcomes Study Social Support Survey (MOS-SSS)
• Construct	Factor analysis performed Items with eigenvalues >1.0 and factor loadings ≥0.30 were retained	Preliminary investigation of construct validity through exploratory factor analysis performed (although small sample, 38 subjects) Items with eigenvalues >1.0 retained LSNS three-factor structure confirmed with loadings >0.6 MOS-SSS to two-factor structure in modification (rather than three) with loadings >0.7 Assessed theoretical basis against psychosocial studies on social networks and functional support
• Criterion		No gold standard against which to assess
Reliability		
• Stability		ICC for modified LSNS were 0.73 (Internet work), 0.76 (family network), 0.77 (friends network), and 0.87 overall ICC for modified MOS-SSS were 0.90 (hyperinterpersonal support) and 0.76 (nonpersonal support) and 0.88 overall
• Internal Consistency	Cronbach's alpha varied on 4 subscales and with test groups Physical, 0.76 and 0.81; Behavioral, 0.91 and 0.92 Economic, 0.69 and 0.79 Psychosocial, 0.84 and 0.89 Split-Half Reliabilities Physical, 1st half 0.79 and 2nd half 0.58 Behavioral, 1st half 0.86 and 2nd half 0.85 Economic, 1st half 0.57 and 2nd half 0.70 Psychosocial, 1st half 0.84 and 2nd half 0.84	Cronbach's alpha for modified LSNS were 0.74 (family network) and 0.78 (friends network) with 0.77 overall Cronbach's alpha for modified MOS-SSS were 0.93 (hyperinterpersonal support) and 0.73 (nonpersonal support) and 0.83 overall
• Rater Reliability		

research study. Attention to validity, in fact, spans three parts of the research process:

1. Research design
2. Data collection
3. Analysis

Reflecting its importance, validity is discussed in chapters 9, 10, and 11. See table 10.5 for an overview of the ways validity and reliability affect the research process.

Structured vs. Unstructured Questions

Questions on instruments are delivered in two different modes: **structured** or **unstructured**. Structured (closed-ended) questions list all the possible responses. Unstructured (open-ended) questions allow free-form responses. The advantages of structured questions over unstructured questions is that structured questions are easier for the participant to complete and for the researcher to tabulate and analyze. The advantages of unstructured questions are that they allow in-depth questions and may uncover

Table 10.5.   Validity and reliability across research design, data collection, and analysis

Research Design	Data Collection: Instrument Development	Analysis
Internal validity	*Validity*	*Statistical conclusion validity*
Integrity of research plan that supports accuracy of findings, threatened by 8 potential occurrences 1. History 2. Maturation 3. Testing 4. Instrumentation 5. Statistical regression 6. Differential selection 7. Experimental mortality 8. Diffusion of treatment	Extent to which an instrument measures what it is intended to measure • Face validity • Content validity • Construct validity (convergent, divergent, and concurrent) • Criterion validity	Extent to which the statistical conclusions about the relationships in the data are reasonable. Threats are lack of reliability and lack of power
	Reliability	
	Extent to which a procedure or instrument is consistent, dependable, and reproducible • Stability • Internal consistency • Rater reliability (interrater and intrarater)	
External Validity		
Generalizability of findings to other groups, settings, or other entities		

aspects of a problem unknown to the researcher. Exploratory and qualitative research often use unstructured questions. The purpose of the research determines whether researchers use structured or unstructured questions.

Numeric vs. Categorical Items

Structured questions may be formatted as numeric items or as categorical items. (See table 10.6.) Numeric items request the respondent to enter a number. Categorical items require the respondent to select the appropriate category or grouping. When feasible, numeric items are preferable to categorical items (Alreck and Settle 2004, 113).

Numeric items result in metric data (**interval** or **ratio**, see chapter 11). Statistical analysis of metric data has fewer limitations than statistical analysis of categorical items. However, in writing a numeric item, researchers must be careful to explicitly specify the unit of measure. For example, the question, "How long ago was your last visit to the dentist?" does not give the respondent an explicit unit of measure. The respondent may write 365 days, 52 weeks, or 1 year.

Categorical items classify respondents into groupings. Categorical items result in **nominal** or **ordinal**

data (see chapter 11). Statistical analysis of nominal and ordinal data has greater limitations than statistical analysis of numeric data. Composing good categorical items requires time and careful thought. Researchers must construct categories that are all-inclusive, mutually exclusive, and sufficiently broad or narrow, and form meaningful clusters, as explained below:

• All-inclusive: All respondents must fit into a category, even if it is "other." Typically, there are unusual or exceptional cases that warrant the

Table 10.6.   Example of numeric and categorical items

Numeric	Categorical
_____ Indicate the number of hours that you work per week (whole numbers)	Mark the number of hours that you work per week: ☐ 19 or fewer hours per week ☐ 20 to 29 hours per week ☐ 30 to 39 hours per week ☐ 40 to 49 hours per week ☐ 50 to 59 hours per week ☐ 60 or greater hours per week

category "other." Moreover, the lack of a matching category, even if it is "other," frustrates the respondents.

- Mutually exclusive: Categories should not overlap, which could confuse the respondents.

- Form meaningful clusters: Categories should make sense and be meaningfully distinct. For example, the following set of categories does not form a reasonable, balanced progression:

    —Kindergarten to 12th grade

    —Freshman

    —Sophomore

    —Junior

    —Senior

    —Graduate school

A more meaningful set of categories is:
    —High school education
    —Associate's degree
    —Baccalaureate degree
    —Graduate degree

- Sufficiently narrow or broad: The number of categories for a question may range from two (yes/no, true/false) to six or eight. Respondents have difficulty seeing shades of meaning beyond eight categories. Alreck and Settle recommend that, when in doubt, use the narrower (greater number) categories (2004, 112-113). These experts explain that researchers can always combine categories, but researchers cannot disaggregate broad categories into fine-grained categories if the detailed data were not collected in the first place. On the other hand, requesting participants to respond to many categories and unnecessarily narrow categories may lower the response rate and introduce inaccuracy.

Scales

A scaled item is a type of categorical item. **Scales** are progressive categories, such as size, amount, importance, rank, or agreement. (See table 10.7.) For example, Garvin used a five-point scale on a 2001 questionnaire that asked respondents to categorize their feelings of capability regarding various skills related to coding. (See figure 10.4.) Research shows that reliability increases steadily from a two-point scale to a seven-point

Table 10.7.   **Common scales**

Scale	Purpose	Example
Two-Point	Dichotomous Question	Yes, No Favor, Oppose True, False
Three-Point	Importance, Interest, or Satisfaction Satisfaction with Amounts	Very, Fairly, Not at All Too Much (Many), Just (About) Right, Not Enough (Too Few)
Four-Point	Generic Measurement of Amounts	Excellent, Good, Fair, Poor Very Much, Quite a Bit, Some, Very Little
Likert (Five-Point)	Indication of Agreement or Disagreement	Strongly Agree, Agree, Neutral, Disagree, Strongly Disagree
Verbal Frequency (Five-Point)	Frequency	Always, Often, Sometimes, Rarely (Seldom), Never
Expanded Likert (Seven-Point)	Extra Discrimination Desirable	Very Strongly Agree, Strongly Agree, Agree, Neutral, Disagree, Strongly Disagree, Very Strongly Disagree

Figure 10.4.   **Excerpt from survey questionnaire**

> **Questionnaire on Coding Skills**
> **Contained in AHIMA's Vision 2006**
>
> On a scale of 1 to 5, 5 being the most capable, please designate how capable you feel in the following areas:
>
> 1. Understanding the current clinical coding systems relevant to the organization:
>   A. ICD-9-CM   5 4 3 2 1
>   B. CPT   5 4 3 2 1
>   C. DSM-IV   5 4 3 2 1
>   D. SNOMED   5 4 3 2 1
>   E. ICD-O   5 4 3 2 1
>   F. ICD-10   5 4 3 2 1
> 2. Ability to gather clinical data from primary data sources   5 4 3 2 1
> 3. Understanding of the elements required for research and outcomes   5 4 3 2 1
> 4. Ability to participate in the design of studies   5 4 3 2 1

Source: Adapted from Garvin 2001.

scale (Cicchetti et al. 1985, 35). After seven points, the improvement is trivial and insignificant. Thus, if the literature provides researchers with no information on the appropriate number of scale points, they should choose a seven-point scale.

Likert Scale

A commonly used scale is the **Likert scale**, named for its developer, Rensis Likert. A Likert scale records the respondents' level of agreement or disagreement. On a Likert scale, the categories are along the range "strongly agree, agree, neutral sure, disagree, strongly disagree." Each category is also called a point. Therefore, a scale with five categories is a five-point scale.

Semantic Differential Scale

Researchers, marketers, and others use a **semantic differential scale** to ascertain a group's perspective or image of a product, healthcare organization, or program. (See figure 10.5.) A semantic differential scale uses adjectives to rate the product, organization, or program. Adjectives that are polar opposites are placed on the ends of the continua. Up to 20 adjective pairs may be used. Half the items should begin with the positive adjective of the pair and the other half with the negative adjective. Identifying polar opposite objectives and capturing the major attributes make this scale difficult to construct. However, a well-constructed semantic differential scale can provide a valuable profile of a product, organization, or program's image (Alreck and Settle 2004, 132–134).

Factors in Selection

Researchers should review several instruments before selecting one for their study. Researchers should allow adequate time for this review because obtaining instruments from companies or from other researchers can introduce delays. Delays also occur in securing permission to use the instrument and purchasing it or its license. Factors that determine the selection of an instrument include:

Figure 10.5.   Semantic differential scale

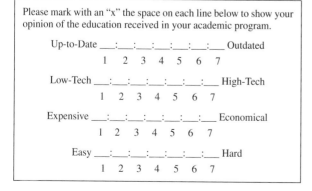

- Purpose, including matches between the theories underpinning the instrument and the researcher's investigation and between the researcher's **operational definitions** and the instrument's operational definitions
- Developed instrument with satisfactory ratings for validity and reliability
- Appropriate format, in terms of clarity of language, brevity and attractiveness, and match between the level of measurement (nominal, ordinal, interval, or ratio scales of data; see chapter 11) and the proposed statistical analyses
- Feasible logistics, such as whether the instrument is in the public domain or is proprietary and any related cost

Purpose

Purpose is the most important of these factors. Researchers should match their purpose to the instrument's purpose. Reading the description and critique in the reference book or database is just the first step. Researchers should obtain the instrument itself and read it closely to ensure that the instrument exactly matches their purpose. They must pay special attention to the instrument's theoretical underpinning and the operational definitions of terms. Merely reading the description and critique in the reference book or database is insufficient. Knowing all the details of the instrument requires careful reading and interpretation of the instrument.

Theoretical Underpinnings

Researchers develop instruments as they work within a theory. Thus, the instrument reflects the theory's assumptions about knowledge and reality. For example, using an instrument evolved from existential psychology in a study using Skinner's behaviorism would be problematic. These two theoretical bases are entirely different.

Operational Definitions

Operational definitions represent concepts in observable and measurable terms. Different researchers operationalize concepts differently. Researchers need to verify that the instrument's use of the terms matches their meaning for the terms so that the instrument is collecting what they want to collect. For example, some instruments measure "social support." If the researcher is studying social support for maintaining personal health records (PHRs) in a household, an instrument about social support from colleagues in the workplace would be unsuitable. A researcher studying the effect of social support on a household's maintenance of the PHR should select an instrument about social support in the home. Selecting an instrument about social support in the workplace would be considered an error. This error is serious because it undermines the entire purpose of the study and negatively affects the validity of the research.

Developed Instrument with Satisfactory Ratings for Validity and Reliability

If at all possible, researchers should select instruments that other researchers have already developed and refined. The validity and reliability of such existing instruments are established. As the studies described in the previous section on validity and reliability confirm, construction of a valid and reliable instrument is a research project in and of itself. Osborn explained that the construction of a **questionnaire** includes deciding on the content, considering the audience, determining the level of measurement, pilot testing, analyzing the validity and reliability, and confirming the scales (1998, 4-9). Researchers should undertake the difficult task of developing an instrument only after they have investigated and verified that an appropriate instrument does not already exist.

Appropriate Format

The format of instruments is also important. Clearly worded instruments are more likely to collect accurate data than vague or imprecise instruments. Confused respondents may simply quit and leave the instrument incomplete, or they may misinterpret the instrument and thereby provide erroneous information. Brevity and an attractive format also increase the **response rate**. Finally, researchers need to inspect the items to determine what format the instrument collects data. Researchers need to collect the data (nominal, ordinal, interval, or ratio; see chapter 11) in a format that matches their proposed statistical analyses.

Feasible Logistics

Instruments may be in the public domain or proprietary. Instruments in the public domain can be copied and used freely. Instruments that are proprietary must be purchased and cannot be copied. Researchers should be aware that hidden costs also exist. For example, some instruments must be scored by the institute or researcher who holds the copyright. The cost of scoring can significantly increase the cost of the study. Other hidden costs include having to purchase the user's manual or the scor-

ing guide. However, researchers often can obtain samples of instruments for review at little or no cost. In addition, researchers must consider the quality of the research. An instrument that collects inaccurate data only tangentially related to the researcher's topic would not be of use. The instrument must match the purpose and contribute to the collection of accurate data that build knowledge.

In summary, obtaining or developing the proper instrument is a key step. Researchers should carefully consider the various factors as they review and select instruments. Carelessness or haste during this step can lead to unusable data that are difficult to analyze. On the other hand, thought and thoroughness are more likely to result in accurate, analyzable data. Purpose should drive the decision.

Techniques and Tools for Data Collection

Techniques and tools to collect data vary by the method of the research. For example, surveys use different instruments than observations. The following section reviews various techniques and tools in surveys, interviews, observations, treatments, and mining.

Response rate is a critical issue for surveys and interviews. There are two considerations related to response rate: overall numbers and **response bias** (also known as nonresponse bias). When researchers first design their study, they need to consider how to achieve the highest possible response rate and, at the same time, how to avoid response bias. These considerations extend into data collection. As researchers collect their data, they must maximize response rates and minimize response biases.

Choice of delivery method—electronic (Web-based) survey, postal mail (paper-based) survey, individual face-to-face interview, telephone interview, or **focus group**— is based on knowledge of the target audiences' habits, preferred means of communication, type of data, and past patterns of response. Early studies of Web-based surveys generally showed response rates equivalent to paper-based surveys at less cost and for less researchers' effort. However, these early results may have been a function of the delivery method's novelty. Current research comparing the response rates of Web-based surveys to paper-based surveys shows less positive results. (See table 10.8.) Moreover, researchers have recorded

Table 10.8. Selected examples of response rates for surveys and interviews

Title (Author)	Year	Target Audience	Study Information
Methods for the design and administration of Web-based surveys (Schleyer and Forrest)	2000	450 dental professionals	• Queried the Internet Dental Forum • Problems included technological incompatibilities, usability, and 1 programming error • Response rate 74.2% (84% of responders used Web and 16% of responders used e-mail or fax) • 38% less cost than comparable paper-based survey
Assessing response rates and nonresponse bias in Web and paper surveys (Sax et al.)	2003	4,498 college freshmen at 14 institutions	• Freshmen divided into 4 groups: Group A, paper-only survey; Group B, paper with Web option; Group C1, Web-only with incentive of comparing their responses to other freshmen e-mail; and Group C2, Web only • Response rates: Group A, 22.0%; Group B, 24.0%; Group C1, 17.1%; Group C2, 19.8%; Overall 21.5% • Women had higher response rates across all modes • Interpretations for low response rates include proliferation of junk mail and spam, students' perception they are excessively surveyed, other demands on students' time, irrelevance to students' lives, length of survey (4 paper pages versus 32 computer screens), number of items (200), uncertainty about students' use of and access to their institutional e-mail accounts, and privacy concerns
Internet versus mailed questionnaires: A controlled comparison (Leece et al.)	2004	442 surgeon-members of Orthopaedic Trauma Association	• Web survey had 45% response rate (3 follow-ups) • Paper survey had 58% response rate (3 follow-ups) • Statistically significant lower response to Web survey • Interpretations for low response rate for Web survey included unsolicited e-mails deleted or easier to ignore than paper • Web survey more expensive than paper survey due to initial Web site set-up costs, although per-participant cost was lower than paper survey
Online consumer surveys as a methodology for assessing the quality of the United States healthcare system (Bethell et al.)	2004	U.S. adult population and sample of adults with diabetes	• Comparison of Web-based survey and telephone survey • 17.3% uncorrected response rate for online survey (13,400 e-mails) • ~20% adjusted response rate, accounting for nonworking or dormant e-mails (10% to 15%) • 9.3% adjusted response for telephone survey, despite 6 follow-up telephone calls • 1-time contact for e-mail survey resulted in higher response rate • Increasing resistance to telephone solicitations make Web-based surveys an efficient, real-time strategy for data collection
The effect of personalization on response rates and data quality in Web surveys (Heerwegh et al.)	2005	2000 first-year students at Belgian university	• 1000 students sent "no-personalization" invitation to participate in survey (Dear Student) • 1000 students sent "personalized" invitation (Dear Student's First Name, Last Name) • 8.6% higher response rate for personalization • Students who received "personalized" invitation also tended to respond with more social desirability bias • Interpretation was that using personalization for sensitive topics should be carefully weighed
Comparison of three tobacco survey methods with college students: A case study (James et al.)	2005	3300 randomly selected students from 11 state colleges and universities (300 students each)	• In-class administration of the survey had highest response rate (66%); 4 institutions selected this mode of administration • Mail surveys had the 2nd highest response rate (25%); 2 institutions selected this mode of administration and also used incentives (various follow-up procedures) • Web-based surveys had the lowest response rate (10%); 5 institutions selected this mode of administration and also used incentives (various follow-up procedures)
Web-based and mailed questionnaires: A comparison of response rates and compliance (Bälter et al.)	2005	All persons ages 20 to 59 in middle-sized Swedish county	• Three groups: Printed questionnaire, Web questionnaire, and Web questionnaire with feedback • Printed questionnaire, 64% response rate (188 of 292) • Web questionnaire, 51% response rate (149 of 293) • Web questionnaire with feedback, 50% response rate (146 of 290) • Continuation rate (to 2nd half on nutrition) greatest for Web questionnaire with feedback group (64%)
E-mail versus Web survey response rates among health education professionals (Kittleson and Brown)	2005	600 professional health educators	• Two groups: 300 received e-mail survey and 300 received e-mail asking them to go to a Web page to complete the survey • No statistical difference in response rates (43% response rate for e-mail survey, 48% response rate for Web-based survey)

several advantages and disadvantages for Web-based delivery. (See table 10.9.) Therefore, researchers should carefully consider their target audience as they choose a delivery method.

To guard against response bias, researchers should again know the characteristics of the group being studied. The following points should be considered:

- Have past studies encountered response bias? If yes, did the researchers recommend means to avoid the bias in future studies?

- Are the researchers able to monitor whether the persons who volunteer to participate in the research differ from those who do not volunteer?

- Are the researchers able to monitor whether the persons who responded to the survey (responders) differ from those who did not (nonresponders)?

- Can the researchers state how similar the participants, nonparticipants, responders, and nonresponders are to the population?

- Can the researchers track both responders and nonresponders?

Researchers are reminded that a low response rate is a threat to generalizability and a biased response is a threat to validity.

Surveys

Surveys are a form of self-report research in which the subjects themselves are the source of data. Researchers collect data about a population to determine its current status with regard to certain factors. Surveys that collect from all the members of the population are **census surveys**; surveys that collect data from representative members of the population are **sample surveys**.

Two techniques of surveys are Web-based surveys and paper-based surveys. In both techniques, researchers commonly use **questionnaires** to query their participants (subjects). The questionnaires are these researchers' instrument to collect data. Questionnaires are printed or electronic lists of questions. Researchers send questionnaires to participants via electronic mail (e-mail or Web-based) or postal mail (paper-based).

Web-Based Surveys

Web-based surveys are becoming more prevalent. They are now being used to gather data on health status, access to care, health outcomes, perceptions of health professionals, and professional issues. As listed on table 10.9, Web surveys have several advantages and disadvantages. Two advantages that contribute to their prevalence are:

- Ability to gather data from large samples relatively inexpensively

- Enhanced efficiency because the subjects' answers are entered directly into the research database or spreadsheet, eliminating a step for the researchers

Researchers should not assume that they can immediately and directly transfer paper-based surveys to the Internet. Paper-based surveys may deal with aspects of face-to-face interactions; these aspects do not exist in virtual interactions. For example, researchers identified the "tangible support" scale of an existing instrument, the

Table 10.9. **Advantages and disadvantages of Web-based data collection**

Advantages	Disadvantages
Useful with computer-savvy populations or populations with computer access	Selection bias
	Lack of e-mails in directories
Time to respond reduced from weeks to days (even hours)	Nonsavvy users of technology
Direct, automated data entry eliminates manual data entry	No follow-up questions from researchers (probes)
Ease of follow-up communication	Traceability may reduce participation and cooperation
Reduced costs (administration and tabulation)	Respondents paying for Internet access and thus paying for participating
Increased user convenience (time zones for telephone surveys no longer an issue)	Technological difficulties (incompatibilities and slow transmission)
Wide geographic coverage	Potential for multiple responses from one participant
Relative anonymity supportive of obtaining sensitive data	
Reduced interviewer bias	
Ease of adjusting for visual impairments	
Flexibility in response medium (e-mail, fax, ground mail, telephone)	
Responses in written format (eliminates transcription)	

Adapted from Klein J. 2002, May-June. Issues surrounding the use of the Internet for data collection. *American Journal of Occupational Therapy* 56(3):340-343.

Medical Outcomes Study Social Support Survey (MOS-SSS) as unrelated to computer-mediated support networks. In the existing instrument, tangible support was operationalized as "provision of material aid and behavioral assistance" (Nahm et al. 2004, 213). The researchers deleted this entire scale from their Web-modified version of the survey. The researchers also modified items from other scales of the MOS-SSS. For example, an item on the "affectionate support" scale was deleted because it asked about "someone who hugs you" (Nahm et al. 2004, 214). Other items were reworded so they included e-mail communication as well as face-to-face communication. Moreover, validity and reliability must be confirmed on the Web-based instrument. The researchers modifying the MOS-SSS for the Internet were specifically testing the modified version's reliability and validity.

Elements of good Web site design affect the design of Web-based surveys. Researchers provided the following guidelines (Dillman 2007, 378–394; Schleyer and Forrest 2000, 418–419):

- Include title of survey on each Web page
- Be consistent in page layout including Clear Form and Next buttons
- Use a small file size for each Web page to minimize download time
- Use multiple sequential screens rather than one long Web page to avoid server time-outs, lengthy uploads, and respondents' confusion
- Format answers in a table for consistency in layout across browsers' operating systems, and window sizes
- Provide a PIN number to limit access
- Make the first question interesting and easy to answer
- Present questions in familiar formats similar to paper questionnaires to which respondents are accustomed
- Allow respondents to skip questions
- Limit use of color and other visual appearances because of differences in screen configurations, operating systems, browers, and other technologies
- Provide specific instructions for computer actions, such as how to change an answer or to enter multiple responses

Strategies to increase the response rate include using an invitation, sending multiple mailings, and using incentives as detailed in the section on paper-based surveys.

This discussion focused on Web-based surveys. However, e-mail surveys also are an electronic data collection method. E-mail surveys are most effective for surveys that are three to five questions in length and that are querying small samples for which the researchers already have a distribution list (Dillman 2007, 372). Typically, the technological capabilities of Web-based surveys make them the preferred means of delivery.

Paper-based Surveys

Paper-based surveys continue to be a popular and common technique to conduct a survey. Reasons for selecting a paper-based survey include:

- The study's population does not have access to computers
- The researchers have reason to believe that the population will consider the e-mail invitation spam and, thus, delete the e-mail
- The researchers have access to a postal mail directory, and an e-mail directory either does not exist or cannot be easily created
- The researchers have reason to believe that using a Web-based survey will result in response bias (or nonresponse bias)

Strategies to increase the response rate for questionnaire research include using a brief cover letter and multiple mailings. The cover letter should explain the purpose of the study and its benefits for the participants. Obtaining the sponsorship of a professional association or officials is desirable, as the association may allow use of its database of members. Moreover, the letter should thank the responder, provide a deadline, and offer access to the study results. In the field of health informatics, ensuring the confidentiality of the response also is particularly important. Multiple mailings in a timed sequence can significantly improve the response rate. For example, the tailored (total) design method can achieve response rates as high as 74 percent (Dillman 2007, 27).

Interviews

Interviews are another type of survey. In interview surveys, researchers orally ask the questions to collect their data. This oral questioning can be focus groups or one-on-one interviews (face-to-face; telephone; or exit polls, such as during elections).

Researchers conducting interviews often use **interview guides** to collect data. Interview guides are written lists of questions. Use of an interview guide ensures that the researchers ask all the participants the same questions. Researchers conducting interviews choose whether they will:

- Strictly follow the guide asking structured questions
- Strictly follow the guide asking unstructured questions
- Ask follow-up questions, known as **probes**
- Conduct a **semistructured interview** that follows a guide but allows additional questions that seem appropriate or triggered by the participants' comments
- Allow the participants to elaborate on their answers and to explain their opinions

Researchers also choose how narrow or free-flowing the conversation will be. They must also determine their level of involvement:

- Low-level involvment does not guide the conversation. The advantage is that participants may reveal information unknown and new to the researchers. The disadvantage is that the discussion may be disorganized and not cover aspects of the topic important to the study.
- High-level involvement follows the interview guide and cuts off extraneous conversation. The advantage is that all the researchers' questions are answered in minimal time. The disadvantage is the potential loss of participants' key insights, unknown to the researchers.

In telephone surveys, the response rates are depressed, even with up to 20 attempts to reach the subjects (Dillman 2007, 28). The public's distrust of telephone solicitation has resulted in no-call directories, caller ID, and unpublished numbers. These practices have made telephone surveys very difficult to conduct. However, for a small, specialized group, such as health information management educators or curators of library medical history collections, a telephone survey on a subject in their area of interst may be appropriate (Salant and Dillman 1994, 38).

In a **focus group**, researchers interview approximately six participants as a group. The researchers have a topic or focus for the group's discussion. Two researchers, one leading the discussion and one documenting events, are often present. Researchers using focus groups should make certain to establish ground rules, which include:

- One person speaks at a time (important for audiotaping)
- Everyone's participation is important
- Outline the group's purpose, its topics, and time frame
- All participants introduce themselves

Data collection can be completed on the interview guide, if structured questions are used. In addition to the interview guide, the interviews often are recorded and transcribed as part of the data collection. If audiotapes and videotapes are made, then they must be coded and transcribed to capture their data. Coding entails transforming the responses into analyzable data. Moreover, taping requires the participants' signed permission. Focus groups are usually audiotaped and videotaped, so data collection includes coding and transcribing these sources.

Interviewing has advantages and disadvantages. Researchers who conduct interviews need to have excellent interpersonal and communication skills. Building a positive rapport with their subjects is a means to obtain data about sensitive topics. While creating this link, however, the researchers cannot allow their feelings or body language to influence the subjects. Unstructured questions that result in greatly detailed and in-depth answers can provide previously unknown insights. A caveat, however, is that the subjects need to be able to articulate their feelings, observations, and opinions. Without the subject's verbalization, the interview will not provide data. Finally, interviewing is time-consuming and expensive.

Observation

Observation is a means to collect data by observing rather than by asking. The researchers observe naturally occurring phenomena as well as staged phenomena. Examples of naturally occurring phenomena include events on nursing stations, emergency rooms, and physicians' offices. These events include use of EHRs, DSSs, interactions with patients, and interactions among members of the healthcare team. Other naturally occurring events are disasters. During the disaster, researchers could observe how rescue and emergency teams obtain health information on residents whose lives depend on medications and special devices, such as respirators, or how healthcare providers document treatment when they have little or no access to EHRs. Staged phenomena include scenarios, vignettes, and disaster drills. As these naturally-occurring and staged phenomena unfold, the researchers collect data by observing and recording what happens.

To collect data, researchers typically use activity lists, case notes, check sheets, logs, observation forms, audiotapes, or videotapes. These tools *must* be developed and tested before the phenomena. Audiotapes and videotapes must undergo the additional step of transcription. Then, the researchers also must code all the recorded observations so they can be analyzed. Moreover, qualitative studies emphasize obtaining data from multiple data sources in order to triangulate (see chapter 2). Finally, observation results in vast volumes of data that must be transcribed and compiled before analysis and interpretation can begin.

As they collect their data, the researchers can be nonparticipant observers or participant observers. Nonparticipant observers adopt a neutral stance. They are more likely to represent a quantitative approach. Participant observers are part of the group being observed. As participant observers, they reflect the biases, assumptions, and blinders of the group. Thus, they may be oblivious to some aspects of the phenomenon that they are observing. This lack of awareness may jeopardize the quality of the study.

One advantage of observation is the depth of data it provides. This depth of data, layer upon layer, is known as **rich data**. These rich data provide a window on the participants' points of view. Observation allows researchers to focus on participants' feelings, behaviors, and perceptions. The disadvantage of observation is that it is resource-intensive in terms of time, energy, and cost.

Treatment

Collection of data about treatments includes experimental and quasi-experimental studies. Questionnaires, interviews, observations, and physiologic measures can be used to collect data about treatments. Physiologic measures include laboratory values (such as increased heart rate or galvanic skin response for stress or anxiety), eye tracking, and brain scans (positron emission tomography for tracking neural pathways and brain activity). For computer activity, researchers can collect data on keystrokes, time spent per screen, and audit trails. One set of researchers collected photographs of the types of health information that people managed in their homes (such as medication lists, blood type cards, and insurance information) and the ways that they stored the health information (such as calendars, folders, and notebooks) (Moen and Brennan 2005, 652). Thus, the data collection tools are as varied as the research questions.

Mining

Mining data comes under the umbrella of secondary analysis. Secondary analysis is the analysis of the original work of another person or organization. Similar to the approach to literary databases, researchers must take a systematic and orderly approach. Conducting secondary analysis is particularly suited to the skills of health informatics professionals.

For mining, researchers have many sources of data available to them. These sources include both **primary sources** and **secondary sources.** (See table 10.10.)

Primary Sources

Primary sources are data that are not aggregated and have not been manipulated by others. Health records, at the individual patient level, are commonly used primary sources. These individual health records exist across the continuum of care (physician office, hospital, home health, long-term care, and hospice). Other sites of health records include public health clinics, health insurance companies, and free health clinics. Healthcare and health-related organizations also have data from operations and business transaction that have not been aggregated. Examples of these data include claims data, patient accounts, complaints, chargemasters, and satisfaction surveys. (See table 10.10.)

Secondary Sources

Secondary sources are aggregated data or data that have been manipulated by others. Aggregate data derived from health records include registries, indexes, and administrative records. Aggregate data also are derived from organizational operations and business transactions. Manipulated data include public databases compiled by governmental agencies or other researchers' data or databases. (See table 10.10.) Specific examples of available data include:

- Labor force, earnings, and prices (Bureau of Labor Statistics)
- Crime, demographics, education, and health (Social Statistics Briefing Room)

- Statistics and information from 70 federal agencies (FedStats)
- Behavorial health (Behavioral Risk Factor Surveillance System [BRFSS] of the Centers for Disease Control and Prevention)
- Health statistics (National Center for Health Statistics, FASTATS A-Z)
- Health statistics, social indicators, and population health research (Area Resource File [ARF] of the Health Resources and Services Administration of the U.S. Department of Health and Human Services)
- Health information national trends survey ([HINTS] U.S. National Institutes of Health, National Cancer Institute)

- Medicare data (Medicare Provider Analysis and Review [MedPAR] of Short-Stay Hospitals
- Demographic data on U.S. population (Population Reference Bureau)
- Business, economic, and trade data from the federal government (STAT-USA)
- Hundreds of files from various state and federal governmental agencies (Statistical Resources on the Web)
- U.S. census data (U.S. Census Bureau)
- Medicaid data by state (see Medicaid programs of each state)

These examples focus on data available in the U.S. Similar data exist in other countries. For example,

Table 10.10.   Selected examples of primary and secondary sources for data collection

Primary Source	Secondary Source
Academic course catalogs	1994 Health Care Cost Utilization Project-3 (HCUP-3)
Accreditation surveys	2000 Healthcare Cost and Utilization Project Nationwide Inpatient Sample
Adjudication decisions	Accreditation reports
Audit trails	American Hospital Association (AHA) data
Certification surveys	Benefit administration reports
Chargemasters and superbills	Certification reports
Claims and claims data	Clinical pathways
Contracts (individual)	Contracts (group)
Cost reports	Cost reports
Credentialing reports	Healthcare administrative databases
Emergency room and clinic logs	HIMSS Analytics databases (Healthcare Information and Management Systems Society)
Health plan enrollment data	Indexes (disease, operative, master person, enterprise, physician)
Health records (paper and EHR)	National Ambulatory Medical Care Survey (NAMCS) data
HEDIS data	National Health Interview Survey Database
OASIS data	National Hospital Ambulatory Medical Care Survey (NHAMCS) data
Obstetrical suite records	New York's Department of Health administrative databases
ORYX data	Medicare Denominator file
Patient (resident, client) accounts	Medicare Provider Analysis and Review (MedPAR) file, Hospice file, and Physician /Supplier Procedure Summary Master file
Patient blogs	Membership lists of professional associations
Quality and risk reports	Quality and risk reports (aggregated)
Remittance advices	Registries (cancer, disease, operation, trauma)
RUGs data	Satisfaction survey database
Satisfaction surveys	Utilization reports
Surgery schedules	
Utilization reviews	

researchers in Canada accessed the following data sets: the membership list of the College of Physicians and Surgeons of Ontario, the membership list of the Law Society of Upper Canada, the Ministry of Government Services' Personal Property Security Registration, and Canadian 411 Telephone Directory (El Emam et al. 2006). Thus, the previous list and table 10.10 are representative of data available in many countries.

Researchers who want to conduct investigations using secondary data must resolve two key issues. These issues are access and transforming the data into a usable format.

Access to data depends on the type of data and their location. Access can range from totally uncontrolled to highly secured. For example, data on the Internet are easily accessed whereas data in health records require approvals from Institutional Review Boards (IRBs). (See chapter 13.) Data can be public or proprietary. Public data often are accessible under the Freedom of Information Act; some have been posted on the Internet. State registry data also are often accessible. Accessing proprietary data requires the permission of the database's owner.

Data that identify one individual are less accessible than aggregate data. Moreover, access to individually identifiable data has become more complex since the advent of the Health Insurance Portability and Accountability Act (HIPAA) of 1996. (See chapter 13.) For example, some healthcare organizations take a conservative view and require a patient's informed consent to review any health data. Researchers should take note that individually identifiable data are protected both under HIPAA and IRB provisions.

Access has developed as an important international problem. Ethical and legal questions have been raised regarding secondary analysis of large data sets. In Europe, ethicists believe that all possible means should be used to obtain the individuals' consent to use the data (Central Ethics Commission 2000, 584; Kluge 2004, 635). In the U.S., the American Medical Informatics Association convened a panel of health informaticians to discuss issues associated with the secondary use of health data (Safran et al. 2007, 1). Researchers are encouraged to review the framework that this panel recommends (Safran et al. 2007, 5-7).

Researchers who want to mine a dataset may need to restructure the data so they can mine them. In order to convert the data into a usable format, the research-

ers must understand the underlying structure of the data and how they were collected. For example, researchers mining hospital databases and researchers mining secondary databases of the Veterans Health Administration both found problems with missing data (Oostenbrink et al. 2003; Long et al. 2006). Thus, each data source has its own unique characteristics with which researchers must become familiar.

The techniques and tools of data collection include surveys, interviews, observations, treatments, and data mining. For surveys and interviews, response rate is a critical issue. Researchers who collect data by interviews and observations must consider the time and costs associated with these techniques. Testing a data collection tool prior to its use is required. The techniques and tools to gather data for treatments include all the techniques and tools of surveys, interviews, and observations, and adds physiologic measures. Access to data is a critical issue for researchers who mine data or combine their primary research with public databases. Additionally, researchers must consider how they can convert these databases into usable format. Researchers who want to mine these rich resources are reminded to obtain appropriate approvals and to allow sufficient time to manipulate the data.

Sampling

Sampling is the process of selecting a set of subjects or units to represent a population. Two major types of sampling are **random sampling** and **nonrandom sampling**. Within the two types, researchers conduct sampling in several different ways.

A sample is a set of units selected for study. It is a subset of a **target population**, which is the large group that is the focus of the study. For example, researchers cannot poll all U.S. citizens for their opinions on storing their health data on the Internet. Researchers can identify a sample, meaning a group of citizens representative of the entire population. Individuals are one set of units. In other studies, the sets of units could be bacteria, mice, families, schools, television shows, historical documents, and Web sites.

In sampling, the **sampling frame** is an important issue. The sampling frame is the list of subjects from which the sample is drawn (Salant and Dillman 1994, 16). The sampling frame must represent all the elements of the target population. A discrepancy between the sampling frame and the population is a **coverage error** (Salant and Dillman 1994, 16). The 1936 presidential election between Franklin Roosevelt and Alf Landon provides a classic example of a coverage error. The *Literary Digest* conducted a mail survey to predict the results of the election. The *Literary Digest* used telephone directories and automobile registration lists to compile its sampling frame. Based on the results of the survey, the *Literary Digest* predicted that Landon would beat Roosevelt by 15 percentage points. However, many people in 1936 owned neither telephones nor automobiles. Apparently, people in lower socioeconomic strata were unlikely to vote for Landon. In the actual election, Roosevelt beat Landon, earning 61 percent of the popular vote and 523 of 531 electoral votes (Salant and Dillman 1994, 16).

A sampling frame based on Web access currently has a high probability of resulting in a coverage error. In 2008, many strata of society do not have access to computers, similar to 1936 when many lower-income people were not included in telephone directories and automobile registration lists. Couper notes that Web-based sampling faces the challenges of drawing representative samples, of including people without access to computers, and of minimizing nonresponse bias (2007, S88). Similar to all tools, the Internet has its advantages and disadvantages, and is better suited to some tasks than others (Couper 2007, S88).

A **sampling error** is a difference between the population and sample due to pure chance. If several samples were drawn from the same population, there would be random variations. These variations are sampling error. A sampling error reduces the reliability of the study (Alreck and Settle 2004, 59-60).

Random Samples

Random sampling is the unbiased selection of subjects. Selection is pure chance; thus, there is no discernible pattern of selection. Random sampling is also known as probability sampling because each subject's probability of being selected is equal. The four types of random sampling are **simple random sampling**, **stratified random sampling**, **systematic sampling**, and **cluster sampling** (See table 10.11.)

Random sampling is associated with the quantitative approach. Random sampling underpins many statistical techniques used to analyze data. To generate random samples, researchers can use either a random number generator in spreadsheet software, an option of statistical packages called select cases, or a table of random numbers from a statistics textbook.

Nonrandom Samples

Nonrandom sampling is *not* the random selection of subjects. Nonrandom sampling also is known as nonprobability sampling because each subject's probability of being selected is unknown, and could be either equal or unequal. Nonrandom sampling is generally associated with the qualitative approach. Five types of nonrandom sampling are **convenience sampling**, **purposive sampling**, **quota sampling**, **snowball sampling**, and **theoretical sampling.** (See table 10.11.)

A discussion of convenience samples is necessary because they are found in both the quantitative approach and the qualitative approach. Convenience samples are the "convenient" use of subjects that are nearby or at hand. Convenience samples are also known as accidental samples or haphazard samples. For example, members of a hospital's health information services (HIS) department investigating physicians' satisfaction with departmental services could use a convenience sample. Their convenience sample could be the physicians who came to the department. Although convenient and easy for the members of the HIS department, this convenience sample ignores the opinions of all the physicians who did not come to the department. These physicians may find services substandard—which could be the reason that they do not visit the HIS department—or those who may avoid using information services. Therefore, the use of convenience samples diminishes the credibility of research studies.

Sample Size

Sample size is the number of subjects that the researcher determines would represent the population and should be included in the study. The adequacy of the sample size is a common concern for quantitative researchers. The size of the sample depends on the purpose of the study, the nature of the population, and the researchers' resources (Chadwick et al. 1984, 67). Some experts state that the general rule is to use the largest sample possible (Gall et al. 2007, 176; Gay et al. 2006, 110). However, Kish factored in utility to arrive at economic samples (1995/1965, 49). An economic sample provides the level of detail needed to answer the question. Although no absolute rule dictates the size of the sample, researchers should strive for a level of accuracy that makes the study worth conducting.

Adequacy

If a researcher's purpose is to explore areas of inconsistency between paper and electronic records, 90 randomly

Table 10.11. Types of random and nonrandom sampling

RANDOM	
Type	**Description**
1. Simple	The selection of units from a population so that every unit has exactly the same chance of being included in the sample. When a unit has been selected, it is returned to the population so that the other units' chances remain identical.
2. Stratified	Some populations have characteristics that divide them. For example, the human population is male and female. The male and female subgroups are called strata (singular, stratum). The percentage of the stratum in the population should equal the percentage of the stratum in the sample. Therefore, the sample should be 50% male and 50% female. Other percentages would cast doubt on the results.
3. Systematic	Units of the sample are selected from a list by drawing every nth unit. For example, health information professionals could choose every fourth surgery on the surgical schedule for surgical case review.
4. Cluster	The sample is clusters of units. The population is first divided into clusters of units, such as family, school, or community.
NONRANDOM	
Type	**Description**
1. Convenience	Use of easily recruited and accessible subjects.
2. Purposive	Selection of subjects based on experts' (researchers') opinion that they are typical of the population or meet a criterion for inclusion.
3. Snowball	Earlier subjects recommend later subjects for the researchers to recruit; in this way the researchers reach their desired number of subjects.
4. Quota	Selection of subjects to ensure proportionate representation of various strata present in the population; increases the study's representativeness.
5. Theoretical	Selection of subjects as topics emerge to ensure representation of those topics; selection of subjects to fill gaps that emerge and to build theory.

selected records at one academic health center may be sufficient (Mikkelsen and Aasly 2001, 125). However, a study comparing the efficacy of various treatment protocols for breast cancer warrants a sample size in the thousands. If the researcher's purpose includes many variables, the sample size needs to be larger. Thus, purpose is a critical concern.

The nature of the population includes **heterogeneity,** and typical response and attrition rates. Heterogeneity means variation or diversity. The more heterogeneous a population, the larger the sample. The sample needs to be larger in order to ensure that the sample includes all the diverse units in the population. Typical response rate is a factor for surveys. In the literature, other researchers report their response rates. The response rate is the number of people who returned the questionnaire or were reached for interview. If the typical response rate is 50 percent, the researcher will need to distribute twice as many surveys to achieve an adequate response. Attrition (mortality) rates refer to the number of subjects lost during the course of the study. (See chapter 9.) Attrition is a threat to internal validity. High attrition rates require a larger sample. Understanding the nature of the population contributes to the accuracy of the research.

Resources, namely time and money, can affect sample size. Sometimes researchers must provide answers in a short time frame. For example, to respond in a timely fashion to a legislative initiative regarding content of PHRs, health informatics professionals may conduct a quick survey of a small sample. Individual researchers often face financial constraints. These constraints sometimes result in smaller samples than purists would prefer.

Calculation

Sample size calculation refers to the qualitative and quantitative procedures used to determine the appropriate sample size. Some experts have offered rules of thumb to calculate sample size. (See table 10.12.) These rules of thumb try to account for frequency of the behavior, numbers of variables, and statistical technique. Statistical formulae also are used to calculate adequate sample sizes (Osborn 2006, 145–149). Formulae depend on the sampling method used, such as simple random sampling or stratified random sampling, and on the amount of information the researcher has about the population. Osborn's text offers detailed examples and step-by-step procedures (Osborn 2006, 145–149). However, specific

Table 10.12.   Rules of thumb for sample size

Rule of Thumb	Source
General: Minimum of 30 cases or responses	Bailey 1994, 97
Pilot study: 20 to 50 cases	Sudman 1976, 87
Descriptive study: Minimum 10 percent of population	Gay et al. 2006, 110
Descriptive study: Population 100 or fewer, survey entire population	Gay et al. 2006, 110
Descriptive study: Minimum 20 percent of small population (~1500)	Gay et al. 2006, 110
Correlational study: Minimum of 30 cases or responses	Gall et al. 2007, 176
Causal-comparative and experimental research: 15 to 30 cases per comparison group	Gall et al. 2007, 176; Gay et al. 2006, 110
Major subgroup: Minimum of 100 each Minor subgroups: Minimum of 20 to 50 each per subgroup	Sudman 1976, 30
General: 200 cases or responses	Chadwick et al. 1984, 68

considerations should override reliance on these rules of thumb and formulae.

The following example outlines the procedure for arriving at an optimal sample size. (See figure 10.6.) Suppose the HIS director at a large academic health center wants to determine the sample size for a study on the medical staff's opinion of a diagnostic DSS. One commonly used formula for determining sample size requires the researcher to know or decide on the size of the population, the proportion of subjects needed, and an acceptable amount of error. In this instance, the director knows that the number of attending physicians on the medical staff is 800 but has little other information. Therefore, using the formula presented in figure 10.6, p = .5 and B = .05. Using the basic formula, the director calculates that, in this situation, a sample of 267 is needed if he or she is willing to accept a 5 percent error due to variability in the sampling.

Readers can also find specific information about minimum sample sizes in Olejnik's classic article (1984, 44–45). In two tables in the article, minimum sample sizes are provided for several statistical techniques (Olejnik 1984, 44–45). For researchers to use the tables, they must know:

- Desired level of significance (alpha, ρ)
- Desired level of statistical power
- Statistical technique (such as ANOVA or t test)
- Effect size (degree to which the null hypothesis is false; small, medium, or large effect; see meta-analyses of the topic in the literature) (Olejnik 1984, 41–42).

Olejnik emphasized that determination of the necessary sample size is a complex question that requires familiarity with the literature (1984, 47).

Procedures

The research plan should consider every logistical detail of the data collection from start to finish. Coiera et al. provide an example of the level of detail necessary in a research plan (2006, n.p.). Lack of attention to detail at this point will breach factors of internal validity. Some issues related to data collection affect many of the methods; other issues are unique to the method. Data collection issues include:

- Obtaining approvals of oversight committees
- Listing each data element required to perform the appropriate statistical techniques
- Training for data collection procedures
- Performing a **pilot study**
- Storing the data securely
- Assembling the data for analysis

Approvals of Oversight Committees

Federal regulations govern research on human subjects. (See chapter 13.) The purpose of the regulations is to protect humans from researchers' abuses. To comply with federal regulations, organizations have institutional review boards (IRBs). IRBs (also sometimes referred to as human subjects committees) are administrative bodies established to protect the rights and welfare of human

Figure 10.6.   Basic example of sample size calculation

Sample size = n

Size of the population = N

Proportion of subjects needed = p

Acceptable amount of error = B

Formula

$$n = \frac{Np(1-p)}{(N-1)(\frac{B^2}{4})+(p)(1-p)}$$

Data from the Case

N = 800

p = .5

B = .05

Calculations

$$n = \frac{(800)(.5)(1-.5)}{(800-1)(\frac{.05^2}{4})+(.5)(1-.5)}$$

$$n = \frac{200}{(799)(.000625)+.25}$$

$$n = \frac{200}{.75}$$

n = 267

subjects recruited to participate in an institution's research activities. IRBs provide oversight for the research studies conducted within their institutions. As specified by both federal regulations and institutional policies, IRBs have the authority to review and approve or reject research studies within their jurisdictions. They also may require modifications to the research protocols.

Prior to conducting studies, researchers must obtain written approvals from the IRB and other oversight entities within their organizations and the organizations controlling the data or database. (See previous section on access to secondary sources.) To obtain approvals, researchers complete the organization's documentation, providing descriptions of their research plan and copies of their informed consent forms. Sufficient time must be allowed in their plan for the board to review the research, meet, and respond.

Listing of Data Elements for Statistical Techniques

Researchers should compile a list of the data elements required for each statistical analysis they plan to conduct.

Prior to beginning data collection, researchers should ensure that their data collection strategies will obtain all the data. Additionally, researchers should ascertain the number of cases needed to run the statistical analyses. This detail is particularly important when there are subgroups of unequal size in the sample. For example, researchers may want to investigate various clinicians' views of an alert system in an integrated delivery system (IDS). For these researchers, the umbrella term "clinicians" could include family nurse practitioners (FNPs), primary care physicians, and physician assistants. If the IDS had few FNPs, a lack of sufficient of data related to the FNPs could limit the statistical analyses that could be performed. The list of analyses compiled by Coiera et al. is an example that other health informatics researchers could emulate (2006, n.p.). Therefore, it is advisable to conduct mock statistical analyses on fabricated data and to create tables and figures for the manuscript early as part of planning the research.

Training on Procedures

It is also advisable to run trial analyses. These trials may identify flaws in the extraction formula or data definitions. For example, one set of researchers investigated conformance with health indicators (Dimick 2007, 59). One health indicator was mammogram screening rates. The numerator was women who had received a mammogram, and the denominator was all women ages 50 to 65 years. The initial analysis of the data showed that 51 percent of the women ages 50 to 65 years had received a mammogram. Upon further detection, the researchers found that the denominator erroneously included deceased patients and patients who had left the practice. After correcting this error, the actual compliance rate was 66 percent (Dimick 2007, 60). Running mock and trial statistical analyses can reveal gaps in the researchers' data collection plan or other errors.

Researchers and their assistants should test the data collection instruments before collecting real data. Such tests will identify ambiguous instructions and inconsistent definitions. Moreover, researchers and their assistants may require special training. For example, publishers of some psychological tests require verification of training to administer the tests. The researchers must obtain this verification or select another instrument. To effectively conduct interviews or to observe vignettes, researchers and their assistants also need training. If the research requires that instruments be scored, training on scoring should occur. Training and testing of the instruments help ensure reliable data.

Pilot Studies

Performing a **pilot study** (trial run) enhances the likelihood of a study's successful completion. Researchers work out the details of their research plan when they conduct pilot studies. The maxim, "The devil is in the details," is only too true. Pilot studies can reveal the following information:

- Biases in sample selection
- Volumes required (forms, envelopes, data entries, and so forth)
- Associated costs
- Performance features of equipment
- Defects, such as poorly worded cover letters of invitations, unclear questionnaire items, leading questions in interviews, Web browser incompatibilities, programming errors, and other inconsistencies and errors
- Possible logjams (gridlock) in the mailing or scoring methods
- Errors in the scoring key
- Discrepancies between the order of items on the data collection instrument and the order on the computer screen

Pilot studies demonstrate that the research study is logistically feasible. Even researchers conducting naturalistic studies perform simulations that test their instruments prior to the event. (See chapter 2.) Pilot studies are as necessary as disaster drills.

Storing and Assembling Data

Researchers must include a mechanism in the plan that addresses how they will safeguard the confidentiality of their data. If videotapes are involved, where will they be stored? Because sensitive data may be on personality tests, where will these documents be stored? How will the confidentiality of data on computer hard drives, laptops, external storage devices, and Web sites be ensured? In accordance with the rules of applicable oversight entities, the plan also must include a mechanism for disposition of the data (storage, archiving, destruction) after the termination of the research.

After researchers collect the data, they must assemble and organize them in a way that allows analysis. In this step, the researchers must decide how they will enter the data into a software package. Who will enter the data? How will they ensure accuracy of data entry? Who will transcribe the contents of videotapes or audiotapes?

Summary and Conclusions

Data collection is a systematic, planned procedure that results in internal validity. Multiple aspects of an instrument's validity are assessed. Two important aspects of an instrument's validity are **content validity** and **construct validity**. **Reliability** involves the consistency of measurements. Researchers state in their studies the validity and reliability of the instruments that they used. Questions on instruments may be structured or unstructured, and may collect numeric or categorical data. Sampling is the process of selecting a sample to represent a population. Researchers should carefully assess their sampling frame to avoid a coverage error. Types of sampling include random sampling and nonrandom sampling. Conducting a pilot study is a key step in ensuring a thorough and carefully conceived plan. Validity and reliability demand careful attention to documentation and vigilant adherence to procedures.

References

Alreck, P.L., and R.B. Settle. 2004. *The Survey Research Handbook*, 3rd ed. New York: McGraw-Hill/Irwin.

Bailey, K.D. 1994. *Methods of Social Research*, 4th ed. New York: Free Press.

Bakken, S., Grullon-Figueroa, L., Izquierdo, R., Lee, N.J., Morin, P., Palmas, W., Teresi, J., Weinstock, R.S., Shea, S., and J. Starren. 2006 (November-December). Development, validation, and use of English and Spanish versions of the telemedicine satisfaction and usefulness survey. *Journal of the American Medical Informatics Association* 13(6):660–667.

Bälter, K.A., Bälter, O., Fondell, E., and Y.T. Lagerros. 2005 (July). Web-based and mailed questionnaires: A comparison of response rates and compliance. *Epidemiology* 16(4):577–579.

Bethell, C., Fiorillo, J., Lansky, D., Hendryx, M., and J. Knickman. 2004 (Jan. 20). Online consumer surveys as a methodology for assessing the quality of the United States health care system. *Journal of Medical Internet Research* 6(1):e2. Available online from http://www.jmir.org/2004/1/e2.

Bowling, A. 2005. *Measuring Health: A Review of Quality of Life Measurement Scales*, 3rd ed. New York: Open University Press.

Central Ethics Commission of the German Medical Association. 2000 (December). Statement: The use of patient-related information in medical research and the health system. *Pharmacoepidemiology and Drug Safety* 9(7):581–585.

Chadwick, B.A., Bahr, H.M., and S.L. Albrecht. 1984. *Social Science Research Methods*. Englewood Cliffs, NJ: Prentice-Hall.

Chun, K-T., Cobb, S., and J.R.P. French, Jr. 1975. *Measures for Psychological Assessment: A Guide to 3,000 Original Sources and Their Applications*. Ann Arbor, MI: Survey Research Center, Institute for Social Research.

Cicchetti, D.V., Showalter, D., and P.J. Tyrer. 1985 (March). The effect of number of rating scale categories on levels of interrater reliability: A Monte Carlo investigation. *Applied Psychological Measurement* 9(1):31–36.

Clark, D.J., and K.H. Frith. 2005 (September-October). The development and initial testing of the Internet consequences scales (ICONS). *CIN: Computers, Informatics, Nursing* 23(5):285–291.

Coiera, E., Magrabi, F., Westbrook, J.I., Kidd, M.R., and R. O'Day. 2006 (Aug. 24). Protocol for quick clinical study: A randomized controlled trial to assess the impact of an online evidence retrieval system on decision-making in general practice. *BMC Medical Informatics and Decision Making* 6:33. Available online from http://www.biomedcentral.com/1472-6947/6/33.

Couper, M.P. 2007 (May). Issues of representation in ehealth research (with a focus on Web surveys). *American Journal of Preventive Medicine* 32(5S):S83–S89.

Dillman, D.A. 2007. *Mail and Internet Surveys: The Tailored Design Method: 2007 Update with New Internet, Visual, and Mixed-Mode Guide*, 2nd ed. New York: John Wiley & Sons.

Dimick, C. 2007 (June). Selling physicians on EHRs: Illustrating the benefits to care, the importance of data. *Journal of American Health Information Management Association* 78(6):58–60. Available online from http://www.ahima.org/infocenter/.

El Emam, K., S. Jabbouri, S. Sams, Y. Drouet, and M. Power. 2006. October-December. Evaluating common de-identification heuristics for personal health information. *Journal of Medical Internet Research* 8 (4):e28. Accessed at http://www.jmir.org/2006/4/e28 8 December 2006.

Gall, M.D., Gall, J.P., and W.R. Borg. 2007. *Educational Research: An Introduction*, 8th ed. Boston: Allyn & Bacon.

Garvin, J.H. 2001 (Summer). Building on the vision: Exploratory research in future skill areas of the clinical data specialist as described in evolving HIM careers. *Educational Perspectives in Health Information Management* 4(1):19–32.

Gay, L.R., Mills, G.E., and P. Airasian. 2006. *Educational Research: Competencies for Analysis and Applications*, 8th ed. Upper Saddle River, NJ: Pearson Prentice Hall.

Heerwegh, D., Vanhove, T., Matthijs, K., and G. Loosveldt. 2005 (April). The effect of personalization on response rates and data quality in Web surveys. *International Journal of Social Research Methodology* 8(2):85–99.

Herndon, R.M., ed. 1997. *Handbook of Neurologic Rating Scales*. New York: Demos Vermande.

Hopkins, W.G. 2000. A new view of statistics. Available online from http://www.sportsci.org/resource/stats/precision.html.

James, D.C.S., Chen, W.W., and J-J. Sheu. 2005 (July 14). Comparison of three tobacco survey methods with college students: A case study. *International Electronic Journal of Health Education* 8:119–124.

Keyser, D.J., and R.C. Sweetland, eds. 1991. *Test Critiques*. Kansas City, MO: Test Corporation of America.

Kim, J-O., and C. W. Mueller. 1978. *Factor Analysis: Statistical Methods and Practical Issues*. Beverly Hills, CA: Sage.

Kish, L. 1995/1965. *Survey Sampling*. New York: John Wiley & Sons.

Kittleson, M.J., and S.L. Brown. 2005. E-mail versus Web survey response rates among health education professionals. *American Journal of Health Studies* 20(1/2):7–14.

Klein, J. 2002 (May-June). Issues surrounding the use of the Internet for data collection. *American Journal of Occupational Therapy* 56(3):340–343.

Kluge, E-H.W. 2004. Informed consent to the secondary use of EHRs: Informatic rights and their limitations. *Medinfo* 11(Pt 1):635–638.

Landis, J.R., and G.G. Koch. 1977 (March). The measurement of observer agreement for categorical data. *Biometrics* 33(1):159–174.

Lawshe, C.H. 1975, Winter. A quantitative approach to content validity. *Personnel Psychology* 28(4):563–575.

Leece, P., Bhandari, M., Sprague, S., Swiontkowski, M.F., Schemitsch, E.H., Tornetta, P., Devereaux, P.J., and G.H. Guyatt. 2004 (Oct. 29). Internet versus mailed questionnaires: A controlled comparison. *Journal of Medical Internet Research* 6(4):e39. Available online from http://www.jmir.org/2004/4/e39.

Lohr, K.N. 2002 (May). Assessing health status and quality-of-life instruments: Attributes and review criteria. *Quality of Life Research* 11(3):193–205

Long, J.A., Bamba, M.I., Ling, B., and J.A. Shea. 2006 (February). Missing race/ethnicity data in Veterans Health Administration based disparities research: A systematic review. *Journal of Health Care for the Poor and Underserved* 17(1):128–140.

Maddox, T., ed. 2003. *Tests: A Comprehensive Reference for Assessments in Psychology, Education, and Business*, 5th ed. Austin, TX: Pro-Ed.

McDowell, I., and C. Newell. 1996. *Measuring Health: A Guide to Rating Scales and Questionnaires,* 2nd ed. New York: Oxford University Press.

Mikkelsen, G., and J. Aasley. 2001 (October). Concordance of information in parallel electronic and paper based patient records. *International Journal of Medical Informatics* 63(3):123–131.

Moen, A., and P.F. Brennan. 2005 (November-December). Health@home: The work of health information management in the household (HIMH): Implications for consumer health informatics (CHI) innovations. *Journal of the American Medical Informatics Association* 12(6):648–656.

Murphy, L.L., Spies, R.A., and B.S. Plake, eds. 2006. *Tests in Print VII: An Index to Tests, Test Reviews, and the Literature on Specific Tests*. Lincoln, NE: University of Nebraska Press.

Nahm, E-S., Resnick, B., and J. Gaines. 2004 (July-August). Testing the reliability and validity of computer-mediated social support measures among older adults: A pilot study. *CIN: Computers, Informatics, Nursing* 22(4):211–219.

Olejnik, S.F. 1984 (Fall). Planning educational research: Determining the necessary sample size. *Journal of Experimental Education* 53(1):40–48.

Oostenbrink, R., Moons, K.G.M., Bleeker, S.E., Moll, H.A., and D.E. Grobbee. 2003 (June). Diagnostic research on routine care data: Prospects and problems. *Journal of Clinical Epidemiology* 56(6):501–506.

Osborn, C.E. 1998 (Spring). A methodology for construction of a survey questionnaire in health information management professional practice. *Educational Perspectives in Health Information Management* 1(1):3–13.

Osborn, C.E. 2006. *Statistical Applications for Health Information Management*, 2nd ed. Sudbury, MA: Jones and Bartlett.

Polit, D.F., and C.T. Beck. 2006 (Sept. 14). The content validity index: Are you sure you know what's being reported? Critique and recommendations. *Research in Nursing & Health* 29(5):489–497.

Ramnarayan, P., Kapoor, R.R., Coren, M., Nanduri, V., Tomlinson, A.L., Taylor, P.M., Wyatt, J.C., and J.F. Britto. 2003 (November-December). Measuring the impact of diagnostic decision support on the quality of clinical decision making: Development of a reliable and valid composite score. *Journal of the American Medical Informatics Association* 10(6):563–572.

Ray, M.N., Houston, T.K., Yu, F.B., Menachemi, N., Maisiak, R.S., Allison, J.J., and E.S. Berner. 2006 (September-October). Development and testing of a scale to assess physician attitudes about handheld computers with decision support. *Journal of the American Medical Informatics Association* 13(5):567–572.

Redman, B.K., ed. 2002. *Measurement Tools in Clinical Ethics*. New York: Springer.

Redman, B.K., ed. 2003. *Measurement Tools in Patient Education*, 2nd ed. New York: Springer.

Rowan, M., and P. Huston. 1997 (Nov. 15). Qualitative research articles: Information for authors and peer reviewers. *Canadian Medical Association Journal* 157(10):1442–1446.

Safran, C., Bloomrosen, M., Hammond, W.E., Labkoff, S., Markel-Fox, S., Tang, P.C., and D.E. Detmer. 2007 (January-February). Toward a national framework for the secondary use of health data: An American Medical Informatics Association white paper. *Journal of the American Medical Informatics Association* 14(1):1–9.

Salant, P., and D.A. Dillman. 1994. *How to Conduct Your Own Survey*. New York: John Wiley & Sons.

Sax, L.J., Gilmartin, S.K., and A.N. Bryant. 2003 (August). Assessing response rates and nonresponse rates in Web and paper surveys. *Research in Higher Education* 44(4):409–432.

Schleyer, T.K.L., and J.L. Forrest 2000 (July-August). Methods for the design and administration of Web-based surveys. *Journal of the American Medical Informatics Association* 7(4):416–425.

Shrout, P.E., and J.L. Fleiss. 1979 (March). Intraclass correlations: Uses in assessing rater reliability. *Psychological Bulletin* 86(2):420–428.

Sim, J., and C.C. Wright. 2005 (March). The kappa statistic in reliability studies: Use interpretation, and sample size requirements. *Physical Therapy* 85(3):257–268.

Spies, R.A., and B.S. Plake, eds. 2005. *The Sixteenth Mental Measurements Yearbook* (Buros Mental Measurements Yearbooks). Lincoln, NE: University of Nebraska Press.

Spreen, O., and E. Strauss. 1998. A Compendium of Neuropsychological Tests: Administration, Norms, and Commentary, 2nd. ed. New York: Oxford University Press.

Sudman, S. 1976. *Applied Sampling*. New York: Academic Press.

Chapter 11
Data to Information

Elizabeth J. Layman, PhD, RHIA, CCS, FAHIMA

Learning Objectives

- To present approaches to analyze the data that result in information

- To weigh factors in the selection of analytical techniques

- To discuss the presentation and interpretation of results

Key Terms

Analytic induction

Bivariate

Box-and-whisker plot

Categorical data

Claim (qualitative research)

Conclusion validity

Confidence interval (CI)

Confidence limits

Content analysis

Continuous (metric) data

Data cleaning

Data mining

Dependent (matched, paired) sample

Discrete data

Effect size

Enumerative systems

Grounded (constant comparative) theory

Heterogeneity (variability)

Heuristic

Homogeneity

Imputation

Independent sample

Inferential statistics

Interval data

Item nonresponse

Knowledge discovery in databases (KDD)

Kurtosis

Metric data

Missing at random (MAR)

Missing completely at random (MCAR)

Missing not at random (MNAR)

Missing values (data)

Missingness

Multiple imputation

Multivariate

Nominal data

Nonparametric (distribution free)

Null hypothesis statistical testing

Ordinal data

Parametric

Power

Primary analysis

Qualitative approach

Quantitative approach

Range of indifference

Ratio data

Risk pattern mining
Secondary analysis
Significance level
Skewness
Standardized observation protocols
Statistical conclusion validity
Stem-and-leaf diagrams
Test statistics

Typological analysis
Unit of analysis, qualitative
Unit of analysis, quantitative
Unit of observation (measurement)
Unit nonresponse
Univariate (descriptive) statistics
Warrant (justification)

Introduction

Information is data that have been organized, integrated, synthesized, and transformed into meaningful patterns and themes. One hundred pieces of data are mute unless someone interprets them. Researchers are the interpreters.

Researchers transform their data into information. This transformation requires analysis, interpretation, synthesis, and presentation. These activities are time intensive. To fully explore the meaning and implications of a study's findings, adequate time must be allocated to each activity. The time and effort will be rewarded with observations and insights that advance the knowledge base of health informatics.

This chapter begins with a discussion of data analysis from the perspectives of both the quantitative and qualitative approaches. The discussion then moves to the presentation of results in narrative and graphic formats. The chapter concludes with the interpretation of the results in the discussion and conclusion of scholarly papers. The chapter concludes with the relationship between research and the creation of new information.

Data Analysis

Researchers inspect, probe, dissect, explore, and examine their data during analysis. Analysis requires thought and time. Allocating sufficient time in the research plan to analyze the data is important. Too often, researchers fall into the common error of allowing too little time for analysis and, as a result, shortchange themselves, their subjects, and their topics. Researchers are encouraged to allow themselves the luxury of fully analyzing their data.

In the research plan, researchers determine which analytical techniques they will perform on their data. This determination is made well in advance of any collection of data. Researchers decide these techniques based on their research question, hypotheses (in quantitative studies), and the literature. The literature presents accepted analytical techniques that other researchers have used to analyze similar data. The literature also includes critiques of analytic techniques. Researchers should inspect these critiques for ways to utilize the criticisms to improve their own study. The analytical techniques are described in the methods section of scholarly papers. The descriptions of the techniques should be so precise and clear

that other researchers could reproduce and replicate the procedures using similar data.

Approaches

Two approaches to data analysis are the quantitative approach and the qualitative approach. The quantitative approach involves counting and numerical data. These data can be aggregated. The qualitative approach is used to interpret nonnumerical observations, such as gestures, activities, space, and perceptions. Both types of analyses are tools for health informatics researchers.

Quantitative

Data collected in studies within the **quantitative approach** can be quantified. The data are typically collected in surveys and tests, structured interview protocols, or standardized observation or check sheets. Data can be aggregated across subjects and cases. The data can be **primary** (collected for this study) or **secondary** (collected by different researchers for a different study). The data are numerical and have been collected in ways consistent with subsequent statistical analysis.

Researchers use the literature to identify acceptable statistical techniques to analyze the data in their own proposed investigation. In published studies, researchers state the statistical techniques used to analyze their data. Subsequent researchers find published studies similar to their own studies and attempt to replicate the published studies' statistical techniques. Researchers also should find any critiques of the published studies in case the critiques provide better statistical techniques than the originally published studies.

Thus, before collecting any data, researchers determine which statistical techniques they will use. These techniques are specified in the methods section of the manuscript. The description of the statistical techniques should be clear and comprehensive so that other researchers can duplicate them on similar data.

Statistical Conclusion Validity

Important to quantitative researchers is the concept of **statistical conclusion validity**. Statistical conclusion validity is the extent to which the statistical conclusions about the relationships in the data are reasonable. Figures 10.4 (p. 226) and figure 11.1 compare the types of validity across research design, data collection (instrument), and data analysis. Statistical conclusion validity

Figure 11.1.   Three prongs of validity: Research design, data collection, and data analysis

Research Design Internal validity–Integrity of research plan that supports accuracy of findings External validity–Generalizability of findings to other groups or settings	
Data Collection (Instrument) Validity–Extent to which the instrument measures what it is intended to measure	Quality Research
Data Analysis Statistical conclusion validity–Extent to which the statistical conclusions about the relationships in the data are reasonable	

Table 11.1.   Null hypothesis

Accept or Reject Hypothesis	True	False
Accept Hypothesis	OK	Type II Error
Reject Hypothesis	Type I Error	OK

A **type I error** is the erroneous rejection of the null hypothesis when it is true; in actuality, there is no difference. **Alpha (α)** levels are associated with type I errors.

A **type II error** is the erroneous failure to reject the null hypothesis when it is false; in actuality, there is a difference. Additionally, **Beta (β)** designates the probability of making a type II error.

judges the soundness of conclusions about the relationship between the intervention (**independent variable**) and the outcome (criterion or **dependent variable**).

Common threats to statistical conclusion validity are lack of power and lack of reliability. Briefly, **power** is the likelihood of failing to reject a false null hypothesis. (See table 11.1 and table 9.11, p. 211.) For example, small sample sizes mask effects of interventions or make their effects undetectable. Reliability is the ability of consistently reproducing similar findings (see full explanations of these terms in chapters 9 and 10, respectively). Thus, researchers compromise reliability when they use faulty instruments or procedures to collect data. Other threats to statistical conclusion validity are:

- Use of inappropriate statistical tests, such as the data violating the underlying assumptions of the statistical test (see selection of techniques later in the chapter and in figure 11.5, p. 255)
- Fishing (use of many statistical tests to find a significance)
- Extreme **heterogeneity** (variability) of the subjects (Farrington 2003, 52)

Effect Size

Relevant information to judge the reasonableness of researchers' conclusions are **effect size**, **confidence intervals (CIs)**, and, to a lesser degree, **significance level,** the likelihood of obtaining the observed effect when the null hypothesis of no relationship is true (Farrington 2003, 52; chapter 9).

Effect size is the "degree to which the null hypothesis is false" (Cohen 1988, 9–10). The "effect size char-

acterizes the degree to which the sample results diverge from the null hypothesis" (Thompson 2002, 25). The larger the value of the effect size, the greater the presence of the phenomenon under study (with *no* attribution or inference of causality). Effect size "is an index that quantifies the degree to which the study results should be considered negligible, or important, *regardless* of the size of the study sample"(Hojat and Xu 2004, 241–242). Thus, for researchers and readers, the effect size is the practical (clinical) significance of the study's findings.

Effect size is important not only because of its relationship with statistical conclusion validity but also because many journals now require that researchers report the effect size (Hojat and Xu 2004, 242; Thompson 2002, 25). Reporting of effect sizes emerged as researchers identified weaknesses of **null hypothesis statistical testing** (chapter 9; Cohen 1994, 997; Wainer and Robinson 2003, 28). Thus, researchers now report effect sizes, CIs (discussed in subsequent paragraphs), and *p* values (rejection of the null hypothesis, chapter 9) with their studies' primary findings to put these findings in context.

Effect size is actually several indices. The appropriate effect size index depends on the nature of the data and the statistical test used (Cohen 1988, 11). Common effect sizes are Cohen's *d*, Glass' delta (Δ), eta squared (H^2), Hedges' g, R^2, and odds ratios (Thompson 2002, 25; Rosnow and Rosenthal 2003, 221). Researchers write of families of indices because some indices are related to statistical tests for differences, others to statistical tests for relationships, and others to differences in ratios (proportions) (Rosnow and Rosenthal 2003, 221-222; Hojat and Xu 2004, 242). Thus, many different ways exist to calculate effect size, each way suited to different situations in research studies (see table 11.2).

Odds ratios are common in research involving clinical interventions (McHugh 2007, 59). Some studies in health informatics research involve interventions. For

Table 11.2. Selected effect size indexes by data type and statistical test

Effect Size (ES) Index	Characteristics	Analytic Technique	Formula	Narrative
Cohen's d	Two independent groups, continuous data	t-test Quasi-experimental (ex post facto) designs	$$ES = \frac{MEAN_{Exp} - MEAN_{Cont}}{STANDARD\ DEV_{Pooled}}$$	Mean difference between experimental and control group divided by the pooled within group standard deviation
Cohen's d	Two dependent (matched) groups, continuous data	Repeated measures designs	$$ES = \frac{MEAN_{Exp} - MEAN_{Cont}}{STANDARD\ DEV_{Pooled}}$$	Mean difference between experimental and control group divided by the pooled within group standard deviation
Hedge's g	Two independent groups, continuous data	t-test Analysis of variance (ANOVA)	$$ES = \frac{MEAN_{Exp} - MEAN_{Cont}}{S_{Pooled}}$$	Adjusts Cohen's d for sample size. Inferential measure computed with mean difference between experimental and control group and square root of mean square error (S) $$S = \sqrt{[\sum(X-M)^2/N-1]}$$ and $$S_{pooled} = \sqrt{MS\ within}$$
Glass' delta	Two independent groups	t-test Experimental designs	$$ES = \frac{MEAN_{Exp} - MEAN_{Cont}}{STANDARD\ DEV_{Cont}}$$	Mean difference between experimental and control group divided by the standard deviation of the control group
R^2	Two groups, continuous data	Pearson product-moment correlation coefficient	$$ES = r^2$$	Magnitude of correlation squared is effect size
Cohen's f^2	Variables	Multiple regression and correlation	$$ES = \frac{R^2}{1-R^2}$$	Magnitude of correlation squared is effect size divided by 1-the squared multiple correlation
Odds ratio	Two groups	2x2 contingency table and binary variables	$$ES = \frac{(A/B)}{(C/D)}$$	Retrospective case-control design. Ratio between two ratios with A and B being the number of yes responses in the control group and experimental group, respectively and C and D being the number of no responses in the control group and experimental group, respectively
Phi Φ	Two groups	Chi-square	$$ES = \sqrt{\frac{X^2}{N}}$$	Square root of the chi-square statistic divided by the sample size

example, implementing a diagnostic decision support system can be considered an intervention. Therefore, researchers often state odds ratios in studies about electronic health records (EHRs), alerts systems, computerized order entry systems, and use of health information technology.

Interpretation of effect sizes depends on assumptions similar to other statistical techniques, such as normal distributions (normal bell curve) within the samples and absence of range restrictions (Coe 2002, 15). As a convention, Cohen cautiously proposed standard operational definitions for each effect size (1988, 12-13; table 11.3 and figure 11.2). This preeminent statistician warned that the definitions were arbitrary and ran the

risk of being misunderstood. Thus, throughout Cohen's book on power and effect size, he provided examples to help researchers put their effect sizes in context (1988, 12-13).

Confidence Intervals (CIs)

CIs are another piece of information used to judge the reasonableness of researchers' conclusions. "CIs are numerical extents on either side of the sample mean that, if properly chosen, enable us to believe, at an appropriate probability level, that the limits of the interval surround μ [population mean]" (Riopelle 2000, 203). In other words, a CI is a range of values for a specific statistic (such as a mean or a regression line) that includes the

Table 11.3. Practical (clinical) importance of selected effect sizes

Effect Size Indexes for Differences	Effect Size Indexes for Pearson Product-Moment Correlation Coefficients	Effect Size Indexes for Multiple Regression and Correlation	Practical (Clinical) Importance
0.20	0.10	0.02	Small
0.50	0.30	0.15	Medium
0.80	0.50	0.35	Large

Source: Cohen 1988.

Figure 11.2. Practical (clinical) importance of log ratios

> Odds ratio = 1.00 = No relationship or equal likelihood (intervention makes no difference)
> Odds ratio > 1.00 = Experimental group affected by intervention
> Odds ratio < 1.00 = Intervention has opposite effect than hypothesized

true population parameter (such as a mean or a regression line) at a given level of certainty.

CIs indicate the reliability of an estimate. Thus, they are written as plus or minus (+ or -). They are margins of error or fudge factors. The ends of the range are the **confidence limits**. The given level of certainty is known as the confidence level. Confidence levels can be set at any percentage, but common confidence levels are (see chapter 9):

- 90 percent confidence level, 10 percent significance level
- 95 percent confidence level, 5 percent significance level
- 99 percent confidence level, 1 percent significance level

However, using the confidence level is the preferred means of notation because this format puts the focus on the effect size (Coe 2002, 8).

Calculating CIs requires specific pieces of information beyond the scope of this text. These pieces of information include knowledge of the population mean or the estimated standard error of the mean, and the magnitude of the difference between sample means (t) by degrees of freedom. Moreover, there are multiple formulae for calculating CIs that vary by the specifics of the research study. For example, there are formulae for calculating CIs for means, for differences between two means, and

for odds ratios. Therefore, readers are referred to any standardized statistics textbook to review CIs.

A general example follows to demonstrate the use of CIs around a mean. For instance, educators in health and medical informatics programs across the U.S. wanted to investigate the statistical proficiency of students entering medical programs. The results of a national statistical proficiency examination were obtained for a random sample of 25 entering students. The mean score was 85.0. For this investigation, the CI, at a 95 percent confidence level, is plus or minus 6.2 (±6.2) or 85.0 (±85.0). The confidence limits are 78.8 (lower) and 91.2 (upper). The educators can state that they are 95 percent confident that the population mean falls between 78.8 and 91.2 (95 percent CI: 78.8 to 91.2).

Factors affect the widths of *calculated* CIs at all confidence levels (Sims and Reid 1999, 189). Narrower CIs have greater precision than wider CIs (Sims and Reid 1999, 189). These factors are:

- Variance in measurements or scores of the sample. Less variance or greater **homogeneity** in the measurements or scores of the sample results in narrower CIs. Thus, greater variance and heterogeneity of the sample's measurements or scores result in wider CIs.
- Sample size. Larger sample sizes result in narrower CIs (greater precision) than smaller sample sizes. Researchers can increase the precision of their study by increasing their sample size.
- Selected level of confidence. Higher confidence levels have wider CIs than lower confidence levels. "With a higher level of confidence, the interval needs to be wider in order to support the claim of having included the population parameter at the chosen level of confidence. Conversely, a 90 percent CI [CI] would be narrower than a 95 percent CI" (Sims and Reid 1999, 190). A CI with a 99 percent confidence level has a wider range than a CI with a 95 percent confidence level. The wider range with the higher confidence level has a greater probability of including the population statistic (value) than the narrower range with the lower confidence level.

These factors may or may not be within the control of the researchers in the design of the study. For example, researchers could calibrate their equipment or train their data collectors prior to collecting data and, thereby, potentially reduce variance in measurements. Often, sample sizes are within the control of the researchers. Finally, the selection of the confidence level is within the control of researchers. Conversely, in other research designs or situations, researchers cannot control variance and the sample size is predetermined by the class size or other feature.

Interpretation of CIs depends on information about the study, such as sample size, knowledge of the field, **range of indifference**, and other aspects. (See figure 11.3.) Range of indifference is a way to consider the effect of a research outcome on practice. The values in a range of indifference form a continuum. The continuum encompasses slight changes that practitioners believe to be meaningless to worthwhile changes. Practitioners believe implementing the slight changes is worthless. At the other end of the continuum, practitioners believe worthwhile changes should be implemented. (Simon 2001, 13; and Simon and Oland 2007 n.p.). Therefore, phrases similar to range of indifference are practical importance, practical significance, and clinical significance. Range of indifference is dependent on the topic and the expertise of practitioners. For example, researchers studying an ICD encoding system could decide that an improvement of 0.5 seconds in the system response time was trivial. This trivial change would be within the range of indifference. However, for other researchers studying transmission of data across fiberoptic cables, 0.5 seconds would be an immense effect. Additionally, CIs are also built on the assumptions that the characteristic or variable is normally distributed in the population and that the samples were selected independently from the population. If these assumptions are violated, the estimate may be invalid,

unless the sample is 100 or more. All these aspects are information to put the CIs in perspective.

Studies in health informatics research apply the concepts of effect size and CI. For example, researchers evaluated the implementation of an EHR within the Indian Health Service (Sequist et al. 2007, 192). Self-report that EHRs improve quality was associated with increased utilization of the EHR (odds ratio 3.03, 95 percent CI 1.05 to 8.8) (Sequist et al. 2007, 191). In this example, the effect size is the odds ratio, 3.03. Odds ratios are understood the same as betting odds at racetracks. These "odds" are 3.03 to 1 or 3.03:1. Therefore, interpreting these results, the clinicians who recorded that they believed EHRs improved quality were 3.03 times more likely to have increased utilization of EHRs than those who did not record that they believed EHRs improved quality. The CI is set at 95 percent. Interpreting this statement, the researchers are also 95 percent confident that the population would fall between 1.05 times more likely to 8.8 times more likely. (**Note:** CIs for odds ratios are standard errors of the logarithms of the odds ratios. Thus, the upper and lower limits are symmetrical to the logarithm of the odds ratio, not the odds ratio itself [Rigby 1999, 148].)

Unit of Analysis

The **quantitative unit of analysis** is the object for which the researchers have collected data upon which to conduct statistical analyses (Tainton 1990, n.p.). It is the focus of the researchers' study – individuals, groups, phenomena, codes, and so forth. Based on their study's findings, the researchers make conclusions about the object. These conclusions are the purpose of the study. Examples of units of analysis are:

- Individuals (patients, physicians, nurses, consumers)
- Groups (cohorts or classes of students, departments, professional societies or associations, nursing floors, governance units)
- Settings (hospital, health plan, healthcare delivery system, clinic, long-term care facility)
- Artifacts (elements of recordkeeping or documentation, codes, transactions, advertisements in newspapers)
- Geographical units (communities, core-based statistical areas, states, countries)
- Social interactions (statements, queries, e-mails, probes)

Figure 11.3. Interpreting confidence intervals from the viewpoint of making a change

- Wide interval generally means poor precision (undesirable, typically inadequate sample size)
- Narrow interval generally means high precision (desirable)
- Inclusion of null value (zero (0) for differences and one (1) for ratios) in interval means interval includes no difference, no change, or no effect (undesirable)
- Range of indifference (trivial effect or not important enough to change practice) includes all of interval (undesirable)
- Interval partially includes range of indifference (undesirable, typically inadequate sample size)
- Interval excludes null value and outside range of indifference (desirable)

Source: Excerpt from Simon and Foland 2007.

For example, in preceding chapters, several studies about physicians' use of diagnostic decision support systems or opinions about electronic health records were described. The unit of analysis in these studies was the physician. The unit of analysis was not the service (departmental governance structure of physicians) or the hospital. Thus, the researchers' conclusions based on their statistical analysis were about the physicians' use or physicians' opinions, not the services' or hospitals' use or opinions.

Frequently, the unit of analysis is the same as the **unit of observation (measurement)**, but not always. The unit of observation is the object upon which the original observations were made (Tainton 1990, n.p.). For example, researchers could be studying the effects of a curriculum on a cohort of students. The issue is the effects of the curriculum on the whole cohort, not its effects on individual students. However, the researchers would gather the students' individual achievement scores and perceptions. Thus, the unit of *observation* is the individual students' scores and perceptions. However, to conduct the statistical analysis for the unit of *analysis*—the cohort, the researchers must aggregate the data prior to conducting their statistical tests.

Often researchers present multiple findings for multiple units of analysis. In the previous example, the researchers could present findings and conclusions related both to individual achievement and to cohort achievement. They would, though, need to explain which statistical test supported each conclusion.

In published studies, confusion exists about the unit of analysis (Lederman and Flick 2005, 382; Tainton 1990, n.p.; Whiting-O'Keefe et al. 1984, 1101). For example, medical researchers examined the statistical techniques of studies published in *Lancet*, the *New England Journal of Medicine*, and *Medical Care* between 1975 and 1980 (Whiting-O'Keefe et al. 1984, 1106). The researchers found that 20 of 28 (71 percent) of studies erred in statistical conclusion validity by making conclusions about provider behavior or performance based on patient-related observations as the unit of analysis (Whiting-O'Keefe et al. 1984, 1110). The researchers observed that generally the studies' hypotheses concerned healthcare providers' behavior or performance, the treatment was aimed at the healthcare providers, and the variability in the outcome variable was related to the providers (Whiting-O'Keefe et al. 1984, 1110). The statistical test, however, used the patient encounter or patient-related event as the unit of analysis (Whiting-O'Keefe et al. 1984, 1110). This incongruity between

focus of the study and the statistical analysis is a unit of analysis error.

Typically, researchers are tempted to select the wrong unit of analysis because the wrong unit has more observations (larger n) than the correct unit of analysis (Silverman 2004, iv). It takes more time and money to obtain more observations to support the correct unit of analysis. Succumbing to the temptation of selecting the wrong unit of analysis, however, has consequences. Consequences of errors in the selection of the unit of analysis are:

- Falsely rejecting the null hypothesis (type I error, when in fact there is no difference) (Whiting-O'Keefe et al. 1984, 1111)
- Failing to detect false null hypotheses (type II error, when in fact there is a difference) (Scaring and Davenport 1987, 128)
- Violating assumptions of the statistical tests, such as independence of samples (Lederman and Flick 2005, 382)
- Selecting the wrong statistical test (Silverman 2004, iv)
- Aggregation fallacy (making conclusions about individuals based on aggregate data) (Levine 1994, 282; Robinson 1950, 357)
- Individual differences fallacy (making conclusions about settings based on individuals' data) (Richards 1990, 308)

Thus, selecting the correct unit of analysis increases the credibility of the research and avoids serious mistakes.

To avoid unit of analysis error, researchers are encouraged to specifically and explicitly state in their research design:

- Population for which the treatment is designated
- Hypotheses about the outcomes of the treatment for the population
- Unit of analysis related to the population

This precision enhances the likelihood of quality research. Furthermore, in scholarly papers, researchers should again specifically and explicitly state the unit of analysis in the methods section. This explicit statement increases clarity and reduces confusion for both themselves and their readers.

Missing Values

Another important issue in quantitative analysis of data is **missing values** (data, observations) or **missingness**

(Schafer and Graham 2002, 147). Missingness is a type of incomplete data or "coarse data" (Heitjan and Rubin 1991, 2244). Other types of coarse data of which health informatics researchers should be aware are grouped, aggregated, rounded, censored, or truncated (Schafer and Graham 2002, 148). Of the types of incomplete (coarse) data, missingness has been the most thoroughly studied and, therefore, is addressed in this chapter (Heitjan and Rubin 1991, 2244). Missingness is important because the missing values must be resolved before the data can be analyzed using statistical techniques.

Missing values are variables that do not contain data values for some cases. Missing values are a common problem for researchers (Donders et al. 2006, 1087). For example, responders to a survey may have completed some but not all of the items. This situation, with partial data, is known as **item nonresponse** (Schafer and Graham 2002, 149). In other instances, subjects may have totally refused to participate. This situation is known as **unit nonresponse** (Schafer and Graham 2002, 147). There are types of missing values, such as **missing completely at random** (MCAR); missing conditional on another characteristic, such as disease (misnamed **missing at random**, MAR); and **missing not at random** (MNAR) (Donders et al. 2006, 1088).

Missingness deserves researchers' attention because improper handling of missing values could corrupt the analyses of the data and invalidate the study's findings. Until proven otherwise, the missing values are considered systematically biased and different from the present data in ways that affect statistical analysis. In their scholarly papers, researchers should specifically state the method they used to address the problem of missing values.

There are multiple methods to address the problem of missingness. Selection of the appropriate methods is related to the type of missing values and features of the study. (See table 11.4.) **Imputation** is the substitution of values for the missing values. **Multiple imputation** (MI) has emerged since the 1980s as an effective method because researchers can conduct complete-data statistical techniques. Two major considerations for imputations are that:

- Imputed missing values should be based on predictions, given all observed values
- Random draws preserve measures of variability and correlation, and do not impose a false linearity on the data (Rubin and Schenker 2006, 1).

Maximum likelihood and multiple imputation are recommended methods of handling missing values (Enders 2006, 435; Haukoos and Newgard 2007, 666; Newgard and Haukoos 2007, 669). Multiple imputation has the added advantages of being "computationally straightforward, versatile, relatively easy to apply, and increasingly available in standard statistical software programs" (Newgard and Haukoos 2007, 669). Moreover, multiple imputation has been used in a wide variety of research settings, such as clinical trials, longitudinal studies, epidemiological analyses, registries, probability samples, and clustered data (Newgard and Haukoos 2007, 669). Thus, given the wide range of types of research studies that health informatics researchers conduct, they should carefully consider multiple imputation as a method to handle their missing values.

Primary and Secondary Analysis

To conduct **primary analysis** or **secondary analysis** is another choice researchers make. The distinction between these two types of analyses is that:

- Primary analysis is the analysis of original research data by the researchers who collected them
- Secondary analysis is the analysis of the original work of another person or organization by a second set of researchers. There are two types of secondary analysis: secondary analysis of data sets and meta-analysis (See chapter 8 for meta-analysis.)

Preeminent researcher Glass defined secondary analysis as "the reanalysis of data for the purpose of answering the original question with better statistical techniques, or answering new questions with old data" (1976, 3). In secondary analysis of data sets, researchers also may reanalyze original data by combining data sets to answer new questions. Researchers in health informatics have many potential data sets for secondary analysis. (See chapter 10 and table 10.8.) Reanalysis of secondary data is a powerful tool for health informatics researchers because of the sheer volume and richness of health data in a multiplicity of data sets.

Early in the history of secondary analysis, Glaser identified critical issues that must be addressed prior to analyzing existing data from past research for new

Table 11.4.   Selected methods to address missing data

Type	Description	Advantage	Disadvantage
Case deletion			
List-wise deletion (LD), complete-case (CC) analysis, or case-wise deletion	Delete cases for which values are missing for any variable	Simplicity	Bias because complete cases may be unrepresentative Loss of many cases
Available-case (AC) analysis, pairwise deletion, or pairwise inclusion	Exclude cases from calculations involving variables for which they have missing data; include all cases having valid data for pairs of variables being correlated	Simplicity	Bias because missing data may not be random
Weighting	Weight remaining cases after case deletion to approximate the distribution of the variable's values in the population	Restores representation (minimizes bias)	Requires knowledge of distribution in population Ignores available data in partial cases
Single imputation			
Mean substitution	Substitute mean of available values for missing data	Simplicity	Bias because missing data may not be random No longer considered robust
Last observation carried forward (LOCF)	Substitute last value (observation) to imput missing values	Simplicity	Bias because requires assumption that no change occurs in profile since last value
Conditional mean imputation or regression imputation	Inferred means based on regression using other participants' values	Optimal for limited cases	Overstates strengths of relationship
Hot deck imputation	Random substitution of missing values with values from other participants (drawing from the deck)	Variability not distorted	Correlations and measures of association distorted
Predictive distribution	Random substitution from conditional or predictive distribution	Nearly unbiased	Easiest for univariate missing-data patterns; other patterns can get complicated
Likelihood functions			
Approximate Bayesian bootstrap (ABB)	Logistic regression to approximate response and nonresponse on the dependent variable creating subgroups and imputing values within subgroups	Adds imputed data before analysis	Does not work for assessing interrelationships among independent variables
Maximum likelihood estimation (MLE)	Draw inferences from likelihood without simulations (as in multiple imputation)	Common and efficient; unbiased with large samples	Requires large sample with normal distribution
Indicator (variable) method	Create new dummy variable for each independent variable that is missing. Recode presence as (1) and absence as (0). Include the new variable(s) in multivariable analyses	Popular	Biased associations (coefficients)
Multiple imputation (MI)	Missing data are imputed two or more times (Monte Carlo simulations) creating two or more data sets derived from the original data set. These complete data sets are then separately analyzed with the subsequent yield of parameter estimates and confidence intervals reflecting the uncertainty from the missing data in the original data set	Greater accuracy and less bias Statistical packages include	Requires sufficient cases to estimate unstructured covariance matrix

answers (1962). Researchers who want to conduct re-analysis should assess:

- Comparability of populations and definitions of variables
- Existence of data relevant to present study, question, or hypothesis
- Generalizability
- Access to data and coding schemes (Glaser 1962, 71–74)

Lack of assessment and resolution of these issues may result in premature rejection of the past data or, conversely, uncritical acceptance (Glaser 1962, 71).

In addition to resolving the critical issues, researchers must extract the relevant data and prepare the database and its data. Preparing the database includes assessing the quality of its data and cleaning the data. **Data cleaning** (data cleansing or data scrubbing) involves checking internal consistency, duplication, and identifying outliers and missing data. Researchers note that data cleaning can consume approximately 80 percent of the time in data mining (Sokol et al. 2001, 2). Adequate time should be allocated for this preparation, which must occur prior to analyzing secondary data.

Researchers have studied the effects of missing values on secondary analysis (Wang et al. 1992, 952; see also general discussion earlier in this chapter.). In addition to the considerations noted previously in this chapter, secondary analysts should know all the imputed values in the data set, the method of imputation, and the type of missing data (MCAR, MAR, or MNAR) (Wang et al. 1992, 960). Once the issue of missing values has been resolved, analytic techniques can be performed on the data set.

Epidemiologists conducted secondary analysis on three databases to investigate seasonal variations in the time to pregnancy (Stolwijk et al. 1996, 437). The three databases comprised data on female unionized textile workers, pharmacy assistants, and pregnant women. Each database was analyzed separately. A logistic regression model that adjusted for age and diabetes mellitus was constructed. Odds ratios were also computed. Seasonal variation in time to pregnancy was found in all three populations. For example, for first pregnancies, the women had long waiting times if they conceived in February to April and short waiting times if they conceived in August to October (Stolwijk et al. 1996, 439-440).

More recently, researchers conducted secondary analysis to evaluate deidentification **heuristics** (rules of thumb) (El Emam et al. 2006, n.p.). These researchers linked public databases. They linked the list of physicians published by the College of Physicians and Surgeons of Ontario, the list of lawyers published by the Law Society of Upper Canada, the Ministry of Government Services' Personal Property Security Registration, and the Canada 411 telephone directory data. These researchers demonstrated that by linking public databases, identification of subpopulations—specifically, physicians and lawyers in Ontario—was possible. They also demonstrated that identification of the entire population of Ontario was not possible.

Data mining is a type of secondary analysis. Data mining is a component of **knowledge discovery in databases** (KDD; Fayyad 1997, 7). KDD is the *"nontrivial process of identifying valid, novel, potentially useful, and ultimately understandable patterns in data* [italics in original] (Fayyad 1997, 7). Data mining is a step in the process of KDD (Fayyad 1997, 7). Data mining is "the algorithmic means by which patterns are extracted and enumerated from data" (Fayyad 1997, 9). There are five classes of methods of data mining:

1. Predictive modeling
2. Clustering
3. Data summarization
4. Dependency modeling
5. Change and deviation detection (Fayyad 1997, 9-11)

Thus, data mining is a way to search for previously undiscerned "patterns or meaningful representations" (Lee et al. 2000, 85).

Components of data mining are model representation, model evaluation, and parameter and model search (Lee et al. 2000, 85). Methods of data mining include:

- Characteristic rule discovery methods
- Classification and clustering
- Dependency modeling
- Deviation detection
- Discovery of associations or sequential patterns
- Inductive logic programming
- Regression (linear and nonlinear)

- Relational learning models (autoregressive models)
- Temporal modeling (Lee et al. 2000, 85; Jones 2001, 666)

Analytic techniques in data mining include:

- Decision trees
- Genetic algorithms
- Nearest neighbor methods
- Neural networks
- Probabilistic graphical dependency models (Bayesian networks)
- Rule induction

Data visualization, such as using box plots, bar charts, and regression curves, is a way to present the findings of data mining. Hybrids exist for both the methods and the analytic techniques (Lee et al. 2000, 86; Jones 2001, 666). Each method and analytic technique has advantages and disadvantages when applied to real-world databases and problems. Finally, data mining is an iterative process. As algorithms are applied and information is derived, validated, and refined, new insights will occur that require the application of new algorithms and additional aggregations, and derived data values (Sokol et al. 2001, 4).

Researchers used data mining to detect healthcare fraud and abuse in the U.S. Medicare payment system (Sokol et al. 2001, 2). The researchers conducted data mining on 800 million records in the Medicare database (Sokol et al. 2001, 2). The researchers used visualization techniques, such as clustering and link analysis (strength and nature of relationship–"link"), to detect fraud (Sokol et al. 2001, 2). Summary data showed that a specialist in maxillofacial (face and jaw) surgery had performed significant numbers of mammographies (breast imaging), which warranted further investigation. Also, the researchers used pattern discrepancy to show that, in Puerto Rico, diagnostic mammographies constituted 86 percent of the mammography claims. (In most states and territories, screening mammographies far outnumbered diagnostic mammographies). The researchers believed the providers in Puerto Rico were misusing the Medicare system rather than committing overt fraud (Sokol et al. 2001, 7–8). In another data analysis, three-dimensional graphing showed an unusually high volume of claims in comprehensive preventive medicine (Sokol et al. 2001,

11–12). Using link analysis, the researchers identified abusive or fraudulent behavior based on patterns of referral and identified potential "professional patients" who conspired with providers to defraud the Medicare system (Sokol et al. 2001, 13). Thus, data mining was used effectively to concentrate federal investigations on situations with the highest probability of being abusive or fraudulent.

In another study, several data mining techniques were applied to survey data to determine factors influencing the decision to breast feed (He et al. 2006, 50). The survey participants were 625 mothers. First, the researchers applied a feature-selection algorithm to identify the factors most related to the dependent variable of breast feeding. Factors selected by chi-square statistical tests were less accurate than factors selected by the features algorithm. They also applied the C4.5 decision tree as a classification model. Regression was less accurate as a classifier than C4.5. With decision trees, the researchers identified breast feeders and nonbreast feeders. In **risk pattern mining**, the resulting rules were used to identify cohorts at risk for not breast feeding. Data mining provided information on which factors were influential for the specific cohorts so educational efforts could be tailored. Application of data mining methods to survey data discovered new knowledge on mothers' decision making.

Another set of researchers compared the capabilities of four data mining techniques to discover new knowledge (Kharbat et al. 2007, 2066). The researchers examined 1,150 cases from the Frenchay Breast Cancer dataset. The researchers compared the performance of the following four modern learning classifers:

1. Bayesian Network Classifier
2. Sequential Minimal Optimization
3. C4.5
4. XCS

The output of the classifiers were classifications and rules that predicted the grade of the cancer based on various independent variables. The accuracy in classification ranged from 70.38 percent (Bayesian Network Classifier) to 80.1 percent (XCS). The classifiers created hundreds of rules, which must be compacted to be useful. After compaction, the size of the XCS ruleset was 300. The researchers concluded that, although the size of the rulesets may be barriers to maximal benefit, learning classifier systems combined with compaction can result in knowledge discovery and rule induction from medical datasets (Kharbat et al. 2007, 2072).

Quantitative analysis is performed on numerical data. Analysis of quantitative data requires significant consideration of important issues prior to the application of statistical techniques. These issues are statistical conclusion validity, unit of analysis, and missing values. After addressing these issues, researchers can perform statistical analysis. Specific statistical techniques are overviewed later in the chapter.

Qualitative

Another approach to scholarly inquiry is the **qualitative approach**. Researchers in the qualitative approach interpret nonnumerical observations. These nonnumerical observations include words, gestures, activities, time, space, images, artifacts, and perceptions. These observations are placed in context. Qualitative analysis does *not* test hypotheses; qualitative analysis generates and verifies hypotheses and theories.

There are multiple analytic techniques appropriate for qualitative research. Qualitative researchers generally use a variety of overlapping techniques rather than just one (Goetz and LeCompte 1981, 56). These techniques include **analytic induction**, **typological analysis**, **enumerative systems**, **standardized observation protocols**, and **grounded theory** (Goetz and LeCompte 1981, 57-64). (See table 11.5.) Grounded (constant comparative) theory will be discussed in greater detail

because the technique is commonly used in healthcare (Bluff 2005, 157). **Content analysis,** another common technique in the field, also will be discussed.

Grounded Theory

Grounded theory is commonly used to analyze qualitative data. Grounded theory refers *both* to the theories that the technique generates and to the technique itself. As theories, they are grounded in data. As the technique, the name emphasizes that the data generate the theories. Through coding, categorization, and comparison, grounded theory results in complex theories that fit the data closely and account for diversity. Grounded theory also is known as the constant comparative method (see chapter 4). Grounded theory evolved from the research of sociologists who studied dying in hospitals (Glaser and Strauss 1967).

The purpose of grounded theory is to discover or to generate theories. These theories explain phenomena, specifically human interactions. Moreover, qualitative researchers generally seek to develop grounded theories unique to the setting or group, contrary to quantitative researchers, who seek to develop general theories.

One of the developers of grounded theories, Glaser, explains that conceptualization is the core of grounded theory (2002, 787). Conceptualization results in the identification of latent patterns; enduring relevance and meaning; and abstractions of time, place, and people (Glaser 2002,787). These conceptualizations form the generalizations of theories.

Table 11.5.   Selected analytic techniques in qualitative research

Technique	Description
Analytic induction	Scanning data for categories of phenomena and categories for relationships.
	Developing working typologies (classifications of types) and hypotheses from initial cases.
	Modifying, refining, and expanding typologies and hypotheses from phenomena of subsequent cases and phenomena of negative (poorly fitting) cases. (Robinson 1951, 815)
Typological analysis	Using theoretical framework or common sense to categorize ethnographic observational data.
	Including in categories (types) kind of event, time of occurrence, participants, and participants' reactions. Recategorizing, coding, and crosscoding reveal patterns of relationships (Goetz and LeCompte 1981, 59)
Enumerative systems	Identifying phenomena or categories of phenomena with precision and consistency
	Employing frequency counts of phenomena or categories for quality control or for development of hypotheses (Goetz and LeCompte 1981, 59-60)
Standardized observational protocols	Using instruments with predefined categories for collection of observational data. Instruments have been piloted so adequate levels of reliability and validity are guaranteed (Goetz and LeCompte 1981, 63)
Grounded theory	Including precepts of analytic induction with additional feature of coding all incidents to all relevant categories, not just the most relevant (Glaser 1965, 439)

In grounded theory and other qualitative analytic techniques, data collection, data analysis, and generation of hypotheses and theories are concurrent, intertwined activities. In data collection, qualitative researchers observe the phenomena. They record and code these observations as incidents. The unit of analysis is the incident. Each incident is coded (Glaser 1965, 439). The coded incidents are the data of qualitative researchers. Often, qualitative researchers represent the data by selecting illustrative or characteristic quotes.

Grounded theory is an iterative process. The researchers develop conceptual categories inductively to fit the coded data (see table 11.6). Some researchers may use preestablished categories that apply to the small group under observation. Redesign, collection, and recoding of additional data are constant (as in *constant comparative method*), as subsequent observations reveal gaps or discrepancies in the categories that need additional observations. Data collection, coding, and analysis

continue until all the data fit the discovered or generated theory.

Researchers used grounded theory to explore consumers' experiences using the Internet to seek and appraise information about medications (Peterson et al. 2003, n.p.). The researchers conducted six focus groups with 46 participants between March and May 2003. Using grounded theory, the researchers analyzed verbatim transcripts of the groups' discussions. The transcripts were entered into a qualitative software package that generated themes. Most participants found information by typing the drug's generic name or brand (trade) name into a search engine. The consumers used the information on the first page of the results, usually from the Web page of the pharmaceutical company selling the medication—an especially likely result because trade names often were used. The researchers concluded that consumers had suboptimal search techniques. Moreover, many consumers believed the pharmaceutical company's product

Table 11.6.   Stages of grounded theory

	Stage	Activities
1	Comparing incidents applicable to each category	Code incidents to all applicable categories (laughter, coughing, inflection, and body language are included as well as statements) (known as "open coding" or "level 1 coding")
		Compare current incident with coding of past incidents
		Compare categories' relationships
		Record "memos" and diagrams of ideas, relationships, noted discrepancies, notions about emerging theory, and other reflections
2	Integrating categories and their properties	Compare, constantly, properties of categories
		Create framework by integrating categories (known as "axial coding" or "level 2 coding")
		Integrate diverse properties
		Make sense of theory expressing relationships as paradigm, model, or "conditional matrix"
3	Delimiting the theory	Solidify theory to core categories as fewer changes are made to integrate incidents (selective coding)
		Modify to increase logical clarity
		Discover underlying uniformities and reduce categories
		Account for differences with higher level concepts ("dimensionalization")
		Achieve "parsimony" of variables and formulation
		Attain "dense" categories and theoretical "saturation"
		Generalize to other relevant contexts
		Delimit list of categories
4	Writing theory	Summarize memos on each category
		Validate theory by pinpointing coded data behind it
		Write theory using categories as major sections (themes)

Source: Adapted from Glaser 1965.

information on the Internet to be trustworthy, and other sources to be of poor quality. Finally, the researchers characterized the consumers' skills in evaluation as meager, because while skeptical, many consumers believed the pharmaceutical company's product information to be trustworthy.

Another set of researchers tested combining two data mining techniques and grounded theory (Castellani and Castellani 2003, 1011-1012). The purpose of the study was to determine the feasibility of combining data mining techniques and grounded theory. Thus, the researchers conducted a hypothetical study about the influence of several factors on the treatment of Hispanic patients. They used a hospital database composed of 200 variables and 1,200 patients. The researchers emphasized that combining data mining with qualitative research was theoretically sound. They explained that data mining techniques are not used to explore data; instead, they are used to test hypotheses. Exploration of databases without hypotheses is known as data fishing, data dredging, or data snooping (Castellani and Castellani 2003, 1007). Thus, combining data mining with qualitative research that emphasizes exploration of data supports the investigation of databases without hypotheses. The two techniques of data mining were:

- The self-organizing map—a neural networking technique
- Decision tree analysis—a classification method

The self-organizing map was used to cluster the data. The decision tree analysis was used to determine the key variables that explain the clusters. The researchers subsequently applied the processes of grounded theory. The researchers concluded that self-organized mapping and decision tree analysis had utility for qualitative researchers (Castellani and Castellani 2003, 1017).

Content Analysis

Content analysis is the systematic and objective analysis of communication. Most often, researchers analyze written documentation. However, they may analyze other modes of communication, such as speech, body language, music, television shows, commercials, and movies. The purpose of content analysis is to study and predict behaviors.

In a study of the perspectives of family physicians, researchers investigated the effect of incorporating patients' Internet-based health information into routine medical consultations (Ahmad et al. 2006, n.p.). Data were collected during six focus groups with 48 family physicians. The researchers combined content analysis and grounded theory to analyze their data. Physicians in the study perceived the Internet-based health information that the patients introduced as problematic. Physicians believed that interpreting Internet-based health information presented by the patients was an unwelcomed expansion of the physicians' role. Yet, the physicians believed that this interpretation was necessary because uninterpreted health information could cause patients distress and confusion. The researchers concluded that better physician-patient communication could be facilitated if physicians acknowledged patients' increasing use of Internet-based health information.

Conclusion Validity

Conclusion validity is an important issue for qualitative studies. In conclusion validity, the observations, patterns, and inferences are assessed for reasonableness. Conclusion validity may be judged by:

- Clarity of the logic in assigning categories
- Exhaustiveness of search for confirming and disconfirming data
- Ability of final interpretation to encompass evidence and patterns
- Inclusion of critical examinations of researchers' perspectives and their potential to bias interpretations
- Convincing **warrant** (justification) for the researchers' **claims** (interpretations)

Conclusion validity is the justified reasonableness of the final interpretation to fit the data. Conclusion validity is the qualitative counterpart of quantitative research's statistical conclusion validity.

Qualitative analysis is performed on nonnumerical data. Analysis of qualitative data is a cyclical process. Researchers collect data, pose hypotheses, find gaps, collect more data, refine hypotheses, and conclude their analyses when the theory accounts for both confirming and disconfirming data. Conclusion validity is the reasonableness of the theory and its conformance to the data.

Quantitative Techniques

Quantitative approaches, using statistical techniques, are prevalent in health informatics research. This prevalence warrants a separate discussion of a few common statistical techniques. For a detailed discussion, see a standard statistical text, such as *Statistical Methods for Health Care Research* (Munro 2005) or *Statistical Applications for Health Information Management* (Osborn 2006). The purpose of this section is to suggest appropriate statistical techniques for general situations. Three broad categories of statistical analysis are addressed

- Descriptive statistics
- Inferential statistics
- Test statistics

Descriptive (Summary) Statistics

Descriptive (summary) statistics describe the data. Generally, researchers begin with descriptive techniques to verify the accuracy of their data entry and to provide an overview of their respondents. Descriptive techniques include means, frequency distributions, and standard deviations. These statistical techniques are also called **univariate** because they involve one variable.

Exploratory data analysis examines the raw data. The raw data are presented in graphic displays. Two techniques of exploratory data analysis are stem-and-leaf diagrams and box-and-whisker plots. **Stem-and-leaf diagrams** show all the individual scores on a particular measure and provide information about the normalcy of the data (Elliott and Woodward 2007, 29). **Box-and-whisker plots** (box plots) are constructed by finding the median, the upper and lower quartiles, the largest and smallest values, and the outliers within a dataset. The median line is in the center of a box formed by the upper and lower quartiles, and "whiskers" extend to the largest and smallest values. The outliers are indicated with asterisks. Box-and-whisker plots are especially useful when the sets of data have hundreds or thousands of scores, or the sets of data have unequal numbers of values. (See figure 11.4.) The shapes of these graphic displays allow researchers to see the range and distribution of scores. Outliers become visible. These displays also show whether the

Figure 11.4. Box-and-whisker plot

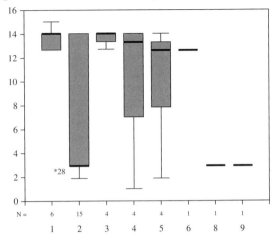

data are normally distributed or nearly normally distributed in a bell curve.

During exploratory data analysis, researchers also assess the **kurtosis** and **skewness** of their data. Kurtosis and skewness are types of nonnormal distributions.

Kurtosis is a measure of the verticality of the frequency distribution as displayed in a normal bell curve. The value of a normal kurtosis statistic is zero. Kurtotic distributions with positive kurtosis statistics are overly tall (peaked). The values are clustered in the middle of the distribution. Kurtotic distributions with negative kurtosis statistics are overly short (flattened). The values are overly represented in the tails of the curve.

Skewness is the nonsymmetrical slant or tilt of the distribution. Skewness occurs when values are overly represented in one of the tails of the distribution. Therefore, the mean, median, and mode are different values. When values cluster in the left tail, the distribution is negatively skewed or "skewed to the left." When values cluster in the right tail, the distribution is positively skewed or "skewed to the right." A skewness value greater than 1 indicates that the distribution is nonnormal.

Inferential Statistics

Inferential statistics allow the researchers to make inferences about the population characteristics (parameters) from the sample's characteristics. Examples of inferential statistics are the paired *t*-test, the analysis of variance (ANOVA), the Pearson's product-moment correlation, and multiple regression.

Test Statistics

Test statistics examine the psychometric properties of measurement instruments. They describe and explore the validity and reliability of tests. Researchers conducting test statistics calculate the validity coefficient (correlation coefficient) and each item's validity. They also could perform factor analysis. Examples of approaches to verify reliability include Cronbach's alpha and Kuder-Richardson formulae (see chapter 10). Finally, test statistics include an index of difficulty, which is the percentage of persons correctly answering each item.

Factors in Selection of Quantitative Techniques

Most research data can be subjected to more than one statistical technique. Tables 11.7 and 11.8 show potential statistical tests for various combinations of data characteristics. The suggested statistical tests in the table are merely a starting point. Appropriate statistical techniques vary by:

- Purpose of the research (research design)
- Number of variables
- Type of data
- Nature of the target population
- Number, size, and independence of the groups

Researchers maximize the use of their data by using a variety of techniques to look at their data from multiple views. Multiple views of the data shed light on different aspects of the issue and expand the body of knowledge.

Purpose of the Research

Researchers match their purpose and their statistical technique. Researchers whose purpose is to investigate the differences between groups use statistical techniques, such as the paired *t*-test and ANOVA. On the other hand, researchers whose purpose is to investigate relationships between groups or variables use statistical techniques, such as Pearson's product-moment correlation, repeated measures ANOVA, analysis of covariance, canonical correlation, and

Table 11.7.   Selected statistical tests by number of groups and distribution of data

No. of Variables	Characteristics	Test
1	One group, normal*	Mean and standard deviation
	One group, nonnormal	Binomial test
	Two groups, normal	*t*-test
	Two groups, nonnormal	Chi-square
	Three+ groups, normal	ANOVA
	Three+ groups, nonnormal	Nonparametric
2	Both continuous	Correlation
	One continuous, one discrete	ANOVA
	Both categorical	Chi-square
3+	One group	Multiple regression, factor analysis, repeated measures ANOVA, analysis of covariance
	Two+ groups	Multivariate ANOVA, discriminant function

*Normal distribution

Table 11.8.   Selected statistical tests by type of data and purpose of study

| Type of Data | Purpose | |
	Difference	Relationship
Nominal	Chi-square goodness-of-fit Chi-square test of independence	Cramer's Phi Cramer's V Lambda
Ordinal	Mann-Whitney U-test Wilcoxon matched-pairs signed-ranks test Kruskal-Wallis test	Spearman rho rank order correlation coefficient
Interval or Ratio	*t*-test Analysis of variance (ANOVA)	Pearson's product-moment correlation Repeated measures ANOVA Analysis of covariance Canonical correlation Multiple regression

multiple regression. These techniques assess whether the data show statistically significant differences or relationships.

Number of Variables

The number of variables also affects the choice of statistical technique. (See table 11.7, p. 259.) Statistical techniques that involve two variables are called **bivariate**. For example, the bivariate correlational coefficient allows the researcher to describe the strength of the relationship between two variables in mathematical terms. **Multivariate** correlational methods involve many variables. For example, multiple linear regression examines the strength of relationship among several independent variables and one dependent variable. Other more complex forms of regression also exist.

Type of Data

Another factor in the choice of statistical technique is the type of data (see table 11.8, p. 259). There are five types of data:

1. **Discrete data** are separate and distinct values or observations. Patients in the hospital represent discrete data because each patient can be counted.

2. **Categorical data** are values or observations that can be sorted into a category; for example, gender.

3. **Nominal data** are values or observations that can be labeled or named (nom = name). Therefore, the data can be coded; for example, Married = Y and Single = N, or Male = 0 and Female = 1. Nominal data cannot be ranked or measured.

4. **Ordinal data** represent values or observations that can be ranked (ordered). Ranking scales are common examples of ordinal data. A common example of a ranking scale is a Likert scale. (See chapter 10.) For example, physicians often ask patients to evaluate the severity of their pain on a scale from 1 to 10. Health informatics researchers could use ordinal data when investigating consumer, practitioner, or user satisfaction. For example, a health informatics researcher could ask physicians how satisfied they were with the new alert system on a scale from 1 to 5. However, because these rankings are subjective, the difference in satisfaction between 2 and 3 may be much less than the difference between 4 and 5.

5. **Metric data** can be measured on some scale. Two subtypes are interval and ratio.

   —The scale for interval data does not begin with a true zero. For example, time, as humans measure it, does not begin with a true zero. Interval data represent values or observations that occur on an evenly distributed scale. Time in years is an evenly distributed scale. The interval between 1985 and 1990 is the same as the interval between 1991 and 1996.

   —On the other hand, the scale for ratio data does begin at a true zero. Height, weight, and temperature are examples of ratio data.

Metric data are **continuous data**. They represent values or observations that have an indefinite number of points along a continuum. For example, measurements made with a ruler can be a foot, an inch, a half-inch, a quarter, an eighth, to infinity. Continuous data also exhibit characteristics of the other types of data; they can be counted (discrete), ordered (ordinal), and grouped.

The type of data depends on the way the variable is measured, not some inherent attribute of the variable. For example, height can be measured in inches, or categorized as short or tall. Therefore, researchers should be careful to collect data in the form that matches their intended statistical technique.

Nature of the Target Population

The nature of the target population also affects the choice of statistical technique. For example, some statistical techniques are based on the assumptions about certain characteristics of the data, such as being normally distributed in the population. (See figure 11.5.) **Parametric** techniques, such as the *t*-test, ANOVA, and Pearson r correlation efficient, are used in cases that meet or nearly meet these assumptions. However, these assumptions are not always true. In these cases, researchers use **nonparametric** or **distribution-free** techniques, for example, the chi-square test and the Spearman rho. Nonparametric techniques also are used for nominal and ordinal data.

Figure 11.5.   Underlying assumptions of parametric statistical tests

- Random selection of samples from population
- Independent selection of samples from population
- Normal distribution of object in population
- Interval or ratio level of measurement
- Homogeneity of variances
- Unrestricted range
- Linearity

Number, Size, and Independence of Groups

The selection of statistical tests also depends on the number of samples or groups. In many instances, researchers want to compare two groups: the control group and the study group. However, in other types of studies, researchers may want to compare results from 10 different communities or all 50 states. The number of groups affects the choice of statistical test. Disparate sizes of groups also sometimes affect the choice of statistical test. Some statistical tests, however, are quite robust and can handle differences in sizes. For example, in many instances ANOVA can handle unequal group sizes. Researchers must take into account the inequality of sizes. For example, the smallest group size determines the precisions of estimates. The independence of the samples is also an issue. An experimental group and a control group are considered **independent samples**. Matched pairs or cohorts, however, are **dependent (matched, paired)** samples. For instance, matched pairs of graduates and supervisors are used when an academic program wants to know the graduates' perspectives on the quality of the education, and the supervisors' perspectives on the graduates' capabilities.

Computerized Packages

Many software packages are available to assist researchers in the analysis of data. For basic descriptive statistics, researchers can use spreadsheet software, such as Microsoft Excel. However, most researchers will choose to use dedicated statistical packages (described in the next section) because these packages require less manipulation of the data than spreadsheet packages, and because they perform many more statistical procedures. Other factors that influence the choice of software are type of data, planned analytical techniques, and cost.

Quantitative

Quantitative researchers have several statistical software packages available to them. There is also freeware on the Internet, such as Amelia II, for more recent techniques such as multiple imputation and Bayesian modeling.

- Epi-Info is freeware from the U.S. Centers for Disease Control and Prevention. This integrated package, which includes word processing, database, and statistics, is designed for public health. The software allows epidemiological data to be handled in questionnaire format; and to calculate the required sample size, analyze data, and present results.

- LISREL is a software package that conducts factor analysis. Factor analysis is used to evaluate the psychometric properties of measurement instruments. LISREL generates test statistics.

- Mathematica is a software package that seamlessly integrates a numeric and symbolic computational engine, graphics system, programming language, documentation system, and advanced connectivity to other applications.

- STATISTICA is a suite of analytic software. The suite provides a comprehensive array of software for data analysis, data management, data visualization, and data mining procedures. The suite includes techniques for predictive modeling, clustering, classification, and exploration.

- Statistical Analysis System (SAS) is a powerful software package that integrates data access, data management, data analysis, and data presentation. Researchers use SAS to enter data, retrieve and manage data, analyze data with statistical and mathematical techniques, write reports, and generate graphics. SAS has powerful programming and syntax languages.

- Statistical Package for Social Sciences (SPSS) offers a broad array of analytical and graphic software. Its many components range from basic statistical techniques to advanced, specialized techniques. Basic statistics packages perform counts and cross tabulations. Advanced techniques include factor, regression, cluster analysis, binomial and multinomial logistic regression, and correspondence analysis.

Qualitative

Qualitative researchers have computer software to assist them. These software support the analysis of the volumes of data obtained during qualitative studies.

- ATLAS.ti is used to code and analyze text-based data from open-ended surveys, transcriptions of focus groups, or other sources. ATLAS.ti can be used to code other types of qualitative data, such as photographs. ATLAS.ti allows the retrieval of specific information based on search criteria. ATLAS.ti also has the ability to export data as an SPSS data set.

- CDC EZ-Text is a free software program from the U.S. Centers for Disease Control and Prevention. EZ-Text assists researchers to create, manage, and analyze semistructured qualitative databases. Investigators can use the software to enter data, create online codebooks, apply codes to specific response passages, develop case studies, conduct database searches to identify text passages, and export data in a wide array of formats for further analysis with other analytic software programs.

- Code-A-Text Integrated System for the Analysis of Interviews and Dialogues (C-I-SAID) is used to code and analyze documents, transcripts, and sound files. Coding is labeling words or word groups (segments) with annotations or scales. These labels are characteristics of the segments. This software allows researchers to specify labels and easily insert them into the document or sound file. Once the researcher has coded what the subjects said, the researcher can analyze the content of the document or sound file using this software. C-I-SAID produces descriptive statistics and tables and charts that support analysis. The software also assists researchers to categorize the segments into themes, known as content analysis. C-I-SAID can be applied to field notes, open-ended questionnaires, and interviews. A multimedia version codes video and pictures.

- NVivo is a qualitative research software used to analyze unstructured data. It is used to code and analyze text-based data from open-ended surveys, transcriptions of focus groups, or other sources. NVivo allows researchers to retrieve specific quotes based on search criteria. The software also can create tabular data representing the counts of specific codes. The data can be exported to quantitative statistical packages.

———————————

Analytic software packages exist for both quantitative and qualitative researchers. Researchers are encouraged to explore the capabilities of several packages. The choice of software depends on the type of data, the planned analytical techniques, and skills of the researcher.

Presentation of Results

Researchers follow a two-step process when presenting their results. In the first step, they report their research findings with no commentary, explanation, or interpretation. This section of a manuscript is called research findings. In the second step, the researchers comment on, explain, and interpret their findings. This section of the manuscript is called discussion. Also included in the discussion are conclusions and recommendations for future research.

Style of Language in Narrative

Researchers describe their results in the past tense; general truths are stated in the present tense. The style of writing for scientific manuscripts is objective, precise, and factual. Researchers avoid subjective interjections and emotional hyperbole. In the research findings, researchers must be very careful to maintain a neutral tone. They are merely recording their findings in narrative form.

In research findings, researchers describe the results for each hypothesis. Restating the hypothesis aids the readers. Researchers state whether or not the results support the hypotheses. They also record characteristics about the sample and describe the results of the statistical analyses that investigate whether the sample is similar to or different from the population. Supplemental statistical analyses also are described. Important findings are described before trivial findings.

Graphics

For research findings, researchers generate tables and graphs to support the readers' understanding of their findings. One rule of thumb is that data should be presented in only one way or mode (Day and Gastel 2006, 88). Researchers present the particular data element in narrative text, in a table, or in a figure, but not in multiple modes. Graphics should clarify the data, not confuse the readers. Figure 11.6 lists 10 important points to remember when constructing graphics. Researchers must carefully consider which mode of communication is most effective for the particular data element. For example:

- Tables summarize data in a grid or matrix. The elements and numbers should be in the columns, not in the rows.

- Pie charts with their segments visually show the relationships among variables and the whole. They also can represent categorical data.

- Line charts show comparisons over time.

- Bar charts show comparisons between and among items. They often illustrate major characteristics in the distribution of data (male or female, age ranges). They can be used to represent categorical, nominal, or ordinal data.

- Histograms are similar to bar charts. They show major characteristics in the distribution of data and summarize data about variables whose values are numerical and measured on an interval scale. Histograms are used for large data sets.

Interpretation: Discussion, Conclusions, and Recommendations

In the interpretation of findings, researchers create new knowledge. Writing the discussion section requires energy and creativity to synthesize the data and turn the data into information. Too often, researchers shortchange this section. The discussion section is not a superficial repetition of the findings section. Researchers explain the significance, implications, and consequences of the findings of their study. Complete discussion of findings advances the body of knowledge of the field of health informatics.

Relationship

In the discussion section, researchers relate their findings to the theory underpinning their study, to the literature,

Figure 11.6.   Considerations for effective graphics

1. Tables, graphs, and figures have titles.
2. Tables have stubheads, spanner heads, and column heads for clarification.
3. Sources are cited.
4. Time frames and dates are noted.
5. Multiple tables, charts, graphs, and figures are numbered.
6. Both axes of graphs are labeled (bar titles, legends, scale captions).
7. Keys show the meaning of shadings and colors.
8. Scales start at zero.
9. Wedges (slices) of a pie chart represent percentages, and the percentages convert to 360°.
10. Graphics are for emphasis; they should not dilute the effect with clutter.

and specifically to the prior findings that prompted their study. Researchers explain how their findings expand and advance the theory underpinning their study. Researchers compare their findings to those in the literature, explaining similarities and differences. More important, they should provide rationale to explain why their findings were the same or different. Of particular importance is comparison to the studies that they singled out as key in the literature review.

In writing this section, researchers should return to why they conducted the study in the first place. They should answer the following questions:

- What theoretical significance or practical worth do the findings have?

- How do the findings explicitly link to the larger body of knowledge?

- How have the findings improved the field's research model?

- How has the study expanded the body of knowledge?

- What new definitions have been added to the field's area of practice?

- How do the findings support practitioners in the workplace?

- What problems do the findings solve?

- What valid conclusions can the researchers and the readers draw?

Researchers also state their assumptions and the limitations of their research. A researcher describing a questionnaire study might state that one assumption is that people are honest and that one limitation is that the study only reflects one point in time.

In their conclusions, researchers frame their findings in the larger body of knowledge. Implications and consequences can be discussed. Also, research always raises new questions. These new questions become the recommendations for further research. Framing the conclusions and recommendations in terms of the theory is an effective closure to the study.

Creation of New Information

The answers to the questions presented in the previous section result in new information. In the discussion, conclusions, and recommendations, the researchers' goals are:

- To put usable information into the hands of practitioners in the workplace
- To specifically note how their findings expanded existing theory by clarifying ambiguities or closing gaps
- To advance the scholarly enterprise by presenting fellow researchers with new information and avenues for continued study

---

The discussion, conclusions, and recommendations should be rich and insightful to accurately represent the time and effort that went into the research study. Sufficient time for reflection and contemplation should be scheduled into the research plan.

Summary and Conclusions

Information is data that have been analyzed and interpreted for the users. During analysis, researchers investigate and probe their data. Statistical conclusion validity is a component of analysis. Unfortunately, as the type of validity that occurs last in the process of research, statistical conclusion validity is often neglected. However, statistical conclusion validity is important because it underpins the reasonableness of the researchers' conclusions. Other important issues are unit of analysis and handling of missing data.

Reanalysis of secondary data is a viable research approach for health informatics researchers because of the wealth of unanalyzed health data in a wide array of data sets. Data mining, a type of secondary analysis, is the application of computational techniques to produce patterns over data.

Multiple analytic techniques are used in qualitative research. These techniques include analytic induction, typological analysis, enumerative systems, standardized observation protocols, grounded theory, and content analysis. Grounded theory is commonly used in healthcare.

Quantitative researchers have a wide range of statistical techniques with which to analyze their data. Three broad categories of statistical analyses are descriptive statistics, inferential statistics, and test statistics. The selection of appropriate statistical tests depends on the purpose of the research, the number of variables, the type of data, the nature of the population, and the characteristics of the groups studied.

Analytic software packages exist for both quantitative and qualitative researchers. Several commonly used software packages were described. Selecting appropriate software depends on the type of data and the planned analytical techniques.

Interpretation occurs during the presentation and discussion of the study's findings. In their conclusions, researchers frame their findings in the larger body of knowledge and make recommendations for additional research. Analysis, presentation, and interpretation require thought and time. These investments, however, are well worth the effort because they advance the body of knowledge.

References

Ahmad, F., P.L. Hudak, P.L., Bercovitz, K., Hollenberg, E., and W. Levinson. Are physicians ready for patients with Internet-based health information? *Journal of Medical Internet Research* 8(3):e22. Available online from http://www.jmir.org/2006/3/e22.

Bluff, R. 2005. Grounded theory: The methodology. In *Qualitative Research in Health Care*, edited by I. Holloway. New York: Open University Press.

Castellani, B., and J. Castellani. 2003, September. Data mining: Qualitative analysis with health informatics data. *Qualitative Health Research* 13(7):1005–1018 Available online from http://qhr.sagepub.com/cgi/content/abstract/13/7/1005 10 August 2007.

Coe, R. 2002 (September). It's the effect size, stupid: What effect size is and why it is important. Paper presented at

British Educational Research Association Annual Conference, Exeter, United Kingdom, Sept. 12–14, 2002. Available online from http://www.cemcentre.org/Documents/CEM percent20Extra/EBE/ESguide.pdf.

Cohen, J. 1988. *Statistical Power Analysis for the Behavioral Sciences*, 2nd ed. Hillsdale, NJ: Lawrence Erlbaum Associates.

Cohen, J. 1994, December. The earth is round (*p*<.05). *American Psychologist* 49(12):997–1003.

Day, R.A., and B. Gastel. 2006. *How to Write and Publish a Scientific Paper*, 6th ed. Westport, CT: Greenwood Press.

Donders, A.R.T, van der Heijden, G.J.M.G., Stijnen, T., and K.G.M. Moons. 2006 (October). Review: A gentle introduction to imputation of missing values. *Journal of Clinical Epidemiology* 59(10):1087–1091.

El Emam, K., Jabbouri, S., Sams, S., Drouet, Y., and M. Power. 2006 (October-December). Evaluating common de-identification heuristics for personal health information. *Journal of Medical Internet Research* 8(4):e28. Available online from http://www.jmir.org/2006/4/e28.

Elliott, A.C., and W.A. Woodward. 2007. *Statistical Analysis Quick Reference Guidebook: With SPSS Examples*. Thousand Oaks, CA: Sage.

Enders, C.K. 2006 (May-June). A primer on the use of modern missing-data methods in psychosomatic medicine research. *Psychosomatic Medicine* 68(3):427–436.

Farrington, D.P. 2003, May. Methodological quality standards for evaluation research. *Annals of the American Academy of Political and Social Science* 587:49–68.

Fayyad, U. 1997. Knowledge discovery in databases: An overview. *Inductive Logic Programming: Proceedings of the 7th International Workshop*. Prague, Czech Republic, (Sept. 17–20, 1997). Book series: Lecture notes in computer science, Vol. 1297. New York: Springer.

Glaser, B.G. 1962 (summer). Secondary analysis: A strategy for the use of knowledge from research elsewhere. *Social Problems* 10(1):70–74.

Glaser, B.G. 1965 (spring). The constant comparative method of qualitative analysis. *Social Problems* 12(4):436–445.

Glaser, B.G. 2002, December. Grounded theory and gender relevance. *Health Care for Women International* 23(8):786–793.

Glaser, B.G., and A.L. Strauss. 1967. *The Discovery of Grounded Theory: Strategies for Qualitative Research*. Chicago: Aldine Publishing.

Glass, G.V. 1976 (November). Primary, secondary, and meta-analysis of research. *Educational Researcher* 5(10):3–8.

Goetz, J.P., and M.D. LeCompte. 1981 (spring). Ethnographic research and the problem of data reduction. *Anthropology and Education Quarterly* 12(1):51–70

Haukoos, J.S., and C.D. Newgard. 2007, July. Advanced statistics: Missing data in clinical research, Part 1: An introduction and conceptual framework. *Academic Emergency Medicine* 14(7):662–668.

He, H., Jin, H., Chen, J., Macaulay, D., Li, J., and T. Fallon. 2006. Analysis of breast feeding data using data mining methods. *Proceedings of the Fifth Australasian Data Mining Conference*, Vol. 61 (Conferences in Research and Practice in Information Technology), pp. 47–52. Sydney: Australian Computer Society.

Heitjan, D.F., and D.B. Rubin. 1991 (December). Ignitability and coarse data. *Annals of Statistics* 19(4):2244–2253.

Heat, M., and G. Nu. 2004. A visitor's guide to effect sizes: Statistical significance versus practical (clinical) importance of research findings. *Advances in Health Sciences Education* 9(3):241–249.

Jones, J.K. 2001 (September). The role of data mining technology in the identification of signals of possible adverse drug reactions: Value and limitations. *Current Therapeutic Research* 62(9):664–672.

Kharbat, F., Bull, L., and M. Ode. 2007. Mining breast cancer data with XCS. *Proceedings of the 9th Annual Conference on Genetic and Evolutionary Computation*, (Real-world applications: papers), London, England, July 7–11, 2007, pp. 2066-2073.47–52. New York: ACM Press.

Lederman, N.G., and L.B. Flick. 2005 (December). Beware of the unit of analysis: It may be you! *School Science and Mathematics* 105(8):381–383.

Lee, I.-N., Liao, S.-C., and M. Embrocates. 2000 (April-June). Data mining techniques applied to medical information. *Medical Informatics & the Internet in Medicine* 25(2):81–102.

Levine, D.W. 1994 (March). True scores, error, reliability, and unit of analysis in environment and behavior research. *Environment and Behavior* 26(2):261–293.

McHugh, M.L. 2007 (January). Clinical statistics for primary care practitioners: Part I, Incidence, prevalence, and the odds ratio. *Journal for Specialists in Pediatric Nursing* 12(1):56–60.

Munro, B.H. 2005. *Statistical Methods for Health Care Research*, 5th ed. Philadelphia: Lippincott Williams & Wilkins.

Newgard, C.D., and J.S. Haukoos, J.S. 2007 (July). Advanced statistics: Missing data in clinical research, Part 2: Multiple imputation. *Academic Emergency Medicine* 14(7):669–678.

Osborn, C.E. 2006. *Statistical Applications for Health Information Management*, 2nd ed. Sudbury, MA: Jones and Bartlett.

Peterson, G., Aslant, P., and K.A. Williams. 2003 (October-December). How do consumers search for and appraise information on medicines on the Internet? A qualitative study using focus groups. *Journal of Medical Internet Research* 5(4):e33. Available online from http://www.jmir.org/2003/4/e33.

Richards, J.M. 1990 (May). Units of analysis and the individual differences fallacy in environmental assessment. *Environment and Behavior* 22(3):307–319.

Rigby, A.S. 1999 (April). Statistical methods in epidemiology. III. The odds ratio as an approximation to the relative risk. *Disability and Rehabilitation* 21(4):145–151.

Repelled, A.J. 2000 (April). Are effect sizes and confidence levels problems for or solutions to the null hypothesis test? *Journal of General Psychology* 127(2):198–216.

Robinson, W.S. 1950 (June). Ecological correlations and the behavior of individuals. *American Sociological Review* 15(3):351–357.

Robinson, W.S. 1951 (December). The logical structure of analytic induction. *American Sociological Review* 16(6):812–818.

Reshow, R.L., and R. Rosenthal. 2003 (September). Effect sizes for experimenting psychologists. *Canadian Journal of Experimental Psychology* 57(3):221–237.

Rubin, D.B., and N. Schenker. 2006 (Aug. 15). Imputation. *Encyclopedia of Statistical Sciences*: 1–7.

Scaring, S.M., and J.M. Davenport. 1987 (May). The effects of violations of independence assumptions in the one-way ANOVA. *The American Statistician* 41(2):123–129.

Schafer, J.L. and J.W. Graham. 2002 (June). Missing data: Our review of the state of the art. *Psychological Methods* 7(2):147–177.

Sequist, T.D., Cullen, T., Hays, H., Taualii, M.M., Simon, S.R., and D.W. Bates. 2007 (April). Implementation and use of an electronic health record within the Indian Health Service. *Journal of the American Medical Informatics Association* 14(2):191–197.

Silverman, S. 2004 (June). Analyzing data from field research: The unit of analysis issue. *Research Quarterly for Exercise and Sport* 75(2): iii-iv.

Sims, J., and N. Reid. 1999 (February). Statistical inference by confidence intervals: Issues of interpretation and utilization. *Physical Therapy* 79(2):186–195.

Simon, S.D. 2001 (January-February). Interpreting negative studies. *Journal of Anthology* 22(1):13–16.

Simon, S., and L. Oland. 2007 (May 15). Confidence intervals. Kansas City: MO: Children's Mercy Hospitals & Clinics. Available online from http://www.childrens-mercy.org/stats/journal/confidence.asp.

Sokol, L., Garcia, B., Rodriguez, J., West, M., and K. Johnson. 2001 (August). Using data mining to find fraud in HCFA health care claims. *Topics in Health Information Management* 22(1):1–13.

Stolwijk, A.M., Olsen, J., Schaumburg, I., Jongbloet, P.H., and G.A. Zielhuis. 1996 (October). Seasonal variation in the time to pregnancy: A secondary analysis of three Danish databases. *European Journal of Epidemiology* 12(5):437–441.

Tainton, B.E. 1990. The unit of analysis "problem" in educational research. *Queensland Researcher* 6(1):4–19. Available online from http://www.iier.org.au/qjer/qr6/tainton.html.

Thompson, B. 2002 (April). What future quantitative social science research could look like: Confidence intervals for effect sizes. *Educational Researcher* 31(3):25–32.

Wainer, H. and D.H. Robinson. 2003 (October). Shaping up the practice of null hypothesis significance testing. *Educational Researcher* 32(7):22–30.

Wang, R., J. Sedransk, and J.H. Jinn. 1992 (December). Secondary analysis when there are missing observations. *Journal of the American Statistical Association* 87(420):952–961.

Whiting-O'Keefe, Q.E., C. Henke, and D.W. Simborg. 1984 (December). Choosing the correct unit of analysis in medical care experiments. *Medical Care* 22(12):1101–1114.

PART IV

Information to Knowledge

Chapter 12
The Grant Process and Proposal Writing

Valerie J. Watzlaf, PhD, RHIA, FAHIMA

Learning Objectives

- To describe the grant writing process, aspects of the grant proposal and methods used to obtain grant funding

- To use grant writing principles to obtain funding of a grant in health informatics

- To describe the different types of funding agencies and application guidelines and how it can be used to seek funding in health informatics research

- To discuss the peer review process, general review criteria, scoring and ranking of the proposal, and the entire panel review process when deciding which grants to fund

- To explain the content sections of the proposal and the application requirements

- To identify why grants are not accepted and funded

- To summarize how grant writing can be used effectively in health informatics research to seek funds in conducting the research

- To describe the process in the management of research protocol data for intervention studies such as clinical trials

Key Terms

Abstract

Approach

Biographical sketch

Budget

Centers for Scientific Review (CSR)

Clinical data manager

Clinical research associate

Clinical research coordinator

Concept sheet

Confidentiality form

Conflict of interest form

Cost sharing

Data and Safety Management Board (DSMB)

De-Identify

Eligibility criteria

Environment

Face page

Grant

Grantee

Innovation

Institute and center (IC)

Integrated review group (IRG)

Investigators

Key personnel

Letter of intent

Matching requirements

National Institutes of Health (NIH)

National Library of Medicine (NLM)

Panel of reviewers

Peer-reviewed research

Principal investigator (PI)

Program officer

Proposal reviewer

Protocols

Request for applications (RFAs)

Request for proposals (RFPs)

Seed money

Significance

Specific aims

Streamlining

Target population

Introduction

Grant writing is an art. To be successful, the grant writer should be creative, immersed in the scientific area at hand, and fully aware of the granting agency requirements and recommendations. Grant writing can be a tedious, arduous task but can provide great rewards if the grant proposal is accepted and the research is funded. If this occurs, then the researcher is able to complete study in an area that may not have been explored before. The researcher becomes a pioneer in a scientific area.

Grant Writing

A **grant,** according to the **National Institutes of Health (NIH)**, is receipt of a financial assistance award for peer-reviewed research (NIH/NIAID 2007a). The **grantee** is responsible for carrying out the research with little or no direct involvement from the granting agency.

Peer-reviewed research is research that is examined and evaluated by experts in the same or related research field or scientific area. Although specific researchers write the grant proposal, if the grant is awarded, the university, healthcare center, or other organization is the entity that receives the funds for the grant award. Therefore, once the grant is awarded, the organization becomes the grantee and must abide by the terms and requirements of the grant. A program officer or grants management specialist will work with the grantees to assist them in managing the award.

Monitor Research Trends and Problems in Areas of Expertise

The investigator should be an expert in the research trends and problems within the area of study. For example, if the investigators are interested in securing a grant award in the area of International Classification of Diseases, 10th Revision, Clinical Modification (ICD-10-CM), then they should know a great deal about ICD-10-CM and its strengths and weaknesses, methods of improvement, and other research that has been performed on ICD-10-CM, and also have a fundamental knowledge base on classification systems in general. The investigator should be able to articulate the advantages and disadvantages of the ICD-10-CM system and be able to explain the gaps in previous research. Providing this evidence to the funding agency will illustrate the need for the proposed research and why it should be funded by their agency.

Build Credibility in Area of Expertise through Publication

The investigator should know the literature related to the specific research area, and should have a track record and credibility through prior publications, presentations, collaborations, and other examples of scholarship and research. For example, in researching ICD-10-CM, investigators should detail their publications and presentations in areas related to classification systems and clinical terminologies, and expertise in the currently used U.S. classification system of ICD-9-CM. Collaborations such as serving on a task force that examines clinical terminologies and classification systems, and serving on committees that examine the effectiveness of ICD-10-CM and International Classification of Diseases, 10th Revision, Procedure Coding System (ICD-10-PCS) also provides strength to the grant proposal. In addition, any preliminary research or previous grant awards in the same or similar area can aid the grantee in securing the grant. Evidence of scholarship in the area of interest is necessary so that the granting agency will accept the calculated risk in providing monies to carry out the proposed research.

Aspects of the Grant Proposal

The content of the proposal is reviewed by the granting agency with several different components in mind. Scientific merit is measured by many components such as the significance or importance of the research area, the methodological approach for carrying out the research, the innovativeness of the research or technologies that are being tested, and the qualifications of the investigators. Other aspects of the grant proposal that are equally important include the programmatic, financial, and administrative requirements. Each of the parts of the grant proposal is discussed in more detail in the following sections.

Science or Scholarship

Granting agencies do not give funds to grantees based on their individual scholarship or expertise, but instead on the scientific merit and scholarship of the actual grant proposal. Peer reviewers or experts in the scientific area, possibly those outside the U.S., evaluate the grant proposal based on specific review criteria. The general review criteria that peer reviewers use for investigator-initiated grant proposals for NIH and the **National Library of Medicine (NLM)** include the following (NIH/ NIAID 2007b):

- **Significance**: Does the study address an important area of research and how will this area be advanced or moved forward if the research is completed?

- **Approach:** Are the conceptual framework, design, methods, and analyses sound and well developed, and integrated in relation to the specific aims or goals of the project? Do the **principal investigators (PIs)** acknowledge potential problems with the proposal and discuss methods to address these problems? (The role of the principal investigator is discussed later in this chapter.)

- **Innovation:** Is the current proposal unique, original, and innovative? Does it challenge existing clinical practice and use novel concepts, approaches, and technologies?

- **Investigators:** Are the PIs and co-PIs well trained to carry out this research? Is the research appropriate to the experience of the personnel listed in the grant proposal?

- **Environment:** Does the scientific environment and physical environment contribute to success of the research proposed? Are collaborative arrangements effective in carrying out the research proposed and is there institutional support?

Request for applications (RFAs) or **request for proposals (RFPs)** may list additional criteria specific to the announcement. The RFA or RFP is the project announcement that describes the project and encourages researchers to apply. (These terms are used interchangeably in this chapter.) Other areas that peer reviewers assess in determining scientific merit include:

- Protection of human subjects (see chapter 13)
- Inclusion of women, minorities, and children
- Care and use of animals in research

Programmatic Requirements

Grants also are awarded on whether they meet the mission of the particular agency and the programmatic requirements. For example, NIH's mission is to lead the way toward important medical discoveries that improve people's health and save lives. Priority is given to children, minorities, women, seniors, and healthy lifestyles. Therefore, it is in the investigator's best interest to include women and minorities in a proposal that is focusing on, for example, developing a database for Parkinson's disease for a specific community in order to detect environmental effects related to the disease. Other requirements may be specific to a particular program within the granting agency. NIH programmatic requirements will be different from NLM, the National Heart, Lung, and Blood Institute, and others. Therefore, it is important for the grantee to carefully review each organization's program and requirements before beginning the writing process.

Financial Requirements

Grant announcements include financial requirements with each RFA. They will usually state the maximum amount awarded and the time period for the award. Some grant announcements will state that the maximum amount is $500,000 per year for a period of three years and encourage the grantee to apply for renewal of the grant at the end of the 3-year period. Others may provide funding of $50,000 for a one-year period with no opportunity for renewal. Because the financial requirements may pose some limitations on how the proposal is written, the requirements should be reviewed before writing of the project proposal begins. For example, the budget may include costs for collaborations with other university faculty for approximately $10,000 per faculty member. If this is known, then the number of collaborating members will need to be limited or expanded depending on the financial requirements of the research grant.

Most granting agencies will state the total funding amount inclusive of indirect costs. Indirect costs can encompass a great amount of the total budget, so it is imperative to read the announcement regarding financial requirements in great detail to determine if indirect costs are inclusive or exclusive of the total funding amount. Direct costs are all costs that coincide with the research project. Indirect costs, or facilities and administration costs, cover such items as office space, use of library resources, electricity, and so forth. Although the indirect costs are not specifically used for a research project, they do represent real costs and expenditures that are paid for by the grantee's employer. Some granting agencies allow no indirect costs. Granting agencies within the federal government allow indirect costs of approximately 40 to 50 percent of the total award, or they allow the indirect rate that has been established for a facility or university. An organization should have a research office that will help prepare the budget and assist in meeting all of the essential financial requirements. A research office representative can answer some of the questions that arise regarding the budget for a research project. Budgetary requirements will vary depending on the granting agency, and it is imperative that the RFA or RFP is reviewed carefully to find this information.

Administrative Requirements

The granting agency will assess various administrative requirements before a grant is awarded. At NIH, these may include meeting NIH's funding principles, review of the project budget, assessment of the applicant's management systems, determination of applicant eligibility, and determination of public policy requirements (NIH/Extramural Research 2003). Additional information may also be requested by NIH before the award is granted. This may include information regarding other grant support (to demonstrate no overlap with other funding sources in regard to budget and commitment by investigators), as well as institutional review board (IRB) approvals for human subjects, animals, and education in the protection of human research participants requirements (see chapter 13). Other administrative requirements include continued eligibility by the investigator for the time period in which grant funds are awarded, cost analysis to determine validation of the budget as proposed in the grant proposal, and other public policy requirements such as financial conflict of interest and age and sex discrimination.

Identification of Funding Entity

An important step in grant writing is identifying the funding entity. This multistep process begins with internal funding entities available through an organization's funding agency or foundation. Once this research is complete, it can continue to the local, state, or federal levels for additional funding sources.

Internal Initiative ("Seed" Money)

For new investigators with little prior experience in grant writing or in the new research area, smaller internal grants exist that provide **seed money** to start exploring the research topic. Seed money is funding that enables an investigator to begin research in a new area of interest. This type of funding entity has specific granting requirements that must be followed. Such limits may include administrative requirements about the types of research funded, travel costs, and the number of graduate student assistants hired. For example, most universities and even some healthcare centers have research monies available for new investigators within their university or healthcare center. These may include research and development funds available from specific university schools or foundations established within the healthcare facility. At the University of Pittsburgh School of Health and Rehabilitation Sciences (SHRS), the SHRS Research and Development Fund is available to students and faculty interested in pursuing research.

Also, approximately $50 million in seed money was provided by the Department of Health and Human Services for the National Healthcare Information Initiative to improve community healthcare information exchanges throughout several states (Klein and Johnson 2004).

Foundations

Some researchers may seek funding through foundations. There are several foundations that provide funding for health informatics. It is best to search for the different funding foundations specific to the area of interest.

For example, the Foundation of Research and Education (FORE) at AHIMA provides funding through its grant-in-aid (GIA) research program. Monies are provided to investigators for such areas of interest as the legal electronic health record (EHR), the personal health record (PHR), data quality, and clinical terminologies. Once this research is complete, the investigators may continue to seek larger sources of funding from other agencies that support similar areas of investigation.

Local or State Entities

The local or state level provides a multitude of funding opportunities for health informatics research. Local and state funding agencies are very interested in funding research that benefits a local healthcare facility, individuals within a particular community, or a local church or school. It is important to emphasize how the proposed research will benefit the community or state because the funding is provided by that local or state entity. For example, a state agency in Pennsylvania provided funding to the University of Pittsburgh Department of Health Information Management for the purpose of enhancing health information technology and systems within the department. Funding assisted with developing seminars for students, faculty, and clinical instructors in the areas of health information technology, privacy, and security. Other parts of the funding assisted with staging recruitment fairs to attract the best and brightest students into health information management (HIM) and health information technology. It is vital to search for all appropriate funding entities that relate to the research idea.

Federal Entities

Federal funding is probably the most sought after and therefore the most competitive. However, it can be more prestigious and lucrative than any other funding agency. It is important to search all of the available federal entities specific to health informatics research. The NLM under NIH provides funding for many health informatics research projects as does the Agency for Healthcare Research and Quality (AHRQ) and the Health Resources and Services Administration (HRSA). Other agencies under NIH provide funding for many research topics that still may deal with health informatics but may focus on a specific group of individuals or a specific disease or condition. For example, a researcher may be interested in determining the effectiveness of the personal digital assistant (PDA) in an elderly group of individuals who record their dietary intake. The National Institute of Aging (NIA), which falls under the jurisdiction of the NIH, may be an appropriate entity from which to seek funding. Other federal funding agencies that focus on a specific condition but also may be appropriate for health informatics research include the National Institute for Disability and Rehabilitation Research (NIDRR). For example, a Web-based disability research registry that includes healthcare services appropriate to the specific disability as well as community and social services may be developed and proposed for funding through NIDRR. Many federal agencies will send e-mails to prospective grantees when an RFA is posted. Similarly, many universities send faculty a monthly list of prospective links of potential funding agencies so researchers can decide which grants to pursue. Some entities, such as NIH, provide automatic notification upon request.

Personnel

Every granting agency has several personnel who work toward achieving the goals of the specific RFA. The RFA is the project announcement that describes the project and encourages researchers to apply. The RFA can be very extensive and should provide project objectives, previous research that has been conducted in a similar area, the major focus of the research project, and names of program officers to contact regarding the grant proposal.

Program Officer

The **program officer** leads a specific RFA or RFP and is the person who will address any questions the investigators may have while developing the proposal. Program officers encourage applicants to call or e-mail with questions early in the grant proposal development process so that they can steer researchers in the proper direction. For example, an investigator may be interested in designing a patient safety education tool that encourages patients to communicate directly with their healthcare providers by using health information technology. However, upon contacting the program officer and explaining their ideas regarding the development of the tool, the researchers may decide to change some of their objectives to better meet the goals of the RFA. In this way, the program officer reminds the researchers to revisit the grant announcement and to pay particular attention to the program goals.

Proposal Reviewers

Another very important group of individuals who play a vital role in the granting process is the **proposal reviewer**. A proposal reviewer is an individual with an extensive background or experience in a particular research area who reviews the grant proposals and provides comments. The reviewer also may develop a score that determines the likelihood of the grant's potential for funding. Steps that the proposal reviewers must follow vary for each granting agency, but for the most part, these steps include:

- Submitting curriculum vitae or résumé with experience listed in specific clinical or science areas

- Reviewing the list of proposal applications to determine which are appropriate for review based on their area of expertise and focus of the proposal application

- Receiving the proposal, evaluation form, and instructions for review via e-mail

- Receiving and completing a confidentiality and conflict of interest form.

    The **confidentiality form** states that all information in the proposal application will be kept confidential. It must be signed and dated by the proposal reviewer. (See appendix 12A, pp. 299–301.)

    The **conflict of interest form** asks the reviewer to inform the program officer if there are any conflicts of interest based on the area of focus for the grant application. This form is also signed and dated by the proposal reviewer. (See appendix 12B, pp. 302–308.)

The confidentiality and conflict of interest forms will be discussed in more detail later in this chapter.

- Reading the proposal and providing comments and a final score based on scientific merit. Usually a score of 1 is highest and 5 is lowest. Some granting agencies use a more detailed scoring range such as 2.5 or 3.3.

Confidentiality

The proposal reviewers should keep every part of the grant review process confidential. Proposal reviewers gain insight into all aspects of scientific research conducted or planned by many different individuals. Reviewers should take utmost care in maintaining confidentiality of information shared during this process.

Before, During, and After Review

Confidentiality of the proposal application must be maintained before, during, and after review. Proposal reviewers should delete electronic copies and shred paper copies of the grant proposal after review, and not share the information with anyone outside of the granting agency. A confidentiality form is completed, signed, and dated by the proposal reviewer attesting to the fact

that all information within the grant proposal will be kept confidential. See appendix 12A for the confidentiality form used by FORE/AHIMA.

Review, Panel Deliberations, and Recommendations

Most granting agencies will have two or three different reviewers evaluate one grant proposal. Once their evaluation forms are submitted with a final score and specific comments, a panel of reviewers (which may or may not include the original proposal reviewers) meets to discuss all of the grant applications received. All of the grant applications are discussed, and final recommendations are determined.

Characteristics

There are certain characteristics that the proposal reviewer should pay keen attention to when assessing the research proposal. In order to perform an effective evaluation, the proposal reviewer should not have any conflict of interest with the proposal application in any capacity. Also, the proposal reviewer should have the same or similar background and expertise related to the topic of the scientific proposal he or she is evaluating. Each of these areas will be discussed in more detail.

No Conflict of Interest

All proposal reviewers must demonstrate that they do not have a conflict of interest with the proposal application that they are reviewing. Conflicts of interest may occur if the proposal reviewer is a consultant within the same organization that is requesting funds, if the proposal reviewer has employed individuals who are listed on the grant application, or if the PI or co-investigator were students of the proposal reviewer. By completing conflict-of-interest forms, proposal reviewers attest to the fact that they have no conflicts of interest with the grant application before them. The conflict of interest form is signed and dated by the proposal reviewer. See appendix 12B (pp. 302–308) for the conflict of interest form used by AHIMA.

Assessment

The proposal reviewers should provide a precise and timely evaluation of the specific grant proposal. To do this, the proposal reviewer should have expertise in the subject matter of the proposal. Reviewers with a minimal background in the subject area still may be suitable if they supplement their expertise with additional reading, and demonstrate interest in that area of health informatics. Some evaluation forms ask the proposal reviewer to rank their reviewer expertise in relation to the subject matter of the proposal. This assists in the final decision, especially if two very different rankings are provided by two different reviewers. Proposal reviewers should thoroughly read the entire grant proposal, but they are asked to focus their evaluation on the practicality, feasibility, relevance, and cost-effectiveness of the proposed project. One of the major areas of focus for reviewers is whether the hypotheses are unambiguous and scientifically plausible. For example, if a researcher's hypothesis is to evaluate the effectiveness of health information technology in improving the quality of care, the first question a reviewer may have is "How is this feasible or practical when assessing the quality of care is such a broad area?" The reviewer will begin to look for other hypotheses or specific aims that narrow the focus of the research. Also, proposal reviewers will focus on the relevance of the grant proposal in relation to the granting agency's goals or RFA. If the proposal is not relevant to the granting agency's mission, then it will be quite difficult to receive a favorable score.

For example, in 2007 NLM sought researchers to provide professional services to design and conduct outreach projects to improve access to HIV/AIDS-related health information by patients, the affected community, their caregivers, and the general public (NLM/RFQ/AIDS 2007). If, however, the researchers focus on health information that is not specific to HIV/AIDS, then the proposal will not be acceptable because it is not relevant to the specific RFA.

The budget is another major area of focus for the proposal reviewer. The budget should be fair in relation to the expected accomplishments. It should not seek the maximum amount that is allocated unless the researchers can show that is needed to meet the project objectives. Also, the researchers should seek from their organization some services in-kind or matching funds. This demonstrates to the proposal reviewer that the researcher's employer may sustain the project after the grant monies are depleted. For example, in-kind services may include providing a computer laboratory or health information systems network so that additional grant monies need not be requested for additional computers or health information technology services.

Review Process

The granting agency is responsible for several steps of the review process. It is the agency's responsibility to select appropriate proposal reviewers, to provide appropriate evaluation criteria that the proposal reviewers use to evaluate the grant proposal, and to organize an effective overall assessment of the proposal. This overall assessment includes initial reviews, meetings, and final recommendations. For investigator-initiated grants, the NIH peer review process consists of having one or more of the **Centers for Scientific Review (CSR)** referral officers review the initial application (NIH/CSR 2007). The CSR referral officers determine the most appropriate **integrated review group (IRG)** to assess the proposal's scientific and technical merit. The application is then assigned to a study section. NIH has many different study sections that consist of more than 20 peer reviewers. If an application may fit into more than one study section, it will be assigned to each of those sections for review. The grantee may state in a cover letter which study sections they prefer to review their application, and these requests are seriously considered within NIH. However, if the grant proposal is in response to a specific RFA, then the study section is listed within the announcement and the application would be reviewed by that group. Steps within the peer review process at NIH include the following (NIH/CSR 2007):

- The application is received and assigned to a study group.

- The scientific review administrator (SRA) reviews the application for completeness, content, and assigns the most appropriate proposal reviewer.

- The application is assigned to three reviewers, and at least two are chosen to provide written critiques and lead the discussion at the meeting.

- The proposal reviewers submit critiques and scores to CSR.

- The reviewers are given a list of proposals that fall in the lower half of the scoring. These proposals will not be discussed at the meeting. This process, **streamlining,** does not mean that the proposal has been disapproved, but grantees are encouraged to resubmit after receiving the critique.

- The members of the study sections meet for about two days, during which time reviewers present and discuss their critiques. Priority scores are marked on the scoring sheet, which is then tabulated by CSR. Scoring is done privately.
- After approximately 2 days, the priority score and percentile ranking is available online to the grantee via e-mail. Summary statements typically are available in approximately 1 month and include the full critique, the SRA's summary of the meeting discussion, study section recommendations, and other pertinent information.

Other aspects of the review process are discussed below.

Initial Independent Assessment

An initial independent assessment is made on every grant proposal received. The initial assessment compares the application to the stated guidelines, such as meeting the objectives of the RFP, page limit requirements, and budget requirements. If these requirements are not met, the granting agency may decide not to move forward to the scientific merit assessment.

Assessment Against Corresponding Entity Application Guidelines

The first step in the review process is to assess whether the grant proposal meets the application guidelines. Application guidelines refer to the organization and construct of the proposal rather than the scientific content. Application guidelines may include eligibility, timeliness (meeting due date), format requirements such as meeting page limitations, budget limitations, required attachments (curriculum vitae for all personnel), and submitting the grant proposal on-line. For example, application guidelines for the AHIMA/FORE foundation are described below (AHIMA/FORE 2007):

> The FORE Grant-in-Aid program is directed toward supporting the development of HIM professionals as leaders in defining and validating the unique body of knowledge encompassed by HIM. The results of these studies not only provide infor-

mation for the HIM professional to apply in meeting current and future challenges, but also support policy initiatives and the redefinition of the roles of HIM practitioners.

The primary or secondary investigator must be an active, associate, or student member of AHIMA. Each recipient shall be limited to one funded grant per year. Ordinarily, the scope of the proposal shall be such that it can be completed within 18 months from the date of funding. There are no minimum or maximum grant request expectations, but the range of grants historically has been between $15,000 and $40,000. Submissions that address one or more of the AHIMA *research priorities* will receive priority consideration for funding.

The Dissertation Assistance Award program supports research undertaken as part of an academic program to qualify for a doctorate in areas relevant to HIM. To qualify for an award under this program the student (**principal investigator**) must be enrolled in an accredited doctoral degree program in an area related to HIM (computer science, business management, education, public health, and so forth) and must be an active, associate, or student member of AHIMA. All requirements for the doctoral degree, other than the dissertation, must be completed by the award date.

Each recipient shall be limited to one funded grant per year. Ordinarily, the scope of the proposal shall be such that it can be completed within 18 months from the date of funding. There are no minimum or maximum grant request expectations, but the range of grants historically has been between $5,000 and $10,000. Submissions that address one or more of the AHIMA *research priorities* will receive priority consideration for funding.

Application Submission and Deadlines

The deadline for submission of proposals is typically in late March for the spring review and late September for the fall review. Resubmissions may be submitted any time within 90 days of resubmission notification. Final award notification will take place within 6 weeks of the application deadline. Applications should be mailed to FORE Grant-in-Aid Awards, Foundation of Research and Education, AHIMA, 233 N. Michigan Ave., Suite 2150, Chicago, IL 60601-5800.

The Grant-in-Aid application is available online at https://secure.ahima.org/fore/gia/login.aspx and is included in appendix 12C (pp. 309–320).

Assessment on Merit

The second step in the review process is to assess whether the grant proposal meets the granting agency's published evaluation criteria. The criteria may be published on the granting agency's Web site and may be part of the RFP. The merit assessment usually consists of the specific components, each of which may be given a weight and maximum score. Evaluation criteria used by proposal reviewers at AHIMA/FORE are included in appendix 12C (pp. 309–320).

Meetings

The review process includes two levels of meetings by the proposal reviewers to discuss the written assessments. The first meeting may include a review of all of the proposal assessments in paper format or e-mail. The second meeting includes the full panel of reviewers and includes discussion of the proposal assessments. This meeting may be conducted in person or via a conference call.

Mail (Traditional or Electronic)

The review of the proposals in paper or electronic format is usually conducted for a specific RFP. Many times, the proposal reviewer is responsible for assessing a certain number of RFPs. It is the granting agency's responsibility to send corresponding assessments to all proposal reviewers. This is done so the reviewers can assess and provide comments, if necessary. Some granting agencies do not have proposal reviewers review all of the initial assessments. Instead, they have one level of reviewers that perform the initial assessment, and then a separate review is performed by members of the granting agency. These assessments are performed independently.

Panel

The **panel of reviewers** consists of individuals who are experts in a scientific area. Sometimes the panel of reviewers are appointed by the granting agency, and other times the reviewers may request participation on the panel. The panel members must demonstrate their expertise by completing an application and submit-

ting their curriculum vitae, which should include their education, certifications, publications, presentations, previous grants funded, and past work experience, consultations, and community service. At NIH, one of the most important criteria is that the panel of reviewers is fair and objective. The reviewers must be able to participate in group discussions, articulate their views clearly and concretely, and work well within the group (NIH/CSR 2006a).

Panel Assessment and Ranking

The panel of reviewers may include the proposal reviewers, or it may include a second level of reviewers different from the proposal reviewers. This depends on the granting agency and their specific requirements. In any event, the panel uses their collective expertise in evaluating the grant proposal and compiling a score. The ranking will enable the funding entity to make a final recommendation on whether or not to fund the grant proposal. At NIH, each application is discussed and then assigned a single overall score based on the five criteria (Significance, Approach, Innovation, Investigator, and Environment). The weight given to each criterion varies depending on the nature of the grant application. Also, the appropriate use and explanation of human subjects, animals, and safeguards against biohazards are taken into account in the priority score as previously described. At NIH, the best possible score is 1.0 and the worst is 5.0. The reviewers can include scores such as 2.2 or 3.3. The scores are then averaged and multiplied by 100 to arrive at an overall score (NIH/CSR 2006b, 1–2).

Funding Entity's Consideration of Panel's Recommendation

After the scoring is complete, the funding entity takes the panel critique, scoring, and recommendations under consideration. It then decides whether to fund the proposal or to seek more information from the grantee. The funding entity may decide that the proposal is not recommended for further consideration. If the decision is made to seek further information, then the proposal is deferred and the panel may make a site visit to the potential grantee. If the decision is to not seek further information, then a priority score will not be made and the budget is not discussed.

Funding Entity's Consideration

The funding entity considers many things before deciding to grant the funding award. A grantee may receive a favorable priority score and the proposal approved for funding, but the award may be different from what is proposed in the original budget. These factors depend on the aspects discussed in the next section.

Entity's Purpose, Emphasis, or Funding Priorities

One of the major items that the funding entity examines before funds are awarded is ensuring that the proposal reflects the entity's purpose, emphasis, or funding priorities. For example, if researchers propose to examine the effects of stroke on family members by developing a Web-based tool that collects the subjects' experiences while caring for a family member who has had a stroke, the funding entity must make sure that this research is in accordance with its purpose and funding priorities. Even if a proposal received an excellent review and recommendation from the panel of reviewers, it may not reflect the mission of the granting agency.

Principal Investigator's or Institution's Past Performance

Another important aspect in the determination of providing the grant award is the previous performance of the PI with the same granting agency. If the PI demonstrates from a prior award that it has good leadership and organizational skills, and promptness in providing reports and updates regarding the grant progression, this is a very good sign that the PI will demonstrate these skills in subsequent research.

Principal Investigator's or Institution's Use of Funds

It is imperative that the PI use the budget appropriately. This will reflect favorably on the PI, and the funding entity will consider this. Many times investigators cannot complete the grant project as written with the funds provided because they did not budget the funds appropriately. Therefore, they may need to curtail the progression of the grant because the monies are depleted. This does not reflect effective management. If this is known from previous awards, then the funding agency may reconsider providing funds again, even if the proposal received a favorable priority score.

Funds Available

Sometimes the funds allocated may be more or less than what was originally stated. For example, a proposal submitted to the Centers for Disease Control and Prevention (CDC) to examine the use of the EHR in physician offices and its impact in improving infectious diseases in the elderly may receive more funds than requested. This may be because the funding entity believes the proposal truly reflects the mission of the agency and does not think that the research will be able to be carried out completely with the amount requested. Therefore, the funding entity may decide to double the request of funds from $20,000 to $40,000. This decision may limit the amount allocated to other proposals, but is justified by the funding entity because it truly reflects its mission, purpose, and priorities.

Following Application Guidelines

Most of what has been discussed so far is from the perspective of the funding agency. There are many steps the investigator or researcher should take to construct an effective grant proposal:

- The investigator should follow the application criteria scrupulously to make sure that the grant is submitted on time, meets eligibility requirements, meets format requirements, and stays within the budget allocated.
- The investigator should align project objectives with the mission of the funding agency, and focus on the entity funding priorities, timelines, and matching requirements.
- The content is of utmost importance and should be written two to three months prior to the due date. The investigator should write a draft of the proposal and form a mock review committee to review the proposal before submission. This mock committee can provide constructive feedback to strengthen the proposal before actual submission.
- The investigator also should discuss how the application, if funded, will change the lives of the target population, and how significant the results will be in relation to health information technology and healthcare in general.

Basic Application Criteria

There are several criteria with which the investigator should become familiar before beginning the grant writing process. Each granting agency will have different application criteria, so the investigator should know the criteria well. In addition, a grant-writing workshop may prove beneficial to the investigator especially if this is the first time he or she is writing a grant. Grant-writing workshops are offered by several universities, healthcare centers, or NIH.

Eligibility

Eligibility criteria specify the types of facilities eligible to apply for funding. The investigator must examine these criteria carefully to make sure that the facility meets the criteria. For example, HRSA, under the Health Information Technology Innovation Initiative, states that several facilities are eligible to apply (HRSA 2007). Eligible applicants include public and nonprofit organizations, and faith-based and community-based organizations. Other examples of eligible categories are more specific and may include: health centers as defined under Section 330 of the public health service act applying on behalf of a managed care network or plan that has received federal grants for two subsequent years. If the investigator has questions regarding eligibility, applicants should contact the program officer or grant representative to be certain that all eligibility criteria are met.

Timeliness

Meeting deadline dates is a very important part of the grant process. Dates are listed for when the application is available, the date and time that application is due, dates for when the letter of intent is due (if required), and the project start and end dates. The application due date is probably the most important date. If the application due date is not met, the application may be rejected by the granting agency.

Letter of intent dates are also very important. A **letter of intent** describes the focus and goal of the research project and enables the granting agency to determine if a full application is of interest. It provides the applicant with feedback regarding the research topic without having to submit a full grant proposal. A one- to two-page letter of intent can save the grant writer precious time and effort if the granting agency determines that the focus of the research project is not in accord with its mission. If, however, the granting agency determines that the research area is one of great interest to them, the feedback received will guide the investigator in framing a better research proposal.

Format

Calls for submissions will state the number of pages, required attachments, and funding limitations. It is imperative that researchers comply with these specific directions.

Page Limits

If the application states that the methodology section should be 20 pages, then the investigator must abide by these rules. Failure to meet the page limitations may disqualify the proposal. Font size and typeface are also essential requirements. For example, if the application states to use 10-point Courier New, then all parts of the grant must be written in this format. The sections of the grant must be labeled as outlined in the application. Proposals must not stray from these requirements. It is recommended that a professional editor review the entire manuscript for grammar, spelling, and punctuation, as well as identify phrasing that does not make sense or could be improved. In addition, many granting entities, including NIH, require that proposals be submitted electronically. Because of this, it is important to work with an administrative assistant or grant writer to formulate the steps needed to successfully submit the grant application on-line. On-line submission may be more complicated and take more time than anticipated. The investigator should be prepared and allot time to this process, especially if it is the first time an investigator is submitting a grant electronically.

Required Attachments

Similar requirements are posed for required attachments and budget constraints. For example, if the grant guidelines state that one-page curriculum vitae (CVs) be included for all personnel listed in the grant as attachments to the application, then it is imperative that the applicant abide by this rule and truncate existing CVs to meet the page restriction. Other financial documentation supporting the grant project may be requested, such as letters of support or Internal Revenue Service (IRS) determination letters of tax-exempt status.

Budget Guidelines

Staying under the maximum budgetary requirements is another important rule. Very rarely will granting agencies examine a proposal if it exceeds the budget limits in the RFA. Sometimes, the budget is listed as an estimated amount. If this is the case, then it is best to stay close to or less than the estimate when framing the budget section.

Minimum Performance Requirements as Specified in Application

This section introduces forms of the minimum requirements typically specified in an RFA.

Project Objectives

Investigators should list all of the project objectives and discuss how the application will meet each objective. Each objective and the proposed activities performed to meet the objectives should be detailed. Start and end dates for completing each activity are necessary, as is listing the personnel who will complete each activity. See figure 12.1 for an HRSA grant application objective to develop an online EHR course for allied health professionals.

Timelines

A grant proposal may include multiple timelines. Timelines may be created for each objective so the proposal reviewers can see the commitment for achieving each objective. An example of a timeline for HRSA's Objective 1 described earlier is shown in table 12.1. The full timeline can be found in Table 12.4.

Some grant applications may state that quarterly timelines be developed with all project activities

and grant expenditures for each quarter. Others may state that timelines be developed for the entire project period, specifying activities, personnel, and outcomes. Table 12.2 displays an example of a project objective with the activities, personnel, time period, outcomes, and evaluation specific to the objective.

Matching Requirements or Cost Sharing

Some grant applications will require **matching requirements** or **cost sharing**. This means that the applicant should discuss use of in-kind contributions and the portion of the costs that would come from an entity other than the funding agency. Some granting entities will state that the matching requirement is, for example, 25 percent of the total project costs. The entity may state that this cost can include nonfederal funds such as state, local, or private funds (Grants Management 2007).

Entity Funding Priorities

Additional priorities one should pay special attention to before writing the content section may include the population, geography, or specific community that the grant will target. Some granting entities will consider only those projects that provide intervention to human subjects, so clinical and community trials may be given priority. Examples of funding priorities are provided below.

Target Population

A **target population** relates to a specific group of individuals on which the granting agency would like the research to focus. For example, NIA targets individuals older than

Figure 12.1.   Example of Objective 1 for HRSA/EHR course grant

Objective 1:   Create EHR course modules with an emphasis on rural and underserved allied health.
Six distance education EHR modules (which will comprise one 3-credit EHR course) will be created by the Project Director and Center for Instructional Development and Distance Education (CIDDE) and assessed by the other members of the Core Development Core Team (CDCT) and the External Advisory Board (EAB) in Year 1.
The modules include:
(1) design, development, management, and administration of the EHR for the rural and underserved allied health professionals;
(2) standards, data elements, structure and content, clinical terminologies of EHR, and how they relate to rural and underserved allied health professions;
(3) safety, security and ethical issues and HIPAA safeguards for EHR;
(4) EHR models/systems with a focus on data exchange for disease prevention and health promotion, geriatrics, long-term care, home health and hospice care, rehabilitation, and behavioral healthcare;
(5) use of the EHR in rural and underserved allied health practice;
(6) outcomes research using the EHR for the rural and underserved allied health professional.
The entire EHR course will also have a course syllabus and course outline created and evaluated by the CDCT and EAB.

Table 12.1.   Example of objective and timeline for HRSA application

Development of EHR course for allied health professionals

Tasks to meet Objective 1:	Year 1	Year 1	Year 1	Year 1
Objective 1: Create distance education EHR modules with an emphasis on rural allied health.				
	Jul-Aug	Sept -Dec	Jan – April	May – June
1. Create EHR course syllabus and schedule	X			
2. Create Module 1	X			
3. Create Module 2		X		
4. Create Module 3		X		
5. Create Module 4			X	
6. Create Module 5			X	
7. Create Module 6				X
8. Review and finalize all modules				X

65 years, and NIDRR targets those individuals with disabilities. Other granting entities will focus only on children with disabilities or individuals with behavioral health issues. The target population or population under study includes who will be in the study, how they will become a part of the study, why these specific subjects will be a part of the study, whether a sample will be used, and why and how the sample will be selected (Watzlaf 1989).

Geography

Some funding entities focus on a certain geographic area. For example, many of the foundations will only fund those projects that will make a difference in a specific community, city, town, or borough. State funding entities may focus on a particular region of the state. Some funding entities may focus on a specific population *and* geographic area. For example, state departments of health may focus on children in need of vaccinations in a low-income region of the state. Because funding entities may focus their attention on a particular region, the applicant must read the RFA carefully to make sure they will qualify for the particular project announcement. The applicant should explain where the study will be conducted and if it will include one facility or multiple facilities and why.

Table 12.2.   Excerpt of the timeline for Objective 1 of the HRSA grant project.

ETHODOLOGY SUMMARY					
(Recommended Format Table)					
Objectives	Activities	Responsible Person/Position	Time Period	Outcomes	Evaluation
Objective 1: Create EHR modules with an emphasis on rural and underserved allied health.	1. Create EHR course syllabus and schedule 2. Create Module 1 3. Create Module 2 4. Create Module 3 5. Create Module 4 6. Create Module 5 7. Create Module 6 8. Review and finalize all modules	Project Director; Associate Director with input from the other members of the CDCT, EAB and CIDDE.	Y 1	An EHR distance education course syllabus, schedule, and six modules will be created.	The EHR course will be evaluated on content, distance education medium, and course evaluation methods.

Intervention

Intervention requirements also may be included in RFAs. This means that the applicant must introduce a health-related intervention of some kind within the target population. In this case, only intervention-based studies will be considered. For example, the Yale-Griffin Prevention Research Center and the Connecticut Health Foundation requested applications to design and implement interventions to improve the prevention and control of diabetes (YGP/CHF 2006). Healthcare centers are encouraged to partner with community organizations to provide prevention programs to minority individuals with diabetes. Objectives include: improving access to quality diabetes prevention and management services in community health centers, improving data collection systems for minorities with diabetes, and developing and testing effective interventions that increase the understanding of diabetes-related complications. Applicants should focus their grant proposal on the intervention to be considered for funding.

Content

Once all of the program announcement criteria have been scrupulously reviewed and the applicant believes that the criteria are met, the content of the grant can be written. It is important to develop an outline of the grant proposal. The outline should contain a timeline that lists what must be done to develop the content of the grant, while at the same time abide by application requirements. The applicant should assess the potential competition in the field and determine the resources needed to compete. In addition, an organizational assessment should be developed and other investigators sought as collaborators. Many granting agencies favor multicenter collaborations when conducting innovative research projects. A mentor to evaluate the grant proposal and provide constructive criticism should be sought. The applicant should establish a niche and then find which grant announcements support the research ideas. Proper training and experience is vital for the PI and co-investigators seek a specific grant announcement. They should peruse grant applications from successful grantees, read the instructions for the grant application over and over again, and refrain from rushing into the grant writing process. It should take at least two to three months to write the grant, and the specific aims should be developed early and reviewed with colleagues, contact persons within the granting agency, and other individuals knowledgeable about the topic of interest (NINDS 2007).

The content of the grant usually includes the following parts (NINDS, 2007 and Watzlaf, 1989):

Section I: Face page, description/abstract, key personnel, budget, biographical sketch, and other support

Section II: Specific aims; background/significance; background, significance, and preliminary studies; research design and methods; approach; results; human subjects; vertebrate animals; literature cited; contractual agreements and consultants

Section III: Appendixes

These sections will be described in more detail in the next section.

Section I: Introductory Materials

The introductory materials consist of five main parts: face page, description or abstract, listing of key personnel, budget, biographical sketch, and other support.

The **face page** is very similar to a title page. It includes:

- The title of the project
- Whether the grant is in response to a RFA
- The name, degrees, position title, and mailing address of the PI
- Dates of the proposed project
- Costs requested for the proposed project
- Performance sites
- Congressional district of applicant and/or other districts that benefit financially from the application
- Applicant organization, type of organization, and official signing for the applicant organization
- Signature of PI

The specific items included in the face page vary based on the specific grant announcement and agency. It is best to complete the items on the face page in the order listed. An example of the face page from the HRSA/EHR course is presented in figure 12.2.

The **abstract** or description of the project is an essential aspect of the grant application. It should be written very carefully because it will determine which peer reviewers will review the application. The abstract serves as a succinct description of the proposed work that can be read separately from the application. Most NIH abstracts have a strict 200-word limit. It can be extremely difficult to include important information in

Figure 12.2.   Example of Face Page of HRSA grant application

DEPARTMENT OF HEALTH AND HUMAN SERVICES Health Resources and Services Administration Grant Application Allied Health Grant Program	Date Received	Grant Number
	CFDA No. 93.191 DUNS No. AHPG 004514360	

1. Title of Proposal (*not to exceed 56 spaces*) *Development of a Course on the Electronic Health Record*		
2a. Project Director, Name (*last first middle initial & position title*) *Watzlaf Valerie J. Associate Professor*	2b. Highest Degree *PhD.*	2c. Social Security No.
2d. Mailing Address (*organization street city state zip code*)	2e. E-Mail Address	
	2f. Department *HIM*	
	2g. School or College: s	
2h. Telephone (*area code number*) : *(412) 383-6647*	2i. Fax (area code number):	

3. Dates of entire proposed project period (This application) *From 7/1/XX To 6/30/XX*	4. Applicant Organization (*name and address*) *University of Pittsburgh* *School of Health and Rehabilitation Sciences* *Atwood and Sennott Street* *Forbes Tower, Suite 6030* *Pittsburgh, PA 15260*

5. Congressional District of Applicant	Other Districts that Benefit Financially from this Application

6. Official in business office to be contacted concerning application (*name title address and telephone number*)	6a. Single point of contact if different from 6
	6b. E-mail address of single point of contact

7. Entity identification no.	8. Official signing for applicant organization (name title and telephone number)

9. Type of organization (*see instructions*) ☐ Private Nonprofit ☐ Public (Specify Federal State Local) _____

10. Project Director Assurance: I agree to accept responsibility for the conduct of the project and to provide the required progress reports if a grant is awarded as a result of this application.	11. Signature of person named in item 2a. "PER" signature not acceptable. _____ . Date
12. Certification and acceptance I certify that the statements herein are true and complete to the best of my knowledge and accept the obligation to comply with the DHHS terms and conditions if a grant is awarded as a result of this application. A willfully false certification is a criminal offense (U.S. Code Title 18 Section 1001).	13. Signature of person named in item 8. "PER" signature not acceptable. _____ . Date

such a small content area. It is recommended that the abstract be written after the major content of the research methods is completed, so all pertinent data are included. The abstract should state the hypothesis, objectives, why the objectives are important and innovative, and how the proposed methods will accomplish the established goals. See figure 12.3 for an example of an abstract for the HRSA/EHR distance education course.

The **key personnel** section lists the name; position title, department, and organization; and role in the project for the PI, co-PI, co-investigators, collaborators, consultants, statisticians, and any other personnel who have important roles in the research project, such as research assistants. Sometimes a summary of key personnel, their role in the project, and percentage of time per person per year are requested in the application guidelines. The actual documents used to display the personnel distribution chart used in the HRSA EHR distance education grant is shown in table 12.3.

The **budget** can be specific or broad-based depending on the grant application. Most grant applications preestablish a format for the budget. The budget normally includes salary and fringe benefits for personnel, and expenses for equipment, supplies, travel, patient care costs, contractual costs, consulting costs, telephone calls, paper, computer usage, and equipment maintenance. The budget must be realistic in relation to the research plan. As with the abstract, the budget should be prepared after the research plan is completed so all costs are included. Overestimation or underestimation of the budget may alert the proposal reviewers that the investigator does not truly understand the research project. Justification for each budget line item is essential. Such items include the specific functions of the personnel, consultants, statisticians, and collaborators. Grants that cover multiple years should contain budgets that reflect each year, and include changes in costs (such as salaries and fringe benefits) over time. A sample of a budget for the HRSA project is provided in figure 12.4.

A standard form for the **biographical sketch** is usually provided. It typically includes the name and title of each key personnel, educational background, key publications, roles in research, and professional experience (including employment history). Although there is some overlap, the biographical sketch includes more detail

Figure 12.3.   Sample Abstract

ABSTRACT

Project Title: The Development of a Course on the Electronic Health Record (EHR) Using Distance Education for Use by Rural and Underserved Allied Health Colleges and Universities

Organization Name: University of Pittsburgh, School of Health and Rehabilitation Sciences, Health Information Management, Emergency Medicine/Emergency Preparedness and the School of Social Work

Address:

Project Director: Valerie Watzlaf   Phone:

Project Period: July 1, XXXX – June 30, XXXX   Fax:

                                                                      Email :

Abstract Narrative:

We will use the power of distance education to develop a course on the Electronic Health Record (EHR) for allied health students in rural and underserved colleges and universities across the country. To our knowledge, there are no courses about the EHR that focus on allied health disciplines in rural and underserved areas. The Course Development Core Team (CDCT) will research EHR technologies, standards, and practices so that a high-quality course on the EHR will be developed. The CDCT is made up of allied health faculty from the University of Pittsburgh who are experts in the areas of EHR, distance education, minority health, and rural health practice. Once the EHR course modules are developed, they will be sent to an External Advisory Board (EAB). The EAB will review the content and provide changes to the course. The EAB is made up of rural and underserved expert allied health faculty and practitioners from across the country. We envision the EHR course to include six modules: design and development; standards and clinical terminologies; safety, security, and ethical issues and HIPAA safeguards for the EHR; EHR models for disease prevention; use of the EHR in rural and underserved areas; and outcomes research using the EHR. The course will then be implemented across several rural and underserved allied health colleges and universities. Faculty coordinators at the sites (who will also serve on the EAB) will integrate the course into their allied health curricula and teach it to their allied health students. Sites agreeing to participate in EHR course implementation include:

Evaluation and analysis of the course will take place and changes will be made.

A final EHR course will be distributed across all rural and underserved allied health schools across the country. Therefore, we will be meeting the following statutory purposes: expand enrollments in allied health professions with the greatest shortages or whose services are most needed by the elderly; provide career advancement training for practicing allied health professionals; develop curriculum that will emphasize knowledge and practice in the areas of prevention and health promotion, geriatrics, long-term care, home health and hospice care, and ethics.

Table 12.3.   Example of key personnel distribution chart

Personnel Distribution Chart	Percentage of Time Per Person Per Year					
	A	B	C	D	E	F
Year 1	Y1	Y1	Y1	Y1	Y1	Y1
Objective 1: Create EHR course modules with an emphasis on rural and underserved allied health.	15	5	5	3	10	0
Objective 2: Evaluate each of the EHR course modules using a Web-based evaluation system.	15	5	5	2	5	0
Year 2	Y2	Y2	Y2	Y2	Y2	Y2
Objective 3: Provide creative ways to incorporate the EHR modules across all allied health programs.	10	2	2	1	5	2
Objective 4: Disseminate the distance education EHR modules to rural and culturally diverse allied health colleges and universities for implementation.	10	5	5	2	5	10
Year 3	Y2/3	Y2/3	Y2/3	Y2/3	Y2/3	Y2/3
Objective 5: Monitor the use of the EHR modules and provide technical assistance where needed.	10/5	3/2	3/2	2/1	5/2	3/3
Objective 6: Evaluate and analyze the competence of students who completed the EHR modules and/or course.	25	8	8	4	13	12
Total percentage of time for all 3 years	90	30	30	15	45	30

Key:

A= Project Director – 30% per year
B = Associate Director – 10% per year
C = Content Advisor – 10% per year
D = Content Advisor/Technical Assistance – 5% (In-Kind) per year
E = External Advisory Board Members – approximately 15% per year
F = Implementation Site Coordinators – approximately 10% over three years

Figure 12.4.   Example of budget for HRSA project for EHR distance education course development

Direct Costs Only						
A. Nontrainee Expenses						
Personnel (Do not list trainees)		Time/Effort		Dollar Amount Requested (Omit cents)		
Name	Title of Position	%	Hours per week	Salary	Fringe Benefits	Total
	Project Director	30%	12			
	Associate Director	10%	4			
	Content Advisor	10%	4			
	Content Advisor	5%	2	In-kind		
	Adm. Assistant	25%	10			
Subtotals				152,038	43,259	195,297
Consultant Costs						42,500
Equipment (Itemize)						3,900
Contracts						
Supplies (Itemize by category)						3,000
Staff Travel						7,500
Other Expenses (Itemize by category)						23,775
Subtotals (Section A)						$ 275,972

Continued

Figure 12.4.   Example of budget for HRSA project for EHR distance education course development *(continued)*

B. Trainee Expenses (Not applicable; DO NOT COMPLETE)	
Predoctoral Stipends	
Postdoctoral Stipends	
Other (Specify):	
Total Stipends	
Tuition and Fees	
Trainee Travel (Describe)	
Subtotal (Section B)	
C. Total Direct Costs (Add Subtotals of Sections A and B)	$275,972

CONSOLIDATED BUDGET				
Direct Costs	**First Budget Period**	**Second Budget Period**	**Third Budget Period**	**Total**
A. Nontrainee Expenses				
Personnel	63,184	65,080	67,032	195,297
Consultant Costs	7,500	17,500	17,500	42,500
Equipment	3,900	----	-----	3,900
Contracts	----	----	-----	-----
Supplies	1,000	1,000	1,000	3,000
Staff Travel	1,000	1,000	5,500	7,500
Other Expenses	9,925	6,925	6,925	23,775
Subtotal Section A	86,509	91,505	97,957	275,972
Stipends				
Tuition and Fees				
Trainee Travel				
Subtotal Section B				
Total Direct Costs (Add Subtotals of Sections A & B)	86,509	91,505	97,957	275,972
Indirect Cost Requested x Yes No If "Yes," at X % rate.				

Estimated Funding	**First Budget Period**	**Second Budget Period**	**Third Budget Period**	**Total**
Federal (Requested in this Application)	93,430	98,825	105,794	298,050
Other Federal				
Applicant Institution				
State, Local/Other				
Program Income				
Total	$93,430	$98,825	$105,794	$298,050

than the key personnel section. All staff, professional and nonprofessional, should be listed, even though salary may not be listed in the budget. Reviewers are looking for a ranking of personnel by the percentage of time each will spend on the project. An example of the biographical sketch form used by most federal granting agencies is shown in figure 12.5.

Other support can include endorsement letters, other applications or proposals pending review or funding, and applications planned or being prepared for submission. Each item should mention the source of support, project title, percentage of time devoted to the project, project period dates, project description, and whether it overlaps, duplicates or is being replaced, or supplemented by the present application.

Additional resources allocated to the project should be described. These would include laboratory, clinical, computer, office, and other facilities and resources.

Section II: Research Plan

The research plan comprises specific aims; background, significance, and preliminary studies; research design

and methods; approach; results; human subjects; vertebrate animals; literature cited; and contractual agreements and consultants.

The **specific aims** are the research objectives and goals for the project. Specific aims should be clearly defined and relate directly to the hypothesis to be tested. The first step in writing the content of the grant proposal is to state the problem clearly and succinctly. The problem must coincide with the project hypothesis and specific aims. An example of the objectives or specific aims for the EHR distance education course is found in Figure 12.1 (p. 279).

Grant applications may ask that objectives or specific aims be listed with outcomes or performance indicators that relate to each objective. Each outcome should be measurable and focus on the problem. Figure 12.6 provides an example of the objectives and outcomes for the EHR distance education course through HRSA. The performance indicator is considered the outcome in this example.

The section on **background, significance, and preliminary studies** details the importance or need of the research project. It states why the research must be done,

Figure 12.5.   Example of biographical sketch format

BIOGRAPHICAL SKETCH
Name:
Title
Education:

Institution and Location	Degree	Year Conferred	Field of Study

APPOINTMENTS AND POSITIONS
Academic

Nonacademic

PUBLICATIONS
Published Articles (related to grant project)

Figure 12.6.   Objectives and outcomes for the EHR distance education course

B.   Objectives/Specific Aims and Outcomes or Performance Indicators:

The six objectives are listed below. They are stated in measurable terms, time-framed, with specific outcomes identified. Each of the identified objectives relates to the project purpose and needs and problems identified with that purpose. Those objectives that address the Bureau of Health Professions (BHPs) National Goals I and/or II, Healthy People 2010, and linkages with relevant health care institutions or community organizations are in bold type.

Objective 1:   Create EHR course modules with an emphasis on rural and underserved allied health (BHP National Goal 1, Healthy People 2010 Public Health Infrastructure goals).

Time Frame: Approximately one module will be created every two months throughout Year 1.

Performance Indicator   Six distance education EHR course modules will be created with an emphasis on rural and culturally diverse allied health education.

Objective 2:   Evaluate each of the EHR course modules using a Web-based evaluation system (BHPs Goal 1 and II, Linkages with Community Organizations, Healthy People 2010).

Time Frame: One course module will be evaluated every two months throughout Year 1.

Performance Indicator: Six distance education EHR course modules will be evaluated by rural and culturally diverse allied health faculty and practitioners.

Objective 3:   Provide creative ways to incorporate the EHR course modules across all allied health programs (BHPs Goal I and II, Linkages with Community Organizations).

Time Frame: July and August of Year 2.

Performance Indicator: Different methods will be created that will delineate how to intersperse the EHR distance education course modules throughout an allied health curricula.

Objective 4:   Disseminate the distance education EHR course modules to selected rural and culturally diverse allied health colleges and universities for implementation (BHPs Goal I and II, Healthy People 2010, Linkages with Community Organizations).

Time Frame: August through December of Year 2.

Performance Indicator: Six distance education EHR modules will be provided to selected rural allied health colleges and universities for implementation.

Objective 5:   Monitor the use of the EHR course and provide technical assistance where needed (BHPs Goal I and II, Healthy People 2010, Linkages with Community Organizations).

Time Frame: September 200X of Year 2 through August 200X of Year 3.

Performance Indicator 1:   Number of allied health students enrolled in the EHR modules.

Performance Indicator 2:   Number of program completers of an EHR module.

Performance Indicator 3:   Number of program completers of an EHR course.

Performance Indicator 4:   Demographics (age, experience, discipline, student level, and so forth.) of students who agree to take the EHR course.

Performance Indicator 5:   Demographics of students who complete any of the EHR modules.

Performance Indicator 6:   Demographics of students who complete the entire EHR course.

Objective 6:   Evaluate and analyze the competence of students who completed the EHR course modules (BHPs Goal I and II, Healthy People 2010, Linkages with Community Organizations).

Time Frame: Beginning September 200X of Year 2 and continuing throughout Year 3.

Performance Indicator 1:   An improvement in the score from pretest to posttest.

Performance Indicator 2:   A grade of 80% or better for students completing each EHR course module.

Performance Indicator 3:   Teaching/course evaluations where EHR course receives a 3.0/5.0 or better.

Performance Indicator 4:   Graduate surveys completed where EHR course receives a 3.0/5.0 or better.

Performance Indicator 5:   Employer surveys completed where EHR course/module receives a 3.0/5.0.

Performance Indicator 6:   Student interviews in which the student evaluates the EHR course positively and believes it should continue to be included in the allied health curriculum.

how it is different from previous research studies, and whom the research will benefit. This section also demonstrates the knowledge of the researcher by citing reviews of existing research and showing the gaps and flaws in that research. Once these deficiencies are explained, the applicant should state how the proposed research would fill the gaps. The key to this section is to be succinct and organized. If the preliminary research is brief, include it in this section, particularly if it adds to the importance of the study. If the preliminary research is extensive, it is included in a separate section under Preliminary Studies. Some granting entities label this section as Impact, Need, or Rationale.

Figure 12.7 provides an example of an excerpt of the Background/Significance section of a grant proposal for the HRSA EHR Distance Education Course.

The applicant should describe the **research design and methods** in detail and provide support for their use. This section should be organized so each experiment or research method relates to a specific aim. If the methods are not innovative, the applicant should describe how established they are and why each method is necessary for this research project. If innovative, then show how the new methods hold promise in moving the field forward, and the soundness and effectiveness of the methods should be shown. If graphics of any kind are used, they should be included in the body of the proposal and also in the appendix. This is recommended because the

research plan may be separated from the rest of the application, and it should contain all relevant information to stand on its own. The methods should be described in logical order, and in relation to:

- Time—when the study will be conducted and for how long
- Place—facilities involved.
- Persons—the population under study

The data collection process also is included in this section. It describes:

- How the data will be collected (questionnaire, interview, abstracting)
- What data will be collected and why
- How the data will be categorized and why
- Who will collect the data
- Training techniques
- Where the data will be stored
- How patient identifiers will be handled
- How the data will be accessed
- How confidentiality of the data will be protected

Why a particular **approach** is chosen should be explained and its methods specified. For example, it is not appropriate to state "Many different health informa-

Figure 12.7.   Excerpt from the Background/Significance/Impact section of grant proposal for the HRSA EHR Distance Education Course

The Department of Health and Human Services (DHHS) Secretary, Tommy G. Thompson is promoting a paperless health care system. On July 1, 2003, he announced two new steps toward building a national electronic health record or EHR. First, he announced that the DHHS has signed an agreement with the College of American Pathologists (CAP) to license their standardized medical vocabulary system, SNOMED, and make it available free of charge to health care facilities across the nation. SNOMED is a reference terminology system that assigns a numbered code to diagnoses and procedures and can be used very effectively in an EHR in retrieving and sending data. Secondly, he announced that the Institute of Medicine (IOM) will be commissioned to design a standardized model of an electronic health record. The standards organization, Health Level 7 (HL7), will evaluate the model once it is designed and the model will be shared at no cost with all types of health care facilities across the United States. The model should be ready in 2004. HL7 is a standards organization that promotes standard formats in the EHR so that different computer applications can talk to each other. These are major steps in the advancement of health care technology and in the improvement of patient care.

However, will allied health professionals of the future, specifically in rural settings, be proficient in all components of the electronic health record (EHR) so that they will feel comfortable in using it to improve their patients' care? Will allied health faculty in rural settings be educated enough in all components of the EHR, especially SNOMED and HL7, to effectively teach it to their students—the allied health professionals of the future?

To our knowledge, there are no distance education courses that include the design, development, safety, security, ethics, complexity, and standards for the EHR that are to be integrated throughout the allied health curricula in rural colleges and universities. Even though the primary goal of physical and occupational therapists, speech pathologists, paramedics, social workers, and other allied health professionals is to provide direct care to patients to improve their level of functioning, the use of the EHR will make them more competent in their professions. Every allied health professional uses or will use the EHR. In order to improve the quality of care for all patients and move toward a paperless health care system, EHR education should be easily accessible and interspersed throughout allied health curricula.

tion technologies in different health information networks across several healthcare facilities will be used to assess differences in the outcomes of care." Reviewers want to know *which* health information technologies, across *what* networks, in *what* type of healthcare facilities. The more specific the information, the more confident the reviewers will be that the applicant understands the research and can successfully carry out the project.

The **results** section should show how the data will be analyzed by describing the type of statistical tests that will be performed and why they are needed. Dummy tables that demonstrate how the data will be displayed may be effective to show understanding of the project's statistical analyses. A statistician should be consulted to help write this section. The applicant should show the limits and the benefits to the kind of results expected, and define criteria for success or failure of a specific test. Specific statistical tests such as frequency distributions, chi-square tests, confidence intervals, sensitivity and specificity, and other validity and reliability tests should be listed, when applicable, for each procedure described.

Figure 12.8 provides an example of an excerpt of the methodology section used for the grant examining EHR distance education course.

Table 12.4 provides an example of the full timeline for the methods of the HRSA grant project.

The **human subjects** section includes a demographic description of the study population, how informed consent will be obtained, how confidentiality will be safeguarded, and how human subjects will be protected during the research process. IRB approval letters are included in this section to demonstrate that the facility where the research will be conducted has approved the study protocol.

If **vertebrate animals** will be used, methods of protection should be described, and IRB letters of approval should be included.

All **literature cited**, discussed, or reviewed in any section of the grant proposal should be referenced in its own section, and also cited at the end of the grant.

There should be an explanation of any **contractual agreements** pertinent to the grant proposal, and any **consultants** that may be used. Letters of support from these individuals or companies should be part of this section. For example, a coding consultant may be needed to code in ICD-9-CM or ICD-10-CM. A letter from this individual stating their support of the project and willingness to provide consultation is beneficial. Table 12.5 is an example of a consultant summary form.

Section III: Appendixes

The appendixes include tables, figures, criteria, lab tests or techniques, data collection forms, surveys, and other such items. It includes anything that is important and relevant to the grant proposal. Appendixes serve to clarify the topic described in the grant proposal. Any information not pertinent to the current research project should be excluded.

Other Considerations

Grant applications have different formats and sections that need to be completed in the body of the proposal. The sections previously described are required by most federal granting agencies such as NIH or HRSA. Some federal and state grants request the applicant to include an extensive evaluation plan. The evaluation description is usually linked to the objectives, activities, responsible person, timeline, and outcomes. The evaluation section is written in relation to each objective, and then summarized as shown in table 12.2 (p. 280). The title of the grant application should stay within any character limitation set forth by the application guidelines. It should clearly and briefly state the major goal of the project.

Sample of Content for Foundation Grant Application

Foundations may include similar content as previously described but with different content headings. Content for the FORE/AHIMA GIA application include the following sections:

  I. Impact: Introduction, Purpose Statement of Need, Objectives or specific aims)

  II. Methodology: Research design, research methods, statistical analysis

  III. Feasibility: Organization/Management Plan, Personnel, and Timetable

  IV. Evaluation: Measurement for Success, Intended Distribution

See appendix 12D (pp. 321–329) for actual documents of the content of a GIA application for FORE.

Figure 12.8.   Excerpt of methodology section used in EHR distance education grant

---

Methodology:

Objective 1:   Create distance education EHR modules with an emphasis on rural allied health.

ACTIVITIES:

We will utilize several different information centers to begin the drafts of the EHR modules. The distance education component used successfully in our Emergency Medicine program and in the Center for Emergency Medicine as well as extensive assistance from CIDDE and OMET at the University of Pittsburgh will be utilized. We will also incorporate the EHR model developed by the IOM, the Vista system of the VHA, HL7 standards, and SNOMED terminology, which were all developed as part of the DHHS agenda. We will also do extensive research on the types of EHR applications that are available for health care facilities in many different settings, especially those that focus on rural and underserved health care.

A syllabus and course schedule outlining the entire EHR course will be developed by the Project Director and Associate Director and discussed with the other members of the CDCT. The syllabus and course schedule will be adjusted by the Project Director based on input by the CDCT. The syllabus and course schedule will be sent to the EAB for their feedback. Changes will be made to the syllabus and schedule, and the Project Director and Associate Director will begin to draft the first module. This will include Power Point slides, links from the Internet, readings, and assignments. The first module will be dispersed via Course Web to the CDCT for their review and comments. Chat rooms, teleconferences, and face-to-face meetings with the CDCT will take place to discuss the changes and revise the content. This activity will take place for each of the six modules. Once the first module is complete, it will be provided to the EAB for their comments. Once their comments are received, a teleconference will be held between the CDCT and EAB to discuss the first module and to make final adjustments to it. A preliminary explanation of the content for each of the modules is described below:

Module 1.   Design, development, management, and administration of the EHR for the rural allied health professional.

This module will include the following components:

A.   A description of different EHR designs and development of such systems will be explored. This module will include vendor, in-house development, vendor and in-house combination systems, a combination of multiple systems, joint ventures between large vendors, and modified vendor EHR systems. Links to appropriate Websites which house some of these systems will be provided so that students can actually see the different designs available. For example, the following Website, http://www.health-infosys-dir.com/yphcmrec.asp, provides a listing of vendor systems available across the country that has an emphasis in EHR systems. Our focus will be to provide successful vendor systems and in-house systems that incorporate the DHHS model vision and work effectively in the rural environment. For example, the Veterans Health Care Administration's EHR system, called Veteran's Health Information Systems and Technology Architecture (VISTA), will be used since it is an effective system that is used across the country in VHA systems and has been cited by the IOM as one of the best in the nation. This system treats about 4 million patients per year in 163 hospitals and 800 clinics and other locations. The VHA system puts patient records online in a confidential environment, which integrates primary care, X-ray records, pharmacy, consultations, and referrals.

Other systems that work effectively in rural health care clinics will be explored. For example, the primary objective in the study by Harris et al in Phoenix, Arizona, was to develop a methodology for customizing an EHR in rural family practice health care clinics. This study is quite important because many rural community health care centers do not have access to a clinic-wide email system nor to the World Wide Web. It is important to include access to these systems as well so students can better understand the obstacles of EHR systems in rural settings and can brainstorm ideas to overcome these obstacles.

B.   The management and administration of the EHR system will also be discussed in this module. Several allied health professionals find themselves managing an EHR system within their facility with very little training in health care technology systems. This is especially true in rural health care settings. Therefore, the focus of this part of the module will discuss how best to manage and administer the EHR system that is currently used in their facility as well as how best to get one started. Power Point materials, case studies, and literature will center on how the allied health professional can do the following: (a) document the business case for an EHR; (b) examine grants for EHR implementation and research; (c) demonstrate the need for adoption of the EHR through case studies, research, presentations, and Websites; (d) establish Websites, such as Health Information Management Systems Society (HIMSS), American Health Information Management Association (AHIMA), and the American Medical Informatics Association (AMIA), as a clearinghouse of information on EHR materials and share these with other allied health practitioners and other clinicians within their facility; and (e) demonstrate a knowledge base in the standards, clinical terminologies, and data elements necessary to develop an effective EHR system within their health care facility. The 25 Most Wired Rural Health Care Facilities listed by the American Hospital Association (AHA) will also be targeted to see how they effectively implemented an EHR system in their rural health care facility.

EVALUATION:

The process of creating the EHR modules will be evaluated continuously throughout Year 1 to determine the following: 1) appropriate content 2) appropriate medium used to deliver the module content and 3) appropriate testing, assignments, and other methods of evaluation.

If any of the above variables need to be changed in order to enhance the content of the modules, adjustments will be made. Our goal is to provide a high quality distance education EHR course that is culturally diverse and can be used by all rural and underserved allied health schools. We will provide this course so that it can be adjusted for use at a 2-year level, a 4-year level or beyond. Again, a major component of the EHR course will include the interdisciplinary interaction of allied health students and faculty through chat room exchanges.

Therefore we envision the evaluation component of the EHR course to include the following:

Evaluation Method	Percent of course grade
1. Pre and post-tests for each of the modules	40%
2. RFP development	20%
3. Outcomes research proposal	20%
4. Participation (chat-room exchanges)	20%

Table 12.4. Example of the full timeline for the methods of the HRSA grant project

METHODOLOGY SUMMARY

(Recommended Format Table)

Objectives	Activities	Responsible Person/Position	Time Period	Outcomes	Evaluation
Objective 1: Create EHR modules with an emphasis on rural and underserved allied health.	1. Create EHR course syllabus and schedule 2. Create Module 1 3. Create Module 2 4. Create Module 3 5. Create Module 4 6. Create Module 5 7. Create Module 6 8. Review and finalize all modules	Project Director; Associate Director with input from the other members of the CDCT, EAB and CIDDE.	Y 1	An EHR distance education course syllabus, schedule, and six modules will be created.	The EHR course will be evaluated on content, distance education medium, and course evaluation methods.
Objective 2: Evaluate the EHR modules using a Web-based evaluation system.	1. Evaluate EHR course syllabus and schedule 2. Evaluate Module 1 3. Evaluate Module 2 4. Evaluate Module 3 5. Evaluate Module 4 6. Evaluate Module 5 7. Evaluate Module 6 8. Evaluate and finalize all modules	Project Director; Associate Director with input from the other members of CDCT, EAB, and CIDDE.	Y 1	An EHR course syllabus, schedule, and six modules will be evaluated.	A Web-based evaluation system will be used to evaluate each of the modules on several variables.
Objective 3: Provide creative ways to incorporate the EHR course across all allied health programs.	1. CDCT and EAB will discuss and develop creative ways to disseminate the EHR course modules across the allied health curricula at the six sites. 2. The CIDDE will provide extensive input. 3. Different methods specific to the sites will be created. 4. The methods will be evaluated by the EAB and implementation sites. 5. Each site will choose one of the methods developed to distribute the course across their allied health curricula within their school. 6. Sites receive the EHR course to disseminate across their allied health curricula using the method chosen.	Members of the CDCT and CIDDE Faculty Coordinators at the Implementation Sites.	Y 2: Jul and Aug	Different methods will be created on how to intersperse the EHR distance education course across an allied health curricula so that students take the course.	The creative methods developed will be evaluated by the EAB members and especially the sites. The EAB members will evaluate the methods via an on-line system.

Table 12.4. Example of the full timeline for the methods of the HRSA grant project

METHODOLOGY SUMMARY
(Recommended Format Table)

Objectives	Activities	Responsible Person/Position	Time Period	Outcomes	Evaluation
Objective 4: Disseminate the distance education EHR course modules to rural and culturally diverse allied health colleges and universities for implementation.	1. EHR course disseminated to sites 2. PD contacts sites 3. Sites complete checklist 4. Sites offer the course 5. Sites contact PD with any problems	Project Director, CIDDE and Faculty Coordinators for implementation sites listed above.	Y 2 Aug – Dec	The EHR course will be disseminated to the allied health colleges and university implementation sites.	Sites will be contacted to ascertain that the course is ready to be offered to students.
Objective 5: Monitor the use of the EHR course and provide technical assistance where needed.	1. Collect data on problems experienced 2. Troubleshoot problems 3. Collect data on number of students taking the EHR modules, program completers and so forth 4. Collect demographic information on students 5. Collect progress reports from faculty at the sites	CDCT, EAB, CIDDE, OMET members as listed above.	Y 2 & Y 3	Several outcomes will be reported such as the number of allied health students taking the EHR course, an EHR module and so forth.	Biweekly progress reports will be obtained from the sites so that problems can be identified and alleviated quickly.
Objective 6: Evaluate and analyze the competence of students who completed the EHR course modules.	1. Collect data on pretest and posttest scores 2. Collect data on course and teaching evaluations 3. Collect data from students who graduated and took the EHR course 4. Collect data from employers 5. Analyze the data collected 6. Discuss analysis with EAB 7. Add changes to EHR course 8. Offer EHR course to all allied health schools across the country	Project Director and Co-Project Director, Content Advisors. All EAB consultant members and faculty coordinators listed above with support from CIDDE and OMET.	Y 2 & Y 3	The average gain in scores on the pretests and posttests; teaching and course evaluations; Graduate surveys completed; Employer surveys completed.	The methods used to evaluate the competence of the program completers will be continuously reviewed and evaluated.

Table 12.5.   Consultant summary table

Consultant	Qualifications	Nature of Work on Project	Assurances that Consultant Agrees to Work on Project
Name	Title and Experience in Relation to Project: for example, Physical Therapist and Director of Health Informatics and Performance Improvement	Provide EHR course content expertise from the allied health professional's perspective	Letter of support

Common Reasons for Rejection

Common reasons for proposal rejection include the following (NINDS 2007):

- The proposal includes objectives that are not specific enough to be measurable.

- The project is overambitious with a large amount of activities proposed.

- The methodology is not detailed enough, does not relate to the objectives cited, and does not convince the reviewers that the investigator knows what he or she is doing by including potential problems or areas of concern.

- There is a lack of alternative methodological approaches in case the first approach is not successful.

- The proposal lacks a thorough review of the literature, which causes the reviewers to think that the researchers do not know the subject area.

- It is not clear which data were obtained by the investigator and which data are from other authors reported in the literature or other reports.

- The hypothesis and goals are not related to the funding agency's priorities and preferred target population.

- The qualifications of investigators are not clearly stated.

- There is an inappropriate or absent evaluation plan.

- There is no itemized budget or the funding limits are exceeded.

Revisions

Reviewers will provide comments and criticisms about the proposal. This information should be used to determine if the application should be resubmitted. If the reviewers thought the idea was needed and interesting,

then it may be worth revising. If it is deemed worthy, the applicant or investigator should reevaluate the existing proposal, then redesign and resubmit it. It is not unusual for an investigator to submit a grant proposal three times before it was accepted and funded. Common problems that can be fixed include (NINDS 2007; Watzlaf 1989):

- Poor writing
- Lack of details or preliminary data
- Significance not powerful enough
- Lack of discussion around problems and how to tackle them with new approaches

More difficult issues include

- The idea is not profound enough
- The work has already been performed
- Hypothesis or purpose is not valid
- Methods are not accurate to test the hypothesis or goals

Research Protocol Data Management

Research protocol data management refers to the methods employed when HIM researchers conduct or assist in conducting extensive research projects such as clinical trials. There are many aspects, such as data and safety monitoring of the clinical trial, that include extensive procedures and data management within the context of the protocol. These concepts are discussed in the next section.

History

On June 5, 1979, the NIH Clinical Trials Committee developed several recommendations for clinical trials. One of these recommendations states "that every clinical trial should have provision for data and safety monitoring." The NIH Clinical Trials Committee acknowledged that the level of monitoring depends on the size, type, and complexity of the clinical trial. Also, the PI may be the one performing the data and safety monitoring (NIH/DSM 1998).

In 1994, the Office of Extramural Research developed the Committee on Clinical Trial Monitoring to review the management of the **institute and center (IC)** for phase III clinical trials. One of the decisions from this extensive review was that all clinical trials should have an outside body oversee the monitoring of the clinical trial (NIH/DSM 1998).

In June 1998, the NIH issued a policy on data and safety monitoring for all NIH-supported intervention studies to ensure the safety of all human participants, and the validity and integrity of the data collected. The policy states that the level of monitoring is based on the potential risks, size, and complexity of the clinical or community trials.

NIH requires **data and safety management boards (DSMBs)** for phase III clinical trials. This policy states that a DSMB also may be appropriate for phase I and II clinical trials, depending on:

- The amount of risk involved
- The number of clinical centers used
- Whether vulnerable populations are involved (such as children or the elderly)
- Whether blinded or masked techniques are used

See chapter 6 for more information on phase I through IV clinical trials and their research design and techniques. The DSMBs are not to be confused with the IRB. The DSMB functions are separate from the review and approval of the IRBs. See chapter 13 for more information on IRBs.

The NIH policy states that clinical trial participants must be fully informed of the study protocol. Participants should either comply with the study protocol or be given the opportunity to withdraw. It is the clinical investigators' responsibility to protect the health and safety of all participants, to inform them of the steps involved to continue their participation, and pursue the research objectives with "scientific diligence." Although there are many benefits to participating in a clinical trial, the NIH and the IRB must ensure the safety of all participants. The NIH and IRB must assess, throughout the clinical trial study period, that the benefits outweigh the risks involved (NIH/DSM 1998).

On June 5, 2000, NIH enacted a policy entitled "Further Guidance on Data and Safety Monitoring for Phase I and II Clinical Trials." This policy requires investigators to submit a monitoring plan for phase I and II clinical trials to the funding IC before the study begins.

All clinical trials require monitoring. Monitoring should be based on the level of risk, and size and complexity of the trial. Investigators must submit a data and safety-monitoring plan as part of the grant application (NIH/Further Guidance 2000).

Sometimes intervention studies are conducted by the healthcare center to determine, for example, if different health information technologies improve the health outcomes of patients. Other times, the primary type of research consists of a clinical or community trial. When this occurs, the academic center, healthcare center, business associates, and industry work together to examine a particular health information technology application or an experimental drug.

Academic

The academic setting may provide the expertise of well-known researchers who can apply the theoretical expertise to the experimental drug or health information application. For example, a researcher who is well known for his or her work in data mining may be able to assist healthcare practitioners in the analysis of healthcare data collected to examine the functional disability levels of patients with osteoarthritis.

Cooperative Groups

Many times a cooperative group of physicians or hospitals can treat a large number of patients quickly using the same protocol. This is usually done with clinical trials because it aids in the evaluation of new treatments, procedures, and medications. Larger samples of patients can be treated than what would be normally be found if only one physician group or hospital conducted this type of study. Clinical trials examining new cancer treatments often use a cooperative group to obtain larger numbers of patients, which may increase the statistical reliability of the data.

Industry-Sponsored Research

The most common type of industry-sponsored research is found with pharmaceutical research. Pharmaceutical research and development is a huge area of research. It incorporates both healthcare centers and university settings to complete their studies. This type of sponsored research tends to focus more on the goals of the pharmaceutical company and the medication or procedure they would like to examine. Researchers frequently are asked to conduct the studies because the research protocols or methods are already written and merely need to be carried out by the researchers.

Organizational Relationships

Organizational relationships for research conducted within a healthcare center are described in the following sections.

Principal Investigator

The **principal investigator (PI)** for the research project is the person in charge and is responsible for carrying out the entire project, meeting the project's budget guidelines, hiring personnel to conduct the project, and monitoring the entire project as it is carried out to make sure it stays within the timeline allotted. The PI is responsible for developing the data and safety monitoring plan.

Institutional Review Board (Academic-Based)

A very important first step that must be conducted before the research project can be started is to submit the research project to the IRB. The IRB consists of a group of experts in research and related health sciences whose goal is to protect the human subjects that may take part in the research proposed. Most universities have IRBs that review all proposed grant projects of all faculty and students. Healthcare facilities also may have IRBs that review research projects before they can be conducted. Any research using human subjects in any way is subject to IRB review and approval. See chapter 13 for more information on the IRB process. The data and safety monitoring plan for clinical trials must be reviewed by the local IRB and the IC, and must be reviewed and approved by these entities before the study begins.

Protocol Review

The research protocol includes the steps to complete the research project. The protocol is normally found within the methodology section of the research grant. The research team should review the protocol before conducting the research. Any individuals or groups that monitor the data and safety of the clinical trial need to review the research protocol, and plans for data and safety monitoring. The IRB also will pay special attention to the research protocol and consent forms. This is done to make sure that the protocol protects the research subjects. Once the PI obtains IRB approval, the project can begin. The protocol should be reviewed continuously throughout the research project. Sometimes changes may be made to the protocol, such as when subjects may have an adverse effect toward a specific treatment or intervention. All changes should be submitted to the IRB for review and approval with justification for changes.

Departments

Education and training of specific personnel will help move the project forward. Clinical departments along with pharmacy and laboratory staff can assist in the overall research protocol:

- Clinical departments such as general medicine, cardiology, anesthesiology, nursing, and oncology help in carrying out the specific research protocol. For example, the staff in the anesthesia department may assist in analyzing the utilization of specific anesthetics for children with asthma in comparison with children without asthma. Data collection from a computerized physician order entry and EHR will assist the PI in following a specific protocol for data collection.

- Pharmacy specialists help with areas related to any type of new medication. These may include changing pharmaceutical procedure, detecting any adverse effects of experimental medications quickly, and determining new side effects of medications.

- Laboratory staff assist in the research protocol by alerting the research project team to specific lab results that may contain inaccurate data, insufficient information to make a diagnosis, or inappropriate laboratory procedures.

Staffing

Other personnel that assist with research protocol are data managers, clinical research coordinators, and clinical research associates. These individuals may be hired specifically for the research project, and may come from outside of the organization. They can assist in developing the data and the safety monitoring plan.

Clinical Research Coordinator

The **clinical research coordinator** is usually the person who runs the research project and ensures that the clinical protocol is followed as written. The researcher or PI delegates and specifies the duties of the clinical research coordinator. The clinical research coordinator may have a clinical, management, business, or information systems background. Clinical research coordinators may oversee the project entirely, and may be responsible for hiring additional staff to help with data collection procedures, data entry, and data analysis.

Clinical Research Associate

Clinical research associates develop new study protocols, hire investigators, write progress reports, write data and safety monitoring plans and subsequent reports of any adverse events, and take part in writing publications once the project is completed. Many times the clinical research associate is a healthcare professional who focuses solely on a clinical or community trial. However, clinical research associates also may participate in other epidemiological or clinical studies other than clinical trials. These may include cross-sectional, case-control, prospective, and historical-prospective studies. See chapter 6 for further discussion of these studies.

Clinical Data Manager

The **clinical data manager's** responsibilities vary depending on the specific research study protocol. The manager's responsibilities consist of managing the data collected during the research project, developing data standards, conducting clinical coding for specific data elements, determining the best database to house the data, choosing appropriate software systems to analyze the data, and conducting data entry and data analysis.

Protocols

There are two basic types of **protocols**:

1. **Disease-specific protocols** examine the disease as it progresses over time. Disease-specific protocols then analyze risk factors associated with individuals who have the disease in comparison with individuals without the disease.

2. **Treatment specific protocols** (pharmaceutical, device, and so forth) usually consist of intervention performed on the specific patients allocated to the study groups.

Process

The specific parts of the research protocol data management for clinical trials are discussed in the next section.

Concept Sheet

The **concept sheet** is used in most pharmaceutical research studies when conducting clinical trials. It is a brief synopsis of the research study and includes similar sections as discussed in the grant application. However, the following parts are contained in one or two pages and include (BCM/CFAR 2007):

- Study title
- Investigators
- Rationale
- Objectives
- Design
- Inclusion and exclusion criteria
- Treatment regiments
- Sample size estimate
- Statistician
- Timeline
- Interested institutions (those clinical sites interested in participating in the study)
- Pharmaceutical company (if applicable)

Full Protocol

The complete study protocol provides detail above each section summarized in the concept sheet. Specific steps for all parts of the clinical trial are included in the full protocol. For more information on clinical trials, see chapter 7.

Initial Review and Evaluation

If a clinical trial or any type of intervention study is funded by a federal agency, such as NIH, an initial review and evaluation is conducted by the DSMB to discuss the research protocol and to establish guidelines for monitoring. The chair of the DSMB, the PI, and other NIH staff prepare the agenda to address the initial, final, and interim analysis plan of the trial.

Study Initiation or Activation

The initial meeting launches the research study. The DSMB meets at specific times throughout the trial study period to review accumulated data on safety and possibly conduct an interim analysis of the data collected.

Protocol Compliance

Once the clinical trial receives funding and is underway, periodic reviews and monitoring are required to ensure that the trial is conducted as stated. NIH states that oversight and monitoring clinical trials is required to ensure the safety of participants, and the validity and integrity of the data. Establishing DSMBs is required for multisite clinical trials involving interventions that include possible risk to study participants. The DSMB functions are separate and distinct from the IRB.

Data collected for the safety of the study participants include the following for the clinical trials:

- Research study protocol
- Informed consent
- Data and safety monitoring plan
- Evidence of data quality and timeliness
- Participant recruitment techniques
- Accrual and retention of participants
- Participant risk versus benefit
- Reports on the safety and scientific progress of the trial
- Evidence of data integrity
- Evidence of confidentiality of all data

Once all the data are collected, reviewed, and discussed, final recommendations regarding the safety concerns of the study participants and recommendations regarding continuing or curtailing the study are discussed in detail. If safety concerns are few, the study continues. If adverse events are found and are not handled appropriately, the study may be halted.

Internal Data Summary Reports, Safety Reports, and Annual Reports

PIs of every clinical trial should complete safety, summary, and annual reports of the current study. These reports include lists of investigators and other key personnel, all affiliated clinical sites, protocol concept sheets, tracking data, and patient accrual and demographics. The annual report includes group activities, accomplishments, performance evaluations, and future directions.

Disseminating Results

Dissemination includes presenting and publishing the study data. Prompt and timely presentation and publication of the research study is key, especially for clinical trials in which the major findings may make a difference in treating a terminal disease, for example. Many times, granting agencies require that a copy of presentation documentation or manuscript be submitted before publication or presentation. In addition, funding agencies require acknowledgment of the support they provided. For more information regarding disseminating results, see chapter 14.

Summary and Conclusions

Conducting research in health informatics is enhanced by obtaining funding to assist in the research process. Writing a grant to secure the funding takes a great deal of time and effort, but it is doable and should be pursued by health informatics professionals. The steps to follow in developing a grant are discussed within this chapter, and examples specific to health informatics are provided. Health informatics professionals may choose to be the PI in a research project, a co-investigator, consultant, grant writer, or a key staff member of an intervention study such as a clinical or community trial. Whatever role is chosen, it is important for researchers to immerse themselves in current research projects. The expertise of the health informatics professional is vital to the success of health informatics research.

References

Baylor-UTHouston, Center for AIDS Research. 2007. Clinical research core, concept sheet development process. Available online from http://www.bcm.edu/cfar/?PMID=2828.

Foundation of Research and Education of AHIMA. 2007. Sample grant application to FORE GIA application. Available online from http://www.ahima.org/fore/research/grantinaid.asp.

Foundation of Research and Education of AHIMA. 2000 (June). AHIMA/FORE Policy/Procedure on Conflicts and Dualities of Interest.

Foundation of Research and Education of AHIMA. n.d. AHIMA/FORE Confidentiality and non-disclosure agreement.

Grants Management, Grants Manual. 2007. General guidelines for grant proposals. Available online from http://

www.vaboard.org/downloads/GeneralGuidelinesGrant Proposals.pdf.

Health Resources and Services Administration, HRSA Electronic Handbooks for Applicants/Grantee. 2007. Available online from https://grants.hrsa.gov/webExternal/FundingOppDetails.asp?FundingCycleId=8ECFB155-CE52-4147-AC5C-6D9540BEB650&ViewMode=EU&GoBack=&PrintMode=&OnlineAvailabilityFlag=&pageNumber=&version=&NC=&Popup.

Klein, M., and K.V. Johnson. 2004. Thompson announces 'decade of health information technology' *Wisconsin Technology Network.*

Available online from http://wistechnology.com/article.php?id=1025

National Institute of Health, Center for Scientific Review. 2008 (Jan. 11). Overview of peer review process. Available online from http://cms.csr.nih.gov/ResourcesforApplicants/PolicyProcedureReview+Guidelines/Overviewof-PeerReviewProcess.

National Institutes of Health, Center for Scientific Review. 2006a (Jan. 6). Peer review meetings. Available online from http://cms.csr.nih.gov/PeerReviewMeetings/Best-Practices/How+Scientists+Are+Selected+For+Study+Section+Service.htm.

National Institutes of Health, Centers for Scientific Review. 2006b (Sept. 21). Review meeting procedures. Available online from http://cms.csr.nih.gov/NR/rdonlyres/C2A9D5DE-8773-456B-A52C-FEC4B15E22C5/11979/ReviewMeetingProcedures092106.pdf.

National Institutes of Health. 2000 (June 5). Further Guidance on a Data and Safety Monitoring for Phase I and II Trials. Bethesda, MD: NIH.

National Institutes of Health, National Institute of Allergy and Infectious Disease. 2007a (July 6). New investigator guide to NIH funding. Available online from http://www.niaid.nih.gov/ncn/grants/new/newpi.htm.

National Institutes of Health, National Institute of Allergy and Infectious Disease. 2007b (Feb. 22). Review criteria standard operating procedure (SOP). Available online from http://www.niaid.nih.gov/ncn/sop/reviewcriteria.htm.

National Institutes of Health, Office of Extramural Research. 2003. NIH Grants Policy Statement. Available online from http://grants.nih.gov/grants/policy/nihgps_2003/NIHGPS_Part4.htm.

National Institutes of Health. 1998 (June 10). NIH Policy for Data and Safety Monitoring. Available online from http://grants.nih.gov/grants/guide/notice-files/not98-084.html.

National Institute of Neurological Disorders and Stroke, National Institutes of Health. 2007 (May 8). How to write a research project grant application. Available online from http://www.ninds.nih.gov/funding/write_grant_doc.htm.

National Library of Medicine Request for Quotations. 2007 (April 2). AIDS Community Outreach Project. Available online from http://www.nlm.nih.gov/oam/AIDS_RFQ_2007.doc.

Watzlaf, V. 1989. The development of a grant proposal. *Journal of the American Medical Record Association* 60(2):37.

Yale-Griffin Prevention Research Center. Connecticut Health Foundation. 2006. Addressing health disparities through systems change for diabetes prevention and management in community health centers. Available online from http://www.yalegriffinprc.org/downloads/chf_rfa.pdf.

Appendix 12A
Confidentiality Form

AHIMA/FORE confidentiality and non-disclosure agreement

THIS CONFIDENTIALITY AND NON-DISCLOSURE AGREEMENT ("Agreement") is entered into this ___ day of _____, 200_, by and between American Health Information Management Association, an Illinois not-for-profit corporation ("AHIMA"), and _____ in his or her individual capacity ("Individual," collectively the "Parties").

R E C I T A L S:

WHEREAS, Individual is the _____ of AHIMA, and has agreed to serve in such capacity; and AHIMA and Individual have entered into an Indemnification Agreement (the "Indemnification Agreement") or Individual is a covered person under any indemnification policy of AHIMA or its affiliates.

WHEREAS, AHIMA has certain confidential and proprietary information concerning its business and operation (the "Business"), which is of great value to AHIMA and which represents trade secrets, to which, in order to perform his/her duties, Individual must have access from time to time.

WHEREAS, the Parties desire to preserve and protect for AHIMA the confidentiality, secrecy and proprietary nature of the information and matters in connection with the information, as set forth more fully in this Agreement.

WHEREAS, in consideration for the application of the indemnification policy and procedures of AHIMA or its affiliates and the Indemnification Agreement, Individual desires to set forth and memorialize Individual's obligations with respect to the confidentiality and non-disclosure of information.

NOW, THEREFORE, in consideration of the foregoing recitals and the mutual covenants and agreements in this Agreement, and for other good and valuable consideration, the receipt and sufficiency of which are hereby acknowledged, the Parties, intending to be legally bound, agree as follows:

1. **Confidential Information.** "Confidential Information" means any books, documents, records, data, facilities, properties, assets and other information relating to AHIMA, its affiliates and their business and operations, which is not generally known except by AHIMA and third parties subject to an express or implied obligation of confidentiality to AHIMA. Without limiting the generality of the foregoing, Confidential Information may also include or relate to technology, products and product specifications, inventions, directors, officers, employees, agents, volunteers, suppliers, membership, members business and market forecasts, research, development, accounting, finances, marketing and other related information pertaining to the Business. Confidential Information expressly includes the strategic

plans and considered business opportunities of AHIMA and its affiliates or joint ventures. Such information may be contained in any form or medium and may or may not be designated or marked "confidential" or the like.

2. **Individual's Acknowledgment.** Individual acknowledges that the Confidential Information is a valuable proprietary asset of AHIMA and constitutes trade secrets of AHIMA. Individual agrees that Individual has a duty to maintain the Confidential Information as confidential and secret. Individual further acknowledges that disclosure to Individual of any Confidential Information is made in the strictest of confidence and that Individual shall maintain the Confidential Information as confidential and secret and shall avoid the unauthorized disclosure, use, publication, dissemination or other communication of the Confidential Information to any third party, including, without limitation, any affiliated or related entity to Individual. Individual agrees that (s)he will not utilize any of the Confidential Information to the detriment of AHIMA during the term of the Indemnification Agreement or thereafter.

3. **Confidentiality and Non-disclosure.**

    3.1.   Individual shall not disclose, use, publish, disseminate or otherwise communicate, directly or indirectly, in whole or in part, at any time or in any manner, any Confidential Information without the prior written consent of AHIMA in each instance; nor shall Individual permit any of Individual's personnel, agents or representatives to do any of the foregoing.

    3.2.   Any Confidential Information which Individual acquires or becomes acquainted with may not be reproduced, copied, summarized or removed from AHIMA's premises without the prior written consent of AHIMA in each instance.

4. **Information Ownership.** AHIMA has and shall retain all right, title and interest in and to the Confidential Information and no license or right of any kind or nature in or to the Confidential Information is granted to Individual hereby.

5. **Return of Confidential Information.** Any Confidential Information that is received by Individual shall be immediately returned to AHIMA when it is no longer required by Individual, upon the termination of any business relationship between Individual and AHIMA, or upon AHIMA's demand at any time.

6. **Remedies.** In the event that Individual breaches this Agreement, AHIMA shall be entitled to all legal and equitable remedies afforded it by law, and in addition to any and all other forms of relief, AHIMA may recover from Individual all reasonable costs and attorneys' fees incurred in seeking such remedy.

7. **Miscellaneous.**

    7.1.   **Binding Effect.** This Agreement shall be binding upon and inure to the benefit of the heirs, successors and permitted assigns of each Party hereto.

    7.2.   **Entire Agreement.** This Agreement constitutes the entire agreement of the Parties with respect to the subject matter hereof and supersedes all prior oral or written representations and agreements between the parties with respect to the subject matter hereof.

7.3. **Waiver.** Any term or condition of this Agreement may be waived at any time by the Party or Parties entitled to the benefit thereof, but only by a written notice signed by the Party or Parties waiving such terms or conditions. The waiver of any term or condition shall not be construed as a waiver of any other term or condition of this Agreement.

7.4. **Amendment.** This Agreement may be amended, supplemented or modified at any time, but only by a written instrument duly executed by the Parties.

7.5. **Governing Law.** This Agreement shall be construed, and the rights and liabilities of the Parties hereto determined, in accordance with the laws of the State of Illinois.

IN WITNESS WHEREOF, the parties hereto have executed this Agreement as of the day and year first written above.

ATTEST

_____

AMERICAN HEALTH INFORMATION
MANAGEMENT ASSOCIATION

By: _____

_____
Print Name

Its: _____

INDIVIDUAL: _____
Title

ATTEST

_____

By: _____

_____
Print Name

"Two copies of this form are enclosed. Please sign both copies, send one back to AHIMA and keep one copy for your files. AHIMA will notify you only if there is a question of accepting your submission. Also, a fully executed copy of this form is available to you upon request."

Source: AHIMA Rev. 6/00

Appendix 12B
Conflict of Interest Form

AHIMA/FORE policy/procedure on conflicts and dualities of interest

1.0 STATEMENT OF POLICY

1.1. Reason for Policy. The articles of incorporation and corporate bylaws of the AMERICAN HEALTH INFOR-MATION MANAGEMENT ASSOCIATION, INC. (AHIMA) and the FOUNDATION OF RESEARCH AND EDU-CATION (FORE) provide that each of these organizations is organized and is to be operated for public, not private, purposes and that the public's welfare shall be an important factor in its operations. Both organizations are not-for-profit corporations and are federally tax-exempt. The boards of directors of AHIMA and FORE have determined that it is in the best interest of these organizations and of the public they serve for each to have a clearly-stated policy and set of procedures to identifying and resolving conflicts and dualities of interest which might occur.

1.2. Definitions. A conflict of interest is a personal and proprietary interest on the part of a person having a fiduciary relationship to AHIMA or FORE (or a member of that person's immediate family, household or business organization) in which the natural pursuit of that interest is or may become in conflict with the financial or business interests of AHIMA or FORE. A duality of interest is the presence of two or more sets of fiduciary duties in one person having a fiduciary relationship to AHIMA or FORE (or a member of that person's immediate household, or business organization) which, if pursued conscientiously, will or may cause others to question the ability of the person to discharge those duties faithfully, provided, however, that concomitant service to AHIMA and FORE shall be deemed not to constitute a conflict or a duality of interest. A philosophical difference of opinion without the other required facts is neither a conflict nor a duality of interest.

1.3. Legal Context. Conflicts and dualities may reflect adversely upon the integrity of AHIMA and legality of AHIMA and FORE and upon all persons who are party to an action or transaction, regardless of whether the conflict or duality is actual or only apparent and not actual. For example, under Illinois law (where both organizations are incorporated), unpaid directors of not-for-profit corporations are immunized statutorily from personal liability only for acts taken in good faith and in accordance with prescribed procedures where conflicts exist. Further, acts which unduly benefit private insider parties with the assets of not-for profit and tax-exempt organizations are surchargeable against the parties having such conflicts, as well as grounds for loss of tax-exempt status.

1.4. Policy Established. Since persons elected and selected to fiduciary positions with AHIMA and FORE are usually active in many related endeavors and it is not realistic to prohibit all conflicts and all dualities of interests, it shall be the established policy of AHIMA and FORE to protect both organizations and their fiduciaries by:

(a) avoiding conflicts and dualities of interest wherever reasonably possible,

(b) requiring effective disclosure of all unavoidable actual or apparent conflicts or dualities of interest appropriately,

(c) proscribing certain conduct by fiduciaries when conflicts or dualities of interest exist, and

(d) establishing a governance review process for routine consideration of whether disclosed conflicts or dualities of interest reasonably require further action, all as set forth herein.

1.5. <u>Intermediate Sanctions Compliance.</u> Among the purposes served by this policy/procedure is the intended compliance with the provisions of Internal Revenue Code §4958, referred to as the "intermediate sanctions" rules. It shall be the policy of AHIMA and FORE, wherever any arrangement is entered into with a person or persons who are "insiders" or who would be classified as "disqualified persons" under Internal Revenue Code § 4958 and the regulations promulgated pursuant thereto, to require that the arrangement be brought before the board of directors for consideration (which may follow a consideration by a board committee if desired). In considering the arrangement, the board of directors shall take into consideration all appropriate comparability data and other factors provided by law. The person or persons identified as disqualified persons may participate in discussion, but shall leave the meeting for final discussion and vote on the matter and shall not vote on the issue. It is intended that this process and the information considered by and retained by the board of directors in its files shall qualify for the rebuttable presumption of reasonableness in each such arrangement, which is approved.

1.6. <u>Additional Definitions</u>. In addition to the foregoing definitions of conflicts of interest and duality of interest, the terms set forth below, when used in this policy and these procedures, shall have the following meanings:

(a) "Board of Directors" shall mean the regularly elected board of directors, including **<u>ex officio</u>** members, of AHIMA and FORE as from time to time serving, whether in executive session or not.

(b) "Committee member" shall include all persons, **<u>ex officio</u>** or otherwise, serving from time to time on a committee, whether standing, special or **<u>ad hoc</u>**, of AHIMA or FORE or of their boards of directors, including committees co-sponsored by AHIMA or FORE as to the representatives on such committees of AHIMA or FORE. Committees by other names, such as task forces, or working groups, are generally intended to be included as committees hereunder.

(c) "Contract" shall mean any agreement, whether in writing or not, by which AHIMA or FORE agrees to purchase or exchange anything of value, either goods or services, whether such agreement is made or authorized by the board of directors or not and whether or not included in an official budget.

(d) "Covered fiduciaries" or "Fiduciaries" shall mean all directors, officers, employees, committee members of all types, and material fiduciary vendors of AHIMA and FORE, together with officers and directors of AHIMA Component State Associations as regards their dealings with AHIMA.

(e) "Disclosure" shall mean a written and attributed revelation of an actual, apparent or potential conflict or duality of interest sufficient to cause same to be announced and published at a meeting of AHIMA or FORE board of directors as required herein.

(f) "Endorsement" shall mean any statement—oral, written or otherwise portrayed—which states or strongly implies that AHIMA or FORE recommend a specific product or vendor which is available commercially. A factually accurate statement that either AHIMA or FORE has purchased or leased a particular product or service for its own use is not an endorsement.

(g) "Material consideration" shall mean an amount which is not inconsequential under the circumstances and which shall in all events include amounts over $500.00. It is not intended that fruit baskets, candies, flowers, most meals or drinks, greeting cards, holiday gifts and most "client entertainment" events constitute material consideration.

(h) "Material fiduciary vendor" shall mean any vendor selling services, including professional services, totaling or reasonably expected to total over $10,000 in any year and who regularly advises AHIMA or FORE on policy matters. Not all vendors of AHIMA and FORE will be material fiduciary vendors.

(i) "Proprietary interest" shall mean any present or anticipatory degree or percentage of ownership, personally or as a fiduciary, or officer or director status, in any applicable business or commercial enterprise, whether incorporated or not, or a salaried or retained advisor relationship with such organization.

2.0 ESTABLISHMENT OF PROCEDURE.

2.1. Coverage. This policy and these procedures shall apply to the following fiduciaries: all directors, officers, employees, committee members of every type, and material fiduciary vendors of AHIMA and FORE, as well as to officers and directors of AHIMA Component State Associations as regards their dealings with AHIMA. This policy does not cover former fiduciaries whose service ended before the effective date hereof or fiduciaries whose service ends and who have already complied with these provisions while in office.

2.2. Disclosures. Disclosures of actual, apparent or even potential or possible conflicts or dualities of interest are appropriate and encouraged whenever they occur or are brought to mind. In addition, the Executive Director of AHIMA and FORE shall distribute disclosure forms and copies of this policy and those procedures to all covered fiduciaries (officers and directors of AHIMA Component State Associations) within thirty (30) days following the annual meeting of each organization and shall further have the duty, together with each director, to educate all those to whom the policy applies of both the need and the procedure for timely and complete disclosures hereunder. Disclosures shall be in writing and shall be delivered to the Executive Director of AHIMA or FORE, as applicable. All disclosures shall be announced at the next meeting of the applicable board of directors of AHIMA or FORE, shall be noted summarily in the minutes of the meeting and, where thought to be only apparent or possible, shall be so identified. Copies of disclosures shall also be forwarded, where applicable, by the Executive Director to the chair of the **ad hoc** committee described below in these procedures.

2.3. Endorsement Policy. Because of recurring requests by outside parties for actions by covered fiduciaries of AHIMA and FORE that are or appear to be the endorsement of AHIMA or FORE, creating continuing actual, apparent or possible conflicts or dualities, and because inappropriate endorsements of commercial goods or services by tax-exempt organizations may create significant legal problems, it is the policy of both AHIMA and FORE that none of its covered fiduciaries individually may endorse goods or services on behalf of AHIMA or FORE and that only the boards of directors may do so expressly by resolution duly adopted pursuant to established criteria. Whenever AHIMA or FORE covered fiduciaries are placed in a position where, regardless of their intentions, a third party is or appears to be soliciting or implying an endorsement, the most appropriate disclaimer is that the fiduciary's participation is personal rather than representative, that it does not and cannot constitute an endorsement by AHIMA or FORE, and that only AHIMA or FORE's boards of directors are authorized to issue endorsements by those organizations. Giving an unpaid speech for, submitting an unpaid article to, or serving as an unpaid member of an editorial advisory board for any party shall not, in and of itself, constitute an endorsement, a conflict or a duality hereunder.

2.4. <u>Bid Contracts</u>. Bidding by price is a procedure for obtaining the best price and not for vitiating the untoward effects of a conflict or duality of interest. Participation by covered fiduciaries in a bidding process by AHIMA or FORE for goods or services is only permitted subsequent to disclosure of the conflict hereunder, regardless of whether the contracting decision is made by the board of directors, the Executive Director, the Chief Financial Officer, or any other management representative and regardless of the amount of the contract.

2.5. <u>Examples of Conflicts</u>. Common examples of actual or apparent conflicts or interest, by no means exhaustive of those possible, are set forth below for the consideration of those fiduciaries covered hereunder:

(a) A covered fiduciary is a stockholder, partner or proprietor of a business which sells videotaping services to AHIMA or FORE for material consideration.

(b) A covered fiduciary is an unpaid director of a business which sells software to AHIMA or FORE for material consideration.

(c) A covered fiduciary is a part-time employee of a business which sells testing forms to AHIMA or FORE for material consideration.

(d) A covered fiduciary is a consultant to a business which sells testing forms to AHIMA or FORE for material consideration and is aware that the business engages in transactions with AHIMA or FORE.

(e) A covered fiduciary receives an honorarium of $600.00 for speaking on behalf of an organization which is seeking the endorsement of two of its products by AHIMA or FORE.

(f) A covered fiduciary and his/her spouse are taken out to dinner, then to the theater, and not charged for an overnight hotel stay or a rent-a-car by representatives of a national hotel chain which seeks to host the annual meeting of AHIMA or FORE, which annual meeting would involve budgetary expenditures of a material amount.

(g) A covered fiduciary receives an expensive piece of jewelry from the engagement partner (with whom he/she is not personally involved) of the law firm which represents AHIMA or FORE.

(h) A covered fiduciary's spouse is a part-time consultant to a consulting firm which bids for a contract with AHIMA or FORE in a material amount.

(i) A covered fiduciary's teen-age son is given a summer job by a business which seeks AHIMA's endorsement for several of its products.

(j) A covered fiduciary who is also a health care consultant requests of the program committee for the AHIMA or FORE annual meeting that she/he be permitted to speak at the annual meeting and distribute materials and that a competing consultant be dropped from consideration as a speaker.

2.6. Examples of Dualities. Common examples of actual or apparent dualities of interest, by no means exhaustive of those possible, are set forth below for the consideration of those fiduciaries covered hereunder:

(a) Service as an officer, director, or paid or unpaid advisor to another not-for-profit organization, whether or not tax-exempt and including an AHIMA Component State Association, which competes with AHIMA or FORE as to revenue sources other than individual memberships.

(b) Service as an officer, director or paid or unpaid advisor to another not-for-profit or governmental organization which competes with AHIMA or FORE as to program and mission.

(c) Service as an officer, director or paid or unpaid advisor to another not-for-profit organization which co-sponsors programs, publications or products with AHIMA or FORE or which exhibits the availability of its goods or services at AHIMA or FORE events or in their publications.

(d) Service in any capacity with or on behalf of any party, regardless of the fiduciary's intent, in which the fiduciary believes that the requested service is to assist the party in obtaining the endorsement of AHIMA or FORE.

2.7. Proscribed Conduct. No person having a conflict or duality of interest as defined herein shall make or second motions or vote other than "present" (abstention) in meetings of the boards of directors or committees of AHIMA or FORE; provided, that this proscription shall not prevent participation in quorum determinations or in debate. Any member of the board or committee may request that the person having a conflict or duality be excused for a portion of the debate. If the affected fiduciary has only learned of the conflict or duality or has not yet had an opportunity to file a written disclosure form, it is appropriate to declare the conflict or duality at the meeting affected to assure its entry in the minutes and to file thereafter the prescribed disclosure form. If there is doubt about whether any disclosed relationship does or does not constitute a conflict or duality, the possibility should be disclosed, and abstention from parliamentary participation thereafter is preferred by this policy. In all cases involving actual, apparent or even potential conflicts or dualities of interest, it is the intent of this policy that the records of proceedings reflect such concern and that the applicable bodies, whether boards, committees, management groups, or plenary meetings, behave more formally in recognition of the importance of the disclosure.

2.8. Ad Hoc Committee. Whenever a covered fiduciary raises a question about whether a disclosed relationship does or does not constitute a conflict or duality of interest or whenever the AHIMA or FORE boards of directors believe that any disclosed or undisclosed conflict or duality should be analyzed in the best interests of the organizations, the President of AHIMA or FORE shall appoint an **ad hoc** committee of two or more disinterested directors to investigate the relationship and to recommend board action or inaction with regard thereto. Any such **ad hoc** committee on conflicts and dualities shall present its confidential written recommendation to the board President or his/her designee for consideration by the board at its next meeting.

2.9. Violation of Policy/Procedures. Negligent or intentional violation of this policy and these procedures shall constitute grounds for removal or discharge of covered fiduciaries from their positions for cause.

2.10. Relationship to Bylaws. This policy and these procedures shall be construed consistently with the corporate bylaws of AHIMA and FORE. As soon as possible after adoption, it is the intention of the AHIMA and FORE boards of directors that their respective bylaws be amended to include these provisions in order further to institutionalize and give effect to them.

AMERICAN HEALTH INFORMATION MANAGEMENT ASSOCIATION, INC.

Approved Form for Disclosure of Actual, Possible or Apparent Conflicts and Dualities of Interest

Date _____, 200___

To the American Health Information Management Association Executive Director:

The undersigned, having a fiduciary relationship to the American Health Information Management Association, Inc. (AHIMA), hereby acknowledges:

(a)   she/he has read the AHIMA policy and procedures on conflicts and dualities of interest,

(b)   that she/he has no actual, apparent or possible conflicts or dualities of interest to disclose (check here if applicable _____),

(c)   that she/he has the following relationships or which should be disclosed under such policy and procedures:

1.

2.

3.

I acknowledge my ongoing duty to disclose conflicts or dualities of interest which may occur in the future.

_____
Signature

AHIMA Title: _____

FOUNDATION OF RESEARCH AND EDUCATION

Approved Form for Disclosure of Actual,
Possible or Apparent Conflicts and Dualities of Interest

Date _____, 200____

To the Foundation of Research and Education Executive Director:

The undersigned, having a fiduciary relationship to the Foundation of Research and Education (FORE), hereby acknowledges:

(a) she/he has read the FORE policy and procedures on conflicts and dualities of interest,

(b) that she/he has no actual, apparent or possible conflicts or dualities of interest to disclose (check here if applicable ____),

(c) that she/he has the following relationships or which should be disclosed under such policy and procedures:

1.

2.

3.

I acknowledge my ongoing duty to disclose conflicts or dualities of interest which may occur in the future.

_____
Signature

FORE Title: _____

Source: AHIMA 2000.

Appendix 12C
Grant-in-Aid Application

FORE
Foundation of Research
and Education of AHIMA

Grant-in-Aid
Research
Application

American Health Information Management Association
233 N. Michigan Ave., 21st Floor
Chicago, IL 60601-5800
(312) 233-1100

American Health Information Management Association
Foundation of Research and Education

Grant-in-Aid
Research Handbook

CONTENTS

American Health Information Management Association
Foundation of Research and Education
Call for Proposals
Grant-in-Aid Research

Statement of Philosophy and Purpose

Grants-in-Aid have been established to encourage and financially assist qualified applicants to conduct research in theoretical and practical aspects of health information practice. Funds are provided through the Foundation of Research and Education (FORE) of the American Health Information Management Association (AHIMA). Researchers are encouraged to submit topics in their established areas of expertise and those within AHIMA's Research Priorities (See page 7 for more details). Submissions that address one or more of AHIMA's Research Priorities will receive priority for consideration for funding.

Scope of Grants

Each recipient shall be limited to one funded grant per year. Proposals may be resubmitted with Research Committee approval. Funding may be requested for supplies and expenses. Salaries and wages of support staff for time spent directly on the funded project may be requested, and must be fully justified in the detailed budget and project plan. Up to a maximum of 10 percent of the primary investigator's salary may be covered by the grant, as calculated by multiplying the individual's institutional base salary by the percent of effort on this project, and must be fully justified in the detailed budget and project plan. Grant funds may not be applied to overhead costs, fringe benefits, or other indirect costs. Grant funding is not available for product development.

Ordinarily, the scope of the proposal shall be such that it can be concluded within 18 months from the date of funding. Exceptions with justifications will be considered. The average range of grants is between $15,000 and $40,000.

Eligibility

The primary or secondary investigator must be an active, associate, or student member of AHIMA.

Proposal Deadline and Submission

Proposals shall be submitted in writing to Grant-in-Aid Awards, Foundation of Research and Education, AHIMA, 233 N. Michigan Ave., Suite 2150, Chicago, IL, 60601-5800. The deadlines for receipt of proposals are March 23, 2007, and September 21, 2007. Award notifications will take place within six weeks of the application deadline.

Applicants who are asked to resubmit proposals may do so at any time within 90 days of notification to resubmit. It is not necessary to wait for the next regular application deadline.

For additional information, contact the Foundation at fore@ahima.org, or at (312) 233-1100.

Format Requirements
- Standard 8 1/2 x 11 inch paper
- 12-point type
- Double spaced
- 1-inch margins required
- Single-side printing

Proposal Content
Each proposal shall be submitted with a cover sheet (Appendix A) and is required to include the following sections:

PROJECT TITLE

IMPACT
Purpose/hypothesis
Statement of Need
Objectives

METHODOLOGY
Research Design
Research Methods
Specific Aims

FEASIBILITY
Organization/Management Plan
Personnel
Timetable

EVALUATION
Measurement of Success
Intended Distribution

APPENDIX
Curriculum Vitae
Budget
Letters of Support

Applicants are strongly encouraged to clearly and specifically address each content area as outlined in the application and to use the Criteria for Technical Review (Appendix D) as a guideline.

Special Requirement for Resubmission: **In cases where the proposal is a resubmission, the applicant must include specifics regarding how the deficiencies cited in the original application have been addressed.**

Proposal Review
Members of the FORE Research Committee will review each proposal submitted according to the Criteria for Technical Review (Appendix D). This includes review of the:

1. Impact
2. Methodology
3. Feasibility
4. Evaluation

Upon completion of the review, the AHIMA Research Committee will make one of the following recommendations:

1. Approve with funding
2. Approve without funding (resubmission encouraged)
3. Disapprove

The Chair of the FORE Research Committee will notify the applicant of approval or disapproval within six weeks following the deadline date for submission of grant applications. The grantee shall agree to the publication of announcement of the grant award. Grant funds will be released after completion of a signed funding agreement.

Reporting

Grantee shall submit a progress report to the designated AHIMA staff liaison at the project's midpoint and a final report within six weeks of the grant completion date.

The midterm report shall state accomplishments to date and explain any deviation from the proposed timetable. The grant fund expenditures to date shall be submitted on the budget form. The grantee agrees to report any circumstances that preclude compliance with the termination date or that constitute any significant change from the proposal as originally approved.

The final report shall be a narrative report of the study's findings, including an executive summary. This shall be submitted in sufficient detail so that the end product can be clearly understood and the research replicated. Final account of expenditure of grant money shall be prepared and submitted on the budget form. Any unused funds shall be returned to AHIMA.

AHIMA shall have first consideration for publication of the primary article or findings forthcoming from funded projects. The grantee shall agree to submit manuscripts intended for publication to the editor of AHIMA's research journal *Perspectives in Health Information Management,* or other AHIMA-sponsored publications, as appropriate. Exceptions to this will be considered for circumstances in which this places a grantee in direct conflict with institutional policies. In such situations, AHIMA may negotiate a separate agreement for funding in which AHIMA shall have simultaneous or subsequent rights to use and publish resultant findings without fee or encumbrance. The editor will submit the manuscript to the Editorial Review Board for review and recommendation regarding publication. All manuscripts emanating from this research for publication must be indicated as having been funded (in part or whole) by a grant from the Foundation of Research and Education of AHIMA.

Curriculum Vitae
Complete this form or attach vitae with the following information.

Name: _____

Home Address (Street, city, state, zip code): _____

_____

_____

Work Address (Position, institution, street, city, state, zip code): _____

_____

_____

Education (College and university. Give dates of graduation and degrees received. If a student, list expected date of graduation and degree to be received.):

Experience (Employers, types of responsibilities, dates of employment):

Present Position Including Title:

Prior Research (Titles and dates of any previous research or publications):

(Append additional information if necessary.)

Grant-in-Aid
Budget Summary

Title of Research: _____

Principal Investigator: _____

ITEM

AMOUNT

Equipment (specify):

Supplies (specify):

Travel (specify):

Other Services (specify):

TOTAL:

Other funding sources: Give name of institutions and amounts contributed.

Grant-in-Aid
Budget Justification

For each category of expense indicated on the budget summary page, provide a brief statement justifying the expense in the context of the proposal and how or why the expense relates to the work required.

Criteria for Technical Review of Grant-in-Aid Proposals

Title of Research: _____

Principal Investigator: _____

The members of the Research Committee of AHIMA will base their evaluation of the proposal on the following criteria for technical review.
1. Impact
2. Methodology
3. Feasibility
4. Evaluation

CRITERIA

A. Impact

1. Does the proposed research support AHIMA's research goals?

2. If the aims of the application are achieved, will health information management practice be advanced?

3. Is there flexibility, adaptability, and diversity in potential applications of the results?

4. Will there be an effect on the concepts or practices that drive the health information field?

5. Will the findings result in any economic impact on the field?

B. Methodology

1. Are the research design and problem statement appropriate and complete? Has a **thorough** literature review been completed?

2. Does the research design attain the data required to successfully complete the project?

B. Methodology (cont.)

3. Are the conceptual framework, design,

methods, and analyses appropriate to the aims of the project?

4. Do the researchers acknowledge potential design problem areas and consider alternative tactics?

C. Feasibility

1. What is the likelihood of meeting the stated objectives? Are the schedule and technical resources available realistic for the scope of the project?

2. Does the proposal contain a realistic budget that will adequately support the study?

3. Are the investigator(s) appropriately trained and well-suited to carry out this work?

4. If there are multiple investigators, has their proposed structure been presented in enough detail to measure its viability for success?

5. Does the proposal contain a staffing plan that identifies key personnel with appropriate experience?

6. If outside data is pivotal to the project, has necessary support and cooperation been documented?

D. Evaluation

1. Does the investigator identify appropriate, effective means of measuring the accomplishment of their objectives?

2. Are the results intended to be submitted for publication or otherwise made known?

3. Do they acknowledge potential problem areas and consider alternative tactics?

Appendix 12D
Sample FORE GIA Application (Completed)

TITLE: Effective and Efficient Public Health Reporting Using ICD-10-CM and ICD-10-PCS

I. IMPACT

Introduction:

The emergence of ICD-10-CM and ICD-10-PCS brings anticipation about future uses, including the accurate capturing and reporting of public health diseases and related procedures. A major issue that needs to be addressed in order to accomplish this task is the need to illustrate how ICD-10-CM and ICD-10-PCS are designed to accommodate changes and additions more easily than ICD-9-CM, especially for public health disease capturing and reporting.

This is extremely important in this day of newly evolved diseases such as AIDS, SARS, and avian flu as well as the acts of bioterrorism. It is expected that the ICD-10-CM system incorporates these newly found public health diseases as well as easily adapting to ever changing public health conditions. However, this may not occur. Thus, it is important to assess if the ICD-10-CM and ICD-10-PCS systems are a more effective and efficient public health reporting system than ICD-9-CM.

Purpose:

The purpose of this research project is threefold:

1. to investigate the completeness of the ICD-10-CM and ICD-10-PCS systems in capturing public health diseases and related procedures;
2. to measure the effectiveness and efficiency of ICD-10-CM and ICD-10-PCS in public health reporting; and
3. to collect feedback from users on how applicable the ICD-10-CM and ICD-10-PCS systems are in relation to capturing public health diseases and related procedures.

Statement of Need:

According to the National Center for Health Statistics (NCHS)[1] and the Centers for Medicare and Medicaid Services (CMS)[2], the ICD-10-CM and ICD-10-PCS have many advantages over the ICD-9-CM coding system. Notable improvements in the content and format include:

1. the addition of information relevant to ambulatory and managed care encounters;
2. expanded injury codes;
3. the creation of combination diagnosis/symptom codes to reduce the number of codes needed to fully describe a condition;
4. the addition of a sixth character;
5. incorporation of common 4th and 5th digit subclassifications;
6. laterality;

7. greater specificity in code assignment;

8. further expansion than was possible with ICD-9-CM;

9. all substantially different procedures have a unique code; and

10. new procedures can be added as unique codes.

However, in the ICD-10-CM Field Testing Project summary report developed by AHA and AHIMA[3], even though ICD-10-CM was felt to be an improvement over ICD-9-CM by 76 percent of the participants, a total of 761 errors or conflicts in the instructions in ICD-10-CM were reported. After eliminating the duplications and other problems, a total of 305 issues remained. In the final list of identified problems, difficulty in locating a diagnostic term in the index was by far the most commonly reported problem. Also, twenty-five of the reported problems pertained to codes for external causes of morbidity, codes that could effect public health reporting. Participants also reported the number of diagnostic statements that were unable to be coded in ICD-10-CM. They were unable to find an ICD-10-CM code for a total of 380 diagnoses. Upon review of the problem identification forms, the reasons why some of the diagnoses could not be coded were eliminated (due to duplication by more than one participant or misinterpretation of instructions etc.) and 151 diagnoses that could not be coded fell into the following categories:

1. Diagnosis was not indexed under the expected main terms or subterms

2. Insufficient documentation to assign a code (clarification with a physician would be necessary)

3. Error in index or tabular

4. Concept does not exist in ICD-10-CM

5. Code choices not applicable to diagnosis (i.e., either a clear "default" code that is broad enough to cover the diagnosis should be provided or additional codes should be made available)

6. Diagnosis is more specific than available code choices

7. Unclear instructions

The reported problems have been submitted to NCHS for review and correction. To our knowledge, however, no studies have been conducted to determine if ICD-10-CM/ICD-10-PCS is effective in capturing public health diseases and related procedures. Furthermore, according to the National Vital Statistics Report[4], the top ten causes of death for 2002 were the following:

1. Diseases of the heart

2. Malignant neoplasms

3. Cerebrovascular diseases

4. Chronic lower respiratory diseases

5. Accidents (unintentional injuries)

6. Diabetes mellitus

7. Influenza and pneumonia

8. Alzheimer's disease

9. Nephritis, nephritic syndrome and nephrosis

10. Septicemia

These diagnoses accounted for 79 percent of all deaths occurring in the United States. Comments received for changes to ICD-10-CM[5] were categorized according to the chapter and recommended disposition. Below, we linked the comment section to the top 10 causes of death for 2002 as stated above. The number of comments that required further study is listed below in Table 1 and includes the following:

Table 1. Cause of Death and Number of Comments that Warrant Further Study in ICD-10-CM

Cause of Death	Number of Comments that have Merit and Warrant Further Study
Diseases of the heart, cerebrovascular diseases	6
Malignant neoplasms	0
Chronic lower respiratory diseases	4
Accidents (unintentional injuries)	19
Diabetes mellitus	13
Influenza and pneumonia	4
Alzheimer's disease	0
Nephritis, nephritic syndrome and nephrosis	2
Septicemia	3
Total	51 Comments need further study

It can be seen from Table 1 that 51 comments for the top ten causes of death were viewed as needing further study. This demonstrates again that ICD-10-CM should be examined to see how well it accurately captures public health related diseases.

Based on all of the above information, it is therefore, important to determine if ICD-10-CM and ICD-10-PCS truly captures public health related diagnoses and procedures.

Objectives:

1. Investigate the completeness of the ICD-10-CM and ICD-10-PCS coding systems in the ability to capture public health diseases and related procedures,
2. Measure the effectiveness and efficiency of ICD-10-CM and ICD-10-PCS in public health reporting.
3. Collect qualitative feedback from users on how applicable the ICD-10-CM and ICD-10-PCS systems are in relation to capturing public health diseases and related procedures.

II. METHODOLOGY

Research Design:

A descriptive, four-part, research study will be performed to investigate the completeness of the ICD-10-CM and ICD-10-PCS coding systems in capturing public health related diagnoses and procedures. First, we will examine the top 10 causes of mortality as well as other infectious and reportable public health conditions such as SARS, avian flu, smallpox, anthrax and so forth. We will also examine the Classification of Death and Injury resulting from Terrorism, which has been added to the ICD-9-CM system. A comparison of the ICD-9-CM codes for these diagnoses and procedures with the ICD-10-CM diagnoses and ICD-10-PCS procedures will be made. Comparison tables that describe the specificity of the coding for ICD-9-CM and ICD-10-CM /ICD-10-PCS for each of the public health diagnoses and related procedures will be developed. Hypotheses about how the coded data affects public health reporting will be developed focusing on the advantages and disadvantages of the ICD-10-CM/ICD-10-PCS systems. The second part of the research study will include using the ICD-10-CM Validity Study data from AHA and AHIMA to abstract public health related codes, for example, the top ten causes of mortality. Agreement levels between the coder and the validator will be determined as well as differences in specific areas in order to demonstrate if ICD-10-CM is more effective and efficient in capturing public health diagnoses. The third part of the research study will include the analysis and organization of the data collected from the previous study parts. The fourth part of the study includes the development of a focus group. The focus group will include experts in ICD-9-CM, ICD-10-CM/ICD-10-PCS and public health. The focus group will review and examine the information accumulated from the first three study parts and provide feedback and recommendations on where changes need to be made in both the ICD-10-CM and PCS systems.

Before any part of the study is conducted, it will be submitted to the University of Pittsburgh's Institutional Review Board (IRB) (as well as any other IRBs required in order to undertake the research) for review and approval either at the exempt or expedited review level. This process should not take longer than two weeks before approval is obtained.

Research Methods:

Part I: Development of Public Health Diagnoses and Procedures Reportable List:

The first part of the methods includes the development and design of all possible public health reportable diagnoses and related procedures. In order to obtain this list we will research reportable diseases for health care providers across the different state departments of health. The website for each state department of health will be reviewed to determine what diseases are required to be reported. Once this list is obtained we will supplement it with two other areas that are very pertinent to public health reporting; the top ten diagnoses for morbidity and mortality and the classification of death and injury resulting from terrorism, a supplemental classification developed after September 11 and made part of ICD-9-CM. Procedures related to the public health diagnoses will also be included. A listing of all the potential public health reportable diagnoses and related procedures will be developed. Comparison tables that describe the specificity of the coding for ICD-9-CM and ICD-10-CM /ICD-10-PCS for each of the public health diagnoses and related procedures will be developed. Hypotheses about how the coded data affects public health reporting will be developed focusing on the advantages and disadvantages of the ICD-10-CM/ICD-10-PCS systems. Table 2 displays an example of how our comparison tables will be organized.

Table 2.   Example of Comparison Table

Public Health Diagnosis	ICD-9-CM Cod/s	ICD-10-CM Code/s	Public Health Related Procedure (if applicable)	ICD-9-CM Code	ICD-10-PCS code	Hypothesis/Explanation

Part II: Validation Study for Public Health Reportable Diagnoses:

The second part of the research study will include using the ICD-10-CM Validity Study data from AHA and AHIMA to examine whether public health reportable diagnoses are easily captured using ICD-10-CM. We have obtained the validity study data from AHIMA and have received permission to use the data in this study. The data includes 359 patient cases in which up to ten narrative diagnoses have been collected. Up to ten ICD-10-CM codes by a coder and then by a validator are also included. Table 3 shows one example of how the data is organized.

Table 3. Description of the AHA and AHIMA Validity Study Data Using ICD-10-CM:

DXNarrative 1	DX Narrative 2	DX Narrative 3	DX 1 Code 1	DX1 Code 2	DX2 Code 1	DX 2 Code 2	DX 3 Code 1	VDX1 Code 1	VDX2 Code 1	VDX3 Code 1	Explanation
Pulmonary edema with respiratory failure	CHF	COPD	I50.1	J96.0			J44.9	J96.9	I50.1	J44.9	DX1Code 1 inconsistent with validator

We will review every diagnosis in the database and extract those diagnoses that are related to public health reporting either by being one of the top ten diagnoses for morbidity, mortality, an infectious disease, a disease related to terrorism and so forth. All public health related diagnoses will then be examined to determine in what areas the coder and validator agreed and disagreed. Agreement levels between the coder and the validator will be determined and a Kappa statistic will be performed to determine if the differences seen are statistically significant. Wherever there are differences between the coder and the validator, that case will be recoded by the researchers to determine if the ICD-10-CM system truly captures the public health diagnoses. Then a new table (Table 4) will be developed and will include the ICD-9-CM codes as well as differences in specific areas in order to demonstrate if ICD-10-CM is more effective and efficient in capturing public health diagnoses than ICD-9-CM. We will have one coder code the diagnoses in ICD-9-CM and then an expert coder (our secondary investigator) recode it in ICD-9-CM to see where differences lie.

Table 4. Description of AHA and AHIMA Validity Data with ICD-9-CM Code Comparison

ICD-10-CM											
DXNarrative 1	DX Narrative 2	DX Narrative 3	DX 1 Code 1	DX1 Code 2	DX2 Code 1	DX 2 Code 2	DX 3 Code 1	VDX1 Code 1	VDX2 Code 1	VDX3 Code 1	Explanation
Pulmonary edema with respiratory failure	CHF	COPD	I50.1	J96.0			J44.9	J96.9	I50.1	J44.9	DX1Code 1 inconsistent with validator

ICD-9-CM											
DXNarrative 1	DX Narrative 2	DX Narrative 3	DX 1 Code 1	DX1 Code 2	DX2 Code 1	DX 2 Code 2	DX 3 Code 1	VDX1 Code 1	VDX2 Code 1	VDX3 Code 1	Explanation
Pulmonary edema with respiratory failure	CHF	COPD									

Once we have complete codes for all public health reportable diagnoses, we will compare the specificity of each coding system, (ICD-9-CM and ICD-10-CM), using a ranked scale. The ranked or ordinal scale will consist of the following values:

5 = Diagnosis is fully captured by the code/codes
4 = Diagnosis is almost fully captured by the code/codes
3 = Diagnosis is partially captured by the code/codes
2 = Diagnosis is less than partially captured by the code/codes
1 = Diagnosis is not captured by the code/codes

A ranked score will be assigned to each public health diagnosis for both the ICD-10-CM and ICD-9-CM coding systems. The mean and median values for each of the patient cases for both I-10 and I-9 codes will be computed and the higher mean and median values (those closer to 5) will constitute the more complete coding system.

Part III: Statistical Analysis of the Data:

The qualitative data (hypotheses and explanations) obtained from the first study, the development of the public health reportable list, will be analyzed using qualitative themes. The hypotheses and explanations will be categorized into five broad themes or areas such as, those explained in the ranking scale. For example, one of the public health reportable diagnoses is HIV and we will code this first in ICD-9-CM and then ICD-10-CM. Then we will develop hypotheses and explanations regarding which system fully captured everything about the disease and provided specific terms and codes related to the disease. The hypotheses and explanations will be categorized into one of the five areas. If we find that a disease is only partially captured, further explanation will be provided as to what should be included in order to fully capture the diagnosis. The same system will occur for related public health procedures. For the second study, agreement levels between the coder and the validator will be determined and a Kappa statistic will be performed to determine if the differences seen are statistically significant. Wherever there are differences between the coder and the validator, that case will be recoded by the researchers to determine if the ICD-10-CM system truly captures the public health diagnoses more effectively than ICD-9-CM. All of the statistical data, both qualitative and quantitative will be organized in tables as demonstrated above. A website will be developed by our research assistant and will include all the tables and information developed from the study. Only those individuals participating in the study will have access to the website. The tables and explanations of the tables will be provided to our focus group (via the website) which will review the information and assist us in making recommendations for changes to ICD-10-CM and ICD-10-PCS.

Part IV: Focus Group:

The focus group will include experts in ICD-9-CM, ICD-10-CM/ICD-10-PCS and public health. The focus group will review and examine the information accumulated from the first three study parts and provide feedback and recommendations on where changes need to be made in both the ICD-10-CM and PCS systems. Focus group experts will be obtained through AHIMA and the American Public Health Association (APHA). The data will be provided to the focus group members through email and through a website that will be established for this study. One conference call will be held and used to discuss more specific information. Basically, the questions that will be posed to the focus group members include the following:

1. After review of the public health diagnoses and procedures reportable list, are there any diagnoses or procedures that you believe should be added, deleted, or changed? If so, please explain.

2. Do the hypotheses and explanations that relate to the coding of the reportable diagnoses and procedures provide enough information so that changes to the coding system can be made? If not, please specify which sections need further detail.

3. Do the ranked scale data and explanations related to differences in the I-10 and I-9 coding systems make sense? Do you need additional information to clarify any cases? If so, which ones?

4. Based on the information provided to you, what recommendations do you have to improve the ICD-10-CM and ICD-10-PCS coding systems for public health reporting?

Information from the focus group emails and from the conference call will be analyzed and organized into a formal report and sent to all members of the focus group for their clarification and additional comments.

Specific Aims:

The specific aims of this research study are to answer the following questions:

1. Are ICD-10-CM and ICD-10-PCS effective in capturing diagnoses and procedures that are specific to public health reporting?
2. Are ICD-10-CM and ICD-10-PCS more effective than ICD-9-CM in capturing diagnoses and procedures related to public health reporting.
3. Can the ICD-10-CM and ICD-10-PCS systems accommodate required changes and additions more easily than ICD-9-CM?
4. Are ICD-10-CM and ICD-10-PCS more efficient systems in coding of public health reportable diseases than ICD-9-CM?

III. FEASIBILITY:

Organization/Management Plan:

This research study will be under the direction of the Principal Investigator (PI) who will be responsible for directing the methodology of the project. The PI has a background in HIM and Epidemiology and therefore will be instrumental in development of the reportable list and coding of the public health diagnoses and procedures, analyzing the validity data to construct the tables, compute percentages of agreement and Kappa statistics, compute the rank scores of both the ICD-10-CM and ICD-9-CM data and compile the data from the focus group and publishing the findings. The Secondary Investigator, with a background in HIM and Public Health will assist the PI in each of the steps outlined above with a focus in the development and distribution of the coding tables, analysis of the data and publishing of the findings. A graduate student with a background in HIM and information technology/systems will be hired to assist with data entry, development of the website, organization of the focus group, typing of tables etc. The Research Coder with a background in HIM and Information Science and an assistant professor who teaches coding to HIM students will assist in the coding of the public health reportable diagnoses, the recoding of the validity study data for public health related diagnoses, and will make recommendations based on the reviews conducted.

Personnel:

Principal Investigator:	Valerie J.M. Watzlaf, Ph.D., FAHIMA, RHIA
Secondary Investigator:	Jennifer Hornung Garvin, Ph.D., FAHIMA, RHIA, CTR, CCS, CPHQ
Research Assistant:	To be Determined
Research Coder:	Patti Firouzan, MSIS, RHIA

Timetable:

The entire research study will take approximately 6 months and the time period for each of the steps listed in the research methodology is categorized in Figure 1.

Figure 1.   Timetable: August 20XX – January 20XX

	Aug	Sept	Oct	Nov	Dec	Jan
IRB submission; I-10 Training; Development/Finalization of Public Health Reportable Diagnoses and Procedures	██					
Development of Comparison Groups		██				
Extract Public Health Reportable Diagnoses from the Validity Database, Assess Agreement Levels, Recode and Assign Rankings			██			
Analyze all Data and Compile Reports for Focus Group Discussion			██			
Develop and Conduct the Focus Group				██	██	
Organize Information from the Focus Group and all Previous Reports and Summarize Findings						██
Submit Presentation Proposal to AHIMA				██		
Submit Manuscript for Publication to PHIM						██

IV. EVALUATION:

Measurement of Success:

The entire research study process will be evaluated as we proceed with the project but the most important evaluation for this project to be successful begins with the development of the reportable list of public health diagnoses and procedures. Every possible research effort will be made to make sure we capture all of the necessary diagnoses and procedures that relate to public health. Also, to make sure that we have accurate coding, an expert coder will recode the original coding. As the data from completed tables is collected, data quality checks will be incorporated by the PI and Secondary Investigator. Finally, the data will be analyzed using SPSS and will be displayed in tables and graphs so that all types of patterns can be seen. Results will then be reported as they compare to our stated objectives and specific aims.

Intended Distribution:

A progress report will be submitted to the designated AHIMA staff liaison at the project's midpoint and a final report on or before completion of the grant. The midterm report will include accomplishments to date and explain any deviation from the proposed timetable. Grant funds used up to this point will be submitted on the budget form. The final report will include a narrative report of the study's findings, including an executive summary. Final account of expenditure of grant money will be prepared and submitted on the budget form. Any unused funds will be returned to AHIMA.

The results will be submitted for publication in AHIMA's research journal *Perspectives in Health Information Management* or other related AHIMA journals. Reports can also be submitted to NCHS and CMS to assist in changes to the ICD-10-CM and ICD-10-PCS coding systems. Results will also be submitted to all members of the focus group prior to publication.

V. CONCLUSION:

This is certainly the time for the use of new, extensive, specific, coding systems such as ICD-10-CM and PCS. With President Bush stating that all Americans should have an EHR in the next ten years, the ICD-10-CM and PCS systems are definitely needed. However, to the author's knowledge, no studies have been conducted that determine whether the ICD-10-CM and PCS systems are effective for public health reporting. This could have great implications for our entire nation since public health diagnoses include epidemics and other diagnoses and procedures that relate to bioterrorism. If a new coding system that is to be used across this country is not able to effectively capture public health reportable diagnoses and procedures, then our country could be in a state of peril. Therefore it is of utmost importance that further study be taken to determine how effective the ICD-10-CM and PCS systems are in fully capturing public health reportable data.

Footnotes

1. NCHS, http://www.cdc.gov/nchs/about/otheract/icd9/abticd10.
2. CMS, http://www.cms.hhs.gov/providers/pufdownload/icd10.asp
3. AHA and AHIMA, ICD-10-CM Field Testing Project Summary Report, September 23, 2003 pgs. 26-30.
4. National Vital Statistics Report, CDC "Deaths: Leading Causes for 2002, Vol.53 No. 17.,March 7 2005, pg. 1.
5. ICD-10-CM Update: From the ICD-9-CM Coordination and Maintenance Meeting, November 2, 1999

Source: FORE/AHIMA 2007.

Chapter 13
Research and Ethics

Laurinda B. Harman, PhD, RHIA and Carol S. Nielsen, MLS

Learning Objectives

- Review important ethical principles and values that are important when conducting or participating in research activities

- Identify ethical issues that are related to the conduct of research

- Review the regulatory issues that affect human subjects' research, including those related to special subjects

- Review research projects that raise important ethical issues

Key Terms

Autonomy

Belmont Report

Beneficence

Bioethics and privacy commissions

Helsinki Agreement

Honesty

Fidelity

Institutional Review Board (IRB)

Justice

National Research Act

Nonmaleficence

Nuremberg Code

Privacy Protection Study Commission

Utility

Introduction

There are many ethical problems that have surfaced over the years with research that involved human subjects. The Jewish Chronic Disease Hospital Study described in figure 13.1 raised important issues of informed consent and truth-telling. There will be several other research studies discussed in this chapter. Even though there are international codes, agreements, government regulations, and institutional oversight activities, there continue to be problems with ethics and research and how human subjects are treated.

Research, Science, and Values

Figure 13.1.   The Jewish Chronic Disease Hospital Study

The Jewish Chronic Disease Hospital Study was conducted in 1963 in New York City and was funded by the United States Public Health Service and the American Cancer Society. The primary stated purpose of the research was to improve understanding of the human transplant rejection process. In fact, live cancer cells were injected into patients who were hospitalized with various chronic debilitating diseases. The consent was oral and not documented, and patients were not told that they would receive cancer cells.

Source: Stanford n.d.

Figure 13.2.   The Manhattan Project

The Manhattan Project, initiated in 1942, and led by Robert Oppenheimer, involved a group of scientists who worked in a secret laboratory in Los Alamos, New Mexico. The goal of this group was to create a nuclear bomb for the United States, with the intention of dropping bombs on Japan in order to end the war. Dr. Oppenheimer and some members of his team began to question the relationship between science and society and the ethics of using a bomb to kill so many people. In 1945, two nuclear bombs were dropped on Japan by the United States.

There are many recent clinical ethical violations with research, such as problems related to the licensure of the anthrax vaccine, the approval of a drug for depression despite the risk of suicide, international clinical trials that take advantage of those who do not have access to healthcare in developing countries, unlawful drug marketing, falsification of data, the use of drug trials on children in foster care (AHRQ 2007). Health information management (HIM)) issues are core to these ethical problems—issues related to privacy, informed consent, what information is collected, how it is used and disseminated, the problems of data integrity and validity, suppression of information, and the misuse of information.

An assumption of western science is that research is lawful and regular, and that the scientific method neutralizes bias. In fact, science and research are value-based and are not value-neutral, and cultural and political values and biases permeate the epistemology, methodology, and conclusions of science (Bronowski 1965; Capra 1982; Imber and Tuana 1988). Western science and research has a vested interest in rationality, objectivity, and protection from values, motives, politics or prejudice—a perspective that has been somewhat misleading to both scientists and society (Gornick 1983; Kerlinger 1979). Science and research inherently embed positive and negative values within the knowledge and technical decisions that are generated (Birke and Silvertown 1984; Longino 1990; Nelkin 1987).

It is important to recognize that science is embedded with the personal and professional values of individual scientists and the cultural values of society that support the research. The interests and concerns of society can influence the research that is conducted and how the information is collected. The role of science is to develop or test theories through the explanation of relationships, laws, and natural phenomena. Society's role has been to assign value to the discoveries and to demarcate appropriate applications of the knowledge. Historically, the criteria of relevance and value was outside the sphere of the scientist and was assigned to philosophers, theologians, and public constituencies; however, "a strong interest in the philosophical and ethical aspects have to be maintained by all concerned, and this is just as important for the scientific elite as for those who make a profession of social concern" (Bulkley 1985, 80). Some of these lines of demarcation of the roles of science and society changed during World War II. Prior to WWII, there was a clearer line of demarcation between the role of science (to help explain nature or discover new things) and the role of ethics (to explain the importance of values, ethical principles, and the competing interests of the many stakeholders when making a decision).

One particular event altered the relationships between science, politics, and ethics. The scientists involved in the Manhattan Project created the capacity to develop a nuclear bomb, and the decision was made by President Harry Truman of the United States to drop the bomb on the nation of Japan in order to end World War II. For the first time, scientists became public with their concerns about what was being done with their scientific inventions. They were concerned about the use of nuclear power to kill so many people and the health care problems that would be faced by the survivors. From that point forward, it became important for the scientists and researchers to recognize the potential ethical issues related to research and new discoveries and to assist in informing the public, or the individual research participant, in understanding the ethical issues that would be related to risk and/or benefit. The Manhattan Project provided the basis for scientists to realize that the results of their research raised issues that surpassed politics alone and required that the ethical issues raises by the discovery be addressed and considered.

The role of the scientist in defining or supporting research that involved ethical issues continues today with the modern-day Human Genome Project (HGP) (figure 13.3).

The Ethical, Legal, and Social Implications (ELSI) Research Program

Figure 13.3.   The Human Genome Project

> **The Human Genome Project** was launched in 1988. Dr. James Watson was the first director of the National Human Genome Research Institute. Watson and Francis Crick discovered the structure of DNA in 1953. One of Watson's first actions was to announce that 5% of the National Institutes of Health (NIH) funding would be allocated to the Ethical, Social, Legal Implications (ELSI) program of the National Center for Human Genome Research (NCHGR).

The National Human Genome Research Institute (NHGRI) was established in 1989 and the Ethical, Legal and Social Implications (ELSI) Research Program was established in 1990 as an integral part of the HGP. This program was organized to foster basic and applied research on the ethical, legal and social implications of genetic and genomic research for individuals, families, and communities. The ELSI Research Program funds and manages studies, and supports workshops, research consortia, and policy conferences related to these topics. (http://www.genome.gov/10001618)

The ELSI Program of the National Center for Human Genome Research (NCHGR) is receiving and sponsoring grants for approximately 5 percent of the total funds allocated for the HGP; thus the availability of the scientific data could far exceed the capacity to deal with the ethical, legal and social implications.

It is within the variability of genetic diversity and values assigned to the diversities that the major ethical, legal and social issues surface. As scientists probe deeper into the smallest units of genetic knowledge, it is apparent that the information cannot be fully understood except within the context of a value-based social construct. As identified by the NCHGR, the ethical, legal, and social implications include (NIH 1990, 2–3):

> . . . questions of fairness in the use of genetic information; the impact of genetic information on the individual; the privacy and confidentiality of genetic information; issues raised by the impact of the Human Genome Initiative on genetic counseling; issues raised by reproductive decisions influenced by genetic information, including questions of: the effect of genetic information on options available, the use of genetic information in the decision-making process; issues raised by the introduction of increased genetic information into mainstream medical practice; the uses and misuses of genetics in the past and their relevance to the current situation, e.g., the eugenics movement and the misuse of behavioral genetics to advance eugenics or prejudicial stereotypes; questions raised by the commercialization of the products from the Human Genome Initiative; conceptual and philosophical implications, such as the problems of determinism and reductionism, and the concepts of health and disease [particularly in view of the high rate of human genetic variability and the large numbers of people who will be found to have genetic vulnerabilities].

Allocating funds for ethical research was radical in that scientists would be supporting and/or participating in the ethics research, heretofore the domain of others—at universities or public policy centers. The grants that are sponsored by the HGP are designed to map and sequence the nucleotide base pairs of the human genome; develop an information system for collecting, storing, retrieving, analyzing, interpreting, and distributing the large amounts of data; sponsor research training; and examine the legal, ethical, and social implications of the HGP (HHS 1990). The HGP is an excellent example of research that requires both technical and ethical expertise.

Conferences sponsored by the scientific community have addressed the application of scientific knowledge from ethical and political perspectives (Engelhardt and Caplan 1987; Etzioni 1975), and although "ethical concerns are certainly not at the top of the worry list for most genomic mappers and researchers" (Davis 1990, p. 261), the commitment was made by the scientific community to fund research on the humanistic and ethical implications that might surface as a result of the scientific findings. The research funded by the ELSI program was separate from the research funded to learn more about the genetic code and the implications for testing and understanding disease.

Although the availability of the scientific data would far exceed the capacity to deal with the ethical, legal, and social implications, this was an important step in the right direction of involving the scientists in understanding the ethical implications of their research. As scientists probe deeper into the smallest units of genetic knowledge, it is apparent that the information cannot be fully understood except within the context of a value-based social construct (Harman 1994).

Ethical Principles and Research

There are several ethical principles that guide those participating in research activities for the methodologies and reporting of the outcomes of the research. These include autonomy, beneficence, nonmaleficence, justice, honesty, fidelity, sanctity, and caring and compassion.

There are four core ethical principles (Beauchamp and Childress 2001):

1. Respect for autonomy (self determination)
2. Beneficence (promoting good)
3. Nonmaleficence (doing no harm)
4. Justice (fairness)

In the research context, **autonomy** refers to the ability of the research participant to understand and authorize the research intervention. Participants need to understand informed consent and approve their participation in the research. This principle does not mean that the participant can control the outcomes of the research or what might happen to them as a result of the research. It does mean that they understand the risks and benefits of the research. This principle also addresses voluntariness: that an individual has control over what they decide to do with their body. They may decline participation in research without explanation.

Beneficence means that the research is intended to help build on the body of knowledge and result in ben-

efit, or the outcomes might help the research participant or future patients. For example, a pharmaceutical intervention might prove to be beneficial for helping or curing a disease. A person dying of cancer may not benefit from the research but may decide to participate in the hope that determining efficacy of the drug or treatment may help others. This ethical principle is often combined with **nonmaleficence**, which means that the intervention should not knowingly harm the participant. A drug study should expose a patient to a drug that could help (beneficence) but should not harm (nonmaleficence). See Figure 13.10 for a description of ethical problems related to beneficience, nonmaleficence, and integrity as it relates to the distribution of the drug Vioxx.

Justice refers to fairness. Are patients treated fairly in terms of enrollment in research studies or with fairness once in the study. It requires that no undue burden for participation be placed on any particular group (prisoners) or race (African-Americans) as a convenience to the researcher. For example, it has been argued that because many African-Americans have poor healthcare, they should be enrolled in clinical trials because a study may provide some healthcare. Clinical studies, though, cannot be substituted for healthcare. Treatment is not an outcome of a clinical study, and once the study is over, the subject does not receive follow-up care. This can hardly be construed as medical care or treatment.

Other Important Ethical Values

In addition to these core ethical principles, there are other values that are important in the context of research. These include honesty, sanctity, utility, and, caring and compassion. **Honesty** and truth-telling are essential to all ethical discourse. Researchers and those funding the research should tell the truth. Failure to tell the truth can involve lies of commission and omission. Truth-telling relates to the researcher revealing any conflicts of interests, such as the financial involvement, in the company testing the drug. Commission would involve intentionally reporting results that are not accurate, and problems with omission could involve failure to fully disclose results, such as potential harm to patients or suppression of unfavorable results. "Duties of **fidelity** are closely aligned with honesty and include keeping promises, honoring contracts and agreements, and telling the truth" (Mappes and Zematy 1991, 22). There is a duty to honor one's words to do something. Healthcare providers, HIM professionals, and researchers all have a duty to perform certain responsibilities, based on their professional roles, and these actions engage the principle of fidelity.

Some research or clinical processes are considered unethical based on the principle of **sanctity**, which supports that human life is holy or sacred (a gift from God) and that all humans have value. Based on this principle, some persons, with or without a faith tradition, would not support research that involves abortion or stem cell research.

Utility is another important ethical principle when applied to research and is involved with the usefulness of an act. "In utilitarianism, an act is right if it helps to bring about the best balance of benefits over burdens . . ." (Purtilo 1999, 48). The principle of utility is engaged when a researcher considers several alternative paths for the methodology or options for the subjects who could be included in the project, then this principle is engaged. There needs to be some assessment or intentionality about predicting the consequences of the research (even though there is no guarantee of those consequences). Examining utility helps researchers to determine if the study will lend itself to the greatest benefit and the least harm.

The principles of **caring and compassion** were introduced as a result of feminist-based research. Gender research has substantiated that the masculine perspective values the importance of self, competition and individualism and is based on the values of fairness, rights, and rules (Kohlberg 1981, 1984; Levinson 1978). Compassion, care, connection between self and others, with an ethic based on the moral imperative of caring for others, are described as important for the feminine perspective (Belenky et al. 1986; Gilligan 1982; Gilligan et al. 1988; Holmes and Purdy 1992; Larrabee 1993; Kittay and Meyers 1987; Lenz and Myerhoff 1985). The ethics of care support the importance of honesty and truth telling, the risks of deception, and failure to report accurate information. Current research needs both masculine and feminine values.

Health Information Management, Ethics, and Research

HIM professionals face many complex ethical challenges in their work environment (Harman 2006):

- The myriad of problems related to privacy and confidentiality
- Compliance, fraud, abuse, and clinical code selection and use

- Quality review outcomes
- The electronic health record (issues such as security, software implementation, and data resource management)
- e-Health (the quality and quantity of information that is made available for patients and issues related to equity and access)
- The protection of sensitive information (such as for adoption, genetic, or behavioral information)
- Management activities, such as, whether to fire an employee

The focus for this chapter is the ethical issues related to research, including problems with research design (Johns and Hardin 2006).

There are two primary reasons why HIM professionals should be concerned about the ethical problems related to research: There are clear and definite ethical obligations to protect patient privacy and confidential information and also to advance knowledge by facilitating the conduct of research. The ethical imperative to protect privacy was identified in the initial pledge of the profession written in 1934 (Huffman 1972, 135), and this ethical imperative continues to be essential to the AHIMA Code of Ethics (2004) (see appendix 13A, pp. 359–366). There are two principles in the 2004 Code that address the importance of these ethical imperatives, Principles I and V:

> *I. Advocate, uphold, and defend the individual's right to privacy and the doctrine of confidentiality in the use and disclosure of information.*
>
> *V. Advance health information management knowledge and practice through continuing education, research, publications, and presentations.*

Principle V is not limited to research conducted on behalf of the health information system and includes the larger scope of clinical research, which is the focus of this chapter. The 2004 Code states that the HIM professional should:

> Engage in evaluation or research that ensures the anonymity or confidentiality of participants and of the data obtained from them by following guidelines developed for the participants in consultation with appropriate Institutional Review Boards (IRBs). Report evaluation and research findings accurately and take steps to correct any errors later found in published data using standard publication methods.

HIM professionals always have had a strong moral voice for the ethical course of action, such as accurate coding, release of information, and assurance of accurate information and reliable interpretation of data. Despite the technical expertise involved in health informatics, it is an insufficient criterion when facing today's complex problems. Ethical expertise must guide the profession. It is important for health informatics professionals to be informed about the appropriate use of the 2004 AHIMA Code of Ethics, which can be used to guide ethical decision-making. It is also important for the health informatics professional to consult with their facility's ethics committee, and in the academic setting, the university's Institutional Review Board (IRB), discussed later in this chapter (Harman 2006, 15).

The health information professional must have knowledge of standards, value systems, and a commitment to interdisciplinary collaboration for effective engagement in ethical decision making. HIM professionals must engage researchers, clinicians, administrators, ethicists, lawyers, policy-makers, accreditation agencies, and patients. No law, accreditation standard, or policy response alone will solve ethical problems in research. In today's arena, health informatics professionals also must look to the ethical framework when considering the best course of action. The core ethical criterion is "what should I do?" This ethical question needs to be added to the list of common criteria for research, such as cost, regulation, policy, technological feasibility, and related issues. The dilemmas faced today require ethical collaboration from many disciplines and from many departments of the organization—informatics professionals cannot do this alone. (Harman 2006). The health information professional has an ethical responsibility to maintain and enhance professional, technical, and ethical competence.

A code of ethics for any profession provides both a public statement to those who might encounter a health information manager in a professional context, and a level of expectation that guides practice. Ethical codes for researchers may differ from professional codes because researchers are not involved in medical treatment. There are several codes that apply specifically to researchers. It is useful to review professional codes of ethics to ground one's thinking about ways to behave and ways to think about potential issues that may arise when assisting researchers with health care data.

The ethical obligation of the health information management (HIM) professional include the protection of patient privacy and confidential information. Core health information issues include what information should be collected, how the information should be handled, who should have access to the information, and under what conditions the information should be disclosed. (LaTour, 2006, p. 274)

Ethical obligations are central to the professional's responsibility, regardless of the employment site or the method of collection, storage, and security of health information. Health information ethical and professional values are based on the obligations to the patient, the healthcare team, the employer, the interests of the public, and oneself, one's peers, and one's professional associations. (Harmon, 1999)

A code of ethics cannot guarantee ethical behavior. Moreover a code of ethics cannot resolve all ethical issues or disputes or capture the richness and complexity involved in striving to make responsible choices within a moral community. Rather a code of ethics sets forth values and ethical principles, and offers ethical guidelines to which professionals aspire and by which their actions can be judged. Professional values could require a more comprehensive set of values than what an individual needs to be an ethical agent in their personal lives. (Harmon, 2006, p. 26)

In the context of conducting research or helping researchers obtain data, other codes may come into play including the Belmont Report, and local guidelines established by institutional review boards.

A code of ethics does not provide a set of rules that prescribe how to act in all situations. Specific applications of the code must take into account and evaluated in the context in which it is being considered and the possibility of conflicts among the code's values, principles, and guidelines. (Harmon, 2006, p 27)

One of the difficulties in the application of codes of ethics in a research context is that every research project is different and may include nuances that one hasn't encountered in the past. For that reason it is important that HIM professionals understand the differences between HIPAA in a patient care setting and a research setting. Institutional review boards and privacy boards provide HIPAA consent for human subjects and the language in the consent may differ from HIPAA authorizations in a medical treatment situation.

Other codes, the International Medical Informatics Association (IMIA) and the American Medical Informatics Association (AMIA) can also be accessed for guidance. See appendices 13A, 13B, and 13C (pp. 359–378) for the ethical codes of AHIMA, IMIA, AMIA.

Research Codes of Conduct

The National Institutes of Health (NIH) have been working for many years to create codes of conduct for researchers. There are various Web sites, manuals, guidelines, and other materials that direct researchers to help them understand ethical behavior when conducting research. The National Academy of Sciences (NAS) published the primary guide in 1994: *On Being A Scientist: Responsible Conduct In Research.* It is available in full text and may be reproduced without permission for educational purposes, indicating the universality of its statements. Most major research universities and institutions share this document with the research faculty and scientists. In addition, most universities have added to the document and created institutional codes of conduct, usually with sanctions for misconduct for the particular institution. Other materials can be found online at from the NIH's Web page, "Bioethics Resources on the Web" (2007a).

Human Subjects: Vulnerable Populations

Figure 13.4.   Tuskegee Syphilis Study

The Public Health Service funded a study, the **Tuskegee Syphilis Study,** 1932-1972, to evaluate the natural history of untreated syphilis in human beings. When the study was conceptualized, the basic concept was considered scientifically important and ethically justifiable because there was no known treatment for the disease. The research population included one of the most vulnerable research populations-approximately 300 mostly indigent African-American sharecroppers in Macon County, Alabama. The reality is that the subjects did not know that they were part of a research study designed to understand the natural progression of the disease. Many thought they were receiving beneficial medical care. Penicillin was discovered in 1928 and was available for mass distribution in 1945. The subjects were followed, untreated, many years after penicillin was known to cure syphilis. In fact, the trial continued until 1972.

Figure 13.5.   Willowbrook State School

Willowbrook State School was a state-sponsored institution for children with mental retardation. It was located in central Staten Island in New York City. Outbreaks of hepatitis were common. Between 1963 and 1966, healthy children were intentionally inoculated, orally and by injection, with the hepatitis virus. The children were then monitored to study the effects of gamma globulin for fighting the disease. The school stayed open for many more years, with many more problems, such as overcrowding, poor sanitary conditions, and physical and sexual abuse of residents by the school's staff. There was a class-action suit filed against the State of New York in 1972 but the last children did not leave the facility until September 17, 1987.

Figure 13.6.   The Holmesburg Prison Study

The Holmesburg Prison Study was a research project in the early 1950's through the mid 1970's, at Holmesburg Prison near Philadelphia, PA. It was designed to capitalize on vulnerabilities of prisoners. This vulnerability can generate multiple opportunities for the misuse of power. Pharmaceutical companies tested many of their products on the prisoners (drugs, chocolate, dioxin, tobacco, eye drops, psychotropic drugs, radioactive isotopes) and many others (Hornblum 1998, 2007). The participating prisoners were paid a lot of money, compared to the normal monies earned as a prisoner, and they got special privileges.

Clinical trials and other research projects involving humans are essential for the advancement of knowledge and the development of improved or new treatment options, such as new drugs or devices that can cure disease or assist patients. Research, by definition, is experimental and will not necessarily result in safe or effective treatments for the people who are involved in the research. Researchers, healthcare providers, and research participants can all walk on ethical "thin ice" as a result. Researchers are not perfect—they will make mistakes, exercise poor judgment, or take calculated risks that ultimately fail. Ethical problems focus on the intentionality of mistakes. Were data suppressed? Were negative results not reported? Did the researchers fail to get informed consent? Were patients harmed? These and other similar questions relate to intentionality.

The Tuskegee Syphilis Study (figure 13.4) was discontinued in 1972 after high-profile stories in the national media generated public outrage over the blatant exploitation of this vulnerable segment of society: poor, often illiterate, African-American men without access to healthcare.

The fact that the federal government directed the Tuskegee study over such a long period of time stained the integrity of the American research enterprise. It catalyzed passage of the National Research Act in 1974. In 1997, President William Clinton issued a formal apology to the subjects of the Tuskegee experiment, and some of the surviving men attended the ceremony.

See figure 13.5 for a summary of a case that involved another vulnerable population—children. There are several ethical issues that surface when trying to protect human subjects, including privacy and confidentiality, voluntary participation, informed consent, and the balance of risks and benefits. There are many issues to consider when including research participants in a study who may be identified as members of a vulnerable population.

Some additional examples of potential unethical behaviors might include the following:

- Approaching a pregnant woman when she is in labor and asking her to participate in a study about her attitude toward the services of the birthing center.

- Studying grown persons with Down syndrome who live in a group home. Are they considered independent? Can they make decisions about their medical care? Can they make informed decisions to participate in research?

- Studying illegal immigrants and asking them to retell their immigration story to begin to analyze differences between age groups.

One of the key issues when considering these study populations center on concerns related to the process and understanding of consent. Some of the issues that should be considered may include how the consent process will be carried out. Some issues to consider in the consent process include:

- Can a person in pain read a consent form and give consent that is voluntary?

- Is there a need for a verbal consent process? Can all potential participants read adequately to understand the consent form?

- Is there a need to reduce the reading level of the consent form?

- Should the consent form be translated in the native language of the potential subject?

- Is a native language speaker available during the study to translate and help the subject understand study processes?

- Should there be a legally authorized representative who would also participate in the study as a "translator"?

See appendix 13D (pp. 379–385) for a sample consent form.

Figure 13.7 explores ethical problems that surface when considering vulnerable populations in research. The list of issues is not all-inclusive and will vary depending on the type of study. It is important to note that vulnerable populations cannot be studied under an exemption certification. Studies that are exempt from review by the IRB are initially determined to be exempt by matching a series of criteria to the requirements to declare a study exempt. Exempt studies do not collect identifiable information and do not pose a risk to the subjects.

Protection of Human Subjects: International and National Initiatives

There always must be a balance between protecting humans involved in research studies with the potential benefit to those who may ultimately use a drug or device, if approved, and marketed. There have been several documents and laws that have contributed to the issue of protection of human subjects, including:

- The Nuremberg Code
- The Helsinki Agreement
- The National Research Act (Public Law 93-348) of 1974
- The Belmont Report
- Several bioethics commissions
- HIPAA

During WWII, atrocious human experiments were conducted by the Nazis in Germany. When these experiments were discovered, the allies developed the **Nuremberg Code.** One of the core principles in the code is the importance of voluntary consent. Another core principle is evaluating whether the research is morally acceptable. In addition to voluntary consent, any experiments involving human beings need to meet other criteria, such as:

- The degree of risk to be taken should never exceed that determined by the humanitarian importance of the problem to be solved by the experiment.

- The experiment should be so designed and based on the results of animal experimentation and knowledge of the natural history of the disease or other identified problems related to the disease so that the anticipated results will justify the performance of the experiment.

- The experiment should be so conducted as to avoid all unnecessary physical and mental suffering and injury.

Figure 13.7. Vulnerable populations

Vulnerable Populations	Issues to consider regarding consent and how attributes of the vulnerable population manifests itself in the consent process.
Children	Protected class of persons who cannot voluntarily consent without parental consent. Children may sign assent form depending on age; See Subpart D of Title 45, Part 46 of the Code of Federal Regulations contain the federal policy on research that involves children: http://ohrp.osophs.dhhs.gov/humansubjects/guidance/45cfr46.htm#subpartd
Cognitively Impaired Persons	Cognitive skills may vary on a day-to-day basis and therefore the ability to understand consent form and ongoing participation may change from week to week; ability to understand consent form may be permanently impaired; judgment and reasoning affected. Assessment must occur so that the investigator knows the condition of each participant. Sometimes assessment must occur each time subject is seen as part of the study. Sometimes a legally authorized surrogate is utilized when research studies include persons with cognitive impairment.
Comatose Persons	Cannot give consent; need appropriate and legally authorized surrogate. Some research with comatose persons could be considered emergency research. See the OHRP guidance from 1996 on this topic: http://www.hhs.gov/ohrp/humansubjects/guidance/hsdc97-01.htm
Drug Addicts	Involved in illegal activities; Certificate of Confidentiality should be considered. Information on Certificates of Confidentiality can be found at: http://grants.nih.gov/grants/policy/coc/ "Certificates of Confidentiality are issued by the National Institutes of Health (NIH) to protect identifiable research information from forced disclosure. They allow the investigator and others who have access to research records to refuse to disclose identifying information on research participants in any civil, criminal, administrative, legislative, or other proceeding, whether at the federal, state, or local level."
Economically Disadvantaged Persons	May agree to be involved in a study only for free medical care or for payment made for participation when it may not be in the best interests of the individual.
Elderly Persons	Cognition levels may vary during the course of the study. Is informed consent still valid throughout the research study?
Employees	May feel coerced by employer to participate. Sometimes lab staff are asked to be "normal subjects". There must not be any requirements of employment that coerce employees to participate if they don't want to.
Hearing-Impaired Persons	If a deaf person wishes to enroll in a study, how will the investigator make sure the consent process has been complete? It is not enough to have the consent form for the subject to read. How will questions be handled? How will future visits be handled? Does someone on the study staff know sign language? Note: The Deaf Pride movement may clash with the IRBs definitions of the hearing impaired and their ability to participate in research studies.
Institutionalized Persons	May not understand consent form, may be cognitively impaired, may not have autonomy, and may not be able to exercise free will (voluntariness).
Low Literacy Persons	May not understand the consent form
Minorities	Not all minorities are considered vulnerable populations. The context of the study, why minorities are included, whether they are the targeted focus of the study are factors that must be considered and may impact informed consent.
Non-English speaking Persons	Even though consent forms must be translated into the native language, without research staff that are fluent in the language, there is difficulty ascertaining whether non-English speaking participants truly understand their study involvement. How are participants informed, if they are illiterate in their native language?
Persons Involved in Illegal Activities	Could include: computer hackers, drug addicts, prostitutes, illegal immigrants, and other types of illegal activities. Collecting data from persons who are involved in illegal activities can be challenging. A foremost consideration must be that by signing a consent form, the subject is, in effect, agreeing to participate in a study about their illegal activities. Therefore the act of protecting subjects, making sure they understand their rights and explaining the study, and executing legally authorized consent may lead to disclosure and place the subject in more harm than non-participation would. Investigators need to carefully weigh what problems may be encountered if subjects are required to sign consent forms. It may be appropriate to ask for a waiver of written consent and employ the use of an information sheet for this type of research. A Certificate of Confidentiality may also be appropriate. See "Drug Addicts" for additional information on COC.
Pregnant Women, Fetuses, Neonates, In-Vitro	In some instances, pregnant women must be included as would any other population; in other instances special protections for pregnant woman must be in place. Investigators who plan to use Pregnant women, human fetuses, and neonates in research should be familiar with the government regulations described in 45 CFR 46. Subpart B. http://ohrp.osophs.dhhs.gov/humansubjects/guidance/45cfr46.htm#subpartb There are specific requirements for the wording in the consent form when using pregnant women in research. Problems with ethical research involving this population occur in "third world research" – promises of pregnancy care, if participate in research.
Prisoners	Do not have free will as they are incarcerated. Prisoners may feel coerced into participating because they think the authorities may grant them special privileges. May agree to participate because they think it will reduce their sentence, earn favors with guards; See Subpart C of Title 45, Part 46 of the Code of Federal Regulations containing the federal policy on research that involves prisoners: http://ohrp.osophs.dhhs.gov/humansubjects/guidance/45cfr46.htm#subpartc
Students (over the age of 18)	May feel coerced because they think their grade may be affected if they don't agree to participate. The professor is always in power position over the student. Usually have another option for participation. Grade cannot be affected by non-participation.

Note: Vulnerable populations cannot be studied under an exemption certification. Additional current ethical violations are online from AHRP (2007).

Source: Carol Nielsen. Reprinted with permission.

- During the course of the experiment the human subject should be at liberty to bring the experiment to an end for any reason including an unwillingness to come to the doctor's office, a desire to stop taking the study medication, or if he or she has reached the physical or mental state where continuation of the experiment seems to be impossible.

- During the course of the experiment the scientist in charge must be prepared to terminate the experiment at any stage, if there is probable cause to believe, in the exercise of the good faith, superior skill, and careful judgment required of him that a continuation of the experiment is likely to result in injury, disability, or death to the experimental subject.

The complete list of principles for human experimentation can be found in *Trials of War Criminals* 1949.

The **Helsinki Agreement,** an ethical code established in 1964 by the 18th World Medical Assembly, is designed to guide researchers beyond the Nuremberg Code. It differentiates between clinical/therapeutic research and nonclinical research, and it addresses problems with those who are legally incompetent and who need "proxy" representation (Mappes and DeGrazia 1996, 199-201).

The principles described in the next section were enacted as laws, and thus researchers can be prosecuted under the laws, although it has been a very rare occurrence.

The **National Research Act** (Public Law 93-348) of 1974 created the National Commission for the Protection of Human Subjects of Biomedical and Behavioral Research. The Commission was directed to consider (National Research Council 2005):

- The boundaries between biomedical and behavioral *research* and the accepted and routine *practice* of medicine

- The role of assessment of risk-benefit criteria in the determination of the appropriateness of research involving human subjects

- Appropriate guidelines for the selection of human subjects for participation in such research

- The nature and definition of informed consent in various research settings

The National Research Act codified the requirement that human subjects in research must be protected. It set the stage for the issuance of the another important set of principles, detailed in the Belmont Report.

The **Belmont Report** was written in 1979 by a commission established under the National Research Act. The Belmont Report focused on the basic ethical principles identified in the National Commission deliberations. Its three main principles include (OHSR 1979):

1. Respect for Persons, which involves recognition of the personal dignity and autonomy of individuals and special protection of those persons with diminished autonomy.

2. Beneficence, which entails an obligation to protect persons from harm by maximizing anticipated benefits and minimizing possible risks of harm.

3. Justice, which requires that the benefits and burdens of research be distributed fairly.

The United States government has established several **bioethics and privacy commissions** formed to specifically address issues related to privacy, electronic systems, and research. In 1972-1973, the Health Education and Welfare (HEW) secretary established the Advisory Committee on Automated Personal Data Systems. This was the first attempt to establish fair information practices for automated personal data systems.

In 1974, the National Commission for The Protection of Human Subjects of Biomedical and Behavioral Research was formed. This commission specifically focused on informed consent for children, prisoners, and the mentally disabled. The framework for establishing IRBs (discussed later in this chapter) was also specified by this commission. There were many precipitating forces for this commission. One of these was The Holmesburg Prison Study (figure 13.6).

Governmental and Institutional Oversight: Roles and Responsibilities

Federal regulations prescribe and guide all the processes of applying for, receiving, and accounting for funding from federal sponsors. Foundations and other sponsors have their own regulations that must be followed. Funding for research projects is rarely given directly to individual researchers. The institution (university, college, medical practice, not-for-profit organization) normally accepts the award and the terms of the funding on behalf of the researcher. The institution appoints someone who signs agreements for the university. This appointee agrees to monitor and enforce the terms of agreements. Investigators cannot sign the proposal submission cover sheet when submitting a proposal for funding, and they cannot sign the "notice of grant award" (NGA)—the official document that executes the agreement between the sponsoring agency and the institution. The signatures are those of the administrators representing the institution, such as the director of grants and contracts or the budget director.

The institution and the researchers are partners in ensuring that grant funding is expended in a manner appropriate to the agreements with the funding agency or sponsor. The fiduciary responsibilities that accompany the receipt of a sponsor's money require application of the highest standards of grantsmanship so that all monies are appropriately expended and accounted for. Grant agreements signed when funding is awarded provide guidance on how amendments to the budget must be submitted. Some changes in research protocols require formal amendments. Minor changes in the budget do not normally require contacting the funding agency, although the details of these transactions must be maintained and submitted upon request of the granting agency.

Grants and sponsored project offices assist researchers in understanding the terms of the grant award and in monitoring the expenses as the project is carried out. Institutions that have robust research programs and receive large amounts of external funding usually have research administration departments to assist investigators in identifying funding, interpreting sponsoring agency regulations, and in preparing proposals for submission. They also assist investigators in managing financial, reporting, and amendment requirements. When research projects are completed, the department assists in "close out" and helps make sure the appropriate reports are provided to the sponsor. Failure to adequately monitor and close out projects can have a negative impact on future funding. In this electronic era, federal agencies, in particular, use sophisticated electronic reporting systems, and it is easy to see when

a project has not been monitored adequately during the life of the funding. Such difficulties could affect future funding allocations.

Most institutions require researchers to participate in seminars about the responsible conduct of research. These training sessions now are required by the National Institutes of Health (NIH) and other agencies. Some institutions have designed their own seminars and others have borrowed from materials organized by NIH. Topics covered by the seminars include:

- publication and authorship
- intellectual property
- conflict of interest
- plagiarism and data fabrication
- misconduct reporting.

The Common Rule was created to reduce overlapping regulations and potentially conflicting regulations for human subjects regulations. The rule is an effort to ensure that humans subjects protections are applied uniformly in all government agencies. This rule restates in the federal regulations for 17 federal agencies whose regulations are promulgated through HHS. It does not apply to agencies who have not signed the agreement, such as the Department of Labor. The main elements of the Common Rule include (ORI n.d.):

- Requirements for ensuring compliance by research institutions
- Requirements for researchers' obtaining and documenting informed consent
- Requirements for Institutional Review Board (IRB) membership, function, operations, review of research, and record keeping.

The Common Rule includes additional protections for certain vulnerable research subjects.

- Subpart B provides additional protections for pregnant women, in vitro fertilization, and fetuses
- Subpart C contains additional protections for prisoners
- Subpart D does the same for children

An institution with a HHS Federal Wide Assurance agrees to apply HHS regulations to all research regardless of the funding source, including research that is internally funded and collaborative research across institutions.

In order to monitor the compliance with federal regulations, the government has set up an office that oversees the government's humans subjects protections program. The Office for Human Research Protections (OHRP) (http://www.hhs.gov/ohrp/)oversees the Federalwide Assurance application process, conducts site visits, and receives complaints from the public regarding research studies. For an idea of what kinds of issues they face, see the list of Compliance Oversight Investigations resulting in restrictions or actions to federally licensed institutions between 1990 and 2000 (OHRP n.d.). It is important to understand that compliance regulations do require a bureaucracy to support review of research activities, but as illustrated by the oversight investigations, there are real ethical breaches that mandate sanctions and intervention. For more information on ongoing investigations see the Web site supported by interested persons outside the government: http://www.ahrp.org/ethical/EthicalViolations.php (AHRP 2007).

The Institutional Review Board (IRB) and Bioethics Committee

The Institutional Review Board (IRB) provides review, oversight, guidance, and approval for research projects carried out by employees serving as researchers, regardless of the location of the research (such as a university or private research agency). The oversight is mandatory for research projects funded by federal agencies.

The IRB is responsible for protecting the rights and welfare of the human subjects involved in the research. Protection is afforded by a careful review of the submission packet, a discussion by board members of issues in conducting the study, requests to make changes to the project that afford additional safeguards for participants, and ongoing monitoring during the conduct of the study.

The role of the IRB is to review all research conducted at a particular institution that involves human subjects or data sources about human subjects (for example, medical records, tumor registry, and Medicare data). It also makes decisions regarding the proposed conduct of the study, the hypothesis, the number of par-

ticipants (statistical analysis), and the procedures for protecting the participants. The IRB takes into account the federal regulations that describe appropriate protections and the risk that may be involved in the study (45 CFR 46.109).

The IRB reviews all items submitted for the research proposal. The review must focus on reducing risk and increasing efficacy based on what is known at the time. Because research results in the creation of new knowledge, it may not be possible to accurately predict what might happen in a research study. The proposal must address risks and benefits with honesty. Risks include physical dangers, and violations of privacy or confidentiality. There must be ensurance of confidentiality and protection. For example, a research participant might be identified as a drug user or alcoholic for purposes of the research, and that information must be protected from subsequent, inappropriate disclosure.

The submission packet is the key component for review. Researchers assemble a packet of materials that includes a submission form from their particular institution, the protocol, the consent forms, and other materials relevant for a review. (See chapter 12.) Figure 13.8 is an example of a complete protocol that will aid in evaluating what may happen in a research study.

Federal and institutional regulations and policies require that all research involving human subjects be reviewed and approved by the IRB before study initiation. This is done to protect the rights and welfare of human subjects. Some smaller colleges and institutions that do not receive federal funds may not be as stringent as larger institutions. However, the current culture of compliance is that any research, whether externally funded or not, should be reviewed by the IRB. An IRB review will help the conduct of the study and should protect humans involved in research, regardless of the funding source.

There are three types of review that the IRB uses to evaluate studies. They are:

- full review
- expedited review
- exempt from review.

Full Review

Full review normally requires review by all members of the IRB. The study is presented to a quorum of IRB

Figure 13.8.   Key elements of a clinical research protocol

A clinical research protocol is the formal design or plan of an experiment or research activity. It is submitted to an Institutional Review Board (or funding agency for research support). The protocol includes a description of the research design or methodology, the eligibility requirements for prospective subjects and controls, the treatment regimen(s), and the proposed methods of analysis that will be performed on collected data.

A clinical research protocol should include the following:

1. Protocol title and date

   Name and address of principal investigator

   Site(s) where study will be performed

2. Background/Rationale/Literature Review: basis for doing the clinical research study

3. Hypothesis/Key Questions: the hypothesis being evaluated: the key questions being asked in the research study

4. Research Objectives and Purpose: an extension of the hypothesis/key questions, can be combined with them

5. Research Methods

   - Study Design (includes some or all of the following)
     - Primary and secondary endpoints
     - Type/design of the study (e.g., double-blind, placebo-controlled)
     - Measures taken to avoid/minimize bias (randomization, blinding)
     - Study treatments or interventions
     - Expected duration of subject participation; what is done and when
     - Stopping rules or discontinuation criteria
   - Selection and Withdrawal of Subjects
     - Inclusion criteria
     - Exclusion criteria
     - Withdrawal criteria
   - Efficacy Assessment
   - Safety Assessment – including recording adverse events
   - Statistical Analysis
     - Statistical methods including interim analysis if appropriate
     - Number of subjects to be enrolled
     - Rationale for choice of sample size (power calculation and clinical justification)
     - Level of significance to be used
     - Criteria for terminating the study
     - Procedures for reporting deviations from the original plan
     - Selection of subjects for inclusion in the analysis

6. Anticipated Results and Potential Pitfalls

7. Discussion of Next Steps

Source: Dr. Lewis J. Smith. Reprinted with permission.

members and may be discussed at length. All elements of the submission packet are reviewed. A primary reviewer system may be used by some IRBs, designating two persons to do a full analysis of the project. The primary reviewer system also encourages all board members to participate in the discussion.

Expedited Review

Expedited review is often considered a quick review, and it may mean that the researcher does not have to wait for an IRB meeting. There are procedures to fulfill fed-eral regulations, and changes that may be required as a result of the expedited review. Expedited reviews are carried out by the IRB chair or a designee. They are not conducted during an IRB meeting. Only projects that involve no more than minimal risk as defined by federal code may be reviewed in an expedited manner (45 CFR 46.110).

Exempt from Review

Projects that qualify as "exempt from review" must meet the requirements of exemption precisely. There are six categories that researchers use as a mirror to assess if their project might be exempt from review (CFR 46.101(b)):

1. Research conducted in educational settings, involving normal educational practices.

2. Research involving the use of educational tests (cognitive, diagnostic, aptitude, achievement), survey procedures, interview procedures or observation of public behavior.

3. Research involving the activities in category 2 and the human subjects are elected or appointed public officials or candidates for public office.

4. Research involving the collection or study of existing data, documents, records, pathological specimens, or diagnostic specimens.

5. Reserved for Federal Government Research: Not available for local IRB Exemptions.

6. Taste and food quality evaluation and consumer acceptance studies.

Investigators cannot determine on their own that a project is exempt. They must submit a packet describing the study and wait for the IRB's approval of the study as exempt. IRB exemptions usually are determined by the board chair or another designated representative. Some institutions require resubmission on a yearly basis to renew the exemption. This is a good idea for a study that will last a long time. Studies can change over time, and it is prudent to have a review after a year, even for an exempt study, as something may have arisen in the study that ultimately changes the review type.

Documentation and Resources

Many academic medical centers, health systems, and hospital IRBs have extensive Web sites explaining the rules for researchers and provide a Frequently Asked Questions (FAQ) page. Since implementation of the law (45 CFR 46 Title 45 Code of Federal Regulations Part 46 Protection of Human Subjects), (http://www.hhs.gov/ohrp/humansubjects/guidance/statute.htm), great progress has been made in synthesizing the massive amount of information and providing understandable documentation. IRBs have local authority, and therefore each IRB must create and make available required documentation and procedures for the local institution they are serving. For example, requirements

for consent forms would include the need to provide information to research participants in an understandable and manageable format, and a large enough font to make reading the text easy. These are examples of the guidance that the IRB's documentation provides so as to avoid unethical behaviors. The IRBs rules and documentation provide guidance so that researchers will create appropriate and legal consent forms. IRBs usually have specific requirements for consent forms regarding the format, content, and reading level, and may reject proposals based on the investigator's inability to follow the requirements.

The institutional culture and the support of deans and vice presidents in response to human subject regulations have an enormous impact on the attitude of researchers. There are complex documents and time-consuming procedures to uphold the regulations that must be in place in order to create an ethical climate for research. Institutions that support a human subjects protections program with a "wink and a nod" make it difficult for IRB staff and signal the possibilities for difficulties down the road. Difficulties could come to light during an audit or an inspection by the Food and Drug Administration (FDA). A serious culture of compliance recognizes that a middle ground must be sought to protect human participants in research. All members of an institution's research community must be serious advocates for the rights of patients and must uphold the ethical guidance outlined in the law.

Whenever possible, a health informatics professional should be a member of the IRB, thus provide the important perspective of health information management (HIM) in its deliberations. The HIM professional's participation can reinforce the importance of privacy, the need to uphold HIPAA and the ethical complexities involved in the collection and use of patient information.

Bioethics Committees

Bioethics committees have a different function from IRBs but may assist in oversight and considerations regarding research. Members can include ethicists, physicians and other healthcare providers, clergy, administrators, patients, and patient advocacy representatives. Normally, bioethics committees provide guidance and education in patient cared receiving medical treatment. They also may provide policies related to clinical ethical issues, such as advanced directives, the withdrawal of life support, and end-of-life decisions. According to Harman (2006, 15):

> Although facility-wide ethics committees typically deal with clinical bioethical decisions, the members of these committees are experts who are well positioned to help create the arguments and counterarguments for HIM issues such as release of the information, sharing data in relational databases, dealing with fraud and abuse issues, and analyzing issues related to problems with computerized software and security.

HIM professionals need to take ethical issues that arise in the treatment setting or in research settings to these committees so that there can be institutional and collaborative support for the decisions that are made.

Health Insurance Portability and Accountability Act (HIPAA)

HIM professionals are very familiar with the Health Insurance Portability and Accountability Act (HIPAA) of 1996, including the regulations and the processes and forms required to uphold the law. When this legislation was passed, the use of personal health information (PHI) was not as important to researchers as it is today. Prior to HIPAA, researchers routinely conducted retrospective medical record reviews without getting the patient's informed consent for access to the information. They often did not notify the patient that the information in their medical records might be included in research projects. It was common that researchers could ask the medical record department for patient records with a particular diagnosis or status, use those records to gather a sample, and analyze the contents of the medical record without patient authorization. Medical students frequently were assigned small research projects involving medical record reviews.

The deadline for compliance with the regulations, commonly referred to as the Privacy Rule, was April 14, 2003. As the deadline for compliance approached, there was concern about how researchers would uphold the law. Because a researcher is not a covered entity (CE), it was obvious that relationships among medical practices or hospitals and the individual researcher would need to be defined. With little guidance, IRBs drafted HIPAA release documents, including authorization documents. IRBs also established processes to ensure compliance.

With the implementation of the Privacy Rule, a new layer of documentation, forms, and processes was added to the existing consent process. In some instances, IRBs added HIPAA information to the consent form itself. There was some despair and handwringing among researchers that prospective research subjects could not possibly review an additional three to five pages of HIPAA language. Researchers felt that patients would not sit through the review of a long consent form in addition to pages of HIPAA information. They were concerned they could not meet study enrollment goals if patients became weary of the many forms that would need to be reviewed, read, and signed prior to entering a study.

For the research participant, HIPAA consent and documentation requires many additional pages of information to review during the consent process. When the Privacy Rule was implemented, there was a movement among IRBs and the federal Office for Human Research Protections offering guidance on how to simplify consent forms by shortening the length, using less-complicated language, and providing clear headers for the various sections of the consent form. The concern remains that a participant in a research study may be overwhelmed with paper and may have difficulty differentiating between the information provided about the study and information about the Privacy Rule.

As institutions became more comfortable with the new rules, some CEs established privacy boards to handle specific data requests. Privacy boards focus on waivers and alterations to authorization requirements for use and disclosure of PHI for a research study. Privacy boards do not have the power or authority granted under federal laws related to the protection of human subjects. Privacy board membership may not meet the same requirements as those for IRBs, and privacy boards usually do not create authorization forms. In effect, their sole focus is to reduce the amount of time IRBs must spend on deliberations regarding use of PHI. Though it may seem cumbersome to have yet another board overseeing researchers, the difficulties of overloaded IRBs is well documented in the literature (IOM 2001).

Researchers should be able to find guidance on their institution's Web site that explains whether a privacy board exists and what the procedures are for applying for waivers and alterations. If a privacy board does not exist, the IRB will handle review and approval of HIPAA requirements as part of the standard IRB application process (Center for Advanced Study 2003).

Department of Health and Human Services and National Institutes of Health

HHS is the administrative home of the NIH, the primary federal agency that sponsors medical and biologic research. In addition to sponsoring the research of other scientists, NIH research laboratories conduct innovative and cutting-edge research in support of both public health, and the scientific/academic and medical/biologic research agenda. Since 1887, the NIH has evolved from a one-room, one-person laboratory to the largest medical research organization in the world (NIH 2008):

> The NIH traces its roots to 1887, when a one-room laboratory was created within the Marine Hospital Service (MHS), predecessor agency to the U.S. Public Health Service (PHS). The MHS had been established in 1798 to provide for the medical care of merchant seamen. One clerk in the Treasury Department collected twenty cents per month from the wages of each seaman to cover costs at a series of contract hospitals. In the 1880s, the MHS had been charged by Congress with examining passengers on arriving ships for clinical signs of infectious diseases, especially for the dreaded diseases cholera and yellow fever, in order to prevent epidemics. During the 1870s and 1880s, moreover, scientists in Europe presented compelling evidence that microscopic organisms were the causes of several infectious diseases. In 1884, for example, Koch described a comma-shaped bacterium as the cause of cholera.

NIH's distinguished record of research is illustrated by the fact that more than 80 scientists have received Nobel Prizes based on the NIH-funded projects (Shilts 1987, pp. 288-298). NIH now supports 28 institutes, centers, and programs. The budget of over $28 billion is calculated at a cost of more than $90 for every American citizen. Though scientists would like more, this expenditure represents great progress in cancer research, reducing the leading cause of death—heart related illness—and addressing medical problems from AIDS to diabetes (NIH n.d., NIH 2007b).

NIH is headquartered in Bethesda, Maryland. It has more than 18,000 employees on the main campus and at satellite sites across the country. With taxpayer support, the NIH annually currently invests more than $28 billion in medical research. More than 83 percent of the NIH's funding is awarded through almost 50,000 competitive grants to more than 325,000 researchers at more than 3,000 universities, medical schools, and other research institutions in every state and around the world. About 10 percent of the NIH's budget supports projects conducted by nearly 6,000 scientists in its own laboratories, most of which are at the headquarters (NIH 2007c).

Though originally focused primarily on public health, contagious and infectious disease, NIH now supports all areas of medical research. As national healthcare agendas have evolved over the years, the focus of the NIH has responded to those changes. During WWII, the primary focus of the NIH research was on war-related injury and illness. After the war, cancer became a focus and has continued to be a focus of research. In 1981 when AIDS emerged as a serious potential epidemic, it took awhile to realize the potential danger of the epidemic, but eventually resources were redirected to begin to address the problem. Congress held hearings to determine whether new funds should be allocated to address AIDS research or whether existing funds should be redirected.

The National Library of Medicine, one of the NIH programs, is the world's largest medical library. It assists in standard setting for terminology development, biomedical communications, and the development of bioinformatics.

Ethical Research Problems

Figure 13.9.   The Tearoom Trade Study

The **TeaRoom Trade Study** was a controversial sociological doctoral dissertation research project that examined the sexual behavior of men in public restrooms. The doctoral student pretended that he was gay and that he was a lookout for the police. He then confirmed that the men had engaged in a homosexual act and then recorded their license plates. Based on this information, he was able to get additional contact information from the Bureau of Motor Vehicles. He subsequently disguised himself and interviewed the men in their homes by pretending that he has conducting a social health survey. When the results were published, some of these men, who were socially prominent and had families, were able to be identified.

In addition to the ethical issues previously discussed, such as adherence to ethical principles and values, and the protection of human subjects and vulnerable populations, several other aspects must be considered. These include informed consent, integrity in research, publication of the results, conflict of interest, research without clinical benefit, and bias.

Informed Consent

The Tearoom Trade Study (figure 13.9) violated the principles of autonomy, informed consent, and the right to privacy. It also raised the issue of the unethical behavior of deception (Citro, Ilgen, and Marrett 2003). Did the end justify the means? Was the knowledge acquired about the behaviors of homosexual men more important than the protection of privacy? This study helped frame the importance of informed consent, the unacceptability of deception (researchers cannot waive the consent of the participants), the risks of the researcher acting as an "insider" and potentially influencing the results of the research, as a result and, the problems with the invasion of privacy for the research participants.

Informed consent is defined by 45CFR46.116. In the regulation, eight primary elements of consent are described. The eight primary elements that must be a part of the informed consent are:

1. A statement that the study involves research, an explanation of the purposes of the research and the expected duration of the subject's participation, a description of the procedures to be followed, and identification of any procedures which are experimental

2. A description of any reasonably foreseeable risks or discomforts to the subject

3. A description of any benefits to the subject or others which may reasonably be expected from the research

4. A disclosure of appropriate alternative procedures or courses of treatment, if any, that might be advantageous to the subject

5. A statement describing the extent, if any, to which confidentiality of records identifying the subject will be maintained

6. For research involving more than minimal risk, an explanation as to whether any compensation and an explanation as to whether any medical treatments are available if injury occurs and, if so, what they consist of, or where further information may be obtained

7. An explanation of whom to contact for answers to pertinent questions about the research and research subjects' rights, and whom to contact

in the event of a research related injury to the subject

8. A statement that participation is voluntary, refusal to participate will involve no penalty or loss of benefits to which the subject is otherwise entitled, and the subject may discontinue participation at any time without penalty or loss of benefits to which the subject is otherwise entitled

Additional points that may be addressed in a consent form include issues with vulnerable populations (figure 13.6, p. 340), the right of the patient to withdraw from the study, and potential costs for the person participating in the study. These elements of consent have been in effect in since 1996.

It would be difficult to turn the elements of consent into a readable form that covers all the procedures, confidentiality issues, and other information and rights afforded the study participant. Most IRBs provide a template prescribing the language and the order of the elements to be included in the consent form. This makes it easier for researchers to prepare readable and comprehensive consent forms. It also provides the IRB with a model to ensure that their consent templates include all the federally required elements. However, the exact wording and order of presentation of the eight elements above are left to the discretion of the individual IRB. Therefore, each IRB, of which there are more than 3000 in the U.S., has its own unique style and language for informed consent. The IRB also may add language that pertains to their institution, and that addresses liability and disclosure.

A consent form must be understandable by the prospective participant. Many IRBs require the consent form to be written between a sixth and eighth grade reading level. Word processing programs can analyze word counts and evaluate the reading level of consent forms. Some IRBs also have a list of words that are suggested to simplify descriptions in the consent form.

Stanford University developed a glossary of simplified medical terms that is the industry standard (2006). It is used by most IRBs. IRBs have difficulty maintaining low readability standards. Often the legal language required in a consent form raises the readability level considerably. If the legal language about confidentiality is removed, often the reading level will drop (Paasche-Orlow et al. 2003).

The consent form is a legal document, and as such it is reasonable that institutions have some concerns that the form provides appropriate protection of the institution's risk. Clinical trials are usually sponsored by pharmaceutical companies, and the company may prescribe particular language to be included in the consent form.

Many IRBs resist a company's recommended language, and often the IRB will not automatically include it. The language may favor the company and not the patient. It may request access to a participant's complete medical record, access to their medical record after the study is completed, or use of blood or tissue samples beyond the study itself. With the implementation of HIPAA, these issues have increased concern about storing samples interminably, access to medical history during the trial, and continued access to medical history after the trial concludes.

It is common practice that an institution's legal department reviews the consent form template. Generally, lawyers are not involved in the review of individual consent forms, other than the review of the template itself. This indicates the great level of trust under which an IRB operates. Recently, IRBs have been named as defendants in some court cases where a research study or clinical trial involved the death of a study participant. If this occurs with more frequency, lawyers may become more involved in the IRB process.

Another reason for template language in a consent form is that the volume of protocols reviewed in a busy academic medical center requires that certain clauses be inserted without changes to help speed the review process.

"A Process, Not a Form"

For many years, researchers and IRBs simply prepared the consent form, presented it to the potential study subject, and then requested a signature. In the late 1990s, events unfolded in the research community that led to great scrutiny of clinical trials. In using human beings as research subjects, it became clear that merely presenting the consent form was an inadequate approach. Many professionals in the IRB community coined the phrase, "a process not a form."

This phrase is used when IRB staff train researchers in the procedures for submitting proposals to the IRB. Researchers rightfully asked, what is the process; how does one obtain consent? Is it only presenting a consent form and asking the potential participant to sign it? The

Path to Consent (appendices 13E and 13F pp. 386–389) outlines all possible steps that could be included, which depend upon the simplicity or complexity of a study. If the study lasts for only a month or so, or does not involve testing drugs or procedures that involve genetic testing, the path might be relatively short and simple. Research involving stem cells, genetics, cancer, and other currently controversial topics in medical research may mean that a person is involved in a study for several years. The path to consent must include all the years of follow-up, tissue banking, or reviewing medical records.

Consent can be considered complete only when all the information relevant to the study has been explained and there has been an assessment that the potential subject understands what will happen and what the risks are in participating. For many years, that explanation took the form of many pages describing the study, the risks, confidentiality clauses and other information within the eight elements listed earlier in this chapter. Informed consent takes place after the process is complete, not just when a signature is obtained. HIPAA requirements complicated the consent forms. Some might argue that virtually none of the consent forms constitute "informed consent" given the large number of pages of a vast amount of detail.

It is important that investigators have a consent process in mind. A flow chart using The Path to Consent can assist in establishing the process. (See appendices 13E and 13F pp. 387–389). All study staff involved in the consent process must have a concept of what will happen from initially approaching the potential study subject until the end of the study. Because consent is more than the process of simply presenting the form to the prospective subject and getting a signature, all research staff need to understand and use a complete process that reflects most of the steps listed above.

All research, even research determined to be exempt from review, should provide a consent form or an information sheet for the prospective study participant. The researcher has a symbiotic relationship with the participant and should recognize their obligation to provide adequate information on the study. Participants give their time, their private information, and possibly their body for the benefit of the research project. Researchers who are blasé in their obligations to the participant are not honoring the covenant of disclosure, "do not harm" clause, are not managing risk, and the need to explain as much as is known about potential side effects and the processes of the study. Because not all researchers are physicians, the ethical principles outlined previously are directed toward anyone who conducts research using human subjects. Therefore, though the "do not harm" principle seems to stem from a medical perspective (for example The Hippocratic Oath) actually any researcher; social scientist, psychologist, economist, or health information manager must be guided by the principle of not causing harm to research subjects.

Understanding

Readability and the general consent process is discussed above, but can be summarized by posing several questions:

- What do the study participants understand about the research?
- Do the study participants understand the potential risks and benefits?
- Do the patients know what their rights are?
- Do they know that they can withdraw from the research study at any time?
- Do they know they can withdraw data or tissue samples?
- Finally, do the participants understand their responsibilities in participating in the trial?

Voluntariness

Informed consent involves the concept of voluntariness. The study participants have the right to make a choice regarding participation in a research study without coercion. Coercion can be very subtle and may not be recognized by the patient. Some ethics experts are of the opinion that physicians should not refer their own patients to a study. This would constitute a conflict of interest in that as a principal investigator (PI), enrollment may have an impact on how much funding is provided for the PI to conduct the trial.

Physicians can amplify the voluntary nature of consent by providing sufficient time for patients to review the consent form, highlighting the sections of the consent form that describe risk, and encouraging the participant to ask questions.

Disclosure

Consent forms must disclose what is known about the effects of the medication, procedure, or device. The forms should carefully describe the potential risks and benefits. In addition, disclosure must cover any conflicts of interest the PI has in relation to the funding or the drug discovery process (Weiss 2007; Guterman 2007).

Competence

Competence is the ability of the participant to make decisions about whether or not to enroll in a research study. It is difficult to declare a specific set of attributes that indicates competence or incompetence. The decisions made by vulnerable populations are inherently affected by the particular condition that may classify them as vulnerable. For example, a person who is marginally literate may not have adequate literacy skills or a knowledge base to make informed decisions about enrolling in a clinical trial. The marginally literate person is also challenged by receiving a consent form in writing and not having the reading skills to navigate the form, the intent, and the often legalistic language. For a list of some of the challenges that apply to vulnerable populations see figure 13.6. A person with mild dementia may not remember from one day to the next what decisions they made. A disabled person may be able bodied and fully capable of making decisions, yet may be regarded within the culture as not competent. Decision making is not a clear-cut path. Courts do declare persons mentally incompetent and then the person who has healthcare power of attorney can make decisions for the incompetent person. (Beauchamp and Childress 1994, pp. 163–170). If a person is not mentally competent and yet involved in a research study, a surrogate may be involved in signing the consent form and interpreting the study to the individual. It would be unusual for a research project to proceed without having patients sign an informed consent. Ethical problems can surface when the typeface is too small for patients to read, or when medical language is used instead of "layman's terms" (Helbig 2006, 604).

Integrity

Figure 13.10.   The deceptive marketing of Vioxx

Vioxx was developed to treat arthritis and acute pain. It was aggressively and deceptively marketed and resulted in huge profits for Merck. Although medical experts had raised some concerns about the safety of this drug and the cardiovascular risks, Merck suppressed this information. The House Committee on Government Reform uncovered Vioxx documents instructing Merck's salesforce to lie to doctors about the cardiovascular risk posed by Vioxx, even though the early research results indicated risk for those who would take the drug for extended periods of time. Merck was considered to be one of the most ethical and profitable companies until this problem occurred.

Instead of drug marketing "detailers" being neutral, the tactics that pharmaceutical company Merck used with physicians can be considered aggressive. Merck told physicians that Vioxx would protect the heart. Though the initial focus of the drug was to relieve symptoms of arthritis, it was thought that protection of the heart would also result from taking the drug. (See figure 13.10.) In fact, trials conducted after the drug was released indicated that heart attacks, strokes, and deaths did occur (more than 55,000). Merck's internal study demonstrated the risks. Widespread advertisements for patients promised that this drug would reduce pain. This ethical problem was exacerbated when physicians who raised concerns were given grants and offered positions as consultants, which effectively "silenced" them.

Vioxx was recalled only after the pharmaceutical company had earned a profit of $2 billion in sales in only two years. The marketing to both the physicians and the patients lacked integrity. This historically ethical and profitable company seriously tarnished its reputation. This incident cost the firm billions in sales and legal fees, and lowered its stock value. This case illustrates that when profit trumps ethics, integrity suffers. Healthcare providers cannot give accurate information to their patients if the information that they are given is not accurate.

Some would argue that the medical research community and its self-regulating system is dysfunctional because it fails to protect the public from hazardous drugs and medical procedures. Another argument would be that the system taints the credibility of the scientific literature with fraudulently manipulated findings (AHRP 2005; Matthews 2004). Is the phrase "business ethics" an oxymoron in the context of profit? Can the company follow moral and ethical principles in the context of financial profits?

The Vioxx Study raised issues of suppression of results, and dishonesty to physicians and the public (AHRP 2007). Ethical action requires adherence to the ethical principle of integrity when reporting research outcomes. Ethical research violations still occur even though there are standards and codes, including The Nuremberg Code, The Belmont Report, and the Federal Policy for Protection of Human Subjects (45 CFR 46)

Publication of Accurate Results

Science has an ethical imperative to publish research that reflects the truth, even if the results are not what is expected. Chan et al. (2004) examined 100 clinical trials and the published reports of the findings. The analysis showed that the system of testing and reporting about drugs and surgical procedures has been corrupted by pharmaceutical industry influence. Even those studies that were not directly funded by pharmaceutical companies were found to be biased. That is because the scientists conducting these trials often have ongoing financial ties to drug companies. The research indicated that harmful outcomes were incompletely recorded, and 62 percent of trials changed, introduced, or omitted at least one primary outcome (Chan et al. 2004; Matthews 2004).

Conflict of Interest

Figure 13.11.   The Jesse Gelsinger Case

Jesse Gelsinger had an inherited metabolic disorder which was the result of a faulty gene. It caused him serious complications as a child but was well controlled with medication. The disorder sometimes was fatal in infants and small children. His family was approached to see if they would agree to allow Jesse to participate in a gene therapy trial when Jesse was 17 years old. His parents decided not to allow his participation. Jesse waited until he was 18 years old—the age of legal consent. At that time, he decided on his own to enroll in the trial. He had the altruistic hope that maybe his participation could help others afflicted with the same disorder. The gene therapy trial involved injecting adenoviruses carrying a corrected gene into Jesse. He received the initial injections on a Monday in September 1999 and was dead by Friday.

The Jesse Gelsinger Case (figure 13.11) was the first publicly reported case of a death in a gene therapy clinical trial. The case resulted in an FDA investigation. Additionally, Gelsinger's father, Paul, filed a lawsuit against the researchers. This case was a landmark in the history of human subject protections primarily because it resulted in the death of an 18-year-old man who was managing his illness with medication. This case was further complicated by the investigator's conflict of interest in that he stood to gain financially if the gene therapy proved to be successful. This example of serious ethical lapses occurred after federal laws were in place. In 1999 universities and hospitals supposedly had fully functioning IRBs, responsible conduct of research training, and oversight programs to protect human subjects. The news rippled through the ethics committee community and intensified discussions regarding ethical treatment of human subjects. These conversations are still occurring.

The outcome of the settlement with Paul Gelsinger, the investigators, and the University of Pennyslvania were confidential; thus, the public was not made aware of what admissions or financial penalties were realized.

In the review of the case, the FDA determined that the researcher in the trial breached ethical principals for human subjects by including Jesse Gelsinger as a substitute for another participate who dropped out. There were several issues for this case that exacerbated the conflict of interest. Jesse Gelsinger had a lab reading that should have excluded him from the study. The researcher failed to report adequately on two patients who already had experienced serious side effects from the treatment. The consent form failed to describe adequately that monkeys given a similar treatment had died. The researcher had a financial interest in the development of the drug used in the trial and if the research was successful, the researcher stood to gain financially from the success. As a result, Jesse Gelsinger was not fully informed of the risks.

This case has affected researchers, IRB staff, and those interested in the protection of human subjects. Not only was the participant young, but he also had his illness under control. Participation in a Phase I clinical trial such as this one is a risky decision. The question exists as to whether an 18-year-old—even though he was at the age of consent—has adequate information and judgment skills to make such decisions.

Paul Gelsinger was very vocal and instrumental in exposing issues related to the case. His work on behalf of other human subjects makes an important contribution for those who are enrolled in clinical trials. Paul Gelsinger went on to work for CIRCARE—Citizens for Responsible Care and Research, an organization devoted to monitoring and detecting abuses in human subjects research (CIRCARE 2007). Accounts of the Gelsinger case are available from Stolberg (1999) and Lehrer (2000).

Research Without Clinical Benefit

Figure 13.12. Human radiation experiments

Between 1944 and 1974, several thousand **human radiation experiments** were conducted by the federal government. In addition, radiation was intentionally released into the environment for research purposes. Over 200 witnesses were interviewed, as well as professionals who were familiar with the experiments and the Ethics Oral History Project captured how research with human subjects was conducted, as told from perspective of prominent physicians.

On January 15, 1994, President Clinton appointed the Advisory Committee on Human Radiation Experiments to investigate reports of possibly unethical experiments funded by the government decades earlier (figure 13.12). Some of the cases compiled involved:

- Experiments with plutonium and other materials used in building atomic bombs: The Atomic Energy Commission's program of radioisotope distribution
- Nontherapeutic research on children
- Total body irradiation
- Research on prisoners
- Human experimentation in connection with nuclear weapons testing
- Intentional environmental releases of radiation
- Observational research involving uranium miners and residents of the Marshall Islands

These studies raised issues of role clarification and the conflict of interest individual for physician researchers. The study lacked informed consent regarding the risks of exposure to radioisotopes, and lacked fairness in the selection of subjects. An additional major ethical breach was that the subjects would also not derive clinical benefit from these experiments (DOE n.d.).

Bias

The following hypothetical case presents the issue of research bias (Fowler 1988, as quoted in Johns and Hardin 2006, 176):

> A research specialist (RS) has been asked to construct a survey instrument to obtain data about how patients feel after receiving a certain treatment modality. The RS designs a three-point ordinal with the rating categories of good, fair, and poor. The principal investigator of the study asks the research analyst to change the scale from a three-point to a five-point scale, with the categories of excellent, very good, good, fair, and poor.
>
> The RS can see that adding excellent and very good does not just break up the good category into three categories. Rather, it changes the whole sense of the scale, because people respond not only to the words in the scale, but also to their placement on the scale. The word fair is now on the

negative side of the scale. Thus, one would expect considerably more people to give a rating of good or better with the five-point scale than with the three-point one.

Technological applications, available through the Internet or electronic systems, facilitate tracking individuals. This also can create problems related to privacy and data integrity. The advances in health information technologies have intensified the ethical challenges in research and decision support. It is important that HIM professionals meet their ethical responsibilities with regard to ensuring data integrity and confidentiality, especially in relation to HIPAA (Johns and Hardin 2006).

Emerging Issues: Misuse of Information and Information Technology

As research increases knowledge and the availability of sophisticated, widespread technology, several ethical issues are emerging, including problems with centralization of data; high-level data mining tools; misuse of sophisticated analytical tools; and utilization of Internet resources.

Science and technology have joined to make possible health products, treatments, and software to store and replicate huge amounts of information. Examples related to the Human Genome Project, aggregated databases, HIPAA, emerging technology (such as geographical positioning systems [GPSs]) and the Internet will be explored.

Availability of information

As discussed previously, the Human Genome Project, which is being researched on a global level, is generating information that will be stored in health information systems. The availability of the information far precedes the ability to deal with the implications from legal, social, and ethical perspectives. As is usually the case, the law lags behind technological developments. The ability to isolate stem cells and the complexities of the EHR (although different in focus) have caused much debate in the medical and ethics community. The opportunities for misuse of information

are tremendous. Can information be protected across the continuum of shared databases and integrated systems and in the context of sophisticated technological interventions?

Large data sets and aggregated health records create ethical dilemmas. The argument can be made that the information collected and used in health information exchanges can only provide meaningful data if many identifiable data elements are included. Do patients who agree to have their data aggregated understand how many transfers may take place as data sets are combined and recombined?

HIPAA, Research, and Census Data

Even with HIPAA, information about a person's prescription data can be gathered from physicians without the patient's knowledge. Data is gathered through data mining techniques, often unknown to the prescribing physician.

The National Physicians Alliance is an organization focused on these complex and serious ethical issues (NPA n.d.). Loss of privacy is an issue that some patients worry about when they agree to share medical records for research purposes. How long will the records be accessed? Might data be compromised if it was not correctly deidentified? If identifiable healthcare data is combined with census data is it possible to identify a person's address and house?

GPS makes it possible to pinpoint and correlate a particular household with census data. Because census data is in the public domain, such techniques could provide private information to a researcher without the knowledge of the person.

The Internet

A notable 1993 *New Yorker* cartoon by Peter Steiner depicts a dog on a chair in front of a computer talking to another dog sitting on the floor. The dog in the front of the computer says, "On the Internet nobody knows you are a dog." This is an example of the difficulty that researchers face when trying to obtain legally informed consent. Who is answering the questions? How does the researcher know if the person is of legal age to give consent? What are the implications of information sharing on the Internet? Do patients begin to understand who they are sharing their health information with? Do they understand that the researchers might share the information collected and who they will share it with? With the massive explosion of the Internet, some social scientists have developed research projects that explore its use.

Issues related to informed consent and the Internet are widely discussed by ethicists. While some IRBs allow Internet research to move forward without consent, or with a process of passive consent, questions regarding data validity come into question. If the sample does not accurately reflect the population because identities can be hidden or altered by Internet users, does the researcher really know who is answering questions in a survey?

Web sites leave tracks on computers that indicate the behavior of users. They leave evidence of what sites persons have viewed. They could be in the form of cookies. Access to the computer would give private knowledge. Cookies allow anyone on the Internet to identify who has looked at a particular Web site. A person's privacy is invaded by capturing this knowledge.

Many Internet users are aware of the use of "cookies" by marketing organizations and others who want to know which computer has visited a particular site. This data gathering without the express consent and sometimes without even the knowledge of the user is an issue in that technology allows the identification of the "computer address." People's surfing habits can be documented. Many people when surfing the Internet may have limited understanding that information may be gathered from their activities.

Uses of data and the creation of new data by applying technological innovation raise new ethical issues for researchers. For example, a new technology under consideration by the Department of Homeland Security, Radio Frequency Identification (RFID), is being considered for use in tracking the movement of human beings. What potential research uses could such a database provide? Even though data are often collected with a limited purpose in mind, the development of data mining techniques and the development of new scientific questions make is plausible that the data could be repurposed for research uses.

The health informatics professional's role is one of advocacy within the context of emerging technological applications that result in the availability of and access to health information. The HIM professional is well positioned to help the public understand the implications of the sharing and use of health information.

Summary

The history of research and ethics presents the HIM professional with many challenges. There are codes of ethics, international agreements, government regulations and laws, and institutional oversight. Despite these initiatives, there are many ethical violations in research. This chapter focuses on the complexities of protecting humans in research.

Ethical deliberations are never theoretical. The discussions are guided by ethical theories and principles. However, action always is required. What should be done? The core ethical questions are: "How should we behave? What should we do in this instance?" HIM professionals must deal with the complexities of ethics and research. HIM professionals may not have time to engage in theoretical discussions but must have ethical principles firmly in their mind and understand them well enough to respond in a reasonable manner when confronted with day-to-day ethical issues regarding using medical information. Should the researchers and providers perform surgery, try something experimental with technology or drugs, forego life-sustaining treatment, limit access to healthcare, or release the information given the risk of discrimination, and the like? The intersection of these questions requires knowledge, values, ethical principles, and interdisciplinary collaboration. Although a group could discuss an ethical problem in theory, "bioethical decisions always require action. Ethical actions at work always require courage" (Harman 2006, 17).

To support ethical processes in research, the HIM professionals can:

- Be a member of the IRB and Ethics Committee
- Be a strong voice in reflecting the principles and guidelines for the professional codes of ethics
- Be a lifelong learner who recognizes the importance of both technical and ethical expertise
- Be an advocate when confronted with new ethical issues in research

HIM professionals need to honor and use their voice of moral agency and continue to be accountable for research that ensures ethical decision making.

References

Common Rule

45 CFR 46.101(b): Basic HHS policy for protection of human research subjects. 2005 (Oct. 1).

45 CFR 46.109: IRB review of research. 2005 (Oct. 1).

45 CFR 46.110: Categories of research that may be reviewed through an expedited review procedure.

45 CFR 46.116. Protection of Human Subjects.

AHIMA House of Delegates. 2004 (July 1). Code of Ethics. Chicago: AHIMA.

Alliance for Human Research Protection. 2007. Ethical violations/investigations today. Available online from http://www.ahrp.org/ethical/EthicalViolations.php.

Alliance for Human Research Protection. 2005. Pharma ethics: Merck CEO resigns—Vioxx deceptive marketing. Available online from http://www.ahrp.org/infomail/05/05/06a.php.

American Medical Informatics Association 2007. Code of Ethics. Available online from http://www.amia.org/inside/code/.

Beauchamp, Tom L., and James F. Childress. 2001. *Principles of biomedical ethics, 5th ed*. New York: Oxford University Press.

Beauchamp, Tom L., and James F. Childress. *Principles of biomedical ethics, 4th ed*. New York: Oxford University Press.

Belenky, M.F., Clinchy, B.M., Goldberger, N.R., and J.M. Tarule. 1986. *Women's ways of knowing: The development of self, voice, and mind*. New York: Basic Books.

Birke, L., and J. Silvertown, eds. 1984. *More than the parts: Biology and politics*. London: Pluto Press.

Bronowski, J. 1965. *Science and human values,* rev. ed.. New York: Harper and Row.

Bulkley, B.H. 1985. Balancing risks and benefits. In *Biotechnology: Implications for public policy* (pp. 41–45), S. Panem, editor. Washington, DC: The Brookings Institution.

Capra, F. 1982. *The turning point: Science, society, and the risking culture*. New York: Bantam Books.

Center for Advanced Study. 2003. The Illinois White Paper: Improving the Systems for Protecting Human Subjects—Counteracting IRB "Mission Creep." Available online from http://www.law.uiuc.edu/conferences/whitepaper/papers/SSRN-id902995.pdf.

Chan, A.W., Hróbjartsson, A., Haahr, M.T., Gøtzsche, P.C., and D.G. Altman. 2004 (May 26). Empirical evidence for selective reporting of outcomes in randomized trials: Comparison of protocols to published articles. *Journal of the American Medical Association* 291(20):2457–65.

Citizens for Responsible Care and Research. 2007 (Oct. 20). Mission statement. Available online from http://www.circare.org/index.htm.

Citro, Constance F., Ilgen, Daniel R., and Cora B. Marrett, editors. 2003. *Protecting Participants and Facilitating Social and Behavioral Sciences Research*. Washington, DC: The National Academies Press.

Davis, J. 1990. *Mapping the code: The Human Genome Project and the choices of modern science*. New York: Wiley Science.

Department of Energy. n.d. DOE Openness. Human radiation experiments: Roadmap to the project. Advisory Committee on Human Radiation Experiments—Executive summary. Available online from http://www.hss.energy.gov/healthsafety/ohre/roadmap/achre/summary.html.

Engelhardt, H.T., Jr., and A.L. Caplan. 1987. *Scientific controversies: Case studies in the resolution and closure of disputes in science and technology*. Cambridge, England: Cambridge University.

Etzioni, A. 1975. *Genetic fix: The next technological revolution*. New York: Harper Colophon.

Fowler, F.J. 1988. *Survey research methods*. Newbury Park, CA: Sage.

Frankel, Mark S., and Sanyin Siang. 1999 (November). *Ethical and Legal Aspects of Human Subjects Research on the Internet*. Workshop report from AAAS Program on Scientific Freedom, Responsibility and Law, June 10-11 1999. Funded by U.S. Office for Protection from Research Risks. Available online from http://www.aaas.org/spp/sfrl/projects/intres/report.pdf.

Gilligan, C. 1982. *In a different voice: Psychological theory and women's development*. Cambridge, MA: Harvard University Press.

Gilligan, C., Ward, J.V., and J.M. Taylor, editors. 1988. *Mapping the moral domain: A contribution of women's thinking to psychological theory and education*. Cambridge, MA: Harvard University Press.

Gornick, V. 1983. *Women in science: Portraits from a world transition*. New York: Simon and Schuster.

Guterman, Lila. 2007 (Aug. 13). Medical professor defends gene-therapy trial in which a patient died. *Chronicle of Higher Education*.

Harman, L.B., editor. 2006. *Ethical Challenges in the Management of Health Information, 2nd ed*. Sudbury, MA: Jones and Bartlett.

Harman, L.B. and V.L. Mullen. 2006. *Professional values and the Code of Ethics*. In *Ethical Challenges in the Management of Health Information, 2nd ed*. Sudbury, MA: Jones and Bartlett.

Harman, L.B. 1994. *Attitudes about the use of genetic information and genetic engineering when making reproductive decisions: Influence of gender, discipline and role*. Unpublished dissertation. Santa Barbara, CA: The Fielding Institute.

Health and Human Services. 2008 (Jan. 8). Office for Human Research Protections (OHRP). 2007 Determination Letters. Available online from http://www.hhs.gov/ohrp/compliance/letters/index.html

Health and Human Services. 1990 (Jan. 26). Ethical, legal and social implications of the Human Genome Initiative. *NIH Guide to Grants and Contracts* 19(4):12–15.

Health and Human Services. 1978 (Jan. 5). Protection of Human Subjects: Proposed Regulations on Research Involving Prisoners. 45 CFR Part 46. *Federal Register* 43(3):1050–53.

Helbig, S. 2006. Advocacy. Ch. 24 in *Ethical Challenges in the Management of Health Information, 2nd ed.*, L.B. Harman, editor. Sudbury, MA: Jones and Bartlett.

Holmes, H. and L. Purdy, editors. 1992. *Feminist perspectives in medical ethics*. Bloomington: Indiana University Press.

Holmes, H., and L. Purdy, editors. 1992. *Feminist perspectives in medical ethics*. Bloomington, IN: Indiana University Press.

Hornblum, A.M. 1998. *Acres of skin: Human experiments at Holmesburg prison*. New York: Routledge.

Hornblum, A.M. 2007. *Sentenced to science: One black man's story of imprisonment in America*. Philadelphia: Pennsylvania State University Press.

Hosford, B. 1986. *Bioethics committees: The health care provider's guide*. Aspen: Rockville, MD.

Huffman, E.K. 1972. *Manual for medical record librarians,* 6th ed. Chicago: Physicians' Record Company.

Imber, B., and N. Tuana, N. 1988. Feminist perspectives on science. *Hypatia* 3(1):139–56.

Institute of Medicine Committee on Assessing the System for Protecting Human Research Subjects, Board on Health Sciences Policy. 2001. *Preserving Public Trust: Accreditation and Human Research Participant Protection Programs*. Washington, DC: National Academies Press. Available online from http://books.nap.edu/catalog.php?record_id=10085.

International Medical Informatics Association, n.d. IMIA Code of Ethics for Health Information Professionals. Available online from http://www.imia.org/English_code_of_ethics.html.

Johns, M.L., and J.M. Hardin. 2006. Research and decision support. Ch. 7 in *Ethical Challenges in the Management of Health Information, 2nd ed.*, L.B. Harman, editor. Sudbury, MA: Jones and Bartlett.

Kerlinger, F.H. 1979. *Behavioral research: A conceptual approach*. New York: Holt, Rinehart, and Winston.

Kittay, E., and D. Meyers, editors. 1987. *Women and moral theory*. Savage, MD: Rowman and Littlefield.

Kohlberg, L. 1981. *Essays in moral development: Vol. 1 The philosophy of moral development*. San Francisco: Harper and Row.

Kohlberg, L. 1984. *Essays in moral development: Vol. 2 The psychology of moral development*. San Francisco: Harper and Row.

Larabee, M., editor. 199). *An ethic of care: Feminist and interdisciplinary perspectives*. New York: Routledge.

Lehrer, Jim. 2000 (Feb. 2). Gene therapy. Available online from http://www.pbs.org/newshour/bb/health/jan-june00/gene_therapy_2-2.html.

Lenz, E., and B. Myerhoff. 1985. *The feminization of America: How women's values are changing our public and private lives*. Los Angeles: Jeremy P. Tarcher.

Levinson, D. J. 1978. *The seasons of a man's life*. New York: Ballantine.

Longino, H.E. 1990. *Science as social knowledge: Values and objectivity in scientific inquiry*. Princeton, NJ: Princeton University Press.

Mappes, T.A., and D. DeGrazia. 1996. *Biomedical Ethics,* 4th ed. New York: McGraw-Hill.

Mappes, T.A., and J.S. Zematy. 1991. B*iomedical ethics*. New York: McGraw-Hill.

Matthews, Robert. 2004 (May 29). Researchers ignore 'inconvenient' drug trial results. *The Daily Telegraph*. Available online from http://www.telegraph.co.uk/news/main.jhtml?xml=/news/2004/05/30/nscien30.xml.

National Academy of Sciences. 1994. *On Being A Scientist: Responsible Conduct In Research*. Available online from http://www.nap.edu/readingroom/books/obas/.

National Institutes of Health. 2008. NIH history. Available online from http://www.nih.gov/about/history.htm.

National Institutes of Health. 2007a (Dec. 14). Bioethics Resources on the Web. Available online from http://bioethics.od.nih.gov/.

National Institutes of Health. 2007b (June 28). FY 2008 Director's Budget Request Statement. Available online from http://www.nih.gov/about/director/budgetrequest/fy2008directorsbudgetrequest.htm.

National Institutes of Health. 2007c (June 19). About NIH. Available online from http://www.nih.gov/about/NIHoverview.html.

National Institutes of Health. 1990 (Jan. 26). Guide to grants and contracts. Bethesda, MD: NIH.

National Institutes of Health. n.d. A Short History of the National Institutes of Health. Available online from http://history.nih.gov/exhibits/history/.

National Physicians Alliance. n.d. Protecting prescription privacy. Available online from http://npalliance.org/Pages/protecting_prescription_privacy.

National Research Act of 1974. Public Law 93-348.

National Research Council Committee for Monitoring the Nation's Changing Needs for Biomedical, Behavioral, and Clinical Personnel; Board on Higher Education and Workforce. 2005. *Advancing the Nation's Health Needs: NIH*

Research Training Programs. Washington, DC: National Academies Press. Available online from http://books.nap.edu/openbook.php?isbn=0309094275.

Nelkin, D. 1987. Controversies and authority of science. In *Scientific controversies: Case studies in the resolution and closure of disputes in science and technology* (pp. 283-294), Engelhardt, H.T., Jr., and A.L. Caplan. Cambridge, England: Cambridge University.

Office for Human Research Protections. n.d. Compliance oversight. Available online from http://www.hhs.gov/ohrp/compliance/.

Office of Human Subjects Research, National Commission for the Protection of Human Subjects of Biomedical and Behavioral Research. 1979 (April 18). *The Belmont Report: Ethical Principles and Guidelines for the Protection of Human Subjects of Research*. (OS) 78-0013, 78-0012. Bethesda, MD: DHEW. Available online from http://ohsr.od.nih.gov/guidelines/belmont.html#gob.

Office of Research and Integrity. n.d. Common rule. Available online from http://ori.hhs.gov/education/products/ucla/chapter2/page04b.htm.

Paasche-Orlow, Michael K., Taylor, Holly A., and Frederick L. Brancati. 2003 (Feb. 20). Readability standards for informed-consent forms as compared with actual readability. *New England of Medicine* 348(8):721–726.

President's Commission on Bioethics. n.d. Available online from http://www.bioethics.gov/

Purtilo, R. (2006). *Ethical dimensions in the health professions (4th ed.)*. Philadelphia: W.B. Saunders Company.

Schulte, P.A., Hunter, D., Rothman, N. 1997. Ethical and social issues in the use of biomarkers in epidemiologic research. *IARC scientific publications* 142:313–18.

Shilts, Randy. 1987. *And the Band Played On: Politics, People and the AIDS Epidemic*. New York: St. Martin's Press.

Shuster, E. 1998. Review of Acres of Skin: Human experiments at Holmesburg prison. *Journal of Criminal Justice and Popular Culture* 6(1):4–9.

Stanford University. 2006 (Jan. 24). Glossary of lay terms for use in preparing consent forms. Available online from http://humansubjects.stanford.edu/general/glossary.html.

Stanford University Office of the Vice Provost and Dean of Research. n.d. Use of Human Subjects in Research. Available online from http://www.stanford.edu/dept/DoR/hs/History/his06.html.

Stolberg, Sheryl Gay. 1999 (Nov. 28). The biotech death of Jesse Gelsinger. *The New York Times, Sunday Magazine*. Available online from http://query.nytimes.com/gst/fullpage.html?res=9C03E4DE1F3CF93BA15752C1A96F958260&scp=1&sq=stolberg+gelsinger&st=nyt.

Thurston, Wilfreda E., Burgess, Michael M., and Carol E Adair. 1999. Ethical issues in the use of computerized databases for epidemiologic and other health research. *Chronic Diseases in Canada* 20(3):127–31.

Trials of War Criminals before the Nuremberg Military Tribunals under Control Council Law 10(2):181–182. 1949. Washington, DC: U.S. Government Printing Office.

Weiss, Rick. 2007 (Aug. 6). Death points to risks in research. *Washington Post*.

Appendix 13A
AHIMA Code of Ethics

Preamble

The ethical obligations of the health information management (HIM) professional include the protection of patient privacy and confidential information; disclosure of information; development, use, and maintenance of health information systems and health records; and the quality of information. Both handwritten and computerized medical records contain many sacred stories—stories that must be protected on behalf of the individual and the aggregate community of persons served in the healthcare system. Healthcare consumers are increasingly concerned about the loss of privacy and the inability to control the dissemination of their protected information. Core health information issues include what information should be collected; how the information should be handled, who should have access to the information, and under what conditions the information should be disclosed.

Ethical obligations are central to the professional's responsibility, regardless of the employment site or the method of collection, storage, and security of health information. Sensitive information (genetic, adoption, drug, alcohol, sexual, and behavioral information) requires special attention to prevent misuse. Entrepreneurial roles require expertise in the protection of the information in the world of business and interactions with consumers.

Professional Values

The mission of the HIM profession is based on core professional values developed since the inception of the Association in 1928. These values and the inherent ethical responsibilities for AHIMA members and credentialed HIM professionals include providing service, protecting medical, social, and financial information, promoting confidentiality; and preserving and securing health information. Values to the healthcare team include promoting the quality and advancement of healthcare, demonstrating HIM expertise and skills, and promoting interdisciplinary cooperation and collaboration. Professional values in relationship to the employer include protecting committee deliberations and complying with laws, regulations, and policies. Professional values related to the public include advocating change, refusing to participate or conceal unethical practices, and reporting violations of practice standards to the proper authorities. Professional values to individual and professional associations include obligations to be honest, bringing honor to self, peers and profession, committing to continuing education and lifelong learning, performing Association duties honorably, strengthening professional membership, representing the profession to the public, and promoting and participating in research.

These professional values will require a complex process of balancing the many conflicts that can result from competing interests and obligations of those who seek access to health information and require an understanding of ethical decision-making.

Purpose of the American Health Information Management Association Code of Ethics

The HIM professional has an obligation to demonstrate actions that reflect values, ethical principles, and ethical guidelines. The American Health Information Management Association (AHIMA) Code of Ethics sets forth these values and principles to guide conduct. The code is relevant to all AHIMA members and credentialed HIM professionals and students, regardless of their professional functions, the settings in which they work, or the populations they serve.

Source: Revised & adopted by AHIMA House of Delegates, July 1, 2004.

The AHIMA Code of Ethics serves six purposes:

- Identifies core values on which the HIM mission is based.
- Summarizes broad ethical principles that reflect the profession's core values and establishes a set of ethical principles to be used to guide decision-making and actions.
- Helps HIM professionals identify relevant considerations when professional obligations conflict or ethical uncertainties arise.
- Provides ethical principles by which the general public can hold the HIM professional accountable.
- Socializes practitioners new to the field to HIM's mission, values, and ethical principles.
- Articulates a set of guidelines that the HIM professional can use to assess whether they have engaged in unethical conduct.

The code includes principles and guidelines that are both enforceable and aspirational. The extent to which each principle is enforceable is a matter of professional judgment to be exercised by those responsible for reviewing alleged violations of ethical principles.

The Use of the Code

Violation of principles in this code does not automatically imply legal liability or violation of the law. Such determination can only be made in the context of legal and judicial proceedings. Alleged violations of the code would be subject to a peer review process. Such processes are generally separate from legal or administrative procedures and insulated from legal review or proceedings to allow the profession to counsel and discipline its own members although in some situations, violations of the code would constitute unlawful conduct subject to legal process.

Guidelines for ethical and unethical behavior are provided in this code. The terms "shall and shall not" are used as a basis for setting high standards for behavior. This does not imply that everyone "shall or shall not" do everything that is listed. For example, not everyone participates in the recruitment or mentoring of students. A HIM professional is not being unethical if this is not part of his or her professional activities; however, if students are part of one's professional responsibilities, there is an ethical obligation to follow the guidelines stated in the code. This concept is true for the entire code. If someone does the stated activities, ethical behavior is the standard. The guidelines are not a comprehensive list. For example, the statement "protect all confidential information to include personal, health, financial, genetic and outcome information" can also be interpreted as "shall not fail to protect all confidential information to include personal, health, financial, genetic, and outcome information."

A code of ethics cannot guarantee ethical behavior. Moreover, a code of ethics cannot resolve all ethical issues or disputes or capture the richness and complexity involved in striving to make responsible choices within a moral community. Rather, a code of ethics sets forth values and ethical principles, and offers ethical guidelines to which professionals aspire and by which their actions can be judged. Ethical behaviors result from a personal commitment to engage in ethical practice.

Professional responsibilities often require an individual to move beyond personal values. For example, an individual might demonstrate behaviors that are based on the values of honesty, providing service to others, or demonstrating loyalty. In addition to these, professional values might require promoting confidentiality, facilitating interdisciplinary collaboration, and refusing to participate or conceal unethical practices. Professional values could require a more comprehensive set of values than what an individual needs to be an ethical agent in their personal lives.

The AHIMA Code of Ethics is to be used by AHIMA and individuals, agencies, organizations, and bodies (such as licensing and regulatory boards, insurance providers, courts of law, agency boards of directors, government agencies, and other professional groups) that choose to adopt it or use it as a frame of reference. The AHIMA Code of Ethics reflects the commitment of all to uphold the profession's values and to act ethically. Individuals of good character who discern moral questions and, in good faith, seek to make reliable ethical judgments, must apply ethical principles.

The code does not provide a set of rules that prescribe how to act in all situations. Specific applications of the code must take into account the context in which it is being considered and the possibility of conflicts among the code's values, principles, and guidelines. Ethical responsibilities flow from all human relationships, from the personal and familial to the social and professional. Further, the AHIMA Code of Ethics does not specify which values, principles, and guidelines are the most important and ought to outweigh others in instances when they conflict.

Code of Ethics 2004

Ethical Principles: The following ethical principles are based on the core values of the American Health Information Management Association and apply to all health information management professionals.

Health information management professionals:

I. *Advocate, uphold and defend the individual's right to privacy and the doctrine of confidentiality in the use and disclosure of information.*

II. *Put service and the health and welfare of persons before self-interest and conduct themselves in the practice of the profession so as to bring honor to themselves, their peers, and to the health information management profession.*

III. *Preserve, protect, and secure personal health information in any form or medium and hold in the highest regard the contents of the records and other information of a confidential nature, taking into account the applicable statutes and regulations.*

IV. *Refuse to participate in or conceal unethical practices or procedures.*

V. *Advance health information management knowledge and practice through continuing education, research, publications, and presentations.*

VI. *Recruit and mentor students, peers and colleagues to develop and strengthen professional workforce.*

VII. *Represent the profession accurately to the public.*

VIII. *Perform honorably health information management association responsibilities, either appointed or elected, and preserve the confidentiality of any privileged information made known in any official capacity.*

IX. *State truthfully and accurately their credentials, professional education, and experiences.*

X. *Facilitate interdisciplinary collaboration in situations supporting health information practice.*

XI. *Respect the inherent dignity and worth of every person.*

How to Interpret the Code of Ethics

The following ethical principles are based on the core values of the American Health Information Management Association and apply to all health information management professionals. Guidelines included for each ethical principle are a non-inclusive list of behaviors and situations that can help to clarify the principle. They are not to be meant as a comprehensive list of all situations that can occur.

I. *Advocate, uphold, and defend the individual's right to privacy and the doctrine of confidentiality in the use and disclosure of information.*

Health information management professionals **shall**:

1.1. Protect all confidential information to include personal, health, financial, genetic, and outcome information.

1.2. Engage in social and political action that supports the protection of privacy and confidentiality, and be aware of the impact of the political arena on the health information system. Advocate for changes in policy and legislation to ensure protection of privacy and confidentiality, coding compliance, and other issues that surface as advocacy issues as well as facilitating informed participation by the public on these issues.

1.3. Protect the confidentiality of all information obtained in the course of professional service. Disclose only information that is directly relevant or necessary to achieve the purpose of disclosure. Release information only with valid consent from a patient or a person legally authorized to consent on behalf of a patient or as authorized by federal or state regulations. The need-to-know criterion is essential when releasing health information for initial disclosure and all redisclosure activities.

1.4. Promote the obligation to respect privacy by respecting confidential information shared among colleagues, while responding to requests from the legal profession, the media, or other non-healthcare related individuals, during presentations or teaching and in situations that could cause harm to persons.

II. *Put service and the health and welfare of persons before self-interest and conduct themselves in the practice of the profession so as to bring honor to themselves, their peers, and to the health information management profession.*

Health information management professionals **shall**:

2.1. Act with integrity, behave in a trustworthy manner, elevate service to others above self-interest, and promote high standards of practice in every setting.

2.2. Be aware of the profession's mission, values, and ethical principles, and practice in a manner consistent with them by acting honestly and responsibly.

2.3. Anticipate, clarify, and avoid any conflict of interest, to all parties concerned, when dealing with consumers, consulting with competitors, or in providing services requiring potentially conflicting roles (for example, finding out information about one facility that would help a competitor). The conflicting roles or responsibilities must be clarified and appropriate action must be taken to minimize any conflict of interest.

2.4. Ensure that the working environment is consistent and encourages compliance with the AHIMA Code of Ethics, taking reasonable steps to eliminate any conditions in their organizations that violate, interfere with, or discourage compliance with the code.

2.5. Take responsibility and credit, including authorship credit, only for work they actually perform or to which they contribute. Honestly acknowledge the work of and the contributions made by others verbally or written, such as in publication.

Health information management professionals **shall not**:

2.6. Permit their private conduct to interfere with their ability to fulfill their professional responsibilities.

2.7. Take unfair advantage of any professional relationship or exploit others to further their personal, religious, political, or business interests.

III. Preserve, protect, and secure personal health information in any form or medium and hold in the highest regards the contents of the records and other information of a confidential nature obtained in the official capacity, taking into account the applicable statutes and regulations.

Health information management professionals **shall**:

3.1. Protect the confidentiality of patients' written and electronic records and other sensitive information. Take reasonable steps to ensure that patients' records are stored in a secure location and that patients' records are not available to others who are not authorized to have access.

3.2. Take precautions to ensure and maintain the confidentiality of information transmitted, transferred, or disposed of in the event of a termination, incapacitation, or death of a healthcare provider to other parties through the use of any media. Disclosure of identifying information should be avoided whenever possible.

3.3. Inform recipients of the limitations and risks associated with providing services via electronic media (such as computer, telephone, fax, radio, and television).

IV. Refuse to participate in or conceal unethical practices or procedures.

Health information management professionals **shall:**

4.1. Act in a professional and ethical manner at all times.

4.2. Take adequate measures to discourage, prevent, expose, and correct the unethical conduct of colleagues.

4.3. Be knowledgeable about established policies and procedures for handling concerns about colleagues' unethical behavior. These include policies and procedures created by AHIMA, licensing and regulatory bodies, employers, supervisors, agencies, and other professional organizations.

4.4. Seek resolution if there is a belief that a colleague has acted unethically or if there is a belief of incompetence or impairment by discussing their concerns with the colleague when feasible and when such discussion is likely to be productive. Take action through appropriate formal channels, such as contacting an accreditation or regulatory body and/ or the AHIMA Professional Ethics Committee.

4.5. Consult with a colleague when feasible and assist the colleague in taking remedial action when there is direct knowledge of a health information management colleague's incompetence or impairment.

Health information management professionals **shall not**:

4.6. Participate in, condone, or be associated with dishonesty, fraud and abuse, or deception. A non-inclusive list of examples includes:

- Allowing patterns of retrospective documentation to avoid suspension or increase reimbursement
- Assigning codes without physician documentation
- Coding when documentation does not justify the procedures that have been billed
- Coding an inappropriate level of service
- Miscoding to avoid conflict with others

- Engaging in negligent coding practices
- Hiding or ignoring review outcomes, such as performance data
- Failing to report licensure status for a physician through the appropriate channels
- Recording inaccurate data for accreditation purposes
- Hiding incomplete medical records
- Allowing inappropriate access to genetic, adoption, or behavioral health information
- Misusing sensitive information about a competitor
- Violating the privacy of individuals

V. *Advance health information management knowledge and practice through continuing education, research, publications, and presentations.*

Health information management professionals **shall**:

5.1. Develop and enhance continually their professional expertise, knowledge, and skills (including appropriate education, research, training, consultation, and supervision). Contribute to the knowledge base of health information management and share with colleagues their knowledge related to practice, research, and ethics.

5.2. Base practice decisions on recognized knowledge, including empirically based knowledge relevant to health information management and health information management ethics.

5.3. Contribute time and professional expertise to activities that promote respect for the value, integrity, and competence of the health information management profession. These activities may include teaching, research, consultation, service, legislative testimony, presentations in the community, and participation in their professional organizations.

5.4. Engage in evaluation or research that ensures the anonymity or confidentiality of participants and of the data obtained from them by following guidelines developed for the participants in consultation with appropriate institutional review boards. Report evaluation and research findings accurately and take steps to correct any errors later found in published data using standard publication methods.

5.5. Take reasonable steps to provide or arrange for continuing education and staff development, addressing current knowledge and emerging developments related to health information management practice and ethics.

Health information management professionals **shall not**:

5.6. Design or conduct evaluation or research that is in conflict with applicable federal or state laws.

5.7. Participate in, condone, or be associated with fraud or abuse.

VI. *Recruit and mentor students, peers and colleagues to develop and strengthen professional workforce.*

Health information management professionals **shall**:

6.1. Evaluate students' performance in a manner that is fair and respectful when functioning as educators or clinical internship supervisors.

6.2. Be responsible for setting clear, appropriate, and culturally sensitive boundaries for students.

6.3. Be a mentor for students, peers and new health information management professionals to develop and strengthen skills.

6.4. Provide directed practice opportunities for students.

Health information management professionals **shall not**:

6.5. Engage in any relationship with students in which there is a risk of exploitation or potential harm to the student.

VII. *Accurately represent the profession to the public.*

Health information management professionals **shall:**

7.1 Be an advocate for the profession in all settings and participate in activities that promote and explain the mission, values, and principles of the profession to the public.

VIII. *Perform honorably health information management association responsibilities, either appointed or elected, and preserve the confidentiality of any privileged information made known in any official capacity.*

Health information management professionals **shall**:

8.1. Perform responsibly all duties as assigned by the professional association.

8.2. Resign from an Association position if unable to perform the assigned responsibilities with competence.

8.3. Speak on behalf of professional health information management organizations, accurately representing the official and authorized positions of the organizations.

IX. *State truthfully and accurately their credentials, professional education, and experiences.*

Health information management professionals **shall**:

9.1. Make clear distinctions between statements made and actions engaged in as a private individual and as a representative of the health information management profession, a professional health information organization, or the health information management professional's employer.

9.2. Claim and ensure that their representations to patients, agencies, and the public of professional qualifications, credentials, education, competence, affiliations, services provided, training, certification, consultation received, supervised experience, other relevant professional experience are accurate.

9.3. Claim only those relevant professional credentials actually possessed and correct any inaccuracies occurring regarding credentials.

X. Facilitate interdisciplinary collaboration in situations supporting health information practice.

Health information management professionals **shall**:

10.1. Participate in and contribute to decisions that affect the well-being of patients by drawing on the perspectives, values, and experiences of those involved in decisions related to patients. Professional and ethical obligations of the interdisciplinary team as a whole and of its individual members should be clearly established.

XI. Respect the inherent dignity and worth of every person.

Health information management professionals **shall**:

11.1. Treat each person in a respectful fashion, being mindful of individual differences and cultural and ethnic diversity.

11.2. Promote the value of self-determination for each individual.

Acknowledgment

Adapted with permission from the Code of Ethics of the National Association of Social Workers.

Resources

National Association of Social Workers. 1999. Code of ethics. Available online from http://www.naswdc.org/pubs/code/code.asp.
Harman, L.B. (Ed.). 2001. Ethical Challenges in the Management of Health Information. Aspen: Gaithersburg, MD.
AHIMA Code of Ethics, 1957, 1977, 1988, and 1998.

Appendix 13B

IMIA Code of Ethics for Health Information Professionals

Preamble

Codes of professional ethics serve several purposes:

1. to provide ethical guidance for the professionals themselves,
2. to furnish a set of principles against which the conduct of the professionals may be measured, and
3. to provide the public with a clear statement of the ethical considerations that should shape the behaviour of the professionals themselves.

A Code of Ethics for Health Informatics Professionals (HIPs) should therefore be clear, unambiguous, and easily applied in practice. Moreover, since the field of informatics is in a state of constant flux, it should be flexible so as to accommodate ongoing changes without sacrificing the applicability of its basic principles. It is therefore inappropriate for a Code of Ethics for HIPs to deal with the specifics of every possible situation that might arise. That would make the Code too unwieldy, too rigid, and too dependent on the current state of informatics. Instead, such a Code should focus on the ethical position of the Health Informatics specialist as a professional, and on the relationships between HIPs and the various parties with whom they interact in a professional capacity. These various parties include (but are not limited to) patients, health care professionals, administrative personnel, health care institutions as well as insurance companies and governmental agencies, etc.

The reason for constructing a code of ethics for HIPs instead of merely adopting one of the codes that have been promulgated by the various general associations of informatics professionals is that HIPs play a unique role in the planning and delivery of health care: a role that is distinct from the role of other informatics professionals who work in different settings.

Part of this uniqueness is centred in the special relationship between the electronic health record (EHR) and the subject of that record. The EHR not only reveals much about the patient that is private and should be kept confidential but, more importantly, it functions as the basis of decisions that have a profound impact on the welfare of the patient. The patient is in a vulnerable position, and any decision regarding the patient and the EHR must acknowledge the fundamental necessity of striking an appropriate balance between ethically justified ends and otherwise appropriate means. Further, the data that are contained in the EHR also provide the raw materials for decision-making by health care institutions, governments and other agencies without which a system of health care delivery simply could not function. The HIP, therefore, by facilitating the construction, maintenance, storage, access, use and manipulation of EHRs, plays a role that is distinct from that of other informatics specialists.

At the same time, precisely because of this facilitating role, HIPs are embedded in a web of relationships that are subject to unique ethical constraints. Thus, over and above the ethical constraints that arise from the relationship between the electronic record and the patient, the ethical conduct of HIPs is also subject to considerations that arise out of the HIPs' interactions with Health Care Professionals (HCPs), health care institutions and other agencies. These constraints pull in different directions. It is therefore important that HIPs have some idea of how to resolve these issues in an appropriate fashion. A Code of Ethics for HIPs provides a tool in this regard, and may be of use in effecting a resolution when conflicting roles and constraints collide.

A Code of Ethics for HIPs is also distinct from an account of legally conferred duties and rights. Unquestionably, the law provides the regulatory setting in which HIPs carry out their activities. However, ethical conduct frequently goes beyond what the law requires. The reason is that legal regulations have purely juridical significance and represent, as it were, a minimum standard as envisioned by legislators, juries and judges. However, these standards are formulated on the basis of circumstances as they obtain here and now; they are not anticipatory in nature and therefore can provide little guidance for a rapidly evolving discipline in which new types of situations constantly arise. HIPs who only followed the law, and who only adjusted their conduct to legal precedent, would be ill equipped to deal with situations that were not envisioned by the lawmakers and would be subject to the vagaries of the next judicial process.

On the other hand, a Code of Ethics for HIPs is grounded in fundamental ethical principles as these apply to the types of situations that characterize the activities of the Health Informatics specialist. Consequently such a Code, centring in the very essence of what it is to be an HIP, is independent of the vagaries of the judicial process and, rather than following it, may well guide it; and rather than becoming invalidated by changes in technology or administrative fashion, may well indicate the direction in which these developments should proceed. Therefore, while in many cases the clauses of such a Code will be reflected in corresponding juridical injunctions or administrative provisions, they provide guidance through times of legal or administrative uncertainty and in areas where corresponding laws or administrative provisions do not exist. At a more general level, such a Code may even assist in the resolution of the problems posed by the technological imperative. Not everything that can be done should be done. A Code of Ethics assists in defining the ethical landscape.

The Code of Ethics that follows was developed on the basis of these considerations. It has two parts:

1. Introduction

     This part begins with a set of fundamental ethical principles that have found general international acceptance. Next is a brief list of general principles of informatic ethics that follow from these fundamental ethical principles when these are applied to the electronic gathering, processing, storing, communicating, using, manipulating and accessing of health information in general. These general principles of informatic ethics are high-level principles and provide general guidance.

2. Rules of Ethical Conduct for HIPs.

     This part lays out a detailed set of ethical rules of behaviour for HIPs. These rules are developed by applying the general principles of informatic ethics to the types of relationships that characterize the professional lives of HIPs. They are more specific than the general principles of informatic ethics, and offer more particular guidance.

The precise reasoning that shows how the Principles of Informatic Ethics follow from the Fundamental Ethical Principles, and that indicates how the Principles of Informatic Ethics give rise to the more specific Rules of Ethical Conduct for HIPs is contained in a separate Handbook and may be consulted there for greater clarity.

It should also be noted that the Code of Ethics and the accompanying set of Rules of Ethical Conduct do not include what might be called "technical" provisions. That is to say, they do not make reference to such things as technical standards of secure data communication, or to provisions that are necessary to ensure a high quality in the handling, collecting, storing, transmitting, manipulating, etc. of health care data. This is deliberate. While the development and implementation of technical standards has ethical dimensions, and while these dimensions are reflected in the Code and the Rules as ethical duties, the details of such technical standards are not themselves a matter of ethics.

Part I.

Introduction

A. Fundamental Ethical Principles

All social interactions are subject to fundamental ethical principles. HIPs function in a social setting. Consequently, their actions are also subject to these principles. The most important of these principles are:

1. Principle of Autonomy

   All persons have a fundamental right to self-determination.

2. Principle of Equality and Justice

   All persons are equal as persons and have a right to be treated accordingly.

3. Principle of Beneficence

   All persons have a duty to advance the good of others where the nature of this good is in keeping with the fundamental and ethically defensible values of the affected party.

4. Principle of Non-Malfeasance

   All persons have a duty to prevent harm to other persons insofar as it lies within their power to do so without undue harm to themselves.

5. Principle of Impossibility

   All rights and duties hold subject to the condition that it is possible to meet them under the circumstances that obtain.

6. Principle of Integrity

   Whoever has an obligation, has a duty to fulfil that obligation to the best of her or his ability.

B. General Principles of Informatic Ethics

These fundamental ethical principle, when applied to the types of situations that characterize the informatics setting, give rise to general ethical principles of informatic ethics.

1. Principle of Information-Privacy and Disposition

   All persons have a fundamental right to privacy, and hence to control over the collection, storage, access, use, communication, manipulation and disposition of data about themselves.

2. Principle of Openness

   The collection, storage, access, use, communication, manipulation and disposition of personal data must be disclosed in an appropriate and timely fashion to the subject of those data.

3. Principle of Security

   Data that have been legitimately collected about a person should be protected by all reasonable and appropriate measures against loss, degradation, unauthorized destruction, access, use, manipulation, modification or communication.

4. Principle of Access

> The subject of an electronic record has the right of access to that record and the right to correct the record with respect to its accurateness, completeness and relevance.

5. Principle of Legitimate Infringement

> The fundamental right of control over the collection, storage, access, use, manipulation, communication and disposition of personal data is conditioned only by the legitimate, appropriate and relevant data-needs of a free, responsible and democratic society, and by the equal and competing rights of other persons.

6. Principle of the Least Intrusive Alternative

> Any infringement of the privacy rights of the individual person, and of the individual's right to control over person-relative data as mandated under Principle 1, may only occur in the least intrusive fashion and with a minimum of interference with the rights of the affected person.

7. Principle of Accountability

> Any infringement of the privacy rights of the individual person, and of the right to control over person-relative data, must be justified to the affected person in good time and in an appropriate fashion.

These general principles of informatic ethics, when applied to the types of relationships into which HIPs enter in their professional lives, and to the types of situations that they encounter when thus engaged, give rise to more specific ethical duties. The Rules of Conduct for HIPs that follow outline the more important of these ethical duties. It should be noted that as with any ethical rules of conduct, the Rules cannot do more than provide guidance. The precise way in which the Rules apply in a given context, and the precise nature of a particular ethical right or obligation, depends on the specific nature of the relevant situation.

Part II.

Rules of Ethical Conduct for HIPs

The rules of ethical conduct for HIPs can be broken down into six general rubrics, each of which has various sub-sections. The general rubrics demarcate the different domains of the ethical relationships that obtain between HIPs and specific stakeholders; the sub-sections detail the specifics of these relationships.

A. Subject-centred duties

These are duties that derive from the relationship in which HIPs stand to the subjects of the electronic records or to the subjects of the electronic communications that are facilitated by the HIPs through their professional actions.

1. HIPs have a duty to ensure that the potential subjects of electronic records are aware of the existence of systems, programmes or devices whose purpose it is to collect and/or communicate data about them.

2. HIPs have a duty to ensure that appropriate procedures are in place so that:
   a. electronic records are established or communicated only with the voluntary, competent and informed consent of the subjects of those records, and
   b. if an electronic record is established or communicated in contravention of **A.2.a,** the need to establish or communicate such a record has been demonstrated on independent ethical grounds to the subject of the record, in good time and in an appropriate fashion.

3. HIPs have a duty to ensure that the subject of an electronic record is made aware that
   a. an electronic record has been established about her/him,

b. who has established the record and who continues to maintain it,

c. what is contained in the electronic record,

d. the purpose for which it is established,

e. the individuals, institutions or agencies who have access to it or to whom it (or an identifiable part of it) may be communicated,

f. where the electronic record is maintained,

g. the length of time it will be maintained, and

h. the ultimate nature of its disposition.

4. HIPs have a duty to ensure that the subject of an electronic record is aware of the origin of the data contained in the record.

5. HIPs have a duty to ensure that the subject of an electronic record is aware of any rights that he or she may have with respect to

a. access, use and storage,

b. communication and manipulation,

c. quality and correction, and

d. disposition

of her or his electronic record and of the data contained in it.

6. HIPs have a duty to ensure that

a. electronic records are stored, accessed, used, manipulated or communicated only for legitimate purposes;

b. there are appropriate protocols and mechanisms in place to monitor the storage, accessing, use, manipulation or communication of electronic records, or of the data contained in them, in accordance with section

c. there are appropriating protocols and mechanisms in place to act on the basis of the information under section A. b. as and when the occasion demands;

d. the existence of these protocols and mechanisms is known to the subjects of electronic records, and

e. there are appropriate means for subjects of electronic records to enquire into and to engage the relevant review protocols and mechanisms.

7. HIPs have a duty to treat the duly empowered representatives of the subjects of electronic records as though they had the same rights concerning the electronic records as the subjects of the record themselves, and that the duly empowered representatives (and, if appropriate, the subjects of the records themselves) are aware of this fact.

8. HIPs have a duty to ensure that all electronic records are treated in a just, fair and equitable fashion.

9. HIPs have a duty to ensure that appropriate measures are in place that may reasonably be expected to safeguard the

a. security,

b. integrity,

c. material quality,

d. usability, and

e. accessibility

of electronic records.

10. HIPs have a duty to ensure, insofar as this lies within their power, that an electronic record or the data contained in it are used only

a. for the stated purposes for which the data were collected, or

b. for purposes that are otherwise ethically defensible.

11. HIPs have a duty to ensure that the subjects of electronic records or communications are aware of possible breaches of the preceding duties and the reason for them.

    a. Duties towards HCPs

    b. HCPs who care for patients depend on the technological skills of HIPs in the fulfilment of their patient-centred obligations. Consequently, HIPs have an obligation to assist these HCPs insofar as this is compatible with the HIPs' primary duty towards the subjects of the electronic records. Specifically, this means that

12. HIPs have a duty

    a. to assist duly empowered HCPs who are engaged in patient care in having appropriate, timely and secure access to relevant electronic records (or parts of thereof), and to ensure the usability, integrity, and highest possible technical quality of these records; and

    b. to provide those informatic services that might be necessary for the HCPs to carry out their mandate.

13. HIPs should keep HCPs informed of the status of the informatic services on which the HCPs rely, and immediately advise them of any problems or difficulties that might be associated or that could reasonably be expected to arise in connection with these informatic services.

14. HIPs should advise the HCPs with whom they interact on a professional basis, or for whom they provide professional services, of any circumstances that might prejudice the objectivity of the advice they give or that might impair the nature or quality of the services that they perform for the HCPs.

15. HIPs have a general duty to foster an environment that is conducive to the maintenance of the highest possible ethical and material standards of data collection, storage, management, communication and use by HCPs within the health care setting.

    a. those formal features of the electronic record, or

    b. those formal features of the data collection, retrieval, storage or usage system in which the electronic record is embedded

    in which the HCP has, or may reasonably be expected to have, an intellectual property interest.

B. Duties towards institutions/employers

1. HIPs owe their employers and the institutions in which they work a duty of

    a. competence,

    b. diligence,

    c. integrity, and

    d. loyalty.

2. HIPs have a duty to

    a. foster an ethically sensitive security culture in the institutional setting in which they practice their profession,

    b. facilitate the planning and implementation of the best and most appropriate data security measures possible for the institutional setting in which they work,

    c. implement and maintain the highest possible qualitative standards of data collection, storage, retrieval, processing, accessing, communication and utilization in all areas of their professional endeavour.

3. HIPs have a duty to ensure, to the best of their ability, that appropriate structures are in place to evaluate the technical, legal and ethical acceptability of the data-collection, storage, retrieval, processing, accessing, communication, and utilization of data in the settings in which they carry out their work or with which they are affiliated.

4. HIPs have a duty to alert, in good time and in a suitable manner, appropriately placed decision-makers of the security- and quality-status of the data-generating, storing, accessing, handling and communication systems, programmes, devices or procedures of the institution with which they are affiliated or of the employers for whom they provide professional services.

5. HIPs should immediately inform the institutions with which they are affiliated or the employers for whom they provide a professional service of any problems or difficulties that could reasonably be expected to arise in connection with the performance of their contractually stipulated services.

6. HIPs should immediately inform the institutions with which they are affiliated or the employers for whom they provide a professional service of circumstances that might prejudice the objectivity of the advice they give.

7. Except in emergencies, HIPs should only provide services in their areas of competence; however, they should always be honest and forthright about their education, experience or training.

8. HIPs should only use suitable and ethically acquired or developed tools, techniques or devices in the execution of their duties.

9. HIPs have a duty to assist in the development and provision of appropriate informatics-oriented educational services in the institution which they are affiliated or for the employer for whom they work.

C. Duties towards society

1. HIPs have a duty to facilitate the appropriate

   a. collection,
   b. storage,
   c. communication,
   d. use, and
   e. manipulation

   of health care data that are necessary for the planning and providing of health care services on a social scale.

2. HIPs have a duty to ensure that

   a. only data that are relevant to legitimate planning needs are collected;
   b. the data that are collected are de-identified or rendered anonymous as much as possible, in keeping with the legitimate aims of the collection;
   c. the linkage of data bases can occur only for otherwise legitimate and defensible reasons that do not violate the fundamental rights of the subjects of the records; and
   d. only duly authorised persons have access to the relevant data.

3. HIPs have a duty to educate the public about the various issues associated with the nature, collection, storage and use of electronic health-data and to make society aware of any problems, dangers, implications or limitations that might reasonably be associated with the collection, storage, usage and manipulation of socially relevant health data.

4. HIPs will refuse to participate in or support practices that violate human rights.

5. HIPs will be responsible in setting the fee for their services and in their demands for working conditions, benefits, etc.

D. Self-regarding duties

HIPs have a duty to

1. recognize the limits of their competence,

2. consult when necessary or appropriate,

3. maintain competence,

4. take responsibility for all actions performed by them or under their control,

5. avoid conflict of interest,

6. give appropriate credit for work done, and

7. act with honesty, integrity and diligence.

E. Duties towards the profession

1. HIPs have a duty always to act in such a fashion as not to bring the profession into disrepute.

2. HIPs have a duty to assist in the development of the highest possible standards of professional competence, to ensure that these standards are publicly known, and to see that they are applied in an impartial and transparent manner.

3. HIPs will refrain from impugning the reputation of colleagues but will report to the appropriate authority any unprofessional conduct by a colleague.

4. HIPs have a duty to assist their colleagues in living up to the highest technical and ethical standards of the profession.

5. HIPs have a duty to promote the understanding, appropriate utilization, and ethical use of health information technologies, and to advance and further the discipline of Health Informatics.

Appendix 13C
AMIA Code of Ethics

A Code of Professional Ethical Conduct for the American Medical Informatics Association
—An AMIA Board of Directors approved White Paper

John F. Hurdle, MD, PhD, Samantha Adams, PhD, Jane Brokel, PhD, RN, Betty Chang, DNSc, RN, FAAC, Peter Embi, MD, MS, Carolyn Petersen, Enrique Terrazas, MD, Peter Winkelstein, MD

Abstract

The AMIA Board of Directors has decided to periodically publish AMIA's Code of Professional Ethical Conduct for its members in the Journal of the American Medical Informatics Association. If you have questions or to provide comments or feedback, contact **Karen Greenwood (karen@amia.org).** The AMIA Board acknowledges the continuing work and dedication of the AMIA Ethics Committee. AMIA is the copyright holder of this work.

MeSH terms: *Ethics, Ethics Committees, Code of Ethics, Bioethics.*

Introduction

The American Medical Informatics Association, in common with other large professional societies, has had a long-standing interest in promoting a strong ethical framework for its membership.* This white paper presents the new AMIA Code of Professional Ethical Conduct, which was approved in February of this year by the AMIA Board of Directors. In an effort to keep pace with the intrinsic dynamism of the field itself, the code presented below is a dynamic document. It will evolve as the field itself evolves. The AMIA Web site (www.amia.org) will continue to publish the most up-to-date version of the code, a process that hinges on continued input from the AMIA membership.

The code is meant to be practical and easily understood, so it is presented in a compact form using very general language. Unlike the ethics codes of some professional societies, the AMIA code is not intended to be prescriptive; it relies on the commonsense of the membership. It provides the broad strokes of a set of important ethical principles especially pertinent to the field of biomedical informatics. The code is organized around the common roles of AMIA members and the constituents they serve and with whom they interact. The AMIA Board and the AMIA Ethics Committee encourage AMIA members to flesh out gaps in coverage and scope. We are especially interested in real-world examples of ethical situations members have encountered. In this way the code will continue to evolve to best serve the informatics community.

* For example, see Robert Greenes' and the AMIA Board of Director's strategic plan description in JAMIA, 1994 May-Jun;1(3):263-71.

Principles of Professional Ethical Conduct for the American Medical Informatics Association.

As a member of the American Medical Informatics Association, I acknowledge my professional duty to uphold the following principles and guidelines of ethical conduct:

Source: AMIA 2007.

I. **Key ethical guidelines regarding patients, their families, their significant others, and their representatives (called here collectively 'patients'):**

A. Patients have the right to know about the existence of electronic records containing personal biomedical data;

1. Do not mislead patients about the how these data are used, about the origin of these data, nor about how and with whom these data are communicated;

2. Answer truthfully patients' questions concerning their rights to review and annotate their own biomedical data, and seek to facilitate a subject's legitimate right to exercise of those rights.

B. Advocate and work to ensure that biomedical data are maintained in a safe, reliable, secure, and confidential environment that is consistent with applicable law, local policies, and accepted informatics processing standards;

C. Never knowingly disclose biomedical data in a fashion that violates legal requirements or accepted local confidentiality practices;

1. Likewise, even if it does not involve disclosure, never use patients' data outside the stated purposes, goals, or intents of the organization responsible for these data.

D. Treat the data of all patients with equal care, respect, and fairness.

II. **Key ethical guidelines regarding colleagues:**

A. Facilitate colleagues' work in a timely, respectful, and conscientious way to support their role in the healthcare or research enterprise;

B. Advise colleagues in a timely fashion about real, or potential, adverse outcomes or adverse situations you discover that could hinder their ability to discharge their responsibilities to patients, other colleagues, involved institutions, or other stakeholders;

C. To the extent you can, foster a professional environment that is conducive to the highest ethical and technical standards;

D. Disclose to colleagues any personal biases, prejudices, technical shortcomings, or other constraints that may hinder your ability to discharge your professional responsibilities;

E. If you work as a leader:

1. Communicate and promote these ethical guidelines to those you lead;

2. Manage personnel and other resources effectively and fairly;

3. Communicate and promote policies that protect the dignity of patients and colleagues.

F. Be forthright in correcting malfeasance or unprofessional conduct on the part of colleagues.

III. **Key ethical guidelines regarding institutions, employers, and clients (called here collectively 'employers'):**

A. In a professional working relationship, employers have the right to expect from you diligence, honesty, and loyalty to common purpose. In return, exercise your right to work in a fair, safe, honest, and productive environment;

B. Work to apply the guidelines for patients (described above in I) to your relationship with an employer (e.g., do not mislead; be truthful; maintain a safe, reliable, secure, and confidential data environment; do not disclose confidential or sensitive information; treat the employer fairly);

C. Likewise, work to apply the guidelines for colleagues (described in above in II) to your relationship with an employer (e.g., facilitate the working enterprise in a timely, respectful, and conscientious way; immediately advise an employer of adverse or disadvantageous circumstances; work to foster an ethical and technically proficient professional environment; and disclose biases, prejudices, technical shortcomings, or other constraints on your ability to conduct your assignments);

D. Learn and respect your intellectual property rights and interests as well as those of your employer, colleagues, and patients;

E. Learn and respect the legal obligations of your employer and comply with local policies and procedures to the extent that they do not violate ethical norms.

IV. Key ethical guidelines regarding society and regarding research:

A. Be mindful and respectful of the societal or public-health implications of your work, ensuring that the greatest good for society is realized by your work under the constraints of your ethical obligations to your patients, colleagues, and employers;

1. The constraints of your ethical obligations to your patients, colleagues, and employers are not absolute, carefully weigh those obligations against the potentially greater interests of society and the public's welfare.

B. Basic human rights, especially as articulated and regulated in conducting research, must remain the highest ethical standard;

C. Know the applicable governmental regulations and local policies that define ethical research in your professional environment. Strive to meet the spirit as well the letter of those regulations and policies.

V. General ethical guidelines

A. Always disclose to any relevant party all real or potential conflicts of interest that may constrain your professional work;

B. Maintain your competence as an informatics professional;

1. Recognize your technical and ethical limitations and seek consultation when needed;

2. Work diligently to meet the continuing education expectations in your field, and if you undertake service obligations (e.g., voluntary participation on technical committees or membership on regulatory boards) discharge these duties with the same care and conscientiousness as you would your regular duties.

C. Take responsibility for your actions and your work, while taking and sharing credit where credit is due;

D. Avoid exploiting professional relationships, especially positions in AMIA, for personal gain beyond those reasonably expected for good service;

E. Respect professional confidences to the extent that it does not hinder other ethical obligations;

F. Strive to encourage the adoption of informatics approaches proven to improve health and healthcare;

1. Strive to make research, development, and evaluation of health information technology a priority;

2. Strive to involve others who have an appropriate expertise in biomedical and health informatics initiatives in your own work.

G. Be mindful that your work and actions reflect both on the profession and on the AMIA organization as a whole.

VI. Enforcement, compliance, and violations. The adoption of a code of ethical conduct naturally raises the questions of compliance. What are the consequences of violating the code? How is the code enforced? The authors have suggested to the AMIA Board of Directors that these are issues best decided by the AMIA membership itself. In future forums, AMIA will initiate a dialog with the membership to seek consensus on this important topic.

Acknowledgments

The authors and the AMIA Ethics Committee would like to thank the AMIA Board of Directors for their continuing interest in refining and publicizing these guidelines. Additional comments on the code were provided by Dan Stein and Kristina Thomas. Other members of the AMIA Ethics Committee who contributed to drafts of the code include: Mureen Allen, MSBS, MS, MA, Joseph Catapano, MD, Oscar Gyde, MD, Carol Hope, PharmD, and Helga Rippen, MD, PhD, MPH.

References

Additional reading and related professional codes that influenced the Ethics Committee's most recent deliberations on this iteration of the Code maybe found in:

American Association of Critical-Care Nurses. Nursing Code of Ethics Resources. 2006 [cited 2006 11/01/06]. Available from: http://www.aacn.org/AACN/practice.nsf/....

American Health Information Management Association. American Health Information Management Association Code of Ethics. 2004 [cited 2006 10/24/2006]; On-line version of the AHIMA Code of Ethics. Available from: http://library.ahima.org/xpedio/groups/public/documents/ahima/bok1_024277.hcsp?dDocName=bok1_024277.

Association of Computing Machinery. ACM Code of Ethics and Professional Conduct. 1992 [cited 2006 11/04/06]. Available from: http://www.acm.org/constitution/code.html.

Healthcare Information and Management Systems Society. Code of Ethics. 2002 [cited 2006 November]. Available from: http://ethics.iit.edu/codes/coe/healthcare.info.mgt.systems.soc.coe.html.

Illinois Institute of Technology. All online Codes of Ethics. 2006 [cited 11/05/2006]. Available from: http://ethics.iit.edu/codes/codes_index.html.

International Medical Informatics Association. IMIA Code of Ethics for Health Information Professionals. 2002 [cited 2006 3/16/2006]; On-line version of the IMIA Code of Ethics. Available from: http://www.imia.org/English_code_of_ethics.html.

Appendix 13D
Sample Consent Form for Medical Research

University of California, Los Angeles
Office for Protection of Research Subjects
MEDICAL INSTITUTIONAL REVIEW BOARD
[*Replace the previous two lines with the name of the department or division conducting the research*]

SAMPLE CONSENT FORM FOR MEDICAL RESEARCH

CONSENT TO PARTICIPATE IN RESEARCH

[*Insert lay title of the study.*] [*If the study involves using different consent forms for different populations, identify the population group as the subtitle of the study.*]

Suggested text:

You are asked to participate in a research study conducted by [*insert names and degrees of all investigators*], from the [*insert department affiliation*] at the University of California, Los Angeles. You have been asked to participate in this study because [*explain succinctly and simply why the prospective subject is eligible to participate*]. [*If appropriate, state the approximate number of subjects involved in the study.*] Your participation in this study is entirely voluntary. You should read the information below, and ask questions about anything you do not understand, before deciding whether or not to participate.

Guidelines:

- *Use simple language.*
- *Be concise.*
- *Use the pronoun "you" consistently throughout (except for the "Signature of Research Subject" on the last page).*
- *If subjects must be patients with a specific disease/condition, and if they must have tried standard treatments without good results, say so in clear terms. For example: "You qualify to participate in this project because you have breast cancer that has not responded well to standard treatment (or that has recurred, in spite of standard treatment)."*

DISCLOSURE STATEMENT

(**Note: If the investigators on this study will <u>not</u> be directly involved in potential subjects' health care, please omit this section and delete the heading.**)

Date of Preparation:
UCLA IRB Number:
Expiration Date:

Your health care provider may be an investigator of this research protocol, and as an investigator, is interested in both your clinical welfare and in the conduct of this study. Before entering this study or at any time during the research, you may ask for a second opinion about your care from another doctor who is in no way associated with this project. You are not under any obligation to participate in any research project offered by your physician.

Guidelines:

- The Human Research Policy Board, Chaired by Executive Vice Chancellor Wyatt R. Hume, issued an April 20, 1999 memorandum "Disclosure of Possible Conflict of Interest to Human Research Subjects" which outlines investigators' obligations to disclose a possible conflict of interest in informed consent forms when (A) the researcher is responsible for the health care of the subject, and/or (B) has a financial interest in the sponsor of the study. The memorandum is available at http://www.oprs.ucla.edu/human/news/item?item_id=119763.

PURPOSE OF THE STUDY

[*State what the study is designed to discover or establish.*]

PROCEDURES

Suggested text:

If you volunteer to participate in this study, we would ask you to do the following things:

Guidelines:

- *Describe the procedures chronologically using lay language, short sentences and short paragraphs. The use of subheadings will help to organize this section and increase readability. Distinguish which procedures are experimental and which are standard clinical treatments.*
- *Define and explain medical and scientific terms .in ordinary language (for example, describing the amount of blood to be drawn in terms of teaspoons or tablespoons).*
- *Specify the subject's assignment to study groups, length of time for participation in each procedure, the total length of time for participation, frequency of procedures, location of the procedures to be done, etc.*
- *For research involving randomization of subjects into different arms of studies, specify the randomization procedures.*
- *For research involving the use of placebo, clearly define the term of placebo.*

POTENTIAL RISKS AND DISCOMFORTS

Guidelines:

- *Identify each intervention with a subheading and then describe any reasonable foreseeable risks, discomforts, inconveniences, and how these will be managed.*
- *In addition to physiological risks/discomforts, describe any psychological, social, legal, or financial risks that might result from participating in the research.*
- *If there are significant physical or psychological risks to participation that might cause the researcher to terminate the study, please describe them.*
- *Include the following statement: [The treatment or procedure may involve risks that are currently unforeseeable.]*

ANTICIPATED BENEFITS TO SUBJECTS

Suggested text:

Based on experience with this [*drug, procedure, device, etc.*] in [*animals, patients with similar disorders*], researchers believe it may be of benefit to subjects with your condition [*or, it may be as good as standard therapy but with fewer side effects*]. Of course, because individuals respond differently to therapy, no one can know in advance if it will be helpful in your particular case. The potential benefits may include:

[*Describe the anticipated benefits to subjects resulting from their participation in the research.*]

Guidelines:

- *If there is no likelihood that participants will benefit directly from their participation in the research, state as much in clear terms. For example:* "You should not expect your condition to improve as a result of participating in this research" *or* "This study is not being done to improve your condition or health. You have the right to refuse to participate in this study."
- *Do not include financial rewards for participating in this section; that will be addressed later.*

ANTICIPATED BENEFITS TO SOCIETY

[*State the anticipated benefits, if any, to science or society expected from the research.*]

ALTERNATIVES TO PARTICIPATION

Guidelines:

- *Describe any appropriate alternative therapeutic, diagnostic, or preventive procedures that should be considered before the subjects decide whether or not to participate in the study. If applicable, explain why these procedures are being withheld. If there are no efficacious alternatives, state that an alternative is not to participate in the study.*
- *If the prospective subjects are suffering from a terminal illness, and there are no alternative treatments available, you should say so; but add that treatment of symptoms and pain control are available through supportive care such as, hospice, home health care, clinics, private physicians, etc. In other words, avoid suggesting that participation in the research is the only way to obtain medical care and attention.*
- *•If prospective subjects have a chronic, progressive disorder, for which no treatment had been demonstrated to be safe and effective, say that, as well. But also describe opportunities for managing symptoms, improving ability to function, etc. so that it does not appear that the patient will be abandoned if he/she does not agree to participate in the research.*

PAYMENT FOR PARTICIPATION

Guidelines:

- *State whether the subject will be paid or offered other benefits (e.g., free care). If not, state so.*
- *If the subject will receive payment, describe remuneration amount, when payment is scheduled, and proration schedule should the subject decide to withdraw or is withdrawn by the investigator.*
- *If the subject will be reimbursed for expenses such as parking, bus/taxi, baby-sitter, travel companion/assistant, etc., list payment rates.*

- *Since subjects should be encouraged to report side effects or intercurrent illness, if subjects will be paid for participating in the research, it is important that they not lose payment if they develop side effects or illness.*

POSSIBLE COMMERCIAL PRODUCTS

(Note: If this does not apply to your research, please omit this entry and delete the heading.)

Suggested text:

Cells obtained from your body may be used to establish a cell line which may be shared in the future with other researchers and which may be of commercial value. A cell line is one which will grow indefinitely in the laboratory. Cell lines may be useful because of the characteristics of the cells and/or the products they may produce.

Guidelines:

- *If any human materials (tumor tissue, bone marrow, blood, etc.) are used for establishing a cell line which may be shared with other researchers and which may in the future be of commercial value, the subject must be informed of the fact in the consent form. The above statement must be included verbatim.]*

FINANCIAL OBLIGATION

(Note: If there is no financial obligation of the subject, please say so.)

Suggested text:

It is possible that your insurance will not pay for all of the treatments and tests you will receive if you participate in the research. That is because many insurance companies, HMOs, and health benefits plans do not cover experimental treatments. If that happens, the charges you will have to pay will be as follows: [*Provide an itemized list.*]

Suggested *alternative* text:

Neither you nor your insurance company will be billed for your participation in this research.

Guidelines:

- *If it is likely or even possible that procedures or tests the subjects will undergo will not be covered by their insurance, health benefits plan, or other third party payers, you should make this clear.*
- *Itemize and estimate the charges that subjects participating in the research will be expected to pay if the charges are not paid by their insurance or other third payer.*
- *If you have had enough experience with similar protocols to estimate which of the charges are likely to be covered, that information may be included, but be sure to make clear that that will not necessarily be true in each case.*
- *Bills should not be submitted to third party payers without the written consent of the subject.*

EMERGENCY CARE AND COMPENSATION FOR INJURY

Note: The following is a required element of informed consent for research involving more than minimal risk. If this does not apply to your research, please omit this entry and delete the heading: "If you are injured as a direct result of research procedures not done primarily for your own benefit, you will receive treatment at no cost. The University of California does not provide any other form of compensation for injury."

If the study is sponsored by a private drug or device manufacturer, the following is a required element of informed consent for research involving more than minimal risk: "If you are injured as a direct result of research procedures, you will receive treatment at no cost. The University of California does not provide any other form of compensation for injury."

Guidelines:

- *Please see http://www.oprs.ucla.edu/human/news/item?item_id=149247 for detailed guidance regarding acceptable wording for this section.*

PRIVACY AND CONFIDENTIALITY

Suggested text:

The only people who will know that you are a research subject are members of the research team and, if appropriate, your physicians and nurses. No information about you, or provided by you during the research, will be disclosed to others without your written permission, except:

- if necessary to protect your rights or welfare (for example, if you are injured and need emergency care); or
- if required by law.

When the results of the research are published or discussed in conferences, no information will be included that would reveal your identity. If photographs, videos, or audio-tape recordings of you will be used for educational purposes, your identity will be protected or disguised. [*Describe the subject's right to review/edit the tapes, who will have access, and when they will be erased. Describe how personal identities will be shielded, disguised, etc.*]

[***When the research records may be subject to inspection by FDA, a funding agency, or an industrial sponsor, you must add:***]

Authorized representatives of the Food and Drug Administration (FDA) [*or a funding agency, such as the National Institutes of Health*] and the manufacturer of the drug [*or device*] being tested [*insert name of company*] may need to review records of individual subjects. As a result, they may see your name; but they are bound by rules of confidentiality not to reveal your identity to others.

Guidelines:

- *Give a brief description of how personal information, research data, and related records will be coded, stored, etc. to prevent access by unauthorized personnel.*
- *Explain how specific consent will be solicited, if any other uses are contemplated.*
- *If applicable, state if and when individual responses to survey questionnaires will be destroyed, following analyses of the data.*

PARTICIPATION AND WITHDRAWAL

Suggested text:

Your participation in this research is VOLUNTARY. If you choose not to participate, that will not affect your relationship with UCLA (or UCLA Medical Center), or your right to health care or other services to which you are otherwise entitled. If you decide to participate, you are free to withdraw your consent and discontinue participation at any time without prejudice to your future care at UCLA.

CONSEQUENCES OF WITHDRAWAL

(Note: If this does not apply to your research, please omit this entry and delete the heading.) [*Explain the consequences of a subject's decision to withdraw from the research and state whether withdrawal must be gradual, for reasons of safety.*]

WITHDRAWAL OF PARTICIPATION BY THE INVESTIGATOR

Suggested text:

The investigator may withdraw you from participating in this research if circumstances arise which warrant doing so. If you experience any of the following side effects [*list and describe*] or if you become ill during the research, you may have to drop out, even if you would like to continue. The investigator, [*insert name*], will make the decision and let you know if it is not possible for you to continue. The decision may be made either to protect your health and safety, or because it is part of the research plan that people who develop certain conditions may not continue to participate.

If you must drop out because the investigator asks you to (rather than because you have decided on your own to withdraw), you will be paid [*insert amount of payment or other remuneration*].

Guidelines:

- *Be sure that this aspect of terminating participation at the request of the PI is noted in the section on Payment for Participation, as well, and that the information in both sections is consistent.*

NEW FINDINGS

During the course of the study, you will be informed of any significant new findings (either good or bad), such as changes in the risks or benefits resulting from participation in the research or new alternatives to participation, that might cause you to change your mind about continuing in the study. If new information is provided to you, your consent to continue participating in this study will be re-obtained.

IDENTIFICATION OF INVESTIGATORS

In the event of a research related injury or if you experience an adverse reaction, please immediately contact one of the investigators listed below. If you have any questions about the research, please feel free to contact [*identify all personnel involved in the research as listed in the IRB Application under the following subheadings: Principal Investigator, Faculty Advisor (if student is the P.I.), Co-Investigator(s), Participating Personnel. Include the daytime telephone numbers and addresses for all listed individuals. For greater than minimal risk studies, include night/emergency telephone numbers.*]

RIGHTS OF RESEARCH SUBJECTS

You may withdraw your consent at any time and discontinue participation without penalty. You are not waiving any legal claims, rights or remedies because of your participation in this research study. If you have questions regarding your rights as a research subject, you may contact the Office for Protection of Research Subjects, UCLA, 11000 Kinross Avenue, Suite 102, Box 951694, Los Angeles, CA 90095-1694, (310) 825-8714.

SIGNATURE OF RESEARCH SUBJECT OR LEGAL REPRESENTATIVE

I have read (or someone has read to me) the information provided above. I have been given an opportunity to ask questions and all of my questions have been answered to my satisfaction. I have been given a copy of this form, as well as a copy of the Subject's Bill of Rights.

BY SIGNING THIS FORM, I WILLINGLY AGREE TO PARTICIPATE IN THE RESEARCH IT DESCRIBES.

_____
Name of Subject

_____
Name of Legal Representative (if applicable)

_____   _____
Signature of Subject or Legal Representative   Date

SIGNATURE OF INVESTIGATOR

I have explained the research to the subject or his/her legal representative, and answered all of his/her questions. I believe that he/she understands the information described in this document and freely consents to participate.

_____
Name of Investigator

_____   _____
Signature of Investigator   Date (must be the same as subject's)

SIGNATURE OF WITNESS (If required by the IRB.)

My signature as witness certified that the subject or his/her legal representative signed this consent form in my presence as his/her voluntary act and deed.

_____
Name of Witness

_____   _____
Signature of Witness   Date (must be the same as subject's)

Appendix 13E
The Path to Informed Consent: A Process, Not a Form (Abbreviated)

The steps below are all considered part of the "process of consent." The "Path of Consent" indicates the steps along the way to fully informed consent that may occur in the conduct of a study.

1. Initial Approach and Contact
2. Introduction to the Study
3. Inclusion and Exclusion Criteria Evaluation
4. Presentation of the Study in More Detail
5. Questions by the Potential Subject
6. Formal Consent Form Review
7. Subject takes consent form home to review
8. Consent form signing and questions
9. Post-test—did the subject understand what he/she agreed to participate in
10. Pre-screening—No pre-screening may take place before the consent form has been signed
11. Enrollment and Randomization
12. The Study begins
13. Study follows procedures outlined in the consent for
14. Revisions to the Study that may impact the consent form
15. Adverse Events and Revisions may dictate reconsenting
16. Reconsenting
17. Annual Review—newly approved consent form—no need to reconsent subjects who are already enrolled if there are not changes to the consent form
18. Drop-out or Withdrawal
19. Drop out of Individual Phases—Blood or Tissue Collection
20. Study Closure
21. Follow-up
22. Data Analysis
23. Research Results
24. Reporting results back to subjects

Appendix 13F
The Path to Informed Consent: A Process, Not a Form (Expanded)

The steps below are all considered part of the "process of consent." The "Path to Informed Consent" indicates the steps along the way to fully informed consent that may occur in the conduct of a study.

1. Recruitment

(please note: No recruitment can occur before IRB approval.)

- Recruitment occurs even when someone is reviewing records and databases to see if there are potential subjects.
- Who is reviewing records?
- Do they have authority for such review?
- Did they receive human subjects training?
- Voluntary recruitment: using posters or flyers to hand-out—advertisements must be IRB approved before they are posted. The potential subject sees the poster and responds to the ad.

2. Initial Approach and Contact

- Who is doing the initial approach to a potential subject?
- What is their background?
- Are they familiar with the study?
- Have they read the protocol?
- Did they take human subjects training?
- What script are they using to introduce the study?

3. Screening for Eligibility

Types of Screening: Records screening; In-person screening—phone calls and walk-ins; use of known subjects who have agreed to be in research studies.

Only brief questions can be asked to determine basic eligibility. Questions should not require participant to self-diagnose. Since person has not signed a consent form yet, this must be somewhat limited.

It is not permitted to record any subject identifiers when performing telephone screening to determine potential subject eligibility unless: 1) the screening questions are not of a private nature; or 2) written informed consent of the subject has been obtained prior to the telephone screening; or 3) the IRB has granted a waiver of the overall requirement to obtain informed consent for participation the telephone screening; or 4) the IRB has granted a waiver of the requirement to obtain a signed, written informed consent form for participation in the telephone screening.

Source: Carol Nielsen. Reprinted with permission.

Screening to determine subject eligibility for biomedical and behavioral research studies often addresses medical information or information of a sensitive nature (e.g., alcohol use, drug use). In these circumstances, exception number 1), above, would not apply.

4. Introduction to the Study

This is a brief overview about what the study is about. Often a short script can be used.

5. Inclusion and Exclusion Criteria Evaluation

Either the research coordinator or the PI carries out this step. The PI is responsible for assuring that all subjects chosen for the study are appropriate and match the inclusion/exclusion criteria.

6. Presentation of the Study in More Detail and Formal Consent Form Review

Either the research coordinator or the PI carries out this step.

7. Questions by the Potential Subject

Be prepared to answer any questions the subject has.
Be consistent with all subjects about answers to questions.

8. Consent form signing and questions

Prior to signing the consent form: subjects may wish to take the consent form home to review or it can be reviewed on site. Subjects must not be pressured to sign a consent form immediately.

9. Post-test

Did the subject understand what he/she agreed to participate in? A solid understanding by the subject of what is involved in the study will result in better compliance, participation, and fewer persons withdrawing.
This does not have to be a test. It can be a few questions.

- Ask the subject about the purpose of the study, the benefits, the risks, alternatives, and reimbursement.
- Be sure the subject understands the length of the study and how many visits are involved.
- Be sure they understand that you are not providing treatment.
- Be sure they understand what they will get to keep at the end of the study.

10. The Study begins

Study follows procedures outlined in the consent form.

11. Adverse Events and Revisions

If there are adverse events (AEs), they must be reported to IRB staff immediately. AEs will be forwarded to the IRB. Adverse events may be expected and are not to be viewed as some lapse on the part of the study managers.

Some adverse events or information that is discovered during the course of the study may require staff to revise the protocol. Revisions to the protocol must be submitted to the IRB and may require a new version of the consent form.

12. Reconsenting

If there are revisions to the study that impact the consent form, they should be reflected in a revised consent form and enrolled subjects must be reconsented.

13. Annual Review

When the annual review occurs there is a newly approved consent form. If the only change is a version date, there is no need to reconsent the subjects who are already enrolled in the study.

14. Drop-out or Withdrawal

If a person decides to drop out or withdraw they are not required to come back to the research center or clinic. Subjects may drop out without giving reasons. You may not collect additional data after a subject drops out but you can use the data that you collected prior to that time.

If there are materials that you must have them return this must be specified in the consent form.

15. Follow-up

The study must remain open if long-term follow-up is part of the study. After a study is closed you cannot recontact subjects.

16. Study Closure

When the study is going to be closed that means that ALL subject contact is completed. After study closure there may be no more study contact.

17. Reporting Results Back to Subjects

Summary of a Study that can be used when recruiting volunteers.

1. Introduction to the organization sponsoring the study
2. Inclusion and exclusion criteria reviewed with potential subject to see if they qualify.
3. Brief overview of what will happen in the study—what are you are trying to do?
4. Time commitment—number of visits, length of visits—important for people with ambulatory issues. Explanation if food is provided or other snacks if the study requires a long visit.
5. Explanation of what they will get. Remember that research studies can't provide answers or cures. They are discovery.
6. Reimbursement or honorarium arrangements.
7. Parking information
8. Time for questions—allow all questions to be answered
9. Appointment set up and how to get to the office to participate in the study.

Chapter 14
Dissemination

Elizabeth J. Layman, PhD, RHIA, CCS, FAHIMA

Learning Objectives

- To present research findings in formats consistent with the purpose of the research

- To present research findings in formats consistent with the guidelines of the modes of dissemination

Key Terms

Abstract

Article (journal article, refereed article, scholarly article)

Impact factor

IMRAD

Manuscript

Paper (research paper, scholarly paper)

Peer review

Poster session

Priority claim

Proceedings

Publication bias

Rigor

Scientific enterprise

Submission guidelines

Introduction

Knowledge must be known before it can affect practice, influence policy, and persuade skeptics (Glass 1976, 4). Therefore, health informatics researchers make their knowledge known through disseminating the findings of their studies.

Health informatics researchers disseminate their research for three reasons. First, disseminating research findings advances the field of health informatics because new knowledge builds and expands its scientific base. Second, this new information moves health informatics practice forward when implemented in the workplace. Finally, disseminating research advances the researchers' own careers. Dissemination of knowledge is essential to its accessibility, availability, and eventual use.

Knowledge is disseminated and examined through **poster sessions**, conference presentations, and publications. This chapter discusses features of all three modes of dissemination.

Presentation

Poster sessions and presentations occur at professional meetings, conferences, symposia, and congresses. These events are planned far in advance. Professional associations will issue a call for session proposals up to 18 months before a professional meeting. (See figure 14.1.) In response to the call, researchers send brief descriptions of their proposed sessions. The meeting organizers and peer-review committees, as applicable, determine which proposals to accept based on the quality, number, and relevance of the topic to the theme of the event.

Researchers whose career advancement depends on presentation should focus their submissions to peer-reviewed events. Feedback and discussions with other researchers at poster sessions and conference presentations provide valuable information on ways to improve the research study. For example, giving a presentation about a pilot study can garner worthwhile suggestions that enhance the later full-scale study. Constructive information flows in both directions at poster sessions and conference presentations.

Abstracts and **papers** associated with poster sessions and conference presentations may be published in the program or **proceedings**. Abstracts are brief summaries of the major parts of research studies (literature review, purpose or problem statement, method, results, discussion, and conclusions and recommendations). Abstracts are used with poster sessions, conference presentations, and journal **articles**. Proceedings are published compilations of the papers delivered at conferences. Published abstracts and conference papers are not as highly esteemed as published journal articles, but they do build researchers' scholarly bodies of work and they do support the field's body of knowledge.

Poster Sessions

Poster sessions are a means of communicating research. The posters contain the key information about research. At these sessions, researchers stand in front of their posters for designated time slots. Typically, poster sessions last three to five hours on one day. Participants at the event read the posters and ask the researchers questions about the study. Researchers have papers available that they can give to interested persons. Poster sessions are sometimes judged (juried). At judged poster sessions, judges mingle with the participants, asking questions and inspecting and rating the research as depicted in the poster.

Researchers' posters must conform to the guidelines of the session. Prior to the event, meeting organizers distribute poster guidelines which state the size of the poster. Common sizes for posters are 3 feet by 5 feet, or 4 feet by 6 feet.

Institutional printing departments offer services that enhance posters. Commercial printing companies with staffs of commercial artists and graphic designers also print posters. A cost-effective alternative are Web sites that offer the printing of posters. These Web sites may have templates that researchers can use. The posters can even be shipped to the conference, a great convenience to researchers.

Researchers need to submit Microsoft Word documents or PowerPoint slides. Posters typically include:

- Banner (header) with title of study, names of researchers, and institutional affiliation
- Abstract
- Purpose
- Method
- Results
- Discussion and conclusions (see figure 14.2.)

Figure 14.1. Sample call for proposals

Call for Research Abstracts

Deadline for Abstracts: October 31, 20**

Abstracts for the Summer Symposium are being solicited.

Topics:

- Workforce initiatives
- Innovations in service delivery
- Organizational or administrative issues in healthcare enterprises
- Best practices or performance improvement
- E-health implementations

Content of the research abstract should include:

- Title of presentation
- Name(s) of author(s) with title, credentials, and organization
- Method
- Brief results

All applicants are invited to submit their abstracts for contributions to the symposium via the online submission form on the symposium Web site www.fictitious-URL.org/symposium200*. The submission deadline is October 31, 200*. Abstracts should be limited to 250 words. Questions should be e-mailed to Professor Qualef (qualefl@fictitious.edu).

Selection of abstracts will be made through a peer-reviewed process. The peer review committee will determine whether the mode of presentation will be oral presentation or poster. Applicants will be notified of acceptance or rejection and the mode of presentation by January 15, 200*. Accepted abstracts will be printed in the Symposium Proceedings, conditional upon payment of the registration fee.

Authors of accepted abstracts will be asked to submit the complete scholarly paper by February 15, 20**. Scholarly papers will be published in *Symposium Proceedings,* conditional upon payment of the registration fee.

Content for the scholarly paper should include:

1. Abstract,
2. Title,
3. Name(s) of author(s) with title, credentials, and organization;
4. Literature review;
5. Purpose or problem statement;
6. Method including analytical technique;
7. Results;
8. Discussion; and
9. Conclusions and recommendations for future research.

Authors of accepted abstracts for oral presentations will be asked to submit their PowerPoint presentations and handouts for their presentations by April 15. Presentations will be limited to 15 minutes, inclusive of questions.

All participants will receive a password that will allow online access to abstracts, *Symposium Proceedings,* and handouts by June 15, conditional upon payment of the registration fee.

Liz Qualef, PhD

Professor and Chair

Fictitious University

Department of Health Informatics

College of Related Professions

City, ST 12345

E-Mail: qualefl@fictitious.edu

Figure 14.2.   Sample poster

SCHOOLS OF ALLIED HEALTH: DO THEY ENHANCE THE ACHIEVEMENT OF FEMALE STUDENTS?

Liz Researcher, PhD, RHIA, CCS, FAHIMA
EAST CAROLINA UNIVERSITY   School of Allied Health Sciences

ABSTRACT

In an era of health care reform, allied health practitioners will need to be leaders. Because women predominate the enrollments of schools of allied health, leaders of these schools need to pay particular attention to factors that advance the goals of educational attainment and future occupational success of female students.

Researchers have demonstrated that women's colleges advance these achievements for female students. Researchers attributed the difference in female success at women's colleges to the numbers of women in administrative and faculty leadership.

METHOD

The sample was schools of allied health at academic health centers in the Southeast. The deans (n = 25) of the Southern Association of Allied Health Deans at Academic Health Centers were surveyed using a researcher-designed questionnaire.

Figure 1.   Comparison of leadership: schools of allied health and women's colleges

ROLE	SCHOOLS OF ALLIED HEALTH	WOMEN'S COLLEGES
Administrative Leader	40	60
Professor	32	43
Assoc. Professor	55	49
Tenured	46	41

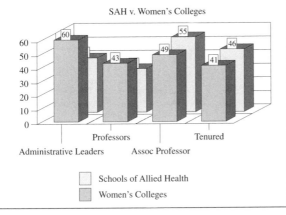

Comparison of Leadership

SAH v. Women's Colleges

Schools of Allied Health
Women's Colleges

PURPOSE

The purpose of this research was to determine whether these same characteristics exist in schools of allied health. The three objectives that guided the research were to identify:

(1)   the proportion of women in positions of administrative leadership in schools of allied health,

(2)   the proportion of women in positions of faculty leadership, and

(3)   the educational preparation of female faculty.

RESULTS

Table 1.   Leadership in schools of allied health

POSITION	% Female
Top Administrative (Dean, Assoc. or Asst. Dean)	40.0
Chair	49.6
Other Admin. (Assoc. Chair)	58.7
Senior Faculty (Professor, Assoc. Professor)	46.8
Tenured Faculty	46.4

Table 2.   Highest degree

DEGREE	% Female
All Faculty	57.2
Doctorate, 1st Professional	46.9

DISCUSSION AND CONCLUSIONS

The characteristics related to achievement of female students are increased numbers of women in positions of administrative and faculty leadership. A comparison of the data of this study and profiles of women's colleges in the literature showed that while schools of allied health did not exhibit the first characteristic, women as administrative leaders, they did show women as faculty leaders.

Schools of allied health could enhance their commitment to the achievement of female students by developing female faculty as administrative leaders.

The study also revealed that female faculty at these schools have earned doctorates at a lower rate than their male counterparts. With increasingly rigorous criteria for tenure in these schools, the doctoral preparation of faculty, and especially female faculty should be supported.

Future studies should broaden the investigation to all institutions in the Association of Schools of Allied Health Professions.

Posters should be colorful and readable at a distance, the banner at 15 to 20 feet and the body at 10 feet. Charts and graphics are particularly striking. The posters can be laminated or mounted on rigid poster board. Web sites created by Hess et al. (2006) and Tosney (2001) provide helpful information on effective posters. In addition to these considerations about the poster itself, researchers also need to think about logistics. Researchers should consider how they are going to transport their posters to the event site and how they are going to mount the posters at the site. Investing time in creating and mounting a poster that looks professional is important.

Conference Presentations

Professional presentations occur during sessions of regional, state, national, and international meetings. As described previously, researchers submit proposals in response to a call, or they may be invited to present if their topic is particularly relevant. Linking the response to the theme of the meeting increases the likelihood that the proposal will be accepted.

Presenters should remember their audience as they create and present their papers and PowerPoint slides. Edirisooriya (1996) studied the delivery of research papers. Over seven years, she attended 126 sessions and viewed 748 presenters (Edirisooriya 1996, 25). Most presenters were allowed 12 minutes, and most found this limit inadequate (Edirisooriya 1996, 25). She found that 42 percent of presenters had not synthesized their data into information and, thus, wasted time on unnecessary and trivial details (Edirisooriya 1996, 27). These presenters never reached the important points of their research. Edirisooriya recommends that presenters prepare for oral presentations by:

- Practicing their presentation
- Bringing all their materials
- Distilling their paper to four or five pages
- Showing eye-catching graphics (not tables with miniscule numbers)
- Focusing on results, discussion, and implications rather than background, theoretical framework, and rationales for analytical techniques (Edirisooriya 1996, 28-29)

A more recent article reiterated these same ideas for effective presentations (Wineberg 2004, 13–14). Generally, presenters should be prepared to talk about their research. Tips on the key points of the study's content to emphasize are listed in table 14.1. Moreover, merely reading the notes is inadequate. Researchers should try

Table 14.1.   Tips for content of conference presentations

Section	Include	Omit
Background	Brief update on status of the *current* body of knowledge with emphasis on gap in the body of knowledge or problem with policy or method	Long discussions of the entire theory and all the related literature
Purpose or problem statement	Clear and explicit statement of purpose or problem Explicit linkage to the issue identified in the Background	Disclaimers Involved qualifiers Claims of primacy
Method including analytical technique	Research design, timeframe, method, sampling stratagem (if applicable), and major analytical technique	Justifications of research design, timeframe, method, sampling stratagem (if applicable), and analytical techniques
Results and discussion	Analyses that resulted in major findings Major findings explained in depth Interpretation of major findings	Trivia Unimportant findings Defense of theory Repetition of literature review
Conclusions and recommendations*	Significance of findings Implications for field, policy, education, future research, or other consequence Recommendations for future research including own directions	Statements, such as "I'm running out of time," or "Just one more point"

* This section is critical and should not be victim of poor planning or execution of other sections.
Source: Adapted from Edirisooriya 1996.

to be animated and talk to the people in the room. Other details regarding the mechanics of creating an effective PowerPoint presentation are listed in figure 14.3.

Publication

Publishing research is critical. Publishing research opens the study's design, method, analysis, and interpretation to the examination and critique of fellow researchers and professionals. This critical examination is known as **peer review**.

Peer review is a long-established part of the **scientific enterprise**. In 1731, The Royal Society of Edinburgh published the society's policy and objectives for its *Medical Essays and Observations* (Kronick 1990, 1321). Also credited with early adoption of peer review is the Royal Society of London. In 1752, it established the Committee on Papers that reviewed all articles prior to publication in its *Philosophical Transactions* (Kronick 1990, 1321). Peer review is essential to the growth of scientific knowledge.

Critical examination serves the functions of gatekeeping, legitimizing, and improving the organization

and logic of the study (Shashok 2005). The gatekeeping function of peer review confirms the significance and relevance of the study to the field and to the journal's mission, respectively. Significant studies are important to the field. Significance may be related to the number of practitioners or sites affected by the study. On the other hand, numbers affected is not an absolute assurance of significance. Some groundbreaking research, such as research related to electronic health records (EHRs), initially affected only a few practitioners and sites. In terms of relevance, journals have defined scopes of interest, and articles must be relevant to the journal's particular scope. (See figure 14.4.)

Legitimizing attests to the face validity and **rigor** of the study—it should have been conducted appropriately using a suitable design, method, sampling stratagems, and analytical techniques. However, peer review is unable to detect falsification or lies. To the best of the reviewers' knowledge, the study should appear to have rigor. Rigor is the strength of the research in terms of strictly following the tenets of quality research. Rigorous research has the highest likelihood of accuracy, validity, and reliability.

Peer reviewers attempt to follow the logic of the study as reported in the manuscript. Sometimes, the structure of the manuscript is illogical and the reviewers can neither understand nor evaluate what the researchers did in the study. Other times, the peer reviewers understand the overall activities of the study but believe that restructuring the manuscript will increase its readability. In this function, publication makes research accessible to readers.

Structure (IMRAD)

Scientific manuscripts follow the structure known as **IMRAD** (Sollaci and Pereira 2004, 364; Huth 1987, 626). IMRAD stands for introduction, methods, results, and discussion. An unpublished paper is known as a **manuscript**. A manuscript or paper published in a journal is an article.

This book has progressed through the steps of research. In each step, the associated documentation was described. This documentation correlates with many sections of a research paper or journal article:

- Problem statement (introduction)
- Literature review
- Statement of hypothesis
- Method
- Results (including discussion)

Figure 14.3.   Guidelines for effective PowerPoint presentations

- High contrast for visibility (black text on white background, or dark blue background with white text and yellow highlights)
- Liberal use of white space
- "6 by 6" rule (6 words per line, 6 lines per slide)
- Upper and lower case (all caps hard to read)
- 18 point size minimum (24 recommended and 28 to 36 preferable)
- 2-inch character height for every 20 feet between visual and audience
- Clear, simple sans serif fonts (Helvetica, Arial, or similar)
- Limit colors to 2 or 3
- Colors' subliminal messages ("in the red")
- Red-green color blindness
- Color opposites on color wheel create "shimmer"
- Inconspicuous slide transitions limited to 1 or 2
- Avoid overuse of sounds
- Bullets represent points of the outline
- No paragraphs
- Consistent verb tenses
- Consistent tense of 1st words of parallel lines
- Simple graphs, charts, and other art elements
- Accurate spelling, math, grammar, and numbering
- Handouts with 3 slides per page and room for notes

Figure 14.4. Varying missions and scopes of journals

The *Journal of Medical Internet Research,* founded in 1999, was the first (and remains the only) international scientific peer-reviewed journal on all aspects of research, information and communication in the healthcare field using Internet and other eHealth technologies. . . This field has also significant overlaps with what is called "consumer health informatics." As the field evolves, despite having "Internet" in its title, the journal also publishes original research on development, evaluation, and application of other (non-Internet) cutting-edge e-technologies in the health care setting.

We are different from other medical informatics journals in that we are targeting a broad readership consisting of health professionals, policy makers, consumers, health informaticians, developers, researchers, hospital and health care administrators, and e-health businesses, rather than reaching only a small medical informatics community. (Available online from http://www.jmir.org/cms/view/jmir_home:scope)

The *Journal of Biomedical Informatics* (formerly *Computers and Biomedical Research*) has been redesigned to reflect a commitment to high-quality original research papers and reviews in the area of biomedical informatics. Although published articles are motivated by applications in the biomedical sciences (for example, clinical medicine, health care, population health, imaging, and bioinformatics), the journal emphasizes reports of new methodologies and techniques that have general applicability and that form the basis for the evolving science of biomedical informatics. Articles on medical devices, and formal evaluations of completed systems, including clinical trials of information technologies, would generally be more suitable for publication in other venues. Papers on applications of signal processing and image analysis are often more suitable for biomedical engineering journals, although we do publish papers that emphasize the information management and knowledge representation/modeling issues that arise in the storage and use of biological signals. System descriptions are welcome if they illustrate and substantiate the underlying methodology that is the principal focus of the report.

(Available online from http://www.elsevier.com/wps/find/journaldescription.cws_home/622857/description#description)

Perspectives in Health Information Management is a scholarly, peer-reviewed research journal whose mission is to advance the knowledge base of health informatics and information management practice. The journal aspires to encourage interdisciplinary collaboration between health information management professionals and others in disciplines that manage and/or use information to support patient-centered healthcare delivery. The primary focus is to promote the linkage of practice, education, and research and to provide contributions to the understanding or improvement of health informatics and information management processes and outcomes. The types of articles sought by the journal are as follows:

- Research papers that report on either qualitative or quantitative research whereby the research problem, question/objective, methodology, results, discussion, and applicability to practice are shared with readers.

- Systematic or meta-analytic literature reviews that cover a specific topic in detail, from research past and emerging to practices related to the topic.

- Education articles that report on academic curricula, case studies, or methodological approaches in curricula and/or instructional design and technology.

- Case studies that report on experiences covering the broad continuum of health information management.

- Methodological and evaluation articles that detail processes or techniques used to implement and evaluate new and/or innovative approaches.

- Theory building papers that advance the discipline of health informatics and information management through the formulation and development of theories and models. Commentary that offers opinions on debates, issues, concerns, future trends, emerging technologies, and/or challenges in the practice of health information management and systems.

Submitted manuscripts are subject to a rigorous peer review process. This review process is designed to help authors improve their manuscripts and to ensure that only manuscripts that comply with general quality criteria, especially originality, clarity, and validity of results and conclusions, are published. AHIMA intends to document the publication's rejection rate.

(Available online from http://www.ahima.org/perspectives/guidelines_authors.asp_)

At this time, the researcher must complete the documentation by writing the abstract, and expanding and detailing the sections already written.

New researchers may find it strange that the abstract, the first section of a journal article, is written last. However, the abstract is written last because it encompasses the entire study. The research study's findings are included in the abstract.

Abstract

An abstract is a brief summary of the major parts of a research study. An abstract generally contains:

- Literature review
- Purpose or problem statement
- Method
- Results
- Discussion
- Conclusions and recommendations

Given that abstracts are generally limited to a certain number of words, authors focus on the most important information in each major part of the study. Brevity and directness are keys to a good abstract.

Some journals have structured formats that researchers must follow. (See table 14.2 for a few examples.) Not only do the formats vary by journal but the formats also may vary within journals by the type of article. Research articles may have a different format than commentary articles. Researchers read the journals' "Information for Authors" to determine exactly how they should structure their abstract.

Table 14.2.   Structures of abstracts for selected journals

Journal	Structure of Abstract
Annals of Family Medicine	• Purpose • Methods • Results • Conclusions
BMC Medical Informatics and Decision Making	• Background • Methods/design • Discussion
Journal of the American Medical Association	• Context • Methods • Results • Conclusions
Journal of Medical Internet Research	• Background • Objective • Methods • Results • Conclusions
Journal of the Medical Library Association	• Background • Purpose • Methods • Results • Conclusions
BMC Medical Research Methodology	• Background • Methods • Results • Conclusion

Abstracts are important because in bibliographic databases they are used to index and retrieve articles. Readers use abstracts to decide whether articles contain valuable information and whether they should read the articles in their entirety.

Titles pique the reader's interest and as such require thought. Consider including these items in the title:

- Subject area (nursing, public health, informatics)
- Type of article or study (systematic review, randomized clinical trial)
- Population or setting (ambulatory care, hospice)
- Implementation, system, or technique (diagnostic decision support system)
- Independent variable(s) manipulated
- Dependent variable(s) measured or observed
- Take-home message (Roderer and McClellan 2003, B4)

Six strategies help researchers to synthesize these items into a readable and clear title. These strategies are using

1. Short (pithy) descriptive phrase (The relationship between quality of research and citation frequency)
2. Gerund phrase (Writing for the informatics literature)
3. Subtitle (Research presentation in a democratic society: A voice from the audience)
4. Indirect take-home message (Developing and evaluating criteria to help reviewers of biomedical informatics manuscripts)
5. Direct take-home message (DISCERN helps consumers evaluate health information)
6. Question (Publication bias in medical informatics evaluation research: Is it an issue or not?) (Roderer and McClellan 2003, B4–B6)

Cautious and judicious use of acronyms is advisable. Brevity, precision, and accuracy are emphasized. Composing a compelling title takes time and work.

Composition Characteristics

The following paragraphs present general insights on expanding and detailing the sections that were already presented. As they begin to write their manuscripts, readers also should review chapter 9 (research question, literature, hypothesis), chapter 10 (method), and chapter 11 (results, discussion, and conclusion). Table 14.3 serves as a final checklist for the composition and revision of a manuscript. Common pitfalls are listed in the companion figure 14.5.

Authors find the metaphor of a funnel helpful. The paper begins with a broad, general question, and then narrows to the researchers' precise problem or question. For example, researchers might begin the problem statement with a general societal concern. Supporting citations would come from the popular literature, opinion commentaries, and journal articles. Then, the researchers concentrate the discussion by explaining how this problem or question affects the field of health informatics. Finally, the researchers state the research problem or question succinctly and accurately.

Authors cannot be too clear or too explicit. The methods section fully explicates the procedure or protocol. In the methods section, authors are writing a recipe for the research. Other researchers should be able to follow the article like the steps of a recipe.

In the results section, researchers must be careful to just document the results of their study. Structuring the

Table 14.3.   Organization of research publications

Section	Contents
Title Page	• Concise and descriptive title • Author and author's affiliation • Grant information • Disclaimer • Author's contact information: Address, telephone, fax, and e-mail
Abstract	• Background, purpose, methods, results, conclusions OR • Context; objective; design, setting, and participants; interventions; main outcome measures; results; conclusions AND • 45 to 250 words dependent upon call for papers or journal instructions • 3 to 10 key words using medical subject headings (MeSH) or key terms
Introduction	• Background • Pertinent literature review that provides rationale for research • Brief statement of research plan • Purpose, objectives, or research question • Hypothesis
Methods	• Protocol with detail for replication • Approach (theory or model), design, method, timeframe, setting, and participants (and controls) • Definition of variables • Reference established methods • Sampling strategy • Intervention • Collection of data • Statement about approval of institutional review board or other oversight entity • Analytical strategy • Subheadings

Table 14.3.   Organization of research publications (continued)

Section	Contents
Results	• Parallel construction to hypothesis • Core • Important results followed by less important results • Neutral reporting • One table or figure for every 1000 words of text • One mode of presentation (text, table, or figure) per major result • Subheadings
Discussion	• Parallel construction to results • Relationship between results and purpose, objectives, or research question • Evidence of relationship • Similarities to and differences from previous research • Inconsistent or unexpected results • New knowledge in terms of theoretical framework • Limitations • Conclusions as related to purpose, objectives, or research question • Implications for future research, practice, or policy • Recommendations as warranted • Summary
Acknowledgment	• Contributors whose level of involvement does not justify authorship
References	• Citations per format in instructions
Tables	• Consistent with narrative • Expand abbreviations • Format per instructions
Figures	• Consistent with narrative • Expand abbreviations • Legend • Format per instructions

Figure 14.5.   Pitfalls in presenting research

1. Allowing insufficient time to write the results or to develop the presentation
2. Interjecting subjective commentary and emotional hyperbole
3. Duplicating information in narrative and graphic forms
4. Creating confusing or inconsistent graphics
5. Substituting verbosity and inflated statements for clarity and accuracy

results to matching the order of the hpotheses is an organization and logic that readers can follow. Researchers must guard against interpreting, explaining, or comparing their results in this section.

In the discussion and conclusion, researchers intrepret and explain their results. Using the theory or model that framed the study is particularly helpful.

Pointing out how the study advanced the theory or filled a gap in the body of knowledge is important. Including unexpected or contrary results is intellectually honest. Researchers should be cautious when making claims of **priority** ("the first study ever to. . .)." In this instance, qualifiers, such as "a comprehensive review of the review of the literature did not reveal a similar study. . . ." are suitable. Lessons learned or mistakes made can result in recommendations for future research.

Selecting the Appropriate Journal

As researchers prepare their manuscripts for publication, they face two major remaining tasks: selecting the appropriate journal and following its submission guidelines. Careful attention to detail at this point has a high return on investment in terms of having journals accept the manuscripts.

There are many journals related to health informatics. (See table 2.7, p. 36.) Moreover, depending on the topic, researchers should consider journals in other disciplines such as allied health, bioethics, biostatistics, computer science, epidemiology, geography, health education, health policy, health services, healthcare management, medicine, nursing, and public health. Researchers can obtain lists of journals from their library's Web site or databases.

Journals are peer-reviewed (also called research, refereed, academic, and professional) or non-peer reviewed (also called popular or trade). Peer reviewed journals have an editorial board and an official and publicized process of review and approval. The members of an editorial review board are experts in various fields and subjects related to the journal's focus. These experts are **peer reviewers** (or **peers**). Peers evaluate the quality of manscripts in their subject area or field. The peers and the editors determine whether to publish a manuscript. Both print and electronic journals are peer reviewed. Information about the status of a journal as peer reviewed is found on the journal's Web site and in the citation information for articles.

The articles in non-peer reviewed journals have not been checked for accuracy. Thus, as information sources for research, non-peer reviewed journals have less credibility. However, non-peer reviewed journals serve an important function as a venue to provide useable information to practitioners.

Selecting the appropriate journal requires thought and investigation, and researchers should take the time to skim through a number of journals. This investigation allows them to match their purpose, topic, research design, and style to the journal's scope, content, and audience. These five considerations are detailed below.

First, researchers should determine their purpose. Is it altruism and service, or promotion and tenure? Certain journals are better suited to one purpose than another. For example, some journals have a practice orientation and others have a research orientation.

For altruism and service, researchers may send their manuscripts to journals oriented to practice, such as the *Journal of the American Health Information Management Association (JAHIMA)*. The researchers want to help their profession by putting effective techniques into the hands of practitioners. For example, if the researcher found that a particular graphical interface increased coder accuracy by 10 percent, he or she may decide to send that manuscript to the *JAHIMA*.

In addition to altruism and service, some researchers must meet work standards for promotion and tenure, and publish as a condition of employment. The gold standard for scholarly publication is an article in a peer-reviewed journal. Sometimes the work standards for publication specify quantity and quality. Quantity is the number of articles. Quality is less easily evaluated than quantity. One indirect measure is the prestige of the journal as indicated by its status as refereed or nonrefereed, and its rejection rate. Another measure is the journal's **impact factor**, a ratio between citations and recent citable items published (Garfield 2005/1994). The impact factor is calculated by dividing the number of current-year citations to the source items published in that journal during the previous two years (Garfield 2005/1994). For example, the *Journal of Medical Internet Research* is ranked second in health informatics journals by impact factor. Researchers publishing to meet work standards should consider the refereed journals that have high rejection rates (recognized as rigorous) or high impact factors.

Second, researchers should match the content of their manuscript with the focus of the journal. For example, researchers should send manuscripts about research on the management of health information services to journals in the field of health information management. If their results have an impact on reimbursement or health policy, the researchers should consider journals with a broader base.

Third, researchers must match the design and method of their research to the types of designs and methods in the journal. Some journals include mostly experimental and quasi-experimental research; others include ethnographies, case studies, and personal histories. Researchers who match the design and method of their study with the typical designs and methods in the journal increase the likelihood of their manuscripts being accepted.

Fourth, researchers should strive for matching their writing style to the preferences of the journal's audience. Journals that are oriented toward practice prefer brief articles written in simple, direct sentences. On the other hand, journals oriented toward scholarly work prefer a more formal and pedantic tone.

Finally, understanding the journal's audience combines the issues of topic and design. Researchers should submit their manuscripts to journals with audiences who would be interested in the topic. If the intended audience includes a broad range of fields, researchers should write manuscripts that are of interest to all potential readers. Moreover, researchers should clearly state how their manuscript affects and benefits the journal's intended audience.

Following the Journal's Submission Guidelines

Researchers must follow the journal's **submission guidelines**. Journals have rules for the format of manuscripts. The rules are both explicit and implicit. Explicit rules are openly stated; implicit rules are unwritten, but important. Editors and peer reviewers assume that researchers will naturally know and follow the guidelines. Different fields tend to have their own unique sets of implicit rules.

Explicit

Journal editors state their explicit requirements for manuscripts in their style manual and submission guidelines. There are four major style manuals, and selection of the style manual relates to the field. (See figure 14.6.) For example, journals in education generally require American Psychological Association (APA) style whereas biomedical journals require American Medical Association (AMA) style. Journals in health informatics typically use AMA style. The variance in these style manuals is illustrated in table 14.4.

Figure 14.6.   Common style manuals

- American Psychological Association. 2001. *Publication Manual of the American Psychological Association,* 5th ed. Washington, DC: APA. [Referred to as APA Style.]
- Gibaldi, Joseph. 2003. *MLA Handbook for Writers of Research Papers,* 6th ed. New York City: Modern Language Association of American. [Referred to as MLA Style.]
- Iverson, Cheryl. 2007. *American Medical Association Manual of Style: A Guide for Authors and Editors.* 10th ed. New York: Oxford University Press. [Referred to as AMA Style.]
- University of Chicago Press. 2003. *Chicago Manual of Style,* 15th ed. Chicago: University of Chicago Press. [Referred to as CMOS or Chicago Style.]

The journal's submission guidelines include details such as the word-processing package, width of margins, length, and organizational structure. (See figure 14.7.) For instance, the editors of AHIMA's *Perspectives in Health Information Management* prefer an organizational structure that generally includes the following elements:

- Abstract (150 words or less and up to 10 key words)
- Introduction
- Background (literature review)
- Research question or hypothesis
- Methods
- Results
- Discussion
- Conclusion
- References

However, most editors do state that the organizational structure is flexible and that researchers should adapt the structure to suit their research. Researchers can find guidelines in journals or at the publishers' Web sites. Most journals provide contact information within the guidelines for researchers' questions on formatting or style. It is wise to call before submission of something questionable.

Implicit

A journal's implicit rules reflect the culture of its audience. Culture is reflected in the use of the first person, anthropomorphism, passive voice, and tone. For example, an audience of qualitative researchers would accept

Table 14.4.   Variation in style manuals

	Book	Journal
AMA	Jencks C, Riesman D. *The Academic Revolution.* Chicago: University of Chicago Press; 1977.	Lloyd SC, Layman E. The effects of automated encoders on coding accuracy and coding speed. *Top Health Inf Manage* February 1997;17(3):72-79.
APA	Jencks, C., & Riesman, D. (1977). *The academic revolution.* Chicago: University of Chicago Press.	Lloyd, S. C., & Layman, E. (1997, February). The effects of automated encoders on coding accuracy and coding speed. *Topics in Health Information Management,* 17(3), 72-79.
CMOS	Jencks, Christopher, and David Riesman. 1977. *The Academic Revolution.* Chicago: University of Chicago Press.	Lloyd, Susan C., and Elizabeth Layman. 1997 (February). The effects of automated encoders on coding accuracy and coding speed. *Topics in Health Information Management* 17(3):72-79.
MLA	Jencks, Christopher, and David Riesman. *The Academic Revolution.* Chicago: University of Chicago Press, 1977	Lloyd, Susan C., and Elizabeth Layman. "The Effects of Automated Encoders on Coding Accuracy and Coding Speed." *Topics in Health Information Management* 17.3 (1997): 72-79.

Figure 14.7.   Content of submission guidelines

- Information needed about the author and contact
- Style manual
- Length and representativeness of title
- Length of abstract in words
- Length of manuscript in maximum number of pages or number of words
- Font and font size
- Line spacing
- Justification
- Margins
- Pagination
- Inclusive (non-sexist) language
- Blinding (names of authors on separate page)
- Format and electronic specifications of charts and tables
- Format of citations in text
- Format of references (sometimes vary slightly from style manual)
- General organizational structure of manuscript
- Word processing software
- Electronic submission

use of the first person, whereas its use probably would cause an audience of experimental researchers to doubt the article's credibility. Purists reject anthropomorphism as giving human traits to inanimate objects. Audiences that reject first person and anthropomorphism also tend to prefer passive voice and a detached, neutral tone. Time spent skimming journals can provide insight into the implicit rules of the various journals.

Researchers also are aware of publication bias. **Publication bias** is the selective publication of studies. Studies with positive results, statistically significant results, or both are more likely to be published than studies with negative results, statistically insignificant results, or both (Machan et al. 2006, 957). Publication bias distorts the body of knowledge because there is a preponderance of favorable results (Abaid et al. 2007, 1091). As

early as 1959, publication bias was recognized (Sterling 1959, 30). Researchers conducted a small-scale study of potential publication bias in health informatics evaluation research (Machan et al. 2006, 958). The researchers found little evidence of publication bias in the health informatics evaluation research. The researchers, however, recommended further investigation (Machan et al. 2006, 962). Researchers should continue to monitor journals and the literature regarding the existence of publication bias in health informatics journals.

Some editors and peer reviewers assume that sloppy writing indicates sloppy research. Moreover, some editors and peer reviewers equate the inability to follow submission guidelines to the inability to follow research protocols. Therefore, attention to detail is important. Researchers seeking more information about writing and publishing manuscripts should read the style manuals and review submission guidelines. Particularly helpful are peer reviewers' criteria that are available online or in print. (See table 14.5.) For grammar and clarity, Strunk and White's book on writing is a classic (1999). First published in 1959 and periodically revised, its succinct discussions and precise examples provide clear guidance. Finally, researchers should carefully read Day and Gastel's 2006 book dedicated to research writing and publishing.

Responding to the Journal's Feedback

Journal editors convey the peer reviewers' decision and comments to the authors. The turnaround time between submission of the manuscript to the receipt of the feedback is highly variable. Authors can make a rough estimate of the turnaround time by carefully reviewing the journal's published articles. Often, a footnote will state the dates of submission, revision, and acceptance. Online journals tend to have faster turnaround times than print journals.

Table 14.5.   Sources of peer reviewers' criteria

Source	Site or article
Canadian Medical Association Journal Checklist for Qualitative Studies	Rowan, M., and P. Huston. 1997, November 15. Qualitative research articles: Information for authors and peer reviewers. *Canadian Medical Association Journal* 157(10):1442-1446. Available online from http://www.cmaj.ca/cgi/reprint/157/10/1442.
International Medical Informatics Association Yearbook Quality Criteria	International Medical Informatics Association. 2006. Yearbook of Medical Informatics: Quality criteria for medical informatics research papers. Available online from http://iig.umit.at/yearbook/.
Perspectives in Health Information Management Manuscript Review Form	*Perspectives in Health Information Management of the American Health Information Management Association*. 2007. Manuscript Review Form. Available online from http://www.ahima.org/perspectives/manuscript_review_form.asp.

Typically, there are five categories of decision:

1. Accept
2. Accept with minor revisions
3. Accept with major revisions
4. Reject, but request resubmission after significant reworking
5. Reject

Note: Categories Number 3 and Number 4 are sometimes merged.

Of course, all authors want to receive feedback stating, "Accept." Unfortunately, this response is rare. Peer reviewers and editors have a responsibility to improve the clarity and impact of the manuscript, and they diligently attempt to fulfill this responsibility. Therefore, reviewers usually make suggestions to authors on how to improve their manuscripts. Thus, authors should be very encouraged when they receive "accept with minor revisions" or "accept with major revisions." Authors are encouraged to turn the revision around quickly in order to maintain the timeliness of their topic.

Authors who receive feedback of "Reject, but resubmit" should follow the suggestion to resubmit. The editor and the peer reviewers found something of value in the manuscript, and they want to see that aspect developed. Authors, though, are cautioned to move expeditiously to return their revised manuscript. Editorial leadership and direction of journals change, and this change could lead to a different and negative outcome.

The author should focus on responding clearly and explicitly to the reviewers' comments. Creating a table that lists the reviewers' comments and the authors' actions is recommended for analyzing necessary changes. When authors disagree or cannot comply with the reviewers' comments, clarifying the passage or issue is a viable strategy.

Once a manuscript is accepted, authors should expect to receive galley (page) proofs. Currently, electronic galley proofs in PDF format are the norm. Journals expect a short turnaround time. Authors should inspect the galley proofs for:

- Grammatical errors
- Typographical errors
- Errors in their address, affiliation, or credentials
- Inaccuracies in editorial changes
- Distortions of facts through editorial changes
- Errors on tables or figures
- Changes in the instrument (survey, questionnaire, and so forth)

Thus, authors should be prepared to review the manuscript quickly and carefully.

Peer review, by its very nature, is critical. Thus, authors will not receive much positive feedback. Therefore, authors should:

- Have thick skins
- Take comments with a grain of salt
- Persevere

Authors will realize, though, much satisfaction and gratification when their manuscript becomes a journal article. The effort is well worth the result as they see their own contribution to the field's body of knowledge.

Summary and Conclusions

Researchers disseminate knowledge to the public through poster sessions, conference presentations, and publications. For the information that the researchers have gained to be useful, it must be available and accessible to other researchers, practitioners, and professionals. Publication is particularly important because other researchers, practitioners, and professionals in related fields can examine and critically analyze the research. A journal's impact factor reflects generally how often articles in the journal have been cited in a particular year. Researchers building a publication record should submit articles to journals with high impact factors and high rejection rates. Journals have both explicit rules and implicit rules for the format of manuscripts. Researchers need to follow both sets of rules. Through publication, the health informatics body of knowledge and its standards of practice become available for and known to the world.

References

Abaid, L.N., Grimes, D.A., and K.F. Schulz. 2007 (June). Reducing publication bias through trial registration. *Obsetrics & Gynecology* 109(6):1434–1437.

Day, R.A., and B. Gastel. 2006. *How to Write and Publish a Scientific Paper*, 6th ed. Westport, CT: Greenwood Press.

Edirisooriya, G. 1996 (August-September). Research presentation in a democratic society: A voice from the audience. *Educational Researcher* 25(6):25–30.

Garfield, E. 2005/1994 (June 20). The Thomson scientific impact factor. Available online from http://scientific.thomson.com/free/essays/journalcitationreports/impactfactor/.

Glass, G.V. 1976, November. Primary, secondary, and meta-analysis of research. *Educational Researcher* 5(10):308

Hess, G., Tosney, K., and L. Liegel. 2006. Creating effective poster presentations. Available online from http://www.ncsu.edu/project/posters/NewSite/.

Huth, E.J. 1987 (April). Structured abstracts for papers reporting clinical trials. *Annals of Internal Medicine* 106(4):626–627.

International Medical Informatics Association. 2006. Yearbook of medical informatics: Quality criteria for medical informatics research papers. Available online from http://iig.umit.at/yearbook/.

Kronick, D.A. 1990 (March 9). Peer review in the 18th-century scientific journalism. *Journal of the American Medical Association* 263(10):1321–1322.

Machan, C., Ammenwerth, E., and T. Bodner. 2006. Publication bias in medical informatics evaluation research: Is it an issue or not? *Studies in Health Technology & Informatics* 124:957–962.

Perspectives in Health Information Management of the American Health Information Management Association. 2007. Manuscript Review Form. Available online from http://www.ahima.org/perspectives/manuscript_review_form.asp.

Roderer, N.K., and D.A. McClellan. Writing for informatics literature. American Medical Informatics Association Annual Symposium, November 8 2003. Available online from http://www.amia.org/mbrcenter/wg/st/documents.asp.

Rowan, M., and P. Huston. 1997 (Nov. 15). Qualitative research articles: Information for authors and peer reviewers. *Canadian Medical Association Journal* 157(10):1442–46. Available online from http://www.cmaj.ca/cgi/reprint/157/10/1442.

Shashok, K., ed. 2005 (Feb. 16). Standardization vs. diversity: How can we push peer review research forward? *MedGenMed* 7(1):11. Available online from http://www.pubmedcentral.nih.gov/articlerender.fcgi?tool=pmcentrez&artid=1681382.

Sollaci, L.B., and M.G. Pereira. 2004 (July). The introduction, methods, results, and discussion (IMRAD) structure: A fifty-year survey. *Journal of the Medical Library Association* 92(3):364–367.

Sterling, T.D. 1959 (March). Publication decisions and their possible effects on inferences drawn from tests of significance—or vice versa. *Journal of the American Statistical Association* 54(285):30–34.

Strunk, W., and E.B. White. 1999. *The Elements of Style*, 4th ed. Boston: Allyn and Bacon.

Tosney, K. 2001. How to create a poster that graphically communicates your message. Available online from http://www.bio.miami.edu/ktosney/file/PosterHome.html.

Wineberg, S. 2004 (May). Must it be this way? Ten rules for keeping your audience awake during conferences. *Educational Researcher* 33(4):13–14.

Glossary

Abstract: A summary of a research study's major parts: context; objective; design, setting, and participants; interventions; main outcome measures; results; and conclusions

Accuracy: The probability that an evaluation's results will be accurate, valid, and reliable for users

Advisory committee: Focus group of experts with experience in survey design as well as the topic of study to assist in phrasing the questions in the appropriate manner

Agent: The actual cause, for example, of a disease

Alpha levels: Significance level; commonly .05 and .01, with lower alpha minimizing the chance of erroneously rejecting the null hypothesis when it is actually true

Alternative hypothesis (HA): A statement of the predicted association or difference between the independent and dependent variables, symbolized as H1 (HA) for the first alternative hypothesis, H2 for the second, and so on, and alternative and null hypotheses in matched pairs

American Hospital Association (AHA): The national trade organization that provides education, conducts research, and represents the hospital industry's interests in national legislative matters; membership of individual healthcare organizations, as well as individual healthcare professionals working in specialized areas of hospitals, such as risk management

American Society for Testing and Materials (ASTM): A national organization whose purpose is to establish standards on materials, products, systems, and services

Analytic induction: One of the many analytic techniques used in qualitative research, along with typological analysis, enumerative systems, standardized observation protocols, grounded theory (commonly used in healthcare), and content analysis

Analytic study: Determines whether there is a relationship between two variables: the **independent variable** and the **dependent variable**. The exposure or risk factor is normally considered the independent variable, and the disease or health outcome is the dependent variable. The **case-control** and **prospective** study designs are examples of analytic observational studies, while the **clinical** and **community trial** are examples of analytic experimental studies

Applied research: A type of research that focuses on implementing scientific theories to improve actual practice, as in medical research applied to the treatment of patients

Approach: Methodology for carrying out research

Area under the curve: A metric of overall model quality

Article: Results of research published in a journal article, also a refereed article or scholarly article

Attrition: Subjects' withdrawing from a study (also called mortality)

Autonomy: The ability of a capable individual to make a voluntary decision about participation in a research study, authorize the researchers' carrying out the study by giving consent, and therefore agree to participate

Basic research: A type of research that focuses on developing and refining theories

Bayesian network: A graphic model representing the probabilities of relationships among a set of variables; *See also* **variable**

Belmont Report: A report written in 1979 by the National Commission for the Protection of Human Subjects of Biomedical and Behavioral Research that focuses on the basic ethical principles for researchers who use human beings in research studies: three main principles are respect for persons, beneficence, and justice; *See also* beneficence, fidelity, justice, National Research Act, Nuremberg Code

Beneficence: Promoting good; indicates that the research is intended to help build on the body of knowledge and may result in benefit, that outcomes might help the research participant or future patients; for example, a pharmaceutical intervention that might prove to be beneficial for helping or curing a disease

Beta: Signals the probability of making a type II error; *See also* **Type II error**

Binning: Categorizing

Bioethics and privacy commissions: Commissions that the U.S. government has formed to specifically address issues related to privacy, electronic systems, and research; for example, in 1972-1973, the Health Education and Welfare (HEW) secretary established the Advisory Committee on Automated Personal Data Systems, the first attempt to establish fair information practices for automated personal data systems

Biographical sketch: A short description of a person, typically includes name and title, educational background, key publications, roles in research, and professional experience (including employment history)

Bivariate: Statistical techniques that involve two variables

Blinding: A method for maintaining objectivity in clinical or community trials; in single-blind design, the study participants unaware of which group (intervention or control) they have been assigned; in double-blind design, neither the participant nor the researcher aware of group assignment; in triple-blind design, the subject, researcher, and statistician all unaware of the group assignments

Box-and-whisker plot: A technique of exploratory data analysis, that is, analysis of raw data, which are presented in a graphic representation; especially useful with sets of data that have hundreds or thousands of scores or with datasets that have unequal numbers of values; constructed by finding the median, the upper and lower quartiles, the largest and smallest values, and the outliers within a dataset; median line in the center of a box formed by the upper and lower quartiles, with "whiskers" extending to the largest and smallest values; outliers indicated with asterisks

Budget: Money allowed for a research project; may include costs for collaboration with other university faculty

Case mix: A description of a patient population based on any number of specific characteristics, including age, gender, type of insurance, diagnosis, risk factors, treatment received, and resources used

Case-control (retrospective) study: Studies with cases and controls to investigate whether exposure to a factor or phenomenon is associated with an outcome; *See also* **cases, controls**

Cases: Individuals who have the disease or condition being studied

Case study observation: An example of nonparticipant observation that is used when the researcher wants to know more about a particular individual; group of individuals; or a particular facility, organization, or institution

Categorical data: Values or observations that can be sorted into a category, for example, gender

Causal relationship: A relationship in which a factor or factors cause an outcome

Causal-comparative research: Studies to investigate whether a particular cause (factor, event, situation, or independent variable) is associated with an effect (outcome, dependent variable)

Census survey: A survey of an entire population

Centers for Scientific Review (CSR): Part of the NIH peer review process that provides referral officers to review applications, assign applications to integrated review group, and receive reviews and scores

Central tendency: A term referring to the center of a distribution; an average or middle value; measured using the mean, median, or mode. In survey research of self-reported data, a potential threat to validity because respondents tend to view themselves and record scores "in the middle"

Chronic disease model: A model quite similar to the infectious disease model except that it focuses on multiple causes of disease and how combinations of risk factors influence the severity of chronic illnesses; *See also* **infectious disease model**

Claim (qualitative research): Researchers' interpretations

Clinical data manager: The person responsible for managing the data collected during the research project, developing data standards, conducting clinical coding for specific data elements, determining the best database to house the data, choosing appropriate software systems to analyze the data, and conducting data entry and data analysis; various responsibilities according to the research study protocol

Clinical research associate: A person who develops new study protocols, hires investigators, writes progress reports, data and safety monitoring plans, and subsequent reports of any adverse events, and takes part in writing publications upon completion of the project

Clinical research coordinator: The person who runs the research project and ensures that the clinical protocol is followed as written

Clinical trial: Studies to help healthcare professionals test new approaches to the diagnosis; treatment, including new medications (most common) and surgical procedures; or prevention of different diseases

Close-ended (structured) questions: Structured or quantitative questions

Cluster sampling: The process of selecting subjects for a sample from each cluster within a population (for example, a family, school, or community)

Cohort study: This study design has two groups of study participants: one with the exposure (independent variable) and one without the exposure (dependent variable). Both groups are then followed forward in time to determine if and when they develop the disease or outcome variable under study.

Community trial: Trials that are very similar to clinical trials except that they take place in a particular community and, therefore, there is less control over the exposure than with a clinical trial; intended to produce changes in a specific population rather than to test diagnosis, treatment, and prevention of disease

Comparison group: A group that receives some other type of intervention (or no intervention) when a different intervention is used as a comparison.

Computerized Physician/Provider Order Entry (CPOE): An online prescription ordering system that also may consist of provider alerts, reminders, and clinical decision support

Concept sheet: A brief synopsis of the research study, including sections similar to those discussed in the grant application; used in most pharmaceutical research studies when conducting clinical trials

Conclusion validity: The extent to which the statistical conclusions about the relationships in the data are reasonable

Concurrent validity: An instrument's ability to discriminate between groups it should be able to differentiate

Confidence interval (CI): A range of values inferred for a characteristic within a sample that has a possibility of including the characteristic's true value for the population

Confidence level: The probability that the confidence interval includes the population's value; usually set at 95 percent or 99 percent

Confidence limits: The ends of the range of the confidence intervals (CI), which indicate the reliability of an estimate

Confidentiality form: A statement that all information in the proposal application will be kept confidential; signature of proposal reviewer and date required

Confirmability: A desirable characteristic of data and their interpretation; external reviewers tracing, analyzing, categorizing, and interpreting the data would agree with the researcher's logic

Conflict of interest form: A form on which the reviewer informs the program officer of any conflicts of interest based on the area of focus for the grant application; signature of proposal reviewer, and date required

Confounding (extraneous, secondary) variable: A variable that confounds (confuses) interpretation of the data

Confounding variable: Extraneous factor

Constant comparative method: A method by which researchers compare and refine results as data are mined

Construct: Theoretical, non-observable concepts; thus "constructed" in language and graphics; for example, psychological concepts, such as intelligence, motivation, and anxiety

Construct validity: The degree to which an instrument measures the constructs that it claims to measure; *See also* **construct**

Content analysis: The ability of the observational researcher to examine all textual data collected and detect the number of recurrent terms to determine emerging themes and factors reflective of the culture or institution examined

Content validity: The rigorous determination that the instrument represents all relevant aspects of a topic; determination that all the content of an instrument is related to the topic and none of the content is unrelated (extraneous) to the topic

Content validity index (CVI): A numerical representation of the experts' aggregate level of agreement for the entire instrument

Content validity ratio (CVR): A representation of the experts' level of agreement in numerical terms

Continuous (metric) data: Another term for metric data; *See also* **metric data**

Control group: Subjects who undergo the intervention that is the subject of the study in order to provide a comparison to the effect of the intervention on the experimental group

Controls: Individuals who do not have the disease or who do not receive the intervention so they can be compared with the experimental group

Convenience sample: The "convenient" use of subjects who are nearby or at hand, also known as accidental samples or haphazard samples

Convergent validity: The degree of correlation between the instrument and other instruments designed to measure similar constructs

Correlational research: 1. Research that studies the existence, the direction, and the strength of relationships between variables; 2. Research that compares the strength of relationships between different variables

Cost-benefit analysis: An analysis that shows the financial benefits of the program from an institutional or a societal perspective; requires an analysis of the costs associated with the program as well as the associated revenues and patient outcomes

Cost-effectiveness: An analysis that can help explore the value of the program in terms of the quality-adjusted years of life gained by patients that can be attributed to the investment in the program

Cost sharing: In-kind contributions and the portion of the costs that would come from an entity other than the funding agency

Covariation: How variables occur or change together

Coverage error: A discrepancy between the sampling frame and the population

Credibility: Procedures of a study supporting the accuracy and representativeness of its findings

Criterion validity: The assessment of an instrument against another established instrument

Criterion variable: Outcome variables

Cronbach's alpha: A measure of internal consistency that determines if all variables within an instrument are measuring the same concept with good reliability being any value close to 1.00; *See also* **reliability**

Crossover design: A study design using one group of participants as both the experimental group and the control group; one group of patients in the intervention group for a specified time and then crossing over into the control group; patient serves as his or her own control

Cross-sectional: A design for research studies that collect data at one point in time; opposite of longitudinal

Cross-sectional study: An exploration of a disease that begins by determining the prevalence in a community or geographic area; describes the disease or health characteristics at one particular point or period in time, such as one month or one year; *See also* **descriptive study**

Cross-validation: A method to assess how well an initial subset of data (training set) performs against other subsets of data called testing sets

Data and Safety Management Board (DSMB): An oversight board to ensure the safety of all human participants and the validity and integrity of the data collected; the level of monitoring based on size, complexity, and potential risks of the clinical or community trials

Data cleaning: Also called data cleansing or data scrubbing; the process of checking internal consistency and duplication as well as identifying outliers and missing data

Data extraction: A review of the full study text for selected articles and information from other data sources; Specific information extracted in a manner that fosters consistency and reliability among reviewers

Data mining: The extraction and analysis of large volumes of data for the purpose of identifying hidden and sometimes subtle relationships or patterns and using those relationships to predict behaviors

Deductive reasoning: Drawing conclusions based on generalizations, rules, or principles; also called deduction

Defining the scope: A directed literature review on background issues, significance of the problem, and legislative or regulatory issues (not a comprehensive literature review) used to develop a framework on which to base the inclusion and exclusion criteria

Defining the terms: An essential step in the process requiring consensus of all involved in the study

De-identify: To remove the names of the principal investigator (PI), co-investigators, and the names of the affiliated organizations to allow reviewers to maintain objectivity

Dependability: Desirable characteristic of data achieved by explicitly tracking and accounting for modifications in the study's design or methods because of changing conditions or factors

Dependent (matched, paired) sample: Matched pairs or cohorts

Dependent variable: Variables that are affected by the independent variable; outcome

Descriptive maps: A structured view of selected studies or user information, usually in the form of a matrix with category keywords or codes allowing a research review team to quickly navigate a complex and in-depth literature review

Descriptive research: Research that determines and reports the current status of topics and subjects

Descriptive study: A study that explores a disease by first determining the prevalence in a community or geographic area; generates new ideas rather than proving existing hypotheses

Diagnostic trials: Studies to find better tests, procedures, or screenings to detect a disease or condition

Direct observation: A method in which the researchers conduct the observation themselves, spending time in the environment they are observing and recording observations

Discrete data: Separate and distinct values or observations; for example, patients in the hospital because each patient can be counted

Divergent (discriminant) validity: The degree to which the instrument does not correlate to instruments measuring dissimilar constructs

Double-blind study: A study in which neither the researcher nor the subjects know who is in the experimental group and who is in the control group

Effect size: 1. The degree to which the null hypothesis is false as represented by the degree to which the sample results diverge from the null hypothesis; 2. The practical (clinical) significance of the study's findings

Eligibility criteria: A specification of the types of facilities eligible to apply for funding

Empiricism: A concept related to scientific inquiry; conclusions based on evidence that has been observed and on validated evidence

Environment: Refers to physical environment or environmental influences, such as disasters (tornado, flood, hurricane, war), crowding, neighborhood density, housing, and occupation

Enumerative systems: An analytic technique employing frequency counts of phenomena or categories; used in qualitative research; *See also* **qualitative research**

Epidemiologist: Researcher who examines the existence of disease or health outcome and determines methods that can aid in the prevention and/or treatment of the disease or health outcome

Epidemiology: The study of patterns of disease occurrence in human populations and the factors that influence these patterns in relation to time, place, and persons

Epistemological assumptions: The synthesis of information based on epistemological (origins of knowledge) assumptions, used in interpretive research

Equitable coverage: A term indicating that a literature review is unbiased, that it includes points of view contrary to the researchers' points of view

Ethnography: 1. A research technique widely used in anthropology that combines participant and nonparticipant observation and quantitative and qualitative approaches to study a particular culture or organization in great detail; 2. The ways of life, or culture, of living human beings

Evaluation research: 1. The systematic examination of the effectiveness of objects, or "things," such as policies, programs, technologies (including procedures or implementations), products, processes, events, conditions, or organizations; 2. A set of methods to explore the impact of new or existing processes

Ex post facto: A term meaning retrospective that is often used to refer to causal-comparative studies

Experimental group: The intervention group

Experimental procedures: Application of the intervention

Experimental research: Studies that involve the creation of environments in which to observe, analyze, and interpret the effects of treatments on phenomena; these studies expose participants to different interventions (independent variables) in order to compare the result of these interventions with the outcome (dependent variables)

Experimental study: Experimental studies are considered the most powerful designs to establish cause and effect. Experimental research studies expose participants to different interventions (independent variables) to compare the result of these interventions with the outcome (dependent variables). Two examples of experimental

research studies in epidemiology include the clinical and community trial.

Exploratory: A category of research that includes descriptive research, historical research, and correlational research

External validity: The extent to which a study's findings can be generalized to other people or groups

Face page: Introductory material on a grant proposal, similar to a title page

Face validity: The extent to which an instrument appears to measure what it says it measures; related to the instrument's apparent coverage of the topic upon an expert's cursory review; technically superficial and a weak measure of validity

Factor analysis: A statistical technique in which a large number of variables are summarized and reduced to a smaller number based on similar relationships among those variables

Feasibility: The realistic likelihood of an evaluation's success given the available time, resources, and expertise

Fidelity: A quality closely aligned with honesty; includes keeping promises, honoring contracts and agreements, and telling the truth

Field notes: Notes that are recorded either immediately after the observation or during short breaks between observations

Focus group: A group of approximately 6–12 subjects, usually experts in the particular area of study, brought together to discuss a specific topic using the focused interview method, usually with a moderator who is not on the research team; *See also* **focused interview**

Focused interview: A type of interview used when the researcher wants to collect a more in-depth, heartier type of information not obtainable from close-ended questions; uses informal conversational, standardized open-ended, or the general interview guide

Formative evaluation: Evaluations that measure or assess improvement in delivery methods with regard to technology used; quality of implementation of a new process or technology; information about the organizational placement of a given process; type of personnel involved in a program; or other important factors such as the procedures, source, and type of inputs

Gap analysis: 1. A review of the collected literature and data to assess whether gaps exist; 2. Advice for those conducting the literature review on additional literature and data sources missed during the initial review

General interview guide: An outline or checklist of issues that the researcher can use for interviews that are a bit more structured than the informal conversational interview, often used with very long interviews that are audio taped so the researcher has time to focus on the interview process

Generalizability: 1. Applicability, that is, the results of a study can be applied to other groups, such as hospitals, patients, and states; 2. A term meaning particular instances that can be developed into concepts or abstract ideas, drawing conclusions based on generalizations, rules, or principles

Grant: Monetary assistance provided to a facility, university, or individual who will then use this monetary assistance to fully carry out and complete the intended research study

Grantee: Recipient of the grant, who is responsible for carrying out the research with little or no direct involvement from the granting agency

Grounded theory: A theory about what is actually going on instead of what should go on

Group case study: Similar to the individual case study except the interviews or observations are performed on a group of individuals instead of just one individual

Health Information National Trends Survey (HINTS): The National Cancer Institute's initiative that was to create a population-based survey that could be repeated biennially to track trends in the use of communication technologies such as the Internet as a source of cancer information

Healthcare Information and Management Systems Society (HIMSS): A national membership association that provides leadership in healthcare for the management of technology, information, and change

Health Level Seven (HL7): A standards development organization accredited by the American National Standards Institute that addresses issues at the seventh, or application, level of healthcare systems interconnections

Helsinki Agreement: An ethical code established in 1964 by the 18th World Medical Assembly to guide researchers beyond the Nuremberg Code; differentiates between clinical/therapeutic research and nonclinical research and addresses problems with those who are legally incompetent and who need "proxy" representation

Heterogeneity: Variation or diversity in a population; variability

Heuristic: A "rule of thumb"

Historical research: Investigations of the past; an exploratory research

Historical-prospective study: Study design used when existing data sources can be used to identify characteristics pertaining to the study groups; groups followed over time, usually from the time the data are first collected to the present or into the future, to examine their outcomes

History: Events happening in the course of the experiment that could affect the results

Homogeneity: Variance in measurements or scores of the sample. Less variance, or greater homogeneity, in the measurements or scores of the sample results in narrower confidence intervals (CIs); greater variance and heterogeneity result in wider CIs; *See also* **confidence interval, heterogeneity**

Honesty: Telling the truth; avoiding lies of omission and commission

Host: 1. The person studied and affected by resistance to the agent and the agent's portal of entry (intact skin or open wound); 2. A host factor, or anything that influences the development or immunity of disease, including age, gender, race, religion, marital status, family history or genetics, ethnicity, anatomy and physiology, social behaviors, and prior illnesses or chronic disease

Hypothesis: A statement that predicts the relationship among variables and can be expressed in measurable data; statements that guide research investigations because they state the predicted outcomes of the study

Impact evaluation: An evaluation that assesses the intended or unintended net effects of a program or technology

Impact factor: A ratio between citations and recent citable items published

Implementation evaluation: An evaluation that essentially consists of monitoring how well the planned events are actually carried out and whether the implementation is meeting the expected timeframes

Imputation: Substitution of values for the missing values

IMRAD: Acronym for introduction, methods, results, and discussion

Incidence cases: New cases with a specific disease

Inclusion/exclusion criteria: Part of the protocol giving explicit parameters for including or excluding studies in a comprehensive literature review or subjects in a study

Independent sample: Samples that do not interact, for example, an experimental group and a control group

Independent variable: The intervention or factor to be measured in order to determine if it will have an effect on the dependent variable or the disease or outcome under study; the factors that researchers manipulate directly

Indirect observation: Research in which the researchers use audio or video recording so that the environment is not changed in any way from the norm

Individual case study: A study in which the researchers record (field notes, tape recording, images, video recording) and collects everything they can on a particular individual as he or she progresses through a certain disease, procedure, treatment, cultural, or health information system change

Inductive reasoning: Drawing conclusions based on a limited number of observations; also called induction

Infectious disease model: A model that examines disease causation and occurrence by examining infectious agents, the host or person, the environment, and how each plays a part in disease development

Inferential statistics: Statistics that allow the researchers to make inferences about the population characteristics (parameters) from the sample's characteristics, for example, the paired t-test, the analysis of variance (ANOVA), the Pearson's product-moment correlation, and multiple regression

Informal conversational interview: An interview that moves forward as the subject converses with the goal of learning as much as possible about the particular situation; no specific topics or questions developed or used

Innovation: 1. Having unique and original qualities; 2. An idea or proposal that challenges existing clinical practice and uses novel concepts, approaches, and technologies

Institute and center (IC): Components of NIH that are involved in the peer review process of specific grant applications

Institutional case study: A study of a particular health-care institution or facility to determine how it conducts a particular process, system, or procedure

Institutional Review Board (IRB): The body that provides review, oversight, guidance, and approval for research projects carried out by employees serving as researchers, regardless of the location of the research (such as a university or private research agency); responsible for protecting the rights and welfare of the human subjects involved in the research; IRB oversight is mandatory for federally funded research projects

Instrument: A standardized, uniform way to collect data

Instrumentation: Effect of instruments on internal validity; for example, changes in instruments, interviewers, or observers may cause changes in results

Integrated review group (IRG): A review group (IRG) to assess a proposal's scientific and technical merit, selected by the Center for Scientific Review (CSR) referral officers

Integrative analytical methods: Methods that combine data through a number of mechanisms, for example, meta-analysis, modeling, consensus development (group judgments), systematic literature reviews, unstructured literature reviews, and expert opinions

Interaction of factors: A combination of factors that might lead to bias in the final results

Interim report: A report that allows the research review team to periodically reassess the appropriateness of the methodology and continued relevance of the research question, selection of the research review team, protocol guidelines, definition of terms, and inclusion/exclusion criteria

Internal consistency: The homogeneity of an instrument's items

Internal validity: An attribute of a study's design that contributes to the accuracy of its findings and can be threatened by factors outside the study (confounding variables)

Interpretive analysis: A rigorous interpretation of data that forces researchers and participants not only to examine themes and patterns but also to recognize and identify relationships

Interrater reliability: The achievement of reasonably similar results when different persons score the same test

Interval: Scales that have true numerical meaning because the distance between the variables relates to the true numerical value assigned

Interval data: Values or observations that occur on an evenly distributed scale, but begin with an arbitrary (not true) zero, examples being years and longitude; can be added and subtracted but not meaningfully multiplied nor divided

Intervention: Independent variable; treatment

Interview: A common tool used to collect descriptive data

Interview guide: Written lists of questions to ensure that the researchers ask all the participants the same questions

Intrarater reliability: The achievement of reasonably similar results when the same person scores the same test at different times

Investigators: Personnel who carry out the research

Item nonresponse: A respondents' completing some of the items on a survey, but not all

Iterative modeling process: A stepwise methodology that allows researchers to compare and refine results as data are mined

Justice: Fairness; applies to enrollment and treatment of participants in clinical trials; requires that no undue burden for participation be placed on any particular group (for example, prisoners) or persons of a particular race (for example, African Americans) for the convenience of the researcher

Kappa statistics: A value that states whether the levels of agreement seen across abstractors are real or due to chance

Key personnel: All staff, professional and non-professional, who are working on a study

Knowledge discovery in databases (KDD): The process of identifying valid, new, potentially useful, and understandable patterns in data; data mining is a step in KDD

Kurtosis: A measure of the verticality of the frequency distribution as displayed in a normal bell curve; positive kurtosis statistics are overly tall (peaked) and negative kurtosis statistics are overly short (flattened)

Letter of intent: A letter that describes the focus and goal of the research project and enables the granting agency to determine if a full application is of interest; enables applicant to get feedback about the research topic without having to submit a full grant proposal

Life table analysis: An examination of the survival of study subjects over time to compare with the length of survival in the control group; used when there is a loss of subjects because it takes into account those subjects who withdrew from the study before it was completed

Likert scale: A scale for recording respondents' level of agreement or disagreement; uses a range of categories, called points, such as "strongly agree, agree, neutral sure, disagree, strongly disagree."

Literature review: A systematic and critical examination of the important information about a topic found in articles in peer-reviewed journals and in magazines, books, book chapters, conference papers, and governmental documents that results in a synthesis of current, important information about a topic

Longitudinal: A design for research studies that collects data from the same participants at multiple points in time; opposite of cross-sectional

Machine learning: A field of computer science that uses intelligent algorithms to allow a computer to mimic the process of human learning

Manuscript: An unpublished paper

Masking: In order for the clinical or community trial to be objective, study participants may not know to which group (intervention or control) they are assigned; *See also* **blinding**

Matching: A concept that enables decision makers to look at expenses and revenues in the same period to measure the organization's income performance

Matching requirements: Cost sharing, either as in-kind contributions or financial support for a portion of the costs from an entity other than the funding agency

Maturation: A factor affecting internal validity that refers to the natural changes of research subjects over time due to the length of time that they are in the study

Meta-analysis: A specialized form of systematic literature review that involves the statistical analysis of a large collection of results from individual studies for the purpose of integrating the studies' findings; combines systematic qualitative analysis with statistical quantitative methods to provide a structure for in-depth research reviews

Metric data: Continuous data that can be measured on some scale representing values or observations that have an indefinite number of points along a continuum; interval and ratio are subtypes

Midtests: Observations that are not administered before or after the intervention but during the middle of the particular study

Missing at random (MAR): A misnomer for a type of missing value in which the missing values are actually conditional upon another characteristic, such as in disease

Missing completely at random (MCAR): A type of missing value in which there is no pattern to the absent values

Missing not at random (MNAR): A type of missing value in which there is a pattern to the absent values

Missing values (data): Variables that do not contain data values for some cases

Missingness: A type of incomplete data or coarse data

Mixed methods research: An approach in which researchers mix or combine quantitative and qualitative research techniques, methods, concepts, or language within one study and across related studies

Model: A representation of a theory in a visual format that includes all of a theory's known properties

Models of causation: A logical framework that can be used when examining concepts within health informatics

Mortality (attrition): The loss of research subjects

Multiple imputation (MI): Missing data are imputed (substituted) two or more times in simulations, creating two or more data sets derived from the original data set, and allowing separate analyses to reflect the uncertainty from the missing data in the original data set

Multivariate: Correlational methods that involve many variables

Multivariate analysis: Analysis of the relationship between more than two variables

Naïve modeling: This process uses a Bayesian theory of conditional independence to predict the conditional probability between input and outcome variables for classification purposes

Narrative analysis: A type of analysis that captures a person's narration, or story, illustrating a particular social, clinical, or medical point and analyzes that story for its instructional value, suggesting causal links between ideas, discovering particular themes in an individual's experiences, and framing the experience in its social setting

National Ambulatory Medical Care Survey (NAMCS): An annual survey on healthcare practice under consideration for use on collecting information on electronic health records (EHRs) by adding a section to the survey on EHR use

National Center for Health Statistics (NCHS): The federal agency responsible for collecting and disseminating information on health services utilization and the health status of the population in the United States

National Health Interview Survey (NHIS): A study from the National Center for Health Statistics that describes the health status of individuals and their families (NCHS)

National Institutes of Health (NIH): The primary federal agency that provides grant funding to researchers so that they are able to conduct clinical research

National Library of Medicine (NLM): The world's largest medical library and a branch of the National Institutes of Health

National Research Act: 1. A law (Public Law 93-348) protecting human participants in research studies, in large part the result of the reaction of the public to information about the Tuskegee Syphilis Study; 2. The law that created the National Commission for the Protection of Human Subjects of Biomedical and Behavioral Research, which was charged with consideration of boundaries between research and the accepted and routine practice of medicine; role of assessment of risk-benefit criteria in determining the appropriateness of research involving human subjects; guidelines for selecting human subjects to participate in such research; nature and definition of informed consent in various research settings 3. The law that set the stage for the Belmont report; *See also* **Belmont Report, Nuremberg Code**

Natural (naturalistic) experiments (research): Observational research

Naturalism: Another term for the qualitative approach; *See also* **qualitative approach**

Naturalistic observation: A type of observation used when the researcher records behaviors or events that occur naturally in the normal environment; may be used when the researcher(s) want to know if individuals are following a specific procedure, rule, law, or policy; best if study subjects are unaware of the researcher

Needs assessment: A process of gathering and analyzing background data related to a given group or process that centers on an ultimate aim of designing an intervention to address high priority needs

Negative (inverse) relationship: The relationship between variables that change in opposite directions

Nominal: Scales that assign a numerical value to a particular response

Nominal data: Values or observations that can be labeled or named (nom = name), but not ranked or measured; allow data to be coded, for example, Married = Y and Single = N, or Male = 0 and Female = 1.

Nonmaleficence: Doing no harm; a term meaning that the intervention should not knowingly harm the participant; *See also* beneficence

Nonparametric (distribution free): A type of statistical procedure, such as the chi-square test and the Spearman rho, used for variables that are not normally distributed in a population; also used for nominal and ordinal data

Nonparticipant observation: Involvement in a study as a neutral observer who neither intentionally interacts with nor affects the actions of the subjects being observed; observation by the investigator of the actions of the study subjects with limited interference

Nonrandom sampling: Selection of subjects that is not random; also known as nonprobability sampling because each subject's probability of being selected is unknown and could be either equal or unequal; generally associated with the qualitative approach

Null hypothesis: A statement that maintains there is no association between the independent and dependent variables; symbolized as H0, usually with a colon following the symbol (for example, H1:); alternative and null hypotheses are matched pairs

Null hypothesis statistical testing: Analysis of the study's data to obtain the probability value and comparing that probability value to a pre-established significance level

Nuremberg Code: A code that the Allies developed after WWII in reaction to the atrocious human experiments conducted by the Nazis; two core principles are the importance of voluntary consent and the evaluation of whether the research is morally acceptable

Object: Also called "things"; for example, policies, programs, technologies (including procedures or implementations), products, processes, events, conditions, or organizations

Objectivist: A term related to, but distinct from, objective referring to the philosophy of evaluation, which suggests the merit and worth of an information resource can, in principle, be measured with all observations yielding the same result and that a quantitative gold standard for performance can be identified and agreed upon

Observation: Neutral exploration, recognition, identification, recording, and analysis

Observational research: Exploratory research that identifies factors, contexts, and experiences; does not attempt to attain generalizability (applicability) to other situations; includes observing, recording, and analyzing behaviors and events

Observer-expectancy effect: Effects of observer's expectations and perceptions on participants; similar to self-fulfillment *See also* **subject-expectancy effect**

Odds ratio (OR): A very useful statistic that quantifies the differences in exposure for the cases versus the controls; can be used in conjunction with the case-control study design; *See also* **relative risk**

Office of Measurement and Evaluation (OME): An office at the University of Pittsburgh that assists researchers and students with the development, design, and content of survey instruments

One group pretest-posttest method: A method similar to the one-shot case study except that the pretest is used before the intervention

One-shot case study: A simple design in which an intervention is provided to one group and they are followed forward in time after the intervention to assess the outcome (posttest)

One-tailed (directional) hypothesis: Hypothesis for which researchers predict the direction of the relationship between the variables; direction is one way and one-tailed hypotheses contain a tail on one end only

Ontological assumptions: Assumptions that are concerned with the nature of knowledge and socially constructed relationships

Open-ended (unstructured) questions: Unstructured questions, used for phone or face-to-face interviews

Operational definition: A representation of concepts in observable and measurable terms

Operationalize: To define a research question or its variables in observable and measurable terms

Ordinal: The scale used when a question can be rank ordered

Ordinal data: Values or observations that can be ranked or ordered, for example, a Likert scale

Outcome evaluation: An evaluation to determine if the program or technology has caused demonstrable effects as defined in the project goals

Outcome variables: Criterion variables, predictor variables

p value: The probability of obtaining the result by chance if the null hypothesis is true

Panel of reviewers: Individuals who are experts in a scientific area

Paper: Abstracts and papers (research papers, scholarly papers) associated with poster sessions and conference presentations that may be published in the program or proceedings

Paradigm: Another term for research frame

Parametric: A type of statistical procedure that is based on the assumption that a variable is normally distributed in a population, for example, the *t*-test, ANOVA, and Pearson r correlation efficient

Parsimony: The elimination of extraneous or unnecessary complications

Participant observation: The involvement of the researcher as a participant in the observed actions, as part of the study group or environment he or she is observing; can be overt (open) or covert (secret)

Peer: Expert reviewers who evaluate manuscripts in their subject area or field

Peer review: Review by the members of an editorial peer review board that ensures that the information reported in the journal is of the highest quality; *See also* **peer**

Peer reviewed: A term indicating that a journal has an official and publicized process of review and approval and an editorial review board comprised of experts in fields and subjects related to the journal's focus.

Peer reviewer: Experts (peers) who evaluate manuscripts in their subject area or field and with the journal editor determine whether to publish a manuscript

Peer-reviewed research: Research that is examined and evaluated by experts in the same or related research field or scientific area

Personal digital assistant (PDA): A hand-held microcomputer, without a hard drive, that is capable of running applications such as e-mail and providing access to data and information, such as notes, phone lists, schedules, and laboratory results, primarily through a pen device

Phase I: Trials that usually test a new drug or treatment for the first time in a small group of people (20 to 80) to evaluate its safety, determine a safe dosage, and identify any side effects

Phase II: Trials that study the intervention in a larger group of people (100 to 300)

Phase III: Trials in which the study drug or treatment is given to even larger groups of people (1,000 to 3,000) to confirm its effectiveness, monitor side effects, compare other treatments, and collect data to confirm that it can be used safely

Phase IV: Trials that include studies to collect additional information after the drug has been marketed, such as the drug's risks, benefits, and optimal use

Pilot study: A trial run on a small scale that enhances the likelihood of a study's successful completion because it provides an opportunity to work out the details of the research plan

Pilot test: *See* **pilot study**

Placebo: A preparation that looks exactly like a drug in a study but which contains harmless ingredients (sometimes called a sugar pill)

Positive (direct) relationship: The relationship between variables that change in the same direction

Positive predictive value: A measure of the probability that a positive is a true positive given a specified probability threshold for the variable of interest

Positivism: Another name for the quantitative approach

Poster session: A means of communicating research using posters that contain the key information, with researchers standing in front of their posters for designated time slots

Posttest: Measurements taken after the intervention or observation

Posttest-only control group method: A method similar to the pretest-posttest control group method except that no pretest is used

Power: The likelihood of failing to reject a false null hypothesis

Predictor variables: Predictors

Preliminary modeling: First phase in a stepwise or iterative modeling process

Pretest: Measurements taken before the intervention or observation

Pretest-posttest control group method: A classic experimental design in which participants are randomly assigned to either the intervention (experimental) or non-intervention (control) group with measurements taken before and after intervention or observation

Prevalence rate: The proportion of people in a population who have a particular disease at a specific point in time or over a specified period of time

Prevalence study: A study that examines existing diseases to generate new hypotheses rather than to prove existing hypotheses; does not answer questions regarding causation *See also* **cross-sectional study**

Prevarication bias: Biased results caused by respondents giving untruthful responses; may occur when collecting salary information for a specific job title or other sensitive pieces of data

Prevention trials: Trials that aim to prevent disease in a person who has never had the disease or to prevent it from advancing or reoccurring

Primary analysis: The analysis of original research data by the researchers who collected them

Primary research: Original gathering of data

Primary source: 1. Original sources, such as health records, patients' blogs, or eyewitness accounts; 2. The original works of the researchers who conducted the investigation

Principal investigator (PI): The person in charge of a project and responsible for carrying out the entire project, meeting the budget guidelines, hiring personnel, and monitoring the entire project, including meeting deadlines; also responsible for developing the data and safety-monitoring plan

Priority claim: Claim that a study or aspect of the study is a "first"

Privacy Protection Study Commission: A commission established to review the weaknesses of the Privacy Act of 1974, evaluate the statute, and issue a report containing recommendations for its improvement to greater protections.

Probabilistic models: Models that can represent complex interrelationships between variables

Probe: Follow-up question

Proceedings: Published compilations of the papers delivered at a conference

Process evaluation: An evaluation that measures the effectiveness of the program

Program officer: The person who leads a specific request for applications (RFA) or request for proposals (RFP) and addresses any questions the investigators may have while developing a proposal

Proposal reviewers: Individuals with an extensive background or experience in a particular research area who review grant proposals and provide comments; may develop a score that determines the likelihood of the grant's potential for funding

Propriety: 1. Appropriate protections for participants; 2. Involvement of appropriate stakeholders

Prospective: Studies in which participants are followed into the future to examine relationships between variables and later occurrences, opposite of retrospective

Protocol: A step-by-step plan for how a clinical or community trial will be conducted

Protocols: A rule or procedure to be followed in a clinical trial, can be disease-specific or treatment-specific

Publication bias: The selective publication of studies, usually in favor of studies with positive results, statistically significant results, or both

Purpose statement: A clear statement of what the researchers are attempting to achieve, also called aims or objectives

Purposive sampling: A type of nonrandom sampling; a strategy of qualitative research in which researchers use their expertise to select representative units and unrepresentative units to capture a wide array of perspectives

Qualitative approach: Interpretation of nonnumerical observations, including words, gestures, activities, time, space, images, and perceptions; also called naturalism

Qualitative research: Investigative studies conducted within the qualitative approach; *See also* **qualitative approach**

Quality appraisal: An appraisal of the studies included in the systematic research review that identifies research methodology of each study, which either strengthens or weakens the credibility of the outcomes; involves weighting so that their level of significance to the research question can be assessed

Quality of life (QOL) trials: Trials that explore methods used to improve comfort and the quality of life for individuals with chronic diseases

Quantitative approach: Combining scientific inquiry and empiricism to explain phenomena; the data can be quantified and result in statistical or numerical results to arrive at objective knowledge

Quantitative unit of analysis: The object for which the researchers have collected data upon which to conduct statistical analyses

Quasi-experimental research: Research that searches for plausible causal factors by exposing one or more experimental groups to one or more treatment conditions with or without control groups and manipulations of the variables by the researcher, does not include randomization of subjects

Questionnaire: Printed or electronic lists of questions that researchers send to participants via electronic mail (e-mail or Web-based) or postal mail (paper-based)

Queue learning: A reinforcement learning methodology where large problems are subdivided into more manageable problems for analysis

Quota sampling: A type of nonrandom sampling

Random sampling: Unbiased selection of subjects from the population of interest

Randomization: Assignment of subjects to intervention or control groups by using statistical techniques to prevent pre-selection of patients into one of the groups

Randomized controlled trials (RCTs): Studies in which subjects are randomly selected and randomly assigned to an experimental group or a control group

Range of indifference: A way to consider the effect of a research outcome on practice; values in a continuum from slight changes that practitioners believe to be meaningless to worthwhile changes

Rater reliability: Consistency in the scoring of tests by one or more raters, indicating the extent to which subjectivity has been eliminated

Ratio: Scales with true numerical meaning because the distance between the variables relates to the true numerical value assigned to observations that have been made

Ratio data: Data that do begin at a true zero, for example, height, weight, and temperature

Recall bias: Bias that is introduced by the fact that the respondent's answer may be affected by his or her memory and, therefore, not completely accurate

Relative risk (RR): A measure of the strength of an association between the exposure (independent variable) and the disease or outcome (dependent variable)

Reliability: The survey consistently produces the same results, also referred to as reproducibility or repeatability; reliability involves the consistency of measurements

Reproducibility: A term that also is known as stability or as test-retest reliability

Request for applications (RFA): The project announcement that describes the project and encourages researchers to apply, may list additional criteria specific to the announcement.

Request for proposals (RFP): *See* **request for applications**

Research: Building a body of knowledge

Research design: A plan for conducting research; a plan determined by type of question or problem

Research frame: The overarching structure of a research project, also called a paradigm, comprising the theory or theories underpinning the study, the models illustrating the factors and relationships of the study, the assumptions of the field and the researcher, the methods, and the analytical tools

Research methodology: The study and analysis of research methods and theories

Research problem: A research question that is stated in a declarative sentence

Research protocol: A definition of the methodology that will be followed in collecting, synthesizing, and analyzing the research literature review or data; enables the research review team to address potential bias because guidelines are established prior to the beginning of any work; includes a brief introductory narrative that links the research question to an identified need or gap in existing knowledge

Research question: An interrogative sentence (that is, a question) about the specific issue that the researcher is investigating

Response (nonresponse) bias: Bias introduced by a low response rate; also called nonresponse bias, minimized by maximizing response rate

Response rate: Percentage of subjects answering surveys, letters of invitation to a study, and so forth

Retrospective: Looking back in time; opposite of prospective

Retrospective study: A study design that looks back in time to determine if the independent variable is causing the dependent variable (the disease)

Rich data: The many layers of data, or depth of data, that observation provides; provide a window on the participants' points of view

Rigor: Strength, exactness, or accuracy as applied to research results

Risk pattern mining: A data mining technique to deal with two unbalanced classes or cohorts and to identify the cohort (usually the minor cohort and the primary study group) at risk for a particular condition

Sample: Representative members of the population

Sample size: The number of subjects in the sample

Sample survey: Surveys that collect data from representative members of the population

Sampling: The process of selecting a set of subjects or units to represent a population

Sampling error: A difference between the population and sample due to pure chance; for example, random variations in samples drawn from the same population; reduces the reliability of the study

Sampling frame: The list of subjects, representing all elements of the target population, from which the sample is drawn

Scientific enterprise: History of science including its revolutions, advances, culture, and effects on society; sometimes associated with collaborations between scientists and entrepreneurs

Scientific inquiry: Making predictions, collecting and analyzing evidence, testing alternative theories, and choosing the best theory

Screening process: A review of study abstracts followed by a second screening of complete articles

Screening trials: Trials to examine the best method for detecting diseases or health conditions

Secondary analysis: The analysis of the original work of another person or organization by a second set of researchers includes secondary analysis of data sets and meta-analysis; *See also* **meta-analysis**

Secondary research: Analyzing other researchers' data

Secondary source: Sources that are based on primary (or original) sources and that summarize, critique, or analyze the primary sources, for example, encyclopedias, textbooks, annual reviews (also sometimes called tertiary sources)

Seed money: Funding that enables an investigator to begin research in a new area of interest

Selection: Systematic differences in the selection and composition of subjects in the experimental and control groups based on knowledge or ability

Selection bias: A type of bias introduced when some participants can choose to answer a survey questionnaire or to be part of a survey research study; responders' reasons may differ

Semantic differential scale: A scale that uses adjectives to rate the product, organization, or program, adjectives that are polar opposites placed at either end of the continuum and up to 20 adjective pairs used (half positive and half negative)

Semantic ontology: A system of describing knowledge for the integration of heterogeneous data sets to be used in modeling; allows the researcher to normalize all of the data sets to a common set of features and values that can support modeling

Semi-structured interview: An interview that follows a guide but allows additional questions that seem appropriate or triggered by the participants' comments

Sensitivity rates: A measure of validity; percentage of all true cases correctly identified where TP/(TP+FN)

Shallow data: Data that are easily collected but are equivocal

Significance: 1. Likelihood that the relationships or differences in their data are pure, random chance; 2. Merit of the research question

Significance (hypothesis or null hypothesis) testing: An analysis of the study data to obtain the probability value for comparison to a pre-established significance level

Significance level: The criterion used for rejecting the null hypothesis, a pre-established cutoff that determines whether the null hypothesis is rejected; the alpha level

Simple random sampling: The most common method; enables every member of the population under study to have an equal chance of being selected

Simulation observation: A type of nonparticipant observation that is usually conducted by observing study subjects in an environment created for them instead of in their natural environment

Skewness: The nonsymmetrical slant or tilt of the distribution that occurs when values are overly represented in one of the tails of the distribution and the mean, median, and mode are different values; value clusters in the left tail indicates a negatively skewed distribution and value clusters in the right tail indicate a positively skewed distribution; skewness value greater that one indicates non-normal distribution

Snowball sampling: A type of nonrandom sampling

Social desirability: Tendency to present oneself in a favorable light by responding in ways thought to be socially approved; a potential threat to validity of self-report data

Solomon four-group method: A method similar to the pretest-posttest design, but with two intervention or experimental groups and two control groups

Specific aims: The purpose or goal of the particular trial; may include both long- and short-term goals and should explain the major aim of the study

Specificity rates: A measure of validity; percentage of all true non-cases correctly identified where TN/(TN+FP)

Stability (test-retest reliability, reproducibility): Also known as test-retest reliability or reproducibility

Standardized observation protocols: One of the overlapping analytical techniques appropriate for qualitative research

Standardized open-ended interview: A format that uses specific questions that are asked across all participants with the same probes for all respondents

Static group comparison method: A study in which two groups are examined, one with the intervention and one without; assessed with posttest

Statistical conclusion validity: The extent to which the statistical conclusions about the relationships in the data are reasonable

Statistical regression: Statistical regression (regression toward the mean) is when extreme scores of measurement tend to move toward the mean because they have extreme scores, not because of the intervention under study

Statistical significance: The probability that an observed difference is due to chance (ascertained by analyzing the study's data to obtain the probability value and comparing that to a pre-established significance level); if not due to chance, the null hypothesis is rejected

Stem-and-leaf diagrams: Diagrams that show all the individual scores on a particular measure and provide information about the normalcy of the data

Step-wise modeling process: In this process, the researcher manually adds variables to the model in order to assess the independent effects of each variable.

Stratified random sampling: A sampling method that separates the population by certain characteristics, such as physician specialties, nursing units, or DRGs before choosing the random samples

Streamlining: Not discussing proposals that fall in the lower half of the scoring at the meeting to discuss proposals, but critiquing them and returning to applicants for resubmission

Structured questions: Close-ended questions, which are used more for self-assessments, Web-based or e-mail surveys, or mail and faxed surveys

Subject-expectancy effect: Effect related to subjects' expectancies; similar to self-fulfilling; *See also* **observer-expectancy effect**

Subjectivist: A philosophy that suggests that what is observed about a resource depends in fundamental ways on the observer and the context of the observation, that observations may be more qualitative, and that legitimate disagreements can exist

Submission guidelines: A journal's guidelines, both explicit and implicit, for the scope and format of manuscripts

Summative evaluation: An evaluation conducted after implementation that is designed to examine areas such as the effects or outcomes of a program, for example, to determine if the program had the intended effect; determine the overall impact of a project or program; evaluation of the cost-effectiveness of the program

Survey: Tools commonly used to collect descriptive data

Survey research: Research that allows the researcher to explore and describe what is occurring during a particular point or period in time; often used for descriptive, cross-sectional, or prevalence study designs

Survival analysis: A statistical analysis that uses data from all participants whether they withdraw from a study or not and examines how certain variables affect survival; *See also* **life table analysis**

Synthesis of data: Combining or integrating data using one of two basic forms, interpretive (qualitative) approaches or integrative (quantitative) methods

Systematic random sampling: A method of random sampling that draws the sample from a list of items, such as diagnoses, ICD-9-CM codes, or discharges, and selects every *n*th case

Systematic research review (SRR): 1. A systematic method of gathering, synthesizing, and evaluating evidence); 2. The method on which policy decisions are often based

Systematic review: A specialized type of journal article that summarizes, synthesizes, and critiques all the literature on a topic

Systematic sampling: The process of selecting a sample of subjects for a study by drawing every *n*th unit on a list

Target population: 1. The large group that is the focus of the study and from which samples are drawn for study; 2. A specific group of individuals on which the granting agency would like the research to focus

Test statistics: Statistics for examining the psychometric properties of measurement instruments, including validity and reliability

Testing: The effect created once participants are exposed to questions that may be on the posttest

Test-retest: A method for determining if an instrument is consistent over time or when given multiple times; same assumptions as the Cronbach's alpha

Test-retest reliability: Stability demonstrated in repeated tests resulting in reasonably similar findings; dependent on constancy in the object being measured.

Theoretical sampling: Type of nonrandom sampling in which selection of subjects is to fill gaps that emerge and to build theory; *See also* **nonrandom sampling**

Theory: 1. The systematic organization of knowledge that predicts or explains behavior or events; 2. The means to organize knowledge and explain the relationships among concepts

Time-series tests: Tests that allow observations throughout the study period as a new policy or law is implemented

Transferability: Degree to which key characteristics of contexts are similar and applicable to other contexts; established by rich and extensive descriptions

Transparency: A term that indicates that someone else could replicate the researchers' process; requires that researchers briefly describe the strategy used to identify the literature and explain the scope of the literature review by explicitly stating their inclusion and exclusion criteria

Treatment: Any action, not confined to therapies; for example, a computer training program, an algorithm to extract medical abbreviations from bibliographic databases, a specific technology or application, or the procedure to implement health information and communication technologies

Treatment trials: Trials to test experimental treatments, new combinations of medicines, different types of surgery, radiation, or chemotherapy

Triangulation: 1. The use of multiple sources or perspectives to investigate the same phenomenon, including data collection (multiple times, sites, or respondents), investigators (researchers), theories, and methods; 2. The use of several different approaches to collect data, answer the research questions, and support the conclusions made

Two-tailed (non-directional) hypothesis: A hypotheses for which researchers do not predict a directions and thus more conservative than one-tailed; hypotheses with tails on both ends of the bell-shaped normal curve

Type I error: An error that occurs when the researcher mistakenly rejects the null hypothesis when it is actually true; associated with Alpha levels

Type II error: An error that occurs when the researcher erroneously fails to reject the null hypothesis when it is false; associated with power

Typological analysis: An analytic technique used in qualitative research

Unit nonresponse: Subject totally refusing to participate

Unit of analysis, qualitative: The coded incident in qualitative research

Unit of analysis, quantitative: The object for which the researchers have collected data upon which to conduct statistical analyses

Unit of observation (measurement): The object of the original observations and purpose of the study; may or may not be the same as the unit of analysis

Univariate (descriptive) statistics: Descriptive) statistics

Univariate association: A term referring to the involvement of one variable

Unstructured questions: Open-ended questions that are often used for phone or face-to-face interviews

Utility: The process of getting the right information to the right person at the right time

Validity: A term meaning that the right thing was measured; accuracy

Variable: A factor

Warrant (justification): Justification for the researchers' claims (interpretations)

Web-based survey: A survey posted on the Web; usually close-ended questions

Index

New York
from the air

ANTONIO ATTINI   PETER SKINNER

vmb
PUBLISHERS

New York
from the air

CONTENTS

1 The pyramidal roof of 40 Wall Street reflects a bygone age of elegant design and detail.

2-3 Extensively restored, with its gold-leafed torch ablaze at night, the Statue of Liberty salutes an American ideal of liberty.

4-5 Historic Battery Park, with its circular Ft. Clinton, dominates Manhattan's southern tip. Here the Hudson River and the East River flow into Upper New York Harbor. On the left rises Battery Park City; to the right the Financial District and Wall Street.

6-7 Central Park, the city's jewel, extends from 59th to 110th Street. Flanking the park are the luxury apartment houses of Central Park West (left) and Fifth Avenue (right), with the Metropolitan Museum just below Jacqueline Kennedy Onassis Reservoir.

8 The Hudson River is flanked by Battery Park City and (right) by older office buildings. The 'beehive' building (bottom left) is the Holocaust Museum.

9 The Empire State Building, at the crossing of Fifth Avenue and 34th Street is the heart of Mid-Manhattan.

vmb
VMB Publishers®
An imprint of White Star S.p.A., Italy

© 2005 White Star S.p.A.
Via Candido Sassone, 22/24 - 13100 Vercelli, Italy
www.whitestar.it
ISBN IO: 88 540 0577 0
ISBN I3: 978 88 540 0577 8
Reprints:
2 3 4 5 6   09 08 07 06
Revised edition in 2005

Printed in Indonesia
Color separation by Chiaroscuro, Turin

Photographs   Antonio Attini

Text   Peter Skinner

Graphic Design   Marinella Debernardi

Introduction

"New York," like other world-cities, defies easy description; it is too diverse and contains too much. For every public image – Wall Street brokers in their office towers, nerve-wracking traffic, crowd-mobbed celebrities, etc. – there's a countervailing private image – the artist in a waterside studio, the solitary stroller in wooded parkland, the serene Chinese calligraphy teacher, etc. Many visitors arriving in New York eager to map their own impressions find that they can't easily get to grips with the city: Just what, they ask, is 'New York'?

Anyone getting a panoramic view of New York City from the air (and quite a few airborne arrivals do) would be looking down on five areas – four of them densely settled. The long, slender island of Manhattan would be instantly recognizable. The massy fingerprint of Staten Island, twice Manhattan's size, would be recognizable. But there's also Brooklyn, Queens and the Bronx, all parts of New York City, all three separated from Manhattan by rivers but variously linked by bridges and tunnels. All in all, the geography of New York City poses problems for the visitor: just where does Brooklyn become Queens? And where is Queens' farther boundary – and what comes next? It's easy to see where the Bronx begins, across the narrow river at Manhattan's northern tip, but just where does it end? And why is Manhattan so often called "New York" if there's so much more that is New York?

A map will help with the city-as-parts and the city-as-a-whole problem, but will not explain governance issues. Each of the five named areas is a borough of New York City but also a county of New York State. Manhattan is New York County; Brooklyn is Kings County; the Bronx is Bronx County, Queens is Queens County; and Staten Island is Richmond County.

So exactly what's meant by "New York"? Though it should mean the whole city, for many residents New York usually means only Manhattan. And that's not all: people in the outer boroughs (particularly in Staten Island) often call Manhattan "the city" . . . and many maps name the Hudson the North River . . .

Today's five-borough New York is a young city; the act of consolidation that created it was passed hardly a century ago, in 1898 – opposed by a fiercely independent Brooklyn. Though in many ways an ultra-modern city, New York – all five boroughs – are proud of their local histories. They differ markedly in one respect, which can be basically stated thus: whereas Manhattan's first southern-tip settlement rolled determinedly north up the 2 mile by 12 mile island (swallowing up a few small villages en route), in all the other boroughs, separate little settlements slowly expanded and finally coalesced into borough-wide urban areas. Actual patterns differed; historically, Brooklyn, for example, maintained an industrial base while Queens was more residential.

More than in any other world-city, New York's growth has been driven by immigration; around the turn of the century each year a million or so immigrants entered the United States via New York. Mercifully, by no means all stayed within the city. But so many did that whole areas of new housing sprang up, particularly along the fast-expanding subway routes, with schools, churches and institutional buildings following. The miracle of New York is its diversity: the boroughs retain strong identities. Each has its own rich array of educational, cultural and recreational facilities, but textures often differ; street layouts, housing, churches, colleges, institutional buildings, parks, and residents reflect different ethnic backgrounds, and result in vibrant and exciting neighborhoods.

Anyone seeing New York from the air in any sort of leisurely circuit would be struck by the fact that Manhattan is the smallest borough. They would also be struck by how much parkland each borough has, quite often at the shore. Of course, the various sections and neighborhoods of each borough are not equally well served, though the creation of miniparks has somewhat improved the situation. Aerial photography over major cities is a challenging business. Security and safety regulations often preclude specific desirable shots and thus the bigger more easily visible sites and features are photographed more often than smaller, more 'hidden' ones. Each of New York's five boroughs has at least one surviving 18th-century house, but not all are freestanding in open setting; they get lost in the mosaic.

The pattern of settlement in New York is not easy to capture as many earlier communities with their farms, mills and churches were simply torn down when the land was bought up for redevelopment. Increasingly the old ethnic enclaves and neighborhoods have become mixed. Time was when Italians, Irish, Scandinavians (particularly Norwegians), Germans, Poles, Czechs, Hungarians, Ukrainians, Chinese, Jews and others lived in quite clearly defined neighborhoods, both in Manhattan and often in the other boroughs, with their own churches, breweries, food stores, newspapers and associations. After World War II, greater

11 A satellite view of the lower tip of Manhattan.

12 This satellite view shows Central Park and East and Upper West Sides.

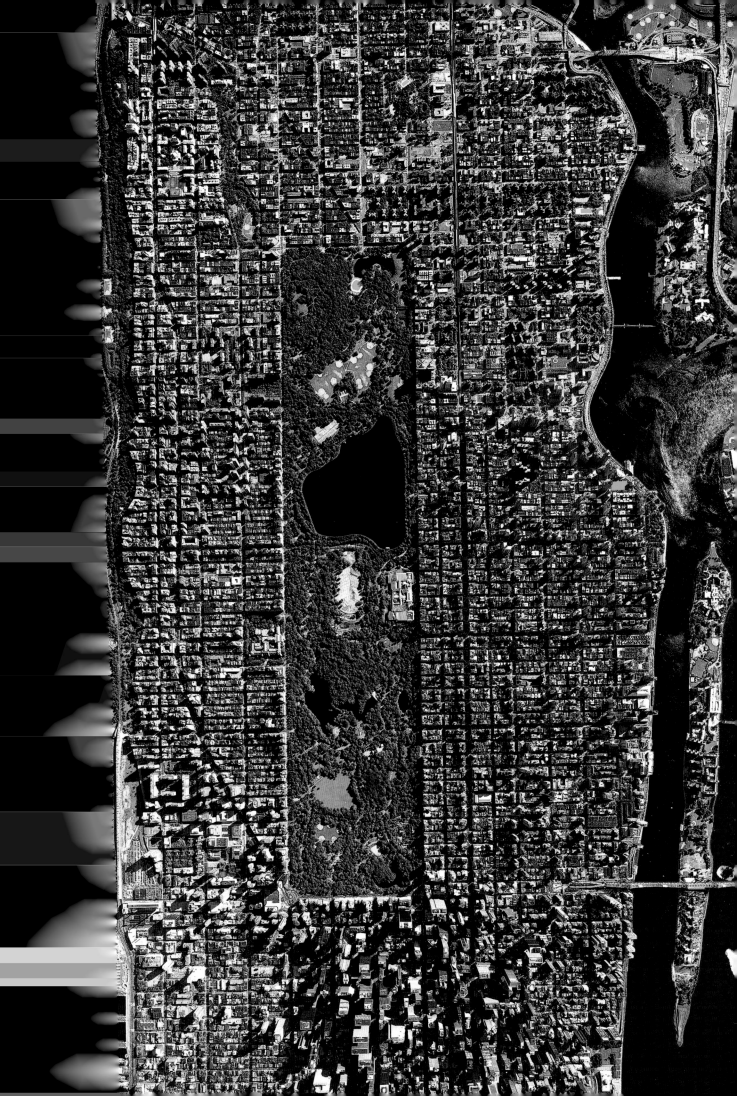

social mobility and the rapid development of Long Island, where new townships sprang up in the potato fields, led to the slow but progressive dilution of most of these ethnic neighborhoods. However, though the German and Hungarian communities may be only a shadow of their previous selves, Chinatown and Little Italy remain vibrant – much helped by being big attractions for visitors. Patches of the old Lower East Side, with its declining Jewish population survive, but largely as specific shopping streets.

Concurrently, new ethnic neighborhoods are developing, particularly in the boroughs. Woodside and Jackson Heights in Queens are remarkably mixed, but within the mix are concentrations of people from specific Latin-American and Caribbean nations, while Flushing is known for Indians from the subcontinent and for Koreans and other Asians. One or two blocks in Central Brooklyn are home to many members of New York's modest Tibetan population, while Bay Ridge, losing its Norwegians, has welcomed newcomers from a number of Muslim nations. Overall, new immigrants are not at all as clustered as those of a half-century ago; the ethnic tapestry has a richer and more varied pattern. Such is the new mix that a school class of 30 children may represent 20 or more nationalities. Some parents may be basically monolingual – and it is not unusual to see their children interpreting for them.

Certain callings attract specific ethnic groups. Many Albanians have become apartment house superintendents; Koreans operate numerous small 24-hour-per day neighborhood groceries; Pakistanis manage an immense number of newsstands; Afghanis are the deft chefs in hot chicken outlets, Uzbeks efficiently repair shoes, Mexican chefs prepare an amazing amount of non-Mexican food, to name but a few. And in almost every case these hardworking individuals are determined to ensure college educations and white-collar careers for their children.

New York's many ethnic groups add greatly to the city's cultural life. Not only is food and other shopping much more rewarding, but cultural festivals and events from Irish theater through Indian dance to Korean opera are a delight, to say nothing of proudly celebrated 'annual days' such as Puerto-Rican Day and numerous exuberant street fairs. Unless a series of pictures is taken over time, photography captures the scene of the moment rather than registering change. It's difficult to convey to any visitor the sheer rate of change – change for the better – that is occurring throughout New York. The mentality that led

to the destruction of Penn Station, deemed by many to have been an act of vandalism, and the threat of a similar fate for Grand Central Terminal, is much less evident. Many fine buildings no longer economically serving their original functions are converted to new uses; notably, the dowager office towers of Lower Manhattan are becoming residential. Similarly, Greek-temple style banks, deconsecrated disused churches, and unneeded fire stations have become housing or retail stores as appropriate.

The architectural design of public facilities has come under the spotlight. No longer will the economic, drab but functional structure suffice. In part, the plans for re-building the World Trade Center site have heightened aesthetic awareness. Notably, the Santiago Calatrava's stunning design for a major subway interchange station at the WTC breaks new ground, as does the design for the neighboring Fulton Street multi-line station, and plans for a new Amtrak terminal in the soon-to-be-relinquished General Post Office on 33rd St. and Eighth Avenue. Recreational facilities are also being upgraded. Central Park has been restored to pristine condition; the lessons learned are being applied to other parks in other boroughs, though funds, particularly private funds, are scarce. Citywide, citizens are finding a new voice – and, if need be, are willing to press their claims in court.

New York City is gaining recreation areas and parks through the continuing transformation of the waterfront into usable public space. Thousands of small irregular plots – even isolated within highway junctions – have been planted, fenced and lit. Increasingly, 'street furniture' – bus stop shelters, phone kiosks, newsstands, waste bins, bike racks and signage – are being upgraded. All these improvements are citywide, involving all five boroughs; they are subject to much discussion and many demands for further civic improvements. One factor has been the huge increase in Manhattan rents. As more and more young professional couples and singles move to areas of the outer boroughs once considered working class, they bring professional expectations and activist skills with them, creating attractive new communities.

This album captures some of Manhattan's historic sections, featuring both the old and the new. It also journeys farther afield, presenting an introductory glance at the immense stretch of Upper Manhattan, and visiting the outer boroughs and some of the city's far-flung waterfronts, a world apart, so different from the Manhattan's urban density.

14-15 Three historic skyscrapers anchor Mid-Manhattan: bottom left, the McGraw-Hill Building; and toward the East River and Queens rises the silver-spired Chrysler Building. To the right, the Empire State Building, with Brooklyn across the East River.

16-17 This spectacular view shows Brooklyn and Manhattan Bridge connecting Manhattan to Brooklyn.

18-19 Warm linght embraces the Empire State Building with its 86th-floor observation deck which draws over 3.5 million visitors annually.

LOWER MANHATTAN

"Lower Manhattan" has rolled north: past wall-less Wall Street; past canal-less Canal Street; past 14th St. and up to 23rd St. A blend of old and new streets and buildings, vibrant ethnic enclaves and distinctive neighborhoods, with water on three sides – the Bay, the East River and the Hudson – it's an exciting area

At the tip of Manhattan sits Battery Park (the city's oldest) and Castle Clinton – not a "castle" but a circular fort built on the Battery to protect Lower Manhattan. It demonstrates New York's genius for recycling buildings, having been a concert venue where Jenny Lind, "the Swedish Nightingale,"sang and where General Tom Thumb was an exhibit. Then, before Ellis Island opened, the building became an immigration station; now it is a fully restored historic site.

In dramatic contrast, nearby Battery Park City is one of New York's newest planned communities. The rock excavated for the World Trade Center was dumped in the Hudson and forms the 20-block development's foundation layer. A broad tree-lined esplanade fronts the Hudson; inland, well-spaced apartment houses stand on green sites extending twenty bocks. At the midpoint are the three towers of the World Financial Center, topped respectively by a mastaba, a dome, and a stepped pyramid, green-tinted against the buff stone facing. In rear is the World Trade Center site. The twin towers' cleared "footprints" are reminders of the tragedy, but to the north of the site reconstruction of the 7 WTC office tower is a symbol of New York City's indomitable optimism.

Anyone walking through the canyons of the Wall Street area should slip into the lobbies of the grand old buildings. No empty rectangles of black marble, no stainless steel and fluorescent-light sterility; instead, handsome spaces with walls of colored marbles, coffered ceilings, chandeliers, and bronze fittings. The external masonry is rich in architectural detailing; the roof lines sport iconic pyramids or Gothic-trim mansards. From the Staten Island ferry, the old vs the new, the spire vs the flat top is seen to advantage. But the tide has turned: the International style is out; newer buildings are not ashamed of decorative features.

The South Street Seaport beckons to all who seek "Old" Manhattan. Here on the East River, rescued and restored vessels are docked against a backdrop of restored 19th-century ship chandlers' and merchants' premises. More than a living museum, the Seaport is a vibrant shopping and dining area, with tables dotting the cobble-stoned slips where in times past men handled the cargoes from which much of the city's wealth derived.

Broadway, which follows an old Indian trail leading north, is always thronged with visitors, and the adjoining City Hall Park is an ideal place for a pause. Set amid the world's most expensive real estate, it is an oasis of calm against an eclectic backdrop of buildings: the Renaissance-style City Hall and the severely Neo-Classical Tweed Courthouse frame the park; just beyond loom the Municipal Building with its Baroque cupola and the Neo-Gothic Woolworth Building. These four icons reflect Lower Manhattan's visual richness and its role as the city's governmental and commercial heart.

Since the first Dutch settlement of 1624, New York has welcomed immigrants from almost every country of the world. Chinatown, with many immigrants arriving in the mid-1800s, remains a thriving community. Smaller, older buildings with shops below and accommodation above is the common pattern; Bayard, Pell, and neighboring streets are perfect examples.

Crossing Canal Street, to the northeast of Chinatown, leads the visitor into Little Italy, also proud of its colorfulness and traditions and drawing visitors to its many restaurants and cafés and to the religious festivals that mark the year. Mulberry and Grand Streets, in the heart of Little Italy, are thronged with visitors year round.

Bridges are one of Lower Manhattan's major visual highlights, the more so because their ramps begin well inland and rise above waterfront streets. Such was the challenge of building spans over the East River that the bridges offer proud, almost triumphal approaches. Leading off Canal Street is the colonnaded approach to the Manhattan Bridge (opened in 1909), the middle one of the three bridges that take Manhattanites to Brooklyn. Farther south is the Brooklyn Bridge (opened in 1889); farther north is the Williamsburg Bridge (opened 1903). All three have popular pedestrian walkways. The Brooklyn Bridge predated the earliest subway, but other two carry subway tracks in addition to their roadways. The bridges' long approach ramps, rising high above the streets, offer a wonderful range of views over and into buildings lying below.

Lower Manhattan is known for its bargain shopping. Flanking the East River is the Lower East Side, with the Delancey Street as its spine. It is no longer an entirely Jewish neighborhood; residents began to seek

less crowded neighborhoods after World War II. Nonetheless, the area's synagogues, kosher butcher shops and restaurants, and its many small clothing stores, gift shops, and other retail establishments, with their wares spilling onto shop-front racks and sidewalk tables, reflect Jewish traditions in serving an increasingly mixed population – often Sunday shoppers from elsewhere in Manhattan or from the outer boroughs.

To the west of the Lower East Side, beyond Little Italy, lies Soho ("South of Houston" [St]), an area of old manufacturing lofts that are now generally avant-garde art and style galleries, high-fashion salons, and expensive restaurants, with multimillion-dollar 'loft' apartments on the upper floors. Joining the scramble for instant fashionability is self-created Tribeca ("Triangle above Canal [St.]," where a similar art-style-fashion-and-dining scene has taken root.

Houston St. (more or less 1st St.), a river-to-river thoroughfare, marks the beginning of two "villages" that continue north to 14th St., also a broad river-to-river thoroughfare. Greenwich Village (extending from Broadway to the Hudson) is a genuine village with 18th-century roots, a country escape for the Dutch and then the British settlers clustered around the Battery. Washington Square Park, host to open-air music and theater programs, with its smaller-scale "Arc de Triomphe" at the foot of Fifth Avenue, is the Village's central meeting place; around it are New York University buildings – whose student population keeps the Village youthful. A mix of handsome town houses, dignified older apartment buildings and turn-of-the century tenements on often charming tree-lined small streets, home to many specialty shops and renowned restaurants old and new, give the Village its special residential flavor.

Along the Hudson Greenwich Village (now called the West Village) is undergoing dramatic change. A continuous strip of waterfront park has been built, with access to restored piers, one sporting a café, seating, and an airy pavilion. Inland, new steel and glass highrises are being heavily criticized as destroying the historic ambience and character of the Village. Many gay couples and single gay men live in the area; their sense of style is reflected in the stores, cafés, and street life.

From Broadway to the East River another "Village" exists: the East Village, a real estate marketing invention. This area of tenement buildings that extends over to the East River is probably home to more one-of-kind stores within a single small area than anywhere else in New York. African art, Burmese restaurants, Tibetan antiques, Ukrainian books, acupuncture, aromatherapy supplies, brass furniture fittings, herbal remedies, macramé work, reflexology and theater, dance, music, and foreign films – the East Village offers them all. It is home to Polish and Ukrainian communities, to Hells Angels, rockers, punk and all else that can be imagined. The East Village draws many of New York's most talented young artists; with them come an army of artsy hopefuls.

The East Village boasts a number of distinguished buildings, among them the Cooper Union (opened as an engineering school in 1853 by Peter Cooper, a cast-iron pioneer). In 1860, President Lincoln gave a speech in the Union's Great Hall. Tompkins Square Park (site of short-lived communes, squatter settlements, and demonstrations) is the community's biggest park.

Lower Manhattan's northern section, from 14th to 23rd Sts, marks the start of "grid-plan New York." Gone are the tight clusters of sometimes curving or dog-leg streets found around the Battery and in Chinatown; gone is Greenwich Village's on-the-diagonal street plan. Here regularity is the hallmark, though the parallel the avenues and streets have much of interest. Union Square at 14th St. and Broadway, famed for protest rallies, is also the site of a Greenmarket selling local fresh farm produce, while the private Gramercy Park on 20th Street, a genteel oasis, erupts into lawsuits if a tree is trimmed. To the east, extending from First Avenue to the East River, are two almost self-contained communities: the immense multiblock housing developments of Stuyvesant Town and Peter Cooper Village, with their brick towers rising in orderly ranks from a green park base. Stuyvesant Square, a park bisected by Second Avenue, is a nearby quiet oasis.

"Big" is the fingerprint elsewhere too. Toward the Hudson, the brick monolith of the Port Authority Building occupies an entire block at 16th St.; north at 20th Street the red-brick Gothic-style buildings of the Union Theological Seminary, occupy another. Extending around a grassy courtyard it seems to be an Oxford or Cambridge college airlifted from Great Britain

At 23rd St, where Broadway (on the diagonal) crosses Fifth Avenue, stands the landmark Flatiron Building, built in 1902 and now named for its shape. New York's earliest true skyscraper, its predates the Woolworth Building, built in 1913. To the north are the massed tower of Mid-Manttan.

24 The multilane highway going north once flanked the Hudson River. Today it separates

Battery Park City (built on landfill in the 1970s) from neighboring Manhattan.

26-27 Battery Park City's Esplanade is a major amenity enhanced by trees, flower plantings and river breezes. Top

left is the 'Gothic' Woolworth building; center top is 40 Wall Street, with its distinctive green pyramid roof.

28 Battery Park City's new apartment houses look onto the tree-lined Esplanade fronting the Hudson River.

28-29 The World Financial Center, with its towers topped by the green dome and truncated pyramid, is the main entry to waterfront Battery Park City. Here one tower is ablaze with light.

29 top North Cove is a yacht-fancier's paradise that offers Lower Manhattan residents a new recreation.

30-31 Two characteristics define downtown buildings: they conform to the old 17th-century curving streets, and the old dowager skyscrapers are known for their decorative and intricately patterned architecture.

32 top and 32-33 The Municipal Building (left and center foreground), City Hall in its wooded park, and the soaring white stone Woolworth Building hark back to an era of gracious architecture and generous ornamentation. The ornate cupola of the Municipal Building is a much-loved landmark.

32 bottom Infinite gradation characterizes the summits of many buildings dated the first decades of last century.

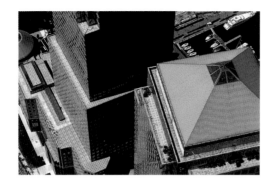

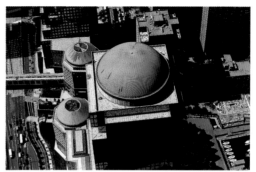

34 top Classical architectural roof treatments in metallic blue are keynotes of the World Financial Center's towers.

34 bottom The narrowing of Lower Manhattan is clearly shown here: top left are the Brooklyn and Manhattan bridges, spanning the East River.

35 The World Financial Center, North Cove and the Hudson offer residents urban life with nature at hand.

36 top Lower Manhattan's clustered towers nod to Brooklyn's piers. Many people working in Lower Manhattan live across the river in conveniently close Brooklyn.

36-37 The Brooklyn and Manhattan bridges link downtown

Brooklyn to Manhattan. The tree-lined Brooklyn Heights Esplanade (above the twin piers) provides a great view of Lower Manhattan.

37 Though appearing delicate, the Manhattan Bridge carries road, rail, and pedestrian traffic.

38-39 The Brooklyn Bridge, the Manhattan Bridge and, far right, the Williamsburg Bridge, all span the East River. Brooklyn is at the base of the photograph.

40-41 In good weather the center walkway across the Brooklyn Bridge is thronged with pedestrians.

42 top The
Williamsburg Bridge
(left) and the
Brooklyn Bridge
(right) demonstrate
the intricate ties and
strengtheners of
early bridges.

42-43 The restored
South Street Seaport
lies just south of the
Brooklyn Bridge; the
slender white spire
of the Woolworth
Building marks
Lower Broadway.

43 The
Williamsburg
Bridge, north of the
Broooklyn and
Manhattan bridges,
completes the trio of
downtown East
River spans.

44-45 The
Brooklyn waterfront
below the
Manhattan and
Brooklyn bridges
has been
redeveloped into
attractive miniparks.

46-47 *The designers of the Manhattan Bridge, completed in 1909, chose steel over stone for the bridge towers and adopted numerous decorative elements to differentiate their bridge from the Brooklyn Bridge, completed in 1883.*

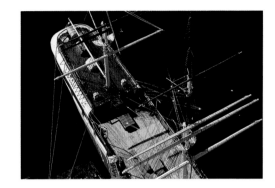

48-49 *The South Street Seaport represents history preserved: center and right on the mainland are restored 19th-century buildings.*

49 top *The afterdeck of a 19th-century sailing vessel. The South Street Seaport's "saved" vessels have been, or are being, expertly restored.*

49 center *Before honorable retirement is 1967, the Ambrose Light Ship was stationed in Lower New York Bay. The light tower that replaced it was hit by a ship in 1996, and had to be replaced by a second one.*

49 bottom *The Seaport's waterfront, with its many restaurants, bars, and stores, is a popular warm-weather rendezvous for New Yorkers and visitors alike.*

50 The masonry-clad, copper-roofed cupola-topped building at 40 Wall Street proudly displays architectural trim too expensive for cut-price modernity.

51 top left The elegant three-story City Hall, combining French Renaissance and Georgian styles, with its delicate cupola, is a happy survival from 1811.

51 top right The flat roofs of modern office towers support an amazing variety of mechanical equipment, invisible from below.

51 bottom The magnificent colonnaded approach to the

Manhattan Bridge has been restored to its former glory.

52-53 The spires of the 70 Pine Street and 40 Wall Street frame the tree-lined Brooklyn Heights Esplanade, behind which rise 19th-century houses.

54 19th- and 20th-century buildings, both high-rise and low-rise, pack the narrow streets of Lower Manhattan, where older office buildings are becoming residential.

55 Lower Manhattan boasts much distinctive architecture: to the left, the curved-façade new Federal Building, to its right the pyramid-capped Federal Courthouse; close by the cupola's Municipal Building, and front right, the Woolworth Building with its 'Gothic' ornamentation.

56-57 The Williamsburg Bridge connects Manhattan and Brooklyn (top); below the four-chimneyed generating plant is the huge Stuyvesant Town-Peter Cooper Village housing development.

58-59 The headquarters of Con Edison (New York's electric utility) with its landmark 'campanile'; to the right is the Zeckendorf Towers apartment building, with its four pyramid-capped towers overlooking Union Square.

60 During the
summer months,
numerous sailing
craft dot the waters
of New York Bay
surrounding Ellis
Island and the Statue
of Liberty.

61 The Statue of
Liberty is seen at
its inspiring and
dramatic best
against the
backdrop of Lower
Manhattan.

62 The Statue of
Liberty, which soars
305 ft., was
dedicated in 1886.
For many visitors,
the inspiring statue
and its park are
"must see"
attractions.

63 Strength,
serenity, and
timelessness mark
the classic features
of the symbol of
Liberty.

MID-MANHATTAN

Mid-Manhattan – from river to river, 23rd St. to 59th St., where Central Park begins. An almost perfect grid. But uniformity doesn't mean dullness. Mid-Manhattan is home to ethnic neighborhoods ranging from Brazilian through Indian to Korean; add in shopping that offers a Diamond District, a wholesale flower market, spice bazaars, and vertical malls in retrofitted department stores, include Macy's, highlight a number of world-famous skyscrapers and magnificent public buildings, throw in a number of handsome parks – and some sense of what Mid-Manhattan offers may emerge.

Take 23rd St. at Fifth Avenue, where Broadway crosses from the east to the west side of Manhattan. Directly ahead, flanking Fifth Avenue on the east side is the verdant oasis of newly refurbished Madison Square Park, its eastern margin is flanked by the elegant Neo-Classical building housing NY State Supreme Court's Appellate Division, in turn overshadowed by the tower of New York Life Insurance Co., in turn dwarfed by the massive bulk of the Metropolitan Life Insurance Co. building.

Straight ahead on the west side of Fifth Avenue at 34th street, the unmistakable Empire State Building (1931) soars skyward. Walking up to 34th St., Broadway takes one through a heady concentration of Korean import stores awash with electronic and photographic equipment, housewares, and fashion accessories. Farther east, Lexington Avenue offers a journey through the Indian spices and foodstuffs area, with restaurants beckoning.

Macy's, at Herald Sq. (34th and Broadway), anchors the retail shopping area. To the west at Seventh Avenue is Madison Square Garden, a squat silo housing convention and sports facilities that in 1963 replaced the majestic Penn Station, whose unrivalled inner halls were based on the Baths of Caracalla. The slender One Penn Plaza tower rises alongside, while the colonnaded Neo-Classical façade of the General Post Office forms a backdrop, occupying the entire 32nd to 33rd St. block.

Trade fairs and conventions are big business in New York,and the vast Jacob Javits Convention Center, a series of glass pavilions already occupying 34th to 37th Sts. off Eleventh Avenue, is slated for further expansion.

Famed 42nd St. is Mid-Manhattan's main cross-town artery. The view of the general area from a plane would include the *USS Intrepid*, an aircraft carrier that is now an Air-Sea Museum, with aircraft on its deck On West 42nd rises a unique green glass Art Deco skyscraper that once housed McGraw-Hill; close by the immense, efficient Port Authority Terminal buildings, sprouting a web of ramps that descend into the tunnel that daily serves thousand of commuters from New Jersey and beyond.

As a vantage point from which to see New York both conserve and reinvent itself, 42nd St. and Seventh Avenue is the perfect place, and dusk is the perfect time. To the south there will be dwindling number of garment district workers pushing dress racks along the sidewalks. But to the east, along 42nd St. are the hypermodern billboard-bearing steel-and-glass towers of the 42nd St.-Times Square revival project: visual excitement, movement and light are the keywords, and the surging crowds spilling off the sidewalks show these aims have been realized.

Looking north up the broad sweep of Seventh Avenue/Broadway toward 52nd St. is a wonderland of blazing, colored light stemming from advertising panels that occupy entire building façades, their messages emphasized by ever-changing scenes drawn in brilliant neon hues. Below are lit-up movie house, hotel and theater marquees.

A block east, Sixth Avenue northbound presents itself as a canyon flanked by office towers in the steel-and-glass International Style, each sitting on a plaza; many of the plazas feature sunken concourses with some featuring a massive piece of modern art. By day the clean lines of buildings and the flows of office workers dominate the scene, but at night, the canyon is ablaze with the light streaming from a million windows.

Toward Fifth Avenue Bryant Park is a needed oasis of trees, lawns and seating, with an elegant café making it a favorite lunch place. It is also the site of annual fashion shows, for which the rear façade of the New York Public Library's palazzo-style building, a magnificent palace of learning, opened in 1911, forms a classical backdrop.

The Library's main front is on Fifth Avenue: here the broad steps and twin sculpted lions provide a meeting place for thousands daily while within is the spectacular Main Reading Room and below are elegant rooms housing special collections serving more arcane scholarship.

To the east on 42nd St. is the magnificent Beaux-Art triumph of Grand Central; Terminal (1913), where a handsome restoration of the great central hall and the shopping and dining facilities draw thousands of non-travelers. A succession of distinctive and absolutely different structures line the street going east. First the black glass box-like masses of the Marriott Hotel, then the Art Deco shaft of the iconic Chrysler Building, with its unmis-

64-65 from left to right Midtown view; the UN; the Chrysler Building spire; dusk, with the MetLife Building in the foreground.

67 For many New Yorkers the Chrysler Building remains their favorite architectural icon.

takable cascade of shimmering crescents below its spire, then, with its tree-studded atrium, the Ford Foundation Building, then Gothic-trim Tudor City.

The United Nations complex, with its Library, Secretariat Building and General Assembly Building, are of course instantly recognizable; the stark simplicity of the Secretariat contrasting with the longer, more sinuous lines of the other two low-rise structures. The campus and attached park (extending to 48th St.) make this a delightful oasis. The free-standing pierced-monolith sculpture in the forecourt of the Secretariat Building is by Barbara Hepworth, a British sculptor.

If Mid-Manhattan has a single central point it is surely Rockefeller Center. The placement of buildings, their unity of design and striking verticals that lighten the masonry cladding, with the GE Building, the tallest in the center, surrounded by ones of lesser height, of which the lowest have roof gardens, makes for a noble complex of timeless appeal. The Mall leading from Fifth Avenue to the central Concourse is a unique feature: plantings change with the seasons and at Christmas achieve high art.

Across the avenue, St. Patrick's Cathedral, designed in the high Gothic style and possessing perfect symmetry, offers a fine contrast between God and Mammon. Both St. Patrick's and Rockefeller Center seen from street level are very impressive; when seen from the air they create indelible impressions of solidity and of lightness respectively. But the traditional Fifth Avenue is visibly changing. New high rises shoehorned in on often quite small sites are thrusting high above the roof lines of their neighbors. Still farther east, on Park Avenue north of Grand Central Terminal, is another canyon of immense office towers. Straddling the avenue is the Met Life Building, whose sheer light- and breeze-blocking bulk is its main characteristic. Modern office towers line both sides of Park Avenue. At dusk, the canyon is filled with white light streaming into the growing darkness; the lack of retail establishments means a lack of colored neon.

But Park Avenue is not only office towers in the 40s and 50s giving way to grand old apartment houses farther north. There's fashionable St. Bartholomew's Church, Byzantine in style and built in brick and stone, and then the great stone pile of the Waldorf-Astoria Hotel at 47th St., temporary New York home to thousands of the world's makers and shakers. Lever House and the Seagram Building, both famous as architectural style-setters, stand nearby. Overall the East 50s is a glamorous area. Madison Avenue is already offering high-class boutiques

and specialty galleries; Lexington, and Third, Second, and First avenues are a mix of brand-new high-rise apartment towers, older 8- to 12-story buildings and century-old 6-story tenements. Every sidestreet has its small restaurants, corner groceries, and old-fashioned laundries.

The West Side is more given to business; residential blocks are farther from the center. On 47th St. diamond dealers cluster; farther west there is an amazing concentration of restaurants serving Broadway and Times Square theater patrons; at 42nd and Eighth Avenue is a high-rise development largely housing people in the theater and the arts. Much of the waterfront is still commercial; not shipping but other businesses.

Almost the northern boundary of Mid-Manhattan, 57th St. has a special character. A landmark Philip Johnson building with an iconic "broken pediment" stands at Madison Avenue. The central blocks still house many long-established art galleries, but the jewel of this broad thoroughfare is Carnegie Hall, New York's best-loved concert hall, known for its fine acoustics that yield a golden tone. It opened in 1859, with Piotr Tchaikowsky conducting the inaugural concert.

Just north, 59th St. is indeed a frontier. At Fifth Avenue, the Plaza Hotel with its green copper roof pierced by mansard windows and set off by corner turrets, stands across from Grand Army Plaza. Across the avenue rises the white-marble clad tower until recently known as the GM Building. But the true glory of 59th St. is Central Park South, extending from Fifth Avenue to Eighth Avenue and opening onto the glories of the park. Columbus Circle (the junction of Eighth Avenue and Central Park South) is now one of New York's finest architectural ensembles. Standing across from the corner of the park is the Time-Warner Building, with twin shimmering curved glass façades flanking a "Window on the Park," planned as a show-case auditorium for jazz events. The huge building is home to world-class high-fashion stores, renowned restaurants and apartments that cost several million dollars.

If Columbus Circle is the focal point of the new and stylish, then the eastern section of 59th St. (together with neighboring blocks) is much-appreciated for its charming townhouses and a quiet, neighborhood air. Just beyond Second Avenue the ramps leading to the Queensboro Bridge begin their ascent. Alongside the cantilevered steel-lattice structure built in 1909 runs a Swiss-style gondola serving residents of Roosevelt Island, a planned community in the middle of the East River.

68 Flatiron Building, erected in 1902 and now named for its shape, stands at 23rd Street, where Broadway (left) crosses Fifth Avenue.

70-71 *An observer looking northeast from the block-sized Port Authority Building on Eighth Avenue and 16th Street (lower right) would see the Empire State Building soaring up at Fifth Avenue and 34th St.,*

with midtown office towers to its north. The East River can be glimpsed toward the top of the photo.

71 top left *The East River Drive is flanked by some of Manhattan's most expensive apartment houses.*

71 top right *Fifth Avenue begins in the exact center of this image and runs north past the Empire State Building.*

72-73 *Washington Square is here depicted with its famous arch; to the right is the beginning of Fifth Avenue, which divides Manhattan's West Side (left) from the East Side (right).*

74 left Many older Mid-Manhattan office towers, like the New York Life Insurance Building are enhanced by pyramidal roofs.

74 right and 75 The Metropolitan Life Insurance Company's 'campanile' (1906) and quasi-polygonal North Building (1931) on Madison Avenue and 23rd St. overlook Madison Square Park. The landmark campanile manages to combine Italianate and

eclectic architectural features, reflecting the architectural confidence of the early 20th century.

76-77 The white ribbon of Fifth Avenue begins at Washington Square Park, immediately north of the famous arch.

78-79 East Mid-Manhattan, looking north with Fifth Avenue on the left. The Queensboro Bridge passes over Roosevelt Island en route to Queens.

80 and 81 The
Empire State
Building remains
an unchallenged
icon; it has no
near neighbors of
similar height. Its
86th-floor
Observation Deck
remains a 'must-
go' for New York's
tourist tide. The
architectural
detailing is very
restrained
compared to that
of the flamboyant
Chrysler Building,
completed a year
earlier.

82 This railcar
parking yard west of
Penn Station and
Madison Square
Garden is under
consideration as the
site for a proposed
Olympic stadium.

83 The circular
Madison Square
Garden arena
presents a low-rise
contrast to the green
roofed General Post
Office to the right.
Below the Garden is
Penn Station,
serving Long Island.

84-85 *The* USS
Intrepid, *anchored
in the Hudson River
against a backdrop
of Mid-Manhattan
highrises, is both a
popular 'Sea-Air-
Space Museum' and
an interesting
setting for social
functions.*

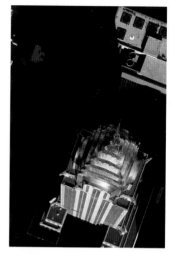

86 top Strong vertical lines increase the Chrysler Building's upward thrust but the structure has a substantial cross-section.

86 bottom and 87 Few if any Manhattan structures can rival the Chrysler Building for the exuberant confidence of its decorative motifs.

88-89 The Met Life Building's uninspired bulk (left) dwarfs Grand Central at its base and the elegant Chrysler Building. As a queen among skyscrapers, the Chrysler Building is known for the silvery facing of its cascading spire. To the right is the UN; to its north is Roosevelt Island.

90 The balance of forms – high-rise Secretariat, the tapered General Assembly Building, and slope-roofed Library in an open setting – give the United Nations a unique visual presence.

91 Dome, crescent and straight lines combine harmoniously in the UN's architectural design. The UN's East River frontage and adjoining park make it a tranquil haven in busy Mid-Manhattan.

92-93 Mid-Manhattan is has a huge variety of highrises. Here the pierced pediment of the AT&T Building (extreme left); the slope-roofed Citicorp Center Building, and the spire-capped Chrysler Building (center) represent distinctly different styles.

94 Visible in the
upper left, the lights
of Times Square, the
area where Broadway
and Seventh Avenue
meet.

95 left The
forbidding bulk of the
Met Life Building
casts shadows over
its elegant neighbors

95 right World Plaza
Building 50th Street
and Eighth Avenue
marks a return to an
earlier architectural
idiom that favored
masonry cladding.

96-97 In a forest of
highrises, the Citicorp
Center on Lexington
Avenue presents an
unusual roof line. In
the background is
Roosevelt Island and
the Queensboro
Bridge.

Lower
Manhattan

Lower Manhattan

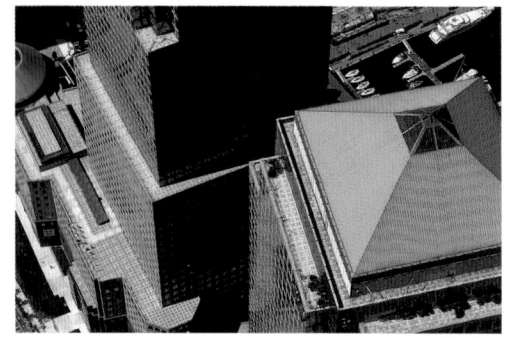

34 top Classical architectural roof treatments in metallic blue are keynotes of the World Financial Center's towers.

34 bottom The narrowing of Lower Manhattan is clearly shown here: top left are the Brooklyn and Manhattan bridges, spanning the East River.

35 The World Financial Center, North Cove and the Hudson offer residents urban life with nature at hand.

106 and 107 bottom right A cone of brilliant light . . . the Chrysler Building spire at night.

107 left 4 Times Square's radio mast soars skyward; top left is the golden pyramid of the World Plaza Building at 50th St. and Eighth Avenue.

107 top right The sun goes down; the lights of Manhattan skyscrapers will soon start illuminating the night.

108-109 Looking north with the MetLife, Citicorp Center, Chrysler, General Electric, and Empire State buildings all lit up.

102 top left and 103 top The Citicorp Center's sloping roof contrasts with the turrets and flat-tops of older buildings. The roof is not an architectural whimsy but a massive solar energy panel.

102 top right The exuberant copper pyramid and cupola of the New York Central Building is a Midtown icon.

102-103 The Plaza Hotel, at Fifth Avenue and Central Park South, reflects European architectural motifs.

103 bottom This triangle is no a work of art but the site of air-conditioning intakes and exhausts.

104-105 The clustered towers of central Mid-Manhattan, looking northwest toward Central Park, flanked by Central Park West and its

luxury apartment houses. The "broken pediment" building with the solar panel is the AT&T Building at Madison Avenue and 57th Street.

UPPER MANHATTAN

From the air, Central Park, flanked by the Upper East and Upper West Sides, each a mix of high-rise apartment buildings, tenements, and retail businesses, seizes the eye. Manhattan's green heart extends from 59th St. to 110th St., on land set aside in 1853, when the city's patricians decided that Manhattan should match the parks of European capitals. Fortunately, the area was too rocky for other uses.

The formidable duo of Vaux and Olmsted, the park's designers, created a masterpiece, taking advantage of topography and sinking and bridging transverse roadways, ensuring a haven for pedestrians. The park's many elements delight all strollers. Looking north, there's the Bird Sanctuary and the Sheep Meadow, a big open area that draws strollers, dog-walkers and child exercisers. Just east is the small Zoo, beloved by local children.. Then there's the great tree-lined Mall ending in a magnificent balustraded terrace overlooking the Bethesda Fountain. Beyond is the Boating Lake, and then almost at the park's center is the Great Lawn, a venue for concerts, overlooked by Belvedere Castle, whose turret provides splendid views of the Delacorte Theater, the Shakespeare Garden and the farther reaches of the park.

North of the Lawn is the huge Jacqueline Kennedy Onassis Reservoir; fitness enthusiasts run around it at dawn and dusk. Toward the park's northern boundary are tennis courts, the elegant Conservatory Gardens, the Meer, the Lasker Pool and Skating Rink, as well as numerous tree-shaded walks and, for the energetic, the Ravine and the Great Hill. Some twenty or so architecturally impressive gates, each celebrating a profession or group, adorn the park's perimeter.

Fifth Avenue forms the park's eastern boundary, one marked by staid but luxurious apartment houses. In the avenue's lower reach, Temple El-Emmanuel, with a typical arched cross-section, breaks the line of residential buildings. The Frick Collection, at 70th St., offers Old Master paintings in the palatial home that Henry Clay Frick, a turn-of-the-century steel millionaire, bequeathed to the nation. From 80th to 84th streets (within the park) stands the massive Metropolitan Museum of Art; now both

a cultural and social venue. Farther north on Museum Mile is the white spiral of the Guggenheim Museum, considered one of Frank Lloyd Wright's masterpieces. Next door is the National Academy of Design, located in an elegant townhouse. In striking contrast to these two institutions is the huge Georgian mansion built for the steel multimillionaire Andrew Carnegie, now housing the Cooper-Hewitt Museum of Design. Also located on the prestigious of Museum Mile are the Jewish Museum, known for outstanding exhibitions, and the International Center for Photography, with its archival collections.

Body as well as soul is catered for: at 98th St. stand the strikingly modern buildings of Mt. Sinai Medical Center; just beyond, at 103rd St. is the dignified older building of New York Academy of Medicine, with its unrivaled library. Those in search of musical and choral offerings can visit St. Nicholas Russian Orthodox Cathedral at 97th St. Then, for the visitor keen to check on questions about the city, at 104th St. is the Museum of the City of New York.

Parallel to Fifth is Madison Avenue, which still retains many smaller buildings, home to many fine antiques, high fashion, and design boutiques, as well as elegant restaurants. It is also home to the Whitney Museum, which Gertrude Vanderbilt Whitney, a sculptor, founded in 1930, after the Metropolitan Museum highhandedly refused her gift of work by living American painters. The museum's current home at 74th St, designed by Marcel Breuer, is a dark brick building that widens as it rises. The Whitney Biennal is a recognized showcase for new American art. Another iconic Upper East Side building is the vast Seventh Regiment Armory; here annual antiques shows and equally prestigious antiquarian book fairs draw thousands of enthusiasts.

The buildings on Park, Lexington, Third, Second and First avenues and their cross streets are home to an innumerable army of New Yorkers determined to live on the "fashionable Upper East Side." Most pay excessively high rents for the privilege - and neighborhood stores, often offering expensive imported food delicacies and glamorous apparel, tempt tastes but burden credit cards. In every way, the Upper East Side is chic designer and tasteful importer territory, with never quite satisfied customers. The Hungarian community, with its tastes and preferences reflected

110-111 from left to right Upper West Side; the Guggenheim Museum; the Century Apartments; the Time-Warner Building.

113 The twin-towered San Remo apartment house offers magnificent views over Central Park. It was

completed just before the Great Depression, and is one of the architect Emery Roth's many luxury buildings.

in shops on the streets just below 86th St, and the German community of Yorkville centered on 86th St. are only a very faint shadow of what they were a half century ago; restauranteurs and storeowners die and their cuisines and businesses die with them.

Beyond First Avenue lie the short stretches of York and East End avenues; they occupy land edging toward the East River. Just beyond East End Avenue, on a bluff at 89th St., is Gracie Mansion in its delightful small park. Built for Archibald Gracie in 1799, it is now the official residence of the Mayor of the City of New York.

The Upper West Side is a narrower swathe of territory than the Upper East Side, but Riverside Park, with the Hudson beyond, gives everyone easy access to exercise and open-air leisure. The area prides itself on its distinctive differences from the somewhat conservative Upper East Side, its urban "neighbor" across the park. Many residents consider the Upper West Side to be more liberal, with more street life and more varied retail businesses; others note the contribution of Jewish residents with their vitality and love of theater and music.

Central Park West in every way matches Fifth Avenue for handsome apartment houses; in fact, many are more architecturally distinctive than those that face them on the Fifth Avenue side. Breaking the skyline are the exuberant twin towers of the Century, the Majestic, the San Remo, and the Eldorado; the Dakota (when built in 1884 it was "in the wilds"), the turreted Beresford, and other palatial buildings are equally prestigious places to live. On Broadway, imagination plays a larger role: for sheer exuberance of detailing the Ansonia at 71st St. and the nearby Dorilton and a dozen other buildings are unrivaled.

The Upper West Side prides itself on its cultural resources, and the severe Classical building of the New-York Historical Society is a solid presence on Central Park West. Farther north at 81st St. is the American Museum of Natural History, a treasure house of magnificent displays and dioramas of wild life that is also famous for its mineral and gem collections. Its new glass-cube addition containing the silver-sphere Planetarium contrasts sharply with limestone and red-tile of the main building.

A brand-new building at 59th St. and Central Park West is already a hub of activity. Two broad towers with curved glass façades overlook the southwest cor-

ner of Central Park; between them is a concert hall high above the park, in which jazz will be the main fare. Just north, on Columbus Avenue, is Lincoln Center for the Performing Arts. New York State Theater, The Metropolitan Opera and Avery Fisher Hall flank the central plaza, while other performance halls and the Juilliard School of Music fill out the complex.

Behind Lincoln Center, West End Avenue runs north. Like Park Avenue, it is flanked by huge old apartment houses. By comparison, Riverside Drive is much more varied; with smaller buildings which offer many architectural delights. Not to be missed is the long-established "floating village" of the West 79th St. Boat Basin, where the hardy live year-round on their water-borne homes.

Upper West Siders enjoy life. The area abounds with ethnic restaurants: Chinese, Vietnamese, Thai, Indonesian, Greek, Cuban, Latin-American of every style. Ask for any exotic cuisine and someone can point out where it is to be had. Theater and music flourish in off-beat venues. Small cafes punctuate many of the side streets, where handsome old brownstones house a burgeoning population of the young and the hopeful. A large number seem to be film-makers, actors, writer, or dancers. They are making their way in New York: what more can they ask for?

Farther north, at 110th St. in Harlem, the massive Triborough Bridge passes over the stadiums, tennis courts, and pool of conjoined Randall and Ward's Island, with its web of elevated highways linking Manhattan, Queens and the Bronx. Still farther north, adjoining Broadway from 114th to 121st Streets is Columbia University's immense urban campus. Seen from above, the intricate geometry of the quadrangle and courtyards and the green copper-roofed buildings, with the circular Low Memorial Library at the center, is truly impressive. Heading north and passing over Harlem's Morningside and Marcus Garvey parks one would look down on a much narrower Manhattan, an urban spine flanked by parks and riverfronts. On the west, the lengthy span of the George Washington Bridge (1931) links Upper Manhattan to New Jersey.

The last sight is the most atypical: close to Manhattan's hilly, wooded northern tip is rugged Fort Tryon Park. In it stands the Cloisters, a gem of a hilltop monastery-museum, one which the New World assembled from religious structures salvaged from the Old World.

114 Columbia University's impressive campus on the Upper West Side extends over eight full blocks from 112th to 120th Streets. The three domed buildings are top, Butler Library; center, Low Memorial Library; and foreground, St. Paul's Chapel.

*116 top and 117 top
The century
Apartments at 62nd
St. and Central Park
West is characterized
by twin towers.*

*116-117 The twin
tower-tops of the
Time-Warner
Building at
Columbus Circle
(59th St. and*

*Eighth Avenue)
support air-
conditioning
equipment. Central
Park can be seen in
the upper corner.*

*117 bottom The
buildings flanking or
close to Central Park
present an amazing
variety of
architectural detail.*

118 top Baseball in the park or strolls along the Hudson: the Upper West Side offers both.

118 bottom Central Park West is one of New York's finest residential avenues, and the Hudson is within easy reach.

118-119 The soaring twin towers of the new Time-Warner Building cast their shadow over Central Park's southwest corner.

119 top The Fifth Avenue Synagogue forms a contrast to the high-rise apartment houses that look onto the park.

120-121 This spectacular image looks down Central Park from 110th to 59th Street, with the circular Lasker Pool and Rink and the Jacqueline Kennedy Onassis Reservoir clearly visible. Fifth Avenue is on the left, Central Park West on the right.

122 top The
Metropolitan
Museum built a new
wing to house the
Temple of Dendur,
acquired when the
Aswan Dam was
constructed on the
Nile.

122-123 In this
image are shown the
Metropolitan
Museum's Fifth
Avenue façade and
steps; the pediments
above the paired
columns have yet to
be sculpted.

123 top and 124-125
The Metropolitan
Museum, one of the
world's great treasure
houses of art, flanks
Fifth Avenue,
extending well into
Central Park.

123 bottom This
elegant addition to
the Metropolitan
Museum houses the
distinguished
Lehman Collection.

126-177 This
panoramic view
shows the West Side
Highway running
north from a new
housing area and
entering tree-clad
Riverside Park at
72nd Street. The
West Side Highway
is flanked by
handsome older
apartment houses,
which are prestige
addresses.

128 top and 128-129 The Guggenheim Museum, the Church of the Heavenly Rest, and the Andrew Carnegie residence (now the Cooper-Hewitt Museum) contrast dramatically with their apartment house neighbors.

129 top The famed Museum of Natural History is a Central Park West landmark and a top-tier attraction for New Yorkers and visitors.

129 bottom The height of most Central Park West apartment houses blocks the view for those living in rear.

130-131 This image looking east, shows the twin towers of the San Remo and the Majestic apartment houses overlook Central Park.

132-133 Looking east from Fifth Avenue, the borough of Queens is visible beyond the three red-banded smokestacks.

134 Churches flourish in Harlem, drawing large congregations. Many serve as neighborhood anchors and provide needed community services.

135 A view north from mid-Harlem with the George Washington Bridge on the upper left.

136-137 The interdenominational Riverside Church, on Riverside Drive and 122nd St., was built in the 1930s with funding contributed by John D. Rockefeller, Jr. It is famous for its carillon and as a liberal forum.

THE OUTER

BOROUGHS

The boroughs have rich histories, impressive architecture, universities, cultural centers, and diverse ethnic communities forming a rich h mosaic. Many of New York's cultural and hishistoric jewels are in the boroughs, together with many of the finest parks and beaches. Each borough contributes vitally to New York's unrivaled attractions.

From the air, the Harlem River stands out, separating the Bronx from Upper Manhattan. The Bronx is indeed "a borough of parks and beaches": Van Cortlandt and Pelham Bay parks are great swathes of turf, woodland, and water. Also visible is the spectacular Bronx Zoo, with over 3,500 animals, many roaming in open habitats. The adjacent New York Botanical Garden is also world class; spectacular hothouses, groves, and climatic zones accommodate an unrivaled wealth of flora.

In the northern Bronx, Fieldston's winding streets adjoining Van Cortlandt Park, and hilly, wooded Riverdale, with its park overlooking the Hudson, will be visible. In the northeastern Bronx, in total contrast, stands a massive monument to mid-1960s Modernism, the 35 huge apartment towers of Co-Op City, containing some 15,000 apartments. Not far distant in Long Island Sound is City Island, a haven of small homes and boat-yards.

The scene changes in the southeastern Bronx; waterfront communities abound. Throg's Neck, fronting onto Eastchester Bay and the East River, is one such community; nearby the soaring Throg's Neck and Whitestone bridges link the Bronx to Queens. Fort Schuyler (now part of New York State Maritime College) faces Fort Totten on the Queens side; both were part of New York's waterway defenses.

Standing proud in the mid-Bronx is the towering new glass-clad County Courthouse, almost adjoining are Fordham University and Bronx Park, through which the Bronx River flows. Atop University Heights is the Hall of Fame for Great Americans, a huge colonnade housing bronze busts that encircles three Neo-Classical buildings, now part of City College.

Though the South Bronx suffered a massive decline in the 1960s, rows of attractive new two-family homes and gardens witness the area's economic rebirth, attracting new immigrants and adding to the quality of life. The Grand Concourse, with its Art Deco apartment houses, is also regaining its former luster. For local baseball fans, Yankee Stadium, once home to the Bronx Bombers and now to the New York Yankees, remains a nearby mecca. Other sports thrive: Van Cortlandt Park hosts rugby (British and Irish), cricket (West Indians and British), hurling (the Irish) and tennis and golf. There is indeed something for everyone: hence the weekend crowds.

From overhead, Brooklyn appears endless, but distinctive features abound. Most dramatic is Prospect Park with its lake, Long Meadow, wooded Ravine, and Concert Grove among other "rustic" attractions. Grand Army Plaza, with a backdrop of handsome apartment houses, provides a fitting entrance to the park, while in easy reach on Eastern Parkway are the modern Brooklyn Public Library and the Classical-style Brooklyn Museum, with its dramatic glass-roofed entry plaza. Once culturally satisfied, visitors can stroll in the attractively planted Botanic Garden. The much smaller Fort Greene Park boasts a distinctive feature: the columnar Prison Ship Martyrs' Monument, honoring some 12,000 American who died below decks on British ships during the Revolutionary War.

Brooklyn has a highly varied series of waterfronts. Above those facing Manhattan are the approaches to the Brooklyn, Manhattan, and Williamsburg bridges. All three are highly photogenic; from-the-air photographs capture them in every sort of light. Brooklyn's most spectacular span is the Verrazano-Narrows Bridge, soaring over the water from Bay Ridge to Staten Island, a undisputed triumph of vision and engineering.

From above, the south and southeastern Brooklyn waterfronts are spectacular. Coney Island (not an island at all!) and Brighton Beach offer huge expanses of sand; in summer thousands of Manhattanites flock there to join the local population. Noticeable from afar are the clusters of new high-rise apartment communities. Looking down to the east, Gateway National Recreation Area swings into view, where extensive parkland runs down to Jamaica Bay, rich in protected wildlife. From the air, Gateway National Recreation Area presents itself as a huge bay, dotted with still wild islands, large and small, across which runs the silver thread of the rail line going out to Rockaway Peninsula, passing a modest on-the-water community of turn-of-the-century houses on stilts. The Bay's sheer size and "a different world" quality remain a constant surprise

138-139 from left to right Jamaica Bay; two views of the Verrazano-Narrows Bridge; Yankee Stadium in the Bronx.

141 The mighty Verrazano-Narrows Bridge, New York's longest span, crosses Lower New York Bay to link Brooklyn and Staten Island.

Arts and education are well served: for eager audiences, the much-loved Brooklyn Academy of Music's three auditoria present often avant-garde music, drama, and dance; and in academia, Brooklyn College, housed in 1930s Neo-Georgian buildings, is held in high respect. Brooklyn is a proud borough - with reason.

Historically, Queens has been known for quiet homes on quiet streets. People flying into either LaGuardia or JFK airports will note whole neighborhoods of private homes and small apartment houses, occasional institutional complexes on landscaped plazas, parkland, and a lot of shoreline. But airports need support services, and industrial facilities are also visible.

Those really wanting to live "at the shore" are well served. From Far Rockaway to Breezy Point, homes look out over the Atlantic; inland lies Jamaica Bay, incorporating Gateway National Recreation Area. In some areas homes have built on pilings, directly over the water, looking like New England fishing-village homes. Jacob Riis Park, named for the great 19th-century crusader against slums, runs from ocean to bay. The park and its boardwalk are favorites among Rockaway residents. At Rockaway's eastern end is Breezy Point, a gated private beach community.

Queens has large and still-growing immigrant communities. Asians are a vibrant presence in Flushing and adjoining areas; temples, clothing stores, and specialty foods are common. In Jackson Heights the note is predominantly Indian, and sari and jewelry stores abound. Other areas have large Latin-American populations, adding another range of restaurants, foodstuffs, and music.

Queens residents are well served by a necklace of parks. Flushing Meadow-Corona Park and nearby Kissena, Cunningham, and Alley parks form a near-continuous greensward, each park offering splendid vistas and walks. Kissena Park is home to Queens Botanical Garden, which houses a fine arboretum. Flushing Meadows-Corona Park, site of the 1964 World's Fair, is graced by a number of striking avant-garde buildings commissioned for the occasion and retained after it ended. They include the Unisphere and the elevated Terrace on the Park, as well as the New York Pavilion, which became the Queens Museum (it has a huge model of New York City), and the imaginative Hall of Science. Queens in also home to the taste-setting P.S. 1 Contemporary Art Center.

Sports are well served in Queens. Shea Stadium, home of the New York Mets, draws tens of thousands of home-team enthusiasts. The borough has long been home to international tennis tournaments; in the past they took place in Forest Hills but now use larger, more modern facilities in Flushing Meadows.

From overhead, Staten Island seems huge, a patchwork quilt of small townships and modest clusters of houses and gardens. Only St. George, with the Ferry Terminal, Borough Hall, and the Island's administrative buildings, looks like a traditional town.

Among the boroughs only Staten Island has real wooded hills. Exclusive Todt Hill is dotted with expensive homes and occasional big mansions. Dongan Hills presents two surprises, Staten Island Lighthouse (well inland and 230 ft high), and the Jacques Marchais Museum of Tibetan Art, housed in a Tibetan-style monastery on a wooded hillside, with descending terraced gardens.

From overhead, Sailors' Snug Harbor, Staten Island's finest architectural complex, is unmistakable. Situated in an 83-acre park of stately trees close to St. George and the Kill van Kull (the waterway separating Staten Island and New Jersey), this haven for "aged and decrepit" mariners was built in the 1830s on a now unimaginable scale. Five enormous Greek-temple style structures face a second row of similar structures across a broad mall. These buildings housed the retired sailors, who had a concert hall, library, church and every other needed facility. Snug Harbor and its well-tended park is now a cultural center, with the buildings sensitively restored for contemporary uses.

Staten Island's many other attractions include High Rock Conservation Area, a 94-acre forest and wild life refuge. Overall, creek-side parks and numerous patches of woodland help give the borough a still often bucolic, occasionally rugged look. Another surprise that Staten Island presents is a whole "village" of historic buildings, the Richmontown Restoration, were some 30 restored buildings, many with furniture, provide a dramatic sense of life in the past. They are survivors of the modest mid-island township that served as the Island's administrative center from the 1750s until the 1850s.

Development came late to Staten Island, and historic survivals are numerous. At the island's southern tip is the Conference House (ca. 1670), a fieldstone manor where George Washington met with the British. Of much later vintage is Austen House in Rosebank, an exquisite Victorian cottage where the pioneer photographer Alice Austen lived. Beautifully sited at the Narrows, the entrance to New York Bay, house and garden are a delight.

143 Yankee Stadium is situated in the Bronx, "the borough of parks, universities, and waterfronts," whose numerous attractive residential neighborhoods are home to many thousands who work in Manhattan.

144 top Parked yellow school buses are a familiar sight in New York's four outer boroughs. Shown here is a bus park in the Bronx.

144-145 In this image is a partly "wrapped" George Washington Bridge. The Little Red Lighthouse on the Manhattan side of the Hudson is a storied icon.

145 top The High Bridge Watch Tower was once part of the Croton Aqueduct system that brought water through the Bronx to Manhattan. The tower (actually on the Manhattan side

of the Harlem River) now overlooks a swimming pool.

145 center More than a dozen bridges span the Harlem River, linking the Bronx to Manhattan.

145 bottom The Bronx has many fine older collegiate and institutional buildings, as shown here. A generally

Georgian style with Classical notes was very popular in the late 19th and early 20th centuries.

146 top and 146-147
Showcase stadiums
and immaculate
patterned turf
(usually artificial)
are all part of the
mystique of
contemporary
baseball.

147 On game
nights, Yankee
Stadium, just
across the Harlem
River from Upper
Manhattan, draws
thousands of
eager New York
Yankee fans.

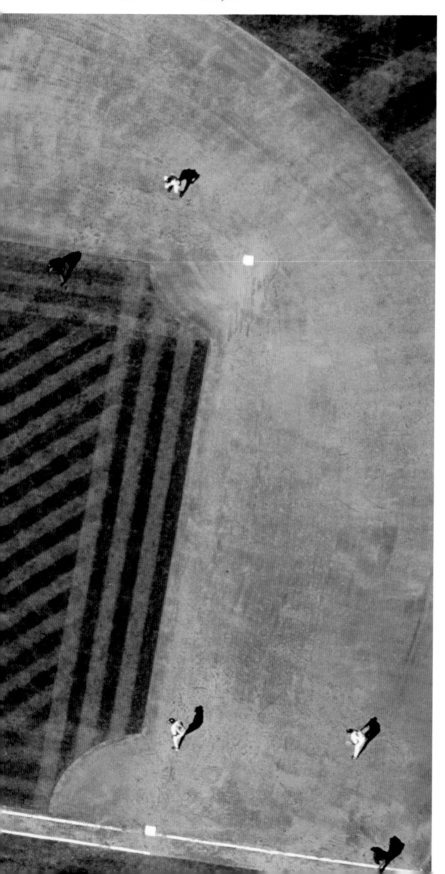

148 top Bronx Park includes a fine piazza and garden forum.

148-149 The Bronx Botanical Gardens' Conservatory

Range houses world-famous plant collections. The extensive Gardens share Bronx Park with the equally famous Bronx Zoo, a pace-setter in animal care.

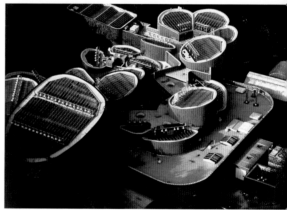

149 top The old Elephant House at the Bronx Zoo is now the Zoo Center; the elephants roam freely on the open range.

149 bottom The Bird House, one of the Bronx Zoo's finest attractions, is an ultra-modern series of buildings.

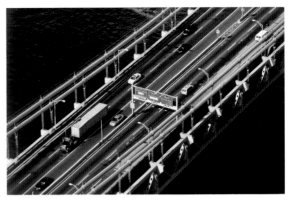

150 top The Verrazano-Narrows Bridge is heavily used by vehicles carrying freight landed in the Brooklyn and Staten Island maritime terminals. Manhattan is no longer a major cargo entry point.

150-151 The Staten Island approaches to the Verrazano-Narrows Bridge. The park is federal land; historic Ft. Wadsworth, guarding the Narrows, can be seen to the left, on the bay.

151 top Spanning the Narrows, the Verrazano Bridge marks the divide between the Upper Bay (north, to the left) and the Lower Bay, opening onto the Atlantic.

151 bottom The Verrazano-Narrows Bridge combines uncluttered design with unrivaled traffic capacity.

152 and 153 On Marathon Day, thousands runners turn out and the Verrazano-Narrows Bridge carries a human tide. Many but not all New York bridges have pedestrian pathways.

154-155 Here is the small community of Foxbury, close to the western end of Rockaway Peninsula. For. Tilden, a historic defense structure, is on the upper left, near the bridge ramp.

156-157 One of the many communities fronting onto Jamaica Bay. Sections of both Brooklyn and Queens face the Bay, which incorporates Gateway National Recreation Area.

157 top For homeowners on Jamaica Bay, parking a boat can be as problematic as parking a car!

157 bottom Many Jamaica Bay homeowners see a private dock as a necessary addition to their homes.

158-159 Handsome older warehouse and commercial buildings, now being renovated, and new miniparks characterize the Brooklyn waterfront below the approaches to the Manhattan and Brooklyn bridges.

160 The Statue of Liberty dominates Manhattan Bay in the orange and warm lights of sunset.

All the pictures inside the book are by Antonio Attini/Archivio White Star except for the following:
Kevin Fleming/Corbis/Contrasto: pages 2-3
Jim Wark: pages 4-5, 8, 24, 82, 126-127
Alan Schein Photography/Corbis/Contrasto: page 9
World Sat: page 11
Hammon, Jensen, Wallen and Associates, NGS: page 12
Alamy Images: pages 60, 68, 106, 160
Jason Hawkes: pages 62 right, 63, 99
David Zimmerman/Corbis/Contrasto: pages 72-73, 104-105
Falke/laif/Contrasto: pages 135 left, 153
Timothy Fadek/Corbis Sygma/Contrasto: page 137
David Alan Harvey/Magnum Photos/Contrasto: page 140, 141, 142-143
Yann Arthus-Bertrand/Corbis/Contrasto: pages 146-147, 152

PHOTO CREDITS

The photographer would like to thank Pegasus Flight
(www.pegasus-flight.com)